Colored Property

HISTORICAL STUDIES OF URBAN AMERICA

Edited by Timothy J. Gilfoyle, James R. Grossman, and Becky M. Nicolaides

ALSO IN THE SERIES

Colored Property

State Policy and White Racial Politics
in Suburban America

DAVID M. P. FREUND

The University of Chicago Press
Chicago and London

David M. P. Freund is visiting assistant professor in the Department of History at Rutgers University, Newark.

The publication of this book was supported by a grant from the Graham Foundation for Advanced Studies in the Fine Arts.

The University of Chicago Press, Chicago 60637
The University of Chicago Press, Ltd., London
© 2007 by The University of Chicago
All rights reserved. Published 2007
Printed in the United States of America

16 15 14 13 12 11 10 09 08 07   1 2 3 4 5

ISBN-13: 978-0-226-26275-8 (cloth)
ISBN-10: 0-226-26275-8 (cloth)

Library of Congress Cataloging-in-Publication Data

Freund, David M.
    Colored property : state policy and white racial politics in suburban
America / David M. P. Freund.
        p.   cm.
    Includes bibliographical references and index.
    ISBN-13: 978-0-226-26275-8 (cloth : alk. paper)
    ISBN-10: 0-226-26275-8 (cloth : alk. paper)
    1. United States—Race relations—History—20th century.   2. Whites—
United States—Politics and government—20th century.   3. Whites—United
States—Attitudes—History—20th century.   4. African Americans—Hous-
ing—History—20th century.   5. Discrimination in housing—United States—
History—20th century.   6. Housing policy—United States—History—20th
century.   7. Suburban life—United States—History—20th century.   8. City
and town life—United States—History—20th century.   I. Title.
    E184.A1F738 2007
    305.896′07300904—dc22
                                                                    2006033989

For family

CONTENTS

ACKNOWLEDGMENTS

So many generous people and institutions contributed to this project and made the book possible. I am grateful to the archivists, municipal officials, librarians, and museum staff who helped me navigate dozens of collections in southeastern Michigan and Washington, D.C. Special thanks to the staffs of the Archives of Labor and Urban Affairs at Wayne State University; the Bentley Library (Michigan Historical Collections division) and Harlan Hatcher Library at the University of Michigan, Ann Arbor; the Hazel Park City Clerk's office; the Michigan Municipal League; National Archives II in College Park, Maryland; the Oakland County Planning Office; the Oakland County Pioneer Museum; the Lawson Room (now the History Collection) at the Royal Oak Public Library; the Troy Historical Museum; and the Troy Planning Office. I could never adequately express my gratitude to the staff of the Dearborn Historical Museum and Archive in Dearborn, Michigan. Winfield Arneson, Mary MacDonald, William K. McElhone, Helen K. Mamalakis, and Bertha M. Miga welcomed me from day one, treated me like a colleague, and eventually (when they saw I wasn't leaving anytime soon) cleared a table in the back room for me. Kirt Gross at the Dearborn Historical Museum and Carol Windorf at the Royal Oak Library were equally generous with their time, providing essential help in the later stages of the project. Special thanks to the late Winthrop Sears Jr. for his volunteer work cataloguing the Hubbard papers and his generosity with a young scholar.

Several institutions provided me with time to read, search, and write. They also created settings where I presented and discussed this project with engaged academic and nonacademic audiences. I want to thank the U.S. Department of Education; the Department of History, the Rackham School of Graduate Studies, and the Center for Research on Learning and Teaching at the University of Michigan, Ann Arbor; the National Museum of American

History, Smithsonian Institution; the New Jersey Council for the Humanities; Princeton University; the Ford Foundation; and the Poverty and Race Research Action Council. Special thanks to the Graham Foundation for Advanced Studies in the Fine Arts for a generous grant that helped defray the cost of producing this volume.

I have benefited tremendously from the commentators and audiences who responded to this project at various stages. Special thanks to the participants in sessions and colloquia at the Center for Afroamerican and African Studies at the University of Michigan, Ann Arbor; the National Museum of American History; the Princeton Public Library; the Shelby Cullom Davis Center for Historical Studies at Princeton University; the Cornwall Center for Metropolitan Studies at Rutgers University, Newark; and at annual meetings of the Social Science History Association, the Organization of American Historians, the American Historical Association, the Department of Housing and Urban Development's National Fair Housing Training Conference and Housing Policy Summit, and the Housing and Development Law Institute's Legal Conference. The other major contributors to this ongoing conversation were students at Princeton University and Rutgers University, Newark. They were very receptive to the idea that subjects like the *mortgage market*, of all things, were important for thinking about American politics and culture. And they constantly challenged me—and each other—to make sense of how race operates in the modern United States.

I am grateful to the teachers, colleagues, and friends who have long contributed to my development as a student, historian, and teacher. Special thanks to David Keightley, Thomas Laqueur, Leon Litwack, Karen McConnell, Marc Steinberg, Janet Thomas, Frederic Wakeman Jr., and Isser Woloch. The Department of History at the University of Michigan is a special place, which allowed me to work with a remarkable group of scholars and educators in Ann Arbor. For their time, ideas, support, commitment to teaching, and *lots* of careful readings of my work, I am grateful to Andrew Achenbaum, Richard Campbell, Kathleen Canning, Barry Checkoway, Geoff Eley, Joseph Gonzales, Carol Karlsen, Marya McQuirter, Sonya Rose, Warren Rosenblum, Ara Sarafian, Julius Scott, John Shy, J. Mills Thornton, Victoria Wolcott, and Ernest Young. Four scholars had a particularly dramatic impact on my development as an historian and teacher during those years, and long since. Thanks to Elsa Barkley Brown, Robin D. G. Kelly, Earl Lewis, and Terrence McDonald for welcoming a wayward Germanist into their line of work and then constantly asking so many important questions.

This is a much better book because of the people who generously gave their time to read and comment on it. Florence Wagman Roisman, Terrence McDonald, Earl Lewis, and Robin D. G. Kelley read early drafts and individual chapters, responding with extremely helpful commentary and suggestions. Arnold Hirsch, Robert Self, David Roediger, Michael Berk, Karen Caplan, series editor James Grossman, and two anonymous readers for the University of Chicago Press read the entire manuscript. Hopefully they will recognize how influential their commentary has been, on so many levels, in producing the final product. Special thanks to the editor of my dreams, Robert Devens, and to Elizabeth Branch Dyson, Jean Eckenfels, Mary Gehl, and Leslie Keros for their remarkable work on the manuscript. I am also grateful to Jason Frank for his tireless work producing wonderful maps and to Ken Music for his attention to detail in reproducing archival sources.

There isn't room to express my appreciation for the colleagues and friends—in New Jersey, Washington, D.C., and other locales—who have supported and engaged me on so many levels in recent years. I am especially grateful to Larry Adelman (and the staff at California Newsreel), Pamela Smith Chambers, Brian Corrigan, Pete Daniel, Hank Dobin, Pamela Groves, Chester Hartman, Arnold Hirsch, Scott Henderson, Andrew Isenberg, Anthony Kaye, Romana Kahn, Tia Kolbaba, Kevin Kruse, Matthew Lassiter, Jan Lewis, Charles McGovern, Michael Mahoney, Robin Parker, Wendy Plotkin, Dara Regaignon, Dave Riddle, David Roediger, Noliwe Rooks, Andy Smith, Thomas Sugrue, Phil Tegeler, Dale Tomich, Florence Wagman Roisman, Kerry Walk, Nancy Watterson, and Pat Young.

It is difficult to thank friends and family on paper. Some of them played multiple roles, as both loved one and colleague-critic. Others knew that this project was lurking out there but didn't focus on it too much. All of them helped me understand why I was writing it and shared much time, thought, attitude, and general play. So while the press would not let me list them on the cover, the book's coauthors include Karen Leon Aponte, Michael Berk, Julia Cole, Michal Ditzian, Jason Frank, Katie Holt, Jerma Jackson, Jay Kaufman, Lisa Lindsay, Elizabeth Meister, Erin Kelly, Courtney McCarthy, Gerard McCarthy, Judy Ruttenberg, Philip Cohen, Robert Self, Stephanie Shaw, Steve Simon, Paul Southworth, and the far-flung (yet always near!) Clemens and Mandel clans. It is difficult to imagine how I'd see the world if not for Ray Clemens, Maud Mandel, Adam Ray, Elsa Barkley Brown, and Mira Geffner. And if not for Arna and Marty Caplan (and the extended Caplan network), who let me borrow their car before they even met me. And if not for the small but fast-growing army of silly people who hang out with us because, well, they have no choice (Benjamin, Sophie, and Reuben

Clemens, Lev and Ava Simon, Owen and Rosalind Holt-Frank, Maggie and Rosie Caplan, Lorelei McCarthy, and Isaac Meister Kelly). And if not for Elaine, Lee, and Mark Freund, whose love and support got me here and sustain me to this day. This book is for Karen, Jonah, and Benjamin, who make it *all* happen.

CHAPTER ONE

The New Politics of Race and Property

On September 9, 1925, one day after Ossian and Gladys Sweet moved into their new house on the east side of Detroit, their neighbors ran them out. Gladys had grown up in the city, from the age of seven, and studied at City College. She was twenty years old in 1922 when she met Ossian, a twenty-six-year-old, Florida-raised, Howard-educated physician who had relocated to Detroit to begin his medical practice. They married that winter, spent a year in France and Austria while Ossian completed additional training, returned to Detroit in the summer of 1924, and began searching for a home to buy. The young African American couple found their choices limited by the city's unofficial but firm residential color line, which restricted the fast-growing black population to a handful of neighborhoods, most of them downtown on the east side, centered along Hastings Street. Overcrowding in the so-called Hastings Street corridor encouraged many blacks, especially middle-class families like the Sweets, to look for property in nearby neighborhoods that were exclusively white. It was in one such neighborhood, three miles east of the city's all-black enclave, that the couple purchased a two-story bungalow at 2905 Garland Street in June 1925.

It was no secret that the Sweets would not be welcomed. There had already been five mob attacks that summer against blacks who settled in nearby all-white east-side neighborhoods, and at least one black homeowner had been forced to sell his property to members of the local "improvement association." Soon after purchasing the Garland Street house, the Sweets heard talk that residents were organizing to force them out, even that some had made threats against their lives. Naturally the couple approached moving day with caution. Accompanying them on the morning of September 8 were Ossian's brothers Henry and Otis, two family employees, Joseph Mack and

Norris Murray, and two family friends, William Davis and John Latting. The Sweets left their fifteen-month-old daughter Iva with Gladys's parents, notified the police of their plans, and, fearing the worst, armed themselves for protection. Their fears were confirmed within hours of their arrival, when dozens of whites gathered on the street in front of 2905 Garland, spurred on, it was later learned, by the newly formed Waterworks Improvement Association. As many as eight hundred people assembled by midnight. The crowd dispersed at daybreak but returned in greater force on the evening of the ninth, eventually filling nearby streets, alleys, and porches—even surrounding rooftops.[1]

At about eight o'clock that night, Ossian Sweet later testified, "something hit the roof of the house." When he heard men outside yelling instructions to surround the property, Sweet grabbed a gun and ran upstairs, threw himself on the bed, and listened as "stones kept hitting the house intermittently." One crashed through the window and struck him. Seventeen Detroit police officers stood by in the street, refusing to intervene. Then, events forced their hand when William Davis and Otis Sweet returned to the home by taxi and were immediately set upon with bricks, chunks of coal, and shouts of "Niggers! Niggers! . . . Get the Niggers!" From his second-floor vantage point, Ossian saw the mob "surge . . . forward 15 or 20 feet"—to him it looked "like a human sea"—while the barrage of projectiles "kept coming faster." Then he heard gunfire. At least two shots were fired from the house by his brother Henry and at least one by Detroit police officer Frank Lee Gill, who later admitted aiming "at two Negroes he saw dimly on the upper back porch of the Sweet home." Two white men in the crowd had been shot, and one lay dead. The police immediately entered 2905 Garland and led off its occupants, charging them with conspiracy to murder and conspiracy to assault with the intent to kill.[2]

The trial was scheduled for October, but the court of white public opinion did not wait to pass judgment, accusing the Sweets of instigating the violence simply by buying a house on Garland Street. Detroit mayor John Smith proclaimed, "any colored person who endangers life and property, simply to gratify his personal pride, is an enemy of his race as well as an incitant of riot and murder." Clearly sharing this view were the white residents who appeared as witnesses for the prosecution. Most were circumspect about their motivations, testifying that they had supported the Waterworks Improvement Association solely to protect their property. But the Sweets' attorney, Clarence Darrow, eventually drew out admissions that homeowners' central preoccupation was excluding black people. "I don't believe in mixing people that way," acknowledged one witness finally, "colored and white."[3]

Nearly four decades later, and about twelve miles west of the house on Garland Street, in the all-white suburb of Dearborn, hundreds of white residents descended upon the home of Giuseppe Stanzione, at 7427 Kendal Street, after learning that he had sold it to black people. It was September 2, 1963, Labor Day weekend, when word spread through northeast Dearborn that two black men, accompanied by a pregnant black woman, were unloading a moving truck on Kendal. The news drew about six hundred whites to the property by early evening. At around six o'clock, they began throwing stones and eggs at Stanzione's home and vandalizing his car, slashing the tires and pouring sugar in the fuel tank. Throughout the evening, Stanzione received anonymous phone calls threatening to bomb the house. None of the Dearborn city police officers on the scene, including the chief, deputy chief, and safety director, attempted to disperse the crowd, despite the intensifying violence and appeals from a local minister and from Stanzione himself. "I called the . . . police at least 20 times Monday night," the homeowner later explained, "but all they did was cruise around the block, never interfering while the mob . . . threw bottles and rocks at my window and yelled insults at me." According to some reports, the police left the scene by 10:00. And it was another hour before Stanzione's attorney subdued the crowd when he appeared on the front porch waving the property's title, documentary evidence that the house had not been sold. The neighbors soon learned that Stanzione had in fact rented the property, to a white man, who in turn hired the black men to move his belongings. One of those movers had been accompanied that day by his wife.[4]

In the weeks that followed, local political leaders and whites from throughout the Detroit region applauded the mob action, the police department's response, and the suburb's commitment to racial exclusion. Dearborn's mayor, Orville Hubbard, told reporters that "there [had been] no need for [municipal] action," adding, curiously, that "Dearborn is one of the safest and cleanest places in the world to live." Meanwhile, whites from city and suburbs alike registered their support for the racial status quo, in hundreds of letters, telegrams, and phone calls to the mayor's office. "We have all seen what can happen to a good, well kept neighborhood when taken over by Negroes," wrote one Dearborn woman in a letter of September 17. "Their treatment of property and their behavior," she explained, "is like a slow disease killing off a once healthy neighborhood." Hubbard's suburban supporters celebrated the homeowners' associations that were maintaining the residential color line and assured the mayor that "property owners back you all the way." A Detroiter joined many others in declaring that he, too, would "love to be a home owner in Dearborn."[5]

––––––––––

This book asks if northern whites' views about racial integration had changed in the four decades separating the attacks on Garland Street in 1925 and Kendal Street in 1963. Throughout the intervening years, urban and suburban whites consistently mobilized to exclude minorities from their neighborhoods. They pressured real estate agents, wrote race-restrictive covenants into their deeds, blocked construction of low income and rental housing projects, and, when these strategies failed, resorted to intimidation and assault. The Kendal Street episode was hardly an anomaly in the post–World War II metropolis. So common was white vigilantism that Arnold Hirsch has described these years, quite appropriately, as an "era of hidden violence." Meanwhile the politics of exclusion was so prominent a fixture of white neighborhood life that housing and development issues became a key site for local battles over race and rights, in cities and suburbs nationwide.[6]

But was there anything new or different during the postwar era about whites' response to the threat of racial integration? Had the years of Depression, war, and suburban expansion changed anything about white neighborhood politics? To be sure the suburban revolution itself had transformed both metropolitan geography and tenancy patterns. During the 1920s blacks and whites in the Detroit region lived in separate neighborhoods, but the vast majority lived within the city itself. Nationwide, both people and commercial activity were firmly centered in fast-growing municipalities like Detroit. And the majority of urban residents, be they black or white, immigrant or "native," rented their place of residence. Neither trend would be long-lasting. Postwar development rapidly drew millions of urban whites and much of the nation's commercial and industrial base out of major cities and into the suburban fringe, and most suburbanites bought their homes.[7] By the 1960s, most of the nation's suburbs were almost exclusively white domains and dominated by a homeowning class. Largely excluded from both the exodus and the new, robust market for real estate were racial minorities, most of whom were restricted to overcrowded and often deteriorating center-city neighborhoods.

The expansion and resegregation of the metropolis after World War II coincided, paradoxically, with an equally dramatic transformation in the national politics of race. In the 1920s, most white public officials and private leaders did not apologize for the nation's stark racial inequalities. Whites openly embraced a racial science that described blacks and other racial minorities as biologically inferior. And most whites openly endorsed the segregation of residential neighborhoods by race and national origin; indeed, even immigrants from southern and eastern Europe were viewed as racial threats and, thus, systematically excluded from neighborhoods occupied by native-born whites. The contrast with the postwar era could not be more striking. The United States' new world-power status, achieved in part through war against totalitarian regimes seen as antidemocratic and intolerant, helped civil rights activists highlight the hypocrisy of the nation's racial caste system, forcing most northern whites to disavow racism and embrace, at least rhetorically, the principle of racial equality. By the time of the Kendal Street incident, racial science had long been discredited, a domestic war was being waged over civil rights, and the federal government had been forced to reassert its role as a protector of racial fairness, in no small part by outlawing practices that had long promoted residential discrimination. By the 1960s, few whites openly endorsed race-based discrimination or justified race-based inequality. And the European immigrants once considered a threat to native-born whites had joined the exodus to the prosperous, all-white suburbs.

In short, we know that between the 1920s and 1960s both the geographical and intellectual settings for white homeowner vigilantism had clearly changed. The mob that descended upon Kendal Street represented a new generation of white resistance to racial integration—ethnically more inclusive, predominantly home-owning and suburban. And postwar whites organized to maintain the color line at a time when it was impolitic, at best, to announce one's racism out loud. Nonetheless, the similarities between the Garland and Kendal Street episodes, and the apparent continuity of white hostility to integrated neighborhoods, raise a fundamental question that this study seeks to answer: If most northern whites had disavowed racism and supported the principle of racial equality, why did so many continue to oppose residential integration? What motivated postwar whites to exclude black people from their neighborhoods?

For decades writers have addressed this question, in a multidisciplinary investigation of residential segregation, suburban growth, and urban decline that has revealed how public policy and private practices encouraged white people to view racial integration as a threat. We know that New Deal–era and postwar housing programs—most famously the programs of the Public Housing Administration (PHA), the Urban Renewal Administration (URA), and the Federal Housing Administration (FHA)—accepted and codified white racial prejudices, in turn facilitating urban and suburban development patterns that systematically segregated populations by race while denying most racial minorities access to homeownership and better quality accommodations. During and after World War II, as employment opportunities drew more and more blacks to northern cities, public policy simultaneously fueled white flight and underdeveloped the black center city. Meanwhile employment discrimination denied most urban blacks the secure, well-paying jobs that were lifting millions of whites into the middle class, and the decentralization of manufacturing and retail drew even more opportunities away from urban centers. The result was a spatial separation of jobs and wealth, with suburban growth and affluence creating a striking, very visible contrast to the physical deterioration, overcrowding, and relative poverty of black, central-city neighborhoods.[8] Many whites concluded that integration would threaten their status, their pocketbooks, and ultimately their way of life. And they felt threatened by the continual expansion of urban black communities and by black people's willingness to challenge their second-class status publicly by moving into white neighborhoods, protesting against discrimination, and using public spaces once the exclusive preserve of white people. If scholars agree on nothing else, there is some consensus that the early postwar era saw the emergence of a new kind of white racial conservatism, a precursor to the better-known backlash politics of the 1960s and the rise of the New Right, fueled by whites' preoccupation with protecting their neighborhoods, status, and privileges from minorities.[9]

There is, nonetheless, considerable disagreement about the role that race per se played in fueling white vigilance. Many argue that while black people were clearly the targets of exclusionary practices, racism played little or no part in whites' decision-making. After 1940, according to this argument, battles over neighborhoods were fueled primarily by whites' economic and class concerns, their desire to protect property values, and their preoccupation with defending local turf.[10] Others, by contrast, insist that racial prejudice continued to shape whites' actions, with recent work exploring how the category of "white" itself grew more inclusive after the war, allowing more ethnic groups to reap its benefits.[11] Finally much of this same work shows that this expanding white population defended segregation in the postwar era by invoking the amorphous language of "rights," which enabled them to cast racial exclusion as a defense of hard-earned, and presumably nonracial, privileges, be it as homeowners, working people, consumers, citizens, or loyal supporters of the New Deal state.[12]

The disagreement about postwar whites' motivations is rooted, I argue

here, in a conceptual assumption that informs most studies of racial conflict in the modern United States. Most commentators treat white racism
as something unchanging and as conceptually separable from other variables that fuel conflict between groups (including racial groups). Scholars
generally portray white racism as a static, though ill-defined, sentiment, an
irrational and misguided antipathy toward nonwhites. They depict white
people as either having racist views or not and describe those views as being expressed or acted upon in different degrees; some racist thoughts or
behaviors are thus more "intense" or "extreme" than others. White racism
after World War II, at least in the North, is usually portrayed as a less potent
and less prominent force than its early twentieth-century predecessor. The
postwar variant is cast alternatively as atavism or ideological relic: either as
a vestige of an intellectual tradition that (wrongly) described black people
as biologically inferior or, at best, as a remnant of a political order that
openly accepted and enforced racial hierarchy. As a result, racism is usually factored in as complementary to, and often secondary to, other points
of contention in postwar America. In most discussions of northern racial
conflict, a latent or lingering white racism resurfaces or is intensified when
other, discrete preoccupations create conflict between racial groups. Some
of these preoccupations are also described as purely ideological, such as
ideas about the family, citizenship, or the more indistinct category of rights.
Other preoccupations are assumed to have a strictly material basis, such as
jobs, or housing, or neighborhood turf. But all of these variables are treated
as conceptually discrete from racism, both in the minds of white people and
for the purpose of historical analysis.[13]

Studies of racial discrimination in New Deal–era housing programs,
for example, usually argue that policymakers and public officials were influenced by racial prejudice (their own and their constituents') but were
also attending to imperatives that had little if anything to do with race:
promoting economic growth, deferring to local authorities, and respecting
the free market for property.[14] The analytical separation of racial and nonracial variables also informs most work on white exclusionary politics after
1940. In case studies of urban, suburban, and workplace conflict, especially,
white racism ebbs and flows; sometimes it is influential, sometimes it is
not. And when racism does matter, it is an exogenous force with a discrete
origins story. Whites are often described as carrying preexisting antiblack
prejudices with them to their new neighborhoods; racism is transferred
from one locale to another, usually from city to suburb or from southern
states to the North. Upon arrival, these static racial antipathies complement
and inflect whites' responses to other pressing concerns, such as enforcing

neighborhood boundaries, maintaining control over local job markets, and above all else protecting property values.[15]

Largely missing from this important scholarship is an investigation of how whites' racial thinking itself changed during the years that the United States became a predominantly suburban and home-owning nation. Like many studies of the postwar metropolis, this book argues that race *did* matter—that whites' racial views and preferences continued to shape struggles over housing and neighborhoods in the 1940s, 1950s, and 1960s. But unlike most studies, it argues that whites' ideas about race were undergoing a fundamental transformation during these years. It explores an important facet of that transformation, by showing how whites grew deeply invested in new ideas about the relationship between race and property. And it argues that this new racial thinking was decisively shaped by the powerful new institutions and private practices that fueled postwar suburban growth while also successfully excluding most black people from its benefits. Rather than describe how other variables interacted with a presumably static white racism, I argue that white identity and white racism were being remade and that these changes were inextricably linked to a revolution in metropolitan political economy.

First, the study argues that whites' rationale for exclusion, that is, the language and logic used to talk about race and housing, was subtly but decisively transformed in a generation's time. Before World War II, most northern whites justified exclusion by invoking a mythical racial hierarchy, claiming that blacks made poor neighbors because they had little in common biologically and, contingent upon this, economically and culturally, with people of European descent. In the words of a Chicago property owners' group active in the 1910s and 1920s, for example, it was "heaven's first law" that whites and blacks live separately. By contrast, after World War II most northern whites justified racial exclusion by invoking what they viewed as nonracial variables: protecting the housing market, their rights as property owners and, linked to both, their rights as citizens. Whites still actively kept blacks out of their neighborhoods, yet insisted, and many apparently believed, that they were merely exercising what they described as the prerogatives of "homeowners," "property owners," and "law abiding citizens." They insisted that whites had a "constitutional right to private property, private attitudes, and personal privacy," as one Dearborn resident explained in 1963. By no means did older, biological myths disappear. But by the time that the mob gathered on Kendal Street in 1963, most whites insisted that their preference for homogeneous neighborhoods had little if anything to do with race per se—and certainly nothing to do with biological difference or racial hierarchies. They claimed to be driven solely by immutable and supposedly nonideological market considerations, in defense of their hard-earned rights as property owners, to choose their neighbors and protect their investments. Of course this claim, when voiced by all-white communities and directed against nonwhites, was still racist. But it was constituted very differently and thus operated very differently from earlier thinking about race. The study argues that whites' ideas about race were not a static, competing variable in postwar metropolitan politics but that whites altered the ways they thought about racial difference during these years and, thus, the ways they understood and acted upon their racial presumptions.

Inseparable from this shift in racial thinking was the means by which residential exclusion was achieved after the Great Depression. Most important, whites' efforts to exclude black people were now supported by and in crucial ways given form by a powerful new public-private alliance that facilitated and guided postwar economic growth. In a series of interventions that began before World War II but had their greatest impact after 1945, the federal government revolutionized both municipal land-use politics and the market for private homes. By standardizing and popularizing restrictive zoning and by creating a series of oversight, regulatory, and insurance programs for the private mortgage market, the state subsidized suburban growth and made it easier to exclude racial minorities, not just from white neighborhoods but also from a robust new market for private homeownership. Meanwhile federal interventions did more than simply structure opportunity; paradoxically, they also helped popularize the idea that government interventions were *not* providing considerable benefits to white people. Public officials, their private-sector allies, and even federal appraisal guidelines assured whites that state interventions neither made suburban growth possible nor helped segregate the fast-growing metropolis by race. They promoted the story that urban and suburban outcomes resulted solely from impersonal market forces. Not surprisingly, white homeowners, particularly in the suburbs, embraced this narrative and made it a central refrain in local debates about housing, race, and inequality. It was this story about market-driven growth and market-driven inequality that enabled countless white people to insist that their support for exclusion was not a racist act.

So in the final analysis, whites' responses to integration had changed significantly in the four decades and twelve miles that separated the incidents on Garland and Kendal streets. By the 1960s, white suburbanites were defending racial separation with an argument very different from that offered by their prewar predecessors. They had developed a new language for talking about race, property, and neighborhood integrity and were engaging in a new politics of race and rights firmly grounded in these new ideas. Their defense of exclusion had changed, in large part, because the federal government had grown so deeply involved in the economics and politics of metropolitan development. When Detroit whites attacked the Sweet family for crossing the city's residential color line in 1925, the state had little influence on land-use politics and the private market for homes. By the time that Dearborn's residents fought comparable battles in the 1960s, the state had been shaping zoning politics and mortgage markets for over three decades.

Much of the impact of the new federal role has been well documented and is quite tangible, even to this day. What has not been fully examined is how state interventions shaped whites' ideas about race, property, markets, and residential segregation. More than simply structuring development and opportunity in the postwar metropolis, federal policy helped transform the ways that countless white people understood the difference that race supposedly made. By the 1960s, far more white people were suburban dwellers and homeowners, changes that empowered them financially and politically. They lived in a newly fragmented metropolis where wealth was increasingly centered in the suburbs and in an era that increasingly viewed homeownership as a prerequisite for full citizenship. By 1960, whites not only talked differently about race and property but also believed what they were saying because their material investment in their homes was simultaneously foundational to a new kind of localized political power and a symbol of success, stability, and "Americanness" in the Cold War era. Whites' investment in homeownership bred a new kind of emotional and economic investment in their own racial privilege. The changing political economy of segregation helped give rise to a new white rationale for exclusion, popularizing new ideas about property, color, and rights that would have important implications for racial politics throughout the modern civil rights era and well beyond.

Comparing White Racisms

What does it mean to argue that whites' ideas about race changed during this era, that the nature of white racism itself was transformed? On one level, this book contributes to an investigation of how racial categories and racial identities are invented and reinvented over time. The book begins with an assumption—shared by scholars of "racial formation"—that race is not a fixed category.[16] Studies of racial formation are informed by both the physical and social sciences. Biologists and physical anthropologists have demonstrated that there is no genetically consistent measure of race: that the visible, hereditary physical traits generally associated with race in the modern world (skin color, facial features, hair texture) do not correspond to any kind of biologically discrete, unambiguously distinguishable human groupings. For example, we know that blood type, foot size, and a propensity for Tay-Sachs disease are heritable traits, as genetically significant as skin color or hair texture. But of course we do not recognize a "Type-AB" race or a "Small Foot" race or a "Tay-Sachs" race and, if we did, each one would be racially "mixed," by modern standards. Likewise if genetic distinctions separated people into discrete biological racial groups, then by definition women and men would belong to different races. The degree of genetic variation between any woman and any man is much greater than that between, say, an Asian man and a white man, or a black woman and a Native American woman.[17]

Just because race is a biological fiction, however, does not make the concept of race irrelevant. For hundreds of years people in the Western world have acted upon the assumption that perceived racial differences do matter and that some so-called racial groups are inherently superior to others. These assumptions have had a dramatic impact on the experience of populations identified along racial lines. Europeans created the modern concept of race during the Age of Exploration to justify the conquest of indigenous peoples in the Western Hemisphere and the expansion of the African slave trade. With the rise of the biological sciences in the eighteenth and nineteenth centuries, explicitly biological theories—Blumenbach's theory of human origins, phrenology, craniometry, eugenics, and others—codified prevailing assumptions about racial difference and hierarchy. So while race is not biologically real, a belief in racial distinctions and, eventually, a science of racial difference helped to justify centuries of discrimination, brutality, and enslavement.

Racial science was finally discredited by the 1930s, in most professional and academic circles. But race had mattered far too long in the United States for this intellectual revolution to erase popular memory, to dissolve communities that self-identified racially, or to undo centuries of race-based discrimination. White racial privilege and the degradation of people considered nonwhite had long been protected by institutions and by popular practice and was still enshrined in the law, reproduced by the class structure, and celebrated in white-produced popular culture. Meanwhile racial minorities in the United States had for generations associated their distinct cultural communities and traditions with people seen as members of their racial group, and regularly turned to those communities to sustain themselves in the face of discrimination and the threat of violence. So while biological race had been proven illusory, people remained invested in racial privileges and in communities long identified as having racial boundaries. Throughout the twentieth century, Americans were constantly reminded, whether they recognized it or not, that long-standing, perceived distinctions between racial groups shaped their behaviors, their social interactions, and their opportunities. To this day, historically constructed ideas about race continue to carry tremendous political, economic, and cultural power.[18]

This study of suburban politics and culture explores one chapter in the constant reinvention of racial meanings and reconfiguration of racial power, by examining how whites in the modern United States came to view the difference between white and black in large measure through the prism of property and neighborhoods. Scholars have demonstrated that the category of white has grown more and more inclusive in the nineteenth and twentieth centuries, now embracing populations once deemed racially different or suspect. As late as the 1930s, federal policy helped to integrate millions of European immigrants into the ever changing category of whiteness. Writers have also explored whites' "investment" in their racial privilege and the way it shaped their understanding of prosperity and inequality after World War II.[19] Whites have defended their identity (or in some cases adopted it) in large part because it pays. But I also argue that whites' assumptions about the meaning of racial difference changed significantly over the course of the twentieth century, that white people developed new ideas about what it meant to be white and how, precisely, nonwhites threatened them. As whites abandoned theories about biological difference and hierarchy, they embraced the argument that racial minorities simply threatened white-owned property. This shift occurred as a majority of whites became property owners for the first time, and as the politics that facilitated this process encouraged whites to view property and property ownership through a powerful but distorted racial lens. New ideas about race were largely born in and sustained by the politics of metropolitan change itself.

This study does not claim that postwar whites no longer held "racist" views. It argues that whites living in northern and western metropolitan areas reimagined the frame of whiteness, blackness, and racial difference and thus constructed new kinds of racism grounded in very different measures of difference. White suburbanites (and urbanites) still discriminated against blacks after World War II because they were black. However, whites increasingly believed that they were discriminating not because black people were inherently different but rather because black people—for whatever cultural or market-driven reason—posed a threat to communities of white property owners. Critically, the argument here is not that whites adopted an economic argument that merely disguised an unchanging, latent racism. Instead, the book demonstrates that the very language and assumptions of white racial thinking, and thus of white racism, were changing.

Nor does this study argue that older, biological myths were simply replaced by a new racial discourse. Those myths did not disappear overnight, and many persist to this day. This book explores how and why the new language about racial difference and racial threats gained currency, gradually supplanting the biological story in public and even private debates over property and neighborhoods. Whites grew invested during these years in a racially constructed vision of the metropolis, collapsing older myths about the permanence of racial difference into a set of powerful new ideas about neighborhoods and homes. This new narrative was significant because it allowed whites to address their racial preoccupations by talking about property instead of people. It was a conceptual move enabling them to claim that discrimination was not driven by personal prejudice, indeed that support for racial exclusion was not necessarily a racist act. Of course it still represented a racist worldview and whites' actions systematically discriminated against certain racial groups. But the language and assumptions were very different and, critically, whites believed what they were saying. Postwar whites did not simply disguise their racism by cloaking it in economic arguments or in a political discourse about property rights. They developed a new language about difference, about metropolitan economics, and about the politics of property that justified exclusion by a means that seemed genuinely nonracist.

―――――――

The history of white racial ideology in the twentieth century cannot be told solely by examining popular ideas about cities, suburbs, and property. But the focus is crucial, because of the remarkable transformations in patterns of metropolitan development, settlement, and tenancy. Between 1910 and 1970, most people in the United States either moved to or within a metropolitan region, often repeatedly. The residential color line remained firm (if shifting), first within the city center itself and then, as suburbs grew dramatically after World War II, between city and the suburb. Meanwhile millions of whites became homeowners for the first time. It was in the context of metropolitan growth, the resegregation of residence, and the birth of a "homeowners' nation" that most people of European descent negotiated both the demise of racial science and a civil rights revolution. They did so, in large measure, by making sense of how and where people lived. Of course the maintenance of racial boundaries in the United States has a long history. But by the 1940s white northerners were increasingly justifying segregation, specifically residential segregation, in a very novel way, abandoning claims about racial hierarchy for arguments about the free market for property.

This represented a stark contrast with the common claim before the Depression that racial segregation was "heaven's first law." Whites' preoccupation with residential exclusion arose in northern cities at the turn of the century and solidified during and after World War I. The migration of over one million southern African Americans to northern industrial centers put enormous strains on existing black communities, encouraging many families like the Sweets to seek housing in white neighborhoods. A popular response was the formation of local "property protective" associations, designed to prevent a "Negro invasion," as Chicago's Kenwood and Hyde Park Property Owners Association wrote in their newsletter, the *Property Owner's Journal*. These groups met regularly, distributed flyers, staged rallies, encouraged adoption of race-restrictive covenants, and constantly pressured both realtors and homeowners to reject black renters and buyers. Whites did not disguise their motivations. The racial integration of neighborhoods, according to the *Journal*, would defy the "laws of nature." "Keep the Negro in his place, amongst his people and he is healthy and loyal," it explained in 1920, but "remove him, or allow his newly discovered importance to remove him from his proper environment, and the Negro becomes a nuisance. He develops into an overbearing, inflated, irascible individual, overburdening his brain to such an extent about social equality that he becomes dangerous to all with whom he comes in contact." A *Chicago Tribune* commentary on black migrants complained about their "childlike helplessness in the matter of sanitation and housing," warned about their "promiscuous scattering," and insisted that blacks were "happiest when the white race asserts its superiority." After Chicago's race riot of 1918, a city commission asked whites to explain their hostility toward black people. "Niggers are different from whites and always will be," explained one interviewee, "and that is why white people don't want them around." "It is a fact recognized by science," noted another respondent, "that Negroes are so different from whites that the two races cannot be amalgamated."[20]

It was these sentiments that fueled the hostility to the Sweets or anyone who challenged Detroit's color line in the 1920s. When blacks were seen house-shopping in all-white neighborhoods, posters quickly blanketed the streets announcing neighborhood-association meetings and warning that black occupancy would threaten the "good health conditions and environment for . . . little children." The Ku Klux Klan boasted over twenty thousand members in Detroit by 1925 and was very active in local housing controversies (its mayoral candidate even stood a chance of winning in the fall elections). The all-white mobs that attacked the Sweets and other black families that summer spoke in the racial shorthand of the day. When Vollington Bristol and John Fletcher attempted to occupy their homes, they faced mobs of 2,000 and 4,000 people, respectively, and listened to whites challenge each other to "move these niggers out" or to "lynch him." Black renters were run out of these neighborhoods, accused of having "more privileges than [they were] entitled to." Jurors at the Sweet trial spoke this language too. "I don't give a God damn what the facts are," announced one member upon learning that the judge declared a mistrial. "A nigger has killed a white man and I'll be burned in hell before I will ever vote to acquit a nigger who has killed a white man." At times racial presumptions and contempt were expressed more subtly. The white-owned *Free Press*, for example, described Ossian Sweet's trial testimony as "raised to scientific level above his fellows by his training," although "his mind was a bit awkward and did not jump as fast as the prosecutor's, so he had to be straightened out at times."[21]

Whites' preoccupation with biological difference and hierarchy did not preclude the emergence of other, complementary narratives about race. These years saw the birth of an alternative theory about the threat posed by black occupancy, one that focused not on race but on economics. It was first articulated formally in the 1910s, when real estate developers and economists, in an effort to gain professional legitimacy for their fields, began standardizing the guidelines governing appraisal and construction practices. All-white real estate boards became fixtures in most major cities, and their members began to outline and codify what they saw as commonsense rules about race and property. In doing so they began to cast racial exclusion as a purely economic or market imperative. Already by 1917, when the Chicago Real Estate Board (CREB) announced a campaign to organize "owners societies in every white block for the purpose of mutual defense," it insisted that realtors were dealing with "a financial business proposition and not with white prejudice." Three years later CREB called for the expulsion of "any member who rented or sold property on a white block to black people," and in 1924 the National Association of Real Estate Brokers (NAREB) added a clause to its Code of Ethics forbidding members from introducing into a neighborhood "members of any race or nationality" whose presence "will clearly be detrimental to property values." NAREB's code was authored by their general counsel, Nathan William MacChesney, who three years later outlined the economic rationale for racial exclusion in *Principles of Real Estate Law*.[22] MacChesney's work was one of several influential publications that would eventually transform the rules governing real estate brokerage and residential property markets.

But this new "market imperative" argument for exclusion was still a novelty in the 1920s that at best complemented a far more commonplace narrative about blacks' fundamental racial incompatibility. The biological story was so powerful that CREB representatives continued to invoke it when speaking to church groups, social clubs, and property owners' associations about the importance of protecting white neighborhoods; they warned that black activists were attempting to "settl[e] a negro family in every block in the city," which would make Chicago a "mecca" of racial mixing. The *Property Owners' Journal* regularly accused blacks of "damag[ing] a man's property and destroy[ing] its value" but insisted that it was biology, in the final analysis, that created the incompatibility. "There is nothing in the make-up of a Negro, physically or mentally," the *Journal* explained in 1920, "which should induce anyone to welcome him as a neighbor." Blacks were "as proud as peacocks, but have nothing of the peacock's beauty," the *Journal* continued. "The best of them are insanitary" and "ruin alone follows in their path." "Niggers are undesirable neighbors and entirely irresponsible and vicious." Meanwhile, in Detroit, race-restrictive covenants defined a "Negro" as any person with "1/8 or more Negro blood." Even Richard T. Ely, regarded as the father of the young field of land-use economics, attributed the impoverishment of black Americans to racial variables. White prejudice played a role, Ely conceded in his textbook *Outlines of Economics*, but equally important was the "economic inertia and shiftlessness of the negroes themselves."[23]

By 1963, when Dearborn residents attacked Giuseppe Stanzione's house on Kendal Street, the language and logic of northern white housing politics had changed quite dramatically. In both public and private forums, whites who defended racial exclusion seldom spoke about biology or racial hierarchy. These traditional racial discourses were overshadowed by a language that openly endorsed segregation while claiming to rise above racism or above ideological or personal preferences of any kind. Typical was a letter from a self-described "housewife and mother," written in 1965 to thank Dearborn's mayor for his support of segregation, yet insisting that her family had moved to the community years earlier "not because of the negroes" but rather because it was a "beautiful clean safe city." She was one of the hundreds of whites from the Detroit region and from cities and suburbs nationwide who contacted Hubbard after the Kendal Street affair to applaud his "stand in [the] Labor Day episode." These correspondents rarely self-identified as white and rarely mentioned race at all. They described themselves as "homeowners," "citizens," and "parents." They assured the mayor that "Dearborn property owners back you all the way." Local insurance agents, builders, and realtors also praised the city's response to the Kendal Street violence, usually without mentioning race or black people. Instead they pointed to facts they "all know," as one Detroit insurance agent noted: that integration would threaten their "home values," and that "do-gooders have nothing to lose as they do not own their own homes."[24]

Notably, when whites' conversations about exclusion *did* mention race, the focus was not on black people per se but rather on property and the rights of people who owned it. "We all know what will happen if [the white sections] are integrated," wrote one Detroiter just days after the Kendal Street attack, predicting "that our home values will drop up to fifty percent." Suburbanites were committed to racial restriction, explained a Dearborn resident, solely to ensure that "property values remain high . . . and neighborhoods stay together in peace." Advocates of racial exclusion regularly used the terms "homeowner," "citizen," "voter," and "white" interchangeably, but then insisted that it was their status as property-owning citizens, not as white people, that afforded them special prerogatives and protections. They thanked the mayor and the Dearborn police for "defend[ing] the rights of citizens" and "upholding [residents'] civil rights." They complained that they were hearing too much about "the rights of Negroes" instead of "our rights." One self-identified "Citizen" criticized Kennedy's fair housing executive order, issued in 1962, by asking if whites were "to be sheep or free people." Then he signed off with what had become, by the time of the Kendal Street affair, a familiar declaration of support for racial exclusion: "Remember," he told the mayor, "all the people who own homes are with you."[25]

And because this narrative focused on property and its privileges—because it claimed *not* to be about race per se—it enabled whites to defend segregation and even to dismiss civil rights protest while claiming to be nonracist. Throughout the postwar decades, whites defended residential exclusion while insisting that it had nothing to do with prejudice and that they had no intent, as one white Detroiter wrote in 1964, to deny anyone their "ordinary rights under the constitution."[26] By the time the modern civil rights movement became a prominent national issue for white people, most northern whites had long collapsed myths about racial character and privilege into a story about the supposed democratization of property ownership and black people's failure to obey the rules of the market. This story celebrated homeownership in general and suburban homeownership in particular, rather than naming it "white privilege." And it warned of the threat posed by racial integration or by federal intervention on behalf of minorities, rather than focusing on black people. Thus it enabled whites to resist important facets of the civil rights revolution while still claiming, quite earnestly, that they did not believe in blacks' inherent inferiority; indeed it enabled them to support segregation without discussing their feelings about black people. Rather than focusing on blacks' abilities or the threat of "mongrelization," whites were now asserting their rights as property holders and responsible neighbors, juxtaposing this to what they described as blacks' unwarranted demands. Rhetorically, at least, whites focused not on the threat that black people posed to white people but on the threat that blacks' presence posed to white-owned property, white neighborhoods, and other supposedly white "places."

Nor can it be emphasized enough that during the postwar decades this story about race and property was a very public and widely accepted one among metropolitan whites, for reasons that the following chapters explore in some detail. This story was discussed among federal housing officials and private developers, realtors and bankers, planners and city council members, homeowners and prospective homeowners. In 1963, it enabled a white housing activist in Detroit to assert, without apology, that racial exclusion was the "inherent right" of the city's "honorable, long-established property owners groups." Open occupancy was "not a moral question," argued another activist in 1964, but rather "political and economic." In 1965 this narrative prompted a white New Yorker to write Orville Hubbard with praise for Dearborn's approach to racial issues. Like so many whites, this man asserted his racial progressivism—he "wish[ed] the negro people a better way of life"—but had resigned himself to the fact that blacks simply "live for today." They never "pool . . . their money to help their own," he explained, or to "start . . . some business" or "build . . . something to call attention to their ability." Blacks had ample opportunity to improve their condition, he insisted, but they unfortunately "have little ambition for that." "They do not care for their home or possessions like most others do and they see nothing wrong with that and resent anything said about it too."[27]

The postwar decades saw most northern whites argue that the American metropolis was segregated and unequal not because blacks were inferior, but because they were unable or unwilling to play by the rules of the marketplace. The debate over integration, whites insisted, no longer turned on questions about race, ideology, or personal preference. What counted was a person's relationship to places and to property, and a person's ability to function properly in what was assumed to be a free market for both. Of course the more traditional kinds of race talk did not disappear from neighborhood politics. Many northern whites continued to focus on what they saw as blacks' character or propensities, and some even continued to invoke a scientific defense for segregation. But they represented a fast-dwindling minority during these decades, certainly in the public debates over residential exclusion but also in those private and informal conversations that have been preserved in the historical record. Replacing the older narrative was a multilayered, and racially coded, story about homeownership and private property, and about the need to protect the vibrant market that had made suburban growth and affluence possible.

This subtle shift in language is critically important to our understanding of postwar racial politics. Starting with the premise that all Americans competed freely in an unrestricted market for housing and neighborhoods, whites concluded that they had consistently demonstrated their ability to own, maintain, and protect the value of homes in that market, particularly in the nation's fast-growing suburban fringe. And because of this, they concluded, whites had the right to protect their investments, their families, and their communities from any kind of threat. Whites had the right, they insisted, both to choose their neighbors and to be free from government interventions that might interfere with the market mechanisms that had allowed them to prosper. Whites now claimed that what distinguished them from black people was their ability to take care of their neighborhoods, to become responsible, home-owning citizens without asking for "government handouts." They concluded that white people, in sharp contrast to racial minorities, functioned quite capably in a robust, free market for residence, an argument reflecting their fundamental misunderstanding of the forces driving metropolitan change.

An important source of this narrative can be found, paradoxically, in the politics and policy interventions of an era that still embraced biological interpretations of racial difference. Planners, economists, federal officials, and businesspeople began articulating this "market imperative" argument in the decades before World War II. During and after the Great Depression, the federal government codified and disseminated the market rationale for exclusion, and metropolitan whites embraced and elaborated upon it. By Labor Day weekend of 1963, the market imperative story was so well rehearsed and so deeply institutionalized that it provided a ready vocabulary for men and women fearful of what black occupancy would do to their neighborhoods, their families, and their investments. It was an argument for exclusion quite distinct from the one used by the white mob that chased eleven black people off Garland Street in 1925. It was an argument that by the 1960s had helped give rise to a radically new politics of racial privilege, enabling countless people of European descent to redefine the measures and the terms of racial difference.

The Local Case Study: Metropolitan Detroit

Commentators regularly note that the whites who filled the post–World War II suburbs vigilantly defended their neighborhoods and their privileges because both were so novel. Millions of white families were finally enjoying a comfort level and partaking in a lifestyle formerly reserved for the affluent. Thus residents celebrated the suburbs and jealously guarded its spoils because these places offered so much and seemed to hold so much promise. There is considerable truth to this characterization. After the war, suburbs did become more affordable and accessible. Rising incomes, cheaper construction costs, easy credit, and the automobile together enabled a much broader cross-section of whites to become homeowners, and the homes available for purchase were almost exclusively detached, relatively spacious single-family dwellings. During these decades the United States became a nation in which most whites owned their homes, in which a plurality of whites lived in the suburbs, and in which most whites considered themselves to be middle class. For countless people of European descent, prosperity (or even economic stability) and suburban life were increasingly seen as inseparable.

But scholars generally assume that it was the novelty of suburban living—its unique spaces, geography, housing, and amenities—that shaped whites' views about the privileges, racial or otherwise, associated with suburban residence. Most accounts describe whites moving to communities physically separated from the central city (often simply carved out of farmland) and physically quite different from the city as well. Aerial photographs of Levittown and pictures of ranch-style homes regularly appear in histories of postwar suburbanization, suggesting that curvilinear streets, public parks, and community centers created a new kind of residential environment,[28] one that shaped social attitudes and eventually political loyalties.[29] Scholars have long shown that early suburban development was in fact far more heterogeneous.[30] Nevertheless, most histories describe whites as settling in geographically and architecturally unique places, most often modern, spacious, and isolated bedroom communities, a characterization that has had important implications for scholars' assumptions about the links between suburbanization and whites' antiblack sentiments. Whites' resistance to integration is often depicted as an understandable sort of reflex action, an attempt to defend their unique, insulated communities from the minorities who had supposedly destroyed the old neighborhood and now threatened the new one. Suburban places, themselves, are assumed to physically manifest whites' new privilege and sense of security.[31]

The story of whites' exodus to suburban Detroit certainly supports important parts of this argument but also challenges one of its core assumptions: that the new suburban havens were always physically and architecturally distinct from the city that whites were leaving behind. Most of Detroit's early suburban development took place in neighborhoods just across the municipal border and often indistinguishable from the city itself. This suggests that place, alone, did not determine whites' views about race and residence. It suggests that the content of local politics played an equally important role in shaping ideas about the distinctiveness of any neighborhood that was populated by white people.

No urban or suburban place is prototypical, and Detroit's history made the region's postwar expansion and politics unique. Most influential was the city's dependence on and association with heavy industry. Detroit's strategic location along regional trade routes and its proximity to iron ore and coal deposits enabled it to dominate early automobile production and to emerge by 1920 as the center of an extremely powerful national industry. Detroit's steel mills, foundries, engine plants, and assembly lines made it a natural center of war-materials production in the early 1940s and thus a magnet for migrant workers, both black and white. Early postwar industrial expansion, much of it in the near suburbs, continued to draw workers and their families to the region. Along with other northern industrial cities, Detroit had long been a destination for migrant African Americans, and the percentage of blacks in the city rose dramatically after World War II. Finally, Detroit was home to a well-organized industrial workforce, and, to many, it was an important symbol of labor's militancy and triumph during the New Deal. Union members were heavily represented in the new suburban subdivisions that took shape after World War II. Unions had a prominent voice in local and regional politics, so they often shaped laborers' responses to racial conflict, even when it was not centered on the shop floor.[32]

Yet in the realms of suburban growth, racial inequality, and neighborhood racial politics, the region's uniqueness was in many ways overshadowed by what it shared with other metropolitan areas, particularly once New Deal policy introduced so much consistency to suburban and urban development patterns nationwide. The Detroit region underwent demographic, geographic, political, and economic transformations repeated in dozens of northern and western metropolitan centers during the 1940s, 1950s, and 1960s. The resultant patterns of growth, relocation, and racial inequality looked familiar to metropolitan residents nationwide.

First, the class divide between whites and blacks, already sharp before 1940, remained so throughout the war and early postwar years. Detroit's industrial prowess created unprecedented opportunities for blacks, and yet most were restricted to less secure and less skilled jobs, and most were excluded from white-collar and better-paying service positions. (In the mid-1950s, for example, fifteen of Detroit's largest department stores simply refused to hire blacks for sales positions.) Making matters worse, after World War II the nation's major industrial firms began simultaneously to disinvest in domestic production facilities and to relocate many of the plants that they did maintain. Detroit's industrial employment sector, like that of most Rust Belt cities, was quickly undermined by the regional mobility of capital and by federal investments (in transportation, research and development, and the military) that further decentralized the nation's economic activity. By the late 1950s, plant closures and relocations (usually to the suburbs or the South) eliminated thousands of jobs in Detroit, including positions that had only recently enabled countless black families to rise out of poverty. By 1963, 134,000 manufacturing jobs had fled the city. As both industry and people headed to the suburbs, retailers and commercial enterprises followed. As early as 1947, Detroit was already losing jobs in the retail and wholesale sectors. In 1958, 66 percent of the region's retail sales took place in the city, and 34 percent in the suburbs. Five years later only 38 percent were urban and 62 percent suburban, and by 1972 urban sales made up 20 percent of the regional total.[33]

Most white people were relocating to the suburbs as well. One of the most powerful forces accentuating racial and class inequality was the physical and demographic expansion of the suburban fringe itself, and the primary motor of this growth was the construction and sale of new housing. After 1945, Detroit's suburbs grew very, very quickly. Flush with government-insured mortgage financing, small builders filled the empty lots of existing subdivisions with single-family homes and constructed thousands more on formerly unimproved land. For a low monthly mortgage payment, an economically stable white family could purchase a new, modern home on a private lot, in a neighborhood marketed as a respite from city life. The flurry of construction activity was spectacular. Between 1940 and 1950, the number of dwelling units in Royal Oak City increased by 277 percent, from 6,500 to about 13,240. By 1960, over 70 percent of the city's homes had been built since 1940 and the population had more than tripled. Dearborn had 16,477 dwelling units in 1940 and 35,063 in 1960, while the population increased from 63,584 to 112,007.[34]

Again mirroring a national trend, the vast majority of these new suburban houses were detached, single-family units owned and occupied by white people. About 93 percent of the new homes built in Royal Oak during the 1940s were detached, single-family dwellings. In Dearborn, the percentage of single-family units rose from 56.7 percent of all dwellings in 1940, to 68.6 percent in 1950, to 79.1 percent in 1960. Only 55.3 percent of Dearborn's housing units were owner-occupied in 1940, but they accounted for 74.5 percent by 1950 and 78.2 percent by 1960. Between 1940 and 1950, Royal Oak's rate of ownership increased from 61.7 percent to 85.7 percent, Berkley's rose from 71.8 percent to 91.1 percent, and Ferndale's rose from 65.9 percent to 84.3 percent. Comparable changes were recorded in most of the Detroit suburbs and in first-tier suburbs nationwide. Each year between 1935 and 1960, between 78.4 percent and 84.5 percent of the nation's housing starts were detached, single-family homes, the lion's share of them privately owned in suburban communities that remained almost exclusively white.[35] In 1968, sixteen of the Detroit region's most affluent suburbs had no black homeowners, and most of the remaining communities had miniscule black populations.[36] The racial segregation of both space and housing equity in metropolitan Detroit suggests how an oft-cited figure—the increase in national homeownership rates from 44 percent in 1934 to 63 percent in 1969—obscures an important racial imbalance. Between 1940 and 1960, the rate of homeownership increased from 45.7 percent to 64.4 percent among whites but from 23.7 percent to 38.4 percent among blacks. Meanwhile blacks owned homes in segregated neighborhoods (both urban and suburban) and a segregated real estate market, property deemed unsalable in the far larger and federally secured market for "white" property.[37]

The people joining the "white" exodus to suburban Detroit were a very heterogeneous lot, at least by pre–World War II standards. Before the Great Depression, first- and second-generation immigrants from eastern and southern Europe, who provided much (often most) of the workforce in major industrial centers, were viewed as a threat to so-called "native" white populations. In most regions they were excluded from both working-class and middle-class urban neighborhoods and from the small, but growing, suburban fringe. Restrictive covenants in Detroit, for example, forbade occupancy by anyone not of the "Gentile and Caucasian race" (such as Jews and Armenians). Nationwide, most Poles, Hungarians, Italians, and Jews remained clustered, by a combination of choice and necessity, in urban, ethnic neighborhoods. The barriers against neighborhood integration did not come down during the Depression.[38] In 1939, when federal appraisers assessed the marketability of immigrant enclaves in Detroit and its near suburbs, they judged most to be risky investments, at best. There was "little possibility of reversal" in the Polish-dominated northwestern section of Dearborn, according to the agent who surveyed the region. Detroit neighborhoods shared by immigrants and blacks (usually in a ratio of about four to one) were rated as unmarketable, in part because of the "grade of residents" who lived there, including the "aliens who not speak English."[39]

Yet in the 1940s, the nation's suburbs embraced and actively welcomed a much broader range of "white" people. Suburban growth helped confirm the whiteness of the "new" European immigrants. Consider the ethnic heterogeneity of Detroit's postwar suburbs. By 1960, the U.S. Bureau of the Census counted 42.5 percent of Dearborn's population as "foreign stock," meaning that they were either foreign born or had foreign or "mixed" parentage. This category described 30 percent of the residents in Royal Oak, 49.8 percent in Oak Park, 33.9 percent in Ferndale, and 29.7 percent in Livonia. Like suburbs nationwide, these communities hosted ethnic mixtures that had been unimaginable in most places during the 1920s and, remarkably, that were deemed financially risky at the outbreak of World War II. By 1960, Oak Park's "foreign stock" included northern and western Europeans but was dominated by people claiming ancestry in Poland, Czechoslovakia, Austria, Hungary, the Soviet Union, and Italy. The largest groups in Dearborn were Polish and Italians, followed by people who traced their heritage to Germany, Syria, Russia, Rumania, Hungary, Austria, Yugoslavia, Czechoslovakia, Ireland, Greece, Lithuania, and Mexico.[40]

Finally, Detroit's suburbs share with many others a lesser-known similarity—a similar geographical, planning, and architectural history—that has received comparatively little attention in the scholarship on postwar America, particularly in studies of white resistance to integration.[41] In the region's fastest growing suburbs, most neighborhoods bore little if any resemblance to the ranch-home ideal rehearsed in postwar magazines and long debated by experts and academics. Instead, most of Detroit's early suburban pioneers lived in relatively small, cottage-style homes, on small lots, and in neighborhoods of gridiron streets designed before World War II. Many lived in places physically indistinguishable from nearby neighborhoods in Detroit, just across the municipal border.

The region's first wave of postwar construction and settlement was centered in the "first-generation" suburbs of Royal Oak, Dearborn, Ferndale, Oak Park, Berkley, Hazel Park, Madison Heights, and Clawson, communities very close or adjacent to Detroit (fig. 1.1).[42] Most of their residen-

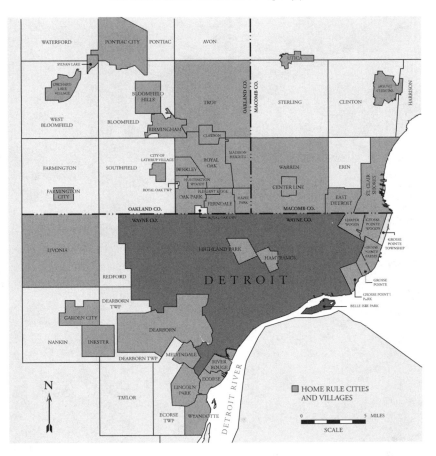

1.1 The Detroit Metropolitan Area, 1955. By the end of 1955, most of Detroit's near suburbs had incorporated as home-rule municipalities. Wayne County municipalities to the east or west of Detroit are referred to as "out-Wayne suburbs." Map by Jason Frank.

tial subdivisions had been platted during a wave of real estate speculation between 1915 and 1926, that saw investors carve up Detroit's immediate hinterland. Those investors designed neighborhoods suited to the era, when the market for private housing was comparatively small and buyers had far different expectations. Relatively few people could afford to purchase a prebuilt house before World War II. Most of these buyers were constrained by the prohibitive terms of debt financing and, finally, most sought homes close to downtown jobs, recreation, and services. So speculators platted gridiron-style subdivisions filled with 30- to 45-foot wide lots, just large enough to accommodate the modest, affordable bungalow-style homes popular after World War I (fig. 1.2). Proximity to the central city

1.2 Aerial photograph of Dearborn, Michigan, August 28, 1925. Much of the land in Detroit's near suburbs was purchased by speculators and subdivided in the 1920s. Most of the homes intended for these subdivisions, however, were not built until the 1940s or later. This survey photograph shows a section of southwest Dearborn, south of Michigan Avenue (running east-west at the top of the image) between South Military and Nowlin streets. South Military is at the right, running two blocks north-south before turning to the southeast. It would eventually be extended northward to intersect with Michigan Ave. Nowlin intersects with Michigan Ave. at the left, then runs south before turning southeast. One of the streets laid out in the southwestern corner was not developed. A park occupies most of that two-block area today. Aerial Surveys, Inc., Cleveland, Ohio. Courtesy of the Dearborn Historical Museum, Dearborn, Michigan.

was a selling point, so developers marketed properties with the promise of easy access, by automobile or streetcar, to "the greatest of [Detroit's] west side industries." Promoters in Ferndale, Pleasant Ridge, Royal Oak, and Berkely offered buyers "all the advantages of a suburban home—coupled with extreme accessibility." The builders of Eastwood Gardens, at Eight Mile Road and Gratiot Avenue (literally adjacent to Detroit), invited people to "Drive Out Today" to inspect "Homesites 40 × 120, Carefully Restricted."[43]

The speculative craze soon ended and boom turned to bust, leaving most of these lots undeveloped throughout the Depression. By the late 1930s New Deal mortgage programs had spurred a modest revival in suburban construction but had meanwhile created other problems for developers. As early as 1938, the Michigan Planning Commission worried that Detroit's existing suburban subdivisions could not accommodate the large-lot housing (requiring lot widths of 50 or more feet) recommended by FHA appraisal guidelines "as a standard minimum for residence purposes." Most of the region's suburban lots were narrow and undeveloped, leading the Commission to conclude that they would "inevitably become . . . obsolete and unsalable as time goes on." A year later, federal appraisers described much of the existing development in Dearborn, Oak Park, Berkely, Ferndale, and other near suburbs as "small housing of mediocre design and construction."[44]

When postwar conditions created a flush market for suburban housing, and eventually made larger homes on larger lots affordable (and more fashionable), local builders found themselves constrained by a prewar land-use schema. But they constructed new homes regardless, defying planners' predictions, because it was easier and far less expensive to build in preapproved subdivisions (rather than submit new plats for approval) and because for many years most homebuyers were still seeking fairly modest accommodations. After 1945, developers filled existing suburban plats with thousands of small, cottage-style homes, like those built in the western and northern sections of Detroit before the war (fig. 1.3). Detroit and its near suburbs share a flat, glacial plain that stretches northward and westward from the Detroit River, and so the division between the city's outermost residential neighborhoods, already dominated by single-family homes, and the new "suburban" subdivisions that cropped up after 1945 was purely jurisdictional, and in most cases invisible to the human eye.[45]

The layout of the new suburban neighborhoods mirrored that across the municipal border, with new housing units arrayed on rows of narrow, parallel streets that divided each neighborhood into a uniform grid. Typical was the postwar development of Section 18 in Berkley, bounded by Eleven Mile Road, Greenfield Road, Twelve Mile Road, and Coolidge

1.3 Aerial photograph of Dearborn, ca. 1965. By the late 1960s, most of the land zoned for residential development in Dearborn had been built up. This photograph shows Michigan Avenue, heading west. The first cross street in the foreground is Oakwood Boulevard. Four blocks west is the intersection with South Military, which by this time has been extended to Michigan Ave. (compare fig. 1.2). Courtesy of the Dearborn Historical Museum, Dearborn, Michigan.

Highway. The homes built there after World War II were in subdivision plats recorded no later than 1928. The units in the Brookline Hills subdivision, for example, sat on a grid of 40-foot wide lots approved by the Royal Oak Township Board in April 1916. This pattern was repeated throughout these communities, giving rise to neighborhoods that boasted few of the design features and amenities associated with high-profile, automobile-oriented developments like the Levittowns or Park Forest, Illinois. Some sections of Detroit's first-generation suburbs looked "classically" suburban, with larger lots and curvilinear streets. But while the national median for single-family suburban lots in 1950 was 11,100 square feet, in Detroit's near suburbs a typical lot measured 40 by 120 feet, or 4,800 square feet.[46] Few newcomers to Royal Oak, Dearborn, or Ferndale lived in homes resembling the expansive and sprawling ranch style designs celebrated in builders magazines, home-design columns, and child-rearing magazines. Only a small minority benefited from the cul-de-sacs and judicious street planning that kept automobile and truck traffic away from homes in more modern, isolated subdivisions.

While there would eventually be more housing choices, and more "classic" suburban development, in the region's second-generation suburbs, most of this construction was a long way off. Early postwar development in places like Troy and Southfield generally created more of the gridiron style neighborhoods familiar to Royal Oak and Ferndale.[47] Meanwhile the lion's share of postwar construction and most of the region's early battles over race and property were centered in the first-generation suburbs. In many cases, mobilizations to exclude blacks or apartment construction took place in subdivisions that bordered Detroit on Eight Mile Road or Tireman Street (which marked Dearborn's northernmost border with Detroit). Suburban residents fighting to protect the homogeneity of their new neighborhoods often lived in places indistinguishable, at least physically and architecturally, from the Detroit neighborhoods that many had recently left behind. At times they fought to protect their suburban havens from so-called urban neighborhoods that were only blocks away and sometimes literally across the street.

This fact did not stop whites from describing and imagining their new communities as distinct, uniquely suburban places that had little in common with Detroit. And this paradox is important for considering the history of whites' investment in ideas about property, neighborhoods, and racial prerogatives. Whites' enthusiasm for suburban living in the postwar era must be seen not simply as a function of living in new kinds of communities but also in light of the ways that whites constructed their ideas about what makes a place suburban at all. The design and physical appearance of so many first-generation suburbs suggest that whites turned elsewhere to convince themselves of the distinctiveness of their new neighborhoods. The map of metropolitan Detroit suggests that suburban political culture, not simply suburban geography, architecture, and amenities, played a crucial role in shaping whites' ideas about the racial character of the places where they lived.

———————

Construction figures and rates of population growth tell an important story but do not capture the everyday drama of suburban expansion, the ways that development constantly unfolded before peoples' eyes. For decades after 1945, residents of Royal Oak, Ferndale, Dearborn, or Oak Park watched as empty lots on their streets were finally filled with new houses, and as entire

Break Ground for First House in Low Cost Home Project

A feature of the low cost project will be varied exterior design. These sketches by Richard B. Pollman, designer, show three of the choices available. All the houses will be completely finished on the exterior, but these will be four choices as to the degree of interior finish depending on how much the purchaser wants to pay and if he wants to do any of the work himself.

10   THE DAILY TRIBUNE
                                Friday, September 10, 1948

1.4 An article, "Break Ground for First House in Low Cost Home Project," in the *Daily Tribune*, September 10, 1948. By the late 1940s, developers were constructing dozens of new subdivisions of modest single-family homes in Detroit's first-generation suburbs. Participating in the groundbreaking for this development of 100 "low cost" homes in Royal Oak were George Duke, president of the Metropolitan Builders Association; William B. Grabendike of the Veterans Administration; N. J. Quickstad, the project's chief builder; Arvid C. Peterson, project general chairman; Henry Fett, project vice chairman; E. M. Schafter, Royal Oak's city manager; and George Zinkey, state director of the Federal Housing Administration. Reprinted with permission of *The Daily Tribune*, Royal Oak, Michigan. Photographed by Ken Music.

new subdivisions—neighborhoods that resembled their own—rose up on land which had for years lain unimproved. The rapid disappearance of open space was most striking to long-time residents, many of whom had settled there decades earlier to farm or simply to enjoy a rural lifestyle. A third-generation Southfield woman later recalled how men and women who had "known everyone" in their township as children in the 1910s, 1920s, and 1930s then watched, after World War II, as "farmland," "sky," and "water" were "cut into [the] lots" that gave rise to countless new neighborhoods. Yet even postwar arrivals could not count on the preservation of the status quo and watched as undeveloped land adjacent to their subdivision gave rise to yet another neighborhood of single-family homes. "Many of you, I know,

—Tribune Staff Photo

Representatives of the Metropolitan Builders association of Detroit, the city and school district attended
ground breaking ceremonies for the first of a 100-home project in Maplecrest subdivision, Royal Oak.
Shown are George Duke, association president, William B. Grabendike, Veterans administration, N. J.
Quickstad, Arvid C. Petersen, builder and general chairman of the project; Henry Fett, vice chairman; City
Manager E. M. Shafter, and George Zinkey, FHA state director.

1.4 (Continued)

have had the same experience that I have," wrote Philip Miller, editor of the
South Oakland County *Daily Tribune*, in 1954. "Twice within 15 years I have
built, not far from the center of Royal Oak, a home on what was at the time
a 'woods road,' a narrow dirt road with trees and woods on each side. In no
time at all the open spaces had vanished and new homes had sprung up all
around us until not a vacant lot was left . . . We have started out living 'in the
country,' so to speak, and ended up very soon in a highly built-up area. That's
true of almost any place in South Oakland county."[48] Construction was everywhere, as if it were a permanent condition of suburban life. Residents
were the daily witnesses to the improvement of undeveloped land. In newer
suburbs like Hazel Park, the "swamps and open ditches that once disposed
of sewage" disappeared. And even in more established suburbs like Royal
Oak, the morning drive to school or work might be interrupted one day by
municipal workers digging an eighteen-foot-deep ditch for a new "modern
disposal system." Throughout the region, a trip to the market might reveal
that foundations were finally being laid on a neighboring residential block,
while the commute to or from work afforded daily progress reports on the
platting of a new subdivision, the paving of a county road, or completion
of a retail strip in a neighboring suburb.[49]

Or on a weekend drive a family might witness a very different kind of
mob scene: white people flocking to preview the homes in a new residential

subdivision. A typical episode occurred in February 1949, when the Builder's Association of Metropolitan Detroit announced an open house for the first units of a development of one hundred homes in northwest Royal Oak. They broke ground the previous fall, and since then the project had featured prominently in news coverage of local efforts to solve the city's dire housing shortage (fig. 1.4). Finally open for viewing, the model homes showcased exciting new features, including a "reverse-circulation" heating system (the builder's innovation) and an "expansible" design, meaning that as a family grew, it could add rooms without compromising the unit's design or structural integrity. The homes were affordable, ranging in price from $4,900 to $8,500, and were FHA-approved. The public response was overwhelming. On one Sunday alone, according to local news coverage, as many as 2,000 people "brave[d] the mud of Normandy Road, east of Woodward Avenue, at the Thirteen and One-Half Mile Road, to get a good look at the low-cost homes." The 100 units sold almost immediately.[50]

Growth was everywhere in metropolitan Detroit in the decades after World War II. And most of the region's white residents believed that enjoyment of this growth and the prosperity it embodied was their racial prerogative. The following chapters explain how the national and local politics of suburban development encouraged many people of European descent to see not only their neighborhoods but even their status as home-owning citizens in these distorted yet persuasive terms.

Overview of the Study

This book is divided into two parts, the first an examination of national development politics and the second a study of local politics in Royal Oak, Dearborn, and similar communities in suburban Detroit. Together, the two sections explore how the national and local politics of exclusion constantly interacted with, built upon, and reinforced one another to shape white people's understanding of metropolitan growth and racial privilege.

Part I: The Political Economy of Suburban Development and the Race of Economic Value, 1910–1970

The chapters of part I examine how the rise of municipal zoning and the creation of the modern mortgage market shaped patterns of suburban growth and the content of suburban politics. They demonstrate that federal involvement in both the zoning and mortgage revolutions spurred three closely related metropolitan transformations, which together helped revolutionize racial politics in the modern United States. First, federal initiatives and policies fueled the resegregation of the nation's metropolitan regions by race and by wealth. The federal government was instrumental in standardizing and promoting a restrictive zoning doctrine that empowered homeowners to exclude "incompatible" development and populations from their communities. And New Deal–era selective credit programs created and subsidized a powerful new mortgage market that made suburban growth and widespread homeownership possible, but for whites only. Together the zoning and mortgage revolutions ensured that after World War II, the nation's housing and development resources would be concentrated in the suburban fringe, in independent municipalities exercising considerable control over land use and populated almost exclusively by white homeowners.

Second, state interventions helped popularize a new rationale for the exclusion of minorities from the fast-growing suburbs. Through its involvement in both zoning and mortgage politics, the federal government put considerable force behind the theory that racial segregation was driven not by white racism but by economic necessity, that exclusion was a "market imperative," required solely by the principles of land-use science. This argument was not new to the postwar era. But federal involvement made it constitutive of a new metropolitan political economy, one in which suburban growth and new patterns of racial separation depended on easy, federally subsidized credit. Government participation in the mortgage industry made the market imperative argument the primary and in most cases the sole explanation among whites, be they federal officials, judges, bankers, realtors, or individual homeowners, for demanding the racial segregation of neighborhoods. Not coincidentally, this shift occurred as older narratives about racial hierarchy and biological difference were being challenged and, eventually, abandoned by most white people.

Finally, federal interventions were instrumental in popularizing a powerful and quite paradoxical myth: that neither suburban growth nor new patterns of racial inequality owed anything to the state's efforts. The federal government insisted that the new metropolitan order was a product of unregulated free-market activity. Public leaders (and their allies in the private sector) actively promoted this story, by writing it into the policies and guidelines that structured the new market for home finance and by constantly touting the market-friendliness of the state's mortgage insurance programs. They even told this story in state-sponsored public relations campaigns designed to draw consumers and businesspeople into a new market for housing debt. This celebration of the era's supposedly market-driven growth, along with the new market imperative defense for racial segregation, would eventually hold powerful sway over countless white homeowners in communities nationwide.

These transformations are explored more or less chronologically, beginning in chapter 2 with the history of land-use planning and zoning in the years before World War II. This topic might seem tangential to the mortgage revolution and postwar racial politics, given the limited nature of federal involvement in the early zoning movement and the fact that planners and developers seldom advocated its use for explicitly racial purposes. Nonetheless, the early zoning movement set the stage for a new politics of race and housing in the United States by establishing public-private networks that would eventually design and staff New Deal–era housing programs and by popularizing a rationale for exclusion—the market imperative defense—that would shape national housing markets and municipal politics throughout the postwar era. The first generation of urban planners, land-use economists, and zoning experts designed restrictive ordinances that intentionally excluded racial minorities but did so, for the most part, without explicitly naming "race" as a motivating factor. The thinly veiled racial rules built into zoning theory and practice were well articulated before the federal government entered the story in the 1920s. Federal involvement quickly standardized and popularized the new zoning science, when the Department of Commerce promoted municipal zoning and the Supreme Court validated its most restrictive and discriminatory powers. The new federal role legitimated a nascent theory about the relationship between race and property and disseminated the theory nationwide, in the process giving it unprecedented exposure, legitimacy, and power.

Meanwhile zoning's advocates, a loose alliance of planners, public officials, economists, and businesspeople, had forged a powerful public-private partnership that would soon reinvent the market for homes. Chapters 3, 4, and 5 explore this reinvention, by reconstructing a structural revolution in the mortgage industry initiated by Depression-era federal policy and sustained by government action throughout the postwar era. Federal policy transformed the market for housing finance, changing the ways that most privately owned homes in the United States were built, bought, and sold. By creating a series of powerful "selective credit programs"—the FHA, the Federal National Mortgage Association (FNMA), and the Veterans Administration (VA) were the best known at the time—the federal government assumed responsibility for the creation of home finance capital in private markets and regulated its distribution. State intervention subsidized the fantastic growth of the housing market in postwar America. And it did so by adopting appraisal and lending standards that systematically denied nonwhites access to easy mortgage credit and to the nation's fast-growing suburbs.

Because versions of this structural argument appear with some frequency in studies of the modern suburb and racial segregation and because the point is still, nonetheless, contested by some observers, it is worth underscoring this book's central claims about federal policy, subsidy, and racial discrimination. On one level these chapters confirm a story familiar to students of suburban history. Federal selective credit programs subsidized the postwar market for housing credit, permitting millions of consumers to gain equity (or to increase existing equity) in residential property. By popularizing, insuring, and regulating use of the long-term, low-interest mortgage, federal policy enabled millions of Americans to become homeowners for the first time. These credit programs were designed, quite self-consciously, to benefit white people. FHA appraisal guidelines, outlined in its *Underwriting Manual*, prohibited realtors (and thus lenders and builders) from introducing "incompatible" racial groups into white residential enclaves, predicting that any "change in social or racial occupancy" would lead "to instability and a reduction in values." In addition, the government refused to insure mortgages for most home purchases in all-black neighborhoods, since these properties were deemed to be of lesser value.[51]

Still most commentators understate the extent of federal subsidy and the depth of the federal role in shaping the private market for housing, because they focus almost exclusively on FHA and VA operations and because they do not examine how selective credit policy transformed the way that wealth in housing is generated in the modern United States. The FHA and VA worked in tandem with other powerful programs that subsidized and regulated the conventional mortgage market (for home loans *not* covered by FHA or VA insurance) and virtually *created* a secondary mortgage market (enabling investors to trade home finance debt like other securities). Taken together, this broad range of federal initiatives did more than shore up a struggling market for housing finance. It created a new kind of mortgage market and a new kind of mortgage industry, which together issued more credit, and thus produced far more wealth than their predecessors. These chapters situate federal mortgage policy within a much larger revolution in U.S. money and credit markets, demonstrating that postwar suburbanization was part and parcel of a fundamental transformation in the mechanics of American capitalism. The postwar era's stunning suburban expansion represented a central, indeed a constitutive, component of the socialization of consumer debt and, with it, the socialization of American economic growth. Because the programs that subsidized the mortgage market systematically excluded racial minorities, suburban growth and its corollary prosperity were not just state-managed but also inherently discriminatory. Federal housing policies did not merely "embrace . . . the discriminatory attitudes of the marketplace," as the FHA's critics have long argued. Selective credit operations created a new *kind* of discriminatory marketplace.[52]

This structural transformation was accompanied by a change in national housing politics, an ideological change of equal importance. State involvement in the private housing sector helped popularize a mythical story about the mortgage revolution and suburban racial exclusion. Supporters of federal intervention insisted that market forces alone were spurring suburban growth and that it was these same impersonal forces that required the exclusion of minorities. Public policy, they claimed, neither facilitated suburban growth nor encouraged the racial resegregation of the modern metropolis. The story was pervasive, shaping Congressional debates over legislation, FHA appraisal guidelines, federally sponsored promotional campaigns to encourage borrowing, and media coverage of the postwar suburban miracle. Throughout these decades, as a result, the state's role in fueling suburban growth and racial segregation largely disappeared from whites' conversations about both.

With this important context in mind, chapter 5 then picks up the story about municipal zoning after 1940, exploring how its meteoric spread and its centrality to postwar suburban politics complemented the racial exclusion being achieved by a federally subsidized market for homes. Restrictive zoning grew enormously popular during these decades—as of 1931, only 800 cities had adopted ordinances, compared with 6,880 in 1968—and land-use restriction became a central focus of local politics in most suburban municipalities. Zoning's guiding principles—its assumptions about the "incompatibility" of certain populations, defined both by race and by class—were adopted and, in the process, adapted to a new era of exclusionary politics. Chapter 5 (and part I) concludes by identifying an important confluence of events in the decades after 1940. In suburbs nationwide, a zoning politics that did not talk about racial exclusion per se but that helped achieve racial exclusion in practice became the focal point of local battles over development. Advocates of restrictive zoning in general and of racial exclusion in particular defended their stance by embracing the argument long advanced by public and private leaders that it was markets, and not whites' preferences, that were fueling metropolitan growth and determining patterns of racial settlement. Meanwhile the state was both

subsidizing white suburban homeownership and abetting racial segregation, all the while insisting that it was doing no such thing.

In the final analysis, part I shows that the federal role in metropolitan
development did not merely endorse and accelerate existing market practices that discriminated against minorities, as most scholars argue, but that
it created a new kind of discriminatory marketplace, one that subsidized
private housing markets, demanded racial exclusion, and simultaneously
popularized an illusory story about the origins of both growth and inequality. Federal policy promoted restrictive zoning and created a flush new
market for housing that required racial segregation, yet encouraged whites
to believe that it was the free market, not racial prejudice or government
policy, that set the rules of competition: that the exclusion of minorities was
not about race per se but about the principles of real estate economics and
homeowners' rights to control their communities.

Part II: Race and Development in Metropolitan Detroit, 1940–1970

The process by which suburban whites came to be invested in this free market narrative is the subject of part II, which examines the politics of race and
property in local places and local contexts. By reconstructing homeowners' mobilizations in several Detroit suburbs during the 1940s, 1950s, and
1960s, these chapters explore the ways that the local politics of exclusion
shaped and in the process helped transform whites' ideas about homes,
race, neighborhoods, and rights. The case studies demonstrate the debt that
the new local politics owed to the nationally standardized policies and practices that were creating a suburban nation.

My focus is on land-use politics because Detroit's white suburbanites—
like their contemporaries nationwide—devoted considerable time and energy to the subject. Most residents opposed the racial or socioeconomic integration of their neighborhoods and viewed their communities as safe havens
from black people. To maintain those havens, they blocked construction of
rental units and low-income housing, elected municipal officials committed to class and racial exclusion, encouraged realtors to steer minority home
buyers away from their neighborhoods, and often resorted to intimidation
and violence to maintain the residential color line. These chapters follow
suburban residents into zoning board and city council meetings, detail the
efforts of property improvement associations, and reconstruct individual
battles over housing, exclusion, and race—ranging from ballot referenda to
the mob action on Kendal Street. The case studies document the centrality

of exclusion to local political life and the methods that residents employed to protect their neighborhoods. Residents' vigilance helps explain why most of these communities remained racially homogeneous throughout these decades.

These chapters also explore a matter of equal importance: how suburban residents understood and described their commitment to exclusion. Race clearly mattered to white people in metropolitan Detroit. But whites' ideas about race and property and their interpretation of racial exclusion were also undergoing important changes during these decades, changes closely linked to the new national politics and economics of exclusion.

First, Detroit's white suburbanites became deeply invested in the market imperative argument for segregation. Whether organizing to run out an individual black family, block apartment construction, or stop zoning reform that would permit commercial development, residents invoked the same argument. They did not distinguish between so-called racial variables (such as an aversion to black people) and putatively nonracial or race-neutral ones (for example, public health, homeowners' prerogatives, or protection of real estate values). They tapped into a discourse about color and property deeply embedded in both the theory and practice of the modern housing market, arguing that their commitment to racial exclusion, like their opposition to apartment construction or drive-in theaters or gas stations, was purely market-driven. They insisted that while they certainly did not want black neighbors, this did not make them racist.

In these chapters I challenge the assumption shared by most writers on suburban politics and culture that whites' racial preferences were simply one of many discrete preoccupations fueling resistance to integration—that racism operated as an exogenous variable, conceptually distinct from whites' ideas about economics, property, municipal autonomy, or homeowners' rights. Whites' ideas about race and their preoccupation with property were relational and mutually constitutive. The political, demographic, and material conditions of postwar growth encouraged whites to view homeownership and suburban neighborhoods in racial terms—specifically, as a prerogative of white people. Conversely, whites' ideas about race were constantly mediated by their investment, simultaneously financial and emotional, in widely held assumptions about the prerogatives of homeowners. The result was a justification for residential segregation that relied almost exclusively on the language of land-use economics and suburban autonomy. It was a political rhetoric that enabled whites to oppose the racial integration of their neighborhoods openly while insisting that their motives had nothing to do with prejudice.

This new theory about color and property was not the sole force driving restrictionist politics, nor was it the only manifestation of white racism during these years. But it was so widely codified, endorsed, and disseminated after 1940, and thus so central to local political mobilizations and conversations, that it fast became among the most consequential forms of racialist thinking. Of course, struggles over development remained local affairs; every suburban community engaged in unique battles shaped by local conditions. But all suburban whites achieved and justified racial exclusion by tapping into state-sanctioned rules for real estate development and employing state-sanctioned land-use instruments. They turned to the same real estate manuals, economics textbooks, federal guidelines, enabling acts, and court rulings. Whites embraced the market imperative defense for exclusion because it was built into the materials that they used, everyday, to exclude. Paradoxically, this standardized narrative simultaneously encouraged whites to ignore the fact that they benefited from racist institutions and lived in a racist culture.

Exploring the Detroit-area case studies demonstrates the elusive but very important interchange between the national and local influences on white suburban politics and racial identity. Whites' investment in the market imperative rationale stems from their experience of, and often their intense involvement in, a series of structural changes, government reforms, and local mobilizations. How urban experts and businesspeople constructed a new kind of discriminatory marketplace can be seen in part I. In part II we can see how suburban residents responded to and acted within this new marketplace and how, in the process, they developed new ideas about whiteness and racial privilege. The federal role was decisive, but the identity of "white suburbanite" or "white homeowner" was not prefabricated or ready-made and then adopted wholesale by a new generation of mortgage holders. Efforts to exclude were initiated locally and fueled by local preferences. Still they were shaped by the federal government's new stake in land-use politics and housing markets because residents embraced and continually reframed what had emerged by the 1940s as a national political language about race, property, and rights. Detroit's white suburbanites constantly inscribed a wide-ranging structural, political, and discursive transformation onto their own neighborhoods, streets, and homes.

These chapters also contribute to an important reappraisal of white backlash politics in the decades after World War II. Recent studies have challenged the common claim that northern, urban whites turned against the New Deal state and the Democratic Party in the 1960s, when civil rights protest threatened white privileges and forced Democratic leadership to embrace racial reform. The year 1964 is often cited as a turning point, when northern whites showed considerable interest in the presidential campaigns of George Wallace and Barry Goldwater and many reacted negatively to changes in the civil rights movement and the Johnson administration's willingness to promote real reform. Scholars have documented the limits of this analysis; northern whites did not wait until the 1960s to mobilize against black civil rights or to restrict blacks' economic opportunity.[53] This book, along with several recent studies of early postwar suburban politics, demonstrates that this earlier white backlash was a metropolitan phenomenon.[54] By the mid-1950s, whites in suburban Detroit had long been involved in and committed to the politics of racial exclusion. In chapters 6 and 7 I reconstruct white neighborhood mobilizations between 1940 and 1955 and document residents' commitment to segregation and their growing investment in the market imperative defense of racial exclusion. In chapters 8 and 9 I detail white suburban politics after *Brown v. Board of Education* and through the heyday of the modern civil rights movement. That movement did not trigger northern whites' resistance and hostility. Whites responded to the rising tide of protest by tapping into the strategies and rhetoric that had sustained white neighborhood politics since the 1940s. They adapted an existing restrictionist politics to the new civil rights challenge, framing resistance as a justifiable defense of their rights as property owners and responsible suburban citizens.

Part II also complicates common assumptions about the political forces that made the early postwar suburb such a racially conservative place. The suburbs are generally portrayed as racially conservative bastions of Republicanism; indeed many observers argue that suburbanization "converted" whites to the Republican Party, especially during and after the 1960s, while racial progressivism is often portrayed as a Democratic issue. But like so many suburban regions, metropolitan Detroit was politically quite heterogeneous and included large and very loyal blocs of Democratic voters throughout the decades discussed here.[55] Suburban Democrats and Republicans fought with equal determination to secure the racial boundaries of their new, all-white communities. This suggests that the well-documented (and much maligned) shift in many whites' party allegiance in the 1960s and early 1970s was a response to the Democratic Party's new willingness to support racial reform rather than a reflection of whites' new preoccupation with racial matters. Whites in the Detroit region did not "turn" on the Democratic Party because they became suburbanites or because civil rights protest changed their minds about racial equality, but rather because the party made a sharp departure from its early postwar acceptance of the racial status quo. Meanwhile white Republicans stood by the party that continued to hold the line against "Negro invasion." So where many scholars portray a liberal consensus on race within the Democratic Party and portray its collapse in the 1960s, these cases confirm the findings of several important recent studies, which show that racial liberalism was not widely embraced by the white Democratic rank and file. These cases suggest that already by the late 1940s and early 1950s, a commitment to racial exclusion was unifying people of European descent across party lines.

This commitment unified whites across class and ethnic lines as well. Royal Oak, Dearborn, and their suburban neighbors were occupied by working class and middle class alike, and both groups participated whole-heartedly in the politics of exclusion. Examining socioeconomically diverse suburbs reveals the limits of some common arguments about the distinction between middle class and working class racism. By many accounts, working class whites were more willing to resort to threats and violence to protect their neighborhoods, while middle class whites relied on economic control or on legal devices such as restrictive covenants or zoning ordinances to keep their distance from undesirable neighbors. Yet in much of suburban Detroit, middle class and working class whites relied on the same strategies and even the same rhetoric, and it was middle class leadership that organized homeowners and often primed them for violence. In the final analysis, the politics of exclusion helped unify a suburban population that was remarkably diverse. It helped bring together Republicans and Democrats, laborers and physicians, secretaries and managers, housewives and shop owners. It united immigrants and their descendants from countries including Italy, Poland, England, Germany, Russia, Hungary, and France. The politics of exclusion created considerable solidarity among a wide range of people who were now considered to be white.

———————

Postwar development politics helped convince a generation of whites that homeownership and neighborhood control rose above issues of class or party affiliation or even personal preference. Ironically it encouraged white people to believe that property had no politics. This fact would have dramatic consequences for metropolitan development, the shape of national electoral coalitions, and the lives of white and nonwhite people for decades to come. During the years that saw metropolitan fragmentation, restrictive zoning, and federal credit policy resegregate the nation's neighborhoods and wealth by race, white suburbanites were immersed in a local politics and a public conversation that described racial and socioeconomic segregation as nothing more than a by-product of impersonal free market forces. By the time the Supreme Court declared race-restrictive covenants unenforceable in *Shelley v. Kraemer*, white suburbanites were dependent on institutions and invested in a popular theory of suburban autonomy and real estate economics that treated racial exclusion as nothing more than a normative principle of land-use management. So by 1948, the year of both the *Shelley* ruling and the groundbreaking of the Builders' Association subdivision on Normandy Road in Royal Oak, suburban whites no longer needed a race-specific tool for excluding nonwhites. In the case of the Royal Oak development, "FHA approved"—together with the City Council's commitment to a "strong" zoning ordinance—said all that white suburbanites needed to hear. The chapters of part I demonstrate that by the year of the *Shelley* decision, the market for suburban home construction and ownership had been racially structured, thus making explicit racial proscriptions largely irrelevant. The chapters of part II show that by the late 1940s, countless white residents of the Detroit metropolitan area had become deeply immersed in a political culture that defined economic value in racially specific terms.

A final word about the relationship between national and local politics and between parts I and II of this study is in order. If the zoning and mortgage revolutions helped create the preconditions for all-white suburban development, postwar suburban leaders and residents used the zoning power and a new market for housing credit to construct countless unique suburban communities. Likewise the arguments used to justify exclusionary zoning and to celebrate the new free market for housing were adapted in myriad ways by local suburban residents. Homeowners did not blindly follow a national template for protecting the suburban ideal. Nonetheless, they created unique homeowners' politics and unique narratives about exclusion out of the political, economic, and legal materials at hand: a vast new system of mortgage finance and the public-private networks that sustained it, standardized home-rule powers to determine and police "compatible land use," and federal court protections for property owners. For this reason whites' commitment to racial exclusion was not simply a locally rooted reflex action, nor can it be attributed solely to class anxieties or turf battles. Instead, it was an historically specific form of white racialist thinking and white racial power, one grounded in a state-sponsored vision of race and property yet one invented and refined, by and large, in countless local places. The chapters that follow begin to explore how and why so many people were exposed to this story and took it to be true.

PART ONE

The Political Economy of Suburban Development and the Race of Economic Value, 1910–1970

CHAPTER TWO

Local Control and the Rights of Property: The Politics of Incorporation, Zoning, and Race before 1940

By the 1960s, most of the nation's suburban dwellers lived in independent political jurisdictions known as "home rule" municipalities. In essence these were suburban cities, empowered by their state government to collect taxes, provide basic services, and regulate land use by adopting comprehensive zoning ordinances. Scholars and critics have long argued that the rapid multiplication of home-rule municipalities facilitated metropolitan segregation in the postwar era because most suburbs used their autonomy, largely through the exercise of zoning power, to monitor the kinds of structures built in their communities and, as a result, who could live there. Postwar zoning practice is critical to understanding the politics of race and housing in the modern suburb. By limiting construction of apartments and modest, affordable private homes, suburban municipalities magnified trends in class and racial segregation already set in motion by private acts of discrimination and federal mortgage programs.

Municipal land-use politics have another, complementary legacy that has largely been ignored in studies of postwar race and housing: namely, the role played by the early city planning movement in setting the stage for New Deal–era housing policy, the modern housing market, and the intellectual foundations that helped defend racially discriminatory practices after 1940 in both the public and private sectors. Zoning's founders fashioned a powerful new rationale for residential exclusion: the claim that exclusion of any "incompatible land use," be it apartments, factories, or occupancy by black people, was motivated not by ideology but by economics. This "market imperative" argument, first outlined in the 1910s and 1920s, eventually became foundational to the legislation, court decisions, and politics that would guide zoning practice in the modern American suburb. This argument would also structure the postwar housing market, when zoning's promoters helped design and manage the New Deal–era programs that reinvented the mortgage and real estate industries. Many of the individuals and organizations in the forefront of zoning advocacy before the Depression helped design and operate the government's powerful New Deal initiatives. And the market imperative defense for racial exclusion was quickly embraced by influential New Deal reformers, regardless of their prior involvement in planning circles. The core principles of pre-Depression land-use science, including the argument that racial mixing undermined property values and economic growth, were written into the more dramatic federal interventions of the 1930s, 1940s, and beyond.

Many commentators argue that the proliferation of restrictive zoning after World War II was not driven by whites' racial preferences. This chapter begins an analysis that challenges this claim, by rooting postwar zoning practice in its pre-Depression history. It shows that zoning had, from the outset, a racialist foundation and a racial intent, one that later, often in unexpected ways, enabled postwar suburbanites to employ municipal ordinances as instruments of racial exclusion. Critically, zoning's original intent must be understood in the context of early twentieth-century racial politics, when enthusiasm for the new science of land-use economics converged with assumptions about racial, specifically eugenic, science. Most early zoning advocates believed in racial hierarchy, openly embraced racial exclusion, and saw zoning as a way to achieve it. But they formulated strategies and sketched out a language for justifying segregation that focused on practical, supposedly nonideological considerations. They seldom talked about racial exclusion in specifically racial terms. This defense of exclusion would eventually be adopted, and adapted, by later generations of white people committed to preserving the homogeneity of their neighborhoods.

Defining the Police Power: Reform Politics, Local Control, and the Invention of Restrictive Zoning

Gaining autonomy and securing local control have not always been the guiding principles of suburban politics. In the mid- to late-nineteenth century, most suburban settlements were small, exclusive residential enclaves for affluent professionals. Because these "streetcar" suburbs lacked the resources and administrative capacity to provide capital-intensive services and improvements (such as sewer systems, electrical grids, paved roads, and parks), their residents usually promoted annexation by richer and bureaucratically established central cities. As a result, early suburban settlement most often led to waves of annexation and the continual expansion of city boundaries. Between 1850 and 1880, for example, Cincinnati grew in size from six to twenty-one square miles, and between 1860 and 1900 Chicago nearly doubled in size every decade. After midcentury, most large municipalities doubled their geographic area about every twenty years.[1]

Three developments gradually made incorporation a more attractive alternative for the growing suburbs, beginning with late nineteenth-century legal reforms that made it easier to achieve jurisdictional independence. After decades of jealously guarding their control over urban areas, state governments awarded cities a measure of autonomy. In 1875, Missouri granted St. Louis the nation's first home-rule charter, and an 1879 amendment to California's constitution permitted localities to petition for similar status. Over the next five decades another twenty states followed suit, enabling suburban residents to petition county or village authorities for the right to create a charter commission, draft a municipal charter, and put it to a popular vote. Once approved, the home-rule charter afforded residents an unprecedented degree of decision-making power. Home-rule municipalities (both cities and villages) did not become truly independent entities, and local government in the United States has remained to this day, in a strict legal sense, a "creature of the states." Nonetheless, incorporation enabled suburban communities to maintain their own streets, parks, and recreational facilities, to provide police and fire protection, to manage water and sewer service, to approve plats and construction standards, and to tax local residents to finance these new responsibilities.[2]

Other developments made suburban autonomy economically feasible and politically attractive. New technologies dramatically lowered the cost of providing basic services, and strong municipal bond markets and elevated incomes during and after World War I enabled otherwise tax-poor communities to finance infrastructural development and services. In addition, some states authorized county governments to provide services for suburban municipalities. Meanwhile suburbs were simply growing, as the extension of streetcar and railroad service made these quiet, spacious, and semipastoral enclaves both accessible and desirable to more and more upper-income Americans. The streetcar suburb's popularity was partly fueled by affluent whites' concerns about the stunning transformation of central cities. Suburban residents, who were, by and large, middle-class professionals and described themselves as "native" whites, were uncomfortable with unchecked industrial and commercial development, with increasing population densities, and with the specific populations that were crowding into major cities: a laboring class dominated by immigrants from southern and eastern Europe and migrant blacks from the American South. Especially troubling to native whites was the supposed "character" of these new arrivals, who were deemed racially inferior both by scientists and politicians to the nation's "Anglo" stock. The home-rule provisions added to state constitutions during this era were by no means designed to segregate the American metropolis by race. Nonetheless, they provided affluent suburbanites with a means to separate themselves jurisdictionally from populations seen as socially and even racially suspect.[3]

Incorporation activity usually came in waves; some metropolitan regions jumped on the home-rule bandwagon in the late nineteenth century and others witnessed little or no activity until after World War I. But by the 1920s, as the automobile began to accelerate the rate of suburban settlement, most metropolitan areas had been carved into multiple minor civil divisions. Between 1850 and 1920, the number of jurisdictions grew from 30 to 119 in greater Philadelphia, from 27 to 49 in Boston, from 56 to 148 in metropolitan New York City, and from 20 to 127 in Pittsburgh. Detroit was among the latecomers, still surrounded by "general law" villages at the end of World War I, before a wave of incorporations created two dozen new suburban governments during the 1920s and 1930s. Nationwide, the race to incorporate revolutionized the structure of regional governance by 1930, dividing most metropolitan areas among 10 to 50 independent jurisdictions. Annexation did not stop altogether. But the wholesale absorption of well-established suburban settlements had largely ceased, ensuring that in most northern and western states, subsequent metropolitan growth would produce an ever-expanding patchwork of autonomous local governments.[4]

During the decades that suburban incorporation grew more popular, its politics and rationales grew significantly more complicated, as the new preoccupation with autonomy coalesced with, and provided critical momentum for, the efforts of urban reformers, architects, and businesspeople to promote the zoning concept. The suburban incorporation trend predates the widespread use of zoning and other modern land-use controls in the United States, in some regions by decades. But during the 1910s and 1920s, as zoning grew in popularity, as its practices were standardized, and as its legal standing was confirmed by the courts, it quickly became a driving force behind most suburban incorporation campaigns. Soon it would also become a focal point of local politics in the nation's new home-rule suburbs. As a result the arguments invoked to promote incorporation neatly dovetailed with the most common defense for restrictive zoning: the need to protect homeowners from development described as incompatible or inharmonious—be it a factory, apartment building, or housing for minorities—in order to protect the value of private property and the fiscal health of municipalities.

———————

In the first two decades of the twentieth century, incorporation politics intersected with a young planning movement that was attracting new advocates and taking on a dramatic new orientation. Planners' focus was shifting from the somewhat rarified, nineteenth-century preoccupation with creating the City Beautiful (by means of monumental urban design projects) to more mundane concerns like managing land use, curbing congestion, and reforming municipal government practices. A range of reform agendas coalesced during these years, giving birth to what was soon called a "city planning" movement. Its proponents proudly devoted equal attention to questions of design, infrastructure, public health, and public administration.

Prominent among this movement's leaders were men and women concerned with three closely related, and increasingly dire, urban problems. Housing reform was the primary focus of settlement house workers, public health officials, journalists, and tenement reformers. The leading figure was Lawrence Veiller, who in the 1890s advocated the adoption of building codes and municipal regulations for apartment construction. Through his leadership of the Tenement House Committee, Veiller helped design New York's Tenement House Law in 1901. Focusing on municipal corruption were activists associated with the National Municipal League, founded in 1894, which called for radical reform of municipal charters. Their Model City Charter, first proposed in 1899, recommended election of a "strong" mayor (with considerable appointment powers) and a nonpartisan city council, elected for staggered six-year terms. Finally, a coalition of public officials, religious leaders, and settlement house workers sponsored educational campaigns to warn about the perils of urban congestion. These reformers found their most influential voice in New York City's Committee on Congestion of Population (CCP), founded in 1907 by social worker and National Consumers League Secretary Florence Kelley and joined that year by progressive reformer and planning advocate Benjamin C. Marsh.[5]

Soon planners were pursuing more radical interventions, including the nation's first experiments with municipal zoning. In 1908, Los Angeles adopted the nation's first citywide land-use restrictions (designating separate municipal "zones" for industrial and residential development). In 1909, Boston set height and bulk limits for new construction and Wisconsin legislators permitted larger cities to appoint planning commissions authorized to regulate the width and placement of new streets. That year witnessed other important benchmarks of planning's new orientation and prominence: Harvard University offered the nation's first university-based planning course, and Marsh's *An Introduction to City Planning: Democracy's Challenge to the American City*, an early manifesto of the zoning movement, was published. Marsh encouraged municipal officials to control future development by buying vacant land on the urban periphery and by emulating European land-use experiments, especially the German "zone" system, which he had studied during two CCP-sponsored research trips. Citing Frankfurt's system as a model, Marsh predicted that "the most important part of City Planning, as far as the future of health of the city is concerned, is the districting of the city into zones." [6]

By the time that *Introduction* appeared in 1909, Marsh was organizing like-minded reformers to promote their planning vision. That May he joined banker and CCP chair Henry Morgenthau to convene the National Conference on City Planning and Congestion, in Washington, D.C., which attracted architects, civil engineers, municipal reformers, landscape architects, social workers, conservationists, and other urban experts estranged from planning's City Beautiful orientation. Among the attendees were municipal tax specialist Frederick C. Howe, settlement house leaders Jane Addams and Mary Simkhovitch, landscape architect Frederick Law Olmsted Jr., editor Herbert Croly, former congressman and real estate lawyer Edward M. Bassett, and two recent converts to city planning, George Ford and John Nolen. Marsh's opening remarks challenged reformers' long-standing preoccupation with urban aesthetics, declaring instead that city planning must be viewed as "fundamentally a health and, hence, an economic proposition." By 1910, the upstart organization had renamed itself the National Conference on City Planning (NCCP). That same year, Veiller created the National Housing Association, which would work closely and share members with the NCCP throughout the decade. [7]

In place of the City Beautiful, this new generation of planners promoted what architect and founding NCCP member George Ford described as "The City Scientific." Ford argued that by applying scientific expertise to the challenges posed by urban growth, planners could ensure metropolitan development that was efficient, orderly, safe, and healthful. Like many of his contemporaries, Ford bridged two planning eras. He remained preoccupied with urban aesthetics and even warned that "science" could be "overdone," yet also became a careful student of European planning models and eventually contributed the technical chapter in Marsh's *Introduction*. And so secure was Ford's faith in this new direction that in 1913 he described city planning to an NCCP audience as "rapidly becoming as definite a science as pure engineering, solely a matter of proceeding logically from the known to the unknown." "In city planning there is, above all," he explained "the necessity for a careful analysis of the conditions," whereby all relevant and necessary "requirements" were "separated into several classes according to their urgency." "Working in this way, one soon discovers that in almost every case there is one, and only one, logical and convincing solution [to] the problems involved."[8]

This new investment in the science of land-use planning found a powerful forum in the NCCP, just as zoning was becoming the centerpiece of that science. It was at the conference that the zoning concept first gained extensive U.S. exposure and began to attract a broad following in both the public and private sectors. Participants at the inaugural NCCP in 1909 heard bankers, architects, and planners, including Morgenthau, Olmsted, and Nolen, portray zoning as a panacea for practical urban problems such as congestion and public health and report on Europe's successful land-use experiments. NCCP leadership encouraged audiences to popularize the zoning concept by sponsoring publicity campaigns or drafting model enabling legislation for state constitutions. Presentations on zoning soon became regular features of the annual meeting. In the first years of the NCCP, the municipal power to restrict land use fast became a primary focus of the city planning movement.[9]

But the young zoning science proved to be quite malleable and quickly underwent an important transformation, as the real estate industry took interest in planning and gained considerable influence at the NCCP. The result was a decisive (and quite rapid) shift in zoning's focus, away from the broad concern with ensuring "best use" and toward a far more narrow preoccupation with protecting property values. Just a year before the first meeting of the NCCP, realtors and developers had founded *their* first national organization, the National Association of Real Estate Exchanges, soon renamed the National Association of Real Estate Boards (NAREB). At first, the NCCP and NAREB had little to do with each other. The conference was founded and dominated by planners and neither solicited nor attracted support from the real estate industry, with the exception of Baltimore developer Edward Bouton. But other businessmen soon followed his lead, private sector interest in city planning grew rapidly, and both realtors and residential developers began to attend national planning conferences. Concerned that private (and thus profit-oriented) interests were beginning to wield undue influence at the NCCP, Marsh shortly abandoned the organization that he had helped found.[10]

The burgeoning alliance between planners and developers was soon formalized. In 1913, pioneering Kansas City developer J. C. Nichols joined the NCCP's General Committee (he would eventually cofound NAREB's independent research arm, the Urban Land Institute). By 1914, state realty organizations were exhorting members to help develop the "Science of City Planning," and NAREB, now just five years old, created its City Planning Committee (CPC), staffing it exclusively with residential developers (Bouton, Nichols, Lee J. Ninde of Fort Wayne, Indiana, Duncan McDuffie of San Francisco, King G. Thompson of Columbus, Ohio, and future NAREB president Robert Jemison Jr. of Birmingham). The CPC urged local and state governments to provide legal and financial support for planning advocacy and worked with the NCCP to popularize planning legislation. Meanwhile, NAREB supported and collaborated with the NCCP on research projects, including a 1914 study, "The Best Methods of Land Subdivision," co-authored by Nolen and Ernest Goodrich, a civil engineer and public works official in New York City. Their report provided the centerpiece of the NCCP's 1915 meeting in Detroit, a conference at which, for the first time, several realtors were scheduled to speak.[11]

Among them was Paul A. Harsch, a residential builder from Toledo, Ohio, who participated in a forum on Nolen and Goodrich's study, presenting the "Point of View of the Real Estate Developer." The CPC's Thompson and Ninde facilitated the discussion that followed. During that exchange, Ninde described his recent conversion to the planning concept and what he saw as a new symbiotic relationship developing between planners and businessmen. He had been introduced to the "subject of city planning" only a year earlier at the 1914 NCCP, Ninde explained, but had quickly grown "quite enthusiastic over its possibilities," so much so that just two months later, when attending a Pittsburgh meeting of the National Real Estate Association, he was disturbed by the indifference of his "brother real estate men." Ninde was shocked that "men who had platted and laid out subdivisions comprising thousands of acres, men whose dealings had run into millions of dollars . . . took no interest whatever in the subject of city planning." The experience "rapidly forced [him] to the conclusion that we needed widespread education along the lines of city planning and that we real estate men had better begin at home." "The propaganda," he told his NCCP audience, "should start with ourselves," recommending that builders "find some point of contact" or a "point of common interest" like the residential subdivision that would enable them to work with "the professional city planners." Ninde was confident that "the experience of real estate men in sales campaigns qualified them to advise, in a practical way, on the educational campaign in city planning." "You all know," he concluded, "that the real estate men spend more for advertising and are more interested in its practical results than any other group of people who have to do with city planning. They advertise to obtain results."[12]

Developers' enthusiasm for the planning concept led to rapid changes in NCCP membership and its strategy. Before 1914, conference leadership rarely consulted or collaborated with businesspeople. They sought the counsel of architects, municipal officials, and charitable organizations, and their campaign—"Popularize the City Planning Principle"—targeted city governments, journalists, and social service clubs. But soon the NCCP focused far less attention on social problems, attracted far fewer social workers and civic reformers, and worked hard to cultivate support from businessmen—since they "pay the bills," as George Ford noted. Already in 1916 at least ten realtors, including NAREB president Henry Haas, sat on the conference's sixty-nine member General Committee, and builders regularly presented papers at the annual NCCP. That year, in "Financial Effect of Good Planning in Land Subdivision," J. C. Nichols framed a detailed primer in subdivision economics with a plea for conference participants "to pay more attention to the planning of residence property," specifically what he called "high-class" homes. "Eighty to ninety per cent of our city property is covered with residence districts," Nichols explained, "and yet ninety per cent of the discussion in city planning conventions I have attended is directed to traction problems and downtown development." In 1917, NAREB representatives took the podium at the NCCP to celebrate their success in popularizing the zoning concept and to announce that its members were hard at work drafting model city planning legislation. "Four or five years ago it was difficult to get the interest of real estate men in city planning," explained NAREB executive secretary Thomas S. Ingersoll. But since then, he continued, Nichols, Harsch, Ninde, and other NAREB members had successfully developed and popularized "the new idea."[13]

The most enduring legacy of developers' involvement was zoning's new focus on protecting the value of residential property. Originally framed as a panacea for a wide range of practical urban problems, by the mid-1910s zoning was portrayed in NCCP sessions primarily as a tool for shoring up real estate markets, especially for "high class" residential subdivisions. At the 1916 meeting, Nichols told real estate developers that by "pay[ing] more attention" to residential planning, they could predict future market prices and thereby determine if a proposed subdivision could "create . . . enough value . . . to take care of the cost of carrying your land long enough to put

it on the market." Good planning would ensure healthy returns on investments. And the key to good planning was zoning and subdivision control.
"Private planning," argued Nichols, "must have municipal aid." "How in
the world can the private developer, without municipal assistance, expect
his property to succeed if he is to work with unregulated development all
around him?" he asked, concluding that "we must have municipal regulations in order to protect [homeowners'] investments." Further blurring the
boundaries between public authority and private motivation, Nichols suggested that restrictive covenants provided a good model for future public
action.[14]

By now businesspeople were not the only ones advocating public intervention to protect property values. When New York City tax official and
National Municipal League president Lawson Purdy spoke before the NCCP
in 1917, he described zoning primarily as a means to "enhance the value
of land [in] the city and conserve the value of buildings." By decade's end,
zoning's most influential public and private sector advocates focused their
attention on insulating middle-class residential enclaves from commercial
development, apartments, and other "undesirable" land uses. Zoning had
come a long way, in a short time, as its most prominent and influential
promoters were no longer preoccupied with general urban land-use issues
but rather with protecting and enhancing the value of high-end residential
real estate. Builders' involvement was instrumental in making this shift, ensuring that NCCP advocacy would promote state interventions designed to
protect private interests.[15] As zoning became more palatable to businesspeople, the stage was set for the dissemination of an influential new theory
about the relationship between private property and public intervention, a
theory that would decisively shape the politics of restriction in the twentieth
century.

Equally important to zoning's popular appeal was the intersection between
the new science of land-use economics and contemporary debates about
racial difference although it is seldom discussed in histories of the early
planning movement. Vocal proponents of the City Scientific built support
for zoning, in part, by invoking racial science and tapping into whites'
anxieties about "alien" peoples, anxieties that suffused the national debate
about unchecked urban growth, a new wave of immigration, and citizenship. Scholars have begun to explore the influence of Progressive-era racial
ideology on the early planning movement. Yet there has been only limited treatment of the centrality of racial thinking to the early zoning move-

ment, and no exploration of its long-term impact on land-use politics in the United States.[16]

Racial science figured prominently in the early planning movement because urban congestion and unregulated development were often associated with migrant blacks, immigrant Asians, and immigrant Europeans, the populations whose cheap labor (and often squalid living conditions) made the era's rapid industrial and commercial growth possible. These populations were considered by both white elites and well-established European immigrant groups to be "nonwhite." An elaborate racial science, first popularized in the early nineteenth century and deeply institutionalized by the Gilded Age, described black Americans, Native Americans, and Asian immigrants as biologically distinct and, in most cases, permanently inferior. Popularized through fields including phrenology, craniometry, and eugenics, the science of racial difference was not simply the preserve of professional intellectuals and the nation's elite but the stuff of popular science, popular culture, and mainstream politics.[17]

In the late nineteenth century, racial science was harnessed to describe the wave of so-called new immigrants to the United States, the arrivals from Poland, Russia, the Austro-Hungarian Empire, and Italy who settled, for the most part, in the industrializing metropolitan areas of the Northeast and Midwest. Together with their American-born children, the new immigrants soon came to outnumber people of English, German, Scottish, and Irish descent in many cities. In the eyes of these self-described whites (or "Americans"), the new immigrants were culturally and even biologically distinct, thus described alternatively as nonwhite, "almost white," or "inbetween." In popular discussions as well as policy debates over immigration, the term "race" sometimes stood in for nation, at times it was treated as heritable, at times it was viewed as acquired. The line separating culture or national origin, on the one hand, and biology, on the other, was not clearly delineated and in the case of European immigrants, especially, the distinctions grew increasingly blurred by the early decades of the twentieth century. The often contradictory legal, cultural, and biological measures of "whiteness" do not lend themselves to a clear, linear narrative about immigrant racial identity. While Italians, Slavs, and Jews were deemed white for purposes of naturalization, there was considerable confusion about their racial capacity and, ultimately, widespread fears that they were incompatible with "native" Americans and incapable of supporting democratic institutions. (In a 1912 congressional debate over immigration restriction, for example, there was some debate over whether or not Italians were "full-blooded Caucasians.") When the nation's constantly shifting racial mythologies intersected with the young urban planning movement, most native whites considered the new immigrants to be distinct and perhaps unassimilable, at best. At worst, they were viewed as genetically incompatible and posing a long-term threat to the polity.[18]

Racial science suffused public debates over "the immigrant problem" and means of addressing it. Since the 1880s, eastern and southern Europeans had been the target of spirited and explicitly racialist campaigns led by prominent publicists, politicians, and their allies in the eugenicist movement. Scientists exerted considerable influence on policy debates, explains Matthew Frye Jacobson, ensuring that discussions of restriction were couched "in a language of 'desirable' versus 'useless' races" and "the important national work of 'breeding.'" "In the mind of the average American," eugenicist Henry Pratt Fairchild commented in 1911, "the modern immigrants are generally regarded as inferior peoples," as "races he looks down on, and with which he does not want to associate on terms of social equality." That year the Dillingham Commission's report on immigration, which included a volume entitled *A Dictionary of Races or Peoples*, embraced a five-tier model of humanity first articulated by eighteenth-century naturalist Johann Friedrich Blumenbach and later popularized in nineteenth-century scholarly debates over human origins. (The Dillingham Commission did acknowledge that racial science had since grown far more sophisticated, noting that the federal government "recognize[d] 45 races or peoples among immigrants coming to the United States," of which "36 are indigenous to Europe.") The immigration debate provided eugenicists with greater visibility in the popular press, where they repeated warnings about the threat posed by "racial intermingling." Demand was so great for Madison Grant's history of Anglo superiority, *The Passing of the Great Race*, first published in 1916, that new editions were issued in 1920 and 1921. And by then, anti-immigration activists had lobbied Congress to consider legislation curtailing the immigration of select national groups. The proposal, authored by the U.S. Committee on Selective Immigration, under Grant's direction, proposed annual quotas calculated as a percentage of each group's presence in the United States as recorded by the 1910 census. This formula heavily favored northern and western Europeans who, the committee noted, were "of higher intelligence."[19]

These were high-profile conversations, by no means limited to academic publications and government reports. Consider Kenneth Roberts's influential endorsement of the quotas, published in the *Saturday Evening Post* on the eve of the 1921 congressional debates over restriction. Unchecked immigration from eastern and southern Europe, warned Roberts, threatened to overwhelm the nation with people from "the other two main races of Europe, which are known to biologists and ethnologists as the Alpine race and the Mediterranean race. The Alpines are the stocky, slow, dark, round-skulled folk who inhabit most of central Europe and whose chief representatives are the large part of the different Slav peoples. The Mediterraneans are the small, swarthy, black-haired, long-skulled people who form the bulk of the population in Southern Italy, Greece, Spain and the north coast of Africa." "Throughout the centuries," he explained, "these people . . . have [never] been successful at governing themselves or at governing anyone else," instead "rush[ing] to the spots where a stronger and hardier people have established successful enterprises"; "by their low standard of living and their willingness to subordinate everything to immediate gain, . . . [they force] out the people who preceded them." Citing Roberts's writings and other expert testimony in support of "race quotas," Congress passed restrictive legislation in 1921, incorporating Grant's recommendations into public policy. This did not stop the hand-wringing over the immigrant threat, and by 1923 Congress was considering additional restrictions and tightening naturalization requirements. That year psychologist Robert Yerkes documented the biological "intellectual differences" between the new and old immigrants in the *Atlantic Monthly,* while Judge Alphonso T. Clearwater urged members of the New York State Bar Association to endorse "the exclusion from citizenship of the southern and eastern European and western Asiatic immigrant." The quality of immigrants had "deteriorated," he explained, as "Native Anglo-Saxon stock" had been "superceded by races of widely different character." In 1924, the Johnson-Reed Act effectively cut off all "non-Caucasian" immigration to the United States and drastically reduced access for "in-between" peoples. President Coolidge applauded the bill, having already cited the "biological" laws and "racial considerations too grave to be brushed aside." "Divergent people," he wrote in a 1921 *Good Housekeeping* article, "will not mix or blend."[20]

Some policymakers and planners resisted the blatant racialization of the immigration debate, but it resonated powerfully with two influential audiences: the millions of "native" whites living in major metropolitan centers and the cadre of urban experts who fashioned early zoning legislation in the 1910s and 1920s. The annual NCCP became an important forum for debates over restriction, race, and property, and served as a key site in which modern zoning's discriminatory logic began to take form. The prominence of business leaders, the focus on a new planning science, and the popularity of eugenics coalesced to help forge a theory and practice of land-use restriction that assumed the relevance of race to protecting private property.

In zoning and the emerging land-use science, race was first collapsed into a unique set of twentieth-century strategies—legal, economic, political, and rhetorical—designed to regulate, protect, and ultimately increase the money value of white-owned residential property.

Planning's most progressive advocates had long accepted the era's assumptions about racial difference. Late nineteenth-century housing reformers were heavily influenced "by a social theory that embraced race-based cultural determinism and arranged different ethnic and racial groups along hierarchical lines." By 1909, Marsh was celebrating the European zoning model "as a means for preventing race deterioration," echoing a transatlantic preoccupation among self-described white people about the threat of racial mixing. (He conceded that "the physique of immigrants may be slightly better [in the United States] than abroad" but added that this was "not a fair test of progress.") Soon these racial preoccupations assumed a new importance, as zoning advocacy shifted away from a focus on best use and public health and toward the protection of expensive homes. In 1913, an audience at the Third National Conference on Housing heard eugenicist Dr. Charles A. L. Reed explain that the "degeneracy" associated with impoverished urban neighborhoods was as much "the cause of the hovel" as "the hovel [is] a cause of degeneracy." Veiller, Olmsted, and other prominent National Housing Association and NCCP leaders offered comparable assessments throughout the debates that created modern zoning, while influential advocates and consultants like Robert Whitten, who would soon help design New York City's comprehensive ordinance, openly celebrated zoning's facility to discriminate by race and class. In *Outlines of Economics*, Richard Ely insisted that the new immigrants "have none of the inherited instincts and tendencies" characteristic of earlier immigrant populations. These were "beaten men from beaten races, representing the worst failures in the struggle for existence."

An occasional dissenting voice was recorded: at the 1910 NCCP, for example, William S. Bennet insisted that "the immigrant" and "congestion" were not "necessarily because of the other." But Veiller's response, essentially a rebuttal, reveals that planners were fashioning a land-use science that simply assumed the legitimacy and relevance of racial science. Veiller criticized urban experts for failing to discern between the causes of "land overcrowding," on the one hand, and "room overcrowding," on the other. The former, he acknowledged, did result from poor planning, but the latter was the product of the "social habits of certain foreign elements of our population," specifically Italians, Russians, and Jews.[21]

If the new immigrants had occasional defenders in the planning profession, most urban experts still viewed blacks and other unambiguously "nonwhite" populations as a categorical threat to sound development. And they viewed zoning as a means to protect property from racial threats. Many northern planners found common cause with a racial zoning movement, formally inaugurated with the passage of a race-exclusionary ordinance in Baltimore in 1910. The Supreme Court struck down racial zoning in its 1917 decision in *Buchanan v. Warley,* but racial ordinances were passed and enforced in some southern states for decades, often by instituting land-planning equivalents of the grandfather clause. As Christopher Silver has shown, advocates of race-specific restriction made little distinction between zoning's larger goal of managing urban growth, in general, and its ability to segregate populations by race, in particular. Planners drafted racial zoning ordinances by drawing upon the same legal precedents used to support the general, and far more common, restrictions that did not specify racial aims. Advocates of racial zoning saw the national planning movement as a natural ally, both before and after *Buchanan,* and hired consultants and NCCP stalwarts Nolen, Ford, and Whitten to design master plans for Roanoke, Norfolk, and other southern cities. Their proposals called for the use of restrictive covenants and other planning tools to create "colored" or "Negro expansion areas." Long after the *Buchanan* ruling, writes Silver, "the racial zoning ideal remained a mainstay of planners" and not simply a "manifestation of misguided southern leaders out of touch with the mainstream of urban reform." As late as 1928, the National Housing Association's *Housing* magazine continued to advocate segregation, noting that covenants offered a "perfectly legitimate method" for dealing with "the Negro problem."[22]

Planners' racial preoccupations would have a lasting impact on twentieth-century suburban politics because zoning's early promoters built networks and devised political strategies that soon popularized their model of municipal restriction nationwide. During the 1910s, zoning advocacy gave rise to a new public-private alliance, a loose network of officials, planners, and businesspeople that promoted restriction at the municipal level while simultaneously lobbying for legislation (and even court rulings) that would eventually facilitate zoning's remarkable spread. The alliance began to take shape when planners and businesspeople collaborated and pooled resources. As early as 1913, realtors helped lobby the Wisconsin, Minnesota, and Illinois state legislatures to empower certain classes of cities to establish residential districts that excluded manufacturing and commercial development (Illinois's governor vetoed the measure). In New York the cities of Syracuse and Utica created "residence districts" that restricted construction to single- and two-family dwellings. In 1914, Duncan McDuffie, the architect and developer who sat on NAREB's City Planning Committee, helped found the California Conference on City Planning, which in turn successfully lobbied the legislature to pass the state's first city planning enabling legislation the following May. Public-private collaboration quickly became the norm nationwide. When the American City Planning Institute was established in 1917, its fifty-two founding members included the CPC's Nichols, Bouton, Jemison, and Ninde. Soon prominent residential developers, including Paul Harsch and Harry Kissell, were actively promoting the adoption of restrictive land-use instruments. Most of these instruments focused on protecting single-family residences from factories, stores, and apartments.[23]

NCCP leadership encouraged such collaboration and applauded the adoption of local ordinances, but feared that most were far too limited in scope. Confirming their fears was the frequency with which judges struck down individual zoning experiments. Planners responded with a concerted, two-pronged advocacy campaign. They encouraged municipalities to adopt comprehensive land-use ordinances, instead of the more limited use and size restrictions. At the same time they set out to educate planners, builders, and public officials, including judges, about zoning and the law. To fashion a legal defense for restriction they turned, not surprisingly, to urban science, arguing that zoning would meet the constitutional test if its advocates effectively marshalled scientific expertise.

Quickly emerging as an influential spokesperson for this strategy was Cincinnati attorney and municipal reformer Alfred Bettman. In 1914 he urged the NCCP to recognize that the "question of protecting residential districts is in the United States today a question of Constitutional law," and predicted that advocates would "win their victory" only if they convinced the courts that zoning represented a justifiable use of the municipal police power. The key would be demonstrating that restrictive ordinances were designed not for an "aesthetic motive" but to ensure "safety or comfort or order or health." Thus "it would seem wise," Bettman explained, "that the courts be educated [about zoning], so to speak, by having the actual enactment of such legislation preceded by some scientific study of the city's plan, so that the residential-district ordinance may bear a relation to the plan of the city, and the plan should be devised with a view to the health or the comfort or the safety of the people of the city." For example, a developer seeking justification to separate residential and commercial districts should hire "leading physicians" to "make a study of the effect of noise upon the nervous system of human beings." If this demonstrated that "the lessening of noises and turmoil and hurly-burly will tend to lessen the extent of nervous diseases in the city, no court could say that the ordinance was passed solely for the promotion of aesthetic satisfactions." Versions of this argument were soon presented regularly by lawyers defending embattled ordinances, a development that pleased Veiller since it presaged what he predicted would be a new kind of "judge-proof" planning law. By 1916, Veiller was encouraging NCCP audiences to tell judges that single-family zoning represented nothing more than a local government's exercise of its police power to protect the public welfare.[24]

––––––––

Both the police power defense of restrictive zoning and its social scientific rationales for exclusion would eventually become hallmarks of zoning advocacy. In the mid-1920s, Bettman would emphasize both in arguments before the Supreme Court, and that Court would cite both when upholding a city's right to adopt a comprehensive ordinance. In the meantime, one local experiment with municipal restriction, passage of New York City's ordinance in 1916, set equally important precedents for zoning's future. By that year many cities had adopted height and bulk restrictions on commercial buildings. But the New York City ordinance marked a significant departure and a watershed in the history of land-use restriction, because it represented the kind of truly comprehensive restriction long promoted at the NCCP, by dividing the entire city into "zones" (on the European model) and regulating land use in each. Of equal importance, passage of the New York City ordinance helped further codify zoning's discriminatory logic and its assumptions about race and property. Scholars and critics have long disagreed about early zoning's intent. Many treat race and class exclusion as an accidental by-product, or at best as a misuse of an otherwise well-intentioned experiment in urban reform. Other scholars have demonstrated, quite persuasively, the race- and class-discriminatory *intent* of the early planning movement.[25] The history of the New York City ordinance shows how zoning helped codify a new kind of racially discriminatory land-use politics, one that targeted racial minorities, in fact—and did so because white elites saw racial hierarchy as normative—but did not rely on race-specific language to do so. The strategies employed to promote New York City's experiment; the assumptions about property, wealth, race, and inequality written into the ordinance itself; and the ordinance's eventual success in the courts: each would prove foundational to modern zoning and housing politics and to whites' efforts to maintain the residential color line.

The movement that created the nation's first comprehensive zoning ordinance first took shape in 1907, when Fifth Avenue luxury-goods retailers,
led by former journalist and publisher Robert Grier Cooke, spearheaded a
campaign to exclude garment factories from the avenue's elite shopping and
hotel district north of Fourteenth Street. Cooke's group, the Fifth Avenue
Association, spoke for proprietors and patrons upset by the proliferation of
garment plants in the loft spaces atop the district's commercial buildings,
plants that drew thousands of garment workers—primarily recent immigrants from southeastern Europe—into the streets before work, after work,
and during the mid-afternoon lunch break. Their presence was particularly
unsettling to the city's affluent consumers, who frequented Fifth Avenue during the "fashionable hour between twelve and one" only to find themselves
"struggling for passage with ten thousand operatives." Cooke's campaign
dovetailed with the aims of local, reform-minded public officials. It was embraced by leaders of New York's ruling Fusion coalition and a number of its
most committed activists, particularly George McAneny and Edward M. Bassett, long-time public servants, reformers, and students of urban planning.
In 1911, Cooke appealed to McAneny when he was serving as Borough President to create a public commission that would determine whether restrictions were needed on Fifth Avenue. McAneny in turn appointed the Fifth
Avenue Commission, all but one of whose members belonged to the Fifth
Avenue Association. In March 1912 the commission proposed a height limitation of 125 feet for structures built on Fifth Avenue and a limit of 300 feet
for buildings to the east and west, a plan clearly intended to prevent the
construction of structures capable of accommodating manufacturing plants.
Two months later, McAneny offered a similar proposal to the city's Board
of Estimate and Apportionment. It ignored his plan, so in 1913 he created
the Heights and Buildings Commission (HBC), directing it to propose a
municipal zoning plan and justify its implementation.[26]

The HBC provided a forum for prominent members of the young city
planning movement. It was chaired by Bassett and included two influential NCCP members, Lawrence Veiller and Lawson Purdy, as well as other
prominent realtors, lawyers, architects, city officials, and Fifth Avenue Association members. Its report, unveiled six months later, clearly bore the mark
of planning's new orientation. The commission surveyed zoning policies in
the United States, Canada, and Europe, discussed American municipalities'
legal right to zone, and emphasized the dangers posed by the concentration of skyscrapers, such as overcrowding and threats to the public health.
Their report singled out the Fifth Avenue district, yet insisted that the "in-
jury" caused by incompatible uses in this district was "not an isolated prob-

lem, but part of a problem that confronts the entire city." In addition to recommending a 125-foot limit for new construction and the exclusion of factories from Fifth Avenue, it proposed that the entire city be "divided into districts," "natural" districts of "different occupation, use and type of building construction," and set restrictions on future development within each. These restrictions should be designed, they argued, "with a proper regard for the most beneficial use of the land . . . practicable under existing conditions as to improvements and land values."[27]

Meanwhile local zoning advocates cultivated support for restriction by appealing directly to affluent New Yorkers, focusing on the danger posed both by factories and the immigrants working in them. In 1912, the Fifth Avenue Association's annual report, cited in the *New York Times*, argued that "restriction and regulation" were the only sure means of stopping the "vast flood of workers which sweeps down the pavement at noon-time every day and literally overwhelms and engulfs shops, shopkeepers, and the shopping public." It was "imperative," the association insisted, "to put an effectual stop to the evil," predicting that the immigrant workforce could otherwise "not be controlled." A muted version of this warning appeared four years later in a full-page *Times* advertisement entitled "Shall we save New York?" which argued that the expansion of factory lofts above Thirty-second Street threatened to "blight" the "finest retail and residential sections in the world," thus "depleting" the area of its "normal residents," a population described in a subsequent appeal as "normal people." Interviewed by the *Times*, McAneny compared the "invasion" of factories and immigrant workers to a plague of locusts.[28] Although the campaign made no explicit references to biological difference, contemporary public debates provided the context for the association's indictment of what it called the "hurlyburly crowd." Clearly, as Raphael Fischler writes, "class- and race-based exclusion was a conscious rationale of building and land-use regulation from its very first days." Again it would be a mistake to describe the early zoning movement as focused primarily on racial exclusion per se. Zoning's advocates were focused on ensuring efficient and profitable urban development. Nonetheless, the restriction of populations viewed as racially suspect was seen as integral to that process, it was regularly taken for granted in early debates over restriction, and it readily became symbolic of zoning's promise.[29]

Cooke's campaign garnered enough support to ensure the appointment in 1914 of a Committee on City Planning, which counted Bassett, Purdy, Whitten, and George Ford among its members. The committee oversaw the drafting of the nation's first comprehensive zoning ordinance, one based directly upon the recommendations of its predecessor, the Heights and

Buildings Commission. Their draft was approved in 1916, creating the first comprehensive measure adopted in an American city.[30]

That ordinance represented the culmination of years of advocacy and a confluence of discrete but complementary interests: the parochial aims of Fifth Avenue merchants and the city's landed elite, the public-spirited zeal of City Scientific reformers such as McAneny and Bassett, and the class and racial prejudices that shaped a vision of cities, property, and populations shared by metropolitan elites in the both the public and private sectors. The ordinance articulated assumptions about the rights of property owners and the nature of compatible populations that had long guided zoning advocacy, and thus marked a notable victory for the NCCP, which, since 1914, had counted both McAneny and Bassett as members of its General Committee.[31] Much like the conference itself, the New York City ordinance embodied a tension long central to zoning politics—an attempt to balance the pursuit of local and blatantly discriminatory interests, on the one hand, with planners' proud investment in the patina of progressive and scientific reform, on the other.[32] Meanwhile, the battle over restriction in New York City reenacted locally what the NCCP had been doing for national advocacy, by conflating ideas about the scientific management of property with arguments for the necessity of segregating populations by race and class. Finally, the New York ordinance was the first comprehensive zoning instrument to give full statutory expression to this new discriminatory land-use science and would serve as precedent for the model eventually codified and reproduced throughout the century. Its passage acted out on a local stage the convergence of two parallel developments that would come to characterize land-use politics in the United States: the articulation of a theory of urban economics and politics that presupposed racial and class difference but did not always address racial topics by name and the inscription of this theory in powerful legislation that enabled whites to segregate metropolitan resources systematically, again without directly talking about race.

With the victory in New York City behind them, NCCP leadership redoubled their efforts to popularize comprehensive zoning and win over the courts. Continuing Bettman's strategy, leading planners replaced aesthetic arguments for restriction with social-scientific ones. Meanwhile they continued to stress zoning's importance for residential planning and development, arguing that the science of restriction was necessary, above all else, to protect the value of private property. In the years immediately following passage of the New York City ordinance, advocates aggressively promoted the zoning concept and made the property value justification the campaign's rhetorical focus. The prominence of this argument was revealed during a 1918 NCCP roundtable on the topic of residential restriction, when National Municipal League president Lawson Purdy announced that "the courts must be educated," so that they "see what we wish them to see." It was critical to "think in terms of value," he explained, to "popularize the idea of preserving the value of a man's house, of a man's lot. Get that talked about." "When you meet one of these judges tell him about it," Purdy concluded, "so that when, bye-a-bye, a case comes before him as a judge, it will be entirely familiar to him." [33]

The audience's response to Purdy's appeal was revealing. Most participants apparently took for granted the urgency of "educating the courts" and immediately turned the discussion toward what was seen as a more pressing problem: using zoning to segregate what one speaker called "different races" (including the "foreign born") now that the Supreme Court had outlawed racial zoning in *Buchanan*. There was some dissent; one participant was outraged that zoning could be used to exclude immigrants from what he called the "family of Americans." But NCCP President Frederick Law Olmsted Jr., had the final word, reiterating a theory about property value and populations that echoed a now familiar discussion about the urgency of race preservation. To ensure the success of a new residential subdivision, Olmsted explained, "one must, of course, consider the requirements and the habits of the people for whom the houses are being built," requirements that were "more or less coincident with racial divisions." "It is a question," he concluded, of "how far one can intermingle houses for people who do not readily intermingle with each other and get away with the thing commercially." [34]

That a planning session on residential restriction was dominated by discussions of legal strategy and racial difference demonstrates just how far zoning advocacy had come since the conference's creation in 1909. In less than a decade, a movement initiated by the impulse to bring order to unbridled and often dangerous urban growth had been transformed into a powerful alliance of public and private figures who championed zoning as a means to protect white property owners in "high class" residential enclaves. Most important, their theory of land-use economics treated racial and class differentials, like other supposedly objective land-use variables, as calculable. Advocating these principles and applying them nationwide was a well-organized cohort of planners and builders hard at work encouraging localities to experiment with restriction. Participation of the real estate industry was particularly decisive, as local real estate boards promoted the adoption of local ordinances, especially outside of city centers. By 1917, the success of the New York City ordinance had prompted campaigns to introduce comprehensive zoning in twenty-one municipalities, including Baltimore, Chicago, Cleveland, Los Angeles, Milwaukee, Minneapolis, Philadelphia, St. Louis, San Francisco, Seattle, and Washington, D.C.[35]

Meanwhile zoning's new respectability further emboldened its promoters, many of whom spoke openly about the necessity of segregation. Robert Whitten followed up his work on the New York City ordinance by returning to his lucrative consultancy business, designing an ordinance for Atlanta with separate districts for residents described as "white," "colored," and "undetermined." To Whitten this was a noble gesture, intended to "promote the welfare and prosperity of both the white and colored races." A less generous interpretation came from journalist Bruno Lasker in 1920, who took Whitten and his fellow planners to task in the pages of *The Survey* for turning restrictive zoning into a tool for excluding "undesirable neighbors." Whitten replied that he was confused by Lasker's assertion "that zoning tends inevitably toward segregation of the different economic classes." "I admit the fact," Whitten explained, "but do not consider this result either antisocial or undemocratic in its tendency." "A reasonable segregation is normal, inevitable and desirable," he concluded, "and cannot be greatly affected, one way or the other, by zoning." Here Whitten previewed what would soon become a familiar defense of restrictive zoning and racially restrictive federal housing policy; the existence of de facto segregation, he insisted, made continued, state-sponsored segregation a necessity.[36]

Meanwhile zoning advocates did not see any conflict in promoting the use of public power to protect private interests. They openly celebrated the new public-private alliance and its potential for shaping metropolitan land-use patterns. At the 1919 meeting of the NCCP, Olmsted used his presidential address to call for even "greater cooperation between private subdividers and local government through the establishment of city zoning and subdivision regulations and planning." His allegiance to this partnership was forged, as it had been for many advocates, by both an intellectual commitment to the planning concept and by more practical, professional considerations. By 1919, Olmsted had worked with a number of prominent "community builders," both as director of the U.S. Housing Corporation's Town Planning Division (between 1918 and 1919) and through his firm's work on residential subdivisions for Bouton, McDuffie, and other NAREB members.[37]

In the decade following their victory in New York City, zoning's advocates gained important new supporters when businesspeople and public officials embraced and popularized the zoning concept and the courts sanctioned, thereby quickly accelerating, the adoption of restrictive ordinances nationwide. In both public and private arenas, meanwhile, the claim that zoning represented a nonideological, scientific approach to development was continually invoked to validate the pursuit of local (and often) discriminatory interests. Zoning's defenders insisted that its aim was solely managerial: to ensure development patterns that protected the health, welfare, and economic self-sufficiency of local residents by separating incompatible land uses. Yet advocates focused considerable energy on the exclusion of renters and other populations from neighborhoods of "homeowners." They also placed the power to make choices about compatibility solely in the hands of those same property owners. Crucially important for the subsequent history of restriction was a series of legislative interventions and court rulings between 1916 and 1920, when public officials outlined, for the first time, the legal guidelines for determining what constituted a compatible use. Inscribed within these guidelines were clearly delineated hierarchies of class and race. The guidelines quickly gained considerable force because they were championed and aggressively promoted not only by municipal leaders and state legislatures but also by Hoover's Department of Commerce and the Supreme Court.

The lower courts had begun to affirm the municipal zoning power, albeit in piecemeal fashion, before 1916, by validating ordinances that restricted establishments or structures deemed harmful to residential neighborhoods. These included brickyards, laundries, carpet-beating establishments, slaughterhouses, and billboards. Municipal officials scrutinized these rulings, acutely aware that there was little consensus about the validity of the zoning concept, few solid precedents, and no clear judicial guidelines for design or enforcement. Local officials were especially sensitive to the fact that even favorable rulings failed to provide clear guidelines for determining what constituted a compatible land use.

For this reason, the constitutional justification invoked to validate early restrictive ordinances had important consequences for subsequent zoning theory and practice. In most of the early, favorable rulings, the courts validated a municipality's right to exclude anything if officials demonstrated that restriction eliminated threats to the public health and safety. And to sort out this ill-defined "health and safety" standard, the courts turned to the law and language of "nuisance" abatement. Nuisance doctrine developed in medieval England to provide a means of redress for conflicts between private landowners, when one proprietor's use infringed upon the use or enjoyment of another's. In the nineteenth century, U.S. industrial expansion and debates over the public good led to the development of a public nuisance law. Not until the 1880s was the doctrine invoked to justify specific land-use restrictions, when the Supreme Court, in *Barbier v. Connelly* (1885), upheld a ban against the operation of commercial laundries in San Francisco's affluent residential enclaves. Notably the ruling treated commercial and human threats to property owners as interchangeable, arguing that the ban protected residents not only from material nuisances, such as street flooding and fire, but also the "moral" threat posed by the presence of Chinese business owners. Few subsequent decisions described racial threats so explicitly, but they did repeatedly refer to the necessity of protecting "public . . . morals," as a California court, in *Ex parte Quong Wo* (1911), described the threat posed by Chinese-owned laundries.[38]

In the meantime, several courts invoked nuisance doctrine to defend a municipality's authority to zone. From its 1909 ruling in *Welch v. Swasey* (validating the use of height restrictions in Boston) to its approval of use restrictions in *Hadacheck v. City of Los Angeles* (1915), the Supreme Court broadened its reading of nuisance doctrine and made it central to legal justifications for municipal land-use control.[39] Zoning advocates closely monitored and celebrated these favorable rulings throughout the 1910s. They remained concerned, however, that by 1916 no court had ruled on the kind of comprehensive regulation outlined in the New York City ordinance. Indeed that ordinance raised very complicated interpretive issues. While earlier rulings had approved specific restrictions or limits on, for example, the size and bulk of structures or the exercise of potentially harmful commercial activities, comprehensive restrictions had not been affirmed nor had their rationale been tested.

Uncertainty about zoning's legal status did not stop city and state officials from promoting it. In New York City, an amendment to the municipal charter permitted adoption of its groundbreaking new ordinance. Meanwhile a number of states, many with the aid of Bettman, Bassett, and other leading zoning experts, began drafting and adopting standard city and state zoning enabling acts that empowered most "home-rule" municipalities to adopt restrictive land-use legislation. By 1922, twenty states, including Michigan, had passed some version of these acts, which in turn "guided the majority of cities" nationwide on land-use planning throughout the decade.[40]

These state-level interventions proved to be very important. The standard acts, many of them drafted by zoning's most prominent national advocates, represented the first attempts by state or federal authorities to standardize and give statutory expression to land-use restriction. Scholars have noted that their passage facilitated zoning's spread after 1916 and fueled efforts to establish national standards for defining the municipal police power. The acts did far more than this, however. By giving state sanction to existing zoning practice, the acts also endorsed the still contested argument that "nuisance" doctrine validated municipal zoning, applied that rationale to comprehensive zoning for the first time, and encouraged hundreds of local communities to embrace this strategy. Almost inadvertently, state legislatures began the process of formally standardizing the municipal power to control land use and the arguments that would support that power. Because the states turned to existing ordinances and precedents, and because they sought direct counsel from the NCCP and other leading planners, the enabling acts promoted the zoning concept that had been designed by the public-private planning alliance during the early years of local experimentation. Building on the New York City model and existing court rulings, state legislators applied the "nuisance" doctrine heretofore used solely to validate restrictions against *specific acts or activities* deemed harmful to a community to the city's authority to restrict *land use in general*. This triggered an important transformation in the application of nuisance law. By applying the lower court's far narrower application of the nuisance doctrine (in *Welch v. Swasey*, for example) to justify comprehensive land-use ordinances, state enabling acts asserted a jurisdictional reach for the local zoning power far broader than that defined in the courts' precedent-setting cases.

The new enabling acts mimicked earlier court rulings in other important ways, by invoking the nuisance abatement justification for zoning without providing guidelines for identifying and assessing harmful land uses. This left localities and the courts considerable leeway to set those guidelines in later years. Meanwhile the acts validated and further promoted the lower courts' implicit (and sometimes quite explicit) conflation of people and property. Like the ordinances and court decisions that shaped them, the state statutes were grounded upon the principle that some populations posed a calculable threat to the affluent and to whites.

Passage of the state acts also put the burden squarely back on the courts, forcing them to rule on the constitutionality of comprehensive zoning. And state judges declared that it was legal, in language that confirmed the new, broader interpretation of nuisance doctrine and its applicability to land-use restriction. Two decisions were pivotal. In a 1920 advisory opinion, the Supreme Court of Massachusetts enthusiastically endorsed a state enabling act authorizing cities to use comprehensive zoning. It cited a host of earlier, but much narrower, nuisance precedents regarding the exclusion from residential neighborhoods of "disagreeable" uses. That same year, in *Lincoln Trust Co. v. Williams Building Corp.*, the New York Court of Appeals approved New

York City's comprehensive ordinance, also citing narrower precedents that had prohibited from residential neighborhoods such nuisances or "near nuisances" as laundries, brick kilns, and billboards.[41]

Thus in just four years, between the adoption of the New York City ordinance in 1916 and the 1920 rulings, the nuisance justification for comprehensive zoning had been written into more than a dozen state constitutions, numerous local ordinances, and finally into state court rulings. Then throughout the early 1920s, state and federal courts continued to uphold and expand the municipal police power, ruling that nuisance prevention provided a legitimate legal foundation for public interventions designed to prevent what the Wisconsin Supreme Court in 1923 called "the deterioration in the desirability of certain residential sections."[42] Just as lawyer and planning advocate Alfred Bettman had predicted at the 1914 NCCP, the courts proved unwilling to strike down zoning ordinances, regardless of their discriminatory intent or impact, when they claimed justification in the science of land-use management. More than this, the courts, with the encouragement of public officials nationwide, had dramatically expanded the legal meaning of nuisance itself. By applying the concept to comprehensive zoning, and by authorizing landowners to determine what, precisely, constituted a nuisance, the courts assigned a legal status to land uses, including types of tenancy and categories of occupants, that affluent homeowners found threatening. This expansion of the nuisance doctrine marked a key step in the process by which property owners and courts fashioned a supposedly economic argument about compatible land use, one that excluded specific types of tenancy arrangements, specific kinds of architecture, or even specific populations while claiming to rise above ideology.

———————

Ultimately it was in thousands of local places that comprehensive zoning would have the greatest impact, because it was at the municipal level that zoning simultaneously shaped land-use patterns and introduced a new rationale for exclusion to local land-use politics. A brief examination of the changes in zoning authority in Michigan and, by extension, in metropolitan Detroit demonstrates how the national politics of land-use restriction was beginning to shape local suburban land-use practices, while also introducing the new planning science and its exclusionary logic to suburbs that would eventually represent the front lines of whites' battle against "racial invasion."

Michigan Public Acts 207 and 5, both adopted in 1921, dramatically increased home-rule municipalities' power to control local land use. They did so by broadly interpreting a municipality's right to both identify and elimi-nate public nuisances.[43] Prior to this, the state's autonomous localities held limited authority, under the 1909 constitution, to regulate or prohibit spe-cific acts or activities such as gambling, liquor sales, "vice and immorality," "noise and disturbance," "anything tending to cause or promote disease," and "the use of toy pistols." Home-rule cities approved subdivision plats, enforced building regulations, and licensed specific commercial enterprises (such as billiard tables, ball alleys, taverns, and butcher shops), but other-wise had no direct control over how people used their private property.[44]

The 1921 enabling acts revolutionized urban land-use politics in Michi-gan by writing into the state constitution the zoning model fashioned by the NCCP, NAREB leadership, and other advocates over the previous decade. The Michigan bills were introduced and promoted by a state senator and his colleagues on the Senate Committee on Cities and Villages (appointed just two months earlier), all of whom were businessmen, developers, and real estate agents from Detroit, Battle Creek, Muskegon, Bay City, and Ann Arbor. With the help of local NAREB representatives and professional plan-ners, they drafted a bill modeled upon existing comprehensive zoning legislation and including provisions and language that clearly anticipated and sought to preempt future legal challenges. The new laws prescribed comprehensive restriction and justified it by citing its goal of maintaining neighborhood "character" and protecting property values. Meanwhile they claimed legal sanction for restriction in the new, expanded interpretation of nuisance doctrine. The restrictions outlined by Act 207 were intended to "lessen congestion on the public streets" and "promote public health, safety and general welfare" and should be designed "with reasonable con-sideration, among other things, to the character of the district, its peculiar suitability for particular uses, the conservation of property values and the general trend and character of building and population development." Lo-cal authorities were given broad discretion to determine what kinds of land uses were harmful to "residential" neighborhoods. Indeed, the act empow-ered local elites to simply designate as "nuisances" any buildings or land uses that they suspected might harm the "public health, safety and general welfare." Section 7 concludes that "buildings erected, altered, razed or con-verted, or uses carried on in violation of any provision of local ordinances or regulations made under the authority of this act are hereby declared to be a nuisance per se." And "the court," it concludes, "shall order such nuisance abated."[45]

With this provision, Michigan's state legislators gave statutory form to a theory about compatible land use first articulated by housing economists,

builders, and reform-minded municipal officials in the 1910s, later validated by the court's expansion of the nuisance doctrine, and finally written into law in individual municipal ordinances, most notably in the New
York ordinance of 1916. Michigan's enabling act, like similar acts elsewhere,
further codified and standardized this zoning model, disseminated it to
localities, and, in the process, gave sweeping powers to local elites without defining precisely which land uses posed a threat, instead giving those
elites the power to simply determine and calculate "compatibility." It was
these powers, and the assumptions inscribed within them, that suburban
residents and leaders in places like Royal Oak, Dearborn, Ferndale, and Troy
would employ decades later, when zoning became the focus of suburban
land-use politics.

Spreading the Gospel: The Department of Commerce and the Standard State Zoning Enabling Act

The zoning model outlined by the public-private alliance would eventually
guide land-use politics in thousands of municipalities, in large measure
because the federal government embraced and promoted that model beginning in 1921. Before that year, zoning advocacy had remained a largely
private affair, and the only public officials involved in land-use debates were
municipal officials, state legislators, and judges. With the election of Warren
Harding, planners and developers found a powerful new ally in the federal
government, and any doubts about zoning's validity or the standards for
determining land-use compatibility would soon be put to rest. Thanks in
large measure to the new secretary of commerce, Herbert Hoover, restrictive
zoning and the arguments used to justify it would soon be standardized and
reproduced nationwide.

Hoover's interest in development politics and public-private cooperation predated his tenure at the Department of Commerce. An engineer by
training, Hoover worked for private companies in the American Southwest,
Australia, and China in the 1890s and 1910s, establishing a reputation as
a first-rate engineer, financier, manager, and promoter. Based in London
when the war broke out in 1914, he was recruited by the U.S. government
to assist with the evacuation of American tourists and later to manage relief efforts in Belgium and France. Hoover was Wilson's logical choice to
become U.S. Food administrator when the nation entered the war in 1917
and served as American Relief administrator to coordinate recovery in postwar Russia.

By the time of his return to the United States in 1920, Hoover was a minor celebrity and a leading figure in a movement to promote a new "corporate" or "associative" state, in which private sector professionals worked with government officials to guide the nation's economic development. The goal was to limit government intervention in domestic affairs, by encouraging business organizations to monitor and regulate economic activity voluntarily, ensuring that American enterprise remained efficient and productive but also humane. Hoover's prominence earned him the presidency of the Federated American Engineering Societies, a new organization committed to promoting industrial efficiency in part by influencing public policy. In 1921 he took over at Commerce, quickly transforming it into a sort of command center of the new "associative" state. Hoover organized the numerous public-private bodies—the committees, councils, and conferences—that studied, published, and advised on a range of topics, including production and safety standards for manufacturing, promoting domestic and foreign markets for American goods, regulating the airwaves and aviation, and encouraging health education in the schools. Prominent on Hoover's agenda was the promotion of home construction, homeownership, and municipal land-use control.[46] His tenure at Commerce marked the beginning of the federal government's extensive intervention in private markets for residence. Ironically, it was an attempt to arrest the growth of federal power and a "statist" regulatory apparatus that helped initiate decades of intensive government involvement in the nation's housing economy and, ultimately, in its suburban politics.

Hoover was not starting from scratch on the housing front; World War I had already prompted some public-private collaboration. It was NAREB that initiated these experiments in 1917, by offering its services to assist the U.S. military (without compensation) in obtaining leases, gathering "intelligent appraisals on leaseholds or property needed by the government," and purchasing property suitable for "housing facilities at any point where government work is being carried on." Anticipating a severe housing crisis for war workers, federal officials accepted the offer. In 1918, J. C. Nichols, Henry Haas, and other NAREB leaders traveled to Washington, D.C., to advise in the creation of the U.S. Housing Corporation (USHC), a division of the Labor Department's Bureau of Housing. By year's end, NAREB members were directing the USHC's new Real Estate Division, a comparable Real Estate Division of the War Department, and the Housing Division of the Emergency Fleet Corporation's U.S. Shipping Board, which subsidized financing for developers who provided housing for shipyard workers. The USHC was up and running by July and eventually provided accommodations (either through construction or the management of existing units) for 110,000 workers. It also drew other prominent planners into the new federal-private partnership. Olmsted directed the USHC's Town Planning Division, while Veiller drafted its recommended standards for war housing design.[47]

NAREB was also busy preparing for future lobbying efforts. In June 1918, it established the War Service Board, designed to promote private-public cooperation after war's end. Three months later the association relocated its national headquarters from Minneapolis to Washington, D.C., providing easier access to legislators when the wartime (and war-driven) construction boom gave way to a postwar slump. NAREB joined other private organizations in lobbying for federal tax credits on mortgages and calling for a system of federal discount operations to promote lending. The organization also sought federal aid to promote the zoning concept. Because the Supreme Court had not spoken on comprehensive zoning's constitutionality, many local officials remained wary of experimentation. So planners and developers called for the drafting of a standard enabling act, a federally sanctioned template for zoning legislation that state legislators could easily incorporate into their constitutions.[48]

The NAREB and NCCP development vision—harnessing public authority to promote robust, orderly metropolitan growth—fit comfortably into Hoover's vision of the associative state. The secretary created the Division of Building and Housing (DBH) and staffed it with NAREB leaders, who in turn helped orchestrate the department's efforts to promote residential development and land-use regulation. Commerce intervened in two important arenas. First, it worked closely with business leaders to promote home construction and homeownership, building in part on an informal, short-lived collaborative effort, the "Own-Your-Own-Home" campaign, organized after World War I by NAREB and the Department of Labor. The DBH was designed specifically, as Dolores Hayden explains, "to stimulate consumption through the standardization of lots, houses, and building materials."[49]

In response to NAREB's urging, Hoover also put the department's authority and resources behind a new nonprofit organization, Better Homes in America, Inc., founded in 1921 by magazine publisher Marie Meloney to sponsor local, volunteer committees that promoted spending in the housing sector. Better Homes was a relatively modest operation before Hoover helped arrange private funding for their work (via a Rockefeller Foundation grant) and reorganized it as a public service corporation in 1923. Meloney agreed to relinquish control, and Better Homes relocated to Washington, D.C., where it was joined by Hoover (as its president), Harvard ethics professor James Ford (executive director), and Calvin Coolidge (who joined its advisory council). The directors of the DBH also served as officers of Better Homes, which began coordinating Better Homes campaigns in local communities nationwide—as many as 7,000 by decade's end. A popular feature of these local promotions was the fully furnished "demonstration house," five thousand of which were built for public viewing. (A demonstration house in Kalamazoo, Michigan, reportedly had nearly 20,000 visitors.) Better Homes volunteers also gave lectures, distributed publications (*How to Own Your Own Home* appeared in 1923), and led discussions on topics including home finance, construction standards, zoning, sanitation, citizenship, "racial strife," and the threat that Communism posed to the private enterprise system. The message was consistent and was echoed in all of Commerce's housing-related promotional efforts: expanding homeownership was vital to the nation's economic health and its cultural ideals, including the maintenance and sustenance of healthy families.[50]

Complementing these campaigns was a series of less public but consequential interventions, as Commerce provided substantial financial and institutional support to planners, developers, and economists seeking to change both how land use was regulated and how housing was financed, built, and sold. Commerce's multifaceted contributions to the residential development sector were largely invisible to the average American, but they fostered a new relationship between the state, business leaders, and academics that set the course for decades of public policy and metropolitan development politics. Hoover initiated the first formal and potentially permanent federal involvement in the public-private alliance that had taken shape in the early planning movement. Commerce promoted public-private collaborations that were purely advisory but, nonetheless, provided zoning's advocates and a generation of housing economists with resources and legitimacy that enabled them to popularize and standardize new strategies for promoting residential development, controlling its use, and explaining any inequalities that these new mechanisms produced.

Receiving by far the least fanfare was the department's support for a group of real estate economists who were outlining a radical new vision of housing markets and metropolitan growth. Its proponents were based at the Institute for Research in Land Economics and Public Utilities, founded in 1920 by Richard Ely at the University of Wisconsin. Ely was legendary, one of the nation's most prominent economic thinkers and a key figure in popularizing economics as a field of academic study.[51] His new institute brought together scholars—most of them his students—to explore how the adoption of new investment and land-use strategies could promote the development of a *speculative* market for housing finance. In their view three essential preconditions would create and sustain such a market: the standardization of property appraisal practices, the widespread use of a more flexible and affordable mortgage instrument, and the widespread adoption of zoning ordinances, restrictive covenants, and other land-use restrictions.

Naturally these economists found allies among real estate developers and public officials anxious to stimulate the production and sale of homes. Since 1918, Ely had been speaking before the meetings of real estate boards nationwide and corresponding with NAREB representatives about the need for collaboration. Ely's dream of scientifically codifying real estate practice (and by doing so spreading homeownership) fit nicely with realtors' ongoing campaign to create professional institutions and a professional culture. They agreed with Ely that real estate practice, which they were now calling "realology," needed to be "just as much an established science as geology and zoology," as Kansas City developer J. C. Nichols told his colleagues at NAREB's annual meeting in 1924. Throughout the 1920s, Commerce joined NAREB in promoting institute scholarship and, as a result, dramatically raised its profile. Together Hoover and the nation's leading residential developers sponsored institute research, hired its economists as consultants, and eventually recruited several into powerful advisory positions; Ely, for example, served as a consultant for the Department of Commerce and the institute produced reports for the U.S. Bureau of the Census. In 1921, NAREB designated the institute as its official "reference organization" and named Ely "adviser for Research and Education." Soon NAREB was copublishing Ely's Land Economics Series textbooks with Macmillan, volumes that would eventually transform college curricula and real estate practice nationwide and popularize the institute's work on appraisal, mortgage markets, and land-use restriction.[52]

Another momentous Commerce intervention began in 1921, with the creation of the Advisory Committee on Zoning. Hoover assigned it two tasks: encouraging municipal officials to adopt restrictive land-use ordinances and drafting a standard enabling act that legislators could adopt in state constitutions. Its staff was recruited from the reformers and businesspeople long in the forefront of planning advocacy: NCCP-stalwart and New York City zoning activist Edward Bassett; NHA-founder and former NCCP executive committee member Lawrence Veiller; subdivision developer and future NAREB president Irving B. Hiett; ACPI president and former NCCP Executive Committee member Nelson Lewis; NCCP and U.S. Chamber of Commerce member and former NHA field secretary John Ihlder; USCC member Morris Knowles; Frederick Law Olmsted Jr., a past president of both the ACPI and the NCCP and currently president of the American

Society of Landscape Architects; and past president of the American Civic Association J. Horace McFarland. The project was overseen by John M. Gries of the Harvard Business School, who had recently been appointed chief of Commerce's Division of Building and Housing.[53]

The Advisory Committee represented the first federally sanctioned and federally supported body organized specifically for the promotion of zoning and the new land-use science. Its members made no secret of their desire to encourage continued collaboration between the public and private sectors and of their intention to build directly upon precedents established in the early years of zoning advocacy. Indeed many of the same men who had for years endorsed a very specific, discriminatory vision of zoning's intent were now given a federal mandate to prescribe a standardized template for municipal restriction. After careful consultation with what they called "practical zoners," the experts "who have been associated with a majority of zoned cities," the committee members drafted promotional brochures, guidelines, and finally the "Standard State Zoning Enabling Act," first circulated in 1922, which codified and disseminated the new zoning concept. The Advisory Committee portrayed land-use regulation as a scientific response to the nation's rapid urban growth and placed special emphasis on protecting single-family homes from incompatible development and populations. Commerce described exclusion not as a choice reflecting property owners' class or racial preferences, but rather as a nonideological, indeed an impersonal, tool for protecting the robust free market for property.[54]

The committee's first promotional effort, *Zoning Primer*, a seven-page pamphlet distributed to municipal officials in 1922, describes land-use control as applied science, that is, a technocratic, public-spirited endeavor representing "the application of common sense and fairness to the public regulations governing the use of private real estate." It was a "painstaking, honest effort to provide each district or neighborhood . . . with *just such protection* and *just such liberty* as are sensible in *that particular* district." It "foster[ed] civic spirit by creating confidence in the justice and stability of the protection afforded." A detailed tutorial portrays zoning as a democratic instrument that strikes a delicate balance between property owners' rights and community interest by relying on planning and legal professionals. Proper zoning, the *Primer* explains, was based on "comprehensive and detailed stud[ies]" produced by experts with "professional knowledge." Good zoning increased municipal efficiency because it was designed to "Protect Property and Health" and "Reduce . . . the Cost of Living" for local residents. Zoning ordinances never discriminated. Indeed, modern land-use science produced regulations that would be *the same for all districts of the same type,"* and that would "treat all men alike." [55]

Yet the land-use model outlined in the guidebook was hardly egalitarian, as the privately owned, single-family home occupies a special status and its protection serves as the measure, in the end, of a "well-designed" ordinance. The committee did distinguish "residential" uses from "business" and "manufacturing" more generally, but not all residential arrangements were considered equal or deserving of the same consideration. Neighborhoods of single-family homes afford the most "healthful" living conditions, the *Primer* explains, even illustrating the principle of compatibility by emphasizing the importance of protecting such neighborhoods. In the section "Property and Health," the authors wondered what would happen if "you have just bought some land in a neighborhood of homes and built a cozy little house." "There are two vacant lots south of you. If your town is zoned, no one can put up a large apartment house on those lots, overshadowing your home, stealing your sunshine and spoiling the investment of 20 years' saving. Nor is anyone at liberty to erect a noisy, malodorous public garage to keep you awake at nights or to drive you to sell out for half of what you put into your home." (Other potential sources of "blight," the *Primer* notes elsewhere, are "sporadic stores, or factories, or junk yards.") The single-family home also serves as practical and symbolic centerpiece when the *Primer* demonstrates that "Zoning is Legal." "Enough favorable decisions have been handed down," it explains, "to show that the courts regard regulation . . . as a reasonable exercise of the police power 'for the public health, safety, and general welfare.'" It cites several precedents, including an Ohio court ruling in *Morris v. Osborn*, which upheld residential zones restricted to one- and two-family houses. Until the higher courts ruled on these principles, the Advisory Committee could "not say whether other States will follow." But the courts (and other states) did soon follow, as even the two-family house fell out of favor. In a revised *Primer*, released in 1926, the committee replaced *Morris v. Osborn* with a discussion of subsequent rulings that supported the "exclusion of two-family houses or multifamily houses in certain districts." [56]

By that year, another Commerce initiative had begun to accelerate zoning's spread nationwide. In 1922, just months after releasing the original *Primer*, the Advisory Committee fulfilled advocates' wishes by issuing the "Standard State Zoning Enabling Act," model legislation designed to be inserted, verbatim if necessary, into the home-rule provisions of state constitutions. Decisively shaped by Bassett and Bettman, the act outlined a now familiar set of local controls, empowering municipalities to regulate land use, the height and size of structures, setback and open space requirements, and population density. For the benefit of legislators, the act was carefully annotated, prefaced by background materials and instructions for use, and filled with testaments to the legislation's pedigree, most prominently Hoover's assurance that the act was issued only after an "exacting and painstaking study [of] existing State acts and court decisions and with reference to zoning as it has been practiced and found successful in cities and towns throughout the country." Municipal officials were advised to "modify this standard act as little as possible," since it "has been prepared with a full knowledge of the decisions of the courts in every case in which zoning acts have been under review." In subsequent editions, footnotes update readers on relevant court rulings. Meanwhile the committee distributed supplementary bulletins summarizing new legal "trends."[57]

The act was essentially a set of federally sanctioned standards for restrictive zoning that legitimated zoning advocates' long-standing assumptions about private residential property, compatible land use, and the supposedly scientific basis of restriction. These assumptions are articulated quite explicitly in the act itself. By "encourag[ing] the most appropriate use of land," it explains, zoning would "promote health and the general welfare" of local communities. It describes the separation of incompatible uses as the centerpiece of zoning practice because to be constitutionally valid an ordinance must be designed to "lessen congestion in the streets," "secure safety from fire, panic, and other dangers," "provide adequate light and air," "prevent the overcrowding of land," and "avoid undue concentration of population." Yet like the statutes and court decisions upon which it was modeled, the act fails to provide guidelines for assessing compatibility, instead instructing municipalities to design regulations "made with reasonable consideration, among other things, to the character of the district and its peculiar suitability for particular uses, and with a view to conserving the value of buildings."[58] Footnotes provide some guidance, defining the "suitability for particular uses," for example, as "a reassurance to property interests that zoning is to be done in a sane and practical way," and explaining that zoning must "encourage the most appropriate use of land" by preventing "depreciation of values such as come in 'blighted districts.'" Still by sidestepping the question of *how* municipal authorities should determine compatibility, and by constantly "reassuring property interests," the Department of Commerce endorsed the widespread assumption that local property owners were best qualified to make decisions about neighborhood "character" and "appropriate use."[59]

These assumptions would soon be written into law in municipalities nationwide, as the standard act facilitated and often accelerated passage of numerous state enabling acts. When the Advisory Committee was formed in late 1921, only 48 municipalities and towns, representing less than 11 million urban dwellers, had adopted zoning ordinances. Commerce distributed the standard act in mimeographed form within a year, and a revised version in January 1923. By the end of 1923, eleven states had passed enabling legislation modeled in part or in its entirety on the committee's draft, and 218 local governments had passed ordinances that governed land use for 22 million residents. So great was demand for copies "from persons in all sections of the country" that Commerce issued the act in published form in 1924 and again in 1926, with only minor revisions. By 1925, a total of 19 states had "used the standard act wholly or in part in their laws," and at least 425 municipal governments with more than 27 million residents—over half of the nation's urban population—had passed local ordinances. In just five years, the number of cities with zoning ordinances had increased twelve times. In 1926, the committee proudly reported that "more than 55,000 copies of the [1924] edition had been sold by the Superintendent of Documents."[60]

More than simply popularizing municipal restriction, the Advisory Committee helped disseminate a particular theory of zoning's intent and function, validating and standardizing a model that was blatantly discriminatory but that cast itself as a scientific, nonideological means of managing metropolitan growth. And while the standard act never explicitly discussed race, committee members' work in other contexts confirmed their investment in a model of property and property rights that assumed the importance of racial hierarchies.[61] Meanwhile NAREB and real estate economists provided the texts and manuals that codified and quantified the racially specific risk structure imagined by the nation's planning and business elites. In 1924, NAREB updated its Code of Ethics to require that realtors maintain the racial segregation of neighborhoods. Institute scholars endorsed the use of restrictive zoning and restrictive covenants, both in articles published in its journal *Land Economics* (including a contribution by NCCP stalwart J. C. Nichols) and in two influential monographs released in 1928: Helen Monchow's *The Use of Deed Restrictions in Subdivision Development* and the institute's textbook *Urban Land Economics.*[62]

The Department of Commerce helped set the stage for decades of exclusionary zoning theory and practice by providing federal sanction to an emerging land-use science that would view black occupancy as a threat to white people. Soon hundreds, and eventually thousands, of cities would adopt legislation modeled on the standard act. Further affirming the Advisory Committee's work, meanwhile, and securing zoning's place in

America's postwar future, was the U.S. Supreme Court. Once again, the NCCP's legacy would be decisive.

The Court Speaks: *Euclid v. Ambler* and the Rights of Property

Commerce encouraged more states and cities to experiment with restriction by the mid-1920s, but zoning had still not received a clear judicial sanction. Standing between its advocacy and its widespread use was a significant legal mystery: would the Supreme Court uphold planners' contention that the Constitution permitted public bodies to comprehensively regulate private property? State courts had validated height and area restrictions as legitimate uses of the municipal police power. Yet nearly ten years after passage of New York City's ordinance, only the lower courts had ruled on the constitutionality of comprehensive zoning, and, of perhaps greater importance, there was little agreement about the constitutionality of use restrictions in particular. In 1926, the Supreme Court's ruling in *Euclid v. Ambler* provided the sanction for comprehensive zoning that its advocates had long hoped for and set the standard by which localities and courts would determine the compatibility of land use for decades to come. Significantly it did so by approving the discriminatory logic invoked for years by zoning advocates: the claim that certain property owners, namely, the owners of "better" homes, had the right to control development patterns and to make determinations about what constituted a threat to their communities.

With *Euclid* the law finally caught up with zoning advocacy and practice. And viewed with the benefit of hindsight, the ruling also proved to be the most influential judicial sanction of the discriminatory presumptions that had informed land-use politics for over twenty years. Ruling on a challenge to a municipal zoning ordinance in Ohio, the Supreme Court put to rest debates over the validity of the zoning principle and the constitutionality of use restrictions. It upheld a comprehensive ordinance for the city of Euclid, Ohio, arguing that municipal zoning was valid if designed to protect the "general welfare." The decision performs a very careful balancing act, one that mimicked efforts by the planners and businesspeople long in the forefront of the zoning movement. On the one hand, the court acknowledged the authority of public corporate bodies to regulate the use of private property, if they did so to benefit the public good. Yet at the same time, the court affirmed the right of homeowners, specifically, to determine which types of development constituted a threat to the "public." The *Euclid* decision deserves special attention because it set the most enduring legal precedent (planners and historians refer to subsequent land-use restrictions as "Euclidian zoning") and it wrote into law assumptions about property and exclusion that would prove foundational to zoning politics in the modern suburb.[63]

The case had its origins in November 1922, when the Village of Euclid, a small, home-rule suburb of Cleveland, passed a comprehensive ordinance restricting construction of commercial and industrial enterprises, apartments, and two-family houses. It also set lot- and floor-size minimums for all residential structures. In a common practice, Euclid established three main categories for residential development, setting aside "U-1" districts, the most exclusive, for single-family homes, public parks, commuter train stations, and agriculture. Two-family dwellings were permitted in the less exclusive "U-2" zone, and "U-3" districts were open to "apartment houses, hotels, churches, schools, public libraries, museums, private clubs, community center buildings, hospitals, sanitariums, public playgrounds and recreation buildings, and a city hall and courthouse." Other commercial, and all industrial uses, were prohibited from residential districts. The new ordinance prevented the Ambler Realty Company from completing an industrial development on a 68-acre parcel, by suddenly dividing Ambler's land between a "U-2," a "U-3," and a "U-6" (commercial) district. Ambler sued the city, challenging the restrictions against industrial use in "U-2" and "U-3" districts. To defend the municipal ordinance, the city hired attorney, Euclid resident, and author of its zoning ordinance James Metzenbaum, who in turn recruited the NCCP's Alfred Bettman to assist him with the case.[64]

The federal district court sided with Ambler in 1924, holding Euclid's ordinance unconstitutional. Its ruling is notable because it devotes attention to two issues not raised by the original suit: single-family homes and race. Rather than simply discussing the "U-2" and "U-3" restrictions against industrial development (the focus of Ambler's suit), the decision speaks at length about residential restriction, accusing Euclid of discriminating against renters and people of modest income by excluding multifamily development from "U-1" zones. "The plain truth," wrote Judge D. C. Westenhaver, was that the ordinance was designed to put the undeveloped land in Euclid in a "straightjacket" by "regulat[ing] the mode of living of persons who may hereafter inhabit it." "The result to be accomplished is to classify the population and segregate them according to their income or situation in life." Westenhaver was not opposed to such exclusion; "many of the restrictions imposed throughout the village may be valid," he concluded, but they did not represent a "reasonable or legitimate exercise of police power."

And to illustrate this, he invoked *Buchanan v. Warley* and discussed the topic of racial restriction, which he accepted in principle. Westenhaver, an active participant in the anti-immigration movement and student of eugenics, insisted that "the blighting of property values and the congesting of population, whenever the colored or certain foreign races invade a residential section, are so well known as to be within the judicial cognizance." If the *Buchanan* court refused to uphold a type of exclusion so widely deemed necessary, he concluded, there was no basis for upholding the restrictions in the Euclid case.[65]

Metzenbaum and Bettman appealed the case to the Supreme Court, which not only read the ordinance very differently but made the right to exclude certain populations, namely, apartment dwellers, foundational to the argument for enforceability. Overturning the lower court's ruling in 1926, the Supreme Court declared in *Euclid v. Ambler* that the city's ordinance met the constitutional test because it found its "justification in some aspect of the police power, asserted for the public welfare."[66] And in a remarkable refutation of the lower court's holding that discrimination against specific groups was not a legitimate use of the municipal police power, the Court defended Euclid's ordinance with a theory of zoning that explicitly validated a city's right to exclude. It did so by invoking an argument long advanced by zoning advocates, and even referenced in Westenhaver's ruling: the claim that certain kinds of residential development posed a categorical threat to neighborhoods of single-family homes. Ironically, it was Westenhaver who articulated popular theories about the specific racial threats posed by unregulated residential development. The Supreme Court's decision by contrast does not mention race but is, nonetheless, grounded in assumptions about urban growth and residential compatibility that had long been foundational to zoning advocacy and key to its popularity.[67]

The ruling in *Euclid* is both a legal justification of zoning and an ode to urban social science. It upholds the general principle of zoning by arguing, as judges had in earlier, more limited cases, that unforeseen but inexorable development patterns, particularly the expansion of industry, had made municipal restriction necessary. Zoning was a technical and managerial issue, the Court explained, required by the "complex conditions of our day, for reasons analogous to those which justify traffic regulations." It repeatedly compared the central legal issue in zoning cases (the need to justify an ordinance "in some aspect of the police power") to the legal issues surrounding "nuisance" law, even ruling that "the law of nuisances . . . may be consulted, not for the purpose of controlling, but for the helpful aid of its analogies in the process of ascertaining the scope of . . . the [municipal] power." For example, "the question whether the power exists to forbid the erection of a building of a particular kind or for a particular use, like the question whether a particular thing is a nuisance, is to be determined, not by an abstract consideration of the building or of the thing considered apart, but by considering it in connection with the circumstances and the locality." ("A nuisance," they added, extending the analogy, "may be merely a right thing in the wrong place, like a pig in the parlor instead of the barnyard.") The court upheld zoning by describing it as a practical, indeed a necessary, tool designed only to protect the "public welfare" from uses that, in certain circumstances, threaten that ill-defined public.[68]

This left the judges with a critical task. By what standards were individual cases to be judged? How were threats to the public welfare to be gauged? The court's answer would have monumental implications for land-use politics in the modern United States. Rather than delving more deeply into Ambler's challenge against "U-2" and "U-3" restrictions, the court raised the topic of residential restriction, just as the lower court had, but here with very different results. The emphasis is particularly revealing in light of the justices' insistence, early in the ruling, that since none of Ambler's land was in a region zoned for single-family homes, it would be "unnecessary to consider the effect of the restrictions in respect of U-1 districts."[69] Nonetheless the court devoted considerable time to "U-1" restrictions (without naming them as such), when it turned to the subject of how municipal authorities could best determine "risk." At this point it addressed "the validity of what is really the crux of the more recent zoning legislation, namely, the creation and maintenance of residential districts, from which business and trade of every sort, including hotels and apartment houses, are excluded. Upon that question this Court has not thus far spoken." Acknowledging that relevant lower court rulings were "numerous and conflicting," the court concluded that "those which broadly sustain the power [to restrict] greatly outnumber those which deny altogether or narrowly limit it," adding that the tendency appears to be "in direction of the broader view."

The court then spoke on the question of residential restriction, in what amounts to a lengthy paean to the physical, economic, and moral superiority of single-family homes and the people who occupy them. It even invoked the science that now defined such communities as deserving of protection. Citing a ruling by the Supreme Court of Louisiana, the judges noted that "the matter of zoning has received much attention at the hands of commissions and experts, and the results of their investigations have been set forth in comprehensive reports." "These reports, which bear every evidence of painstaking consideration, concur in the view that the segregation of residential, business, and industrial buildings will make it easier to provide fire apparatus suitable for the character and intensity of the development in each section; that it will increase the safety and security of home life; greatly tend to prevent street accidents, especially to children, by reducing the traffic and resulting confusion in residential sections; decrease noise and other conditions which produce or intensify nervous disorders; preserve a more favorable environment in which to raise children, etc."

While the Louisiana ruling describes the goal of zoning as the "segregation of residential, business, and industrial buildings," it also distinguishes single- and two-family zones from all other residential uses. "With particular reference to apartment houses," the citation continues,

> it is pointed out that the development of detached house sections is greatly retarded by the coming of apartment houses, which has sometimes resulted in destroying the entire section for private house purposes; that in such sections very often the apartment house is a mere parasite, constructed in order to take advantage of the open spaces and attractive surroundings created by the residential character of the district. Moreover, the coming of one apartment house is followed by others, interfering by their height and bulk with the free circulation of air and monopolizing the rays of sun which otherwise would fall upon the smaller homes, and bringing, as their necessary accompaniments, the disturbing noises incident to increased traffic and business, and the occupation, by means of moving and parked automobiles, of larger portions of the streets, thus detracting from their safety and depriving children of the privilege of quiet and open spaces for play, enjoyed by those in more favored localities—until, finally, the residential character of the neighborhood and its desirability as a place of detached residences are utterly destroyed. Under these circumstances, apartment houses, which in a different environment would be not only entirely unobjectionable but highly desirable, come very near to being nuisances.

The *Euclid* decision collapses multifamily housing into a category of development that threatened healthful "residential" life. And while insisting that the nuisance standard did not directly apply to zoning's constitutional test, the court seemingly could not help itself from invoking the comparison, even suggesting that apartments, in certain circumstances, "come very near to being nuisances." "These reasons, thus summarized," the justices concluded, "are sufficiently cogent to preclude us from saying . . . that such provisions are clearly arbitrary and unreasonable, having no substantial relation to the public health, safety, morals, or general welfare."[70]

Equally revealing are the Court's decision to focus on residential restriction and the terms in which it does so. Protection of elite residential neighborhoods was not the focus of Ambler's suit, yet the Court considered that subject essential to establishing a judicial standard for assessing threats to the public welfare. Thus, the Court outlined standards for the determination of incompatible uses and risks that invoked and further codified zoning's long-held discriminatory presumptions. It deemed zoning a justifiable exercise of the municipal police power if used to protect the public welfare. And to clarify how cities should assess threats to the public welfare, it cited zoning's ability to protect homeowners from "invasion" by multifamily developments, describing an apartment building as a potential "parasite" and referencing the nuisance precedent to clarify the point. Like zoning itself, the nuisance doctrine had come a long way. A decade earlier, the designers of New York City's comprehensive ordinance refrained from creating separate districts for single-family homes, unsure whether the courts would consider apartment buildings to constitute a "public nuisance."[71] The *Euclid* court did just that, not by formally invoking the nuisance standard, but by stressing the parallels, and arguing that apartments could, in certain cases, "come very near to being" one. Years of zoning advocacy proved to be decisive here; the Supreme Court's invocation of the nuisance metaphor came directly from a lower court ruling.

The role of zoning's advocates in the *Euclid* decision was even more dramatic. The Supreme Court was originally prepared to uphold the lower court's 1924 ruling, by a vote of five to four. But after Ambler's attorney presented his final argument, Metzenbaum filed a reply brief that led the Court to order the case re-argued. During this delay, Bettman submitted an *amicus curiae* brief on behalf of the NCCP emphasizing zoning's ability to suppress nuisances; Metzenbaum's brief, by contrast, focused on protecting the general welfare. Bettman's argument encouraged the Court to reconsider its finding and, critically, served as a primary source for the majority's ruling in *Euclid*.[72] With the intervention of the man who had long urged the NCCP to "educate" the courts about the scientific basis for restriction, the Supreme Court declared zoning to be a defensible exercise of the municipal police power by comparing it specifically with nuisance abatement. The ruling validated decades of theorizing about the relationship between land-use science, compatible land uses, compatible populations, and the rights of certain white property holders.[73]

Subsequent court rulings extended the logic of *Euclid* and further codified its standard for determining incompatible uses. Federal courts soon made explicit what earlier decisions and what Hoover's Advisory Committee had long implied: that local bodies, elected or appointed, were best suited to determine which land uses were compatible and which ones constituted a nuisance. The post-*Euclid* courts agreed, writes Beverly J. Pooley, that "a legislative determination declaring that a given field is reasonably connected with the preservation of the public safety, etc., is itself *prima facie* evidence of such a conclusion." In other words, if a city council or zoning board declared a particular land use to be a threat to the community's safety and welfare, and if it created restrictions that outlawed or controlled that use, the courts were instructed to accept the community's judgment. Once local elites identified a particular land use to be inharmonious, the law said that it was so.[74]

———

As these precedent-setting cases wound their way through the courts, the national alliance of developers and planners grew stronger and its advocacy efforts even more focused. Its leaders also began directing their gaze beyond the city limits, to the stretches of undeveloped (and potentially quite lucrative) land in the near suburbs. Most suburban enclaves were still sparsely populated after World War I and accessible primarily to the affluent. But the automobile was changing that, enabling residential developers to build farther from streetcar and interurban lines and enabling more skilled workers and middle-class professionals to consider residence outside the central city.[75] One result was a surge in speculative real estate investment and subdivision platting on the peripheries of major cities. NAREB responded by accelerating efforts to popularize restrictive zoning. In 1923, it established the Home Builders and Subdividers Division, soon to serve as the "organized voice for the homebuilding industry," which in turn created the Committee on Subdivision Control in Metropolitan Areas in 1925. NAREB invited planners from the ACPI to serve as consultants, a role that spurred the ACPI, in turn, to create the Committee on Subdivision Control "to work together with NAREB in hopes of defining a consensus position." NAREB's committee was headed by Ireneus Shuler, who told the NCCP that planners must lobby for public intervention; he believed that most subdividers were promoting responsible development, by adopting deed restrictions, for example, but that there were still many who did not "exercise proper private control." That year the organizational bonds of the planner-builder alliance grew stronger in other arenas as well, as three NAREB leaders, Jemison, Shuler, and attorney Nathan William MacChesney, joined J. C. Nichols on the NCCP Board of Directors.[76] MacChesney, author of the racial clause in NAREB's Code of Ethics and CREB's model race-restrictive covenant, also served as NAREB general counsel.

Two years of collaboration between the NAREB and ACPI subdivision committees produced the *Joint Statement on Subdivision Control* in 1927. It promoted adoption of state planning enabling acts that empowered cities to appoint planning commissions and "prepare general plans" for future development, including regulations for the "nonmunicipal territory [beyond the city limits] which will sooner or later be developed." Hoover's Advisory Committee on Zoning, which had welcomed Alfred Bettman to its ranks in 1926, received the NAREB-ACPI recommendations enthusiastically and used them as the basis for its *Standard City Planning Enabling Act,* issued by Commerce later that same year. Like its zoning predecessor, this was draft legislation as well as a technical and procedural manual that carefully defined municipal powers, discussed officials' responsibilities, and monitored case law on planning and zoning.[77]

While there is some debate over the *Planning Act*'s impact,[78] there can be little doubt that by 1927 the efforts of zoning advocates, together with the ruling in *Euclid,* had encouraged hundreds of municipalities to exercise their zoning power, while encouraging countless communities to pursue home-rule status so that they could zone. A year before the *Euclid* decision, 425 cities had adopted restrictive ordinances. This grew to 565 by 1926, and by 1927 nearly 400 cities had established city plan commissions as well. At the annual NCCP that summer, Nolen attributed the spike in zoning activity to a unique collaboration between public and private leaders, listing the NCCP, NAREB, the National Municipal League, the American Civic Association, other professional associations, the nation's city managers, and Hoover's Department of Commerce. Nolen was no doubt little surprised that by 1930 zoning ordinances had been adopted in 800 cities.[79]

But the impact of the public-private alliance cannot be measured by numbers alone. Of equal importance, its theory of urban economics and its portrayal of restrictive zoning as a purely managerial land-use strategy had become guiding principles of zoning politics. Its advocacy efforts had focused the young zoning science on the protection of exclusive residential neighborhoods from specific kinds of development and specific populations. The *Euclid* court's preoccupation with elite residential neighborhoods is perhaps the most revealing example and also proved to be the most enduring legal precedent. By the late 1920s, public officials, development professionals, and the courts had agreed on a series of zoning standards that made two closely related conceptual moves: they defined restrictive zoning as a pragmatic, nonideological developmental strategy, and they defined the segregation of certain land uses (and by extension of certain populations) as a requirement dictated by impersonal market imperatives. NCCP organizing and the federal government's interventions were only the most visible evidence of the public-private alliance's impact on shaping both the statutory zoning power that would be so widely exercised after World War II and the zoning logic that would justify exclusion by invoking the hard and fast laws of metropolitan growth.

This same alliance would also sustain support for restriction and city planning throughout the Depression. Most important, its representatives literally wrote this theory about property and neighborhood stability into a new market for private residence, by designing and implementing the New Deal programs that revolutionized metropolitan development patterns and politics (see chap. 3). In the meantime, the alliance continued to promote municipal zoning. Although the collapse of the construction market stifled zoning activity and left most city planning commissions "completely inactive" by 1930, planners and federal officials continued to promote the zoning concept. The Department of Commerce continued to tutor and encourage, with publications including *The Preparation of Zoning Ordinances* (1931), *Model Subdivision Regulations* (1932), and its annual report "Zoning Progress in the United States." In 1933, President Franklin Delano Roosevelt appointed ACPI members Alfred Bettman, John Nolen, Jacob Crane, Frederic Delano, and Charles Elliot to the National Land Use Planning Committee. Among their recommendations was a call for a federal agency to coordinate a national planning policy, soon realized in the short-lived National Resources Planning Board. The NRPB proved to be both unpopular and relatively powerless, yet it helped establish planning authorities in 41 states, 500 regions and counties, and 400 towns and cities by 1937. It also produced, according to Marion Clawson's calculations, over 370 reports on topics including housing, urban government, and natural resources. So while residential construction remained relatively stagnant throughout the early and mid-1930s, municipal zoning and planning were underwritten with federal relief funds. In 1937, the National Resources Committee reported that 1,322 zoning ordinances were in effect in the nation's cities and counties, 954 of which were comprehensive (another 235 regulated use only). By 1940, some kind of planning was in place in every state and every major urban area, including 1,500 counties, metropolitan regions, and cities.[80]

On the eve of the war that would force white Americans to alter the way they talked about racial difference, the men at the forefront of zoning advocacy continued to promote a vision of urban planning rooted in eugenicist assumptions about the threats posed by unregulated urban development. Among "the general objectives of all social planning," wrote Bettman in 1933, was "to conserve human resources and maintain the nation and the race."[81] Meanwhile, the zoning concept that Bettman had helped to popularize at the NCCP, in his decisive brief to the *Euclid* court, and in his work at Commerce and the NRPB was by then established in practice and in law. By the late 1930s the public-private alliance's vision of property, populations, and appropriate land use was foundational to the manuals, the statutes, the individual ordinances, and the court rulings that now validated a municipality's authority to zone. It was this authority, along with the assumptions about real estate and segregation upon which it was founded, that millions of white suburbanites would mobilize when the war was behind them.

Michigan's experience illustrates how the federal role helped municipalities learn about zoning and employ it. The state had adopted zoning enabling legislation in 1921, before Commerce issued the standard act, but few Detroit-area municipalities exercised their zoning authority until the late twenties and thirties, by which time Hoover's efforts and the *Euclid* ruling had laid to rest doubts about the municipal police power. By then it had also become standard practice to invoke the "nuisance" doctrine, as a 1925 amendment to Michigan's enabling legislation did, to designate a land use as incompatible. "Any building erected or constructed in violation of any of the provisions of this act," the act concludes, "is hereby declared to be a nuisance."[82]

The handful of Detroit-area suburbs that adopted zoning ordinances before World War II did so after *Euclid*. For example, in July 1928, Oak Park's village commission held its first public hearings on a proposed ordinance, drawn up by Detroit planning engineer T. Glenn Phillips. Finally adopted in February 1929, the ordinance reserved virtually all residential areas for single-family homes, designated three types of business zones, and prohibited industrial development within the village borders. The ordinance would guide Oak Park's land use until the drafting of a master plan in 1950. In 1929, Ferndale, Pleasant Ridge, and Huntington Woods adopted their first ordinances as well, and the Royal Oak city commission appointed a committee to draft zoning guidelines for the city.[83]

The Royal Oak ordinance, adopted in April 1931, reveals how the standards established by decades of zoning advocacy shaped land-use policy in countless suburban localities. Following a lengthy definition of terms, including the stipulation, notably, that a "family" was both small and nuclear, it established five residential districts (A, AA, AAA, B, and C), five business districts (A, B, BB, C, and D), and two industrial districts (A and B). It defined appropriate uses for each. Residence A districts limited construction to "detached single family dwellings" and to nonresidential construction deemed compatible: churches, public or parochial schools, parks, playgrounds, public golf courses, small clubs, boardinghouses, servants' quarters, farms and stables, and "professional offices" (for "physicians, dentists and other professional persons.") The rules for each succeeding zone grew increasingly permissive. Residence AA zones permitted construction of "semi-detached single family dwellings [and] detached two-family dwellings or income bungalows," and residence AAA zones allowed for "the construction of semi-detached homes and duplexes with separate entrances." Residence B districts permitted "single-family terrace dwellings in groups of not more than eight" and "apartment dwellings containing not more than twelve housekeeping units." And residence C districts, finally, permitted "terrace dwellings in groups of not more than twelve," as well as larger apartment buildings. The ordinance set lot area minimums, requirements for frontage and the "percentage of lot occupancy," and height limitations. Both business and industrial districts were permitted to include any residential uses. Article VIII established a Zoning Board of Appeals and defined its operations.[84]

Most revealing are Royal Oak's rules about compatibility. Districts designated for single-family and two-family homes forbade most commercial activities, in sharp contrast to zones designated for apartments and "terrace" type dwellings. Residence B zones were open to "public hospitals, convents, [student] dormitories and residential clubs . . . homes for the aged or infirm . . . boarding houses . . . public utility structures [including sewage pumping stations] . . . extensions of existing cemeteries . . . [and] public stables and garages." And residence C zones—when viewed in light of the *Euclid* court's description of "environments" that would "increase the safety and security of home life"—presented inhabitants with real hazards, such as parking garages, motels, "penal or correctional institutions," and "institutions for the care, treatment or training of the mentally defective, or of liquor or drug addicts." Echoing well-established, national zoning precedents, Royal Oak's ordinance defined single-family homes as a superior type of residence, deserving municipal protection from commerce, convicts, and renters. Local officials relegated apartment dwellers, both physically and ideologically, to regions of the city deemed a danger to health, family, and property.

If any Royal Oak officials had doubts about zoning's legality, they received constant encouragement from the planners and federal officials who literally campaigned on behalf of the zoning concept. Harry W. Jones and his colleagues on the Royal Oak commission were among those quite wary of this new experiment with the municipal police power. "Zoning was so new," Jones recalled years later, "that many attorneys still thought it invaded the private rights of individuals." Yet by the early 1930s, zoning's advocates had helped create enough precedents and had circulated enough promotional materials to encourage even the tentative to dive headlong into the new politics of restriction. Confidence in the zoning power would soon grow so widespread that by the 1940s, most of Detroit's elite suburbs were excluding all "inharmonious" land uses from the regions' new bedroom communities.[85]

The Race of Property Value: Racial Covenants, Comprehensive Zoning, and the New Logic of Restriction

It should come as little surprise that Nathan William MacChesney, author of the racial clause in NAREB's Code of Ethics and an early model race-restrictive covenant, was a prominent NCCP member and committed zoning advocate. For while covenants and zoning operated in discrete legal domains—covenants in the realm of private contracts, zoning in the realm of public regulatory authority—most of their supporters shared a similar set of aims, interests, and political predispositions, particularly regarding the need to maintain racial segregation. (This fact was clearly demonstrated by efforts to promote race-specific zoning laws.) Yet scholars have devoted little attention to the intellectual parallels and very concrete legal and institutional connections between early covenant politics and early zoning politics. Most studies treat zoning ordinances and racially restrictive covenants as discrete if sometimes complementary legal instruments of exclusion because zoning law addresses the right of public bodies to regulate the uses of privately owned property, whereas covenant law addresses the right of private persons to regulate uses of their own property. Zoning ordinances established and defined public powers, while covenants governed interactions between private individuals.[86]

Largely unexamined, as a result, are the ways that zoning and racial covenants shared an intellectual, cultural, and even legal provenance, a shared history documented by the courts' defense of both. The laws protecting a city's right to zone and a landowner's right to restrict the use of his or her property came of age simultaneously, shared many key assumptions, and often relied on similar precedents. Both restrictive zoning and racial covenants received their most important legal challenges during the same quarter century, and both were consistently upheld, until the Supreme Court judged racial covenants to be "non-enforceable" in 1948. The courts upheld both by advancing a sometimes interchangeable argument about nuisances and property values. Early zoning politics was heavily influenced by the theory that certain kinds of development (industrial, high-density residential) and certain populations (renters, racially suspect groups) posed a calculable threat to private homeowners. During these same years, the courts upheld restrictive covenants with comparable (and sometimes complementary) arguments about the threats posed to communities of affluent property owners, people assumed to be white. Both racially restrictive covenants and restrictive zoning laws were legally grounded upon the assumption that certain land uses and certain populations categorically threatened the value of private property and the "health and welfare" of white property owners. The covenant cases provide further evidence that zoning was justified, legally and politically, with a theory about property and urban growth that assumed the necessity of racial exclusion.

————

Restrictive covenants are legal instruments, included in a property's deed or stipulated by a separate agreement, that dictate how the parcel may be used. In legal parlance, many covenants, including race-specific ones, "run with the land," that is, they are contracts between the property and its owner that mandate how any current or future owner can use it. Once the grantor of the covenant signs it, the instrument is legally enforceable against subsequent grantees. In short, restrictive covenants effectively define the rights of specific properties and, thus, the responsibilities of property holders to uphold those supposedly intrinsic rights.

Covenants have a long history in American urban and suburban development. First used by antebellum builders as land planning tools for exclusive residential subdivisions like New York City's Gramercy Park, they were frequently employed, by the late nineteenth century, to control both land use and appearance in luxury developments. By the 1910s, their adoption was commonplace in higher-priced residential subdivisions. Covenants generally established rules for new construction (for example, requiring minimum square footage), for the alteration of existing structures (such as architectural details), and for the use of land and buildings (prohibiting commercial uses in residential neighborhoods). Quite commonly, the creation of mandatory-membership "homeowners' associations" enabled residents to sue neighbors who violated a covenant's terms.[87]

It was also at the turn of the century that racially restrictive language began to appear in covenants with increasing frequency, notably before economists and realtors began to quantify racial integration as a "risk" factor.[88] Yet the two developments soon converged and became mutually supportive, as industrial expansion drew millions of blacks and European immigrants to American metropolitan areas. Racial covenants appeared with increasing frequency in the 1910s and 1920s, just as real estate professionals were outlining the new economic, or market imperative, defense of racial exclusion. The Supreme Court ruling on racial zoning in 1917 made covenant use even more attractive. Racial covenants withstood important challenges in state and federal courts during the 1920s and 1930s. By 1928, according to one estimate, as many as half of the homes owned by white people had covenants written into their deeds, and virtually all of the newer subdivisions were restricted to Caucasian occupancy.[89] By the time the Supreme Court ruled race-restrictive covenants to be "non-enforceable" in 1948, as many as 85 percent of the nation's newer large residential developments were racially restricted. Virtually *all* of Detroit's new subdivisions, for example, included racial covenants.[90]

Some racial covenants remained circumspect about their intent, merely prohibiting occupancy by people whose "ownership and occupancy would be detrimental or injurious to the neighborhood." But white property owners understood their purpose. Most deeds were far more candid, restricting occupancy to a "person of the Caucasian or white race," as one Dearborn contract specified or simply listing prohibited "racial" groups. These commonly included "Negroes" (alternatively described as members of the "Ethiopian race" or "every person who is commonly known as a colored person"), "Indians," "Asiatics," "Mongolians," "Jews," "Japanese," "members of the Balkan races," "South Europeans," and, particularly in the Detroit region, "Armenians."[91] The language used in covenants reveals how the new land-use science was shaping restriction politics, as whites portrayed the threat of racial integration as interchangeable with a host of palpable, indeed measurable nuisances. For example, a covenant filed by residents of the Bonaparte Heights Subdivision of Detroit stipulated that "at no time shall any part of said land be used or occupied for the manufacture, brewing, distilling, or selling of spirituous or malt liquors . . . or occupied as a bone-boiling establishment, tannery, slaughter house, glue, soap, candle, starch or gunpowder manufacturing unit or for other offensive or dangerous purposes, or for the keeping of pigs . . . That no barn, stable, garage, coop, or other outbuilding shall be erected nearer to any road or avenue than 10 feet, nor shall any of said lots be occupied by a colored person." "All of [these] restrictions," it concluded, "shall be in full force and effect until January 1, 1950." In his comprehensive study of Detroit covenants, Harold Black notes that "restrictions barring the twin evils of liquor and an unwanted race are common, particularly in deeds dating to the prohibition era."[92]

By seeking justification for racial restriction in the language of nuisance law, landowners were in part following the courts' lead. With the proliferation of covenants in the 1920s came numerous legal challenges against them. And courts upheld them by invoking the nuisance doctrine that was simultaneously influencing key zoning decisions. The courts regularly interpreted generic exclusionary language—for example, prohibitions against populations whose presence would be "injurious" to homeowners—as restrictions against black people. Meanwhile, in 1924, the D.C. Court of Appeals upheld restrictions against sale to or occupancy by blacks, arguing that private parties were not prohibited from entering contracts regarding the use of property. And by the time of the *Euclid* ruling, most courts hearing covenant cases were accepting defendants' contention that the mere presence of "nonwhites" posed a threat to private property, a standard frequently invoked over the next two decades. As late as 1945, three years before *Shelley v. Kraemer,* many courts were upholding racial covenants by invoking late nineteenth-century precedents pertaining to the restriction of "unpleasant sights, noxious vapors, or disturbing noises."[93]

Other influential covenant cases that did not address the question of racial restriction provide further insight into prevailing assumptions about property and race in the age of *Euclid.* In *Sanborn v. McLean* (1925), for example, the Michigan State Supreme Court ruled in favor of property owners who sued Christina and John McLean for building a gas station in a neighborhood of single-family and two-family homes. Unbeknownst to the McLeans, most of the neighboring lots included restrictive covenants, filed by the original subdivider in 1892, which specified that "nothing but residences shall be erected upon said premises." (Their parcel was covenant-free.) The McLean's neighbors argued that the gas station would be "detrimental to the enjoyment and value of its neighbors," and the court agreed, citing the deeds in the *neighboring* properties. A restrictive covenant operates as a "reciprocal negative easement" that "runs with the land," the court explained, and "is not personal to owners but operative upon use of the land by any owner having actual or constructive notice thereof."[94]

The ruling reveals two important assumptions about covenant law, the first concerning deedholders' right to determine land-use patterns, and the second concerning how determinations of appropriate use should be made. The court ruled that a covenant "originates for mutual benefit and exists with vigor sufficient to work its ends." The rights of restriction, once established, did not belong to individual property owners, but rather became intrinsic to the property and thus bound all subsequent owners to it. Put another way, whoever first owned property could assign to that property specific social values with regard to how it could be used and even who could occupy it. Accordingly, the ruling asserts that the original owners were best suited to determine which land uses were appropriate and should thus be granted the power to police development in their neighborhood—even on lots not covered by a restrictive deed. Indeed while acknowledging that some of Green Lawn's parcels, including the McLeans', were not restricted, the court, nonetheless, explained that Mr. McLean simply should have known better. "Considering the character of use made of all the lots open to a view of Mr. McLean when he purchased," they argued, "we think he was put thereby to inquiry, beyond asking his grantor whether there were restrictions." "We do not say Mr. McLean should have asked his neighbors about restrictions," the ruling continues, "but we do say that with the notice he had from a view of the premises on the street, clearly indicating the residences were built and the lots occupied in strict accordance with a general plan, he was put to inquiry, and had he inquired he would have found of record the reason for such general conformation."[95] The court argued that the defendant should have inferred the appropriate use of land by looking around the neighborhood. The ruling assumes that the appropriate uses for specific properties, that is, those deemed suitable for what it termed the community's "mutual benefit," were visible.

In subsequent rulings, including *Snow v. Van Dam* (Mass., 1935) and *Neponsit Property Owners Association, Inc. v. Emigrant Industrial Savings Bank* (New York, 1938), the courts consistently validated covenants that restricted the uses of private property,[96] in the process buttressing planners' and economists' arguments about the appropriate use and control of private property. Judges asserted, on the one hand, that property rights were enforceable against the claims, desires, or rights of individuals. Yet at the same time they fudged the question, giving current owners (defined as neighboring community members with a common interest) the right to determine appropriate uses. Property rights were sacrosanct, but certain owners were granted the power to define appropriate use. As in the precedent-setting zoning rulings, the courts asserted the rights of property owners to both identify incompatible uses and devise means of excluding them. It was this logic that by the 1920s and 1930s was collapsing the threat posed by "members of the Ethiopian race" and other "non-Caucasian" groups into a generic category of tangible and calculable threats, like congestion or gas stations or barn animals. When judges upheld covenant and zoning cases, they regularly suggested that property owners, specifically, homeowners or the "corporate form" that represented them, had the right both to designate what, exactly, constituted a threat to their property and, once they identified that threat, to police it. By doing so, they might, as the New York court of appeals ruled in *Neponsit,* "advance their common interests" and thus fully enjoy the "common rights of property."[97]

This line of thinking would sustain covenant law and practice until the courts reversed themselves in *Shelley v. Kraemer* in 1948. And while it requires jumping ahead chronologically, it is worth looking briefly at a covenant adopted just months before that ruling, in the Detroit suburb of Troy, to see how the pre–World War II history of racial restriction would help postwar whites conflate racial values with property values. In February 1947, the owners of a 133-acre parcel of farmland in southeast Oakland County incorporated as "The Golf Estates Company" and platted the property for residential development. In July, they filed a lengthy and detailed document, entitled "Restrictions," in order "to establish and maintain the desirable character of said lands . . . for its future benefit." The document describes the territory and the plat filed with the Oakland County Register of Deeds, before listing a number of "protective covenants, restrictions, and reservations imposed upon said lands." Among them were the following:

> No land included herein shall be rented to or occupied by any person or persons other than of the Caucasian Race.
>
> All lots in said subdivision, excepting Lots 36 to 43 inclusive, shall be used for residence purposes only.
>
> On Lots 1 to 8 inclusive and 25 to 35 inclusive the dwellings to be erected on each, shall have a ground floor area of not less than 720 square feet. . .
>
> When of wood, building for residence or business purposes shall be sided and painted 2 coats before being occupied . . . No building of any kind or purpose shall have an exterior covering of tar paper, roll roofing, composition board, nor any makeshift material. . .
>
> No part of this land shall be used or occupied by a slaughterhouse, glue, starch or gunpowder manufactory nor for other offensive or dangerous use or purpose; nor for an auto wrecking or junk yard or a storage place for old, wrecked or broken down automobiles; nor for the commercial raising or keeping of dogs, pigs or goats.

Employing a logic that was by then codified in land-use science, real estate manuals, and court decisions, these owners described the threat posed by non-Caucasians as on par with that posed by roll roofing, goats, glue factories, and junk yards. The restrictions "shall run with the land," the deed concludes, and "if any current or future owner violated them, any other land owner reserved the right to prosecute, to prevent the violation, or to recover damages."[98]

This early postwar contract owed its language, its rationale, and its institutional legitimacy to the prewar politics that had created and sustained legal forms of restriction since at least the 1910s. It previews how postwar whites would inherit tools for restriction and a concomitant housing politics, both of which allowed them to collapse racial threats into a broader category of tangible, measurable, and calculable nuisances. Like zoning law and practice, the covenants bridge the pre- and postwar eras and, by doing so, helped fashion an economic and legal discourse that defined the exclusion of so-called inharmonious populations not as acts of prejudice but rather as sound land-use practice. And the fact that zoning and covenants relied on comparable arguments helps explain why the latter were no longer necessary by 1948, and why *Shelley v. Kraemer* did so little to dismantle patterns of residential segregation in the postwar period. For by the 1940s a community's right to discriminate against any use deemed "incompatible" was firmly ensconced nationwide in both zoning law and practice. Indeed zoning law described the exclusion of certain nuisance populations as a necessary and justifiable act, required by the immutable laws of land-use science to protect a community's "general welfare." In part because of this, the court's prohibition against race-restrictive covenants would do little to abate the exclusionary practices of white suburban homeowners.

Of even greater importance in understanding *Shelley v. Kraemer*'s failure is the creation in the 1930s and 1940s of a revolutionary new market for mortgage loans, a market fashioned and sustained by federal intervention, that systematically denied nonwhites access to most suburban housing for at least three decades. And this market, too, owes a great deal to the zoning politics that predated it, to the racialized land-use science that zoning helped to codify, and to many of the public and private advocates who helped spread the zoning gospel in the years before the Depression. What distinguished restriction in the new market for mortgages, surprisingly, was its designers' willingness to identify white people's racial preferences by name.

CHAPTER THREE

Financing Suburban Growth: Federal Policy and the Birth of a Racialized Market for Homes, 1930–1940

Beginning in the 1930s, the economics and politics of homeownership were fundamentally transformed in the United States when federal interventions simultaneously restructured the market for residential mortgage lending and popularized a very distorted narrative about that process of restructuring. Confident that public policy could shore up the private market for housing debt and jump-start several housing-related sectors of the economy, the Hoover and Roosevelt administrations created a series of oversight, insurance, and reserve programs that reinvented and actively subsidized the nation's home finance industry. Meanwhile advocates of the new federal presence insisted that intervention did not fundamentally alter the existing free market for property. This combination—extensive federal influence in credit markets coupled with the claim of noninterference—has remained a hallmark of state involvement in residential development to this day.

The new federal presence in the mortgage market was designed by leaders of the public-private alliance that had promoted the zoning concept since the 1910s, and its agencies were in large part operated by them. Subdivision developers, housing economists, and institutional lenders began lobbying for federal intervention in the debt market after World War I. The urgency of the Great Depression drew the federal government to their ideas and initiated decades of experimentation, beginning with creation of the Federal Home Loan Bank system (FHLB) in 1932, creation of the Home Owners Loan Corporation (HOLC) in 1933, and the government's most decisive intervention, passage of the National Housing Act (NHA) in 1934. The NHA fundamentally altered the ways that housing credit was created and distributed in the United States, by putting the government's stamp of approval on the long-term, low-interest, self-amortizing mortgage and creating an administrative and regulatory body, the Federal Housing Administration

(FHA), to insure lenders experimenting with these loans. Eventually these programs worked in concert with the Federal National Mortgage Association (FNMA), created in 1938 to purchase and resell existing mortgage debt. FNMA operations provided a federally run "secondary" mortgage market that sustained FHA operations and eventually ensured the long-term expansion of the nation's home finance industry.

By decade's end, government programs had created a new kind of home finance market, one that made it safer for lenders to issue mortgage loans and economically feasible for more people to borrow. The market became more stable, far more flexible, and, for institutional lenders in particular, far more lucrative. The result was the creation of more home finance capital (i.e., the creation of new wealth), which in turn accelerated borrowing, construction, and the sale of related goods and services. The revival was gradual, and by no means was the home finance market fully revolutionized during the Depression. But by the time American industry retooled for wartime production, an infrastructure capable of supporting an expansive market for private residences was in place, and key national industries, especially home finance, home building, construction materials, and real estate, were poised to benefit from the fantastic growth that would soon follow. Monitored by quasi-public regulatory bodies and secured by U.S. Treasury funds, the new mortgage market would soon create billions of dollars in credit earmarked almost exclusively for the construction and purchase of private homes. This state-supported market would soon bring homeownership and equity to millions of American families when the war ended.[1]

Federal intervention not only facilitated lending and construction, but also determined what kinds of dwellings would be built, where they would be located, and who could purchase them. The new mortgage market was designed to promote the construction and purchase of detached, single-family homes. Federal programs insured suburban properties, yet denied insurance for most urban ones. And the appraisal guidelines that served as the linchpin of the new system required realtors and lenders to segregate residential neighborhoods by race *and* to deny loans to most racial minorities. From its inception, federal intervention promoted the expansion of a particular kind of suburban growth focused on the automobile-centered subdivision of single-family homes and secured almost exclusively for white people. The market's development preferences and its racial rules were firmly in place by 1940 and provided a template for metropolitan growth and segregation throughout the decades of postwar "boom."

No single agent fueled the expansion of the housing market and shaped the geography of metropolitan growth more decisively than the public-private alliance that drafted federal housing policy and administered its programs. Before the nation's entry into World War II, this alliance had assembled most of the agencies and designed the procedures that would finance the postwar suburb and segregate metropolitan populations by race. Depression-era legislation also laid the groundwork for decades of future interventions. Much of this story has been documented by activists, critics, and scholars; the literature on the revolution in housing policy and politics is as old as the programs themselves. Specific programs have been studied in great detail, and yet there is a dearth of attempts to synthesize their impact on housing markets, little research on the day-to-day operations of the FHA, and only minimal work on the important links between the early zoning movement and the New Deal–era programs that revolutionized the mortgage market.[2] Equally important, scant attention has been devoted to the ways in which the architects of federal intervention envisioned the new housing market.[3] Examining their vision is critical for understanding the shape of the postwar metropolis and the white racial politics that would help define it. Most public officials and business leaders insisted, and apparently believed, that Depression-era housing programs did not interfere with or alter the existing market for residence. They insisted that the stunning growth of suburbs and homeownership rates and the corollary segregation of neighborhoods and capital owed little if anything to state interference. They also went to great lengths to *popularize* this view through a multimillion-dollar, government-sponsored promotional campaign to educate consumers about the new mortgage programs. Government officials literally marketed a national experiment in mortgage lending to American consumers, in part by assuring that the housing industry's revival was nothing more than a result of healthy, free market activity.

This chapter discusses the programs and the political alliances that reinvented the market for home finance in the 1930s. Chapter 4 then looks carefully at the influential political and economic language used to describe the mortgage revolution. Together these chapters highlight two developments central to the history of race and property in the modern American suburb.

First, they challenge a common (though certainly not uncontested) claim: that federal mortgage programs neither subsidized suburban growth nor encouraged whites to leave urban areas. The government's insurance, reserve, and regulatory programs actively subsidized home construction and homeownership, while assuring that both would be concentrated in the suburban fringe. The history of federal collaboration with the development industry, both to fashion federal policy and to encourage lending, borrowing, and construction, demonstrates that there was nothing inevitable or preordained about whites' new preoccupation with suburban living. Indeed, the FHA's concerted promotional efforts suggest that to ensure the new mortgage market's solvency and stability, the state had to do much more than simply insure and regulate the new system—it had to persuade businesspeople and consumers to participate and constantly guide them through its operations. Of course, millions of families were anxious to repair existing homes or buy new ones, and the prospect of suburban residence, long an ideal among so many metropolitan residents, appealed to countless Americans. Yet there is no evidence that borrowing for that purpose or relocating to suburban neighborhoods would have become a national obsession, or even economically *possible* for most people, if not for the public-private alliance that designed, implemented, and managed a revolutionary new market for mortgage debt.[4]

Second, these chapters explore the influential narrative about government intervention that accompanied the new mortgage initiatives, and its impact on national conversations about property and race. Advocates of federal intervention and the officials who ran the new selective credit agencies insisted that the government's new stake in the private housing market was *not interventionist;* that it did not disrupt natural economic processes or distort the "free market" for property. In speeches, congressional debates, promotional materials, and countless direct appeals to consumers and business groups, advocates portrayed the FHLB, FSLIC, FHA, and FNMA as market-friendly initiatives designed to "unleash" the free market for housing. This story was not mere window dressing for publicity efforts. It was constitutive of a multifaceted, national effort to legislate a new federal role in the housing market and promote borrowing and spending in specific sectors of that market.

Because this story was so pervasive, the coincidence of the government's promotional efforts, on the one hand, with its requirement of segregation, on the other, would have momentous consequences for racial politics in the twentieth century. Simultaneously, the government masked its role in transforming the market for housing, promoted appraisal guidelines that required racial exclusion, and defended that exclusion by claiming that the free market for housing simply required it. Federal interventions subsidized suburban growth and set new rules for sustaining metropolitan inequality, while insisting that the state's presence did not alter natural market operations. With the encouragement of the federal government, whites began to endorse discrimination not by discussing the "problem" of race or their personal feelings about racial minorities, but rather by invoking the supposedly hard and fast rules of real estate economics.

Restructuring Home Finance: FHLB, HOLC, and FHA

Early Depression-era housing legislation was emergency legislation, a response to the swift collapse of regional markets for home finance debt. Unregulated real estate speculation during the 1920s had sustained a grossly inflated market for housing credit, which was quickly undermined after 1928 by the collapse of wages and property values. Black Monday accelerated the crisis. In 1930, mortgage lenders foreclosed on approximately 150,000 residential (nonfarm) properties, triggering a precipitous drop in new lending and construction. This sent shock waves through the national economy, further undermining already fragile financial institutions and destroying millions of jobs in construction and other housing-related industries. Herbert Hoover's election to the presidency was soon followed by the stock market's collapse, and during his first year in office he presided over an unprecedented housing and credit crisis that by all indicators was only deepening.[5]

He responded in August 1930 by convening the President's Conference on Home Building and Home Ownership, to which he invited many of the nation's leading architects, builders, bankers, realtors, insurers, economists, educators, and social workers. Their task was to examine the nation's housing sector, analyze the origins of its collapse, and propose legislation to revive the market for homes. Participants were divided between twenty-five fact-finding committees that prepared reports on topics including home design, construction, financing, ownership, planning and zoning, slums and blighted areas, Negro housing, rural housing, and the role of private business in promoting residential development. Their findings then provided the centerpiece for the December 1931 conference in Washington, D.C., attended by 3,700 men and women.[6]

Hoover had sought counsel, not surprisingly, from the economists, real estate professionals, and publicists with whom he had collaborated during his years at Commerce. Among the most influential participants at the conference were men and women long committed to promoting restrictive land-use practices and expanding the market for private homeownership. The Planning Committee included NCCP president Harold Bartholomew, Better Homes in America founder Marie Meloney, and James Ford, who served as Better Homes executive director when it was absorbed by the

Department of Commerce. Richard Ely, John Nolen, John Ihlder, and Lawrence Veiller helped prepare some of the conference's most influential research reports and legislative proposals. The Committee on Large-Scale Operations included NAREB executive secretary Herbert Nelson and Coleman Woodbury of Ely's Institute for Economic Research. Meanwhile, Ely and institute economist Arthur J. Mertzke sat on the Committee on Business and Housing. The Committee on Subdivision Layout included John Nolen and Robert Whitten and was otherwise dominated by NAREB members (including two past presidents) and builders or planners closely associated with the organization. It was chaired by the NCCP's Bartholomew, long associated with Ely's institute and currently serving as NAREB's director of research for city planning.[7] The conference provided an institutional and intellectual bridge between the pre-Depression zoning and planning movement and the decades of federal involvement in the housing market that would follow. Hoover created a presidential mandate for the promotion of a unique vision of housing economics and metropolitan development. Housing and development experts then used the conference to initiate what would become their decades-long role in designing, promoting, and managing a new kind of private market for housing: a federally subsidized market that promoted suburban expansion and homeownership and that catered, by design, almost exclusively to white people.

The influence of Ely's institute stemmed largely from its scholars' work on the mortgage market. During the 1920s, institute publications celebrated the savings and loan industry's experimentation with a new, more flexible kind of mortgage instrument, a loan with comparatively low interest rates, longer repayment terms, and full amortization (meaning that the borrower paid off the principle and the debt simultaneously). The loan enabled institutions to lend up to 75 percent of a home's value (the average was 58 percent) and to allow borrowers between 10 and 15 years to repay the debt (the average was 11). By comparison, loans granted by insurance companies and commercial banks covered between 46 percent to 54 percent of the purchase price, rarely had full amortization, and required repayment in as little as two or three years, leaving borrowers with a huge lump-sum payment or, more commonly, negotiating costly (and generally nonamortized) second and third mortgages.[8] Institute economists believed that widespread use of the long-term, low-interest mortgage would expand the market for credit and make homeownership feasible for more Americans. The loan's terms, they predicted, would make borrowing more attractive for households, thereby increasing demand. Increased demand would draw more institutional lenders into the home finance field, thereby providing more capital for the purpose of construction and purchase. Finally, competition between lenders would further reduce the cost of borrowing for consumers.[9]

It is true that the S&L industry's use of long-term mortgages was reducing the cost of purchasing residential real estate in the 1920s. Nonetheless, the institute economists' enthusiasm for this experiment—and what Marc Weiss calls the "distinct bias of their research . . . toward a policy of promoting homeownership"—cannot be separated from their close collaboration with public and private leaders deeply committed to expanding the housing market. During the 1920s, Ely served as a consultant to NAREB, the U.S. Savings and Loan League (USSLL), the National Association of Building Owners and Managers, and the Department of Commerce. Publication of his influential "Land Economics Series" textbooks for Macmillan was cosponsored by NAREB. Prominent institute scholars, many of them Ely's students, served these same organizations as officers, staff members, or research consultants. They worked in industries that by 1920 had already floated proposals for a government role in restructuring mortgage markets. Mortgage bankers and NAREB officials, for example, responded to a postwar slump in housing starts by calling for federal tax reform designed to stimulate construction, and several congressional bills were introduced after 1919 to create federal or state-run mortgage banks, including a USSLL proposal to create a federal system of regional banks, modeled on the Farm Loan Bank System, to provide extra liquidity for private mortgage bankers.[10]

In short the institute's theories about land values and mortgage markets took shape in the context of a constant interchange between private industry, research economists, and the federal government, with all participants focused on promoting the expansion of the home finance market and creating a nation of homeowners. Institute scholars juggled their work for the private and public sectors throughout the 1920s, as they produced their influential studies on land-use restrictions, mortgage lending, and real estate appraisal. In 1923 the institute issued "Real Estate Mortgages as Investments for Life Insurance Companies," a report for NAREB that predicted high yields for anyone entering the home loan market, prepared *Mortgages on Homes* for the U.S. Bureau of the Census, and released Ernest Fisher's *Principles of Real Estate Practice* in the "Land Economics" textbook series. Updates of the life insurance studies were prepared by Fisher and Mertzke; both of them soon thereafter served as research directors for NAREB. Mertzke conducted research for the Committee on Finance at the 1931 President's Conference and Ely contributed an essay on limited dividend companies. Fisher, meanwhile, worked on the Department of Commerce's real property inventory and later joined the FHA as a consultant. Institute economists

Morton Bodfish and A. D. Theobald actively promoted the expansion of S&L-style mortgage lending, the latter in his influential *Financial Aspects of Subdivision Development* (1930), and both as leaders of the USSLL.[11]

Promotion of the long-term, low-interest mortgage would prove to be the institute's most enduring legacy. These economists neither invented the instrument nor were they the only ones to endorse its use, but their targeted advocacy would be decisive, and their work on property valuation and appraisal would shape both the national mortgage market and mortgage politics for decades to come. Most important was their novel approach to the concept of real estate value. At the time, economists generally equated the market price of real property with its market value. Institute scholars, by contrast, saw that by creating an environment conducive to speculation in real estate, investors could actively increase market values (and thus prices). To ensure the stability and continual expansion of this market, they proposed comprehensive (and purportedly universal) guidelines for appraising real estate, arguing that a speculative market required standardized rules for the assessment of individual properties. Frederick Babcock's *The Appraisal of Real Estate* (1924), also part of Ely's "Land Economics Series," articulated the institute's position. Subsequent contributions by Mertzke in 1927 in a study written for NAREB and Horace Clark in 1930 in his textbook for the American Savings, Building and Loan Institute built directly upon Babcock's work, introducing the claim that assessment of the borrower's financial stability was essential to the appraisal process.[12]

The institute's ideas would eventually wield considerable influence because the President's Conference of 1931 gave its economists and their allies a prominent stage and a presidential mandate, which they used to promote public programs grounded in their theory of property and urban growth. Not all housing experts shared their vision; there were competing strategies for solving the nation's housing crisis and providing adequate shelter to American citizens.[13] But by the time that the Depression pressed federal officials to seek radical solutions, institute economists and influential developers had forged a powerful network of activists promoting a vision of economic growth that had long appealed to Herbert Hoover. Along with the president, they shared a faith in the transformative power of homeownership. They subscribed to a social science that seemed to account for the current mortgage market's inability to satisfy demand for privately owned homes. They agreed that careful federal interventions would promote efficient land-use patterns and stimulate lending and construction, without distorting the free market for housing. It was this faith and these priorities that dominated the President's Conference, the research sponsored by its twenty-five fact-finding committees, and their legislative proposals.

The committees' research appeared in a final conference report, eleven encyclopedic volumes edited by John Gries and James Ford that marshal survey evidence and social science theory to explain the collapse of the nation's housing market and prescribe strategies for reviving it. The reports detail the nation's housing stock, explore the links between urban "blight" and community instability, and discuss trends in construction, financing, regional industrial development, taxation, and home repair. They calculate average household budgets nationwide, catalogue images and floor plans of "model" small homes, and recommend policies to promote the financing of new construction. Throughout the reports, there is a general consensus about the nature of the crisis and the best solution. It was urgent, most authors agreed, to improve housing conditions and revive markets for housing, household goods, and related products and services. Most insisted that the problem was not that producers were unable to supply the needed goods and services nor that consumers did not desire them. The problem, these experts argued, was the inadequacy of the institutional structure that facilitated exchange.

This distinction was important. Conference committees repeatedly cited the substandard condition of the nation's housing stock as evidence that financial markets were not permitting suppliers to meet existing demand—not, by contrast, that existing financial instruments and market conditions were incapable of *producing* adequate housing. They concluded from this that interventions designed to stabilize and revive existing, private-market mechanisms offered the best model for any future action. There were dissenting voices, most prominent in the remarkable volume on *Negro Housing* (prepared under the direction of Charles Johnson), which presents a cautious but scathing critique of leading economists' explanations for black poverty and slum housing. But these were minority voices, overshadowed by the conference's celebration of the free market and its unflagging support for pursuing what it considered to be private-sector solutions to the nation's economic crisis. Two recommendations follow logically, providing a virtual chorus for the reports. Most authors insisted that recovery would require extensive rehabilitation of existing housing, the construction of new, modern, spacious homes, and, most important, the growth of widespread private homeownership. Second, they insisted that these were tasks not for the government but for private industry. "The building of homes," explained the Committees on Slums, Large-Scale Housing, and Decentralization, "must be carried on as a business operating for a legitimate profit."[14]

Conference participants had a flexible understanding of how markets operate and insisted that the free enterprise system would reach its full potential only if the federal government intervened in the market for credit. Most consequential was the conference's endorsement of proposals supported by NAREB and USSLL leadership to establish a system of federal mortgage discount banks. Under the plan, private lenders would be invited to join the regional branches of this new system. The regional banks would regulate member institutions and, crucially, provide them with liquid capital by discounting prime paper. A federal presence would enable members to lend more money, that is, to create more credit for home construction and purchase, on better terms, than the current system permitted. Leading the effort to promote this discount system was institute economist Morton Bodfish, who since 1929 had also served as chief executive of the USSLL. Bodfish drafted the proposal that was endorsed by the conference. Meanwhile, months earlier, Hoover had been approached directly by NAREB representatives with a proposal for a similar regional system, designed specifically to promote the use of long-term, amortized mortgages. Developers and the S&L industry had been floating these ideas since the end of World War I. Now a national economic crisis provided them with unprecedented leverage to create a significant federal role in the private market for homes.[15]

Yet to hear Bodfish and others describe it, federal discount operations would not alter existing market mechanisms and thus posed no threat to the free enterprise system. It was "distinctly not proposed that the Federal Government itself act directly," explained the Committee on Slums, Large-Scale Housing, and Decentralization in their endorsement of the USSLL proposal. The government would merely "set up enabling machinery and establish general policies." Most important (and technically true), the proposed federal banks would not "directly lend money."[16] In what became a common refrain at the conference and in Depression-era debates over federal selective credit programs, the committees described the government's proposed new role as that of intermediary, as a force that would correct and free up sluggish markets, without disrupting or changing them. They also described federal involvement as temporary, necessary only until industry resumed its normal operations and consumers regained their confidence.[17]

Hoover was persuaded, under considerable pressure from the USSLL, to take action. He presented a compromise version of the proposal to Congress and in July 1932 signed the Federal Home Loan Bank Act, legislation drafted by Morton Bodfish. The act authorized creation of the Federal Home Loan Bank system (FHLB), consisting of twelve regional banks and the body that would both oversee and partially finance their operations, the

Federal Home Loan Bank Board (FHLBB). As prescribed by the conference, the twelve regional banks lent money to private institutions (primarily savings and loans associations) to compensate for sudden, often seasonal, fluctuations in their capital reserves. The board, meanwhile, stabilized regional credit markets by regulating the branch banks and providing them with short- and long-term loans. Assigned primary responsibility for administering FHLB operations were the business leaders who had the most to gain from state intervention. The act required that eight of the twelve directors for each regional bank must be "officers or directors of the thrift and home financing institutions affiliated with the Bank." The remaining four were to be selected by the board from "representatives of the general business and professional community." With passage of the Home Loan Bank Act in the summer of 1932, the S&L industry was asked to design and operate a federal regulatory apparatus, dependent on both U.S. Treasury funds and federal authority, that enabled local thrift and home finance associations to increase their mortgage lending and thus to make more profits. With creation of the FHLB, the lines between the "public" and "private" home finance markets first began to blur.[18]

The legislation represented an important victory for the public-private housing alliance first forged in the 1910s, a victory best symbolized by Bodfish's appointment to the first FHLBB. The act also marked a radical new phase in that alliance's influence, since the board was a federal body that used public money to manage and inject funds into the private market for housing. Its leadership remained tentative at first, experimenting cautiously with a state presence unimaginable just three years earlier. But the discount banks would eventually become an essential component of a much larger federal system that subsidized lending, construction, and homeownership. The act also established an important precedent for future government intervention in the home finance and construction markets, laying the groundwork for the far more aggressive New Deal initiatives soon to follow. Creation of the FHLB foreshadowed what would become trademarks of the alliance's approach to metropolitan issues: a heavy reliance on private industry to draft and then lobby for federal legislation; an almost exclusive focus on the implementation of government-run, funded, and/ or regulated programs designed to expand the market for housing credit; and the administration of these programs by quasi-public agencies staffed largely by representatives of the industries poised to benefit from a new and ever expanding federal presence.

In the short run, however, the FHLB could not abate the deepening housing crisis. For while it insulated institutional lenders by stabilizing credit supplies, it did virtually nothing to encourage people to take out loans. Most important, the terms of most mortgages, the high interest rates and short repayment periods that concerned institute economists, made borrowing prohibitive if not impossible for most households, particularly in light of the devastation wrought on family budgets by the Depression. The FHLB was designed to promote the flow of credit, but it could not create sufficient demand. And by 1933, the collapse of demand continued to expose the fragility of the existing mortgage system and its profound structural limitations. Again the origins of the crisis lay in the speculative real estate boom of the 1920s, when high-interest, short-term mortgage loans looked like attractive investments to the nation's savings and loans, mutual savings banks, commercial banks, and insurance companies. Rapid inflation and rampant real estate speculation, most of it suburban, had drawn institutional lenders into the mortgage market throughout the decade; by 1930 they held about 60 percent of the nation's home finance debt. When the real estate bubble burst, and when unemployment and inflation destroyed consumers' purchasing power, defaults threatened a serious liquidity crisis for scores of lenders. During the summer of 1932, as many as one thousand mortgage defaults were being recorded every day, and the FHLB proved powerless to stop the trend. Over 270,000 borrowers defaulted that year, three times the 1926 total, and by early 1933 about half of the nation's home mortgages were in default, placing the "entire system of home finance," writes J. Paul Mitchell, "on the verge of collapse." The ripple effect was devastating. In 1933, builders began work on fewer than 100,000 private dwelling units, compared with the 973,000 starts recorded in 1925. By 1934, two million of the nation's twelve million unemployed were in the building trades, and one third of the families receiving government aid were connected in some fashion to the construction industry.[19]

The impact was especially dire in metropolitan areas, home to most of the nation's at-risk real estate investments and, not unrelated, a concentration of the newly unemployed. In areas heavily dependent on a single industry, such as metropolitan Detroit, the housing market's collapse was particularly abrupt and devastating. Layoffs in the auto industry precipitated thousands of mortgage defaults in Wayne, Oakland, and Macomb counties, eventually leading to a run on the so-called "group" banks that controlled 87 percent of the region's loans and investments. The collapse of the home finance market and of real estate values triggered a flurry of bank failures statewide, and again Detroit-area institutions were hit especially hard, particularly those specializing in financing residential construction for autoworkers. Of the thirty Michigan institutions that collapsed in the first eight months of 1931, eighteen were in Oakland and Wayne counties, most of them suburban banks with heavy commitments in real estate mortgages and construction bonds. The regional crisis also led to an epidemic of tax delinquency on subdivided suburban lots, prompting the state to confiscate 40–70 percent of the residential parcels in each of Detroit's unincorporated suburban townships by 1935 (64.2 percent in Royal Oak Township and 41.4 percent in Dearborn Township, for example). Virtually all of the tax delinquent lots in unincorporated suburban regions were *not* developed, further evidence that the speculative frenzy of the 1920s had taken its toll on developers and bankers alike.[20]

The Detroit region's crisis, while particularly severe, was part of a national one that left most metropolitan economies reeling by 1933. The precipitous collapse of the housing finance industry, coupled with Roosevelt's election the previous fall, created support for more radical experimentation. With the new president's mandate, the public-private housing alliance set to work designing federal programs that would rescue financial institutions and revive the market for homes, by simultaneously transforming the mortgage instrument itself, the institutional structure that regulated and fueled mortgage lending, and, critically, the risk environment for private lenders. It was through these interventions that the modern mortgage market was born and the market imperative rationale for residential segregation received its most important validation.

The first step came on June 13, 1933, with passage of the Home Owners' Loan Act. Created with the urging of the FHLBB, the savings and loan industry, and the real estate lobby, and passed with bipartisan congressional support, the act created the Home Owners' Loan Corporation (HOLC), a public agency administered by the board. A familiar group of industry experts crafted the new agency, including Bodfish and NAREB's Herbert Nelson. The latter was invited by Senator Cordell Hull, chair of the Senate Banking Committee, to use his office to design the legislation. FHLB general counsel Horace Russell drafted the final version. The HOLC was assigned a singular task: purchasing delinquent home loans from banks, S&Ls, and other lenders, and refinancing them with new long-term, low-interest, fully amortized loans. (The first HOLC mortgages allowed 15 years for repayment, with interest rates as low as 5 percent; subsequent amendments increased the term to 25 years and lowered the interest rate to 4.5 percent.)[21] The agency was designed to rescue both lenders and borrowers by offering homeowners a particularly liberal version of the mortgage instrument long-promoted by institute economists. These were loans that struggling borrowers could pay off.

With the Home Owners' Loan Act, the federal government took on a much more direct role in shaping private housing markets. HOLC operations were government financed. The Treasury was instructed to provide a maximum capital of $200 million, interest free, from the Reconstruction Finance Corporation. The HOLC was authorized to sell up to $2 billion in bonds, which it would exchange with private lenders for mortgages on one-to-four-family homes. The agency issued and sold the bonds itself until 1934, when the Treasury Department began participating in the sales. Eventually the HOLC received its funds directly from the Treasury; after 1934, it borrowed another $375 million, at 0.25 percent interest, "repayable at any time." From the program's inception, the federal government insured the interest on HOLC bonds and after 1934 insured the principle as well.[22]

Not surprisingly, the new program was enthusiastically received by lenders and homeowners alike. Lenders had little faith in the government's credit and were troubled by the HOLC's below-market interest rates, but they counted on receiving a better return from the state than from the nation's desperate mortgagors. And evidence of homeowners' desperation was compounding daily. In just its first four months of operations, the HOLC received over 400,000 applications for refinancing. By the time the agency stopped accepting loans in June 1935, after just twenty-one months of operations, it had received 1,886,491 applications, 1,017,821 of which it processed. In less than two years, about 40 percent of the nation's eligible homeowners applied for assistance from the HOLC.

The program's impact was swift and decisive. The agency accepted and closed on over 50,000 loans by December 1933. When it stopped its active loan program in 1936, it had purchased and refinanced $3.1 billion of delinquent debt from banks, S&Ls, and other lenders, in the process protecting more than 800,000 homeowners from losing their property. It granted loans to 54 percent of applicants. By 1936, more than 20 percent of the nation's nonfarm, owner-occupied dwelling units that had carried mortgages were now mortgaged to the HOLC. The benefits were felt nationwide. The local HOLC office in Detroit received more than 58,000 applications by April 1934. By June 1936, over 30 percent of the state's eligible homeowners had applied, 56 percent of the applicants had been approved, and the HOLC had refinanced 81,126 private mortgages. When measured by state, Michigan was a big winner, with only Ohio receiving more home loans from the agency. But in metropolitan areas around the country, the HOLC rescued borrowers and lenders and put housing markets, if only temporarily, on a more stable footing. In the process it provided a federal bailout for mortgage lenders, both individual and institutional. Of the $3.1 billion in HOLC loans granted nationwide, institutional mortgagees received about $2.2 billion. More than $1.5 billion of this total went to building and loan associations, cooperative banks, commercial banks, and other institutional lenders.[23]

Although short lived, the HOLC would have a profound impact on metropolitan development patterns and the national politics of race and housing. First, it demonstrated the potential of the long-term, low-interest mortgage not only to shore up but also to expand the market for privately owned homes. Before 1933, the terms of most mortgages made homeownership prohibitive for most families; the HOLC demonstrated, as institute economists had predicted, that the long-term, low-interest mortgage had the potential to sustain a far larger market for private housing. Second, HOLC operations set a crucial precedent for further state involvement in the private credit system, suggesting that a federal regulatory and financial presence might create and sustain expanded consumer spending. In the eyes of many contemporaries, most prominently Franklin D. Roosevelt, creation of the HOLC marked a declaration "that it was national policy to protect homeownership."[24]

Of equal importance, the HOLC set in motion both a new means of achieving the racial segregation of neighborhoods and a new rationale for defending it. Built into the agency's appraisal procedures and lending policies was an explicit commitment to racial exclusion, which was eventually codified in a series of Residential Security Maps commissioned by the FHLBB in 1935. Working in concert with local realtors and lending institutions, the HOLC drew up maps for most metropolitan areas, which ranked neighborhoods on a scale of A (most desirable and, hence, most valuable) to D (in "decline," and least valuable). The rankings were also color-coded, with the D neighborhoods in red, giving rise to the term "redlining." A racial and ethnic calculus explicitly guided the rating process. As Kenneth Jackson explains, if the structures in a neighborhood were relatively new, and the neighborhood was populated by middle-class white Christians, it generally received an A rating. But if homes were older, if they showed signs of physical deterioration, *or* if the neighborhood was populated by a significant number of racial or ethnic minorities, it usually received a C or D rating. In one St. Louis suburb, for example, HOLC officials assigned an A rating to an elite residential enclave in 1940, citing residents' affluence, the widespread use of restrictive covenants, and the absence of "foreigner[s] or Negro[s]."[25]

The assignment of a C or D rating was also contingent on indices of race and class. To be sure, many of the C- and D-rated neighborhoods contained dilapidated homes or were "congested," by agency standards, because their lots were small or lacked adequate setback requirements. Many of these neighborhoods were occupied by poor whites, especially immigrants from southern and eastern Europe. But the majority of the residential sections receiving the D rating had an African American presence, and, most important, virtually every majority-black or racially mixed neighborhood, regardless of its physical characteristics and housing stock, received this rating. Among these was St. Louis's Lincoln Terrace, a black neighborhood of new and structurally sound bungalow homes, which in the eyes of one agency official had "little or no value today, having suffered a tremendous decline in values due to the colored element now controlling the district." In the HOLC's 1939 survey of Detroit, neighborhoods described as having a "Negro concentration" or viewed by appraisers as an "area developing as a negro colony" automatically received a D rating. A summary filed with the Detroit survey explained that agents gave greatest consideration to "homogeneity, general appeal, location, protection from adverse influences, uniform social groups and mortgage risk for long term investment."[26]

Why did HOLC guidelines require racial separation, and what is the significance of the agency's decision? Long before the federal government entered the home finance market, most urban and suburban whites preferred to live in racially segregated neighborhoods, and white realtors respected their wishes. It was whites' strong preferences that led most realtors to require segregation and that encouraged housing economists to endorse racial exclusion in their studies of real estate appraisal, zoning, and deed restrictions. Many scholars have emphasized the similarities between pre-Depression real estate practices and subsequent federal appraisal guidelines and concluded that the HOLC was simply building upon well-established sentiments and protocols. The HOLC's guidelines, according to this argument, institutionalized existing prejudices. There is much truth to this argument. The HOLC was a federally funded (yet only quasi-public) administrative body that accepted the existing segregation of metropolitan areas as well as realtors' commitment to maintaining it. Adopting the theory that a free market for property demanded segregation, the federal government required that its programs further promote it and, thus, began the creation of a new kind of mortgage market that systematically discriminated. The HOLC, as Kenneth Jackson writes, "exhorted segregation and enshrined it as public policy" and by doing so created a much more powerful discriminatory marketplace.[27]

But the HOLC did much more, for it initiated a fundamental transformation in the way that whites' racial preferences shaped the market for housing. Beginning with the HOLC, federal intervention created a market for privately owned homes that simultaneously changed two things: *how* most people bought their homes (and how wealth was created in housing), and the *means of determining who could participate*. More than simply "embrac[ing] the discriminatory attitudes of the marketplace,"[28] the HOLC initiated the creation of a new kind of discriminatory marketplace, one that functioned very differently and that achieved and justified discrimination in a wholly new manner. Much more effectively than the FHLB, the HOLC created new wealth by investing federal funds into an unprecedented experiment in debt spending (the terms of pre-Depression S&L loans were never as liberal and thus as accessible as HOLC loans). Meanwhile, the HOLC provided a powerful forum for the argument, first codified by economists and realtors, that racial discrimination was not a matter of ideology or personal preference but of economics. The agency did not merely make it easier for business people and consumers to discriminate by race. It helped give birth to a market that created more wealth for whites while providing a state-sanctioned platform for housing experts to argue that racial discrimination was simply a by-product of impersonal economic processes.

This market imperative argument was central to the HOLC because the real estate industry figured so prominently in the agency's creation and operations. It was designed by many of the urban experts and professionals long affiliated with the NCCP, Ely's institute, and the Department of Commerce who had been promoting a racially specific model of land-use restriction since the 1910s. By the early 1930s, Babcock's study of real estate appraisal and the revised NAREB Code of Ethics had codified racial exclusion as a principle of real estate science. In 1933, NAREB founded the American Institute of Real Estate Appraisers (AIREA), assigning it the task of training a generation of professional appraisers. Then in 1934, it asked AIREA president and future NAREB president Phillip Kniskern to design the HOLC's appraisal standards. The new federal agency gave state sanction to a vision of property markets that had been articulated by members of the public-private planning alliance for over two decades.

Of equal importance, the HOLC's day-to-day operations, such as coordinating local operations, making individual loans, and, beginning in 1935, preparing appraisal maps, were handled by thousands of white businessmen receptive to the racial rules outlined in the new urban science. The HOLC recruited local realtors, financial officers, and builders, hiring them either as full-time, salaried employees or as part-time appraisers paid on a fee basis. When the agency struggled to fill staff positions in the first months of operation, it consulted with the AIREA to establish uniform qualifications for HOLC staffers. In December, the HOLC announced that it would only consider candidates with considerable appraisal experience (be it in the public or private sector) or with other suitable professional qualifications (such as AIREA membership). By June 1935, the HOLC had processed over 6,000 applications and hired 1,300 salaried and 2,700 part-time appraisers from local pools of private realtors, assessors, bankers, and builders nationwide. These local representatives put into practice a system of appraisal that would soon become the focal point of a state-regulated and state-funded system of home finance, one that explicitly required appraisers and lenders to maintain and further promote residential segregation.[29]

The inscription of the market imperative rationale for racial exclusion into HOLC operations marks a notable transition between two distinct eras of housing economics in the United States. While neither the segregation of neighborhoods nor its legal sanction were new to the 1930s, HOLC operations initiated a decisive shift in the means of achieving residential segregation and—inextricably linked to this—in the rationale advanced to justify it. The means changed because the public-private alliance, in the process of expanding the capital market for housing credit, put the fiscal and administrative powers of the federal government behind a long-standing tradition of private market discrimination. For decades, restrictive covenants and informal real estate practices had segregated neighborhoods on a case-by-case basis and had done so through private market operations. HOLC appraisal and lending practices, by contrast, offered whites a means to segregate neighborhoods universally and systematically, following standardized procedures, and with the blessing and financial support of the federal government.[30] Second, and very consequential for the subsequent politics of race and housing, the HOLC justified segregation not by commenting on the supposed racial differences between residents, but by claiming, as white realtors and economists had for years, that homes and neighborhoods occupied by minorities were worth less money. Beginning in 1933, federal programs promoted the racial segregation of housing resources by embracing, codifying, and thus further validating the new science of urban development, a science that subsumed myths about racial difference within a supposedly objective analysis of housing markets and property values.

A comparison of HOLC operations with race restrictive covenants highlights the change initiated by the new federal role. Before 1933, covenants in northern cities had served as the only legal instrument that explicitly required racial exclusion. And whites defended the use of racial covenants, both in the private sector and in the courts, by describing them as an expression of an individual's (or a community's) preference for racial homogeneity. Homeowners and the courts justified this choice, in part, by claiming that mixed-race neighborhoods threatened property values. But this economic argument was neither central to nor in any way necessary for justifying covenants' use, and thus for justifying racial exclusion, either in popular discourses on the subject or, in many cases, in the law.[31] By sharp contrast, HOLC guidelines justified racial segregation solely by invoking the economic argument. Then that economic argument, implicitly at least, helped explain and validate the individual's or community's preference for exclusion. It was this subtle distinction in emphasis or in point of departure between personal preference, on the one hand, and economic necessity, on the other that would have long-lasting consequences for metropolitan geography and political culture, as the federal government grew more deeply involved in the mortgage market and as a spirited defense of its supposedly market-friendly programs became a touchstone of postwar political debates. The form that federal intervention took after 1933, and the enormous impact that it would soon exert on housing markets, helped initiate a subtle transformation in the ways that white officials, businesspeople, and eventually homeowners understood the importance and the necessity of segregating neighborhoods by race.

The 1933 act deepened the state's role in private housing markets in other ways. By expanding the FHLBB's reserve and oversight authority, it allowed the board to make larger credit advances to its regional banks and, in a dramatic departure from its original design, to charter and regulate individual savings and loan banks. By awarding vast new powers to an agency originally conceived of as a reserve system, federal officials made the FHLBB "the chosen instrument," as Milton Semer has written, in its effort to "bring into existence and institutionalize sound and progressive home mortgage lending practices through a national system of local savings institutions," with "federally chartered associations" serving both "as leaders and examples." In April 1934, legislators also agreed to guarantee the bonds of the HOLC and authorized the agency to invest over $223 million in the shares of savings and loan associations that were FHLB-affiliated.[32]

The HOLC stopped purchasing loans in June 1936 and began to liquidate its holdings. Its lending record has struck many commentators as surprising, since the agency refinanced a considerable number of mortgages in C and D neighborhoods, in large measure because low-income borrowers had a better record of repayment. The 1940 census reports that 24,290 nonwhites held HOLC loans and that about 5 percent of the total mortgages were held by African Americans.[33] Comparing this activity to the FHA's subsequent record of insuring very few loans for nonwhites, scholars argue that federal mortgage programs at least had the *potential* to be equitable. Jackson argues that the FHA, unlike its predecessor, allowed "personal and agency bias in favor of all-white subdivisions in the suburbs to affect the kinds of loans it guaranteed," evidence that "the [FHA] bureaucracy influenced the character of housing at least as much as [its] enabling legislation did." The government's role in shaping subsequent patterns of residential segregation, this argument suggests, was as much the product of bureaucratic preference as it was of the specific legislative acts that revolutionized the market for homes.[34]

Of course, the fact that the HOLC required the racial segregation of neighborhoods regardless of which applicants qualified for loans shows that the agency was hardly colorblind. But beyond this, the agency's lending record is far less significant, in the long run, than the mechanisms and the appraisal logic that it introduced to the national mortgage market and for the precedent that it set. Government bureaucrats, regardless of their personal racial views, had limited room to maneuver once the federal government defined minority homeownership as an actuarial risk to white people. HOLC operations attached to the long-term mortgage a standardized system of real estate and neighborhood appraisal that demanded racial segregation while defining it as nothing more than an economic necessity. Meanwhile, by rescuing a significant portion of the nation's nonfarm housing sector so efficiently, the agency suggested the potential of a specific tool—the long-term, low-interest, self-amortizing home loan—to further jump-start the home building and related industries. The combination would be devastating. The new mortgage instrument, soon adopted by the FHA for the purchase of new homes, would revolutionize lending practices in the home finance industry, spur the resegregation of metropolitan areas and capital markets by race, and help transform the ways that whites would rationalize segregation itself.

––––––––

The FHA embraced both the new mortgage instrument and the market imperative argument for racial exclusion. With the passage of the NHA on June 27, 1934, the Roosevelt administration created a program that, it argued, could revive the private building industry without requiring direct public investment in housing. Supporters described the new agency as an economic stabilizing force and referee that would bolster lenders' confidence and permit consumers to satisfy pent-up demand for housing.

Throughout the 1930s, and well beyond, the FHA was designed, sold to legislators, and then operated on the premise that federal intervention would stimulate existing market activity, not alter it and that FHA programs in no way posed an "unwarranted and competitive intrusion by the Federal Government into [the] legitimate private business sphere," as Administrator Abner Ferguson explained to a meeting of the American Title Association in 1935. A year earlier, Roosevelt appealed directly to the nation's governors to pass legislation that would permit FHA operations in their states, stressing that the program was designed "to encourage the investment of private capital in the home mortgage field" by "eliminat[ing] as far as possible exorbitant and usurious rates charged in many places." Supporters of selective credit programs portrayed the pre-Depression mortgage market as simply prone to abuse, rather than structurally incapable of supporting affordable loans and widespread homeownership, while the federal government's role in creating and sustaining these new, more favorable conditions was effectively erased.[35]

Whites' investment in this narrative would have momentous implications for the government's approach to racial equality. The FHA openly and systematically discriminated against racial minorities for decades and yet insisted that exclusion was necessitated by impersonal market requirements. Racial segregation was a function, the agency insisted, or at worst a symptom of a healthy free market for property. And federal intervention, according to its champions, was not interfering with the free market for property.

Like the legislation that created the FHLB and HOLC, the National Housing Act was viewed as an emergency measure, designed to jump-start the economy and create jobs, particularly in the building and related trades, which by 1934 accounted for one third of the nation's unemployment. Like its predecessors, the NHA was drafted and passed under intense pressure from building, real estate, financial and labor groups, which saw state involvement as a way to rescue their industries. The initial plan was sketched out in a twelve-day conference, called by the National Emergency Council, to which NAREB representatives were invited. Morton Bodfish and Herbert Nelson helped prepare the legislation and lobbied for its passage. FHA staff was largely recruited from the white private sector: builders, bankers, realtors, and housing economists.[36]

No group of urban experts had a more profound impact on FHA operations and the agency's vision of housing economics than members of the Institute for Research in Land Economics and Public Utilities. By the early 1930s, Ernest Fisher's work on appraisal, *Principles of Real Estate Practice*, which first appeared in Ely's "Land Economics Series" in 1924, was extremely influential and, together with his colleagues' scholarship, informed Homer Hoyt's important 1933 study, *One Hundred Years of Land Values in Chicago*. Of more immediate importance, the FHA hired Fisher as a consultant, and he in turn recruited Frederick Babcock to serve as the agency's chief appraiser and "Assistant Administrator in charge of underwriting." It was Babcock who "recognize[d] the need . . . to set up an underwriting system," agency officials would recall in 1960, and "wrote the underwriting manual that has been the FHA bible ever since." Babcock's contribution to the new agency, alone, supports Marc Weiss's conclusion that "the FHA represented the policy fulfillment of Ely's homeownership vision." [37]

Central to this vision, for economists and New Dealers alike, was the conviction that federal intervention would not simply rescue but transform the market for residence. While modeled on the HOLC, the FHA was intended to be much more than a stop-gap measure. It was assigned the ambitious tasks of fostering new lending activity, creating a national market for mortgages, and, by doing so, expanding the market for home finance—in short, creating new market conditions that would generate far more credit. The key was making the long-term, low-interest mortgage the industry standard for all home purchases. To accomplish this, the agency offered to insure institutional lenders who agreed to experiment with the instrument on new home sales. So whereas the HOLC purchased and refinanced existing mortgages at risk of default, the FHA encouraged private lenders to initiate new mortgages and thus create more credit. FHA operations were straightforward. Private financial institutions, including insurance companies, mortgage companies, and savings banks, issued mortgage loans to individual borrowers. If a loan met the FHA's terms and conditions, the institution would qualify for (and almost surely receive) FHA insurance on each individual loan. This put the lender in an enviable position, because if the borrower defaulted, the government indemnified the lender, using funds collected from premiums paid by participating institutions and ultimately backed by U.S. Treasury notes.

Instrumental to the program's effectiveness was the standardization of mortgage lending, achieved by creating detailed terms and conditions for FHA approval. The agency only insured the long-term, low-interest mortgage loans celebrated by institute economists and later popularized by the HOLC. The first program, established under Title I, insured loans for home improvement; within a few months, Title II operations began the agency's much more extensive support for home purchases. An FHA-insured mortgage covered at least 80 percent of the purchase price (later up to 90 percent) and allowed 20 years (eventually up to 35 years) for repayment. All federally approved loans were fully amortized, which enabled borrowers to pay off both the principle and interest, gradually, over the life of the loan. In short the FHA put the generous terms of HOLC refinancing within reach of new borrowers, while simultaneously removing federal responsibility for directly purchasing and issuing the loans.[38]

What impact did the government's significant new stake in credit finance have on the nation's private markets for housing? There is consensus that the FHA, together with related selective credit programs, facilitated the widespread use of the long-term, amortized mortgage, and with it the remarkable expansion of the private housing market. But there is still considerable disagreement about the terminology that best describes the government's sustained presence in that market. Many observers argue that these programs "subsidized" businesspeople and consumers, by creating market conditions that would not otherwise exist. Others argue that federal intervention only "stimulated" private market activity, providing a neutral, stabilizing force that shored up existing market mechanisms. The subsidy characterization is by far more common, at least in most urban histories and studies of racial inequality—so common, in fact, that one writer recently felt compelled to dismiss the claim as "the hoary granddaddy of all urbanist sprawl criticisms."[39]

But there is another disagreement, or at least an unresolved tension, within the scholarship that identifies FHA programs as a subsidy, for many of these same works portray the larger mortgage revolution as the product of free market forces. It is often unclear in these discussions whether the home finance market that emerged from the Great Depression was underwritten by the federal government with federal dollars or not. Certainly the authors in the "subsidy" camp would reject Robert Wood's claim, in 1963, that the FHA's political philosophy could best be described as "Manchesterian liberal."[40] Still there are echoes in their writings of Wood's insistence that FHA mortgage programs "proceed[ed] on the same philosophy of supply and demand that governs the behavior of private firms." Lizabeth Cohen recently captured the prevailing yet ambiguous consensus, explaining that the FHA and VA were "heavily subsidized by the federal government," but nonetheless represented "private market solutions" to the housing crisis by providing "encouragement and assistance" and thus "broaden[ing] [the] potential consumer market." State involvement in home finance operations, she concludes, illustrated New Deal liberals' reliance on "unregulated private markets" to revive construction and meet consumer demand.[41]

Housing economists, by sharp contrast, have long described selective credit operations as creating new kinds of market structures and market relationships, which together sustained lending, borrowing, and consumption that otherwise would not have occurred. They describe the modern housing market as highly regulated, heavily subsidized, and unimaginable without sustained federal involvement. "The effects of government participation in the residential mortgage market," concluded Raymond Goldsmith in 1965, "were so strong, pervasive, and intricate that it is impossible to visualize the form this market would have had in the absence of government intervention."[42]

Did the FHA and other selective credit programs subsidize homeownership, and if so, what did this subsidy mean for the housing market and postwar economic growth? Since the government's role in fueling suburbanization as well as popular ideas about metropolitan change is central to postwar racial politics, it is worth examining the question more closely. Such a discussion requires a brief consideration of postwar selective credit programs. This long view reveals that, from the outset, Depression-era programs actively subsidized the mortgage market and helped create new wealth for targeted populations. Subsequent interventions, beginning during and after World War II, introduced additional, and often more direct, subsidies for consumers and the businesses that catered to them. It is true that mortgage lending had expanded considerably in the three decades preceding the Great Depression, as more institutional lenders entered the market, as lenders experimented with new types of loans, and as the growing middle class invested in mortgage bonds. These pre-Depression developments set precedents soon adopted by New Deal programs.[43] But federal involvement in the mortgage finance industry significantly altered and dramatically supplemented existing lending practices. Beginning in the early 1930s, there was no pure, "private market" for homeownership in the United States, because the supply of and demand for credit were decisively shaped by an activist state.

Key to understanding the government's subsidy function is recognizing how federal insurance programs created new market conditions that created new wealth. At the heart of the new market was the long-term, low-interest mortgage instrument and the elaborate federal infrastructure that sustained its exchange. Again the thrift industry had experimented with a version of this mortgage, and it was their success that had piqued housing economists' interest in the loan. But the pre-Depression market was relatively limited in scope, the terms on its loans were far less attractive than those created by the FHA (and thus accessible to a far narrower cross section of the American public), and the experiment was destroyed by the economic crisis (by some measures, real estate speculation contributed considerably to the economy's collapse). Federal intervention not only revived the market for this experimental mortgage but also expanded and significantly redesigned it, by creating and funding a new fiscal and institutional infrastructure that enabled a more attractive version of the long-term mortgage to thrive by facilitating it and accelerating its exchange. The state designed a very attractive new market for credit, established the rules for its operation, and by regulating, insuring, and supplementing its operations ensured at least its short-term survival. It was this new, state-supported market that eventually created an unprecedented amount of credit, available exclusively for the repair and purchase of housing.

It is true that the FHA seldom loaned money directly and covered most of its administrative costs with borrowers' fees and other income. Indeed, the agency eventually turned a profit, a point that helps to convince many critics that FHA operations provided no subsidy. But the FHA's administrative efficiency reveals little about the government's larger impact on the mortgage market, both because it masks the FHA's larger impact on credit markets and, of equal importance, because FHA insurance represented only one facet of a multifaceted federal operation. It was only after the federal government redesigned, validated, and promised to underwrite the long-term, low-interest mortgage that lenders and consumers were able to benefit from it. The NHA and other legislation created and sustained conditions that made a new type of borrowing and lending possible, in both the government-insured and conventional (or noninsured) mortgage markets. Federal programs enabled lenders to grant more home loans and encouraged more types of financial institutions to enter the market. On top of this, federal programs invested millions of dollars annually into the mortgage industry, largely through its S&L reserve system and secondary market operations. Taken together, this range of programs enabled all mortgage lenders to "break unmistakably with the past," as Sidney Robbins and Nestor Terleckyj write, by encouraging more and more housing consumers, especially middle-income consumers, to go into debt so that they might own a house. Not surprisingly, eligible consumers jumped at the chance and created sufficient demand to sustain the new mortgage market's astronomical postwar growth. Continually regulated by federal authorities and both insured and supplemented by U.S. Treasury funds, that market went on to produce untold wealth in housing and related industries. Consumers benefited by gaining access to affordable credit, and thus to housing, which eventually translated into substantial home equity. Lenders benefited through their largely risk-free participation in this fast-growing and lucrative market. And, of course, the real estate, construction, and related industries benefited because more homes were built and sold.[44]

In the final analysis, the FHA and related mortgage programs created and sustained conditions in the home finance market that accelerated the creation of credit. Abundant credit, in turn, expanded consumption and production. And this activity eventually created wealth, by introducing substantial equity into the portfolios of millions of families and by supporting myriad housing-related industries. Working in concert with other important programs, the FHA succeeded where the FHLB had earlier "failed," by transforming the structure of the housing credit industry itself, making mortgages affordable for individuals and lucrative as well as safe for private lenders.[45] These programs were integral parts of a larger New Deal–era restructuring of the nation's credit markets, a process well under way by 1935, years before the "Keynesian" revolution, according to most historians, marked the beginning of federal intervention to promote the growth of consumer markets.[46]

An early commentator on the transformation of housing markets during and after the Great Depression was Miles Colean, co-author of the National Housing Act and later the FHA's chief economist. Colean wrote that when policymakers debated strategies, during World War II, to meet the anticipated postwar housing demand, they simply assumed "that the housing needs of the country could not be properly satisfied by the undirected operation of the building and financing markets." So officials emphasized "further liberalization of the mortgage insurance device," together with federal aid for slum clearance and public housing. Colean explained that even the early postwar "emergency" housing measures, including the mortgage provisions of the GI Bill, which eventually put homeownership within reach for millions of returning servicemen, represented "an elaboration of devices developed before and during the war," including "the direction of credit into certain lines, through insurance and guarantees." Depression-era and subsequent interventions created a situation by 1946, Colean concluded, which found the housing market "more completely under [government] surveillance and control" than it was during the war itself.[47]

In studies published between 1950 and 1975, housing economists explored the ways that selective credit programs created new market structures and market relationships, which together made possible new kinds of economic activity that generated considerable wealth. Their work describes, for example, how New Deal–era programs "create[d] and [kept] in operation a greater number of banks and S&Ls than a purely competitive process would have permitted." James Gillies calculated in 1963 that selective credit programs "increased the flow of funds into residential construction" by billions of dollars, without, he added, "materially improv[ing] the housing status of the very low-income groups in society." Institutional lenders, according to these writers, were well aware of the state's influence on the market for debt. They had to be, explained R. J. Saulnier, because by the mid-1950s selective credit operations had made "the problem of investment analysis . . . less one of judging the risk quality of individual mortgages than of understanding and correctly anticipating the loan insurance and guarantee policies of the federal government." Institutional lenders recognized that "market forces do not set the return" for investment in the mortgage market, noted Gillies, so "when it is out of line with other earnings . . . lenders shift out of such lending." These studies also demonstrate that federal programs attracted more lenders into the mortgage finance business. Soon after World War II, life insurance companies assumed a commanding position in the market. The biggest winners by far were mortgage companies, which "developed to meet a need that was created when FHA and VA operations were successful in creating (at least partially) a national market for mortgages." In short housing economists agreed that government programs gave birth to and actively sustained a new kind of housing market. Their debate focused on whether or not selective credit policy—as opposed to, say, direct payments—offered what William Silber called the "appropriate method of subsidization."[48]

The depth of the FHA's subsidy function is further demonstrated by the agency's constant collaboration with the private development industry. Federal mortgage programs did not exist "outside" of the market for credit, like a rule-maker or referee, but rather worked hand in hand with the same private interests that benefited most from state involvement. To ensure the new mortgage market's success and promote its expansion, housing officials worked closely with leaders from the building, home finance, real estate, and other industries, including many of the people and organizations that designed and promoted selective credit operations. The FHA was primarily staffed, at the local, regional, and national levels, by bankers, builders, and real estate agents, and it coordinated virtually every facet of its operations with national business groups and their local representatives. Administration officials kept constant counsel with business leaders, to assess the program's impact on local markets and consider adjustments to current operations. This constant collaboration was no secret. Officials frequently acknowledged their debt to business leaders and openly solicited what one FHA administrator called their "help and cooperation."[49]

For example, the agency constantly turned to business groups to discuss needed legislative reform, to solicit specific language for legislative drafts, and to help promote new bills before Congress. Illustrative were the debates that began in 1937 over renewal of the Title II insurance program, which included support for mortgages on preexisting residential units. The program had its opponents, including legislators uncomfortable with the financial risk that selective credit agencies seemed to pose to the U.S. Treasury. On top of this, there was considerable competition among institutional lenders over the spoils of the new mortgage market. The S&L industry (and their representatives at the FHLBB) were anxious to end federal support for these purchases, since it threatened to draw more types of lenders, and thus unwanted competition, into the mortgage field. Supporting the program's renewal, meanwhile, were the trade, building, and financial interests who had been reaping substantial profits from Title II insurance for existing homes and who saw expansion of this market as inextricably tied to the larger project of reviving housing-related business. Also supporting extension was institute economist and now FHA chief underwriter, Frederick Babcock, who told the agency's administrator Stewart McDonald in 1936 that the agency's insurance programs for new and existing construction were inseparable. Existing "houses must be readily salable," he explained, "in order to make possible and encourage . . . new construction." In 1938, FHA officials lobbied for extension, noting in an internal memo that the "best advised land developers, operating builders, etc., feel that any slowing up of facilities to finance existing homes [on current terms] will have a marked retarding effect on the building and selling of new homes." Congress also followed the recommendation of NAREB president Paul E. Stark, extending the amortization period on FHA-insured loans for small homes to 25 years and permitting a 90 percent loan-to-value ratio.[50]

The S&L industry reconciled itself to this new status quo, but continued congressional skepticism over Title II forced its defenders to remain vigilant. As a new set of renewal hearings approached in 1941, industry leaders and FHA officials mobilized for what Administrator Abner Ferguson anticipated would be "a rather spirited fight" with legislators. Local realtors and real estate boards contacted their congressmen and President Roosevelt, urging them to sustain the program. From Asbury Park, New Jersey, for example, came an appeal from a bank president, who insisted that the "distress" in the regional property markets "cannot be corrected if the Federal Housing Administration withdraws from the field of insuring mortgages on existing construction." Meanwhile, Ferguson consulted with NAREB president Herbert Nelson, who suggested that his members could "approach Congress in support" of renewal and "ask for a hearing," ideally to coincide with the national real estate conferences in Washington, D.C., scheduled for April and May. This way, Nelson explained, NAREB could "bring some men who are well known to members of Congress and particularly to the Committee on Currency to reinforce the necessity of maintaining this phase of FHA." Ferguson agreed that NAREB's efforts "should be very helpful," and promised that he would "do everything possible" to push for a spring hearing date, since it "would be highly important for a number of prominent real estate men to appear before the Committees."[51]

The role of government programs and public-private collaboration in creating new supply, new demand, and new wealth was sometimes openly acknowledged by FHA leadership. Its first administrator, James Moffett, a former official of Commerce's Housing Division, told business audiences in 1934 that the FHA was "creating a year-round market" by "creating an all-season demand for modernization and all the products needed in repairing and furnishing homes." ("The time has come," he told an audience of advertisers, "when any season is *the* season for advertising all the countless lines that profit from modernizing, furnishing, equipping and decorating the American home.") Moffett boasted that the FHA was "educating the banks to carry on indefinitely a tremendous amount of lending," providing "an opportunity to develop far more business than in the past." (Few lenders had previously loaned on "character credit," he explained, but "thousands of them are [now] learning that there is no better credit in the world than the reliable, employed American citizen who promised to pay back what he owes.") And Moffett promised industry that there would be "billions and billions of dollars to be taken out of" the new market for home purchases, noting that "no such market has ever before in all history been offered industry." Over time FHA officials toned down this rhetoric and downplayed their role in restructuring the market, especially when addressing consumers. Still they continually reminded business organizations that government programs were fueling market activity and increasing profits. "The fact of a property's eligibility for mortgage insurance under the FHA plan," explained Administrator Stewart McDonald to a 1937 meeting of Ohio mortgage lenders, "confers distinct sales advantages upon the property." Builders who disregarded federal construction guidelines were "under a distinct handicap in the home mortgage money market and the residential building field."[52]

The most candid assessments of the federal impact on private markets were reserved for internal correspondence and appear frequently whenever Congress threatened to end or limit specific insurance programs. In defending Title II insurance for existing construction, for example, FHA officials described it as "throwing the market open to lenders in general" and "greatly increas[ing] the capital available for home financing." Frederick Babcock asserted that the current program "does make existing construction marketable." The federal presence, one memo concludes curiously, "has created a competitive market," an assertion common among supporters of selective credit operations, betraying perhaps their struggle to reconcile these programs with the administration's investment in pursuing "market friendly" policies. More often these internal conversations suggest that officials were unfazed by the contradictions. A 1939 memorandum estimated that elimination of insurance for existing construction would "remov[e] what amounts to 90 percent of the potential mortgage funds" currently available for purchase of these homes, adding that this would "discriminate against large numbers of people." McDonald also predicted that discontinuation would enable the S&L industry to monopolize the market for existing construction. This would be a disaster, he concluded, "because the people have been taught to avoid the old style short term first, second and third mortgages which were so largely responsible for the crash." He was equally aware of the S&L industry's dependence on federal largesse, referring to the FHLB as "almost entirely financed by the government." "Almost a Half Billion Dollars of government funds have been invested in the Home Loan Bank System," he noted in 1939, "for the benefit of privately owned associations."[53]

––––––––––

The new federal stake in suburban development would have a long-lasting influence on the politics of race and housing in the United States, for two closely related reasons. First, the opportunities and the wealth created by these programs were not made available to most racial minorities; federal policy subsidized an almost exclusively white suburban growth, simultaneously transforming and accelerating the racial segregation of housing and wealth in metropolitan America. Second, the FHA constantly denied that it subsidized, or even that it significantly shaped, the market for homes, especially when presenting its programs to the American public. The agency insisted that the mortgage market's fabulous growth and the racial segregation that accompanied it were solely products of free market activity.

And the evidence suggests that most housing officials and their supporters believed this to be true. The importance of this cannot be underestimated. Public and private leaders did not use state policy, surreptitiously, to achieve "racist" goals. Rather, they sincerely embraced and promoted programs grounded in a racially constructed theory of property. Commentators have long shown that the FHA refused to insure mortgages for most racial minorities and thus excluded them for at least three decades from a fast-growing and lucrative market for suburban homeownership. To fully understand the agency's impact on metropolitan development and the politics of exclusion, it is important to recognize that the FHA discriminated not simply because its agents were "racist" but because they were invested in a theory of race and property that defined racial exclusion as an economic necessity. Rather than manipulating federal authority and using the FHA in a discriminating way, housing officials simply operated a stimulus program that defined minority occupancy as a threat to property values. Thus, in the final analysis, federal policy excluded black people solely by remaining true to its own appraisal guidelines and assessment procedures. This meant that the FHA's major accomplishment—reinventing the mortgage market so that it fueled economic growth and created a nation of homeowners—was undermined by the same standardized procedures that ensured the program's remarkable success.

This has important implications for understanding metropolitan racial segregation after World War II. First, it makes transparent the means by which the FHA structured the housing market along racial lines. Guiding agency operations was a theory about race and property values first articulated in planning and real estate circles before the Depression. NAREB adopted rules about racial restriction in its Code of Ethics in 1924, the same year that Frederick Babcock outlined the market imperative for segregation in *Real Estate Appraisal*. The HOLC gave state sanction to these principles in its appraisal policies and, eventually, its Residential Security Maps. Finally this theory guided FHA operations. When the agency completed its first national real property surveys in 1934, it selected eight variables, each highlighted on agency appraisal maps, considered to be "the factors most pertinent in revealing housing conditions." The variables were average rents, the number and age of residential units, rates of ownership, the physical condition of the structures, the presence of private bathroom facilities, and the percentage of persons "living in the block that are of a race other than white." "These eight factors," explained FHA housing economist Homer Hoyt in 1939, were "shown in each of over 150,000 blocks in the 142 cities for which block data maps have been made."[54]

By then, Frederick Babcock had joined the agency and wrote racial restriction into the *Underwriting Manual*, which was already circulating in 1935 and appeared in published form as early as April 1936. This volume (and subsequent editions) set out the rules that quickly standardized appraisal practices nationwide and set the course for generations of metropolitan development in the United States. Designed to tutor officials and realtors in what a later edition called the "fundamental principles of mortgage lending," the *Manual* emphasizes the need to assess all structures by analyzing the "two major considerations . . . of residential mortgage financing—dwelling properties and borrowers."[55] Then it outlines requirements for judging both property and people, in detailed, technical discussions of topics including construction and design standards, topography and service provision, loan-to-value ratios, and borrowers' creditworthiness. The rules for assessing value focus largely on impersonal variables, such as construction materials, service provision, and lot spacing requirements. Other sections introduce more subjective considerations such as "neighborhood character" and "appeal." And it is here that the FHA introduces explicit rules about race. "If a neighborhood is to retain stability," explains the 1936 edition, "it is necessary that properties shall continue to be occupied by the same social and racial classes," since a "change in social or racial occupancy generally leads to instability and a reduction in values." The chapter "Rating of Location" explains that one of the important "Protection[s] from Adverse Influences" was the presence of restrictive covenants, which, "to be really effective," should include a "prohibition of the occupancy of properties except by the race for which they are intended."[56]

Regardless of the terminology used (which would grow far more muted by the late 1940s), related considerations were structured into every stage of the assessment and approval process. FHA agents compiled data files on 140 metropolitan areas, rating their neighborhoods with the same A through D system pioneered by its predecessor and designating all minority or mixed-raced neighborhoods as economically unstable. For appraisers, the "Completed Established Ratings of Locations" worksheet (FHA Form No. 2082) included a "Racial Occupancy Designation," with space to indicate if neighborhoods were "White," "Mixed," "Foreign," or "Negro."[57] The standard "Report of Valuator" form required for each property asked if "inharmonious racial or social groups [are] present in the neighborhood," and if not, whether there was "any danger of infiltration of such groups." The "Description of Real Estate" form submitted by the home buyer asked if the property had "Deed restrictions, etc.," to which the FHA's first accepted applicant, a man in Alexandria, Virginia, replied with one word: "Racial."[58]

Using these resources as their guides, FHA agents refused to insure loans for home purchase or improvement in most C and all D neighborhoods, and turned down minority applicants seeking to purchase a home in A or B neighborhoods. Standard FHA procedure defined nonwhites as a permanent, calculable risk to stable property values. Standard procedure, in turn, shaped lenders' decision making. In 1941, for example, Harry D. Kramer, of Kramer Realties in New York City, visited the offices of the Hudson Trust Company to secure a loan on a development in Fanwood, New

Jersey (Union County). He presented about a dozen applications from his buyers and "was told by the gentleman in charge that every applicant was worthy to receive a loan." "They asked me if I had an F.H.A. approval. I told them NO, the reason was that it is a colored development. He then said 'I am sorry I cannot do anything for you.' On the Q.T. he said word had been passed around that no loans will be given to colored developments." Outraged, Kramer turned to Prudential Life, which also felt that "the type of applicants that I submitted was above the ordinary, but when I informed them that it is a colored development, they told me they could do nothing unless we had the F.H.A. approval." Kramer recounted this story in a letter to Franklin D. Roosevelt that summer and appealed for help. "Knowing the feelings of Mrs. Roosevelt and yourself in the matter," he continued, "I wish to state that I represent [people] who are loyal and patriotic citizens, but any member of them are bitter in their hearts to think that this great and glorious country should discriminate against them on account of color." "Mr. President," he concluded, "is there anything you can do to assist us in getting a loan?"[59]

The centrality of these standardized procedures to the mutual insurance programs helps explain how state intervention helped popularize the market imperative theory of racial discrimination. In the eyes of government officials, racial considerations were secondary to the urgent task of revitalizing the housing sector and resuscitating the national economy. Racial exclusion was a fundamental premise of FHA operations, to be sure, but by no means a primary focus. The focus was stimulating economic growth, and Depression-era political imperatives required creation of a program that would, first, produce rapid results and, second, be palatable to officials and businesspeople suspicious of governmental interference in the private market. It was essential to create a program that would be (or at least be seen as) market friendly. Advocates placed considerable emphasis on the FHA's uniform underwriting guidelines, which promised to attract lenders (thus quickly spur growth) and protect the federal government against loss. In the eyes of the FHA's supporters, federal appraisal guidelines, including its racial proscriptions, were informed not by ideological preference but economic principle and necessity. Its racial rules were viewed as a minor component of a program designed to accommodate the market's needs. It was this investment in the program's market friendliness that eventually translated into a public discourse about the FHA's supposedly nonideological nature and the corollary assertion that racial discrimination was driven not by prejudice but by a market imperative. Vanishing from the discussion was the fact that state interventions were inventing a new market for residence, subsidizing that market, and dictating the distribution of its resources to some people but not others. It was by this means that FHA operations began to racialize whites' vision of housing economics during the 1930s, as the agency's story about race, property, and housing was rapidly inscribed in a very powerful state apparatus, whose representatives insisted that it was economics and the market, not individuals and their prejudices, that were setting the rules.

For this reason, the FHA's impact on racial politics is greater than previously recognized. By adopting HOLC appraisal guidelines and applying them to a pump-priming operation, the government began to actively promote, indeed to help pay for, the systematic segregation of residential neighborhoods and to deny certain federally subsidized housing opportunities to minorities. Critically, it justified discrimination not by specifically discussing so-called racial issues, but by invoking a theory of market behavior and housing economics that assumed the necessity of racial segregation. Again the contrast with earlier mechanisms of racial exclusion is telling. Racial covenants (as well as racial zoning ordinances) had a singular purpose: to exclude racial minorities. Moreover, they cited the financial threat posed by nonwhite occupancy as *only one of many variables fueling their decision-making.* By sharp contrast, New Deal programs made the economic argument *the primary, and in most circles the sole, justification* for racial exclusion. Meanwhile they achieved racial segregation with a program that was not focused on segregation. By the time the country mobilized for war in the late 1930s, federal programs had created a new kind of market for both credit and suburban residence, a market explicitly grounded in the assumption that race was an economic variable relevant only because of its impact on property values. The rise of this new mortgage market made the market imperative rationale the cornerstone of restrictionist politics, in both theory and practice. While covenants simply legalized segregation, federal housing policies validated (and elevated) the economic rationale for segregation by creating a market designed to sustain it.

Beginning in the 1930s, as a result, racial exclusion was no longer simply pursued by white homeowners and defended as a requirement imposed by the everyday workings of the market for homes. Exclusion by race was now firmly situated, by government statute, within the everyday workings of a newly designed market for homes. The act of excluding minorities from neighborhoods now had a very different relationship to the actual market for residence, both because exclusion was now constitutive of the market (the rules governing its operations literally *required* it) and because that market was dependent on federal support and oversight. Race restrictive covenants (as well as individual acts of discrimination) expressed the wishes of individuals and communities to live separately from "non-Caucasians." While the economic rationale informing private decisions was implicit, and often given indirect sanction by the courts, that rationale did not systematically structure the market for home finance. To be sure, covenants, as well as other discriminatory practices limited minorities' access to housing credit and to certain neighborhoods. But they policed neighborhoods within the parameters of an existing (and limited) market for home finance that catered mostly to the affluent. Racial covenants operated based on the *assumption* that a free market for housing could not support integration but did not systematically shape the creation or circulation of housing credit. The segregationist mechanism built into federal mortgage policy operated very differently, because state intervention created a new kind of market for home finance that simultaneously created more credit and structured the ways in which it was distributed. By accepting the myth that the market for housing demanded segregation, the government in turn forged a new market for housing that actually required it.

The new federal presence in housing markets did not merely institutionalize segregation by putting state authority and state resources behind the impulse. It codified and then administered a racially exclusionary system of housing economics. Passage of the National Housing Act wrote the market imperative argument for exclusion into a new market for credit, one with the potential to create an enormous amount of wealth. And it set the government on a course that it would steer for at least three decades: facilitating both the racial segregation of neighborhoods and the denial of mortgage credit to racial minorities exclusively in the name of protecting the "free market" for homes, while insisting that this market was neither created nor subsidized by the federal government.

———

The FHA's impact on suburban racial politics would not be very visible until the 1940s. But by the time that the nation entered World War II, agency operations had begun to exert their influence. Employing the *Manual* and its market logic as their guides, regional FHA offices committed to hundreds of thousands of loans. Mortgage money soon flowed as never before; the annual rate and total amount of lending quickly matched pre-Depression levels and soon far surpassed them. In just its first year, the Title I program enabled private institutions to issue more than 70,000 home improvement loans. Under Title II, the agency insured 23,397 home mortgage loans during its first calendar year of operation, 77,231 in 1936, 102,076 in 1937, and

168,293 in 1940. Purchasers of new homes benefited the most; beginning in 1935, housing starts increased rapidly nationwide, and the agency backed an ever larger percentage of the nation's new, nonfarm housing starts each year (6 percent in 1935, 16 percent in 1936, 26.7 percent in 1938, and 33.4 percent in 1940). By 1942, the FHA was serving 1 in 4 of the residential mortgages in the United States. And in accordance with the "fundamental principles of mortgage lending" outlined in the *Underwriting Manual*, this fast-growing market channeled virtually all of its resources to people of European descent. City Survey maps filed as late as 1939 document the government's assumptions about which neighborhoods and which populations were deemed "safe" investments.[60]

Fairly typical was the program's impact on metropolitan Detroit. Home-building was almost nonexistent in the early years of the Depression. (Indeed, it was "not unusual," noted one observer from Hazel Park, "for a vacant house to disappear from a lot over-night when a neighborhood was short of fire wood.") But FHA operations turned the tide by insuring mortgages at a slightly higher rate in midwestern states and, within this region, devoting considerable resources to the Detroit area. By 1940, borrowers in the metropolitan region had received insurance on 44,434 mortgages on one-to-four-family homes, or 7.5 percent of the region's total occupied dwellings.[61] Nearly 35,000 of these units were new and accounted for 35.1 percent of housing construction completed in the previous ten years. Over that same period, the agency issued 104,574 property improvement notes, worth over $37 million. Together these programs translated into substantial benefits for individuals and families. For most eligible borrowers, buying a new, FHA-eligible suburban house suddenly became the least expensive alternative, often cheaper than renting an apartment in the central city: 97 percent of the FHA-insured units sold in the 1930s cost between $3,000 and $8,000, and the vast majority (90 percent) required only a 10 percent to 19 percent down payment. Eligible borrowers became homeowners by investing between $300 and $1,520 and committing to a monthly mortgage payment of $39.74 (equal to about 19.6 percent of the average family's monthly income).[62] By comparison, the same family would pay, on average, only $5 less per month or $33.80 to rent housing in Detroit.[63] Purchasers of preexisting homes fared very well too, putting $600 to $2,320 down on their purchases. In 1940, the average buyer of a preexisting home paid $43.37 per month on the mortgage, or about 17.5 percent of their monthly income.[64]

Following the rules that guided FHA practice nationwide, the Detroit-area office focused almost exclusively on promoting the construction, purchase, and repair of privately owned homes—by *certain* white people. There is no evidence that blacks qualified for FHA-insured loans before World War II. The government's City Survey maps assigned a D rating to any neighborhoods in Detroit and its suburbs that had a notable minority presence. In the comments section of the Area Description forms, appraisers noted "Negro concentration" or even "Area of Negroes and aliens who do not speak English." As late as 1939, "Poles" and "Hungarians" and "Italians" were in some contexts not fully white, even in the eyes of the agency that would soon do so much to secure their new racial identity after the war. Meanwhile, in the five years that saw the FHA insure 44,434 home purchases and 104,574 property improvement loans in the Detroit region, it committed to a total of ten mortgages for rental projects (all under Sections 207 and 210 of Title II). Together this added 462 units of rental housing to the metropolitan area.[65]

Restructuring the Conventional Mortgage Market: FSLIC and FNMA

The state's impact on home finance markets, and on popular ideas about suburban growth, reaches far beyond the operations of its well-known mortgage insurance programs. The National Housing Act also helped transform and dramatically expand the "conventional," that is, noninsured, market for mortgage debt, which would eventually account for the majority of the nation's home finance activity. Expansion of the conventional market was inextricably linked to the revolution started by the FHA. New Deal policymakers hoped to promote new kinds of economic growth, by encouraging more institutional lenders to enter the mortgage market and encouraging all participating lenders to issue far more credit than they had in the past. The state created a system in which the insured and conventional markets constantly fueled and provided critical support for each other's operations. Because of this interdependence, the lenders of noninsured mortgages adopted the same racial proscriptions that guided FHA appraisal and lending activity.

Included in the National Housing Act were most of the provisions that would ensure the long-term expansion of conventional lending. First, FHA Title II insurance constantly introduced new loans to the national pool of mortgage credit. As the FHA-insured mortgage became the safest and most attractive loan around (and thus the most competitive), conventional lenders gradually moved toward the long-term, low-interest, self-amortized mortgage. Meanwhile the federal government extended its oversight powers for the S&L industry, and with Title IV created a program of federal insurance for it. The new Federal Savings and Loan Insurance Corporation (FSLIC) was an FHLBB-governed body that insured individual savings accounts in savings and loan associations up to a value of $5,000, providing protections analogous to the FHA-insurance that protected other institutional lenders. Like the FHA, the FSLIC was the product of the private sector's close ties to the new activist state. Worried that FHA insurance operations would challenge S&L dominance of the home mortgage market, the industry lobbied aggressively for inclusion of Title IV in the initial NHA. And while individual savings and loan institutions warmed to FSLIC insurance quite slowly, the program eventually helped attract more funds to the industry and generate far more lending by the late thirties. Federally affiliated savings and loans reaped the most benefits, accounting for only one third of the member S&Ls yet controlling more than half of the assets held by members nationwide.[66]

The NHA also began to foster a vibrant "secondary mortgage market." This is a market for the purchase and sale of existing mortgage loans, as opposed to the "primary" mortgage market, in which mortgage loans are originated, that is, where credit is initially extended. In a secondary mortgage market, investors trade existing loans, often between geographical regions. FHA standardization of appraisal and lending practices was essential to creating this secondary market. Because mortgages were extended based on uniform and thus transferable appraisal guidelines, investors felt confident trading mortgage loans without ever seeing the mortgaged properties. The federal presence made standard appraisal procedures, rather than actual houses, the ultimate measure of value in the secondary mortgage market. The long-range goal was to encourage investors, especially institutional investors, to treat the long-term, low-interest mortgage loan like other capital instruments, so that they traded them much like stocks or bonds. It was hoped that this secondary market would encourage mortgage originators, many of whom were still quite wary of the new mortgage instrument, to deal in a "new and untested type of investment." Advocates also calculated that secondary market activity would eventually help move mortgage loans to credit-starved regions and constantly increase the circulation of housing debt. More circulation would translate into more speculation, attracting more lenders into this potentially lucrative field and creating infinitely more credit. More credit would translate immediately into increased borrowing, sales, and construction.[67]

To jump-start secondary market activity, Title III of the NHA authorized the FHA to charter private national mortgage associations. Officials expected these privately owned and operated entities to trade the long-term, low-interest mortgage; they counted on private institutional lenders, in other words, to initiate the much-needed market activity. As early as 1935, FHA officials described "the operation of such associations" as "vital to the effective and rapid growth of the mutual mortgage insurance plan," predicting that they would "constitute an enduring part of the new home financing system which this administration is fostering." Unfortunately, few lenders took the bait, and those that did failed to qualify for charters. Subsequent incentives did not help. Amendments to Title III offered generous tax exemptions and lowered the minimum capitalization requirements. Meanwhile, the RFC Mortgage Company was created in 1935; in addition to directly purchasing FHA-insured loans (again to stimulate interest in the new market), it was authorized and encouraged to buy stock in national mortgage associations out of its $10-million revolving fund (later expanded to $25 million). But Depression-era conditions made the risks for private investors too great. The private sector was unwilling to take the chance, Oliver Jones and Leo Grebler explain, because "the investment quality of the insured mortgage was yet unproven."[68]

So in early 1938, Roosevelt instructed the RFC to create a federal body that would do the work that the private sector had failed to perform. The new Federal National Mortgage Association (FNMA, or Fannie Mae) was chartered on February 10, under authority of the original NHA provision, with a capital stock of $10 million and an additional $1-million surplus as well as considerable potential reserves. The FNMA was designed to buy existing FHA-insured mortgages to make them more attractive investments by increasing their circulation. To pay for these purchases, FNMA could issue notes or bonds valued up to $200 million dollars, calculated as twenty times the value of its initial $10-million capitalization. The new agency quickly attracted funds from the capital market. Within months FNMA issued $30 million in low-interest, five-year notes, and the following January it issued another $56 million. By the end of 1938, it had purchased and continued to hold more than $80 million in FHA-insured mortgages from the primary market. This activity proved to be essential for the Title II program, which had not yet convinced enough lenders to experiment again with mortgages. By some accounts, initial FNMA purchases helped keep the more visible FHA program on a firm footing during the prewar years.[69]

Critics regularly note that a true secondary market for residential mortgages was very slow in coming. By most calculations, it did not take shape until the 1970s.[70] Technically, this is true. But in its stead, the federal government created public bodies to fill in for the wished-for private market activity. By 1940, the FNMA and RFC together had purchased almost

$247 million of FHA-insured loans, sold $32 million worth back into the market, and still held mortgages valued at $201 million. By 1942, FNMA alone held mortgage debt valued at $211 million. Their activity accounted for nearly 23 percent of all FHA-recorded purchases before World War II. By then legislators had made stimulation of conventional lending an important focus of federal housing policy. Through Federal Reserve policy, the HOLC's investment of about $300 million in the S&L industry, and the centralization and coordination of housing agency activities in 1939, the government continued to enhance and consolidate an institutional support system designed to stimulate lending in both the government-insured and conventional markets. And with the advent of FNMA, especially, it was spending considerable money to do so.[71]

The impact was tangible. By 1940, selective credit programs had drawn hundreds of institutional investors into the mortgage market for the first time. In Detroit, for example, insurance companies, state banks, national banks, and mortgage companies together held 87 percent of the region's mortgages on one-to-four-family properties, while S&Ls held 7.7 percent.[72] After 1940, and especially after World War II, the government's selective credit operations would sustain a "federalized" secondary market for decades. Private sector support for the NHA must be seen in light of the transformation of both the conventional and secondary markets for mortgage finance. The housing and housing-goods industries rallied behind the NHA not simply because it promised to rescue a market on the verge of collapse but also because the government outlined and was clearly committed to sustaining activity that promoted capital formation throughout the home finance industry.

Federal involvement in the conventional market also prompted the near universal adoption of FHA appraisal and lending guidelines, including its racial proscriptions. By the mid-1930s, the *Underwriting Manual* was setting the standard for appraisal practices nationwide. Thus, most conventional loans were restricted, purportedly for economic reasons, to white borrowers. By the time the United States reorganized domestic industrial production to support the war effort, the Hoover and Roosevelt administrations had created a federal infrastructure that transformed the market for home finance capital, continually subsidized and regulated that market, and required that it systematically deny most of its benefits to racial minorities.

———

Meanwhile, government involvement in the mortgage market helped popularize two surprising claims about the nature of government intervention:

one, that federal programs played a minimal (if any) role in reviving and transforming the housing market, and two, that the FHA's racial restrictions were products not of agency prejudice but economic necessity. During the decade that saw public policy revolutionize the market for private housing, public officials promoted the story that the government was not altering normal market operations and, therefore, that it was not culpable for the racial segregation that ensued. By the time the United States entered World War II, lenders, builders, and realtors nationwide were deeply involved in a mortgage industry that required racial segregation and insisted that immutable market forces made it necessary. It was a free market for property that was supposedly creating new wealth in real estate, and it was market mechanisms that dictated the unequal distribution of that wealth.

Thus, with the government's entrance into the mortgage industry came the widespread dissemination of the market imperative rationale for discrimination. A story about the market-friendliness of selective credit programs was rehearsed in the professional conferences and legislative debates that gave rise to modern U.S. housing policy during the Depression. The market defense of racial exclusion was outlined in federal publications and then fully articulated by agency officials when civil rights activists challenged the government to alter FHA appraisal and lending practices. Perhaps most remarkably, champions of the new selective credit programs celebrated the free market for housing in direct appeals to businesspeople and consumers of European descent, by sponsoring a massive promotional campaign designed to encourage lending, borrowing, and spending. It was the perseverance and hard work of businesses and consumers alone, the FHA told its audiences, that would fuel the nation's economic recovery.

CHAPTER FOUR

Putting Private Capital Back to Work: The Logic of Federal Intervention, 1930–1940

It was almost accidental that the market imperative argument became such a prominent defense for residential discrimination in the 1930s. The national economic crisis demanded a level of federal involvement in financial, labor, and consumer markets that drew considerable opposition from business groups and legislators.[1] Early initiatives, such as the FHLB, were fashioned before Roosevelt's election produced a legislative climate more conducive to experimentation. And even during the heyday of New Deal reform, selective credit programs faced resistance from Congress and skepticism from wary businesspeople and consumers alike. Thus, advocates naturally stressed what was seen as the programs' compatibility with the free enterprise system. What made the reserve, regulatory, and insurance efforts unique, they explained, was their ability to spur market activity without altering or disrupting it. Widespread investment in this claim then shaped the government's argument for accepting and encouraging racial segregation. If selective credit operations respected impersonal economic forces, any race-specific outcomes were an unfortunate but unavoidable by-product of efforts to rejuvenate the market for housing.

The story about these programs' market-friendliness was told in many conventional and expected settings. Advocates invoked this argument to persuade reluctant legislators at congressional hearings on the FHLBB, HOLC, and FHA. The story was faithfully reproduced in national media coverage of New Deal reform. Meanwhile, the market defense of racial restriction, in particular, was outlined in the FHA's *Underwriting Manual*, which standardized property evaluation practices nationwide. Other celebrations of the programs' respect for free enterprise appeared in venues far more self-conscious and elaborate. Beginning in 1934, federal officials worked closely with business leaders to cultivate public interest in the long-term mortgage, through a multimillion dollar public relations campaign designed to stimulate lending and borrowing for housing purchase and repair. In print advertisements, publicity films, radio addresses, national speaking tours, and elaborate local campaigns, including door-to-door canvassing, the federal government literally marketed its new mortgage insurance program to eligible borrowers. It did so by assuring consumers that it was the forces of supply and demand, and not the federal state, that were reviving the housing market and making widespread private ownership possible. When the topic of racial integration came up—as blacks demanded equal access to the new mortgage market, or when whites defended the FHA's racial rules—the programs' defenders claimed that it was market forces, alone, that required the racial segregation of neighborhoods. The free market for homes, they explained, simply could not withstand racial mixing. Advocates for the new credit programs assumed a picture of the American property owner that usually excluded, and at best marginalized, large segments of the nation's population.

An analysis of Depression-era policy and legislative debates, FHA appraisal standards, and the agency's promotional activities illustrates the market imperative rationale for racial segregation and the way it was popularized during the Great Depression. The public-private alliance's conception of the free market, specifically its assumptions about profit and value, was firmly rooted in a racialized vision of the market for housing. For this reason the new federal stake in the mortgage industry facilitated a decisive shift in whites' debates over residence and race, a shift in focus from "race" to "economics," by codifying and implementing the market imperative rationale developed by planners and land-use economists in the early twentieth century. New Deal housing policy literally wrote the racial rules of the new land-use science into a new market for residence, in turn giving birth to a market that treated racial separation as a fundamental tenet of metropolitan growth. Federal mortgage programs collapsed popular myths about the character and capacities of racial minorities into a discussion of the market for housing, ultimately assigning supposed group tendencies or impacts a calculable economic value.

Myths about race and real estate were not new; for generations whites had seen nonwhites as a threat to their property and communities. But beginning in the 1930s, federal mortgage programs began to legitimate these fears in a very new way, and in the process subtly redefined whites' assumptions about the relationship between color and property. Federal policy codified, sanctioned, and put tremendous force behind the theory that the mere presence of black people tainted a neighborhood and reduced its monetary value. Meanwhile, selective credit programs created an economic environment that enabled whites to support racial exclusion while insisting, quite earnestly, that their preferences had nothing to do with prejudice.

The rationales for federal intervention and racial segregation remained fairly consistent between the President's Conference on Home Building and Homeownership in 1931 and the nation's entry into World War II. Most supporters of the new federal role agreed that property ownership was the most desirable form of tenancy, because in addition to producing wealth, indeed as a corollary to the production of wealth, ownership produced strong, morally upright families and responsible citizens. It followed naturally from this that individuals, if given the choice and let loose in the free market, would purchase their own homes if possible. Thus, only the revival of a healthy free market for privately owned homes could properly address the nation's housing crisis. But the severity of the Depression, the argument continued, had short-circuited the economy's normal operations, necessitating action that would resuscitate its moribund sectors. This would best be accomplished by the federal government, if and only if its programs did not disrupt natural market mechanisms. Judicious federal action would repair the market and allow it to perform its natural, curative function.

This vision of the housing market was organized around a detailed picture of the homeowner: a responsible, hardworking white man, a man of "character," who was financially stable and supporting a wife (and probably children). It cannot be stressed too much that the urban experts who designed and controlled selective credit programs did not create a new housing market and *then* deny racial minorities access to it. Instead they conceived of the new housing market as exclusively serving white, male-headed families. Their vision of the free market for homes, and of the citizenry deemed capable of thriving in it, simply had no place for racial minorities (or female-headed households). The centrality of this vision to legislative debates and industry standards tells us a great deal about the role that racial ideology played in the operations of the new market for housing. The public-private alliance created and directed home finance capital exclusively to white, suburban families because it could not conceive of a lucrative market for homes that included minority participation. The alliance's very notions of value and profit, specifically in the realm of housing and metropolitan economics, were racially constructed. For this reason federal reform gave birth to a postwar housing market grounded in these principles.

Market-Friendly Interventions and the Homeownership Ideal

Few Depression-era discussions of the housing crisis were free from pae-ans to the free market and celebrations of the privately owned home. Para-doxically, perhaps no voices celebrated free enterprise and private prop-erty more insistently than those calling upon the state to intervene in the market for credit. Proposals for state involvement in the housing market predated Black Monday. As early as 1918, realtors and builders lobbied for tax reform and federal support for home finance markets. Throughout the 1920s, housing reformers, including Edith Elmer Wood and leaders from the National Housing Association, floated comparable proposals, often in the pages of Harold Buttenheim's *American City* magazine. Their ideas at-tracted considerable attention by decade's end, as debate over the economic crisis focused on the nation's moribund real estate market. Government in-tervention did not sit easily with most private and public leaders, however, so reformers carefully worded and qualified their proposals. When Wood opened the 1929 meeting of the NHA by endorsing a federal support pro-gram for "limited dividend housing companies," she assured her audience that state involvement would not cut a path toward socialism. "The root of most of the emotional hostility to government aid to housing in the United States," she began, was the "erroneous impression . . . that government aid is equivalent to government subsidy." By contrast the proposed program, she explained, was designed simply to stimulate demand and supply; it would *"involve no subsidy."* [2]

She was followed by Buttenheim, who spoke on "Slum Improvement by Private Effort." He conceded that "public effort of certain kinds is essential to the efficient functioning of private effort." He saw particular promise in the growing popularity of city planning, zoning, density controls, and build-ing codes and he even acknowledged that it would be difficult to "draw . . . the line" between public and private initiative. But he assumed that "all—or most all—of us would draw it this side of government housing." "We want our public bodies to stimulate slum improvement and better housing by prohibiting the bad and encouraging the good; but we prefer to leave to private effort, rather than to the state or municipality, the actual building and ownership of houses." Buttenheim was willing to entertain proposals for tax incentives and direct government loans, but stressed that there was no need to resort to "actual subsidy from the public treasury." [3]

As calls for aggressive federal action grew more common following the stock market collapse, so, too, did the claim that government intervention could be wholly compatible with the free enterprise system. The consensus position held that well-designed public programs would revive a natural market for ownership that had been disrupted by a crisis in business and consumer confidence. In 1931, James Ford previewed the findings of the President's Conference on Home Building and Homeownership in the *Journal of Home Economics* by focusing on the existing demand for housing and the salutary effects of ownership. "Adequate housing goes to the very roots of the well being of the family," he wrote, "and the family is the social unit of the nation." "Nothing contributes more for greater happiness or for sounder social stability than the surrounding of their homes," so "it should be possible in our country for anybody of sound character and industrious habits to provide himself with adequate housing and preferably to buy his own home." "It is obviously not our purpose," he assured readers, "to set up the Federal Government in the building of homes."[4]

This turned out to be a very understated preview of a refrain about free enterprise and the citizen-homeowner that dominated the conference proceedings and subsequent legislative debates. In a general foreword to the conference report, Secretary of Commerce Robert Lamont, who had served as Hoover's assistant during the 1920s, accused policymakers and businesspeople of underestimating "the effect of home ownership on citizenship" and giving "no thought to [housing's] influence in aiding or obstructing self-government." He speculated that it was "doubtful whether democracy is possible where tenants overwhelmingly outnumber home owners." "Democracy is not a privilege," he explained, but "a responsibility, and human nature rarely volunteers to shoulder responsibility . . . [Rather it] has to be driven by the whip of necessity. The need to protect and guard the home is the whip that has proved, beyond all others, efficacious in driving men to discharge the duties of self-government." Variations of this narrative appear throughout the conference proceedings, as, for example, when the Committees on Homeownership and Dwelling Types report on a disturbing development, which they call the "strong trend toward multifamily housing," and attribute it largely to the "disappearance of the neighborhood or community as a civic and social center." Offering no data to document this "disappearance," the authors still conclude that "there is less pride in home ownership and less centering of the activities of the family in the home." Only by increasing rates of homeownership, they insist, could the nation reverse this trend.[5]

The conference's investment in the homeownership ideal and its debt to pre-Depression development politics are highlighted by some of its experts' more suspect claims. Consider the study "Home Ownership, Housing Economics, and Construction," prepared by the Committee on Types of

Dwellings. That group was led by John Ihlder, former NCCP member, field secretary for the National Housing Association, and member of the Department of Commerce's first Advisory Committee on Zoning. The report that Ihlder helped prepare for the President's Conference relentlessly celebrates the detached, single-family home and attempts to document the benefits of owning over renting. But to make this case, his committee was forced to ignore some of its own research findings. They conducted a survey of 789 "native born" homeowners in Buffalo, New York, for example, to demonstrate that property ownership saved families money, which they could devote in turn to education, cars, household items, clothing, and recreation. The focus group, however, reported "no change" in their budgets for most types of expenditure, so the committee dismissed the results as "hav[ing] very little value." Readers should "be aware," the authors explained, "that a great deal of inaccuracy is to be expected in the [survey]. The opinions given will naturally be biased because past events in retrospect will usually take on content in terms of present conditions. Since the present condition is one of economic stress for a majority of these families, it follows that a mental attitude of stress will be present in the form of bias in the answers to the questions." The authors again had to disregard their survey results in a discussion of the "Advantages and Satisfactions Arising from Home Ownership." Only 69 percent of their respondents agreed that homeownership had "increased interest in community affairs," a number that these experts viewed as suspiciously low. They concluded that "the informants [likely] understood this . . . question to refer to social affairs such as picnics, booster days, women's clubs, politics and the like, whereas the intention was to include questions such as taxation, sewers, garbage removal, public utility services, etc." If the question had been "rightly understood, one would suppose the percentage of affirmative answers to the question would be higher." Generous readings of other survey results further bolstered their case. When 83 percent of the respondents agreed that homeownership had enabled them to "have [the] kind of house [they] desired," the committee concluded that "an affirmative answer to this question probably also subsumed that imponderable attitude designated as 'pride of ownership.'"[6]

Such unbridled enthusiasm for the privately owned, single-family home anchors most of the conference reports, and contributors predicted that expansion of this market would address a host of economic, political, and social problems. Yet critically, the committees' analyses and prescriptions were grounded in a set of untested assumptions about the nature of demand, supply, and the private market. The reports assume that most people would buy a home if they could—in other words that there was an untapped, preexisting demand for privately owned homes. And they assume that a healthy private market could easily meet that demand—that the wealth necessary to finance and build these homes already existed. This wealth "existed" in what these experts refer to as "unused credit." Starting from these assumptions, the authors argue that the key to solving the nation's housing crisis (and related woes) was overcoming the forces that were inhibiting the supply of housing credit.

Best positioned to do this, these experts agreed, was the federal government. Here the narrative about the government's respect for free markets received an important early hearing and gained influential supporters. Conference leaders argued that to mobilize latent (but presumably extant) market resources, it was necessary to expand the federal role. It was the job of private lenders to "meet reasonable demands of their home owning and home buying clients," according to the Committee on Home Ownership, but it was the responsibility of the federal government to assist this process, specifically by operating a credit reserve system for home loan associations that would supplement and regulate the market for finance capital. By creating this federal apparatus, credit shortages "might be reduced substantially through a system whereby local lending institutions could, through a well-recognized procedure, obtain a more liquid supply of credit with which to meet reasonable demands of their home owning and home buying clients." Months later the committee's recommendation was incorporated into the conference's endorsement of the Federal Home Loan Bank Act, drafted by Morton Bodfish and signed by President Hoover.[7]

Proposals for slum clearance and new housing construction also called for a federal role while predicting purely market-driven outcomes. The Committee on Slums, Large-Scale Housing, and Decentralization argued that because neighborhood blight was inhibiting housing construction nationwide, it was necessary for public officials (municipal and federal) and private interests (industry, lenders, labor unions) to promote the mass production of new housing. Construction had to be completed, however, according to the principles of corporate organization, or what the authors called "large-scale operations." In a discussion highlighting a tension that runs through these reports, the authors argued that public-private collaboration was necessary to "place the construction and management of dwellings in the category of big business." Their policy recommendations, which foreshadow operations of both the FHLB and the FHA, reveal the often tortured logic used to characterize the new state-market relationship. To revive the free market for housing, the committee called for the creation of a publicly funded federal housing agency that would (1) coordinate "large scale operations,"

(2) reduce costs to business enterprise by regulating home building and operating a reserve system for the home finance industry, and (3) publish information on housing market fluctuations. Public policy would unleash the private sector so that it could fulfill consumers' demands. Slum clearance, in the final analysis, remained "a problem for private initiative, for business cooperating with the community." The authors even warned that if the private sector "fail[ed] to accept its responsibility," the government would be forced to step in. "The choice lies with business."[8]

The report never addresses the apparent conflict between government involvement and market autonomy, a conflict particularly striking given that the authors were not promoting mere stopgap measures. A federal presence was necessary in the long run, the authors explained, "aside from the exigencies of the immediate situation." Still it was the private sector that would shoulder the burden of solving the nation's housing crisis. "The building of homes," the report concludes, "must be carried on as a business operating for a legitimate profit."[9]

Developers and urban experts were not troubled by such an unprecedented government role in private markets because they viewed credit not as something that was created but rather "unleashed." In fact, the programs they were about to design created new wealth by creating and sustaining a lucrative market for finance capital. But leading voices at the President's Conference, many of whom would design and run the FHLB, the FHA, and other federal programs, viewed the government's role very differently. They described selective credit programs as corrective actions that harnessed existing market resources and mechanisms to create homes, jobs, and profits. They drew sharp distinctions between their programs and competing proposals for "subsidies" and "public housing," portraying these as dangerous steps on a path toward socialized banking and housing. This sharp (and in many ways illusory) differentiation between selective credit programs and the more controversial "subsidy" programs served as a refrain for the congressional debates over housing reform. The legislative hearings during Hoover's term and the early years of the New Deal demonstrate how the expertise, networks, and precedents developed in the pre-Depression decades helped give form to New Deal–era policy and the new logic of intervention that would characterize it.

A particularly revealing moment was also an exceptional one. It came when William F. Stevenson, chairman of the FHLBB, appeared before the Senate in 1933 to endorse the expansion of his agency's powers and creation of the HOLC. In his testimony Stevenson came closer than perhaps any advocate to publicly acknowledging that state policy was designed to *create* wealth. "It is hoped," he told senators at the June hearings, that an enhanced FHLB would "be able to expand the available capital for the financing of homes [by] several hundred million dollars in the next few months." By chartering federal S&Ls and appropriating funds for them, "it is hoped that . . . new capital may be developed." Perhaps recognizing the implication of his remarks, Stevenson quickly qualified them. "It must be kept in mind," he assured legislators, "that the Federal home loan bank system and Federal savings and loan associations must be made to function in the normal mortgage market or there will be more and more distress cases." [10]

It was this reticence to describe federal programs as transformative that set the tone of legislative debates over housing policy throughout the 1930s. Experts speaking in support of the FHLB, HOLC, FHA, and FNMA stressed, instead, that the programs would "function in the normal mortgage market." Typical were the remarks in 1932 of John Sprunt Hill, a banker from Durham, N.C., who testified before the Senate Subcommittee on Banking and Currency as it debated creation of the FHLB. He was especially interested in the bill's promise of "permanent relief," because it was urgent to create "a permanent method by which [S&Ls] can do business on business principles in a sound, plain, honest way." What made the proposed bill "sound," he explained, was its recognition of the "two essential things in this whole land mortgage business": "sound appraisal and ability to sell your bonds." Hill predicted that the new body would "help provide some place to which worthy home owners can go, through proper channels, to get accommodations which a sound banking system ought to give them." The bill would enable lenders to meet existing demand in towns like his own, where "we have few vacancies," a growing population, and "therefore [the] need for home construction." There was "nothing wild about the bill," Hill insisted. "It is on sound principles. It is very sound." No man involved in drafting it "wanted any charity, or wanted the Government to give him something." [11]

Calls for untapping the market's potential grew especially pronounced in congressional debates over the far more radical interventions proposed by the National Housing Act. Endorsing the FHA and related operations at the 1934 House Subcommittee hearings, Federal Emergency Relief Administration director Harry Hopkins predicted that selective credit operations would create jobs, refurbish aging housing stock, and spur demand for industrial products, all while respecting private markets. They would succeed by "unloos[ing] private credit rather than public funds." "If we are going to get home with the return of the unemployed to employment," Hopkins explained, "it can only be done, in our judgment, by the releasing of private credit through some appropriate channels and appropriate methods." He urged that "every possible effort be used to get the money out of the banks: because there are plenty of surpluses in the banks to be used for socially useful purposes."[12] The hearings showcased a stream of equally creative metaphors. Winfield W. Riefler, executive council and chairman of the Central Statistical Board and co-author of the NHA, described the new programs as "directed toward unlocking the [economic] keys which have stopped practically all new residential construction." He predicted that the FHA would "permit that residential construction to go forward which is economically needed and desirable," by "set[ting] in motion the forces" that "spread the demand for new construction." It would "open the mortgage market," while only requiring "a very small fund to operate from a mechanical point of view." The FHA would "not disturb the relations between borrower and lender that exist in the market today."[13]

Illustrating the urgency of getting wealth "out of the banks" were stories about the nation's desperate consumers. FHLBB chairman John H. Fahey explained that when a savings and loan association in one town (which he did not name) recently opened its doors, it received 200 mortgage applications in just three days. In another (also unnamed) community, an announcement by a group of cooperative banks of plans to issue $40 million in loans quickly generated 1,400 applications. To Fahey these episodes demonstrated that the economy did not lack resources but rather that consumers lacked access to them. "This matter of using money if you can get it, and spending if you have it," he concluded, "is the same in [the field of home repair] as it is in nearly every other." Thus Senate inaction on this bill, Fahey worried, threatened to plunge the nation deeper into crisis. "The funds at the disposal of the private lending institutions of this country," he told legislators, "must be brought into action."[14]

Few spokesmen expressed faith in the economy's latent powers more forcefully and creatively than Marriner Eccles, the influential Utah banker and assistant to the secretary of the treasury who co-authored both the National Housing Act and the Emergency Banking Act of 1933. There was not "any doubt in the minds of most informed people," Eccles explained at congressional hearings on the NHA, that "we have adequate facilities for producing in this country most everything that everybody wants." The challenge facing government was to mobilize these "facilities" properly by encouraging spending. "It has been a question of the means of payment, known as money, being sufficiently adequate to provide the exchange necessary." "There is in the banks of the country an excess of reserves over requirements of more than a billion and a half dollars," Eccles explained. "There is no lack of money. It seems to me, however, that it lacks velocity." What made the mortgage insurance program so valuable, in his mind, was that instead of selling government securities to increase the money flow, it recognized "the need of getting a private flow of . . . funds from where they are, by short-circuiting them, to where they are needed in the community." By "induc[ing] existing agencies . . . to extend credit," he argued, the NHA would help "unchannel . . . those funds directly into the field of employment where they are needed." Fahey conceded that the Title I program (for property improvement loans) was not without risk, since it required an initial federal investment of $200,000,000. But he reminded legislators that Title I would release $1 billion of credit into the economy, while stressing that Title II insurance involved no comparable risk and promised even greater returns.[15]

Praise for the economic and social benefits of homeownership and for the limited federal role outlined in the legislation framed testimony by banking officials, federal agents, realtors, business leaders, and average citizens. Henry Harriman, president of the U. S. Chamber of Commerce, acknowledged that "the first suggestion that was made on this homing [sic] question was for the Government to make large expenditures" and declared that he was "personally very strongly opposed to that." "The time has come," he explained, "when we have got to use private capital and put private capital to work." NAREB president Hugh Potter announced that his association would not support legislation currently under debate in a House-Senate conference authorizing the Federal Reserve or "any other institution [to make] direct loans from the Government," because he wanted "to see loans made through existing instrumentalities of a private nature." "I want to see mortgage companies, building and loan associations, savings banks, and insurance companies stimulated in the making of loans directly to individuals, and not the Government making loans." The FHA would "set up an instrumentality," he explained, "which will give to those private institutions a greater feeling of confidence, resulting, as I see it, in a loosening of the present semifrozen market." Fahey introduced several creative descriptions of the new federal role. State policy must focus upon "making money available . . . at lower costs." FHA operations were necessary if mortgage lenders "are to be brought fully into action to render the service of which they are capable." Asked to explain why insurance companies had been unable to meet the demand for housing credit, Fahey insisted that insurers had "an abundance of funds." "The great difficulty," he concluded, "is that these funds have not been widely stampeded into action."[16]

Massachusetts Republican Robert Luce was among the legislators unconvinced by selective credit policy. During the House debate over the NHA, he accused Secretary of Labor Frances Perkins, another co-author of the bill, of encouraging dangerous new levels of consumer debt spending. She countered that the expansion of debt would strengthen the free enterprise system, since it would only be accrued by "those who could afford to do so." "I am told," she continued, "that there is at present a great amount of money not finding a useful and profitable investment, which is in the possession of people who can well afford to make additions to the permanent improvement of their homes, and the permanent social improvement of their communities." Debt spending had become a perfectly justifiable, indeed a necessary, component of economic growth, she explained, because it was "to the social and economic advantage of the whole community that [certain consumers] should spend as much as they can afford to spend" to improve their homes and neighborhoods. Attuned to the concerns of her fiscally conservative critics, however, Perkins emphasized that selective credit programs posed a limited risk to the U.S. Treasury because they were designed to be self-supporting and that the private sector would ultimately revive and sustain the housing market. Asked by Massachusetts Democrat Thomas Jefferson Busby how lending for home improvement loans under Title I would continue once the initial $200,000,000 allocation was spent, Perkins predicted "that private capital, through the banks, will be made available for the extension of this same kind of work."[17]

What troubled Representative Luce so much about Title I was the fact that it did not require borrowers to put up security for their loans. In his mind, he explained in an exchange with Harry Hopkins, the program offered no protection for the "interests of the taxpayer." Hopkins was indignant at the charge. "It seems to me," he replied, that "the very best security there is in America is the integrity of the American home owner. I cannot think of any better security than that." Character was collateral, Hopkins argued, reaffirming the point moments later when asked again why a man should receive a loan to repair his garage without offering security against the debt. Hopkins did "not agree . . . that [the borrower] had not given some security. I think a man's name on his note is as fine a security as there is."[18]

This defense of the prospective homeowner reflected a conviction central to public policy debates over housing reform since the outset of the Depression: namely, that it was the government's responsibility to foster conditions that would enable certain male heads of household to operate freely in the market for homes. At the Senate hearing on the FHLB Act, for example, NAREB president H. S. Kissell explained why the S&L industry needed a federal reserve system. "There is no reason," he told Congress, "why a man who has saved for 5 to 10 years to buy a home and put every dime he and his wife could scrape together into the home, and then when we get into a period like this, when this man is out of employment, can not pay his interest or his mortgage falling due during this period of stress, and he can not refinance it, should not be given a certain amount of time to get together enough to save that home which he has been through this long period of time striving to buy." At those same hearings, John Sprunt Hill invoked the model male homeowner to demonstrate that FHLB operations would be even safer than those of the Federal Reserve Bank. In the mortgage market, Hill explained, "you know exactly what the condition is." "A man has his home. It is a small home, and the loan is on a 40 to 50 per cent basis . . . and the last thing he is going to give up is his home and roof over his wife and his children. It is a case of something that you see, as against something that you do not see." In the eyes of NAREB's Hugh Potter, home-owning men like these deserved the trust of investors and the government alike. During debates over the NHA, Potter conceded that the Title I insurance program entailed some risk, yet described it as "a temporary expedient aimed at the unemployment situation." It was an expedient, he explained, that was "a practical application of our theory of banking that has been used for generations, that we may at certain times and in certain instances, and to certain types of men, make loans without security, limited amounts, for a purpose that is socially good."[19]

The urban experts and businesspeople who fashioned modern housing policy argued that judicious state intervention could address the economic crisis by encouraging certain individuals to own homes. The state could revive markets, families, and even civic pride by simply unleashing the "pent-up" demand of the nation's most stable and productive citizens. It could achieve these ends without building houses itself or directly loaning funds or resorting to "charity." Harry Hopkins captured this message succinctly at the NHA hearings when he predicted that mortgage insurance would encourage a healthy type of consumer debt spending. "There is nothing I know of in the United States that is more socially desirable than a house to live in," he told legislators. Ownership "actually increases the wealth of the Nation at the very time the debt is incurred and, at the same time, puts people to work." "It is altogether a desirable thing to permit people to go into debt to buy a house."[20]

This claim was simultaneously social and economic and must be read in light of the widespread assumption made clear in testimony about men of "character" and in FHA appraisal guidelines that the people who should be "permitted" to go into debt were white. By identifying a "certain type" of male breadwinner as the driving force behind healthy free market activity and by endowing homeownership with the power to create better families and citizens, the leading voices in these discussions were advancing a race- and gender-specific theory of the market for residential property. In the eyes of Hopkins and other officials, allowing certain male consumers to become proprietor-debtors offered the best strategy for promoting long-term economic recovery. "Instead of having the Government continue to pour its money into [recovery] through the use of Government loans," he explained, this "bill permits the use of private credit through ordinary channels, obviates the need of an army of people all over the United States to police it and to make these loans, and gets private credit going—money that is now in the banks."[21]

———————

Whether or not the money was actually "in the banks" is a matter of some debate and depends on how one interprets the operation of credit markets. Likewise the call to promote private homeownership over other housing alternatives was challenged by numerous housing, welfare, civil rights, labor, and civic organizations during the Depression.[22] Nevertheless, it was the argument presented by Hopkins and his colleagues that dominated mainstream press coverage of New Deal legislative debates. Mainstream journalists agreed that selective credit programs were market-friendly, or at least reprinted this claim uncritically. Some contributed new metaphors to the public conversation; for example, a *Business Week* writer saw the NHA as proof that Roosevelt wanted to "pick out the key log in the credit jam, induce banks to make loans for renovation, and stimulate employment." The new programs, the article continued, are "described as the first designed by the Administration specifically to give John Citizen a chance to do his bit for recovery." Within a month of the bill's passage, the magazine reported that the FHA's first administrator, James A. Moffett, was working "to harness the energies of construction and building supply interests" and that he was confident Title I would benefit all industries "by churning up private funds."[23]

That summer a four-part *Literary Journal* series by Wayne Parrish introduced readers to the mechanics of the mortgage insurance system and reported on its reception by the nation's businesspeople and journalists. The NHA was one of the Roosevelt administration's "most important programs,"

Parrish explained, and had "clarified one bitterly contested housing issue" because it "does not in any direct way place the Government in the housing business." Instead "all initiative is placed in the hands of private enterprise and the individual home owner. Indirectly, the Government is participating by guaranteeing certain proportions of loans and easing the entire home-mortgage machine. It is the power-house generating the current, but the use of the current is in private hands." Parrish also reported on the warm response that the FHA was receiving from commentators and private industry. According to the Omaha *World-Herald,* passage of the NHA indicated that the key to "real recovery" is "up to business itself." Parrish elaborated, noting that while business interests were "pleased that the Government has kept its fingers out of the housing program," some commentators "have pointed out that if private business fails to make use of the Government's support" there would likely be "a further drift toward government regulation." Next he reported that the *Architectural Forum* considered the act less of a "recovery plan" than a "reform bill," one that "provides a permanent reorganization of the mortgage-market." Parrish explained that many commentators were praising the program for encouraging homeownership. NAREB announced at its recent convention, for example, that "wide-spread home-owning is the bulwark of democracy." The Association of Operative Plasterers and Cement Finishers used their trade organ, *The Plasterer,* to remind members that "the home is the back-bone of the nation," and that "the home owner is the highest type and the most valuable citizen. He is interested in his community and his nation." Parrish celebrated the American homeowner as well. To qualify for a Title I improvement loan, the author explained, a property owner need only "go direct to his local financial institution . . . and give his personal note on his own character to secure a loan."[24]

This vision of the homeowner and assumptions about his rightful place in the free market would long shape the debate over housing policy and other influential New Deal interventions.[25] Throughout the decade, as Congress broadened the FHLB's and FHA's authority, liberalized the terms of mortgage lending, and created the FNMA to directly purchase existing mortgages, advocates described government intervention as essentially noninterventionist. Selective credit programs were market-friendly, designed only to harness the demand and productive energies of the nation's homeowner-citizens. FHA administrator James Moffett repeated the story in a 1935 article in *Scientific American,* when he attributed Title I's success to the initiative of consumers and businessmen. "At the call of the builders," he explained, "sleeping capital is waking up and employing more workers and creating new wealth."[26]

Defining the Homeowner: The Private Market
for Housing and the Race of Economic Value

This national conversation about federal policy, free markets, and private property casts the FHA's demand for racial segregation in an important new light. For decades critics and scholars have criticized the agency's blatantly discriminatory appraisal guidelines, noting that the *Underwriting Manual*'s racial proscriptions, as Charles Abrams famously wrote in 1955, "could well have been culled from the Nuremberg laws."[27] Most critics describe federal mortgage insurance as a well-intended stimulus program sidetracked, in the final analysis, by the racial preferences of white homeowners, realtors, policymakers, and bureaucrats. Yet when viewed in the context of the era's housing politics, FHA appraisal guidelines emerge as more than a racist atavism that undermined an otherwise fair-minded economic intervention. FHA policy illustrates whites' investment in a vision of the market, and ultimately of the polity, that allowed, at best, a marginal role for racial minorities. It was this racialized vision of the market for homes, embraced by whites during and long after the Great Depression, that would help justify countless mobilizations to protect neighborhoods against "racial invasion."

Federal involvement in the mortgage industry racially structured the market for residential property. Beginning in the early 1930s, and for over three decades, the public-private alliance facilitated and justified the racial segregation of housing and housing wealth by insisting that exclusion was an inevitable by-product of impersonal economic forces. The HOLC and FHA outlined and enforced appraisal and lending guidelines that promised to protect investments secured by the federal government. Central to these agencies' understanding of real estate economics was the assumption that nonwhite occupancy destabilized property values. Granting a loan to a minority, according to this theory, was under most conditions a risky investment. And since federal programs were intended to revitalize free market activity, they had to respect the market's requirements. The result was a series of government-mandated rules for real estate appraisal that described racial exclusion not as a matter of choice, preference, or prejudice, but rather as an economic expedient, as a market necessity. At the same time, of course, federal intervention was creating and sustaining a new market for homes, the same market that policymakers declared their commitment to protect. The circularity was invisible in public debates over federal intervention, so the government's insistence on respecting free enterprise became the primary defense for denying mortgages to black people (see chap. 3).

It is important to look closely at the government's argument for racial exclusion, because this rationale would have lasting consequences for white housing politics in postwar America. Building on an intellectual framework developed in decades of public-private collaboration and advocacy, the FHA made no distinction between a "racial" and an "economic" justification for segregation. It subsumed the former in the latter. In public forums, officials made no attempt to address questions of racial difference per se. Instead they began with the assumption that different racial groups were socially incompatible—the reason for this, they insisted, was not their concern— and then designed a new market for mortgage finance grounded in this assumption. Put another way, the FHA did not first create an institutional framework that would mechanically and impartially create finance capital, and then, once that system was in place, distribute that capital in a discriminatory fashion. They did not create a race-neutral program and then use that program in a racially biased way. Federal policies created an institutional and fiscal architecture that defined racial minorities, from the outset, as incapable of maintaining private property and thus as ineligible to receive benefits. In what might be seen as the culmination of decades of work by economists, planners, municipal officials, and private businesspeople, the FHA defined housing economics in racial terms, and allocated economic resources accordingly. Taking this a step further, and following the internal logic of the new free market rationale for exclusion, federal housing policies defined most people of color as incapable of achieving full citizenship.

It is misleading to describe the FHA's discriminatory practices as an anomaly, as an unfortunate distortion of an otherwise ideologically neutral program of home finance. A careful reading of FHA guidelines and other real estate publications reveals that federal home finance policy assumed, and therefore was instrumental in structuring, an all-white market for homes.

———

The assumption that minority housing was a separate (and separable) issue was reflected in the organization of Hoover's 1931 Conference on Home Building and Homeownership. The reports on "Planning for Residential Districts," "Home Finance and Taxation," "Housing and the Community," and dozens of other topics addressed the needs of white people. Meanwhile the Committee on Negro Housing, under the direction of Charles Johnson, investigated topics assumed to be relevant to African Americans, and published its findings in a separate volume. Even the special report on rural housing issues treated the subjects of "housing special groups such as migratory labor, Indians, Mexicans, and other racial groups" as discrete topics. Robert Lamont revealed the conference's assumptions in his forward to the *Negro Housing* volume, a study that defied conventional wisdom by exploring the structural and ideological forces that had kept blacks both impoverished and ill-housed. Lamont, by contrast, describes "the Negro's housing problem" as "part of the general problem of providing enough housing of acceptable standards for the low-income groups in our society."[28]

Racial minorities were marginalized much more profoundly by FHA operations, a fact that makes the agency's treatment of racial issues particularly revealing. In contrast to the conference, the FHA rarely, and in its general publications never, spoke directly about the housing of special "racial groups." Instead it subsumed questions about race into purportedly normative, social scientific guidelines for protecting the free market for housing. It defined that market as only serving white families, thus systematically, if quietly, writing people of color out of the very logic of homeownership.[29]

This was achieved through the *Underwriting Manual*'s almost singular focus on the scientific principles of property evaluation and the mathematical, reproducible methods that would ensure accurate appraisal. The preface to the 1938 edition described the *Manual*'s purpose: "to prescribe uniform and sound underwriting techniques," so that "those who process and analyze mortgages . . . adhere to sound underwriting practices."[30] Critically, the manual treats the separation of populations by race as one of many, indistinguishable techniques and practices required to maintain neighborhood stability and protect property values. Racial proscriptions receive absolutely no special attention in the *Underwriting Manual*. There are no subsections devoted to "racial restriction" or "the housing of minority groups." Instead it discusses segregation in passing, treating it as one of many principles of sound land-use practice. Prohibitions against introducing "inharmonious racial groups" into stable neighborhoods alternate seamlessly with detailed discussions of "Structural Soundness," "Resistance to Elements," and "Mechanical and Convenience Equipment."

Appraisers are instructed in the chapter on "Rating Location," for example, to examine the age and design of dwelling units, the "stage of development of a neighborhood," and occupants' income level. They are told that neighborhood stability can be ensured by the adoption of well-designed zoning ordinances and deed restrictions; zoning, the *Manual* explains, "is becoming almost universal." The subsection on "Protection From Adverse Influences" notes a preference for deed restrictions: they are "apt to prove more effective than a zoning ordinance in providing protection," because they can specify "types of structures, use to which improvements may be put, and racial occupancy." Racial rules continue to appear, sporadically, in the course of detailed discussions about architecture, setback require- ments, facilities, neighborhood trends, and even topography. The "geo- graphical position" of a property may also "afford in certain instances reli- able protection against adverse influences," the manual explains, noting that "natural or artificially established barriers," such as public parks, hills, and ravines, "will prove effective in protecting a neighborhood and the locations within it from . . . the infiltration of business and industrial uses, lower-class occupancy, and inharmonious racial groups." Instructions for determining a property's market price tell appraisers to compare neighborhoods with similar characteristics, but warn against using minority neighborhoods, since the "racial aspects render the locations actually noncompetitive." Other possible "adverse influences" include "narrow streets," "inadequate light and air," the "intermixture of [building] types or price levels," "flimsy construction," and "locations whose properties present freakish architec- tural designs." A separate section adds "nuisances" to this list, which the text defines as "anything, whether temporary or permanent, which is considered objectionable to any or all of the occupants of residential structures in the neighborhood." [31]

At times the *Underwriting Manual* struggles to maintain the logical coher- ence of its racial calculus. Guidelines for "Rating of Location," for exam- ple, sometimes describe racial proscriptions as interchangeable with other "adverse influences" and at other times suggest a hierarchy of negative in- fluences. Section 233 explains that "the Valuator should investigate areas surrounding the location to determine whether or not incompatible racial and social groups are present, to the end that an intelligent prediction may be made regarding the possibility or probability of the location being in- vaded by such groups. If a neighborhood is to retain stability, it is necessary that properties shall continue to be occupied by the same social and racial classes." [32] Again the section on "Appeal" collapses black people into a list of otherwise material "nuisances." "The utilities and conveniences available to a location will have a pronounced effect on [neighborhood and property] appeal. A lack of desirable conveniences exerts a negative effect which must be reflected in the rating. Presence of noisy and high-speed traffic arteries, railroads, commercial or industrial properties, or the presence of incompat- ible racial elements results in a lowering of the rating, often to the point of rejection." But there are exceptions to this rule, with race and class variables sometimes trumping other considerations. Some neighborhoods, while they "may lack in accommodations or conveniences usually regarded as requisites for stability," will, nonetheless, "possess an appeal created by the social class of occupants, or prestige created by associations"; the residents' status "will make properties at [these] locations as marketable as any similar value range location within the city." Likewise the presence of a good public school is necessary, but not sufficient, to establish neighborhood appeal, for "if the children of people living in such an area are compelled to attend school where the majority or a goodly number of the pupils represent a far lower level of society or an incompatible racial element, the neighborhood under consideration will prove far less stable and desirable than if this condition did not exist."[33]

Standardized FHA forms and the reports filed by government appraisers during the 1930s document the agency's racial calculus in action, while suggesting how other sections of the *Manual* could reinforce explicit directions regarding racial proscription. To assess individuals, for example, "Social Characteristics of Neighborhood Occupants" instructs agents to measure the "abilities and the social, educational and cultural backgrounds of the people residing in the immediate neighborhood." Status and "culture" are revisited again in "Rating the Borrower" and "Methods of Dwelling Valuation," which call for analysis of a borrower's "character, family life and relationships, associates, [and] maturity." That a borrower associates with ethical people and that his family "pursues the accepted moral and economically sound courses in its everyday life" indicate its "general stability." FHA appraisers—white men drawn from the communities they served—followed these directions. In December 1934, for example, a mortgage risk examiner in Alexandria, Virginia reported that Amos E. Herbert, an applicant for an FHA insured loan, "appeared interested and ambitious and is reported to have a high regard for his obligations." (The appraiser apparently spoke with the banker and retailers listed on the application as "trade" and "bank references.") The region's chief valuator agreed, noting that Herbert appeared to be "a steady, industrious type," "a good type of citizen," who was "anxious to keep his home, and interested in his family's welfare." The valuator also filled in responses to the following question under the category "Neighborhood (d)": "Are inharmonious racial or social groups present in the neighborhood"? Answer: "No." Of this he was no doubt confident, since the applicant had indicated, on Exhibit C, the one type of deed restriction listed on the property's title: "Racial."[34]

A borrower's character was even factored into the *Manual*'s instructions for calculating "obsolescence." In contrast to "depreciation," a structural variable, caused by the "decay and disintegration which takes place . . . with the passage of time," obsolescence had multiple origins. These included "new inventions," "changes in the preferences and tastes of the public," the failure of owners to maintain their homes, and "the infiltration into residential districts of people whose living standards are lower than those of the people who already inhabit these districts." In Amos Herbert's application, the property in question received a rating of 20 (out of 25) on "Stability of the Neighborhood" and a 16 (out of 20) on "Protection from Adverse Influences." Other documents suggest how local appraisers might factor racial or ethnic background into calculations about a borrower's character. A "Standardized Factual Data Report" distributed to FHA agents in the 1930s included sections for indicating an applicant's "racial descent" (e.g., "Anglo-Saxon, Hebrew, Italian, Negro"), his "Reputation," and a general section for "Remarks," with instructions to "amplify his business history" and "amplify fully all unusual and unfavorable information."[35]

The FHA's assumptions about color and property receive a telling treatment in the *Manual*'s discussion of "Owner-Occupancy Appeal." In order to "ascertain the degree to which [a] property exerts owner-occupancy appeal," the text explains, the appraiser must "study the property and the environment" and determine if the "desire for ownership" would be "aroused on the part of a typical person or family which could afford to own the property and which is in the market to purchase and occupy a home." Next it details the conditions, "with reference to a property, neighborhood, and neighborhood inhabitants," that "such typical persons or families" would find acceptable. The manual privileges the owner over the renter, noting that the former "will be more exacting in his requirements, more discriminating, and more critical of the property and its surroundings." "Nearly all individuals at some time or other have a desire to own and occupy their own homes," it explains, so it was important for the appraiser to examine a property from an owner's perspective, "rather than from that of the relatively tolerant and superficial attitude of a typical tenant-occupant."[36]

The homeowner's potential satisfaction was calculable, through a careful assessment of the variables that shape "Owner-Occupancy Appeal." A property with strong appeal, the *Manual* explains, "will arouse an intense desire for both ownership and occupancy," a desire that "would be aroused as the person or family would approach the neighborhood. It would be stimulated upon approach to the property, and would attain great intensity upon inspection of the property and the gaining of knowledge that the neighborhood inhabitants were considered very desirable." The *Manual* lists "significant factors in estimating the degree of owner-occupancy appeal":

a. The appearance of the immediate neighborhood and of the approach to it . . .

b. The life-stage of the immediate neighborhood . . . The tendency is for owner-occupancy appeal to go up, level off, and then go down as the life-stage progresses.

c. The degree of prestige associated with the neighborhood as a place for owner-occupancy in contrast with tenant-occupancy.

d. The degree of social and racial compatibility of the inhabitants of the neighborhood. The pressure of socially or racially inharmonious groups in a neighborhood tends to lessen or destroy owner-occupancy appeal.

e. The extent to which the subject property in its external aspects and interior finish and appointments are especially attractive to the eye . . .

f. The extent to which the functional quality of the property, as evidenced by the ratings of the "Function" features in Rating of Property, would be satisfactory . . .

g. The relative newness of the building improvements . . .

h. The extent and effect of neighborhood detractions . . . A dilapidated or ugly or obsolete building would lessen the . . . appeal of adjoining and nearby properties . . .

i. Any inappropriateness of the subject property to its immediate neighborhood.

Equally measurable and of comparable significance, according to FHA calculations, are a neighborhood's appearance, the age and condition of structures, the "functional quality of the property," and the race and class of people who live in the vicinity. By carefully analyzing and weighing these variables, an appraiser could calculate "Owner-Occupancy Appeal": "The conclusion takes the form of a percentage expression which represents the degree of appeal for owner-occupancy."[37]

Few documents capture the new housing market's racial assumptions more dramatically. If a property is going to appeal to the "typical" owner-occupant, it must be well maintained, structurally sound, and free from the threat of the "pressure of socially or racially inharmonious groups." The FHA did not exclude racial minorities (or poor people) by imposing its race and class preferences upon a mechanical, ideologically neutral system of economic analysis. Rather, the system of economic analysis, in the course of assigning value, assumed racial and class differentials. The manual states that the current and future value of homes is shaped directly by the racial and socioeconomic characteristics of the neighborhood and of surrounding neighborhoods. It grounds this economic rule in the assumption that the "typical" owner-occupant, who is presumed to be white and comparatively affluent, has higher expectations and moral standards, especially when compared to low-income inhabitants and "socially or racially inharmonious groups," a category for which "typical tenant-occupant" occasionally serves as shorthand. An appraiser who turned to the *Underwriting Manual* to consider strategies for "Rating the Borrower," for "Methods of Dwelling Valuation," for gauging "Depreciation" and "Obsolescence," and for determining "Owner-Occupancy Appeal" would learn that certain social and racial groups lack the prerequisites, and perhaps the character, deemed necessary to own and properly maintain private property. So when an appraiser filled out FHA form no. 2082, "Completed Established Ratings of Locations," and checked off the choices for "Racial Occupancy Designation" ("W—White, M—Mixed, F—Foreign, N—Negro"), he was not merely describing or designating race. He was acting upon a new theory of housing economics, one informed by whites' preconceptions about the relationship between race and property, about the best means of determining a property's value, and ultimately by assumptions about the "character" of the "typical homeowner" and "typical renter."[38]

Marketing the Free Market

On April 18, 1941, nearly a decade after the government first intervened in the private market for home finance, FHA administrator Abner Ferguson spoke before a meeting of the Negro Business Conference, in Washington D.C. The topic was his agency's influential mortgage insurance programs. Ferguson apparently had little enthusiasm for this appearance, since the FHA did virtually no business with black lenders or consumers and, no doubt, because black leaders had protested against FHA racial policies since the program's inception. Ferguson was not receptive to their critique. As the date of his appearance approached, Ferguson suggested to his speechwriter that his talk focus on *residents'* responsibility for their poor living conditions. He even suggested sample text, borrowed from a newspaper article on urban ghettos: it was "occupants who make slums far more than the structures in which they live."[39]

While that language did not make it into Ferguson's prepared remarks, his speech no doubt left members of the Negro Business Conference unsatisfied. To an audience looking for evidence that the FHA would extend its benefits equitably to minority businesspeople and consumers, Ferguson instead offered a refrain familiar to black leaders. "In any consideration of how the FHA program can benefit Negroes," he began, "certain things must be kept in mind." "The law is one providing insurance of loans made by private capital to property owners for the repair . . . [or] purchase . . . of homes . . . Nowhere in the law is there any compulsion upon financial institutions to make these loans. And, of course, in our form of Government the Federal authorities cannot dictate to whom a private financial institution shall or shall not lend its depositor's [sic] funds." His agency was "enjoined by the law," Ferguson continued, "to insure only those mortgages which are economically sound," and this required, among other things, that eligible properties be located in neighborhoods that are "desirabl[e] as a place of residence over a long period of years." Black occupancy, Ferguson insisted, had been deemed undesirable by the market itself—not by the FHA.

Indeed, he repeatedly declared the agency's commitment to racial fairness, promising that it would give all qualified borrowers "the same consideration . . . regardless of race, color or creed." Then he coupled this promise with an important qualification, the logic of which is vital for understanding postwar racial politics. When the FHA applied its programs "to Negroes," Ferguson explained, it encountered "two specific problems," the first of which he named "marketability." "FHA operations, of course, do *not create* the market. The national income, general business and industrial activity, the shortage or supply of materials and labor, local customs and many other conditions of a given moment are the barometers of the real estate market." And because of this, "the FHA can only follow the trends in the existing market and accept it as we find it, giving reasonable consideration to what changes may be expected in the future." The second problem, he continued, was "income," explaining that since most blacks were poor, they could only "be provided adequate housing . . . through Government subsidy." Ferguson concluded by reiterating that "what we *can* do for [Negroes] is limited by the law, and in no sense are those limits to be construed as discrimination because of race."[40]

Ten days later, the Department of Commerce's adviser on Negro affairs, Emmer Martin Lancaster, wrote Ferguson to request a copy of the speech. Ferguson replied without apology that his remarks "were entirely extemporaneous and I have no manuscript whatever containing the substance of what I said."[41] The archival record shows that Ferguson was lying, no doubt to avoid further scrutiny from black leaders. Far more difficult to assess, however, are Ferguson's motivations for his seemingly calculated defense of FHA operations. Did he believe that the FHA did "not create the market" for mortgages or, at the very least, that it did not shape behavior within that market? And did his knowledge of eight years of federal mortgage insurance operations convince him that the agency's refusal to insure black borrowers was not a result of "discrimination because of race"?

A definitive answer is impossible. But the agency's early operations and its efforts to popularize the new market for suburban housing demonstrate that the FHA presented a fairly consistent story about the relationship between race, housing markets, and government policy. We have already seen that, throughout the 1930s, the free market rationale was regularly invoked to justify federal intervention, consumer debt spending, and urban experts' rules about race. This alone, however, does not fully explain why whites grew so deeply invested in the market imperative for racial exclusion. Of course, one of the ways in which federal interventions popularized a powerful new narrative about color and property was the mortgage revolution itself, which provided whites nationwide with what seemed to be incontrovertible physical evidence that the free enterprise system was determining residential patterns. Selective credit programs set in motion a massive new housing market, one that changed countless lives. Already by 1940, the government had drawn hundreds of institutional lenders into the mortgage market for the first time. The FHA alone had insured $1.25 billion worth of loans for the purchase of 600,000 private homes, in addition to millions of dollars of home improvement loans. Because the rules governing this market required racial restriction, virtually all of the new housing credit, both federally insured and conventional, had been issued to whites. As a result, white people were daily witnesses to a modest but discernible revival of the market for homes, particularly in outlying urban and suburban areas, and to the continued decay and impoverishment of minority, central city neighborhoods. If nothing else, it appeared that whites, alone, were the ones capable (or willing) to buy new homes and repair existing ones.

But at best this was an indirect, and perhaps unintended, lesson of federal intervention. Far more direct was a multifaceted promotional campaign, waged by the FHA and its allies, designed to draw producers and consumers into the market for housing credit. Beginning in 1934 and continuing into the 1950s, the agency sponsored speaking tours, produced radio and film advertisements, distributed promotional literature, hosted regional "home" fairs, and sent canvassers to millions of individual residences. The goal of these efforts was to increase lending, borrowing, and spending on home construction, purchase, and repairs, by convincing Americans that the new, government-insured market for credit was safe. The FHA aggressively encouraged borrowing and lending nationwide, literally promoting and marketing the new opportunities for home improvement and homeownership.

A massive public relations campaign instructed white Americans how to benefit from the state's new selective credit operations.

But the campaign's rhetorical refrain was a celebration of the free market for homes and its untapped curative powers. Uniting the speeches, pamphlets, and other appeals in this ambitious PR gambit was a consistent reminder that federal mortgage programs were wholly compatible with free enterprise, that they did not disrupt or alter existing market mechanisms, and that the American consumer and American businessman held the keys both to national recovery and sustained economic growth. The campaign insisted, as Ferguson would later insist to an audience of black business leaders, that federal programs did "not create the market" for housing.

The most visible promotional activities targeted consumers and businesspeople in local communities. They began on August 9, 1934, when the FHA kicked off its "Better Housing Campaign," a multi-million-dollar effort to stimulate borrowing and spending for home improvement (under Title I of the NHA) and new home construction (under Title II). FHA administrator James Moffett called the initiative a "massive education campaign," describing the "business of the Housing Administration" as "a vast, nation-wide selling job, an educational campaign to sell the public on Better Housing." Key to ensuring the new mortgage market's success, he believed, was spreading the word about FHA programs. Within a week, the agency supplied 28,000 financial institutions with copies of the rules and regulations for Title I insurance. Meanwhile its "public relations division" initiated Better Housing campaigns in thousands of communities, appointing regional, state, and district directors who in turn supplied educational materials to the businesspeople, chambers of commerce, and civic groups that eagerly solicited advice. By early December, the FHA had appointed 4,513 community chairmen, who had initiated 3,245 community campaigns. And by then house-to-house canvasses were underway in over 1,100 municipalities, where volunteers tried to "persuade property owners," Moffett explained, to get started on "the modernization and repair work they need." The campaign was enthusiastically embraced by municipal officials, local businesspeople, and average citizens, many of whom contributed novel promotional ideas of their own. In Fairfax, Oklahoma, for example, fifteen "church women" involved in the house-to-house canvass "decided to modernize their own homes as an example to the rest of the town."[42]

In the first three months, the agency spent $1.3 million on the "Better Housing Campaign" and mailed out more than 52 million pieces of

literature. By November, according to agency estimates, the campaign generated between $145 million and $210 million in business nationwide. This
rapid impact was attributable, in large part, to the unique institutional environment created by the federal government's new stake in credit markets.
Because FHA operations involved constant public-private collaboration, on
both the national and local levels, the agency had a ready-made platform for
its promotional efforts. The collaboration that made FHA operations possible (and cost-effective) facilitated its efforts to promote lending, borrowing,
and spending. By year's end, those efforts had organized 4,000 communities and initiated 3 million household visits. By March 1935, campaigns
were underway in 6,000 communities, which together contained about
65 percent of the country's population, and house-to-house canvasses in
over 2,000 locales had reached 5.6 million individuals. The canvassing,
alone, secured pledges for over 1 million home improvement jobs.[43]

The agency enlisted the nation's newspapers and magazines as well, supplying news and editorial writers with "education copy" and inviting dailies
and press associations to use the FHA's "spot news and feature service." By
December 1934, over a thousand newspapers, 55 percent of the nation's
dailies, were running "Better Housing" sections or supplements, some of
them reaching 33 pages in length. Meanwhile over half of the nation's
1,600 trade publications, according to Moffett, were "cooperating with [the
FHA] in a fine spirit." Half of the nation's 2,000 dailies had already requested additional promotional materials—exclusive articles, or features
tailored to their communities—while another 2,500 weeklies, mostly from
rural areas, had asked to be included in the campaign. Moffett called the
press "a godsend to the Housing Administration," claiming that news coverage and advertising was providing "invaluable help in telling American
industry and the public generally what we have to offer them." This cooperation was translating into sales and profits, especially for the advertising
industry. By March 1935, 41 of the 44 dailies in Oklahoma had run "Better
Housing" articles and more than half had carried entire sections or supplements. Newspapers in Oklahoma City and Tulsa had each devoted 40 pages
to related news and advertisements. Thanks to the FHA, 750 banks, over
200 manufacturers, and 100 large department stores were already "carrying
additional ads because of the Modernization Program."[44]

Other media and venues were equally influential. The agency prepared
films, radio promotions, flyers, and posters for national distribution and
broadcast. So popular was an FHA-produced weekly radio feature, "The
Master Builder," that the agency drafted a form letter to expedite responses
to fan mail. Institutional lenders "approved and eligible" for participation

received a free subscription to the FHA's *Insured Mortgage Portfolio*, which featured testimonials from lenders and articles stressing the safety and potential profitability of government-insured loans. In the December 1936 issue, institute economist and FHA chief underwriter Frederick Babcock contributed "Risk Rating from the Lender's View," in which he explained how "mortgage risk rating establishes the economic soundness" of government-insured debt and the "marketability" of these loans. "There is no attempt," he assured lenders, "to insure unsound mortgages or to create soundness in mortgages by insurance." In "Building a New Mortgage Portfolio," savings and loan president C. W. Grove of Cleveland, Ohio, explained that "the insured mortgage plan is well adapted to federal savings and loan operations." The *Portfolio* also featured sample promotional flyers available to institutional lenders, designed to "inform the public about the possibilities of homeownership under the National Housing Act." Proofs and mats of the artwork could "be obtained through local newspapers" (see fig. 4.1).[45]

The FHA's "Better Housing News Flashes" introduced Depression-era film audiences to the benefits of federal insurance and images of a promised good life attainable by renovating or buying property. Imitating the newsreel format, the shorts juxtapose film and animated images of home construction, repair, floor plans, new subdivisions, urban street scenes, and even historical reenactments (of premodern accommodations). A narrator, occasionally joined by an expert guest, discusses the advantages and the necessity of spending money on housing. In a promotion for Title I insurance, a professional decorator offers tips on remodeling ("every woman would love to modernize her living room"), and a fire chief demonstrates how homeowners can remove fire hazards by "taking advantage of [the] National Housing Act." Efficiently designed kitchens cut down on walking, viewers learn, "free[ing] the housewife of fatigue" and thus helping her "keep young and beautiful." Other segments update audiences on the increase in construction-related employment, show men hard at work in the building and material supply trades, and reenact the transformation of a "shabby" brownstone or an "ugly Victorian home" into a new "modern" residence. The engine of this new economic activity, the FHA explains, was the American consumer. The narrator asks audience members if they have an old attic: "Let's apply a little ingenuity, a few workmen, and a modernization loan and see what we can do." "Business is awakening," explained a segment featuring newly renovated homes in Key West, Florida. "Ask Yourself These Questions," notes another: do you need a new roof, gutters, insulation, more closet space, or new plumbing? "Take advantage of the National Housing Act to repair and modernize. Do it now."[46]

GOING UP!

New homes—*and home standards*—are going up!

The average family can now afford to build—and enjoy home comforts our grandfathers never dreamed of—on the FHA monthly payment plan which this institution offers.

We'll be glad to explain how you can build the home you want—and pay most of its cost by the month, conveniently, out of your income.

Even though you are not a client of this bank, don't hesitate to call on us for information.

FINANCIAL INSTITUTION
SIGNATURE

1323 MAIN STREET   **Phone North 2584**

4.1 Sample promotional flyer featured in *Insured Mortgage Portfolio,* December 1936. The FHA produced these flyers and provided lenders easy access to the proofs and mats. They were designed, the agency explained, to "inform the public about the possibilities of home ownership under the National Housing Act," and represented one part of a multifaceted promotional campaign to draw customers into the new market for Title I home improvement loans and Title II loans for home purchases. The FHA's *Insured Mortgage Portfolio* was sent to all institutional lenders deemed eligible to participate in the mortgage insurance programs. RG 31, National Archives, College Park, Maryland.

4.2 "Better Housing News Flash No. 7," motion picture, 1936. The FHA's Depression-era public relations campaign included exhibitions at home fairs, radio addresses, door-to-door canvassing, and a series of short films produced between 1935 and 1936. RG 31, National Archives, College Park, Maryland.

Later installments focus on the Title II program and the benefits of the single-family home. The narrator discusses the advantages of suburban living for family life as the film juxtaposes footage of children playing in a crowded city street and almost struck by oncoming traffic to a pastoral baseball game with a handful of kids playing in a boundless field. In one segment a subtitle announces that "Modern houses will replace traditional dwellings, according to predictions of architects and engineers." followed by animated floor plans that highlight the efficiency and improvements of the new designs. While viewing a montage of newly constructed homes, audiences were reminded that "it's easy to join this army of new homeowners." "Homeownership is the basis of the happy, contented, family life," the narrator explains, "and now through the use of a National Housing Act insured mortgage," this life "is brought within reach of all citizens on a monthly payment program no greater than rent." Viewers even get to experience one young couple's realization that they, too, can join this new "army." The segment depicts a white husband and wife, perhaps in their late twenties, touring a model home. They marvel at the modern kitchen, ample closet space, and other innovations. Then they leave, resigned to the fact that homes like this were beyond their means. But a well-placed sign tells them otherwise, listing the down payment and terms available with a "National Housing Act Insured Mortgage." The narrator adds that this is "less than they now spend for rent" (see fig. 4.2).[47]

The FHA also exhibited at conventions and fairs. Its installation for the "Palace of Better Housing" at the 1935 San Diego World's Fair, which opened on May 29, 1935, included architectural plans and models of homes and neighborhoods. The highlight was "Modeltown," a quarter-acre lot filled with fifty-six scale models of single-family homes, each about 3 feet high. A real-life version of such a home, the exhibit explained, could be built for only $30-60 per month, "inclusive of interest, taxes, fire insurance and amortization of principle." In the agency's "Modernization Magic" exhibit, a model of an older, blighted town was transformed (by means of individual mechanical turntables) into a modern, well-kept community. Moffett visited the San Diego exhibit that year, declaring that "California leads the nation in the campaign to 'bring back prosperity.'"[48]

Perhaps the most far-reaching effort to interest American consumers was initiated in August 1934, when FHA officials began speaking over NBC and CBS affiliate radio stations, introducing listeners to the mortgage insurance system and assuring them that it was now safe to borrow. These broadcasts served as primers in the new housing economics, instructing consumers how the new long-term mortgage worked and how to take advantage of it. They were always bracketed, however, by assurances that the market revival was driven solely by free market forces and the laws of supply and demand. In the first national broadcast, entitled "New U.S. Housing Plan," aired over NBC on August 15, Moffett introduced a rhetorical strategy that would barely change over the next two decades. The bulk of the talk was a fairly technical discussion, focused on the mechanics of the mutual mortgage insurance programs. Framing the discussion were reminders that Title I and Title II would not disrupt normal market activity, but rather "invite capital once more into the home-mortgage field, . . . restore normal real estate values, [and] . . . permit new construction to proceed again." FHA operations would achieve this not through government spending but rather by "loosen[ing] up frozen credits in the form of existing mortgages." "The programs assigned to us," Moffett assured his listeners, "is [sic] a straight business proposition, to be financed almost wholly out of savings deposits and other funds in the hands of private lending institutions." "This is a sound business plan," he concluded, even apologizing for repeating himself. The agency "intend[s] that it shall be carried out on sound business principles."[49]

Moffett and his successors spoke on the air regularly throughout the decade, sticking close to this format. It was altered only by increasingly aggressive appeals to spend ("every owner of home or business property [would] be wise to modernize and repair while present prices prevail," he explained to one audience) and increasingly detailed instructions for soliciting the agency's help. By 1938, Administrator Abner Ferguson was telling listeners over WCFL, Chicago, that the FHA was "prepared to see you all the way through your construction from the time that you first consider building a home until the last nail is driven and the final papers are signed." He encouraged listeners to visit local agency offices, where they could obtain "a list of those private institutions which are lending FHA insured mortgage funds in your locality." He instructed consumers to ask subdivision builders if their units qualified for FHA insurance. "If the answer is yes," Ferguson explained, "then you need have no further worries concerning the stability of that neighborhood." Finally he assured qualified borrowers that the agency would not only "insure your mortgage," but also "guide you until you own your home outright." These direct offers of agency stewardship did not stop officials from insisting upon the program's compatibility with the free market for property. "Remember," Ferguson concluded, "the Federal Housing Administration has no money to lend. It is not competing with private capital, rather it is bringing private capital back into the mortgage field."[50]

Parallel to this public campaign was a largely private one in which FHA administrators spoke before the meetings of trade and municipal associations around the country. By December 1934, Moffett had introduced the mortgage insurance system to gatherings of the Chicago Association of Commerce, Pittsburgh's Duquesne Club, the New York Chapter of the American Institute of Banking, and to a builders' convention in Knoxville, Tennessee. The following spring, he spoke before the Advertising Club of New York, the Oklahoma Chamber of Commerce, and a meeting of the National Retail Lumber Dealers' Association in Washington, D.C. His successors toured the country throughout the 1930s and beyond, addressing hundreds of audiences: real estate groups; chambers of commerce; local, state, and regional associations of bankers, mortgage bankers, and builders; and the national conferences of groups including the American Title Association, the National Association of Mutual Savings Banks, the Home Builders Institute, the American Bar Association, and the Institute of Cooking and Heating Appliance Manufacturers.[51]

The goal was to educate business people about the new mortgage market, update them on amendments to the National Housing Act, and encourage lending, advertising, building, and spending. Individual presentations were tailored to their audiences; lenders and real estate professionals, for example, were repeatedly assured of "the safety of their loans and . . . the potential liquidity of their mortgages." Otherwise the speeches followed a standard format. In often excruciating detail, speakers described current

FHA operations and pending or recent legislation. They reeled off statistics demonstrating the program's impact on borrowing, spending, and employment, often by providing local and regional figures. And speakers exhorted their audiences to encourage consumption, either by spreading the word about FHA programs informally, or through direct participation in the agency's promotional campaign. Moffett urged an audience of advertisers in New York City, for example, to "persuad[e] industry that it does a fine job for itself and for all business through liberal use of its advertising space to point out how and why its products can be used in modernizing and repairing buildings." Later he exhorted a national conference of lumber dealers to "advertise more . . . [and to] try new methods of promotion. Make every property owner in your community conscious of the program through which a responsible citizen can either improve an existing building or build a new home."[52]

These presentations constantly celebrated the FHA's compatibility with the free enterprise system. Federal mortgage insurance, Moffett told the Oklahoma Chamber of Commerce, was merely "an alarm clock for sleeping capital which should be up and about the business of employing workers and creating new wealth." "People are ready," he declared, "to put their sleeping capital to work." "Together we'll show the world that individual initiative and private enterprise are still capable of action which will result in decent housing for the American people and recovery from the depression." In a talk before the American Title Association in 1935, Ferguson outlined what he called the "fundamental premise" of the agency's insurance operations:

1. That private capital operations in the housing field are both necessary and desirable.
2. That private capital in that field can and must be made effective upon a far wider scale than has ever been possible heretofore.
3. That the collapse of our real estate and mortgage market under the impact of the depression was not caused by any defect in the theory of private capital operation, as such, but by the unsound, unrealistic and disastrously short-sighted system of appraisal and finance [under] which those operations were conducted.

Ferguson added that he was "somewhat puzzled by talk, emanating from certain quarters," that the FHA represented "an unwarranted and competitive intrusion by the Federal Government into [the] legitimate private business sphere." The program was in no way "an attempt by the government to infringe upon private businessmen," he insisted. "To private business it offers not a threat but an opportunity."[53]

―――――――

It was seven years into this promotional campaign, in the spring of 1941, that Ferguson defended the agency's racial protocols to an audience of black business leaders, explaining that the government's hands were tied because the FHA "did not create the market."[54] Ferguson's talk came after years of concerted effort by the NAACP and other civil rights activists to remove racial language from the *Underwriting Manual* and end the FHA's endorsement of race-restrictive covenants. Their protests had limited impact on the agency's lending practices but did force officials to defend their stance repeatedly and, in the process, refine their rationale for racial exclusion. And officials' responses suggest that many were wholly convinced of the logic of their position. When NAACP secretary Walter White called upon the FHA to remove references to "incompatible racial and social groups" from the *Underwriting Manual* (paragraph 233 of the 1936 edition and paragraphs 935 and 937 of the 1938 edition), chief appraiser and the *Manual*'s author, Frederick Babcock, insisted that White had misread the agency's intent. "No possible interpretation of these paragraphs," explained Babcock to FHA administrator Stewart McDonald in 1939, "could lead to the conclusion at which Mr. White arrives, namely that the FHA discriminates against negroes or fosters their segregation." "Our treatment of this problem," he concluded, "has been realistic and unbiased." Responding to a complaint from NAACP assistant secretary Roy Wilkins that New York banks were refusing loans to blacks, the FHA drafted the following response: "There is no power in the National Housing Act which permits us to determine the lending policy of those institutions." "If at any time you can [provide] details of any specific cases where it appears there has been any evidence of racial discrimination," the note concluded, the FHA would "see that an absolutely impartial investigation is made" to "straighten the matter out."[55]

In 1940, McDonald's office responded to a query from NAACP special counsel Thurgood Marshall about the FHA's endorsement of racial covenants, again deflecting culpability to the private sector and inexorable market forces. It was true that the agency advised developers to use covenants, in general, he noted, but "the use of the covenant referred to is purely optional with the subdivider, land-owner, or sponsor of the development." "In no instance does the Federal Housing Administration specify the manner in which the covenant shall be completed . . . Accordingly then, [its use is] the prerogative of persons other than persons administering the operations of the Federal Housing Administration." And "the purpose of the covenant, of course," the letter continued, "is to assure the continuing marketability of properties." The agency also took exception to Marshall's claim that the government provided financial support for restricted dwelling units; his letter apparently referred to "FHA grants" and "Federal funds." McDonald's office reminded Marshall that "the Federal Housing Administration lends no money . . . The nature of our business is similar to that of an insurance company."[56]

———————

The FHA's origins, and the popular interpretations of its operations, help explain why the program's racial policies had, and continue to have, many defenders. The mutual insurance system was designed not as a racially proscriptive instrument but rather as an economic stimulus program. Thus FHA operations have long been seen, first and foremost, as a tool of economic recovery and growth. And since racial exclusion was by no means the agency's primary purpose, many observers have argued that comparisons with traditional, more explicit discriminatory mechanisms are unwarranted. But the comparison is very revealing. For decades whites had been excluding minorities from their neighborhoods, employing strategies and rationales explicit in their racial intent. Racial covenants, racial steering, countless episodes of antiblack vigilantism: these acts were not only designed specifically to exclude—indeed, this was their *only* purpose—but were openly pursued and legitimated as racially motivated actions. By contrast, when federal agencies codified rules for housing segregation in the 1930s, they did so indirectly, practically as a policy afterthought. In that sense the FHA-insured mortgage *was* radically different from a restrictive covenant or a mob attack.

But the federal mandate of racial exclusion was not any less decisive. Indeed, the distinction between race-focused strategies and FHA appraisal policy grossly distorted whites' understanding of the government's role in creating a new *kind* of segregated housing market during and after the Depression. New Deal housing programs initiated the propagation of two powerful, closely related myths: first, that the state's mortgage insurance and reserve system did not create new supply, demand, or wealth; and second, because of this, that federal policy could not be responsible for encouraging racial discrimination in the market for homes. In the eyes of most housing officials, their private sector allies, and eventually countless benefactors of government largesse, it was not federal policy but the free market for housing that demanded segregation. Finally, officials distanced themselves even further from culpability, completing their circular claim by insisting that while the market demanded segregation, it was not because of *race*, per se. Rather it was just that the presence of inharmonious racial groups was one of the "adverse influences" that undermined property values.

When considering the impact of Depression-era policy and politics on suburban growth after 1940, it is critical to recognize that this conversation about race and housing markets was not window-dressing for legislative efforts or an effort to "disguise" motivations that we might view, with the luxury of hindsight, as "racist." This narrative figured prominently in policy debates and public conversations throughout the 1930s and well beyond. Far from an effort to mask the inequities of a new system for creating and distributing home finance capital, public and private leaders believed that racial exclusion was necessary to sustain the free market for property and ensure its growth. The architects of FHA policy believed that racial minorities were excluded from the new mortgage market not necessarily because they were unable to afford it, and certainly not because the government condoned inequality or advocated segregation, but because minorities were incapable of engaging the market on its own terms. This vision of the metropolitan economy was constitutive of a multifaceted legislative, administrative, and promotional effort, which after 1940 created a very powerful new market for housing and convinced white people of their rightful place within it.

CHAPTER FIVE

A Free Market for Housing: Policy, Growth, and Exclusion in Suburbia, 1940–1970

The modern American metropolis, and the suburb that is omnipresent in the iconography of postwar America, began to take shape in the 1940s. They did so as the federal programs created in the 1930s were updated—their loan programs liberalized, their regulatory power extended, their appropriations increased—and supplemented by powerful new initiatives. And they took shape as local communities actively sought out the statutory authority to zone, aggressively deployed this new power, and carefully monitored regional land-use patterns. The postwar metropolis was built with the institutional support, appraisal standards, and legislative tools established by over two decades of public-private collaboration and federal action. The unprecedented growth and wealth accumulation that followed were uniquely post-1940 developments. But the economic, legal, and administrative architecture that facilitated and sustained this growth was inherited from the interwar period.

U.S. involvement in the war altered the machinery of federal housing policy in important respects but did not change its emphasis or assumptions. To help accommodate the influx of "war workers" to major industrial centers, Congress liberalized existing FHA programs to promote construction of moderately priced housing. The Title II program, meanwhile, insured new suburban home purchases until restrictions on building materials virtually halted new construction between 1943 and 1945. By then Congress had created an important new housing program in the Veterans Administration (1944), the centerpiece of the GI Bill of Rights. Anticipating a postwar surge in housing demand and hoping to accelerate the mortgage revolution initiated by earlier federal efforts, Congress created the VA's mortgage guarantee program, which extended the benefits of FHA insurance on even more generous terms to returning servicemen. Meanwhile the government's already limited efforts to promote housing development for low-income residents were scaled back further, as the politics and economics of war, prosperity and, soon, the Cold War shifted government priorities decisively. The postwar focus on promoting ownership was not new. The Roosevelt administration had always devoted more attention and political capital to reviving the market for private homes than to providing housing for low-income populations. Still the Depression-era housing debate acknowledged, however tentatively, the government's responsibility to help all citizens find adequate shelter. By war's end, Congress had tabled proposals to create an extensive system of federal public housing, denouncing the concept as "socialistic," while redoubling efforts to expand the market for housing debt. By 1949, when President Truman declared the government's commitment to providing "a decent home and a suitable living environment for every American family," the state's most influential housing programs focused on subsidizing the construction and sale of single-family homes, in the suburbs, for white people.

The legislative and administrative machinery supporting these subsidies would be only slightly modified over the next two decades. The basic architecture and procedures of federal mortgage insurance programs remained intact, the lending terms grew increasingly generous, thus inviting a larger pool of prospective borrowers into the market for homeownership, and Congress constantly increased the FHA's and VA's spending power and authority. Of equal importance the government extended its influence over conventional mortgage market operations, in part by accentuating its secondary market activities. The result was a dramatic increase in the amount of available housing credit and further consolidation of the public-private alliance's authority to dictate its distribution. Following that alliance's preferences, the vast majority of this credit was issued to white people for the purchase of suburban homes. The federal government did not totally dismiss the concerted protest against its racial policies. Beginning in 1950, two years *after* the Supreme Court ruled the use of race-restrictive covenants unenforceable, the agency stopped endorsing them, and by then it had removed explicit references to race from its *Underwriting Manual*. But these were largely cosmetic changes that had a very limited impact on lending patterns. The state's focus on financing ownership of single-family residences in suburban locales, its continued support for the de facto racial segregation of residence, and its ideological preoccupation with the prerogatives of property owners only grew more pronounced. It was in the two and a half decades following World War II that the government's Depression-era policies and the rationales that had shaped them exerted their most visible and lasting impact.

This chapter examines the expansion of the federal role in the private housing market, exploring the policies and political contexts that set the stage for restrictionist politics in white suburbs nationwide between 1940 and 1970. The federal government continued to underwrite the market for privately owned homes and encouraged the fantastic spread of zoning activity in thousands of local jurisdictions. Federal intervention also led to important changes in both the mortgage market and zoning practice, changes that further benefited the affluent and white, usually at the expense of the poor and nonwhite. Postwar mortgage and zoning politics also continued to obscure the state's role in fueling metropolitan growth and segregation. Housing officials insisted that federal intervention neither created new market conditions nor discriminated, for "racial" reasons, at least, against minorities. The FHA's promotional efforts, resumed after the end of hostilities, continued to encourage white people to lend, borrow, and spend. And they assured whites that market forces, not federal intervention, promoted growth and required exclusion. Dissenting voices were occasionally acknowledged, and sustained protest eventually forced the president and Congress to assert a rhetorical commitment to fair housing, beginning in 1962 with Kennedy's issuance of Executive Order 11063. But the federal response was halfhearted, and its strongest measures were not enforced.[1] Throughout the 1940s, 1950s, and 1960s, neither the concerted efforts of civil rights activists, nor the Supreme Court's ruling on restrictive covenants, nor federal fair housing legislation significantly altered governmental practices. By the mid-1960s, three decades of federal involvement had sustained a racially exclusive market for housing credit, while strenuously denying that government involvement decisively shaped suburban development or that discrimination against nonwhites within that market was motivated by race.

Throughout the postwar decades, housing officials and their private sector allies remained deeply invested in a series of powerful fictions about metropolitan growth and change. They believed that the state had done nothing to alter the natural market for property—that it did not subsidize homeownership and suburban growth. Following logically from this, they believed that the state had done nothing to actively promote racial segregation in the fast-growing market for residence. And when pressed on the issue of racial restriction, they brought the argument full circle, insisting that the state's endorsement of exclusionary practices had nothing to do with race per se but rather that public policy simply had to respect the laws of the free market. It turns out that many average white Americans were equally invested in these fictions. If nothing else, their daily lives told them it was true. By the 1960s, federal programs had helped create cities and suburbs sharply segregated by wealth and by color. A host of experts and officials had insisted that public policies were merely unleashing natural forces of supply and demand, rather than creating new opportunities for production and consumption. Selective credit operations and the spread of municipal zoning helped create the metropolitan geographies, the built environments, and an ideological environment that together helped convince whites that it was the market alone determining the winners and losers in postwar America. For this reason, it is not accurate to describe the politics of race and housing in the fast-growing suburbs as a case of white people *hiding* their racism. Rather white suburbanites failed to recognize that their good fortune was sustained by racist institutions and that they lived in a racist culture.

Building the Segregated Metropolis

An economic emergency had drawn the federal government into the housing market early in the 1930s. The war in Europe encouraged it to extend and refine its Depression-era interventions. Adolph Hitler's invasion of Austria in 1938 accelerated the United States' conversion of industry for war production and helped erode the nation's isolationist consensus. Meanwhile an economic downturn in the United States, the "Roosevelt Recession" of 1937–38, made lawmakers and business leaders particularly receptive to policies that might spur industrial production and consumer spending. By the time the Nazi army overran Paris in June 1940, the United States had significantly reorganized domestic production to supply the Allies. And the men and women migrating to American cities to fill new production jobs needed places to live. Congress responded on June 28, just six days after Germany's occupation of France, with the first in a series of wartime measures designed to promote housing construction for defense workers (and eventually veterans). An amendment to the United States Housing Act of 1937 authorized the U.S. Housing Authority to either subsidize housing construction for defense workers or provide loans for that purpose. With the Lanham Act, passed in October 1940, the Department of War, the Department of Navy, and the Housing Authority began coordinating public housing provision for enlisted men and defense workers. Three days later, the Soldiers and Sailors Civil Relief Act authorized the first direct federal aid to enlisted men for mortgages and other debts. On NAREB's recommendation, Congress also extended the FHA's reach with the Defense Housing Amendment to the National Housing Act (Title VI), passed in the spring of

1941, which provided incentives to private builders by liberalizing the terms of mortgage insurance on homes built for defense workers. The Section 603 program was designed to finance construction of one-to-four family homes. In May 1942, Congress authorized FHA insurance for rental housing under Title VI.[2]

By war's end, federal programs had housed hundreds of thousands of Americans. Section 603 facilitated construction of 373,124 units, in most years between 83 percent and 93 percent of them single-family homes. Meanwhile the existing, prewar programs insured over 410,000 mortgages nationwide, until material restrictions brought new construction to a virtual standstill in 1943. Altogether, FHA-insured purchases represented the majority of wartime construction: 55 percent of all housing starts in 1942, 79.6 percent in 1943, and 67.2 percent in 1944; 95 percent of the units financed with government insured loans were intended for private ownership. By contrast the government insured loans for the construction of 36,006 rental units, while pressure from local authorities and real estate lobbies undermined legislative efforts to increase federal spending on public housing, widely viewed as a "subsidy" program that would slow the market's recovery. The mandate for construction of 114,000 public, low-rent housing units stipulated by the Housing Act of 1937 was abandoned during the war. The FHA's Title II program, by contrast, was immune to criticism, and there was no hand-wringing about the additional subsidy provided by the Defense Housing Amendment, by which the agency insured residential mortgages deemed to be risky investments. According to NHA co-author Miles Colean, the Title VI program "created a nonmutual insurance system (from which the concept of 'economic soundness' was omitted)" and "provided a special fund for the purpose of insuring 90 percent mortgage loans on housing for war workers." "Most of the privately built wartime housing," Colean concluded, "was financed this way."[3]

The designation of a federal housing program as "subsidy" was very selective, a point cast in sharp relief by passage of the Servicemen's Readjustment Act on June 22, 1944. Popularly known as the GI Bill, the act's housing provisions authorized the administrator of Veterans Affairs to help veterans secure financing for home purchases by guaranteeing their loans with U.S. Treasury funds. The VA program was modeled on the FHA insurance program, but its terms were even more generous. The agency guaranteed up to 50 percent of a home loan (with a maximum of $2,000) made to a returning veteran. When combined with a conventional mortgage, veterans now had access to 100 percent loans on dwellings valued up to $6,000. The act also authorized the VA to guarantee up to 20 percent of the value of a second mortgage (again with a $2,000 maximum) on houses that carried FHA-insured first mortgages. On nonfarm properties, VA-guaranteed loans had terms of 20 years and carried interest rates of 4 percent. The agency initially offered to pay the interest on the guaranteed portion of the loan for one year. If a borrower defaulted, the VA could delay foreclosure proceedings for a month while it placed a bid on the property or arranged refinancing "with any other agency or by any other means available."[4]

Several program features expanded the reach of federal subsidy to the private housing market. First, the VA waived down payment requirements. It essentially gave eligible veterans housing equity, an opportunity to become a homeowner, and access to the generous terms of the new long-term mortgages. Next, the agency's losses were covered by direct federal appropriations through fiscal year 1961, and the VA did not charge fees to borrowers or lenders for its services until 1966, and those were nominal. By June 30, 1959, the government had paid $448 million to private lenders for losses on defaulted VA loans and for acquiring properties, of which $315 million represented net expenditures. Administrative expenses were paid by the U.S. Treasury. (The FHA's defenders, when accused of interfering with private markets, could at least argue that the agency generated sufficient income to cover operating costs.) Finally, the VA offered institutional lenders generous incentives to participate. When a borrower defaulted on an FHA-insured loan, the lender was compensated with long-term debentures. By contrast the VA paid lenders with cash up to the amount of the original guarantee. As Miles Colean observed, the VA provided "full debt financing for the acquisition or refinancing of real property with what was in effect a guarantee by government of the lender's risk. It resulted in a financial procedure in which the function of the lender was reduced almost to that of a disbursing and collecting agency of the government." In the final analysis, the GI Bill created another layer of government subsidy, even more direct than that provided by Depression-era selective credit programs. Working in concert with those programs, the VA rapidly expanded the government's role in creating finance capital for the purchase of privately owned homes.[5]

It did so by adopting FHA appraisal standards, including its rules about color and property. Following the guidelines outlined in the FHA *Underwriting Manual*, the VA guaranteed very few mortgages to racial minorities and refused to back loans for blacks buying homes in white neighborhoods. The Servicemen's Readjustment Act did not include appraisal and lending procedures, but rather instructed lenders to determine the "reasonable normal value" of applicant properties according to "proper appraisal." And it stipulated that first mortgages obtained with FHA insurance would not be invalidated by the VA act nor by securing a second mortgage through the VA, a clear indication that the same appraisal and lending procedures would be followed for both.[6]

———

Beginning in 1945, VA operations dovetailed with existing federal credit programs to help spur a stunning transformation of the nation's market for private housing and, with it, the racial and class geography of metropolitan areas. By 1970, more Americans lived in suburbs than in cities, most white Americans were now homeowners, and most homeowners lived in detached, one-family, suburban homes. Selective credit programs did not single-handedly reinvent the housing market. These were years of unprecedented prosperity, generated in large part by increased consumer and government spending. They were years of spectacular demographic growth, coupled with significant regional migrations of populations. And during these years technological and managerial innovations facilitated construction of housing quickly, inexpensively, and on a mass scale.[7] But the government's well-entrenched statutory power and administrative capacity to subsidize, stimulate, and regulate mortgage lending provided the credit that paid for growth and established the guidelines for what got built and who was permitted to buy it. Linking these together and ensuring both legislative support for selective credit programs and opposition to public housing was the Cold War era's passionate rhetorical commitment to free enterprise. Against the backdrop of unprecedented and conspicuous affluence, policies claiming to respect free markets for housing held enormous, virtually ineluctable appeal. The wartime experiments with rental and low-income housing that suggested alternative, or at least complementary, approaches to addressing the postwar housing crisis were quickly abandoned in favor of the politically more attractive mortgage initiatives. Meanwhile World War II had created an additional rationale for federal intervention: the urgency of aiding veterans and their families.

In light of the state's growing involvement in housing markets and its pump-priming expenditures in so many sectors of the postwar economy, from defense spending to the construction of the Interstate Highway System, it is misleading to describe reconversion and postwar expansion as a return to normalcy. Rather than returning to prewar or pre-Depression market conditions, the nation consolidated and built upon a private-public nexus that had fueled and often dictated production and consumption patterns throughout the Depression and war years. Postwar economic growth depended upon a market for consumer debt that had been socialized by early Depression-era banking, monetary, and credit programs. The dramatic expansion of consumer spending for housing and other goods was made possible by a federal state that now underwrote and regulated the creation of wealth in the form of consumer debt.[8] In the case of housing, by 1945 public-private collaboration was firmly ensconced in the federal bureaucracy and in the nation's home finance market. Tested and refined in the emergency conditions of Depression and war and backed by a willing Congress in the postwar years, public programs and private business leaders were positioned to accommodate millions of Americans seeking a new home and the industries that would profit by meeting this need.

Leaders of that alliance applied themselves to the task. In August 1945, FHA administrator Raymond Foley appointed a committee to examine how the agency could "be of help to private enterprise in all broad phases of the postwar housing market" and specifically to determine "what further authorities may be necessary and desirable to put us fully in [that] market." He began to solicit advice from industry leaders. By October, Foley was discussing proposals for liberalizing existing FHA insurance programs with the leadership of the Mortgage Bankers Association, the American Bankers Association (ABA), the National Association of Home Builders, NAREB, and several life insurance companies. Building upon these consultations, the FHA's Planning Committee filed detailed recommendations for pending legislative bills throughout the winter. Representing the ABA at the fall meetings was Ernest Fisher, former institute economist and FHA consultant, who in private correspondence with Foley spoke candidly about the government's influence on the market for residential property. Emphasizing that "this letter is in [no] way an official communication," Fisher warned that inflation might distort housing prices and costs in the immediate postwar period. Since the state's interventions "do have an influence on the market, both direct and indirect," he continued, it was necessary to explore "ways in which this influence can be made effective in restraining the market in the immediate future."[9]

The Congress and the president were also focused on what most feared would be a dire postwar housing shortage. According to a 1945 estimate by the Senate Banking and Currency Housing and Urban Redevelopment Subcommittee, the United States would have to produce about 1.25 million new housing units each year, for ten years, to satisfy anticipated demand. Meeting this demand, Truman reminded Congress that September, was essential for ensuring postwar prosperity. "The largest single opportunity for the rapid postwar expansion of private investment and employment lies in the field of housing," the president explained. For this reason housing was "high on the list of matters calling for decisive Congressional action."[10]

Congress responded quickly, although partisanship and red-baiting forestalled "decisive" action on some programs. In November, Senator Robert A. Taft introduced the Wagner-Taft-Ellender bill, which would liberalize the terms on FHA-insured loans, initiate federal sponsorship of urban redevelopment programs, and provide federal support for the construction of rental housing and 500,000 units of public housing. The provisions for redevelopment and affordable housing troubled leaders of the real estate, finance, and construction industries, who helped defeat the bill in 1946. Two years later the House and Senate reached a compromise with the McCarthy-Wolcott bill, by abandoning funding for public and rental housing. Support for the compromise owed a debt to years of coordinated opposition to public housing by conservative legislators and business organizations that peaked during five months of Senate hearings on the national housing shortage led by Joseph McCarthy between 1947 and 1948. In thirty-three cities nationwide, a professional PR firm (also employed by NAREB) helped spread the message that the expansion of public housing programs threatened the nation's democratic institutions, effectively drowning out appeals by veterans, labor, and community groups that promoted affordable housing alternatives. "The modern private mass builders emerged from the hearings," write Rosalyn Baxandall and Elizabeth Ewen, "as heroes who promised to lead the country out of crisis and build dream houses for all." The campaign also helped secure passage of the Housing Act of 1948, signed by Truman on August 10. The legislation lowered the required down payment on FHA-insured home purchases from 10 percent to 5 percent and extended the maximum repayment period on some loans from 25 to 30 years. It provided no additional money for public housing or revitalization of homes in the nation's central cities.[11]

Like most postwar housing policy, the legislation was a product of well-coordinated public-private effort. Collaboration had become so integral to FHA operations by the late 1940s that staff members repeatedly turned down offers of honorary membership in private building and financial institutions; acceptance would not be "illegal," noted one official, but would be "embarrassing" and seen as a conflict of interest. The FHA continued to work closely with business leaders to assess market conditions, measure activity generated by federal programs, and discuss pending legislation.[12] And it cosponsored forums and regional meetings that updated the business community about changes to the NHA and agency operations. On the day before Truman signed the 1948 housing act, for example, the FHA and the

National Association of Home Builders (NAHB)—a lobbying group formed in 1942 by NAREB's largest subdividers—agreed to cosponsor nationwide educational sessions designed to inform builders and lenders about the liberalization of government-insured mortgages and reauthorization of the FNMA's secondary market operations. On August 19, FHA assistant commissioner Warren J. Lockwood instructed regional directors to recruit local home builders associations for early planning sessions. Together they would plan meetings to "afford you the opportunity of making the benefits of the National Housing Act, as amended, as widespread as possible." The NAHB told its local and regional directors that "we have assured FHA of our enthusiastic cooperation" and instructed them to recruit local institutional lenders to participate.[13]

Collaboration produced impressive results. On the weekend of September 14–16, more than 13,500 people attended at least 110 one- or two-day meetings, held in 60 cities nationwide, that were paid for by industry but that followed an agenda distributed by the FHA's regional commissioners. Each meeting began with a summary of the new Housing Act and a statement from a local NAHB representative; then local FHA officials explained the amendments' impact on the mortgage insurance application process. After lunch, local mortgage bankers, builders, FHA officials, and NAHB representatives participated in panel discussions, which were regularly punctuated by calls for greater cooperation between government and private business. In 1949, another set of meetings held in "all principal cities" promoted the FHA's new "economy housing" campaign, launched that January to encourage lending in both the government-insured and conventional markets for "middle-income" families.[14] Throughout the 1940s and 1950s, business groups communicated with FHA officials about pending legislation. Builders, lenders, and materials suppliers were now *urging* extension and liberalization of existing programs and offering to secure legislative support. An association of building suppliers, for example, promised in 1954 to "vigorously support" proposed amendments to Title I "before the Banking and Currency Committees and Congress" and to "influence Congress to enact in 1955 legislation which will give permanency to FHA."[15]

Meanwhile congressional action made the FHA's promotional efforts considerably easier. First, in December 1945, a series of amendments to the GI Bill made homeownership or refinancing even more attractive by raising the maximum limit for VA mortgage guarantees from $2,000 to $4,000. Now eligible veterans had access to 100 percent financing on dwellings valued up to $12,000 or on a second mortgage for dwellings valued up to $20,000. The amendments also extended the repayment period to 25 years, matching the FHA amortization period on certain properties. Meanwhile, Congress repeatedly liberalized the terms on FHA-insured loans and increased the maximum capitalization of its insurance fund, helping make homeownership feasible for most eligible middle-income applicants. The already generous terms of FHA-insured financing grew even more so. To purchase a $7,500 home in 1934, an FHA-approved borrower needed to pay $1,500 down and commit to a 20-year repayment schedule; four years later, the down payment was $900 and the loan spread out over 25 years. By 1950, the down payment had been reduced by almost half, to $500, and by 1957 it was cut in half again, to $225, with repayment extended to 30 years. By 1964, FHA loans had 35-year amortization periods. White workers with stable monthly incomes were prime candidates for government-insured debt.[16]

Neither rental properties nor public housing were completely forgotten. Some legislators, together with welfare, civil rights, and labor organizations, continued to call for a federal commitment to providing for low-income and minority households. Changing party fortunes in 1949 saw a brief revival of congressional support, as well, with a bill that would reintroduce the public housing and urban renewal components of the Wagner-Taft-Ellender bill. Most controversial was the new Title I, authorizing federal grants to localities to pay for slum clearance and redevelopment, and Title II, authorizing construction of 810,000 low-rent public housing units over a period of six years. Scores of labor, veterans, housing, municipal, consumer, and welfare groups lined up in support of the measure, while most construction, real estate, and financial lobbies marshaled their forces against it. The bill passed, but a sustained lobbying campaign undermined its most progressive provisions. Industry groups sabotaged the Title I and Title II programs for decades. The White House never authorized enough construction nor did Congress appropriate sufficient funds to meet the bill's public housing targets. In 1954, the Omnibus Housing Act formally signaled a shift in federal urban policy away from funding public housing to funding slum clearance and urban renewal. By the late 1950s, the public housing role in renewal projects had been virtually eliminated. In 1964, only about 370,000 of the projected 810,000 public housing units had been completed.[17]

Meanwhile the FHA, in response to sustained pressure from civil rights activists, focused some time and resources on what it called "minority housing," "the non-White market," or what an internal report in 1954 referred to as a "problem area" for the housing industry. The FHA treated housing for blacks as constituting a separate market. It promoted a limited number of subdivisions for black homeownership, mostly in the South and always in sharply segregated residential areas. In northern states, government-insured projects intended for minority occupancy were most often apartments.[18] The NAACP and other organizations challenged FHA policy and practice relentlessly, eventually forcing the agency to disavow support of race-restrictive covenants and remove racial references in the *Underwriting Manual*. Further encouraging reform was the HHFA's Race Relations Service (RRS), the postwar descendant of an advisory group created in 1938 to ensure that blacks benefited from New Deal programs. Under the leadership of Frank Horne, the postwar RRS worked to expand federal insurance activity in the "minority" housing market while challenging the presumption that the white and black sectors should remain distinct. But the RRS was never given more than an advisory role and its agents were received with indifference or hostility by most white officials. Its campaign to encourage open occupancy was either ignored or, more often, dismissed as untenable because of existing market conditions. Finally the RRS was effectively silenced by HHFA administrator Albert Cole when he demoted Horne in 1953. Horne was fired in 1955.[19]

Throughout the postwar period, both during and after Horne's tenure, the FHA declared its commitment to nondiscrimination while claiming that its ability to address patterns of racial settlement was constrained by forces beyond the government's control. On the rare occasion that it considered promoting a housing development open to minorities, it assumed the necessity of segregation. In 1951, for example, an FHA official requested a study of a 129-acre redevelopment area in downtown Detroit, bounded by Gratiot, Lafayette, and Hastings avenues and the Grand Trunk Railway, which had recently been cleared with federal urban renewal funds. An internal agency update on the site's prospects was entitled "Preliminary Report on Non-White Housing Market, Detroit Area, 1952–1953." The report itself—circulated within the agency in 1955 and often dubbed the "Negro housing market analysis"—focused on collecting "material on the potential rental market." But even insuring apartments, the FHA's market analyst insisted, had its risks because the "problem of integration" was the "most critical marketability question posed by the redevelopment project. In an area which is about to be rebuilt from the ground, with the constant glare of community-wide publicity attending every step of the process, an analyst cannot avoid attempting to assess effects upon marketability of deliberate efforts to attain integrated occupancy." If the redevelopment area "were uncomplicated" by this issue, the report continued, the agency could insure construction of at least 500 residential units. "However, the facts of the situation must be recognized and accorded realistic consideration," leading the analyst to conclude that "these problems introduce risk factors which in the aggregate constitute a high degree of risk."[20]

These assumptions structured FHA operations and its self-presentation at every level. A 1954 draft of the agency's Racial Relations Handbook stated programmatically that applications for FHA insurance make "no distinction . . . as to race, color, or creed" and that "underwriting considerations and conclusions are never based on discriminatory attitudes or prejudice." At the same time, FHA officials described the handbook as a tool for instructing appraisers how to examine files "maintained in the Insuring Office which pertain specifically to housing available to minority groups." Moreover the handbook qualifies its nondiscrimination stance with a lengthy citation from the new, revised Underwriting Manual to emphasize that market forces, in the final analysis, are the final arbiter of compatibility. When FHA agents considered granting insurance for properties open to black occupancy, they invariably returned to what Franklin Richards described in 1949 as the agency's "major problem"—"locating and laying out acceptable sites."[21]

During the decades of the nation's spectacular postwar growth, the housing needs of underrepresented groups remained marginal issues to most federal officials and business leaders. Instead they focused on, and constantly sang the praises of, the selective credit programs that were reviving the "free market" for homes. These initiatives, supporters argued, helped deserving citizens get back on their feet. They rewarded veterans for their service and assisted their reintegration into civilian life. They enabled all hard-working, eligible heads-of-household to develop a stake in their communities. And they addressed the desperate postwar housing shortage while stimulating consumer markets that would sustain housing-related industries. Legislators and business leaders saw the practical need of housing American families as inextricably linked to a far-reaching plan to transform postwar credit markets and spending patterns and couched both as an effort to help eligible citizens readjust to and fully participate in postwar society. The rhetorical defense of state economic intervention continued to collapse visions of deserved entitlement into a larger discussion about the nation's productive capacity and the best means of promoting prosperity. Ensuring the well-being of certain sectors of the consuming public, according to this calculus, in no way constituted subsidy or welfare.

Further coloring support for selective credit policy was the Cold War itself. Against the backdrop of communist and totalitarian threats to democracy and the free enterprise system, spirited appeals for market-friendly interventions were as easily defended as condemnations of public housing proposals were politically expedient. There was little risk in decrying public housing as "socialistic" (as Representative Jesse P. Wolcott of Michigan did in the debates over the Housing Act of 1949) or to liken it to "creeping socialism" (in the words of the U.S. Chamber of Commerce). "No home in America," predicted Representative Eugene E. Cox of Georgia, would be "free from its invasion or sacred from its trespass." So seductive was the rhetorical appeal of the homeowner ideal, and so powerful were the real estate and building lobbies, that the market for privately owned suburban housing emerged from early postwar debates as the primary beneficiary of federal largesse. In the decade after World War II, even FHA Section 608 financing for apartment construction was gradually phased out. Section 608 operations had insured mortgages for 280,000 rental units by 1950, before losing congressional support. The program helped build fewer than 6,000 units in 1953 and then just 287 over the following two years, before spending ended altogether in 1955.[22]

That year the FHA and VA, by comparison, combined to insure or guarantee 968,000 mortgages on new and existing privately owned homes, the largest total since implementation of the GI Bill. This accounted for 51 percent of the nation's private nonfarm housing starts that year. In each year between 1947 and 1956, the two programs combined to back loans on no less than 38 percent of all housing starts and as much as 52 percent. Meanwhile the FHA recommended the construction of bigger and bigger homes—with more square feet and more rooms. Throughout the postwar decades, the terms of FHA and VA-backed loans were adjusted in response to recessions, inflationary pressures, or evidence of a drop-off in housing starts. For example, when mortgage originations tapered off in the late 1950s, the FHA stopped requiring borrowers to pay closing costs in cash and the VA removed its already minimal down payment requirements. The Emergency Housing Legislation of 1958 removed the discount controls from both programs while also reducing the required down payment on mid-range FHA-insured homes. A year earlier, Congress raised the FHA's maximum interest rate to 5.25 percent and the VA's maximum rate to 4.75 percent, hoping to draw more lenders into both markets.[23]

By 1960, the FHA had insured over $57 billion worth of home loans ($45 billion of this through Title I and Title II) and the VA had guaranteed loans worth over $45 billion. By 1964 these two programs, alone, supported loans for almost twelve and a half million privately owned homes, both existing and new, providing a stimulus that helped turn real estate, mortgage lending, and house building into major growth industries. Between 1945 and 1958, the nation's total debt in residential mortgages grew by $110 billion, with 90 percent of that amount committed to one-to-four-family homes, and 90 percent of *that* total for single-family homes. Almost 50 percent of this increase was FHA-insured or VA-guaranteed.[24]

Most of the remaining increase was also facilitated by federal intervention. Government involvement in the conventional mortgage market—the market for mortgages not supported by the FHA or VA programs—continued to be equally decisive after World War II, if far more difficult to measure. Housing economists agree that federal programs spurred the fantastic growth of conventional residential mortgage debt after World War II and ensured that institutional lenders would dominate this market. Two interventions proved essential: federal insurance and oversight operations for conventional lenders, and the federal purchasing operations that created a secondary market for mortgage debt. Both were well underway by 1940 but really began to bear fruit after 1945, when the standardization of the mortgage instrument, coupled with FSLIC and FNMA operations, dramatically increased the flow of capital in the market for home finance, enabling lenders to grant more conventional loans on far better terms. And following the precedent set in the FHA-insured market, conventional lenders privileged certain kinds of development and certain populations. While these lenders were not required to follow the FHA's appraisal and lending guidelines, prevailing market conditions strongly encouraged them to do so. By the 1940s, FHA guidelines had effectively structured appraisal, lending, and even construction standards throughout the private housing market. Most white realtors, builders, and appraisers continued to focus on suburban sales and on single-family home construction. They continued to discriminate against nonwhite applicants, but now with an indirect federal sanction and in a federally structured market that allowed little room for racial experimentation. The racial proscriptions written into federal underwriting policy, in short, exerted an influence on national mortgage lending that extended far beyond the loans that carried a federal guarantee.

FHA activity continued to make it easier for private institutions to trade home finance debt—to exchange this debt, for profit, in a national market for loans. Because government-backed mortgages were standardized and insured, private lenders felt confident transferring them, without careful scrutiny, between institutions and even between geographic regions. By standardizing mortgage lending in virtually half of the market, FHA and VA activity helped transform the entire market from a local or regional one, with relatively high risks for investors, into a national one, grounded in shared rules, much of it protected by U.S. Treasury funds. As Leo Grebler writes, by the early 1950s the markets for both insured and conventional mortgages had taken on "some of the characteristics of national capital markets," so that it had "become quite customary to quote premiums and discounts for FHA and VA loans offered and sought in this market." "Deviations from par," he explained, were "largely determined by general mortgage market conditions rather than by the quality of the underlying security of specific loans." Federal intervention allowed investors to speculate in home mortgages without ever visiting actual properties.[25]

One result was that insurance companies, mutual savings banks, and commercial banks bought and traded government-insured mortgages as never before, dramatically increasing their residential holdings as well as their share of the nation's total mortgage debt. Between 1930 and 1950, the amount of commercial banks' mortgage debt held in residential loans increased from 10 percent to 18 percent, while their share of the nation's total mortgage debt on one-to-four-family nonfarm homes increased from 10.1 percent to 16.4 percent. Only half of these holdings were in FHA- and VA-insured loans. Insurance companies' share of the debt on private homes increased from 7.7 percent in 1938 to 14.8 percent in 1948. Institutional lenders, taken together, had held only 50 percent of the nation's nonfarm residential mortgage debt in 1920; by 1954, they held almost 90 percent. Between 1939 and 1954, they were responsible for 86 percent of the net increase in the market for home loans. Key to this growth was the fact that selective credit operations liberalized the terms of conventional home mortgages. Never quite as affordable as FHA or VA approved loans, conventional mortgage financing still came within reach of millions of American families. The long-term, self-amortizing mortgage became the industry standard, while FHA and VA interest rates forced conventional rates down markedly. Before creation of the HOLC and FHA, first mortgages generally carried interest rates of 6–8 percent, short repayment periods, and limited (if any) amortization. Following the war, the terms of conventional loans edged closer to those of federally insured loans. When Carl Behrens studied interest rates on home mortgages held by 170 commercial banks in 1947, he reported an average of 4.0 percent on VA guaranteed loans, 4.5 percent on FHA insured loans, and a range of 4.7 percent to 4.9 percent for conventional, noninsured loans.[26]

Another important stimulus for conventional lending was provided by the FNMA (commonly known as Fannie Mae), established in 1938 to create a secondary market for government insured loans. The new body was unable to foster the hoped-for (and necessary) private-sector activity, and instead provided a cushion for the selective credit experiment by purchasing existing FHA-approved (and eventually VA-approved) mortgages. It was especially active buying loans deemed "risky" by these agencies, offering firm, advance commitments to repurchase such mortgages once they were originated by private institutional lenders. By 1947, Fannie Mae had purchased FHA loans worth $272 million. That year Congress began increasing the FNMA budget and authorizing its purchase of more *types* of mortgages, including, in 1948, loans for defense and veterans' housing. From this point the FNMA basically became a source of government financing for institutional lenders. VA purchases quickly became the centerpiece of the FNMA portfolio, especially after Congress authorized it to issue advance commitments on VA mortgages.[27]

By late 1954, FNMA had purchased $4.6 billion in FHA and VA loans—$4.2 billion of these purchased after 1948. And that year the Housing Act rechartered FNMA, separating its secondary market operations and assigning it the functions "usually assigned to a central mortgage bank," that is, buying, selling, and holding federally underwritten home loans, in addition to raising additional funds to supplement its purchasing activity. FNMA also made advance commitments, at below-market prices, to encourage their sale. This increased activity required a new funding stream, so Congress repeatedly authorized the U.S. Treasury to increase its investment in FNMA preferred stock, and, after 1955, the agency drew more money from the private market to finance its purchases. By 1960, its insured mortgage portfolio accounted for 4 percent of the nation's total nonfarm residential mortgage debt, including 10 percent of outstanding FHA debt and 9 percent of outstanding VA debt. During the 1950s, FNMA purchases accounted for up to 26 percent of the nation's housing starts and 68 percent of all FHA and VA starts in any single month. In 1969, FNMA was involved in 24 percent of all home mortgage sales. Since the vast majority of its purchases (as much as 80 percent in most years) were made from mortgage companies, the FNMA had essentially become a primary lender and was widely seen as a "source of funds to be tapped by mortgage companies when regular clients are out of the market."[28]

FNMA activity made both the government-insured and conventional mortgage markets far more flexible and thus more attractive to lenders in the postwar decades. Charles Haar put it simply: Fannie Mae's "willingness to buy FHA mortgages encouraged lenders to make them." It also enabled lenders to "offer commitments to builders even when they were hard to obtain in the private market." "The mortgage companies," writes Sherman Maisel, effectively used the FNMA's secondary mortgage operations "as an emergency backstop." An agency originally designed to draw private lenders into a secondary market for home finance had instead taken on the task of ensuring that loans unsalable on the private market would be purchased. FNMA advance commitments on VA mortgages, according to Henry Aaron, "assured windfall gains to private borrowers or lenders." By some calculations, FNMA activity both encouraged lenders to accept lower interest rates *and* increased housing costs nationwide. Fannie Mae had become another instrument with which the federal government could promote and subsidize the growth of specific housing sectors. Its interventions were carefully calibrated, with purchasing activity tied to current conditions in the credit market. In 1958, for example, Congress responded to a sudden drop in housing starts by giving FNMA a new revolving fund of $1 billion for the purchase of FHA and VA mortgages on small single-family homes. Agency purchases then provided liberal refinancing for private builders and real estate owners, directly subsidizing their participation in the market.[29]

Finally, the conventional mortgage market received considerable support from the Federal Home Loan Bank system, which helped S&Ls compete with lenders participating in FHA and VA programs. Chartered in 1932 to provide credit reserves for thrift and home-financing institutions, the FHLB quickly initiated the HOLC, which by rescuing hundreds of thousands of private lenders (by refinancing delinquent mortgages) also directed $224 million to savings and loan associations. Meanwhile the FHLB's normal operations, including its insurance program, the FSLIC, continued to subsidize the S&L industry. The 1932 act and subsequent amendments established a regulatory structure for thousands of private home-financing institutions, a structure that remained largely unchanged until 1966 and employed tens of thousands of people in hundreds of national offices. In 1950, Congress authorized the Treasury to make $1 billion in credit available to the regional Federal Home Loan Banks, as well as $750 million to the FSLIC. By 1954, 4,234 private institutions claimed FHLB membership (all but twenty-five of them were savings and loan associations). By the mid-sixties, the FHLB had almost 4,800 member institutions, half of which borrowed funds from regional Federal Home Loan Banks in any given year. The system's regional branches also issued bonds, notes, and certificates in the general money market, attracting additional capital into the FHLB and helping to distribute home finance credit from capital-rich to capital-poor regions. As Jones and Grebler write, the FHLB acted "as a substitute for a private secondary market."[30]

These reserve, insurance, and oversight functions helped foster an exponential increase in S&L lending and the astronomical growth of the industry's assets. Federal support for S&Ls had already been significant during the Depression and World War II, with the twelve regional FHLB banks advancing between $38 million and $158 million to members in any single year. Then in 1944 alone they advanced over $239 million and in 1948 that total rose to over $359 million. In 1954, the system contributed over $734 million to its member institutions. The S&L industry's assets nearly doubled every five years after World War II, and increased more than seventeen times by 1968. (During this time the total number of associations actually decreased.) More assets translated into more mortgage lending. Beginning in 1945, the value of S&L mortgage recordings for one-to-four-family nonfarm residential properties skyrocketed, far exceeding even the impressive increases recorded by life insurance companies, mutual savings banks, and other private lenders. By 1952, the nation's S&Ls overtook life insurance companies (the leader in FHA-insured loans during the forties) as the largest single source of residential mortgage funds.[31]

Other lenders benefited as well, both in the conventional and insured markets. For the new stability and security provided by FSLIC insurance, working in concert with other selective credit programs, continued to draw more investors and more money into the national market for mortgages. Sometimes the agencies' efforts were complementary. In the 1960s, for example, simultaneous increases in both FNMA and FHLB purchasing activity helped to counteract a tight money supply, preventing a sudden drop in residential investment. Meanwhile FHA, VA, FSLIC, and other programs made both the insured and conventional markets remarkably safe and lucrative. Together, writes J. Paul Mitchell, they "attracted deposits to mortgage lending institutions, diminished the reluctance of thrift institutions to make mortgages, stimulated the participation of commercial banks in mortgage financing, facilitated more liberal mortgage terms (lower down payments, lower interest rates, longer contract terms, and hence lower periodic payments), and enabled higher risk households to contract for mortgages." Looking back from 1970, Aaron concluded that the government's system of "loss protection may have perfected the market for home mortgages." "The benefits of the liberalized mortgage market"—which he describes as "widely diffused, impossible to measure accurately, and probably very important"—"accrued to all homebuyers and lenders, not just those who used mortgage insurance or loan guarantees." On top of this, changes to the Internal Revenue Code allowed homeowners to deduct mortgage interest from their personal income tax bill, "subsidiz[ing] nearly every homeowner in the United States." By one estimate, tax deductions subsidized homeownership by $2.9 billion in 1962 alone—that year the federal government spent $820 million on public housing, by comparison—and by another $7 billion in 1966. Postwar federal policy made it much easier, indeed possible, for some Americans to own homes and gain wealth.[32]

Excluded from this market—as they had been before 1940—were the vast majority of racial minorities. There were small black suburban enclaves in the United States before 1940, and these continued to grow, especially in the South. Meanwhile black homeownership rates continued to increase (again with much higher rates in suburban communities). But neither trend benefited significantly from the new federally subsidized mortgage market. Federal policy forced most blacks to turn to smaller institutional lenders, to pay more for their loans, and often to simply build homes themselves.[33] After 1940, the FHA's racial proscriptions continued to structure conventional lending as well because most lenders, brokers, and builders carefully followed FHA appraisal guidelines on design, construction standards, and occupancy. They had considerable incentive to do so, since a subdivision that met government requirements was more likely to qualify for FHA- or VA-backed loans or, alternatively, for an advance repurchase commitment from the FNMA. Federal appraisal standards fast became national standards for the most powerful actors in the home construction and real estate industries. The degree to which builders and realtors adjusted their operations to meet FHA requirements is difficult to calculate, but it is clear that they paid close attention to government guidelines and that real estate associations instructed members to follow federal appraisal procedures, generally making no distinction between properties that carried federally insured mortgages and those financed conventionally.[34]

The government's influence on construction and appraisal is visible in both the federally sponsored and private publications that guided the nation's builders, lenders, and realtors. Among the FHA's offerings were its Land Planning Bulletins, guidebooks for platting and architectural design intended to "acquaint developers with the benefits of neighborhood planning." These brochures encouraged developers to meet with local FHA land planning consultants who would "aid developers in the economical solution of their land planning problems" and to turn in "all pertinent information" about their proposal to the local insuring office, including a zoning map, a certified copy of current or proposed restrictive covenants, a preliminary subdivision plan, a topographic survey, and photographs of "existing structures, streets, and open lands in and surrounding the tract." "Zoning and protective covenants," explained Successful Subdivisions (Land Planning Bulletin no. 1), "safeguard future character of the neighborhood." "Zoning is a protective measure to assure the planned use of land over large

areas just as protective covenants safeguard developments in smaller areas."
Meanwhile private-sector manuals defer to federal guidelines and recommend federal services. The *Community Builders' Handbook,* published in
1947 by the Urban Land Institute, advised developers to prepare "market
analyses" for proposed subdivisions by consulting with local planning
commissions, zoning boards, county officials, and "the local FHA office,"
an especially good source for "maps, charts and future plans." The volume
features an annotated sample of a model residential plat, "prepared by the
FHA," which "illustrates many of the [planning] standards advocated by
the [ULI's] Community Builder's Council." Included in the appendix were
sample restrictive covenants, "Recommended by the Federal Housing Administration for Developments of Single-Family Detached Dwellings."[35]

Similar advice came from a host of professional organizations. In 1953,
an edited volume on *Mortgage Banking,* sponsored by the Mortgage Bankers
Association of America, credited the FHA and VA programs with forging "a
whole new set of public expectations" about minimum property standards,
as well as popularizing valuable subdivision requirements, including the
use of "appropriate deed restrictions." Federal guidelines, wrote contribu-
tor William B. Thompson, a Kansas City banker, "constitute an authorita-
tive guide to nearly all phases of residential planning and construction."
Throughout the postwar years, the American Institute of Real Estate Appraisers (AIREA) directed its members to the FHA *Underwriting Manual* and
to the guidelines followed by the VA and "other government agencies." In
1960, in the third edition of *The Appraisal of Real Estate,* the AIREA continued to recommend the FHA's *Underwriting Manual* in its list of "suggested
readings."[36]

It would have been difficult to ignore the mortgage revolution's impact on
the nation's postwar cities, suburbs, and neighborhoods. The growth of
Detroit's suburbs illustrates some of the tangible results of state intervention.
By 1958, the FHA alone had insured 318,209 home mortgages in Michigan,
worth $2,400,320,000, and it had issued 1,853,234 property improvement
loans valued at $908,888,060. The VA secured even more home mortgages,
while FNMA purchases further supplemented both FHA and VA activity. Between November 1954 and December 1958, for example, the FNMA bought
19,326 mortgages in the state, worth over $239 million. By the latter year it
held $187,884,000 in mortgage loans, 80 percent of which were VA commit-
ments. By contrast the state's renters received few benefits: the FHA insured

construction of only 16,744 rental units statewide by the late 1950s. Meanwhile the government's reserve and insurance policies, coordinated through the FHLB's District 6 bank in Indianapolis, provided an enormous boost to Michigan's conventional mortgage market. Between 1948 and 1958, the total assets recorded in Michigan savings and loans and cooperative banks, both state and federal, increased by 387 percent, from $301,199,000 to $1,467,182,000. The stunning growth of local institutions then translated national policy into finance capital for individual families. Between 1944 and 1951, the assets of the First Federal Savings and Loan Association of Dearborn (est. 1935) increased by 170 percent (from $1,602,873 to $4,331,387). Assets at the People's Federal Savings and Loan Association of Royal Oak (est. 1934) increased by 278 percent (from $1,034,332 to $3,908,102). The Dearborn Federal Savings and Loan Association (est. 1941) saw an incredible gain of 600 percent (from $386,900 to $2,700,239).[37]

Government programs did more than simply create wealth and promote construction. Federal insurance required localities to heed federal planning and appraisal guidelines. Standardized appraisal procedures clearly identified federal preferences, and housing officials actively reinforced them. In 1942, for example, Hazel Park officials were instructed by the FHA to follow its "Minimum Building Requirements for New Dwellings and Property Standards (for Defense Housing)," outlined in direct correspondence with municipal officials. Those guidelines, in turn, dictated the city commission's recommendations to increase the square footage minimum in the suburb's residence A districts, first in 1942 and again in 1948. Meanwhile the FHA's chief underwriter for the district promised to give advance approval for residence subdivision construction in Hazel Park, again specifying the types of development that would qualify for federal support.[38]

Public policies generated comparable market activity, development patterns, and wealth creation in metropolitan regions nationwide. Meanwhile advocates for and defenders of the new federal role continued to describe government programs as wholly compatible with free enterprise. It was this combination of the state's growing influence on metropolitan development, on the one hand, and its insistence that federal programs were *not* distorting free markets for property, on the other, that would have a profound impact on the nation's racial politics. While more and more whites were becoming financially stable, suburban homeowners, so too were they growing invested in a public narrative about the origins of suburban prosperity and metropolitan inequality that masked the complicated origins of both.

The Myth of the Free Market for Residence

On one level, whites' investment in neighborhood segregation should come as no surprise. The steady transformation of suburbs and cities—the growth, affluence, and racial homogeneity of the former, coupled with the apparent stagnation, visible deterioration, and concentration of minorities associated with the latter—confirmed whites' longstanding suspicions that black people posed a threat to their communities. The built environment of the postwar metropolis, alone, told whites a story about housing, neighborhoods, and populations that they had long believed to be true.[39] But this story was also undergoing a subtle transformation in the postwar years, as whites increasingly portrayed exclusion solely as an economic or market imperative rather than a means of satisfying whites' racial preferences. The federal government continued to help popularize this new narrative about race and property, in two ways. It did so directly, by reviving the Depression-era campaign to promote mortgage lending and borrowing, and with it the message that federal involvement did not alter normal market operations. Meanwhile it continued to provide the standards for subdivision design, appraisal, and mortgage lending that mandated racial discrimination throughout the industry and justified it by invoking land-use science. The FHA stopped officially endorsing racial exclusion after 1950, but lenders and builders continued to employ the racial calculus built into its housing and mortgage operations, while FHA agents continued to accept and openly defend systematic discrimination by institutional lenders.

In 1944 and 1945, the FHA was already using its regular zone meetings, which brought together regional directors, chief underwriters, and participating lenders, to revive interest in the mortgage insurance programs, while organizing smaller conferences with lenders "in cities and towns not on [the] Washington staff schedule." The "objective" of the "Mortgagee Conference," according to a handbook distributed to regional and local directors, was to introduce "approved lending institutions and those eligible for approval how they may increase their present business" by familiarizing themselves with FHA programs and "keeping in close contact with the local office." The FHA instructed its representatives to prepare for the local conferences by studying local conditions. Who are the institutional lenders in the area? What is the potential market for mortgages? What "type [of] resistances [have been] shown to Federal Housing insurance"? "Each mortgagee within the area designated for the conference should be called upon," the handbook explains, noting that personal contact was preferred and should be followed up with a phone call—it "may be necessary to sell the idea of the conference to each representative." It was also recommended that the conferences be sponsored and publicized not by the FHA, but by local bankers or mortgage associations. Agency participation was still crucial, however. A state or district director was instructed to speak at each session about the FHA's success in increasing the volume of mortgage lending, both locally and nationally. About twenty minutes into the program, an agency underwriter should "discuss underwriting procedure and explain in detail the use of the various forms, samples of which have been distributed throughout the audience."[40]

Conference participants were also introduced to new promotional materials. The FHA distributed scripts for radio talks, "to be delivered by Realtor" or "by Mortgagee," with blanks where the speaker should insert the name of their city. One segment asked how realtors could join forces with consumers to "buy wisely" and thus prevent rampant inflation in the housing market. "The best way we can work together is through the FHA. That you know is an agency of the Federal Government set up ten years ago to help restore confidence in home ownership after the utter chaos produced by the Depression . . . It does not lend money. It does not build houses. It simply insures mortgage loans made by local approved financial institutions to responsible potential home owners." The radio spots informed consumers that the FHA "makes an impartial appraisal of the property" and thus can determine whether a neighborhood "is stable or beginning to go down hill." If the FHA approves, "then you know that it is a good neighborhood for you to buy in and that the value of your property is protected against destruction through deteriorating neighborhood influences." New promotional brochures were distributed to lenders as well, with instructions for reproducing them (fig. 5.1). A series issued in the mid-1940s featured FHA logos and illustrations, usually depicting some combination of home-buyer, family, and property, with room to insert text and the lender's "signature" below. Sample language was distributed separately, presumably so that institutions could tailor materials to their preferences. The text made homeownership sound hassle-free: "When you finance on the FHA Plan you are on the straight road to debt-free homeownership." "Ask us about the FHA Insured Mortgage Plan. FHA appraisals are expert, unbiased . . . It's the sensible way to buy a house today. Come in for full details."[41]

By the summer of 1945, the NAHB and other industry groups were pressuring the FHA to accelerate its PR efforts, calling for a campaign "wholly devoted," insisted one lobbyist, "to the benefits of mortgage insurance and modernization loans to the individual." Acknowledging that "the FHA-insured Mortgage Plan has been unpublicized and unadvertised . . . for

LAYOUT FHA 471-6

5.1 FHA brochures, 1944–45. When the FHA revived its promotional activities at the end of World War II, it produced and distributed a new series of brochures for participating institutional lenders. The text sections were blank; the agency distributed sample scripts for each layout and invited lenders to adapt them to their preferences. The sample texts usually mentioned the pressures created by the national housing shortage: "an FHA analysis will give you the greatest measure of protection against possible inflated values in real estate." Most scripts detailed the terms of FHA mortgages and concluded by inviting consumers to "let us explain this plan more fully to you—without obligation, of course, on your part. Come in anytime." RG 31, National Archives, College Park, Maryland.

5.1 (Continued)

nearly four years," the agency assigned its Subcommittee on Promotion the task of developing plans to revitalize its prewar promotional campaign. That fall it recommended "an aggressive, nation-wide publicity and advertising program to reestablish FHA-Insured Mortgages to their prewar position as a dominating factor in the mortgage market." "Not only the public, including returning veterans, needs re-education in its advantages," the committee explained, "but also, mortgagees, builders, dealers in building materials and

Doubtful about
buying a home in
today's market ?

5.1 (Continued)

realtors, most of whom must train new personnel, and will require assistance from FHA in this training." It called for reestablishment of the Public Relations Activities office, publication of the *Insured Mortgage Portfolio,* revival of the FHA's "Clip Sheet," Press Digest, Advertising Digest and other related services, and for reassembling a shop to build exhibits featured at home shows and other public fairs. It projected a two-year budget of $755,000 for new staff and $300,000 for production costs, since the "supplies of printed materials are near exhaustion." A week later the subcommittee proposed a nationwide Title II program "to re-educate" consumers and businesspeople. "Its general theme should be 'Now You Can Buy or Build.'"[42]

FHA officials also revived their speaking campaign, appearing before hundreds of industry groups and general business audiences in the 1940s and 1950s.[43] Officials guided builders, lenders, advertisers, lumber suppliers, appliance manufacturers, and other audiences through the constant legislative revisions to the National Housing Act, updating them on new programs, increased authorizations for existing programs, the repeated liberalization of lending terms, and occasional cutbacks in federal insurance activity (during the Korean War, especially). Audience members received copies of "Digest of Insurable Loans," which detailed the terms, construction requirements, and current interest rates for the range of mutual mortgage insurance programs. The speeches themselves grew even more technical and laden with appeals tailored to specific audiences. One group might learn about a new "ten year debenture" for emergency veterans housing, while another received a primer on the insured mortgage's "internal liquidity" (which made them "similar to serial bonds" and thus attractive to retirement funds interested in entering the mortgage market). In the fall of 1952, investors were encouraged to keep their money in the FHA-insured mortgage market, rather than experimenting with "selected issues of current high grade corporate bonds," for while these bonds were "competitive with FHA mortgages," officials explained, their supply was "quite limited and could not possibly fulfill the purchase requirements of those investors who have depended upon FHA mortgages for a large portion of their . . . portfolio."[44]

All audiences were exhorted to contribute to the promotional efforts, and some were reprimanded for not doing their part. In 1951, Richards expressed his disappointment with Texas mortgage bankers about their "continued resistance . . . to make loans under Section 8 and Section 203 (d)." He thought it would be to their advantage to "give study to the internal organization of your companies, whereby you can make and service these low interest mortgages efficiently and on a profitable basis." But most often these appearances were very congenial celebrations of public-private collaboration. By now the speakers were often quite familiar with their audiences, frequently acknowledging the "period of many years" or the "15 years" that the FHA "has been working with your industry" and meeting "in both regional and national conferences." Meanwhile, business organizations contacted FHA administrators in advance of their appearances, specifying what the "best topic would be" for their prepared remarks (a "summary of the FHA program," for example, and "suggestions as to how best mortgage lending institutions can utilize FHA facilities").[45]

Revival of collaborative efforts and this aggressive promotional campaign did not stop the FHA from insisting upon the sanctity of the free market for housing. During an era that saw business and political elites constantly tout the capacity and moral superiority of the free enterprise system, the FHA's celebration of its market-friendliness grew even more pronounced.[46] Raymond Foley set the tone in a speech before New York financial and building interests in September 1945 at the Waldorf Astoria Hotel. "Never in recent years," he explained, "has there been a more generally expressed agreement that the housing task of this nation is one to be done for the most part by private enterprise." He confidently predicted that once government restrictions on building materials were lifted, the nation would quickly meet its citizens' housing needs solely "through the channels of private enterprise." Variations on this story provided a chorus for the FHA's postwar talks and publicity efforts. In 1948 and 1949, builders in Illinois, Oklahoma, and Texas learned that their industry's fate would be determined solely by "competitive supply and demand economics" and heard predictions about a spike in residential construction that would be a testament to the "determination of private industry to surmount the current difficulties in . . . housing American families." Mortgage bankers in New York City and builders in Wisconsin and North Carolina learned that it was "up to private industry as a whole" to jump-start the housing economy and to produce more affordable housing. California mortgage bankers were told that since "adequate funds [were] available" for financing new construction, it was up to private industry to build. When housing starts picked up considerably in 1951, realtors in Georgia and mortgage bankers in Washington, D.C., were reminded that the surge in development had "been accomplished with private funds by private investors," and that "every dollar" spent on government-guaranteed homes "is private capital and every property is privately owned." Reinforcing the message were occasional threats to introduce so-called nonmarket alternatives if necessary. Administrator Franklin D. Richards told builders and lenders in Tennessee that if the nation's businesses did not meet the needs of moderate-income families, they would have to acknowledge that "private enterprise is not equipped to do the job."[47]

Despite the stunning postwar growth of the mortgage market, federal officials continually expressed concern that their promotional efforts were insufficient. In 1954, one official compared the FHA's campaign to the work of a hypothetical local advertising man who has to convince a local lumber dealer to "advertise his wares." Addressing a group of local and regional FHA directors assembled in Washington, D.C., that summer, he explained, "We've got to ring the bell in the FHA from now on and we've got to ring it loudly enough and often enough for everyone to hear." It was the agency's mission, he continued, to help people "obtain homes" by using available federal programs, so it was up to agency directors to "let the people know about them." "I think you will find it fun, as well as exceedingly helpful," he added, "to meet the press regularly."[48]

The message about the FHA's compatibility with the free enterprise system continued to appear in more mundane venues, as well. In legislative hearings, advocates still portrayed selective credit operations as means to "unleash" frozen markets and awaken "sleeping capital." When Richards endorsed renewal of the Title II program before the House Banking Subcommittee in 1952, he stressed that his agency "does not make loans and does not plan or build housing," that "every cent of money advanced under any FHA plan is private capital of private lenders," and that "this is a completely voluntary system." The "$25 billion in loans that the FHA has insured is solely because of the confidence of lenders and borrowers in the system." This narrative accompanied policy debates throughout the postwar period, both in legislative chambers and popular commentary on the suburban housing boom. National press coverage of federal programs dutifully repeated the message, in part by drawing upon FHA press releases. Fittingly, the FHA's self-published history, issued in 1960 to commemorate its twenty-fifth anniversary, described its mortgage operations as a "do-it-yourself program." The FHA was "a helper only," it explained, and its achievements were those of "the builders, lenders, realtors, and other members of industry with whom it has worked, and the American families whose enterprise and integrity have made the program succeed." The agency's narrative about metropolitan growth complemented a national celebration of American affluence and consumption patterns that constantly placed the single-family home at the material and symbolic center of postwar culture and politics.[49]

Finally the story of government noninterference was reproduced in the real estate industry's trade publications, a source viewed by a small minority of Americans but illustrative of this narrative's centrality to postwar development politics. McMichael and O'Keefe's *How to Finance Real Estate*, published in 1949 and revised in 1953 and 1967, explained that "government activity in real estate credit has been confined largely to support of the market rather than to direct participation in the market." Or consider William B. Thompson's *Mortgage Banking*, first published by the Mortgage Bankers Association of America in 1953 and reissued in 1965. His chapter on the FHA acknowledges the program's influence on mortgage markets but stresses that "all this progress has been achieved at no cost to the taxpayer." The agency, he explained, has "used the credit of the government in insuring mortgages so effectively that an abundance of private capital has been forthcoming. In fact the whole FHA experiment has proved to be a model of cooperation between government and private enterprise, each playing the role for which it is best fitted." Notably when Thompson turned to the subject of VA mortgage guarantees, there is no discussion of "cost to the taxpayer," despite his concession that the GI Bill "was not meant to be self-supporting." On the other hand he did distinguish FHA Title II mortgage insurance (for single-family homes) from the newer "complex schemes designed to serve special groups," such as federal support for construction of rental properties to accommodate low-income families and the elderly. "These programs," he concluded, "are clearly subsidy measures foreign to the FHA program as originally conceived."

Preston Martin's *Real Estate Principles and Practices*, published in 1959, perhaps best captures the free enterprise narrative recited by real estate professionals, developers, and homeowners. The volume attributes the spectacular wave of postwar suburban growth to "the unprecedented prosperity of the country" (which was rooted in "increased productivity"), to increasing birth rates, and to a "changed attitude of young American families toward saving and consumer debt." Martin explains that the FHA contributed as well, by "encourag[ing] lending" and working "through private financial channels." He conceded that the VA program, by contrast, demanded the government assume "far more liability." But since the Revolutionary War, he noted, the nation has always been "committed to aiding veterans."[50]

––––––––––

These convoluted warnings about the perils of subsidized housing suggest how whites' understanding of the suburban property market was shaping their defense of racial segregation. Whites genuinely believed that their good fortune owed nothing to federal largesse. They believed that blacks posed a categorical *economic* threat to their property. Thus they insisted upon their right to exclude, purely on economic grounds.

Prominent among the forces encouraging this thinking was the FHA itself, and its new parent agency, the Housing and Home Finance Administration (HHFA), created in 1947. Strictly speaking, the FHA had reversed course on race and restriction by 1950, by removing references to race from its *Underwriting Manual* and announcing that it would no longer insure properties with race-restrictive covenants. But the FHA and other HHFA agencies did little to enforce the government's new commitment to nondiscrimination, while also doing a great deal to flout it. To defend their noncompliance, officials invoked the market imperative argument already embedded in the theory and practice of selective credit programs. Forced by activists in the 1940s and 1950s to address the impact on housing markets of racial prejudice and the government's endorsement of it, officials continued to claim that racial exclusion was not about race but about normative and unchangeable market mechanisms. The market imperative principle now became the standard defense of discrimination in an era that rejected both racial science and, eventually, state-endorsed exclusion. Meanwhile by 1950, federal programs gave birth to and sustained powerful new markets for housing, home finance, and real estate services that operated on the principle that racial integration was destructive. Given these markets' centrality to the nation's postwar prosperity, it is little surprise that federal housing agencies and white business leaders continued to defend segregation long after the government renounced its formal support.[51]

For most of the 1940s, federal housing policy defended racial exclusion and segregation openly, by describing racial minorities as an actuarial threat to white neighborhoods. Until it was revised in 1947, the *Underwriting Manual* clearly outlined the racial rules for property appraisal. The standardized forms distributed to FHA agents and lenders included questions about applicants' "racial descent"; in one completed sample, handed out to appraisers in 1945, the response was "Anglo-Saxon." At regional zone conferences, FHA underwriters told audiences about the importance of adopting restrictive covenants, to "keep out detrimental influences that depress values the minute these influences enter."[52] Meanwhile other agency publications reinforced these warnings. The FHA's first Land Planning Bulletin, *Successful Subdivisions* (1941), instructed builders of "modest cost" homes to avoid "the development of slums, blighted residential areas, and the depreciation of property values" by applying "the [same] fundamental principles used in planning high-priced neighborhoods." Any subdivision was likely to succumb to "blight" if it was poorly designed or improperly located (for example, "on the wrong side of the city"), if it was not properly zoned, if its streets were not adequately improved, or if its properties "lack . . . suitable protective covenants." Repeated reference to covenants appears in a treatment of subdivision design as a technical problem, best addressed through the "application of certain fundamental principles of planning and development."[53] During these years, private-sector manuals also referred builders and realtors to FHA guidelines, while assigning the highest value—at once both social and economic—to neighborhoods of white-owned, single-family homes.[54]

The FHA's investment in the market imperative defense was illustrated by its response to continued protest against the agency's racial protocols. Civil rights activists sustained their campaign, initiated in the early 1930s, to remove the *Underwriting Manual's* racial references and to stop the FHA from insuring properties that contained race-restrictive covenants in their deeds.[55] Federal officials continued to insist that racial restriction was simply out of their hands. In response to a formal NAACP statement on FHA racial policy, presented in October 1944, the agency presented a now familiar defense. "FHA does not . . . create market conditions," the agency wrote, "but has the responsibility of accurately evaluating them and determining for mortgage insurance purposes the extent to which such conditions will react favorably or unfavorably upon any certain parcel of realty." It compared the issue of racial balance to other measurable variables, such as "the provision" or the "lack" of good "public transportation" or "high grade modern schools." If "[racial] infiltration will be unacceptable to the local real estate market," the memo continues, "then this Administration has no alternative but to so recognize the conditions in its valuation." The FHA concluded that "contrary to allegations made in the [NAACP] memorandum, the underwriting operation does not encourage or discourage segregation of races but records conditions as the market reflects them." FHA's New York office reiterated this claim in a response to NAACP assistant special counsel Milton Konvitz, who called upon the agency to deny insurance to properties that carried race-restrictive covenants. "This Administration had no authority to prevent an owner from placing such a restriction on his property or to deny him the benefits of the National Housing Act," wrote the FHA's Warren J. Lockwood in 1944. "I think you will agree" that this "would be a serious encroachment upon the prerogatives of attorneys and title companies throughout the country." Lockwood assured Konvitz that "this Administration does not discriminate in anyway against any race, color or creed but applies the same standards, requirements and benefits to all."[56]

Parsing the language in the *Underwriting Manual* after the FHA removed discussions of race for the 1947 edition poses a more complicated interpretive challenge. The word "race" disappears. But according to officials writing in 1944, when the agency had already decided to delete the *Manual's* "specific references to race," this cosmetic change did not alter the government's "fundamental responsibility of recognizing market conditions." That "responsibility," the agency told the NAACP, "will be fully retained."[57] Meanwhile, the 1947 volume still endorses the use of "protective covenants"—universally recognized as a private means for maintaining racial exclusion. (Notably, the FHA removed references to racial occupancy from its discussion of covenants in 1939 but continued to accept their use. In response to *Shelley*, it announced its intent to accept racial covenants until February 15, 1950, while noting privately, to the shock of civil rights activists, that a lender's "violation [of the new rules] would not invalidate insurance.") Moreover, the revised *Underwriting Manual* discusses covenants in the course of broader discussions about the risks posed by "inharmonious uses." In the section "Study of Future Utility of Property," for example, the manual explains that "it is necessary to recognize the presence of any adverse influences which lessen or destroy desirability, utility, or value, or the absence of safeguards intended to protect against declines in value or desirability." These include: "(a) a declining population in the neighborhood . . . ; (b) a decline, or danger of decline . . . through introduction of commercial, industrial, or manufacturing enterprises, or nuisances or inharmonious uses of any kind; (c) lack of appropriate protective covenants and effective provisions for their enforcement; and (d) lack of appropriate zoning regulations." Guidelines for analyzing both property and borrowers instruct appraisers to view real estate "from the point of view of typical buyers" and to determine if the neighborhood is likely to undergo "any change in occupancy relating to income and other characteristics of occupants which would tend to change desirability for residential purposes." In latter editions, the language regarding inharmonious uses, including instructions to maintain "homogeneity" and "compatibility," remain largely unchanged.[58]

White realtors made little distinction between the type of racially explicit rules outlined in the early FHA manuals and the more ambiguous guidelines that replaced them. The Chicago Real Estate Board, for example, saw the new rhetoric of exclusion as an instruction to continue long-standing practice. Largely in response to the *Shelley* ruling, CREB changed Article 3, Part III, of its Code of Ethics, which for a quarter century had instructed realtors "never [to] be instrumental in introducing into a neighborhood a character of property or occupancy, members of any race or nationality, or any individuals whose presence will clearly be detrimental to property values in that neighborhood." In 1950, a revised instruction, moved to Article 5, Part I, now told members "not [to] be instrumental in introducing into a neighborhood a character of property or use which will clearly be detrimental to property values in that neighborhood." In interviews conducted in the 1950s, realtors and CREB officials acknowledged that "the meaning of Article 5 remains the same and that 'a character of property or use' covers the introduction of Negroes."[59]

Always responsive to the real estate industry's preferences, federal officials also continued to follow the FHA's original racial directives. Senior officials initially balked at the *Shelley* decision and then for two decades refused to stand by the government's new (albeit tepid) commitment to fair housing. And they did not consider alterations to the *Underwriting Manual* as indicative of a fundamental change in FHA policy. In 1948, Assistant Commissioner Warren Lockwood responded to complaints of agency discrimination in appraisals by citing from a much-used memorandum: The agency does not "create market conditions" and "the FHA underwriting operation does not encourage or discourage segregation of races but records conditions as the market reflects them." That year Commissioner Franklin Richards insisted, "it is not the policy of this Administration" to refuse insurance when "occupants are to be of more than one race" but added that when "infiltration of minority groups will be unacceptable to the local real estate market," the agency must "recognize the conditions in its valuation." During his 1953 confirmation hearing to head the HHFA, Albert Cole announced that he would not stop local authorities from maintaining racial segregation in federally funded programs and then proceeded throughout his six-year term to obstruct enforcement of nondiscrimination. The government, he insisted, could not "legislat[e] acceptance of an idea." When challenged about the Public Housing Authority's refusal to require open occupancy in its facilities, Cole explained that discrimination was a "peculiarly local" problem, "deeply rooted in local institutions and emotions." White housing officials continued to echo Cole's argument, despite the 1962 Executive Order banning discrimination in federally supported housing, despite passage of Title VI of the 1964 Civil Rights Act, and despite Robert Weaver's tireless efforts, both as HHFA administrator and secretary of the new Department of Housing and Urban Development, to enforce the new fair housing mandate. At the height of the modern civil rights era housing officials repeatedly declared their commitment to racial equality, while insisting, in the same breath, that market dynamics and "local custom" trumped the government's fair housing obligations.[60] As a result most blacks were denied access to federally supported mortgage financing.[61]

Further complicating matters, private acts of racial discrimination in the sale or rental of property were not legally prohibited until 1968, and real estate publications, used nationwide in college and university courses and by practicing realtors, continued to outline the original market imperative defense of segregating "inharmonious" populations, long after the FHA abandoned explicit discussion of racial exclusion. Many of these texts follow the FHA's lead, replacing race-specific language with more open-ended recommendations for maintaining "common characteristics of population" or ensuring that "population characteristics are qualitatively homogeneous." Revised editions of Homer Hoyt's *Principles of Urban Real Estate*, meanwhile, repeatedly altered and toned down but did not totally abandon instructions about the need to protect "Caucasian" neighborhoods.[62]

Other private-sector publications were even more direct, and picked up where the original *Underwriting Manual* left off, by openly discussing racial exclusion as a normative principle of land-use science. Immediately after the *Shelley* ruling, several texts specifically addressed the "blow that racial restrictions have received" from the Supreme Court and recommend alternative methods for protecting neighborhood homogeneity.[63] The AIREA, meanwhile, cautiously reproduced the FHA's original theory about race and value. In its *Appraisal of Real Estate* (1960), the section on "Neighborhood Analysis" summarizes the "principle factors which improve value in private dwelling neighborhoods," including adequate planning, "good schools," "a homogeneous population with a sense of civic responsibility," "prestige and visual appeal," and "sensible zoning." Among the "factors which depreciate value" were a "mixture of architectural styles," "the movement of commercial and industrial uses into the area," "nuisances such as smoke, noise, and traffic," and the "tendency on the part of a neighborhood's present inhabitants to think of it as losing desirability because of an influx of people of a different economic, social, or cultural status." "The value levels in a residential neighborhood," the text continues, "will be influenced more by the social characteristics of the people occupying or in prospect of occupying the area than by any other factor. Therefore, too much importance cannot be attached to the social data which the appraiser must consider . . . No matter how attractive a particular neighborhood may be from every other angle, it will not possess maximum desirability unless it is occupied by people who will be happy in one another's company and unless it provides the right setting for the rearing of children . . . Thus a wide tolerance or mutuality is involved in matters of race, religion, income, cultural standards, and ways of living."

Racial, religious, or cultural variables are important, the manual emphasizes, only insofar as they impact the current or future estimated value of property. In other words while "social data" was important, any purely ideological component of these considerations was separable from the standpoint of land-use economics. "Race and religion are both touchy subjects," the text continues, and "the reasons that this is so are not the appraiser's responsibility." His responsibility was to predict property values, thus "he must recognize the fact that values are likely to change whenever people different from those presently occupying the area, advance into and infiltrate a neighborhood."[64]

Perhaps no volume reduces social values and whites' racial presumptions to calculable science more clinically than the AIREA's *Handbook for Appraisers*, a dictionary of real estate concepts and terminology first published in 1948. Here an appraiser learns that neighborhoods declined into "blighted area[s]" because of the presence of "destructive economic forces, such as encroaching inharmonious property usages, infiltration of lower social and economic classes of inhabitants, and/or rapidly depreciating buildings." A cross-reference takes the reader to the entry for "slum area," defined as a "squalid, dilapidated, over-crowded area inhabited by the lowest social and economic class of the population . . . [and] characterized by a coincidence of over-crowding in old, obsolete, dilapidated structures." The financial risk created by blight was calculable. "Nuisance value," the *Handbook* explains, was the "price which probably would be paid for the avoidance of, or as a relief from, an objectionable condition." Of course readers were interested in learning how to identify and assess the most valuable properties. A parcel was "improved to highest and best use," the AIREA explained, when improvements "develop[ed] the maximum effective net income which may be imputed to the land."[65]

It cannot be overemphasized that these publications were technical volumes focusing on building, assessing, and selling property, not primers for racial exclusion or strategic memos instructing realtors how to explain away whites' racial prejudices. These manuals reflect ongoing debates among economists and real estate professionals about the proper, scientifically tested methods for assessing property. Like the *Underwriting Manual*, they treat appraisal as science—it was an "orderly procedure," explained the AIREA's *Appraisal of Real Estate*, an "intellectual operation" that "requires clear thinking and sound judgment." The AIREA even cited the FHA as a model of this "orderly" approach, noting that the *Underwriting Manual* outlined "techniques for neighborhood analysis which are well organized and have proved an effective method of property and neighborhood rating since 1934."[66] These manuals illustrate the degree to which the private real estate and development industries pursued development strategies simultaneously shaped and fueled by the state's massive interventions in the market for homes. These were strategies predicated on a belief that sound real estate practices required the segregation of populations by race and class, and that certain populations were incapable of participating in a lucrative market for single-family homes. It was a vision of the market, in the final analysis, that programmatically required the exclusion of *any* structures or populations deemed inimical to a property's "highest and best" use.

The professional guidebooks also reveal just how pervasive this logic had become. Early formulations of this argument had been articulated prior to federal involvement in private housing markets. But the new federal role advanced a specific variation of this argument: the claim that it was market considerations alone that required exclusion and that the *reasons* for racial antagonism were not relevant. Moreover, the new federal presence codified and widely disseminated this argument. This shift in methods of exclusion and rationales for exclusion would decisively shape whites' approach to the politics of race and housing in the decades after 1940, as the market imperative defense quickly became the standard explanation for racial segregation. Whereas race restrictive covenants had directed whites' attention to the issue of "race," New Deal and postwar interventions focused on construction and homeownership and treated racial exclusion virtually as an afterthought, solely as a means of sustaining healthy market activity. According to government officials, residential segregation was a logistical variable, an unavoidable side effect of their commitment to protecting free markets for property. As a result, for three decades the racial segregation of housing equity and of American metropolitan areas was systematically guided by and subsidized by federal programs, yet portrayed simply as an economic inevitability, as the product of natural market mechanisms. Because federal programs focused on housing and growth—and not on race—they further masked the fact that state policy was fueling residential apartheid.

Indeed selective credit programs made it imperative for whites who built, sold, or purchased homes to subscribe to this racialized theory of the market for property. The state's central role in sustaining the insured and conventional mortgage markets made this logic foundational to the operations of the postwar housing economy, an economy that resegregated the nation's metropolitan regions by race and class. Federal interventions set the stage, both structurally and ideologically, for the political mobilizations that arose in countless suburbs nationwide, as white homeowners worked to protect their property and their neighborhoods from "racial invasion" and a host of other "incompatible land uses."

Zoning the Segregated Metropolis

Local suburban mobilizations did not focus on the mortgage market but rather on municipal control and land use. It is not surprising that white suburbanites were little concerned with selective credit operations and the home finance industry. Most residents were comfortable with the benefits they received and the segregation that lending practices helped maintain. Moreover the average suburban dweller had limited influence over the selective credit programs that sustained the modern mortgage market, programs originally designed and later administered by a group of public- and private-sector elites. It is true that the day-to-day operations of the FHA and complementary agencies were managed by local whites in the building, finance, and real estate industries, people who supported the government's racial rules wholeheartedly. White preferences ensured that the new restrictive market for housing remained politically sustainable. Still, the statutory machinery that segregated the mortgage market was not local but federal. It was the federal state that sustained the most powerful instrument of exclusion during this era: a market for housing that deemed nonwhites a calculable threat.

White suburban dwellers did actively shape settlement patterns and land-use politics, nonetheless, by using tools that they did control, especially the zoning power, to monitor local development closely. Before *Shelley v. Kraemer*, whites could employ a direct, contractual method for excluding minorities; race-restrictive covenants were adopted widely nationwide, especially in the suburbs, throughout the 1940s. But of greater importance for understanding postwar racial politics was residents' and officials' growing preoccupation with municipal incorporation and restrictive zoning. This preoccupation has complicated origins and was not simply about race, yet once residents marshaled the zoning power, they consistently used it to protect the racial homogeneity of their neighborhoods, by limiting or totally excluding apartments and moderately priced homes.[67] The municipal zoning power was not designed as a tool of racial exclusion. Moreover zoning could be, and often was, used by whites and nonwhites alike to achieve other kinds of exclusion: keeping unwanted commercial activity or poor people of any race, for example, out of affluent neighborhoods.[68] But after World War II, zoning proved to be a very effective tool for white suburbanites committed to maintaining the residential color line. Most suburbs were dominated by white homeowners, and so suburban zoning quickly became associated with racial exclusion in particular.

Because zoning is a flexible instrument with multiple applications, there has been considerable confusion when scholars attempt to identify and isolate homeowners' motivations for supporting restriction. Were suburbanites who preferred large-lot, single-family zoning driven by practical or ideological considerations? There is good reason for the confusion, since racial exclusion was by no means the sole—or even the primary—intent behind the careful monitoring of development in the modern American suburb. Land-use controls were not employed merely to satisfy the whims and fears of the affluent and white. Zoning's rapid spread is largely attributable, instead, to the fiscal requirements created by the unprecedented, spectacular growth of American metropolitan regions after World War II. Building and managing fast-growing municipalities posed daunting technical, administrative, and budgetary challenges for communities suddenly faced with managing capital-intensive infrastructures and services. Suburban governments had to install and maintain sewage systems, roads, and water mains. They had to build and manage parks, playgrounds, and city hospitals. They had to dispose of garbage, provide police and fire protection, and address a new national disease: the congestion of streets and highways. This was a tall order for inexperienced village and township leaders and even for veteran suburban officials. Between 1948 and 1949, for example, Royal Oak, Michigan's Engineering Department paved 16.23 miles of street, resurfaced another 3.64 miles, and completed work on 3.6 miles of sidewalk, 2.5 miles of water main, and 3.23 miles of sewer line, at a total cost of $1,003,925.61. Monitoring new construction became a full-time job for Royal Oak's understaffed department of building inspection, working out of a 15-by-8-foot office in city hall.[69] Land-use controls—the zoning power, especially—were essential tools for local officials struggling to develop, maintain, and pay for their communities' growing infrastructures.[70]

Still the meteoric spread of suburban zoning and the significant postwar changes in zoning practice cannot easily be separated from the politics of exclusion. Whites' ideas about race and property shaped their land-use decisions, in no small part because they operated in a fast-growing suburban housing market that required racial separation. In the 1940s, the market imperative defense of racial exclusion—already widely embraced by real estate professionals and federal housing officials—was well suited to justifying zoning practices that reinforced existing patterns of discrimination. Meanwhile suburban whites inherited land-use tools, including the zoning ordinance itself, grounded in a racialized conception of real estate values. Although zoning's founding generation seldom addressed racial issues explicitly, they designed land-use ordinances that considered "nonwhites" to be among the nuisances that threatened "high class" residential neighborhoods (see chap. 2).

Important postwar changes in zoning practice and zoning politics must be seen in this light. Both the design and implementation of zoning grew far more complicated during the 1940s and 1950s because of the rapid growth of a planning industry—itself the product, both directly and indirectly, of federal intervention. Residential zoning ordinances grew far more restrictive, favoring larger homes on larger lots and further limiting multiunit development. They also grew far more technical and complex. Meanwhile the courts further validated zoning's most discriminatory presumptions, giving local governments even more discretion to exclude "undesirable" development patterns and populations. It was this new, postwar variant of land-use science—more restrictive, expressed in a language even more technical and impersonal, and increasingly identified with a growing cohort of professional planners—that white suburban residents embraced when they used zoning to protect neighborhood homogeneity. Zoning continued to be grounded in a race- and class-specific vision of property, economic stability, and urban growth. And after 1940, supporters of restriction—public officials, judges, and suburban residents—tapped into zoning's scientific and legal standing to argue that exclusion was not driven by racial or class preference per se but by the need to manage the municipality properly and protect the public health. And now zoning's discriminatory assumptions were even more thoroughly shrouded behind a discourse of urban expertise.

The meteoric growth of all-white suburbs, the influx of African Americans to urban centers, and the simultaneous deterioration of housing stock and services in those cities further affirmed whites' investment in the social science of property. Zoning law and zoning science provided a useful language with which a mobile, increasingly affluent, and fast-growing white middle class could explain its desire for certain kinds of exclusion without invoking the ideologically loaded language of race. Meanwhile, zoning itself provided a powerful, court-tested tool for excluding types of residential development—apartments and public housing, especially—that might give racial minorities access to white neighborhoods. Postwar zoning was not simply a tool of racial exclusion. Most white suburbanites saw it as a means to protect homes and families, indeed the new suburban way of life, by balancing municipal revenues with spending and eliminating "incompatible" development. Suburban residents wanted to be surrounded by like-minded homeowners, in residential neighborhoods with a robust tax base, minimal industry and commercial traffic, and good schools and services. Yet the record clearly shows that countless whites also saw zoning as a means to police the racial boundaries of their communities because they saw racial integration as a threat to the delicate economic and social balance required to maintain the suburban ideal. In the final analysis, whites connected zoning with racial exclusion—as zoning's founders had done decades earlier—by collapsing "nonwhites" into a normative analytical category of development that supposedly threatened natural patterns of metropolitan growth. As postwar whites addressed what many saw as one of their most pressing political challenges, namely, separating their homes, schools, and families from the minority populations that were migrating to northern and western cities, they did so with statutory instruments and a corollary political discourse that categorically denied that ideology shaped *any* decisions about suburban land use, including decisions about who could settle in the new neighborhood.

Zoning Spreads

After 1940 zoning was suburban governments' most important tool for controlling development and managing municipal service provision. Planners and city officials calculated, correctly, that extensive single-family home construction balanced by selective industrial and commercial development would produce sufficient tax revenues while also keeping population densities—and thus costs for services, upkeep, and schools—in check.[71] In order to zone, suburbs usually had to incorporate, so both incorporation and zoning activity increased at a stunning rate. The 1950s saw the most dramatic wave of city formation; two studies (using the same data) reported the creation of 1,074 new governments nationwide. According to this conservative estimate, a new municipality was created every three days, and in 1960 at least one out of every seven metropolitan municipalities was less than a decade old (with one out of five chartered no earlier than 1940).[72] In metropolitan Detroit, thirty-one new home-rule governments were created between 1940 and 1965 (eighteen of these in the 1950s), and ten home-rule villages reincorporated as home-rule cities. Between 1950 and 1965, incorporation consumed territory from thirteen townships and brought more than 215 square miles under the authority of new home-rule governments. The activity often came in waves, with five new cities formed in each of the years 1950, 1954, 1955, 1957, and 1958. Between 1954 and 1955, at least 150,000 residents found themselves living in one of ten new cities: Franklin, Keego Harbor, Walled Lake, Wolverine Lake, Bingham Farms, Madison Heights, Troy, Gibraltar, Northville, and Warren.[73]

Nationally, the communities jumping on the home-rule bandwagon were both younger and smaller than their prewar predecessors. Almost 90 percent of the cities created between 1940 and 1965 were home to fewer than ten thousand people each, yet taken together included 2.5 million people, or 87 percent of the population living in cities incorporated since 1950. By the late 1960s, two-thirds of the nation's metropolitan cities had populations of fewer than 5,000 people, and half of these were smaller than one square mile. The Detroit-area communities that gained home rule before 1940 were usually long-settled, with fairly sizable populations and an existing jurisdictional identity, in most cases a village government. After 1940, by contrast, new home-rule suburbs were younger, smaller (both geographically and demographically), and had no tradition of local government. Twenty-one of the new cities, or 57 percent, were simply new inventions, small enclaves carved out of existing township jurisdictions by local petition. There were important exceptions, as these decades saw the creation of large suburban municipalities including Southfield, Warren, Livonia, St. Clair Shores, and Roseville. Far more common, though, were the twelve new home-rule municipalities that boasted populations under 2,800 in 1960. In that year, Woodcreek Farms was three years old and home to 687 residents. Bingham Farms was five years old and home to 394.[74]

The pace of suburban growth, both real and anticipated, exerted new pressures on localities, pitting jurisdictions against one another over valuable resources, either existing or potential. The cycle was self-perpetuating. As communities raced to secure control over development and revenues, local authority grew increasingly fragmented. Interjurisdictional competition precipitated new waves of incorporation as well as annexation campaigns. After 1940, central cities and well-established suburban municipalities aggressively pursued the annexation of adjacent territory, to capture potential revenue sources (especially land suitable for industrial and commercial development) and to control future residential development. In a flurry of activity reminiscent of the late nineteenth century, suburban governments brought millions of people under their authority in the 1950s. In the Detroit region, suburbs in Wayne and Oakland counties together annexed nearly 4,000 acres of unincorporated territory. Older municipalities usually initiated the cycle; Royal Oak City, for example, annexed 22 acres of Royal Oak Township in 1954, a small section of Berkley in 1955, and 6.5 acres of Troy Township in 1957. Birmingham absorbed 50.6 acres of Troy Township between 1950 and 1954. In the latter year, the City of Clawson attempted to annex a 109 acre parcel on Troy's southeast.[75]

In the areas targeted for annexation, most of them, like Troy, unincorporated, residents responded by petitioning for home-rule status and quickly joining the annexation game. Troy Township's supervisor, Norman R. Barnard, blocked Clawson's annexation bid, convincing county authorities that it would deprive the city of land suited for industry and create an "unbalanced tax base." Troy township's homeowners, meanwhile, had launched an incorporation campaign and by 1955 approved a municipal charter. Within a year, the new *city* of Troy joined the regional scramble over land and tax revenues when it successfully annexed part of Birmingham, its neighbor to the west. This cycle was repeated nationwide, as the announcement of annexation proceedings or simply the fear of future annexation campaigns set off chain reactions of city building. Home-rule campaigns often began as stopgap measures. In metropolitan regions throughout Texas and Missouri, for example, petitions for incorporation were filed in rapid succession, within months or sometimes days of one another. Some were eventually dropped, but most communities followed through. Between 1945 and 1951, fifty-seven incorporations carved up the St. Louis area into a puzzle of independent suburban governments. Forty-four of them were created either to prevent annexation or to bypass county zoning and building codes.[76]

The most powerful catalyst behind the surge in suburban incorporations was residents' desire to acquire the zoning power. Increased zoning activity in turn fueled more city-building. As larger cities and suburbs adopted increasingly comprehensive zoning, subdivision, and planning instruments, neighboring communities defended themselves by assuming home-rule powers and drafting their own land-use ordinances. Larger suburbs then responded by continually revising existing regulations in anticipation of forecast changes in the region's commercial, industrial, and residential development. Meanwhile established suburban municipalities jockeyed for position over unincorporated territory. In 1952, for example, the residents of Hazel Park began proceedings to annex a two-mile long strip of Royal Oak Township. Royal Oak City responded by proposing annexation of that same parcel. A vocal supporter of Royal Oak's bid was Ernest Finnegan, a member of the Red Run Home Owners Association, who reminded city commissioners that annexation was essential if the city hoped to "control future development in the area."[77]

After 1940 zoning became the centerpiece of a new kind of competitive local politics in metropolitan America. It was well suited to the task, for zoning practice was more or less standardized, and the courts had confirmed a city's right to control uses of private property. As millions of people moved to suburban areas, thousands of local governments, both new and old, learned that the municipal police power enabled them to achieve two inseparable goals: gaining control over local land use and striking a balance between revenues and expenditures.[78] Suburban officials and homeowners learned to see political autonomy and land-use control as practically synonymous. This connection was not new, but postwar land-use politics were distinguished by three important developments. First, both the number of jurisdictions and the amount of zoning and planning activity increased very rapidly. Second, proliferation was encouraged, coordinated, and often sponsored by powerful networks of public officials and private leaders.

Finally, and largely as a product of zoning's new prominence, land-use controls grew more complex and restrictive.

Many suburbs had adopted zoning ordinances before 1940, but after that year only a small minority did not, and now there were simply more local governments empowered to do so. When the Supreme Court validated comprehensive zoning in 1926, only 564 cities nationwide used zoning ordinances, and five years later there were just 800. By 1968, 6,880 municipalities and another 2,004 townships were policing local land use, most of them with comprehensive ordinances. The result was the rapid fragmentation of suburban land-use authority, particularly in metropolitan areas and especially in the decade after 1950. By the late 1960s, over 90 percent of the nation's independent metropolitan governments had adopted zoning ordinances, including 97 percent of those with populations of 5,000–50,000 (hereafter referred to as "smaller SMSA cities") and more than half of those with populations of 1,000–5,000.[79]

By deciding to zone, suburban governments committed themselves to an ongoing process of updating and policing existing regulations. Postwar ordinances were seldom left unaltered. In most cities, the zoning board of appeals spent over thirty hours a year considering revisions to existing ordinances and proposals for their comprehensive overhaul. Minor revisions were quite common, with about sixteen requests per year in smaller SMSA cities and about ninety requests in larger cities, of which about 80 percent were approved. Meanwhile between 1940 and 1967, 94.3 percent of the smaller SMSA cities either adopted their first zoning ordinance or comprehensively revised an existing ordinance. Planning and code enforcement were equally time-consuming. By 1964, 92 percent of cities with 10,000 or more residents, or 1,261 cities nationwide, had planning agencies, an increase of more than 60 percent since 1957. And by 1968, 91 percent of the smaller SMSA cities reported the use of local building codes, 90 percent monitored residential development with subdivision regulations, and 93 percent had appointed municipal planning boards, which met, on average, for over sixty hours a year. Almost 70 percent had drawn up and adopted comprehensive (or "master") plans, often through a consultancy with a professional planner. Like zoning ordinances, master plans were regularly revised; more than half of those reported in 1968 were no more than three years old.[80]

This flurry of city building and zoning activity redrew the land-use authority and the land-use maps of metropolitan areas nationwide. In the Detroit region, where few suburban governments had monitored development before 1940, land-use authority was totally fragmented by the mid-1960s, as prewar suburbs adopted their first ordinances or comprehensively revised existing ones, and as virtually every new suburb joined in the zoning game. Of the twenty-four new government units established between 1950 and 1965, twenty established planning commissions. By the later year, seventy-four municipalities—thirty in Oakland, thirty-one in Wayne, and thirteen in Macomb—controlled land use with zoning ordinances or planning commissions, and most often with both. Between 1940 and 1960, meanwhile, the population of the Oakland County and Wayne County suburbs alone grew by over 400,000 persons, or over 60 percent. Comparable transformations took place nationwide. All of the forty-six municipalities in Westchester County, New York, for example, employed zoning ordinances as early as 1957, and 80 percent of these had been either revised or newly adopted since 1945. During that same period, the number of local planning and zoning agencies in New Jersey increased from 120 to 389. By 1956, only 85 municipalities in the greater New York City area did *not* employ restrictive ordinances, and virtually all of these "lay in the outer counties."[81]

The race to incorporate and regulate, and the resultant political fragmentation of metropolitan areas, was not, as many observers claim, the inevitable outcome of population growth and competition over suburban resources.[82] Metropolitan areas splintered into competing units because suburban residents had few legal alternatives and, critically, because public and private leaders encouraged fragmentation. Most state constitutions offered small communities the home-rule option, but no comparable means of organizing metropolitan-wide governmental or planning authorities. There was little to prevent the endless division of suburban jurisdictions, and little incentive to seek metropolitan cooperation either in land-use planning or service provision. Meanwhile, private and public efforts aggressively promoted both incorporation and restrictive zoning, all but ensuring that efforts to promote metropolitan alternatives would fail. Professional planners, national and state associations of municipal officials, and federal officials canonized suburban localism, preached the zoning gospel, and provided valuable resources that enabled cash-poor localities to assume local control over land use. Localities were bombarded with encouragement, practical advice, invaluable resources, and even federal funding to help them incorporate and to zone.

Instrumental to zoning's rapid spread was the growth and reorientation of the planning industry itself, changes attributable in large part to the federal government's continued subsidization of the private planning industry. Selective credit programs established strict guidelines regarding zoning, covenants, and rules for residential "compatibility," making both

planning and coordinated subdivision development an economic imperative for any municipality hoping to attract developers and homebuyers.
The HHFA intervened more directly under Section 701 of the Housing Act
of 1954, by making grants to local governments and regional authorities
to defray the cost of preparing land-use plans, renewal programs, zoning
ordinances, subdivision regulations, economic studies, and population
forecasts. In its first five years, Section 701 supported planning efforts in
over 11,000 municipalities in 94 metropolitan regions. By 1964, the HHFA
had approved $79 million in grants to localities, the lion's share of which
funded preparation of comprehensive plans, including the design or revision of local zoning ordinances and subdivision regulations. Other federal efforts accelerated the planning craze: more than half of the 43 federal
grant programs for urban development "attempt[ed] to shape local efforts
in the direction of functional or comprehensive planning." Yet the 701 program was the engine, according to the American Society of Planning Officials, that "stimulated" the rapid expansion of local, regional, and state
planning activity throughout the 1950s and 1960s. The main benefactors
were suburban municipalities. Seventeen of the thirty cities in Oakland
County, Michigan, that engaged in planning activities by 1965 received Section 701 funds, as did sixteen of thirty-one cities in out-Wayne County and
eight of thirteen in Macomb. After 1965, the influence of federal subsidies on local planning and redevelopment activity would grow even more
pronounced.[83]

Equally "stimulated" by HHFA grants was the planning profession itself,
as enthusiasm for land-use science coupled with generous federal funding
quickly translated into more planning jobs and the rapid development of
educational and professional institutions. Only seven American universities
offered planning programs before 1945; by 1964, there were thirty-one. The
profession and its organizations expanded apace. Of the 2,272 planning
degrees awarded between 1931 and 1969, over two-thirds were granted after
1963. The American Institute of Planners (AIP) was founded in 1917 with
twenty-four members and counted only 200 members in the late 1940s. By
the late 1960s, it boasted 3,400. Membership in the American Society of
Planning Officials grew from 1,525 in 1946 to over 4,500 by 1969.[84]

While it would be a mistake to attribute cities' interest in planning and
zoning solely to federal intervention, the state's involvement clearly fueled
the rapid growth of planning and zoning as well as their emphasis. Many
critics accuse the 701 program of funding unnecessary or ill-conceived
projects and distorting the profession's priorities. By one estimate, the program facilitated the tenfold expansion of the planning industry by 1968,

by encouraging consultants to inflate their fees and encouraging local governments to commission high-priced plans that were either extraneous or unnecessary. During this period of rapid expansion, argue Marion Clawson and Peter Hall, the planning industry's "professional standards" were "vague, often meaningless to those who are not members of the fraternity, and often lacking logical or empirical foundation."[85]

Making matters worse, most local, especially suburban, planners were not qualified for their positions. Summarizing a critique heard repeatedly in the mid-1960s, Richard Babcock described the typical municipal plan commission as "neither expert nor responsible," often run by local residents without formal training and serving on a part-time basis. Paradoxically, most planning agencies lacked the statutory power to pass or enforce land-use laws. Legally speaking, as Beverly Pooley writes, "planning" signified nothing more than "the drawing up of plans upon which regulatory ordinances may be based." Most municipalities had the option of transferring zoning authority to the planning commission, but few exercised it, leaving local planners with nothing more than an advisory role. And while most state constitutions insisted that local zoning ordinances comply with "comprehensive plans," they did not require zoning commissions to follow the advice of planning bodies. Most state zoning laws did "not refer to the master plan of the same state's planning law," according to a 1969 report by the National Commission on Urban Problems, but the courts did nothing to clarify matters. In many cases planning requirements could often "be satisfied by the zoning ordinance itself," so that local zoning could be exercised, the commission concluded, "without a guiding master plan, or, what is more absurd, in disregard of such guidance where it is available." Not surprisingly, a 1955 study of land-use controls reported that as many as half of the municipalities with comprehensive zoning ordinances had not adopted master plans.[86]

This led regularly to the duplication of planning efforts, with local planning boards advising on land-use decisions but with city councils or zoning boards exercising final authority. Planning boards were often asked to approve (and if necessary modify) new subdivision plats and general land-use guidelines, and many boards drafted comprehensive plans, but few had the authority to enforce their own recommendations. Local planners often did little more than provide the patina of expertise for local development agendas, while serving as conduits for federal planning aid. Few planners objected to their new advisory role. The years that saw the rise of the professional planner also witnessed most planning theorists abandon their commitment to the independent planning commission. Instead, planners were encouraged to cultivate local officials' support and, whenever their views conflicted, to defer to local authority. This new approach was more than just theory. Of the cities that employed full-time planners between 1948 and 1965, the number appointed by planning commissions fell 31.9 percent while those appointed by executives rose 28.2 percent.[87]

Taken together, the increase in federal funding and the ascendancy of the politically powerless, nonexpert planner gave suburban residents considerable control over local development. It further reinforced a land-use politics, developed through decades of public-private collaboration, that encouraged property owners and local officials to dictate land-use decision making, while discouraging experiments with comprehensive regional planning. Reform efforts such as the 1962 Highway Act and the 1966 Model Cities and Metropolitan Development Act failed to encourage cooperation between local zoning authorities. Lacking authority to shape land-use patterns within home-rule cities, most of the nation's metropolitan agencies could do little more than consult, advise, and provide planning resources.[88]

Widespread criticism of regional planning's failures, however, has distracted from one of its perhaps unforeseen accomplishments. Paradoxically, regional planning sometimes facilitated the very fragmentation that critics have long decried. Regional planning bodies encouraged localism in two ways. They produced expensive land-use studies that enabled revenue-poor localities to plan more efficiently. In addition, regional planners often embraced a vision of "regionalism" that explicitly encouraged localities to pursue exclusionary land-use strategies.

The history of metropolitan planning in southeast Michigan demonstrates that regional efforts often provided a catalyst for fragmentation. In 1947, two years after passage of a state Regional Planning Act, the Michigan State Planning Commission created the Detroit Metropolitan Area Regional Planning Commission (DMARPC). Funded by a $25,000 state public works grant matched by thirty regional private business interests, the DMARPC was designed by a committee of twenty-seven local officials and business leaders to serve the 126 municipalities and townships of Wayne, Oakland, Warren, and eastern Washtenaw counties, an area of 2,000 square miles and home to three million residents. Its governing board included county, municipal, metropolitan, and school board officials, as well as businessmen, bankers, lawyers, architects, religious leaders, newspaper editors, and educators. The DMARPC was envisioned as an umbrella organization that would promote regional cooperation and coordinated planning by producing land-use studies ("showing the best locations for industry, homes and retail business"), by developing regional plans for water, sewers, and parks, and finally by "providing information and services to the region's local governments."[89]

The commission had no enforcement authority, but in its role as advisor it produced invaluable data and resources, including maps, land-use surveys, and reports on regional land-use trends, which enabled local governments, short on capital or expertise, to plan and zone. By October 1949, it had produced regional baseline maps and had begun collaboration with the Detroit Edison Company to produce detailed aerial photographs of the region. It was preparing a regional land-use study and reports on population growth and future water needs. Studies such as "Movement of Industries from the City of Detroit, 1937–1949" projected industrial, residential, and commercial development patterns and estimated future transportation needs. Finally, the DMARPC provided "advice to county and local planning and zoning agencies in technical planning and zoning matters," as well as assistance in preparing a land-use plan. Vital to these consultations were the regional maps depicting river basins, the location and type of treatment for sewers, drains and other outfalls, and "generalized zoning compiled from all local zoning ordinances." In 1950 the commission reported that it had already distributed 600 copies of its zoning maps and 9,000 copies of other reports, notices, and minutes.[90]

Public funding soon accelerated the commission's efforts. The DMARPC received its first federal grant in 1955, which together with state money dramatically expanded its activities and those of its successor, the Southeast Michigan Conference of Governments (SEMCOG), created in 1968. According to an internal DMARPC report, a Michigan P-2 grant "pushed the[ir] program[s] ahead significantly from a technical standpoint and added greatly to the stature and respect for the program and the agency among both governmental and nongovernmental organizations in the region." An HHFA grant funded the DMARPC's "Survey of Existing Land Use" in 1958, which mapped current zoning districts throughout the SMSA and calculated the "amount and location of urban and suburban development in the region since 1949." By then the DMARPC was able to keep "lot by lot land use data, by municipality . . . on file for use by local government officials and other people." Its "1958 Land Use in the Detroit Region" map was used widely by municipal officials and businesspeople. Together DMARPC and SEMCOG produced a veritable library of invaluable planning resources, including such reports as "Development Area Sketch Plans," "Employment of Women in the Detroit Region," "Mass Transit and Trucking," and "The Detroit Area Economy: Characteristics, Trends, Regional Mix of Basic and Non-Basic Industries, with 1970 Employment Projections." DMARPC's massive

"Profile of Developed Land," its most exhaustive study of regional land use, was completed in 1965 with an urban planning grant from the Department of Housing and Urban Development. Beginning in 1950, the DMARPC also organized annual regional planning and zoning conferences. Throughout the 1950s and 1960s, both bodies encouraged local governments to apply for federal funds, including Section 701 grants to defer the cost of preparing comprehensive plans and zoning ordinances.[91]

In addition to providing resources that enabled municipalities to pursue local interests, the DMARPC and SEMCOG actively encouraged suburban parochialism. Both organizations paid lip service to the idea of regional planning, and both helped coordinate county and regionwide service provision. When it came to questions about local land use, however, they refused to intervene. Indeed, a 1949 DMARPC circular assured municipal officials that one goal of regional planning was the protection of local autonomy. Specifically, it encouraged suburbs to adopt "local zoning and subdivision regulations" since "planning, like any other governmental function, is most effective at the municipal and township level." The DMARPC was "not designed, financed, or staffed to do local planning," it continued, and should not "in any way duplicate the logical operation of local planning agencies. It serves merely to make the work of these agencies more effective and of more lasting value to the communities they serve." The commission encouraged municipal officials to create planning boards, hire professional planners, and draft master plans, all in order to "promote efficiently the best development of the area." Another circular exhorted municipal governments to "*Prepare a zoning ordinance and subdivision regulations* that will protect what you have and *promote what you want*" and instructed them "not [to] hesitate to recommend changes in the Master Plan as new developments indicate the wisdom of such a move." "*A planning board should not plan*," the memo explained. "Its function is to represent the various sections of the community and [its] various economic and social groups and interests." Local officials with questions about zoning were encouraged to call the DMARPC or to visit its office.[92]

Zoning Refined

Empowered to zone and provided with powerful incentives to do so, the nation's suburban governments pursued land-use strategies that had three related effects. First, zoning further facilitated the segregation of the postwar metropolis by reinforcing and extending development patterns fueled by federal housing policies and private acts of discrimination. Scholars and critics have long documented this part of zoning's postwar legacy. Writing in 1976, Michael Danielson concluded that the postwar fragmentation of land-use authority had permitted localities to pursue policies that "played a central role in the development of a spatially differentiated metropolis," one in which "blacks are separated from whites, the poor from the more affluent, the disadvantaged from economic and educational opportunity, and local jurisdictions with the greatest public needs from communities which possess the greatest share of public resources."[93] Municipal fragmentation and the rush to zone provided yet another obstacle to populations already written out of the new market for suburban homeownership.

Second, regional competition over tax revenues coupled with planners' investment in land-use science combined to make restriction seem increasingly urgent to suburban residents while reinforcing their investment in the market-imperative justification for all types of exclusion. Postwar zoning practice built directly on prewar precedents yet was altered in important ways. The surge of homebuilding and city building placed municipal governments in constant competition to control revenue-producing development. One result was that "fiscal zoning"—long foundational to land-use science—became the trademark strategy of local officials nationwide. Meanwhile the new status of the professional planner, coupled with federal support for suburban growth and racial segregation, helped institutionalize increasingly complex standards for distinguishing between types of residential neighborhoods and for measuring the compatibility of different development patterns. Postwar zoning guidelines continued to assign greater value to privately owned, detached homes, but now identified even finer distinctions between types of private housing. They calibrated compatibility and identified nuisances with far greater precision.

Finally, zoning's preference for single-family homes—when seen in the context of a racially segmented mortgage market—meant that most ordinances effectively prescribed racial restriction without ever addressing the issue of race directly. They did so by promoting a well-developed, prewar theory of metropolitan development that described certain groups of people—namely, tenants and racial minorities—as a threat to the "health" and "stability" of neighborhoods of single-family homes. Postwar zoning promoted this vision in concert with a state-sponsored mortgage market that addressed racial issues far more directly—ironically, by institutionalizing a racialized land-use calculus originally formulated by zoning's pioneers.

The result was an unintended, but momentous transfer of both ideas and a regulatory architecture, from the age of eugenics, when zoning was first codified, to the age of modern civil rights protest, when a "zoned

America" became a reality. In a flurry of postwar regulatory activity that brought about the adoption of land-use controls in thousands of suburban municipalities and townships, the machinery and the logic of earlier zoning experiments were introduced to every suburban region in the nation. At the same time, land-use controls grew more precise and often quite arcane, shrouding restriction in a social scientific planning language that further obscured zoning's discriminatory presumptions. Cast solely as a pragmatic response to natural patterns of metropolitan growth, zoning's discriminatory logic grew even more invisible. Meanwhile a decades-old zoning model—both its institutional form and legal reasoning—was used to explain the economic and political necessity of segregating homeowners from renters, the affluent from the poor, and whites from nonwhites. Thousands of local zoning ordinances enabled a racially constructed theory of urban economic development to provide the legal and rhetorical foundation for a new kind of exclusionary politics. A federally subsidized mortgage market, meanwhile, reinforced the new zoning politics by restructuring the housing market along racial lines, and even sometimes saying race out loud.

———

Whether revising existing zoning ordinances or designing their first, local officials built directly upon precedents established before the Depression. After 1940, zoning practices were grounded in the prewar statutory authority codified by the Department of Commerce in 1924 and sanctioned by the Supreme Court two years later. Most state enabling statutes were based on Commerce's standard act, and so most new cities copied its language into their charters. The standard act provided a bridge between an earlier era of zoning experimentation and an era that saw virtually every autonomous local government embrace land-use control. As a result, zoning's postwar practitioners invoked the prewar judicial precedents, most notably the courts' validation of the municipal police power to protect "health and general welfare," to defend local ordinances that excluded renters, the poor, and, by extension, racial minorities.

In most places, the design and administration of zoning ordinances followed well-established patterns. Municipalities established planning departments or boards empowered to draft an ordinance, often with a professional planning consultant. City charters usually required a public hearing on proposed ordinances, and those ordinances generally divided the city into use districts. Once adopted, the zoning ordinance was administered by the city building inspector or a zoning administrator with some background in planning. Existing ordinances could be altered or bypassed in several ways. City councils could amend or totally revise them. Wholesale revision was quite common, but far more routine was the granting of a variance or an amendment. In most cities the Zoning Board of Appeals, appointed by the mayor or staffed by council members, held regularly scheduled public hearings, where community members could object to, or request exemption from, specific provisions. The board could grant a "variance," exempting a property owner from a specific use restriction, while leaving the larger ordinance itself intact; for example, an owner might be permitted to exceed a floor-space maximum or granted an exemption for a nonconforming use. If denied, the owner could petition to amend the ordinance, which would alter the use designation only for the parcel in question, a practice known as "spot zoning." According to contemporary observers, spot zoning served the politically influential quite well. Of the more than 1,000 amendments made to the Chicago zoning ordinance between 1942 and 1953, for example, "a large percentage . . . show[ed] evidence of political pressure or personal influence."[94]

Restrictive zoning also retained its focus on separating "incompatible" land uses, privileging the single-family home, and maximizing the ratio between revenues and costs (i.e., "fiscal zoning"). What changed during these years were the precision and language of the typical municipal ordinance. Beginning in the 1940s, professional planners, federal funding, and heightened metropolitan competition combined to make comprehensive ordinances more complex, technical, and restrictive. The "relative simplicity of early statutes," as Beverly Pooley writes, gave way to a new emphasis on planning language, administrative procedure, and court review. Meanwhile large-lot zoning fast became the trademark suburban land-use strategy. Setting a minimum size for residential plats—generally a quarter acre or more, or twice the size of the typical prewar lot—helped communities maintain low population densities and required the construction of larger, more costly homes. The result was reduced expenditures for services and infrastructural investments, fewer schoolchildren, and properties with higher assessed valuations (which generated greater tax revenues). Few suburbs totally forbade smaller lots. But by the late 1960s, over 40.3 percent of the nation's smaller SMSA cities included some districts requiring a minimum lot of a quarter to a half acre, 20 percent had areas requiring a half- to one-acre minimums, and 22 percent included areas with one-acre minimums. The most uniform and restrictive standards were usually found in newer suburbs with large tracts of undeveloped land—in places like Troy and Southfield, Michigan, for example—and in the most affluent enclaves. In New York's Westchester County, 78 percent of the vacant land zoned for residential uses required a minimum lot size of one acre, and 52 percent of the total had a two-acre minimum. Meanwhile, most rezoning for apartments was done on a case by case basis, giving local jurisdictions further control over design, size, number of bedrooms (to discourage families with many school-age children), and often the race of the occupant population. Another large-lot zoning tactic was termed "overzoning," or the creation of "holding zones," whereby officials set enormous lot minimums in undeveloped areas with the sole purpose of prohibiting development until regional growth patterns could be predicted. In Washington, D.C., for example, ten-acre minimums helped assure that favored developers would eventually gain access to chosen parcels.[95]

Refinement of the zoning ordinance itself provided another means for exercising tight control over development patterns. Most notable was the proliferation in the number and types of use districts, as a finely calibrated hierarchy of zones began to segregate uses once deemed compatible. Whereas most prewar regulations defined four categories of use ("single family residential," "general residential," "business," and "industrial"), postwar ordinances usually established multiple residential subdistricts. By the late 1940s, detached dwellings were usually placed in the new residence A zone, while semidetached units were relegated to the separate residence AA zone. Similarly, general residential zones gave way to residence B for multiple-family or townhouse-style structures and residence C for large apartment complexes. Chicago's ordinance of 1957 defined sixteen major use categories and over seventy subdistricts. Further complementing the lot-size requirements were minimums for setbacks, frontages, the space between buildings, floor space requirements, and the ratio or amount of open space permissible on each lot. Most communities adopted one of four standard national building codes, yet often amended these with requirements that exceeded minimum health and safety standards, dramatically increased building costs, and excluded middle- or low-income residents.[96]

The net result was the limitation, strict segregation, and often total exclusion of multiple-family dwellings in the nation's fast-growing suburbs. In 1958 the Regional Plan Association discovered that eleven of the sixteen communities examined in Westchester County, New York, had set one-acre minimums for all of its residential zones, while four of the remaining five did so for half or more of their territory. With comparable patterns curtailing apartment construction nationwide, by 1960 there were only 2,674,000 apartment units in the nation's suburbs, compared with 15,180,000 single-family units. Apartment construction did increase in the late 1960s, but existing zoning ordinances (and new variances) restricted it to older and less affluent suburbs, while continuing to segregate rentals sharply from detached homes. By 1970, municipalities in Bergen County, New Jersey, had zoned 27,000 acres of undeveloped land exclusively for single-family homes, compared with 131 acres for apartments.[97]

The rationale for limiting apartment construction would sound familiar to zoning's founding generation: protecting the "public health and welfare" and eliminating "nuisances." By the 1970s, writes Danielson, "almost all zoning ordinances consider[ed] apartments an inferior and therefore more restricted land use than single-family residences." Multiple-unit dwellings purportedly undermined residential environments. The courts agreed, consistently validating the new array of postwar zoning tools in the face of numerous challenges. Beginning with the first challenge to lot-size minimums, *Simon v. Town of Needham*, in 1942, courts consistently upheld "large lot" zoning,[98] defending the practice, as did the *Simon* court, by arguing that lower residential densities would protect the "public health and welfare."

But that court went further, reversing earlier decisions that forbade municipalities from considering "aesthetic" variables (or what it called the "character" of the neighborhood) when making designations about compatible use. In the wake of *Simon*, rulings on restrictive zoning focused increasingly on protection of the "public welfare" while liberally expanding the term's meaning. Setting perhaps the most influential precedent was *Lionshead Lake, Inc. v. Wayne Township* (1952), in which the New Jersey state supreme court validated large-lot zoning and minimum floor-space requirements by invoking the public health argument long central to zoning advocacy. Arguing that overcrowding threatened "the well-being of our most important institution, the home," the court ruled that urban housing standards could not be applied to suburban residential areas and that they were especially inappropriate for the rearing of children. Most courts followed the *Lionshead* ruling, disregarding an earlier Michigan decision that struck down the aesthetic argument. By the early 1960s, courts generally defended restrictive ordinances by interpreting "welfare" to embrace "the community's interest in appearance and preservation of property values."[99]

Judicial support for zoning also fueled the continued transformation, or at least liberal reinterpretation, of the nineteenth-century nuisance doctrine. Just as prewar courts cited local preferences as *prima facie* evidence that a use was nonconforming, more and more postwar courts accepted the claim that anything deemed by community members as a threat to property values was, by definition, a nuisance. By the 1960s, a legal doctrine originally established to protect individuals and neighborhoods from fire, disease, unpleasant odors, or exposure to toxins had become the legal standard for protecting homeowners from the threat posed by commercial development, apartment buildings, or even modest detached dwellings. Writing in 1975 about the first half century of Euclidian zoning, Michelle White noted that its justification in the nuisance doctrine had been "stretched beyond recognition," invoked to ban motels, trailers, discount stores, and even modern architecture. Citing the need to protect the community's "health and welfare," she concluded, officials were now effectively eliminating any objectionable land uses by simply labeling them "public nuisances." [100]

————

It was in individual suburbs and metropolitan regions that the rapid spread and increasing complexity of restrictive zoning shaped patterns of development and settlement as well as whites' ideas about the necessity of exclusion. Detroit area land-use politics revealed zoning's impact on both the physical and ideological suburb. After 1940, its municipalities adopted ordinances that reinforced the class and racial homogeneity created by mortgage lending practices and private acts of discrimination. Meanwhile local zoning politics immersed residents in very public, technical battles over development and the rights of homeowners. Everyday land-use politics provided an ongoing primer in the rules of healthy suburban development, the urgency of separating incompatible land uses, and the supposedly impersonal market forces that required exclusion, whether of apartment buildings, factories, or black people. Local politics simultaneously abetted racial and class exclusion while reminding residents about zoning's supposed fairness and impartiality.

It would have been very difficult for any Detroit suburbanite, whether a long-time resident or newcomer, to ignore the politics of zoning, planning, and exclusion. There was simply too much activity, too many controversies, and too much political maneuvering, both within individual municipalities and between them. The adoption or revision of a municipal zoning ordinance, numerous spot zonings, battles over proposed commercial or multiple-unit development, and ongoing debates over municipal master plans: these topics regularly dominated news headlines, council sessions, and neighborhood association meetings. In older, first-generation suburbs the topic was often the comprehensive revision of an existing ordinance to accommodate regional growth patterns and changes in the postwar real estate market. Royal Oak created a nine-member City Plan Commission in 1940 to consider zoning reform and appointed a Zoning Revision Committee the following year. Its 1943 recommendation for a comprehensive redesign was welcomed enthusiastically by residents and quickly adopted by city officials. Dearborn followed suit in 1945, creating its own Plan Commission and asking it to draft a master plan and revised zoning map. Meanwhile in neighboring communities, incorporations created the new suburbs that immediately exercised their authority to zone. Clawson incorporated in 1940 and within a year adopted a citywide land-use ordinance. The Troy Township residents who drafted and campaigned for home-rule status in 1954 simultaneously commissioned a new study of area land use, in anticipation of adopting a zoning ordinance. The new City of Troy published that ordinance in 1956. The following year, it adopted subdivision control regulations and, already looking ahead, hired a planning consultant to prepare a "Thoroughfare Study," the first component of the suburb's new Master Plan Study. Clawson published its new General Development Plan in 1957, produced in collaboration with a private consulting group.[101]

Passage or comprehensive revision of a zoning ordinance rarely provided closure, however, as council and zoning board meetings became the sites of ongoing and contentious battles over development. Often the complainant was a property owner frustrated by new restrictions that prevented commercial uses or even the construction of a modest (i.e., less expensive) home. Yet most battles and most high-profile controversies involved challenges by homeowners and their neighborhood associations to proposed rezonings that would allow business development or apartment buildings near neighborhoods of single-family homes. In 1947 a suburban columnist reported that fights over Royal Oak's new ordinance caused a "continual row" at the regular city commission meetings, practically turning the sessions into a "courthouse." (By year's end, the suburb's zoning map—adopted sixteen years earlier—had been revised ninety-two times.) The *Independent* reported a similar scene at Dearborn's council meetings the following year: "Just as sure as a [zoning] change is proposed or petitioned for, so there is an objection made to that change." Meanwhile, officials were required by statute (and by the practical requirement of sustaining electoral support) to solicit feedback on proposals for comprehensive zoning revision. So suburban officials and residents were constantly debating development in public settings. In 1956, the Oak Park Planning Commission issued studies and plans for land use, zoning, neighborhood planning, and parking, while acting upon ninety zoning requests. It approved construction of nine new residential subdivisions. Soon after Southfield incorporated in 1958, its Planning Commission began work on a comprehensive land-use plan by commissioning technical studies, meeting with community groups, and holding public hearings on its draft proposal. This work eventually produced a Master Plan, made public in May 1961, designed to serve as a template for a new zoning ordinance.

That was a busy year for the suburbs of southeast Oakland County. In August, Berkley published a Future Land Use Plan, and weeks later its Planning Commission held public hearings to solicit community responses. In October, the Madison Heights City Council held a joint meeting with its Planning Commission to begin work on the Comprehensive Master Plan Program, funded in part by a federal Section 701 grant. Hazel Park's Planning Commission was already hard at work on its new Master Plan, which it released in 1962. And by then Southfield had initiated a "comprehensive 701 program" to consider changes to its Master Plan and Zoning Ordinance, both of which were just one year old. Sparsely populated neighboring suburbs watched regional developments carefully, and several initiated preliminary stages of the planning and zoning process. In the fall of 1961, the residents of Northville Township voted to create its first Planning Commission.[102]

Each suburb's battles over planning and land use were unique, yet two outcomes—one developmental and one ideological or political—were repeated throughout the Detroit metropolitan area. First, most suburbs reserved the lion's share of land for residential development and set increasingly restrictive terms for the homes that could be built. Royal Oak's revised 1943 ordinance (combined with subsequent changes) divided the suburb into 33 distinct zones, reserved virtually all residential areas for single-family homes, meticulously segregated land uses deemed nonconforming, and set detailed construction standards designed to further reinforce the suburb's self-proclaimed image as a "city of homes." It rezoned many residence B districts, which had permitted low-density apartment construction, to business use or to a new designation, residence AA, which allowed two-family dwellings. Notably these units were required to be of the "single front entrance type, to preserve the same appearance as a single-family residence." (The goal was to "prevent the influx of any apartment houses, duplexes, terraces or other multiple family dwellings.") In 1952, the city increased the lot size requirements for single-family homes from 4,500 to 5,000 square feet in residence AA, AAA, B, and C districts. It also overruled Plan Commission recommendations under pressure from a local homeowners group, the West Wood Community Association, by rezoning several lots to single-family residence and a residence C district to business B (see fig. 5.2).[103]

Changing expectations, federal mortgage requirements, and homeowner activism combined to ensure similar outcomes in most of the region's fast-growing suburbs. During the war, Hazel Park increased floor space minimums in residence A districts to meet the FHA requirements for defense housing. Oak Park was largely undeveloped at war's end, so in 1948 city

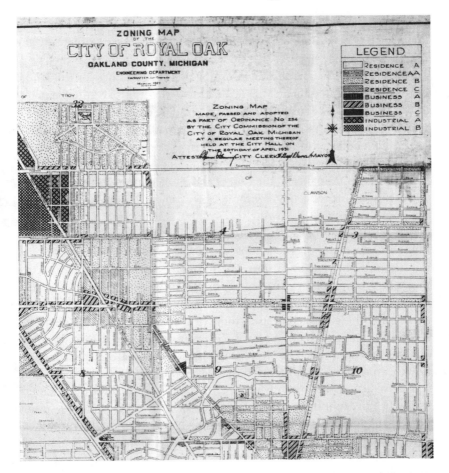

5.2 City of Royal Oak Zoning Ordinance and Map No. 254, April 20, 1931, as amended to January 1, 1949. Many suburban zoning maps were drafted and adopted before the period of dramatic suburban growth following World War II. During the 1940s and after, most suburbs adopted zoning ordinances or comprehensively revised existing ones. Pictured is a close up of the revised map for Royal Oak. By the late 1940s, the vast majority of the suburb's territory had been restricted to residence A development. Visible at the top left and bottom center are two areas of the city reserved for concentrated business and industrial activity. Much of this land, too, was eventually rezoned for residential use. Royal Oak Public Library, History Collection. Photographed by Ken Music.

officials revamped the existing zoning ordinance (originally filed in 1929), creating five grades of residential use, one grade for business, and one for "light industry." The dividing line was Nine Mile Road; most of the land to its north was reserved for residential development, primarily single-family houses, and industrial construction was restricted to the south. Within a year, the council and planning commission were already at work on what they called a new, "modern," and even more restrictive city plan. By the time it was unveiled, with some fanfare, at the city Fire Hall in the fall of 1950, its guidelines had already informed two spot zonings for residential development south of Nine Mile Road. One of the rulings rezoned a parcel to residence AA, so that William Feld, a Ferndale developer, could build a $5,000,000 project of single-family homes, separated by a greenbelt from nearby light industry. Oak Park's master plan was repeatedly debated at public hearings, but never officially adopted. Still it provided the guidelines for a new Zoning Ordinance of the City of Oak Park, approved at the March 3, 1952, City Council meeting, "without objection" from the audience.[104]

More than simply redrawing the region's land-use maps, the ongoing debate over spot zonings and comprehensive ordinance revision constantly immersed residents in discussions about local control, property owners' rights, and residential exclusion. The technical details of zoning practice might be footnotes in the history of postwar racial politics if land-use battles had not been such a prominent fixture of suburban life for millions of Americans. These local contests introduced white residents to the scientific, seemingly race-neutral rationale for segregating both land uses and people. The sheer amount of activity associated with zoning—the debates, consultations, proposals and counterproposals, referenda, hearings, meetings, and legislative actions—constantly exposed residents to tested formulas for ensuring healthy suburban development, to experts' rationales for separating incompatible land uses, and to invocations of the supposedly impersonal market forces that made exclusion essential. By partaking in local planning debates or simply following the land-use controversy of the moment in the local press, average residents quickly became familiar with the language of zoning and the most common justifications for restriction of any kind.

Key terminology and concepts of this planning language dated back to the era of zoning's creation. The ordinances adopted in metropolitan Detroit after 1940 borrowed heavily from the statutory language set out by Michigan's original zoning and planning acts, largely unchanged since their passage in 1921. Thus local suburban statutes required that regulation be part of a plan designed "to promote public health, safety, and general welfare," and they stipulated that all land-use decisions be made "with reasonable consideration" of a district's "peculiar suitability for particular uses, the conservation of property values and the general trend and character of building and population development." Statutory language quickly found its way into political speech as well. When Royal Oak announced the creation of the City Plan Commission in 1940, it described its action as "an emergency ordinance necessary for the public welfare and safety." Existing subdivision regulations were either outdated or expired, officials added, which meant that "large areas [of the city] are inadequately protected by restrictions."[105]

And when zoning ordinances were proposed, revised, or challenged, the ensuing debates turned on the language of land-use economics, law, appraisal, and marketing, a language produced by decades of federal intervention, court rulings, and the expansion and professionalization of the real estate industry. For this reason Detroit's suburban residents not only came to share assumptions about what kinds of properties or people were most valuable and which kinds of properties or people posed a threat; residents also came to use the same technical, normative language to describe both value and threat. They heard this language in multiple venues. Social scientific rules concerning compatibility were a staple of land-use reports and studies produced by professional planners for suburban governments. Detroit's suburban councils and planning bodies commissioned zoning ordinances, building and subdivision regulations, comprehensive plans, applications for HHFA Urban Planning Assistance Grants, and studies of water supplies, recreation, traffic, parking, urban renewal, population, industrial development, and central business district development. Meanwhile when officials or homeowners' groups argued their cases for or against a rezoning, they hired planners and lawyers to present their cases. Throughout the postwar decades, council and zoning board meetings, plan commission meetings, and public hearings exposed residents to a constant stream of urban experts who argued over the merits of restriction and exclusion.[106]

What urban experts said in their reports, recommendations, and testimony was that neighborhoods of single-family homes represented the "best use" of residential property and that homeowners could justifiably exclude a wide range of uses and people from view. Suburban officials and residents adopted expert guidelines and invoked their terminology. They learned that multiple-family developments threatened their well-being by looking to the zoning enabling legislation and court rulings that described apartments as a nonresidential land use. They turned to federal appraisal manuals and real estate handbooks that described apartment complexes, factories, or "incompatible" populations as an actuarial risk. Thus when Royal Oak did make room for apartments—it was one of the few suburbs in the region to do so—it only allowed them in areas deemed "nonresidential." In July 1951, the council rezoned 93 acres for industrial use, included a provision allowing for residence C apartment construction and added a requirement that a "buffer zone" be established "between residence and industrial areas." Royal Oak homeowners adopted the same language and rationales when they organized to block rezonings that would permit apartment construction in residence A neighborhoods, arguing in one 1955 episode that the parcel in question would be better off left vacant. Popular support for restrictive zoning was constantly shaped and reinforced by professional planners. When Royal Oak's city commission denied a rezoning for apartments near a residence A zone in 1964, they cited the advice of the private consultants and planning commission members who recommended against extending "the multiple-family zone into the residential area." Throughout suburban Detroit, exclusion of development and populations deemed non-compatible was viewed as a practical necessity and regularly became a point of pride. Southfield's 1961 Master Plan boasted that the suburbs' "homes consist almost wholly of single-family residences occupied by their owners" and that both percentages were "considerably above the Detroit tri-county area average." "These two characteristics," the planning commission concluded, "point to an absence of multiple units and rental units." [107]

When examining the local politics of suburban land use after 1940, it is important to keep in mind two of the foundational assumptions that guided white builders, lenders, housing officials, economists, appraisers, realtors, and homeowners when they entered debates over land use, restriction, and exclusion. First, they viewed the rules for land-use regulation and real estate practice as objective science, as a set of practices codified by experts, endorsed by the courts and federal officials, and monitored by an army of professional planners. Second, they believed—and that same land-use science confirmed this—that neighborhoods of single-family homes, and particularly the new suburban enclaves devoted exclusively to such development, must remain all-white. The record suggests that most whites generally agreed that excluding any incompatible development or population—a drive-in theater, a factory, a low-income housing development, or an individual black family—was simply good land-use management. The well-established fields of land-use economics and planning said so. The courts echoed this view. And federal officials endorsed it wholeheartedly. Reasonable exclusion of *any* kind was viewed not as an ideological matter, but rather as a means to protect the health and public welfare of people who owned their homes. And virtually all of the people who owned their homes in the fast-growing suburban fringe were white.

So widespread was this logic—so self-evident the assumption that good planning and zoning ensured the maintenance of prosperous, stable, and racially homogeneous communities—that the Royal Oak Chamber of Commerce casually invoked it in a 1954 promotional brochure designed to attract retailers and industrial enterprises to their suburb. Entitled "Royal Oak: Michigan's Most Promising Community," the sixteen-page booklet introduced potential investors to the suburb's infrastructure, local government, population, and neighborhoods. The text offered a capsule history of Royal Oak's good fortune, explaining that the auto industry had sparked the community's stunning growth while good planning and city management kept the suburb a nice place to live, work, and, therefore, invest. Next to a reproduction of Royal Oak's "Business and Industrial Zone Map," the brochure explained that Royal Oak's rapid growth had "none of the earmarks of a boom town" because it was managed by the efforts of "professional city planning engineers, architects, and topographers." The result was a city that attracted residents who mostly "fall into highly-skilled worker brackets" (especially in the automotive, chemical, rubber, and steel industries) and who were relatively affluent ("41% of the [retail] sales made in Oakland County are made in the Royal Oak market area," and Royal Oak city "has an effective buying income per family that is 62% above the national average"). And good planning, the ROCC explained, ensured that "a high percentage of workers residing in this area own their own homes." "Strong pride in property ownership is indicated by the maintenance and improvement of their residences. This sort of pride results in a permanent labor force of much higher than average skill and efficiency, in whom initiative is an inherent trait." Employers would "find in Royal Oak the prime human ingredient necessary to success in industry and commerce." And they could expect the suburb's "nearly 100% white" population to grow to 65,000 by year's end. "This unusual and rapid growth is due not only to the automobile but also to the kind of living and community advantages Royal Oak residents enjoy."[108]

Writing about the "Zoning Game" in 1966, Richard Babcock decried the fragmentation of local power in the nation's metropolitan regions, attributing it in large measure to the desire of white and affluent suburban residents to control zoning, and thus to exclude. Their "overriding motivation," he wrote, "is less economic than it is social," less about *what* to exclude than *whom*. "When they protest that a change in dwelling type will cause a decline in the value of their property," Babcock explained, "their economic conclusion is based upon a social judgment." Many postwar critics have echoed this criticism, arguing that the constant interplay between social and economic factors fueled the politics of exclusion in postwar America. In 1968, the American Society of Planning Officials attributed the spread of large lot zoning to the overlap of what it called "economic" and "racial" motivations, noting that calls for the preservation of community "character" and the maintenance of "high standards" served as euphemisms for maintaining racial homogeneity. In 1965, James Coke and John Gargan popularized new terms, explaining the relationship between the "fiscal" motivations for zoning and the "amenity" or "homogeneity" motivations. "The fact that [these motivations] operate in the same direction," they concluded, "complicates matters considerably. It is not at all certain that removing the fiscal dilemma would produce significant alterations in local land-use policies. It could well be that the striving to maximize amenity and homogeneity values would continue to be enough to maintain the widespread demand for low density development enforced through zoning." [109]

What these critics share, even with uncritical defenders of restrictive zoning, is the assumption that the economic and ideological motivations that fueled zoning's popularity—the "fiscal" and "homogeneity" values—were conceptually discrete in the minds of the residents and officials who promoted exclusion. Yet the origins of racial segregation in the postwar suburbs, both in the mortgage market and in municipal land-use politics, are not rooted in "ideologically" motivated decisions about "economics" or in a "racially" tinged "localism." Whites constructed a discriminatory mortgage market and employed discriminatory land-use strategies because they came to understand the economics and the politics of suburban growth in racially specific terms. For countless whites, ideas about metropolitan growth, housing, and property were racially constructed.

It was the racial assumptions of white planners, businesspeople, local officials, and homeowners—captured, for example, in a Chamber of Commerce promotional brochure—that made the politics of exclusion so intractable in the postwar suburbs. And it was the promotion of this calculus by myriad local, regional, and national bodies, both public and private, that made whites' desire for racial exclusion both an enormously powerful political force and, in important ways, a largely invisible one. At times the market imperative defense of exclusion was outlined explicitly, for example in early editions of the FHA *Underwriting Manual* and private-sector appraisal handbooks. At other times the calculus was more coded or simply assumed, as postwar zoning law and practice reveal. In either case, suburban residents were invested in assumptions about property, neighborhoods, and the nature of the free market for housing that enabled them to construct a well-organized, and sometimes quite fierce, defense of their privileges—as homeowners, as citizens, and as white people.

PART TWO

Race and Development in Metropolitan Detroit, 1940–1970

CHAPTER SIX

Defending and Defining the New Neighborhood: The Politics of Exclusion in Royal Oak, 1940–1955

It is surprising that Royal Oak's business leaders, when marketing their suburb to potential investors in 1954, described it as "virtually 100% white." Boosters, residents, and local officials were constantly promoting and celebrating the fast-growing community after World War II, yet they rarely talked openly about race. The suburb did manage, along with its Oakland County neighbors, to keep black people out. Almost without exception, racial minorities were prevented from renting or purchasing homes in Royal Oak. But there was seldom a need to discuss this fact or to acknowledge residents' racial preferences. Federal selective credit programs ensured blacks' exclusion from the suburban mortgage market, restrictive zoning excluded most renters and low-income families, and residents joined realtors in steering or scaring away minorities who had the means and will to settle there. Royal Oak was never asked to accept construction of federal projects for low-income residents or war workers—housing generally open to black people—and so it never experienced the kind of controversies that forced other white communities to defend their homogeneity openly.[1]

Instead during the postwar years Royal Oak and most of the region's suburban municipalities remained almost exclusively white, without much fanfare. In 1950, the census bureau counted two Royal Oak housing units occupied by blacks, one of them rented and the other privately owned. There were five black people living in Hazel Park (population 17,757) and nine in Oak Park (population 5,258). Typical residents of the Oakland County suburbs seldom had contact with black people unless they spent time in Detroit or employed a domestic servant. Or driving along a section of Eight Mile Road, the border between Ferndale and Detroit (see fig. 6.1), they would see black day-laborers gathered near the intersections at Wyoming and Livernois avenues on most mornings, hoping to be hired by white contractors

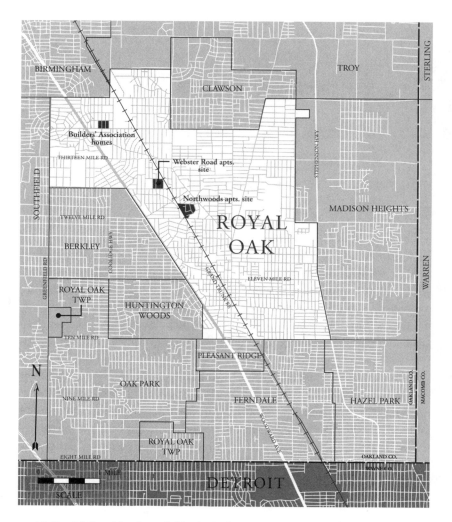

6.1 Royal Oak and Southeast Oakland suburbs, 1955. Because most of the subdivisions
in these first-generation suburbs were platted before the Depression, most of their
residential blocks, especially in neighborhoods closer to Detroit, were designed like
those in Detroit's residential districts, just across the border in Wayne County. Easy
access to Detroit was a selling point for the Oakland County suburbs when developers
marketed their housing in the 1920s. The Eight Mile–Wyoming neighborhood, a black
enclave in northern Detroit, bordered Ferndale and Royal Oak Township. Livernois
intersects with Eight Mile Road in Ferndale, just west of Woodward Boulevard.
Wyoming runs parallel, a mile to the west. Map by Jason Frank.

seeking help for suburban construction sites. Whites referred to the scene as the local "slave market."[2]

Despite suburbanites' increasing isolation from black people, the region's rapid demographic transformation did not go unnoticed. Jobs in Detroit's war production industries drew thousands of African American migrants to the city between 1940 and 1944, mostly from Arkansas, Alabama, the Carolinas, Georgia, Mississippi, and Louisiana. During those years the city's black population increased from 149,119 to 213,345. After the war, Detroit's industrial base and the deterioration of the southern sharecropping economy helped sustain the growth, and by 1950 the city's black population had doubled to just over 300,000. White people were very conscious of this fact. Many of those with jobs in Detroit found themselves working with or around black people for the first time. Meanwhile overcrowding in the city's black residential enclaves intensified. When war broke out, Detroit's black residents were largely restricted to a handful of neighborhoods; most lived downtown, along the corridor just east of Woodward Boulevard, and there were small enclaves in the northern and western sections of the city, such as the Eight Mile–Wyoming neighborhood, home of the daily "slave market." But these neighborhoods could not accommodate the newcomers, and so more and more blacks were forced to move into sections of northwest Detroit previously viewed as "white." Residential blocks sometimes changed from all-white to mostly black occupancy in just three or four years. White Detroiters responded with vigilance, forming nearly two hundred "neighborhood improvement," "homeowners'," or "protective" associations, most created for the sole purpose of policing neighborhood racial boundaries. Resistance was especially fierce in the Northeast Side, the Wyoming Corridor, and the Lower West Side, where white homeowners intimidated realtors, vandalized dwellings built for or purchased by blacks, and terrorized black families brave enough to make the move. In the 1949 mayoral contest, Albert Cobo defeated the prolabor candidate George Edwards by promising homeowners that he would oppose the racial integration of housing and neighborhoods.[3]

Because blacks faced even greater obstacles entering the suburban housing market, the region's suburban whites rarely felt the same sense of urgency. Still a black population desperate for quality housing continued to test the residential color line, so homeowners in places like Royal Oak remained vigilant. Blacks knew that they were not welcome in most of the region's suburbs. Occasionally a well publicized act of harassment or brutality would remind them; in 1956, for example, a black woman in Royal Oak Township was beaten at her home by masked men and later threatened with death. Far more common were neighborhood mobilizations similar to those in Detroit to prevent the sale of a home to a black family or to halt construction of rental housing. As the editors of the South Oakland *Daily Tribune* acknowledged in 1956, "many residents here prefer to live in all-white communities."[4]

Residents' racial preoccupations were also revealed by their enthusiasm for what might be called "recreational" racism—the open embrace of degrading racial parody common in the 1940s and 1950s. The *Amos 'n' Andy* show is only the best known of the radio and television programs, popular films, novelty items, advertising campaigns, cartoons, and even federally funded minstrel programs scripted by the USO that disseminated racial caricature to white audiences virtually every day. These were the texts that taught self-described white people about black people's character and capacity, portraying them as unsophisticated, irascible, dirty, prone to criminality, licentious, and simple minded.[5] Detroit's white suburbanites were not passive recipients of this imagery. Many felt comfortable donning blackface at public fairs and club functions. Local radio programs, advertising campaigns, and popular amusements regularly traded on minstrel imagery. On the weekend of February 9–10, 1948, for example, the Royal Oak chapter of the Lions Club raised money for blind children by staging a minstrel show. Family and friends gathered in a local middle school auditorium to watch club members, dressed in blackface, perform a traditional minstrel chorus and end men skits. A select few took turns singing solos. Joining this annual event two years later was Floyd Miller, the publisher and chief editorialist of the *Daily Tribune.* He and his son, Philip (who took over the paper in 1954) participated throughout the 1950s and early 1960s. Philip often served as musical director. Beginning in 1953, the performances were directed by William Spence, a Lions member from the neighboring suburb of Birmingham. The *Tribune* regularly updated readers about the club's preparations, announced upcoming performances, and provided extensive news coverage of the annual shows (see fig. 6.2).[6]

Most of Detroit's white suburbanites were invested in maintaining their communities' racial homogeneity and protecting—even celebrating—the privileges that came with their whiteness. Yet only on occasion did they openly discuss race in the context of housing and development, at least in a language commonly regarded as racist. Scholars have reconstructed numerous examples of suburban mobilizations that explicitly targeted racial minorities in places such as Dearborn and Grosse Point, Michigan; Cicero, Illinois; and the San Fernando Valley in Los Angeles.[7] But suburbs like Royal Oak, where homogeneity was assumed and enforced but rarely discussed,

'Ladeez, Gen'mun,' Be Seated!

Presenting the sixth annual Lions club Minstrel and Fun Show, a collection of acts, skits and entertainments skillfully blended by an all-star (and male) cast of 40 affable, amiable members of the Royal Oak Lions club. Opening performance for the re-creation of the oldtime blackface review will be at 8 o'clock tonight in the Royal Oak high school auditorium, and successive performances will be given Tuesday and Wednesday nights. All proceeds are used by the Lions for their national project of sight-saving.

WILLIAM SPENCE

LYLE BROWN   ARTHUR L. SNOW

6.2. *Daily Tribune* coverage of the Lions Club's annual minstrel show, 1953 and 1959. Beginning in 1948, the Royal Oak chapter of the Lions Club staged an annual minstrel show to raise money for blind children. Hundreds of residents participated as performers, set designers, and musicians. Among the regular cast members were Floyd and Philip Miller, the editors and publishers of the *Daily Tribune*. They used their editorial column and the paper's news section to promote the programs and update South Oakland County residents on the annual preparations. The shows were performed in blackface until 1960. Reprinted with permission of *The Daily Tribune*, Royal Oak, Michigan. Photographed by Ken Music.

The entire company lines up for a portrait.

He's Harry Hewitt — from businessman to blackface in four smudgy steps.

6.2 (Continued)

were far more typical, a fact that has created considerable confusion in studies of postwar racial politics. With the exception of enforcing race-restrictive covenants (which the Supreme Court struck down in 1948), suburbs like Royal Oak were very quiet about their racial preferences in the postwar era. So is it appropriate to describe the politics of exclusion in these places as racially motivated or, at least, racially informed, when there is little obvious evidence of racially discriminatory intent? Does race matter even when there are few race-specific documents or racist tirades to illustrate it?

The case studies that follow demonstrate that the politics and economics of postwar suburban growth required suburban whites to consider racial variables, encouraged them to demand homogeneity, and helped shape their understanding and defense of residential segregation itself. In metropolitan Detroit, whites participated in a regional and ultimately a national politics that assumed the necessity of racial exclusion and, corollary to this, the racial intent of restrictive land-use practices. Racial intent was not always expressed in familiar racial terms. Blatant expressions of bigotry do not, alone, tell the story of white racism in the postwar suburb. Countless people of European descent expressed, acted upon, and in the process helped to transform their ideas about race and property by living in a resegregated metropolis and participating in local political mobilizations that effectively policed racial boundaries. In all-white communities like Royal Oak, where the need for racial exclusion was assumed and racial homogeneity openly celebrated, residents grew invested in a development politics that described all incompatible land uses, whether buildings or populations, as actuarial risks. For this reason, whites' support for restrictive zoning seldom represented a self-conscious attempt to hide or mask "racist" goals. Large-lot zoning was not a thinly veiled stand-in for instruments that achieved racial exclusion more openly, embraced because it deflected attention from whites' "real" motives. Rather, whites supported restrictive zoning because they saw it as articulating and defending their rights, as homeowners, to make decisions about compatibility, at a time when most whites were encouraged to understand racial segregation as little more than a principle of real estate economics. Whites' participation in suburban growth politics was instrumental to making the "market imperative" narrative about racial exclusion the dominant narrative, part of whites' everyday, commonsense understanding of metropolitan change.

One result was that the prewar history of zoning and real estate economics yielded an unintended postwar outcome. Zoning's founding generation had been motivated by many goals: reducing urban congestion, protecting public health, maintaining property values, and safeguarding comfortable residential neighborhoods. Yet what eventually unified its most influential advocates was the principle that certain categories of development and tenancy posed a risk to white homeowners. Racial integration was seen as one of those measurable, calculable risks, in part because race was still officially seen as a marker of heritable difference. Because zoning's founders simply assumed that the "more favored" environment for family life, to cite the court's ruling in *Euclid,* was a white neighborhood of detached dwellings, racial prerogative was subsumed in early twentieth-century discourses about property markets and property law. Meanwhile whites monopolized the residential real estate industry and had other legal means to exclude unwanted populations, and so early zoning ordinances rarely needed explicit racial rules.

After 1940, in a radically different economic and political environment, existing zoning statutes and land-use theory provided suburban communities with the authority to exclude entire classes of people as well as a social scientific logic that enforced whites' racial preferences. And they did so in ostensibly race-neutral terms—indeed in a language that claimed to rise above ideology altogether. Prewar zoning politics created legal instruments and a body of economic and legal knowledge that empowered postwar homeowners to exclude a wide range of developments and populations, while describing all threats, physical or human, as interchangeable. As more and more whites became suburban homeowners after 1940, and as mortgage markets and private-sector discrimination rapidly created new patterns of metropolitan segregation, the existing zoning machinery and the body of work in real estate economics proved especially useful for accentuating and justifying discriminatory patterns of settlement and property ownership.

Converging during these years in suburban Detroit, and in fast-growing suburban communities nationwide, were ideological and political transformations with discrete, if also interconnected, histories. Metropolitan growth and its particular sociospatial formation were governed after 1940 by a mortgage market and municipal land-use instruments that reduced racial exclusion to actuarial terms, thus divorcing it, rhetorically at least, from issues of personal preference or "ideology." At the same time, whites in the public and private sectors were convinced that postwar economic growth, along with the pattern of inequality that it produced, was solely a market-driven rather than a state-subsidized phenomenon. Finally the national politics of prosperity and Cold War celebrated the sanctity of the nuclear family, its refuge, the single-family home, and consumers' power to sustain Americans' freedom and unprecedented good fortune. This convergence resonated quite powerfully in the nation's fast growing suburbs, and in the battles to protect these new "sanctuaries" for the American family. In places like Royal Oak the seemingly mundane politics of restrictive zoning and residential exclusion helped shape residents' ideas about their property and their rights, as suburban homeowners and as citizens, and, uniting both, as white people.

Detroit's white suburbanites supported restrictive zoning after 1940 not because it was a tool of racial exclusion per se. Rather, they understood zoning as a means to protect communities of property owners, and they believed that racial mixing was a threat to property. Postwar suburban zoning politics was an exercise of municipal power that confirmed and protected the property status quo, in an era that assumed the need for racial separation. Meanwhile whites' investment in the new land-use science encouraged them to view racial exclusion not as a matter of personal preference or ideology but as a market necessity. While scholars generally draw sharp distinctions between residential exclusion that was ideologically motivated and exclusion motivated by economic interest, a careful examination of land-use politics in the Detroit suburbs reveals that few whites made sharp distinctions between economic and racial threats to their communities.[8] They endorsed a range of exclusionary practices that targeted minority populations in practice without necessarily specifying racial intent. Meanwhile they relied upon a real estate and home finance market that followed strict racial protocols. In both cases, whites insisted that exclusion was not about race per se but about markets for property. They did so by invoking and refashioning a story about property and exclusion built into zoning statutes, land use, and the national market for mortgage credit.

Blocking the Webster Road and Northwood Village Apartments

If you lived in Royal Oak it was difficult, after 1940, *not* to be preoccupied with land-use issues. Rapid growth and regional competition over tax revenues immersed its residents in constant debates over development, zoning, and strategies for maintaining neighborhood character. This was a national phenomenon, for millions of families bought homes in suburbs that inherited the home-rule option and its political protocols and in metropolitan regions that fast became patchworks of municipalities vying for control over income-producing development. Each suburb had a unique history, unique exigencies, and unique preferences. But their local battles over land use played out in the context of a more or less nationally standardized zoning politics and a national mortgage revolution. And those national transformations created a new, fairly uniform kind of suburban exclusionary politics and political culture, creating considerable support for restrictive zoning and in the process drawing residents into sustained, technical debates about suburban growth and the rights of people who owned their homes.

In Royal Oak two high-profile battles over apartment construction created a powerful new coalition in favor of restriction. Between 1947 and 1949, homeowners blocked rezonings that would have permitted construction of two large developments, the first on Webster Road, the next just blocks away on Vinsetta Avenue. The battles energized the suburb's homeowners' associations, which in turn organized homeowners and ensured election of a sympathetic city commission. Local development controversies created and then sustained communities of protest and a stable electoral coalition, which curtailed construction of more affordable housing options in Royal Oak for two decades. Homeowners led the way, forcing local officials and publicists to follow, often in the face of powerful countervailing pressures to promote more intensive, revenue-producing land use. These two battles over apartment construction quickly made the protection of single-family homes a central focus of local political culture.

They also drew residents into a national and federally standardized conversation about the rights of homeowners and about the relationship between color and property. Royal Oak's apartment controversies were unique contests over neighborhood control, development resources, and political power. But they immersed residents in the prevailing national politics of restriction, exposing them to the planning science, real estate professionals, urban experts, appraisal manuals, and court rulings that dictated postwar development in every metropolitan region. Royal Oak residents engaged in sustained, and often sophisticated, debates over the municipal police power, the rights of property owners, real estate values, and the "laws" of suburban development. They invoked the principles of sound real estate practice outlined in enabling legislation, appraisal manuals, and zoning law. Here they found affirmation for their growing conviction that property owners were threatened by any kind of development or population deemed "incompatible" with their neighborhood. They also learned expert or legal language with which to describe the threat.

Exposure to this practical primer in land-use economics does not, by itself, explain white resistance to residential integration or their rationalization of it. Whites had long defended their right to "live among their own." But in the context of rapid metropolitan change and whites' rhetorical commitment to racial liberalism, zoning politics and land-use economics provided a coherent, purportedly nonideological defense for restriction of any kind. In an era that relentlessly celebrated the power of capitalism to enrich and liberate all American citizens, a narrative about market-driven suburban growth and the rights of property owners enabled whites to defend their new privileges without identifying its specific racial character. Making this rhetorical feat possible and, to many, commonsensical was the fact that the federal government's role in creating that privilege had been written out of the public narrative about suburban growth and postwar affluence. The politics of suburban exclusion was much more than a simple reflexive resistance to the claims of disenfranchised populations, and the language of homeowners' "rights" was not an amorphous invocation of class or racial privilege. A decades-old, national politics of suburban development and land-use control set the stage for the myriad local battles that helped define postwar suburban development patterns and politics. Local actors engaged in local battles within this context, and made that larger national narrative their own.

Land use had not always been such a contentious issue in Royal Oak. When the village gained home-rule status in 1922, its leadership and residents generally shared a planning vision for the community's rapid growth. With the automobile industry drawing thousands of workers and professionals to the Detroit region, Royal Oak envisioned itself, in the words of its first mayor, George A. Dondero, as "a center and a magnet" for development in South Oakland County. Within sixteen months, the new city annexed enough territory to triple its size. Meanwhile real estate speculation and steady population growth kept officials focused on financing and managing structural improvements. By April 1926, Mayor Harold E. Storz proudly announced that his city contained "over 30 miles of paved streets." Four years later, the zoning commission presented the city's first comprehensive ordinance, designed to make the suburb "a natural residential area for Detroit's excess population." By 1940, that ordinance and capable city management had created a sizable and primarily residential community, home to just over 25,000 professionals, white collar workers, skilled industrial workers, and their families.[9]

Consensus on zoning broke down when wartime and postwar growth created sharp conflicts of interest between homeowners, developers, renters, and public officials. Royal Oak's population nearly doubled, to 46,898, between 1940 and 1950 and grew to 65,500 by 1955. The majority of these residents were homeowners, and the percentage grew rapidly: 61.7 percent of the dwelling units were owner-occupied in 1940, and 85.7 percent just ten years later. An increasingly assertive coalition of property owners hoped to preserve Royal Oak's self-proclaimed status as a "city of homes." But the community was plagued by a housing crisis and unprecedented demands on the municipal budget, creating support for zoning reform to permit construction of more multiple-unit homes, apartment buildings, and commercial development. Complicating matters further were new pressures created by the Detroit region's ongoing transformation. The decentralization of both residence and industry raised the stakes of suburban growth politics, pitting young municipalities against one another for control of revenue-producing development. Meanwhile the expansion and increasing assertiveness of the black community made suburban homeowners wary of any residential development that might attract some of Detroit's racial minorities who desperately needed places to live. Royal Oak's homeowners claimed an early victory by pushing through a revised zoning ordinance, in 1943, which reserved most of the city's unimproved land for single-family residential development. That ordinance then set the stage for repeated postwar controversies, as city commissioners, developers, and homeowners fought over challenges to or proposed enhancements of the new restrictions.[10]

It was one of the challenges to Royal Oak's restrictive zoning ordinance that triggered the suburb's first mass mobilization of property owners. In January 1947, the Royal Oak Land Company petitioned to have its 13.5 acre parcel on Webster Road rezoned from residence A to residence C, permitting construction of a $1.25 million, 265-unit apartment complex. The project would occupy three city blocks north of Webster Road, between Linwood and Maplewood avenues (see fig. 6.1). Outraged homeowners, represented by several property owners' associations in the vicinity of the Webster Road site, "led the fight of North Royal Oak Residents" to block the rezoning.[11] Their first step was to leverage the power given them by Michigan's zoning enabling act. If 20 percent of affected property owners petitioned to stop a rezoning, the proposal required approval by three-fourths of the city commission rather than a simple majority, meaning that opposition by just two voting members would block the change. Using a meeting at the Shrine School to drum up support, members of the Northwood, Royal Oak–Beverly Hills, Vinsetta Park, Woodward Hills, and Woodwardside homeowners' associations quickly gathered the required signatures. Mayor William Hayward and Commissioner S. J. Christie provided the necessary "no" votes. (Commissioner H. Lloyd Clawson, a partner in the Royal Oak Land Company, recused himself.) Christie claimed to support the apartment project,

but noted that he "represent[s] the people" and "the overwhelming majority . . . were against it."[12]

Christie was not alone in recognizing Royal Oak's need for both more
housing and the tax revenues that it would bring. Many residents publicly
endorsed the rezoning and accused homeowners' associations of misrepre-
senting them. Even the *Tribune* endorsed the apartment project, noting that
prewar real estate speculation had left the city with huge tracts of undeveloped land, saddling property owners with a hefty municipal tax burden.
The only way to pay for "long deferred" infrastructural improvements, the
editors insisted, was to increase tax revenues, and new construction was "the
clear course to municipal well-being." "Inflexible zoning regulations . . .
should not be an obstacle to its realization," unless "they can be proven
beyond any doubt a necessary protection for present homeowners."[13]

The paper's deference to homeowners was revealing. It did not endorse
apartment construction for its own sake, but rather because the city's "present homeowners" needed a new municipal income stream. It also argued
that the Webster Road parcel was simply unsuitable for residence A homes.
On the latter point most officials and homeowners agreed. When the Royal
Oak Land Company proposed a compromise plan, a subdivision of 95
small, single-family homes, the city commission struck this down as well,
at its February 17 meeting. Commissioner Price joined the majority, arguing that the proposed plats were too small for proper detached dwellings.
He was confident that Royal Oak residents "who can afford to pay a good
price for a home are not going to build there next to the railroad," adding
that even "FHA officials told me [that] they thought an apartment project
would be much better." Joining this chorus was a local resident, Charles P.
Holliday of Woodward Avenue, who testified that the proposed 55-foot-
wide streets and 43.5-foot-wide lots were inappropriate for a neighborhood
with 60-foot-wide streets and private homes on 50-foot-wide lots. Commissioner Clawson also supported his company's original apartment project, not surprisingly, but his comments nonetheless capture widely held
assumptions about the sanctity of single-family homes. "From the city's
standpoint," Clawson argued, "well-planned apartments there would be
better than this housing project," since the parcel "goes up to the railroad
and properly should be industrial."[14]

Voters were not asked to approve either plan, so it is difficult to measure
popular support for multiple-unit housing in early 1947. It is clear, though,
that the Webster Road battle and ensuing controversies raised the profile
and influence of Royal Oak's homeowners' associations, which made zoning a prominent electoral issue and cultivated a powerful coalition in favor

of restriction. As a result, just months after 5 of 7 commission members voted in favor of the Webster project, 5 of 7 rejected another apartment proposal for a site on Vinsetta Avenue. A two-year battle ultimately settled by the Michigan Supreme Court over the so-called Northwood project provided the rallying point for the activists, organizations, and average citizens who made local control and exclusion focal points of Royal Oak politics.

The new controversy began to take shape during debate over the Webster Road project at the February 17 commission meeting. Lowell M. Price, architect for the Royal Oak Land Company, was describing their alternative, "small homes" proposal when, to the audience's great surprise, he "very abruptly stated that they really did not want to build the houses but wanted to build the apartment somewhere." "Speaking both in a sense of professional duty and as a citizen of Royal Oak," Price urged commissioners to reconsider the company's original apartment project. Mayor Hayward told the developers to consider a new location, suggesting that the city would consider exchanging a municipal park site for the lot on Webster Road. The Royal Oak Land Company countered by announcing its desire to revive an older apartment project, originally proposed in the late 1930s, for a lot between Vinsetta Boulevard and the Grand Trunk railway. Hayward welcomed this idea as well, telling Price that "if you can sell the people in that area on not objecting to it, I will go along on the zone change." Apparently the mayor was counting on community support, after hearing that members of the Northwood subdivision association had met with the developers' lawyers and that "there seemed to be very little objection." That spring, the city and the Royal Oak Land Company reached a tentative agreement on the Vinsetta site. "Objections," Hayward later recalled, "developed later." [15]

The depth of local opposition took many elected officials by surprise, because in the spring of 1947 when the original deal was struck, it seemed as if the local passion for restrictive zoning would be trumped, at least temporarily, by Royal Oak's desperate housing shortage. The housing crisis was a national phenomenon. Depression and war had severely limited home repair and new construction, leaving most cities and suburbs struggling to find adequate accommodations for returning veterans, growing families, and a constant stream of new arrivals. Nationwide, two and a half million families found themselves doubling up with relatives or friends. Royal Oak's thirteenth city commission, taking office in December 1945, declared that addressing the local crisis would be their "first order of business," and the ongoing struggle figured prominently in local news coverage and political debate throughout 1946 and 1947. Not only was demand far outstripping supply, but the new zoning ordinance's construction standards made homebuilding prohibitive for many residents. Among them was World War II veteran Floyd Cline, who in March 1946 requested exemption from a minimum floor space requirement of 750 square feet for single story homes, 30 more square feet than he could afford to build on his lot on Windemer Avenue. "How many veterans," he asked when requesting a variance, "can afford to pay $7,000 or $8,000 for a home?") [16] The crisis continued to dominate local news in 1947, during the battle over the Webster Road project and the opening salvos of the Northwood controversy. The *Tribune* regularly interviewed homeless veterans and their families, reported on municipal efforts to publicize information about rental opportunities, and ran urgent appeals from local realtors: "Wanted . . . 50 homes immediately . . . Any type, any place." [17]

Many local officials believed that the dire shelter crisis would be a decisive issue in the November 1947 municipal elections. Among them was J. B. Sparks, a five-time commissioner, local radio personality, and prominent businessman (he operated a funeral home, built homes and apartments, ran a local hotel, and managed local radio station WEXL). So confident was Sparks that residents would support more intensive land use that he made his reelection campaign a virtual referendum on restrictive zoning. At an August commission meeting, Sparks presented a scathing critique of Royal Oak's existing ordinance, describing it as "discriminating, unjust, illegal, mostly unconstitutional and very wicked." He claimed that it was driving industry from the city, blocking apartment construction (an important source of desperately needed municipal revenues, he added), preventing young men from starting small businesses, and causing "humiliation, loss and poverty to many by requiring them to build a larger building than they can afford." The problem was not political mismanagement, Sparks continued, but "the document itself," which was "contrary to the principles of democracy." "What is needed most of all are men with ability and brains to conduct and manage our cities, not unlawful zoning ordinances and city planning commissions to enforce such cruel, unjust laws on law-abiding citizens who want to live and let live." Sparks announced that he was speaking out on the issue "in order to educate residents before the November commission elections" and stated that because the ordinance was "doing more harm than good" he could not "conscientiously put [his] stamp of approval on such a document." [18]

Events of the next few months revealed that Sparks had misjudged popular sentiment or at the very least underestimated the ability of homeowners' associations to mobilize Royal Oak's residents. The drama began in mid-September, when Clawson's firm, now renamed the Northwood Property

Company, unveiled its plan for the Vinsetta parcel: a 27-building project of "modified colonial architecture" designed to accommodate up to 350 families. Northwood petitioned the city commission to rezone the site from residence A to residence C status. Local officials responded cautiously and with little enthusiasm. The Planning Commission considered the proposal on September 16 and referred it to the city's private zoning consultant, Malcolm Waring. He reported back to the city commission three weeks later, on October 6, calling for a residence B rezoning to allow apartments of a much more modest scale, with each structure limited to twelve units, and reaffirming that multiple-unit development was the only appropriate residential use for land abutting a railroad.[19] A public hearing was set to take place at the next regular commission meeting, scheduled for the following Monday, October 13.

Waring's report set off a week of furious organizing and speculation, as officials, homeowners, the builders, and the press prepared for the hearing. A day after Waring's announcement, the *Tribune* predicted that the upcoming session "promised to be one of the most controversial facing the present city commission." Waring's proposal immediately drew criticism from council members wary of offending Royal Oak's homeowners. Commissioner Christie, who in January claimed to oppose the Webster Road project out of deference to voters, now firmly rejected construction on the Vinsetta site. He had no doubt heard from his constituents again. At a meeting of the Northwood Subdivision Improvement association, homeowners from the area adjacent to the Vinsetta Street parcel announced their opposition and began planning strategy. Meanwhile Royal Oak's Plan Commission met to revisit the Northwood proposal. They refused to vote on it, instead requesting detailed architectural plans. This forced the city commission to call its first special session in four years, where it voted to proceed with the October 13 hearing, ignoring the statutory requirement that the Plan Commission be given ninety days to consider and vote on proposed zoning revisions. Christie went so far as to accuse the Plan Commission of "getting into things over which it has no jurisdiction."[20]

On Friday night, October 10, members of the Northwood, Royal Oak–Beverly Hills, Vinsetta Park, Woodward Hills, Woodwardside, and Vinsetta Heights improvement associations, whose combined membership was reported to include "several thousand homeowners," met again at the Shrine School "to pledge mutual cooperation in their fight against the proposed 350 family structure." They also announced their intent to use the Monday hearing to block the rezoning. On the morning of the scheduled meeting, the *Tribune* predicted that the controversial "apartment issue" would "reach a climax tonight," when "many organizations and individuals," many of them "instrumental," it added, "in defeating an apartment house . . . north of Webster Road," were "expected to proclaim their support or opposition to the project and to rezoning in general." The paper predicted that homeowners might pursue the strategy of requiring three quarters support from the city commission, the tactic that had killed the Webster project.[21]

The 125 people who "jammed the commission chamber" that evening did not see the issue resolved, but instead participated in the opening skirmish of what would be a two-year-long electoral and legal battle. The commissioners opened the hearing by announcing that they had reconsidered their decision to bypass the Plan Commission; they adopted city attorney W. C. Hudson's recommendation that the rezoning issue be tabled until city planners filed their report. Still local property owners insisted on speaking their minds. Patrick McIntosh, a homeowner and lawyer representing six area improvement associations, presented a petition signed by 41 percent of the residents with property facing the Vinsetta site to block the rezoning and a formal resolution opposing the change. McIntosh reminded commission members that this was "the second time we have had to come here to oppose such a change" and that homeowners' objections had remained consistent since the battle over Webster Road. He added that the homeowners' associations had "nothing against apartments" per se but rather did "not want apartments in a residential area" and were "relying on the zoning ordinance for protection." Apartment construction would lower their property values, he argued, thus "lowering" the zoning ordinance and depriving property owners of their rights.[22]

The response of Northwood Properties' supporters revealed a great deal about the strength and strategies of their opponents. Defending the proposed rezoning was FHA agent Harry Steffe, who was invited to speak by city officials to ease homeowners' fears about the "encroachment" of apartments into their neighborhood. Their properties would be safe, Steffe assured the audience, because the Grand Trunk railway and Vinsetta Boulevard would clearly demarcate the boundary between their subdivisions and the new development. The depth of residents' suspicion toward renters was dramatically displayed by Steffe's decision to defend them. "The inference that a man who rents is not a good citizen is wrong," he noted. "While we think of the United States as a land of home ownership, on a national average 54 per cent of the people are renters."[23]

This appeal no doubt fell on many deaf ears, because Royal Oak in the late 1940s, like most first-generation suburbs nationwide, was a city of neither renters nor apartment dwellers. Two months earlier, the city issued a record high 154 permits for single-family dwelling starts; by year's end it would issue a record 851 permits for single-family homes yet only two for two-family residences and none for apartment buildings. The following year, 808 out of 810 permits were for one-family structures. Renters had always been in the minority in Royal Oak, but they now represented a rapidly shrinking one because of a national transformation of metropolitan settlement patterns and a revolution in the mortgage industry. In 1940, 42.5 percent of Royal Oak's dwelling units were renter-occupied, including 29.1 percent of the single-family homes. Just ten years later, only 13.6 percent of the city's dwellings were rented and only 6.6 percent of the single-family homes. The privately owned, single-family home now clearly dominated. In 1940, 81.2 percent of the city's 5,455 dwelling units were single-family detached structures, but only 69.7 percent of these were owner-occupied. By 1950 the number of housing units had more than doubled, to 12,218, 87.9 percent of these were detached single-family dwellings, and now over 95 percent of these were owner-occupied. More than 70 percent of them carried mortgages.[24]

So while Royal Oak was still plagued by a housing shortage in 1947, it was also rapidly becoming a city of white homeowners, notably at a time when Detroit's African American community was growing and asserting itself in ways that made whites in the region, both longtime residents and newcomers, very uncomfortable. Between 1947 and 1949, it was this community of white homeowners that engaged in a contentious public debate about the future of their neighborhoods, the threats posed by "incompatible" residential development, and the centrality of homeowners' rights to local politics.

Royal Oak's homeowners led the effort to make restriction a defining issue of the November 1947 elections. Again they collected signatures, hoping to use the state enabling act's three quarters provision to block the rezoning. The *Tribune* highlighted their campaign in its weekly news roundup, reminding readers that the outcome of the Northwood controversy would "Depend on Two Votes: Two Negative Votes Would Bar Rezoning." Accompanying the article were two large sketches of Northwood's proposal, with a caption noting builders' promise to include landscaped courtyards, a playground, and adequate off-street parking so that the complex would "harmonize with the neighborhood." But the project's opponents "particularly dislike the idea of an apartment project in an area zoned for the highest type of homes," the article continued, insisting "that it would lower property values." In late October, a pair of editorials revealed how large the controversy loomed for Royal Oak residents. By tabling the Northwood issue at the public hearing, the paper claimed, the city commission had "provided the voters with a clear cut election issue."

> The controversy over the Northwood site is only the latest in a series that has plagued the present city commission and which has occupied more than half its time. In every section of the city, building schemes have come acropper over zoning restrictions, and the builder has turned to the commission for relief. Twice this year alone, plans for large scale apartment buildings have failed because of zoning barriers. Yet there is hardly a section in the city where the zoning hasn't been changed since the ordinance originally was adopted . . . Homeowners in the Northwood apartment site vicinity truthfully have declared that enforcement or relaxation of present zoning restrictions is of paramount importance to the whole city. And the mayor has commented that zoning hearings often are swayed by the pressure of the "noisy minority" because the majority is passive.

It was now up to candidates and voters, the editors continued, to resolve a debate over "how . . . they want the city—still half vacant land—to develop." An upcoming poll would allow the presumably silent majority to speak up. "In the municipal election Nov. 4, then is the opportunity for expression of popular will . . . And all 21 candidates for the commission in that election owe it to the public to say now and unequivocally, how they stand on the issue."[25]

A decisive majority of Royal Oak voters supported restriction. Proposition 1 ("Zoning"), which protected the existing ordinance by requiring a referendum to repeal it, passed by a wide margin in all eleven electoral precincts, and by a vote of 2,788 to 1,516 citywide. Meanwhile voters rejected candidates who had challenged the city's zoning ordinance or supported the Northwood project, replacing them with men who campaigned to uphold restriction. Clawson and Sparks, both outspoken supporters of rezoning the Northwood site for apartments, lost their bids for reelection. Commissioner Hering lost as well, and Christie did not run. In their place, voters returned to office two former commissioners, Evert M. Bangham and Samuel K. Truswell, and elected two new members, Arthur H. Fries and Walter R. Eames, both of whom had campaigned for a "strong zoning ordinance." Local press accounts noted that the property owners' associations were instrumental in securing these victories, and that the Northwood controversy had "furnished a major election issue." It clearly energized local voters, producing "record balloting for an off-election year."[26]

The new importance of restriction to Royal Oak politics was theatrically displayed on December 1, at the inauguration of the new City Commission. The carefully choreographed, unusually conciliatory event belied the rancor of that fall's campaign. After the mayor recognized the "retiring" commissioners for their years of "public service," Rev. Gilbert H. McGeehan of the Community Memorial Church described the Northwood controversy as a victory for local political institutions, praising, in the words of a local journalist, "the traditions of democracy in which difference in opinions are ironed out around a table." Then in a remarkable political about-face, former Commissioner J. B. Sparks conceded defeat by embracing restriction in a message sent from Oklahoma City, where he was attending the National Poultry show (Sparks raised black Minorca chickens, for exhibition). Voted out of office after describing the city's ordinance as unjust, Sparks now declared that "like some of the newly elected commissioners, I believe in a strong zoning ordinance." No doubt weighing the influence of local homeowners' associations against his business and political future in Royal Oak, Sparks now asserted that the suburb's ordinance was "too weak." "It needs amending at most every meeting," he complained, and "the only strength it has left is in the associations," which "appear to wield considerable power on election day."[27]

On the following Monday, the lame-duck city commission tabled another motion on the Vinsetta rezoning, leaving the matter for the incoming commission. Patrick McIntosh appeared on behalf of the homeowners' associations, reminding officials that "the people of the city spoke very clearly . . . at the last election" through their "militant disapproval to spot zoning." In January 1948, new commission members Fries, Eames, and Bangham joined Hayward in rejecting Northwood Property's zoning request, preserving the parcel for residence A development. Commissioners Horn, Laidlaw, and Truswell voted in favor of the more permissive rezoning.[28]

The battle soon entered a new and far more public stage, when Northwood Properties took the city to court. On February 2, the developers filed a mandamus suit at the Oakland County circuit court, charging the City of Royal Oak, City Inspector Owen C. Perkins, Mayor William Hayward, and the commission members with depriving them of their rights as property owners without due process. Their petition challenged a 1939 amendment that had rezoned the Vinsetta parcel from residence C to residence A status, claiming that the change represented "an unjustifiable and unreasonable exercise of the police power." Plaintiffs also challenged the state zoning enabling act provision that empowered residents to petition for a three quarters commission majority on zoning revisions. This provision, argued Northwood, represented an unlawful delegation of authority. The next day, Perkins and the six commissioners were served with a circuit court order signed by Oakland County judge H. Russell Holland to show why a writ of mandamus should not be issued against the city.[29]

Emboldened by their recent successes, Royal Oak's homeowner-activists attempted to enter the fray. The Vinsetta Park improvement association petitioned Judge Holland for permission to participate on behalf of area homeowners, arguing that the rezoning would "materially and adversely" affect the health, safety, and welfare of the subdivision's property owners. Russell Knister, an attorney and neighborhood resident, filed the request on behalf of the association's 130 members, many of whom owned property adjoining the Vinsetta parcel. Other subdivision associations considered participating, but in the end the Vinsetta Park group and twenty-two individual petitioners presented the case for restriction. Fletcher L. Renton and H. Eugen Field, attorneys for Northwood Properties, responded that residents' participation was unnecessary. Judge Holland agreed, ruling in late February that the city attorney would adequately represent local citizens and protect their interests.[30]

A divided municipal government spoke next, when the city attorney, W. C. Hudson, prepared his answer to the suit and asked the commission to endorse it. In a brief echoing numerous post-*Euclid* court decisions on restrictive zoning, Hudson asserted that the residence A designation was most appropriate for property along Vinsetta Boulevard because of the area's general development patterns. The site had been rezoned to residence A in 1939, Hudson argued, "in good faith to promote the public health, safety and welfare of the city," adding that since then several beautiful homes had been constructed on the boulevard and on Twelve Mile Road, which intersected with Vinsetta. Horn, Laidlaw, and Truswell continued their opposition, refusing to endorse the city's brief. Hudson announced that their endorsement would be preferred but was not necessary. The commission authorized Royal Oak's city manager, E. M. Shafter, to sign the answer in the name of the city.[31]

In the dissent of Horn, Laidlaw, and Truswell, local housing activists saw an opening. The Vinsetta Park association and sixteen individuals again petitioned the court to participate, arguing that Hudson could not properly represent homeowners' interests since he would be advising council members who supported the Northwood project. Moreover, they used a careful reading of the original writ, the city's response, property law statutes, and

Michigan's zoning enabling act to argue that their participation was legally required. They insisted that because Northwood Properties was challenging the constitutionality of the enabling act's three quarters provision, which enabled homeowners to shape local planning decisions, the case directly addressed their rights. They also invoked the rights of individual property owners under the Fourteenth Amendment, claiming that the defendants (city officials) could not speak to those rights, since they were acting only as representatives of a municipal corporation.[32]

The Oakland County court denied them for a second time. But the unsuccessful appeal and the events that followed received extensive and prominent coverage in the local press, enabling readers throughout the Oakland County suburbs to follow the court actions, the local mobilizations, and the arguments for and against restrictive zoning. They learned that a circuit court judge would hear the case on April 1 and had ordered the city to produce the city's building code, its original zoning map, its charter, and all ordinances and regulations pertaining to municipal sanitary regulations, fire prevention, public safety, and police powers. Officials were also required to produce records of city commission proceedings regarding the adoption of three city ordinances: Ordinance 301 (an earlier amendment changing the Vinsetta parcel from residence A to residence C in the early 1930s); Ordinance 361 (which reinstated the residence A status on September 5, 1939); and Ordinance 448 (adopted May 15, 1944, which specified size and space requirements for the parcel). Finally, the city had to produce the city plan commission's recommendation advising the city to rezone the parcel to residence B and a record of city commission proceedings regarding Northwood's request to rezone the property to residence C.[33]

The trial was held at the Masonic Temple in Pontiac, Michigan, with Judge Leo T. Brennan, of Michigan's Twelfth Circuit Court, presiding. The testimony and briefs demonstrated how central land-use science and legal debates had become to the everyday politics of exclusion. Testifying for Northwood, Harry Jones, who as chair of Royal Oak's first plan commission had helped draft its original zoning ordinance in 1931, argued that the site was ill-suited for single-family homes. Royal Oak's police chief added that the empty parcel represented a threat to public order, a threat that development would end. The Northwood brief reiterated the legal argument: that Royal Oak had arbitrarily exercised its police power, that the zoning ordinance itself was unconstitutional, and that the three quarters clause represented an unlawful delegation of legislative power. The lawyers even turned the language of restriction on its head, arguing that apartment construction would *benefit* the public health, safety, and welfare. Witnesses for the city countered that the project would depreciate home values; among them were two local real estate dealers and a professional contractor who lived near the Vinsetta parcel. Also testifying for the city was its zoning consultant, Malcolm Waring, who in February had recommended rezoning the parcel to residence B. Under cross-examination he described that earlier recommendation as tentative, noting that he had been "on the fence because of public opinion."[34]

Anchoring the city's case were two arguments, one regarding home-rule authority and the other determination of compatible land use, that had been used to legitimate comprehensive zoning at least since the Supreme Court's *Euclid* decision of 1926. Defense witnesses explained that the city commission's decision to deny rezoning represented nothing more than a reasonable exercise of the municipal police power in order to protect the public welfare. And as Waring's testimony made clear, the city was most concerned with protecting the "character of the neighborhood," or what he called its "intangible values." Former city commissioner S. J. Christie, a building contractor by trade, attempted to calculate those values, predicting that apartment construction would depreciate the value of nearby homes by 10 to 20 percent. He also noted that there were sixty single-family, detached dwellings just south of Twelve Mile Road, only blocks from the Vinsetta parcel, further confirmation that the property was ideal for "class A" homes.[35] Hudson's brief placed this line of argument firmly in the context of prevailing land-use law. Both the existing zoning ordinance and the city's defense of it, he explained, were reasonable exercises of the municipal police power, because the city was working to protect residents' health, safety, and welfare by preventing the dangers posed by multiple-unit dwellings. And the ordinance was reasonable, he added, because it was designed to protect property values.

Particularly revealing was Hudson's decision to support the public welfare argument by pointing to the neighborhood's physical, architectural character. The brief explained that Vinsetta Boulevard was one of Royal Oak's finest residential streets, filled with expensive single-family homes, and that the proposed apartments would be clearly visible to its residents. It mattered little, Hudson wrote, that the developers' planned to divide the two neighborhoods with a landscaped parkway, for "the record shows that a multiple dwelling development would depreciate property values in the immediate area"—that visibility alone, in other words, would undermine homeowners' investments. Finally, Hudson cited Supreme Court principle, "that where the matter is reasonably debatable, even though the court might incline to doubt the reasonableness of the ordinance, it is still the court's duty to sustain the discretion of the city governing board that has jurisdiction." Directly invoking court decisions from the heyday of litigation over zoning and the municipal police power, Royal Oak argued that communities of property owners reserved the right to make decisions about what constituted compatible use. It claimed that the city's designations of "value" and "risk" were *prima facie* grounds for upholding restrictive legislation. They had clear federal court precedents to support this claim.[36]

————————

As Royal Oak residents awaited the court's ruling during the summer of 1948, the *Tribune* noted that the battle over the Northwood case, "one of the most controversial and important questions in the city's history," had "found the city commission as well as residents divided." In September, Brennan ruled for Northwood Properties, arguing that the suburb's zoning ordinance, as it applied to the parcel in question, was unreasonable and arbitrary. He ordered city inspector Perkins to issue a building permit and ordered the Royal Oak city commission to rezone the Vinsetta parcel to residence B, the original "compromise" suggested by Waring and the city plan commission a year earlier.[37] Four days later and under considerable pressure from homeowners, the city commission voted 5–2 to appeal the ruling. Only Laidlaw and Horn dissented, charging that an appeal would be a "waste of taxpayers' money," while the commissioners who rode into office on a restrictionist campaign in 1947 voted in favor. "North Royal Oak residents," reported the *Tribune*, "applauded" the commission's decision.[38]

To assist Hudson with the appeal, the city hired Glenn C. Gillespie of Pontiac, a former Oakland County circuit court judge and county prosecutor. Hudson and Gillespie's strategy is quite revealing, again demonstrating how prewar zoning politics shaped postwar battles over local control. Their petition for a new trial invoked key principles of the Supreme Court's ruling in *Euclid*. The lawyers invoked the presumption that a municipal zoning ordinance was valid because it reflected the community's judgment about compatible development; specifically, they charged that the circuit court erred when it held that Northwood Properties had offered sufficient evidence to rebut the "presumption of validity." To support this claim, they again turned to the central post-*Euclid* justification for restrictive zoning: the claim that local ordinances were designed to protect the public health, safety, morals, and welfare. The circuit court had erred, they argued, in ruling that Royal Oak's ordinance had not been designed with these standards in mind.[39] Invoking another well established zoning defense, Hudson and

Gillespie asserted that multiple-family dwellings threatened communities of homeowners. This move came only after the plaintiffs and defense agreed to send a request for a retrial directly to Brennan, and after the city announced its willingness to appeal the case to the state supreme court. In late October, Royal Oak's attorneys raised the stakes further, filing a brief charging that the circuit court decision threatened to undermine the city's entire zoning ordinance. If the circuit court decision were to stand, they argued, it would be difficult or perhaps impossible for any municipality to protect neighborhoods of single-family homes from encroachment by multiple-dwelling units. The attorneys emphasized, again, that Vinsetta was one of the better residential streets in the city and that only single-family homes had been constructed there.[40]

Brennan denied the city's motion for a retrial in mid-November, prompting Royal Oak's city commission to appeal the case to the Michigan State Supreme Court. That court agreed to hear the case, and because the circuit court had denied the retrial request, the Supreme Court was empowered to treat the matter as a new case, to review circuit court testimony, and to gather new information. The justices began to hear oral arguments the following June. On September 8, 1949, they reversed the Oakland circuit ruling in a unanimous decision and quashed the writ of mandamus.[41]

The Michigan Supreme Court ruling, written by Justice J. Dethmers, dramatically illustrates how prewar zoning politics were shaping land-use battles in the postwar suburbs. The court affirmed Hudson and Gillespie's arguments about the municipal police power and the presumption of validity. It confirmed that the city of Royal Oak had adequately demonstrated that its zoning ordinance was designed to protect public health and safety. And the court determined this, just as the defense had, by invoking the sanctity of privately owned, single-family homes—the yardstick that had served as an organizing principle for debates over restriction since the 1920s. "Testimony for the defense," wrote Dethmers,

established that the property in question fronts on Vinsetta Boulevard, one of the best streets in Royal Oak, wide and divided by a beautiful, well-kept parkway, and that the area is one of the choicest and nicest residential districts in the city; that lots in the area are all restricted to single residences; that no violations of the zoning ordinances or restrictions have occurred and that all dwellings built in the area are single residences. In our view plaintiff did not establish by competent evidence that the ordinance's classification of plaintiff's property is unreasonable or bears no relation to public health, safety or the general welfare.

The court assumed that a neighborhood of single-family homes was by definition deserving of protection from apartments. Dethmers referred readers to the U.S. Supreme Court's opinion in *Village of Euclid v. Ambler Realty Co.* for a "cataloguing and consideration of the respects in which such ordinance provisions bear a relationship to public health, safety, morals or general welfare." He highlighted that court's discussion "involving the validity of provisions of a city zoning ordinance excluding apartment houses from residential districts."[42]

Given the prewar history of *Euclid v. Ambler*, this is a remarkable moment in the postwar history of suburban land-use politics. While the original Ambler suit had nothing to do with residential restriction, both the lower court and the Supreme Court had justified their rulings (in 1924 and 1926, respectively) by focusing on Euclid's restrictions against apartments. Of course, the latter court established the enduring precedent, so its lengthy treatment of the "threat" posed by multiple-unit dwellings helped provide the legal justification for all subsequent rulings on the defensibility of restriction in general and on the legality of comprehensive use zoning in particular. More than two decades later, a Michigan court invoked the U.S. Supreme Court's preoccupation with protecting single-family homes to uphold a residence A zone in Royal Oak. City attorneys and local housing activists had wisely focused on that argument since the first shots were fired in the Northwood controversy in early 1947.

Further evidence of zoning's prewar legacy could be found in the Michigan court's discussion of restriction's larger intent. First, the court addressed the three quarters clause of the state enabling act, the tool that Royal Oak improvement associations had repeatedly used to block rezoning requests and drum up opposition to apartment construction. Dethmers explained that the provision of the enabling act did not, as Northwood Properties claimed, "constitute a delegation of legislative power to private individuals." Meanwhile Hudson and Gillespie had argued for the validity of the city's zoning ordinance by asserting that it had been designed to protect the public health, welfare, morals, and safety. The court agreed, citing an earlier Michigan decision (*Austin v. Older*, 1938) asserting that "exclusion of nonconforming businesses" from "residential districts" had a "reasonable relationship to the public health, welfare and safety."[43] Dethmers's ruling explained that "the burden was not on the defendants to establish the relationship, but upon the plaintiff to show the lack of it. This burden plaintiff did not sustain. While the ordinance must stand the test of reasonableness, the presumption is in favor of its validity and courts may not invalidate ordinances unless the constitutional objections thereto are supported by competent evidence or appear on their face . . . Invalidity does not appear on the face of the ordinance merely from its classification of certain property for use for single residences only."

In ruling for Royal Oak, the Michigan court was not categorically supporting a city's decision to exclude multiple-unit dwellings whenever it chose. Indeed, the decision draws a sharp distinction between the Northwood case and other cases that deemed municipal actions confiscatory, for example, when a city prohibited apartment construction on a parcel that was deemed "unsuitable" for "residential" purposes.[44] But in overruling the lower court, the Supreme Court *was* confirming a municipality's right to make decisions about compatibility. It reaffirmed the assumption that certain sites were "suited" or "not suited" for specific types of residential arrangements and that the "reasonable" judgment of homeowners could be used to ascertain how compatibility would be measured.

The culmination of the Northwood controversy illustrates how decades of national zoning politics and mortgage policy influenced the discrete, local battles over restriction that shaped suburban residents' understanding of exclusion. When Royal Oak residents organized to keep apartments or other undesirable developments out of their neighborhoods, they were not reflexively defending their turf or local resources, nor were they simply tapping into immutable class or racial prejudices. And if suburban restrictionist politics was homegrown, it was not invented out of whole cloth.[45] Instead, whites' prejudices and preferences, regardless of their origins, were now being confirmed and validated by an army of urban experts in both the public and private sectors. Local officials and homeowners learned from realtors, developers, lawyers, and government officials that certain kinds of land use and certain populations posed a threat to their property and communities. Suburban residents pursued the politics of exclusion by turning to these experts, to abundant federal resources, and to legal instruments that both told this story consistently and determined the design, tenancy patterns, and racial composition of metropolitan neighborhoods. In the process of preserving a suburb for single-family homes, residents rehearsed the market imperative language about property, rights, local government, and the need for exclusion. After 1940, white suburbanites turned to legal instruments and real estate guidelines long grounded in a discriminatory theory of residence and metropolitan development. Tapping into a land-use science that had always claimed to be above the ideological fray made whites' new investment in exclusion all the more powerful, intractable, and invisible.

Ever more visible, by contrast, were new single-family homes. Four months before the State Supreme Court began hearing testimony in the

Northwood case, the Homebuilder's Association began previewing the model homes in its new subdivision in Royal Oak's northwest. That spring, residents learned that Royal Oak had issued 157 permits for single-family homes in April, breaking the previous high of 154 set in August 1947. The new units represented over half of the new homes approved in all of South Oakland County that month. Fifty of the new Royal Oak homes were located in subdivisions east of Campbell Road at Ten Mile Road in the city's southeast, bordering Ferndale and just blocks from its borders with Hazel Park, Pleasant Ridge, and Royal Oak Township. These subdivisions would be two of the many that area residents would soon watch rise up on undeveloped land as they commuted to work, visited a neighbor, or drove their kids to school.[46]

The day after Dethmers issued his ruling, the *Tribune* reported on Northwood Properties' response. The headline quoted the developers' announcement: "Northwood Issue Dead." In the article, the firm noted its intention to "make the best use of the property possible within the structure of the zoning ordinance." The reporter finished the thought: "That means single-family homes."[47]

Land-Use Politics in a "City of Homes"

The battles over the Webster Road and Northwood projects were not isolated incidents in metropolitan Detroit, nor were the strategies pursued by Royal Oak residents and officials uncommon. One indication was the dramatic increase after World War II of legal challenges to municipal and township zoning laws throughout Michigan, cases that occasionally wound their way up to the State Supreme court. Between 1949 and 1957, alone, that court heard at least sixty-one such cases, two-thirds of which involved the protection of lots for residential use. Half were challenges to the rezoning of residential parcels for commercial uses and another ten involved residents' complaints that the local zoning ordinance was "not strict enough." In most cases, municipal authorities sided with residents demanding more restrictive zoning. And both invoked the legal arguments cited by Royal Oak homeowners in their battles against the Northwood apartments: the "presumption of validity"; using the police power to protect the "public health, safety, and morals"; and, most frequently, the claim that down-zoning would threaten "residential character" or "neighborhood character" and, by extension, property values.[48]

The intricacies of court challenges were not lost on residents. In Royal Oak, improvement association members and anyone following the case in the local press were constantly exposed to debates over the municipal police power and homeowners' legal right to dictate land-use patterns. The *Tribune* devoted considerable space to the Northwood Properties suit, the responses filed by the city and local protective associations, the briefs and counterbriefs, and individual court rulings. Coverage of the state supreme court decision included detailed discussions of Dethmers's rulings on the presumption of validity, on whether or not the residential A classification was confiscatory, on the power of courts to "compel" legislative bodies to rule on the ordinance's validity, and finally on Northwood's challenge to the three quarters clause. Notably, the paper printed a lengthy quote from the court's discussion of the "presumption of validity."[49]

When Northwood conceded defeat in September, the *Tribune* observed that the controversy could no longer serve as a "possible campaign issue" in the upcoming commission elections. Still some candidates hoped to gain advantage with Royal Oak's homeowners. S. J. Christie made residential restriction central to his reelection campaign, warning the Royal Oak Home Owners Protective League that an "unfriendly" city commission could challenge the supreme court's Northwood ruling. Clawson, now retired from the commission, criticized Christie for trying to "scare our people in hope of attracting support." But this did not stop him from trying to curry favor with property owners in his role as developer. Hoping to distance himself from the Northwood fiasco, Clawson now claimed that Mayor Hayward had initiated the apartment proposal and arranged for Northwood Properties to meet with area homeowners. It was not until the months leading up to the elections, Clawson explained, that Hayward spoke out publicly *against* the apartments.[50]

The original Webster Road site made it "Back in the News" in February 1950, with a report that the parcel was being platted for 70 single-family homes, each on lots ranging from 60 to 70 feet in width. For the benefit of newer Oakland County residents, perhaps, the *Tribune* recalled the Northwood battle, noting that "rezoning from residence A to C was rejected . . . after neighbors vehemently protested and submitted objecting petitions." But for most readers this resistance would appear commonsensical. By 1950 Royal Oak's property owners had established firm control over local development politics and calls by public officials to dismantle the city's "discriminatory" zoning ordinance were distant memories. It helped that anxieties about the housing shortage were tempered by repeated announcements that "record numbers of permits" had been issued for new construction and the appearance of advertisements for new FHA-approved subdivisions (see fig. 6.3). Following resolution of the Northwood Properties case,

6.3 Subdivision advertisement, *Daily Tribune,* September 10, 1948. Advertisements
for FHA-approved or FHA-insured homes were common in the suburban press by
the late 1940s. This advertisement for 101 units in northern Royal Oak invited readers
to visit the furnished model for further information. It also listed the payment terms
for both veterans and nonveterans. Reprinted with permission of *The Daily Tribune,*
Royal Oak, Michigan. Photographed by Ken Music.

the public discourse about land use in Royal Oak focused almost exclusively
on the protection of detached single-family dwellings, the advantages of
living in a "city of homes," and the character of the people who purchased
and maintained them. There were dissenting voices, but not widespread
advocacy for construction of multifamily dwellings. The controversy in late
1949, instead, was over how *big* the suburb's homes should be. Arvid Peterson and his colleagues at the Homebuilder's Association complained that
the lot and building size requirements in Royal Oak's zoning ordinance
discriminated against residents unable to afford larger homes. But public

officials could not risk supporting Peterson's views. And by the early 1950s, local homebuilders were no longer staking such a position.[51]

By then there was little need to do so. Among the forces enabling home-owners to consolidate control over local land-use politics was the continual expansion of the market for homes. By the late 1940s, congressional ac-tion on selective credit programs was accelerating lending and borrowing for single-family homes nationwide. Mortgage credit was soon flowing at record rates, in both the government-insured and conventional markets, as reappropriations and repeated liberalization of the FHA and VA programs made ownership accessible to even more white people. For many eligible families these benefits were slow in coming, however. Peterson's comments on Royal Oak's ordinance reflected the fact that in 1949, even an FHA-in-sured home still remained out of reach for many aspiring suburbanites. A house valued at $7,500 required an $800 investment and allowed 25 years for repayment—a bargain compared with pre-Depression mortgages, but still prohibitive for families with modest or insecure incomes. That would soon change. Just a year later, that same house could be purchased for $500. Down payment requirements continued to drop throughout the 1950s, es-pecially on more expensive properties, while repayment was extended to 30 years. Federal interventions accelerated housing starts and promoted the construction of larger dwellings, leading builders to focus their attention on this new market. Local officials, eager to please constituents and local businessmen, were happy to demonstrate their support for both.[52]

––––––––

Following resolution of the Northwood case, supporters of restrictive zon-ing won most battles over Royal Oak's ordinance and built a powerful con-sensus about the need to preserve the suburb as a "city of homes." Home-owners were particularly successful at stopping construction of apartments or commercial enterprises near single-family dwellings and even blocked subdivisions of detached homes that did not meet cost or size minimums. Between 1947 and 1953, the city granted 8,199 permits for the construc-tion of new single-family residences and only 31 permits for apartments. Of course local land-use battles were not exclusively about apartment build-ings. Spot zonings were requested for the construction of nursery schools, municipal parks, and other projects. Nor did local homeowners win all of their battles, and yet notably even in defeat, property owners spent con-siderable energies debating land-use economics and reminding officials of their preferences. (They also commanded considerable respect. In 1949, circuit court judge Frank Doty ruled against twenty-two homeowners who petitioned to halt construction of modest, wood-frame houses near their larger brick and masonry homes, yet openly sympathized with the plaintiffs and encouraged them to appeal his ruling to the Supreme Court.)[53] Nonetheless, mobilizations to protect single-family homes against apartments or commercial development were the most common, the most publicized, and the most controversial. They set the tone of local politics and, as the Northwood controversy demonstrates, even the balance of power.[54]

Most of these contests followed a familiar pattern. A property owner would request rezoning of a parcel to business, industrial, residence B, or residence C status, and the plan commission granted the request. This triggered protests by area homeowners, leading the city commission to overrule the plan commission's recommendation. In the spring of 1951, for example, planners approved rezoning the west side of Woodward Avenue, between Harrison and Lincoln avenues, from residential to business, to permit construction of a $250,000 dollar shopping center. The site, in the far southwest corner of Royal Oak, just east of its border with Huntington Woods and just north of its border with Pleasant Ridge, would span three city blocks of Woodward frontage. At a May commission meeting, one hundred property owners from Royal Oak and Huntington Woods "jammed the commission chambers to protest the rezoning." The attorney speaking on the homeowners' behalf argued that the area "was always [zoned] residential," that the shopping center would pose a hazard to schoolchildren, and that it would create a drainage problem. He offered signatures documenting residents' unanimous opposition. "Several members of the audience were anxious to speak on the matter," according to one reporter, but the mayor did not allow debate, perhaps anticipating that their testimony was unnecessary. By a vote of 4 to 1, the city commission refused to schedule a public hearing on the proposal, effectively killing the plan.[55]

When city planners proposed enlarging the business zone on Woodward Avenue in March 1952, they were again "met with strenuous protests" by local homeowners. The West Wood Community Association objected to the rezoning and made several new requests: that an existing residence B zone on the avenue's south side be changed to residence AA, that Coolidge Highway's east-side business frontage be zoned residence AAA, and that its west side be divided between residence A and residence AAA. In early April, the city commission rejected the plan commission's recommendations for Woodward Avenue, instead rezoning the lots in question to single-family residence A and changing a residence C section to business B. "The commission's actions," reported the *Tribune*, "satisfied nearby property owners who had objected to the planners' recommendation except those in areas intended for residence A." That year a plan commission proposal to nearly double the existing industrial zone on Royal Oak's north side, between Normandy and Fourteen Mile Road, also "ran smack into opposition" from area homeowners and the city parks and recreation board. Proposals for motels and drive-in theaters also sparked considerable protest. In July 1953 residents blocked a rezoning to permit construction of a 130-unit motel on Woodward north of Twelve Mile Road. Homeowners were even looking beyond Royal Oak's municipal borders. In August 1952, members of the Red Run Home Owners Association encouraged the city commission to preempt Hazel Park's efforts to annex a two-mile strip of Royal Oak Township, which bordered Royal Oak City's southeast. They suggested that Royal Oak annex the land, as a member of the Red Run Association explained, in order to "control future development of the area." In 1955, the 800-member Northwood Association blocked apartment construction on another parcel near the Grand Trunk Railroad.[56]

The depth of opposition to revenue-producing development created a quandary for city officials. How could the suburb balance its revenue needs with homeowners' preferences? Regular reminders of this problem appeared in the annual municipal reports, simple brochures mailed to residents that detailed Royal Oak's tax receipts and the costs of government and services. The 1948 report was entitled "How Will We Get It?" and continued in the text: "Money, we mean, to pay the cost of maintaining local government." It encouraged residents to support excise, wheel, or luxury goods taxes. Local news coverage and editorials also stressed the need to accommodate some business, industry, and multiple-family residential development. In a 1954 commentary on recent controversies over industrial development, the *Tribune* asked simply: "City of Homes Enough?"[57]

What suburban officials had learned from architects, planners, realtors, federal officials, local commentators, and especially from their homeowning constituents was that intensive land uses were acceptable in a "city of homes" if they were physically separated from those homes. Industrial, commercial, and even apartment construction would be tolerated if it did not intrude upon residence A neighborhoods. Royal Oak's improvement associations rarely objected to apartments relegated to the city's commercial or industrial districts. In summer 1951, for example, the city commission held a public hearing on a plan commission proposal to rezone 93 acres on Fourteen Mile and Crooks roads to accommodate business, industrial, and apartment development. While a "new residence C area" would "permit the construction of multiple dwelling projects," the *Tribune* reported, the rezoning "establishe[d] buffer zones between residence and industrial areas." It is unclear if the *Tribune* was suggesting that multiple-unit dwellings fit in the category of "residence" or "industrial." But the apartments eventually built there were largely separated from single-family homes by streets, local retail strips, and green space. Royal Oak's Chamber of Commerce endorsed the rezoning, citing the need to supplement municipal income streams. There is no evidence of significant opposition to the plan.[58]

By then Royal Oak officials were pursuing new strategies for encouraging acceptance of revenue-producing land uses. In 1949, in the wake of the Northwood controversy, the annual tax pamphlet was replaced by a far more elaborate, professionally produced annual report modeled on a format recommended by the Michigan Municipal League. Royal Oak's report couched appeals for "balanced" development in a relentless celebration of homeownership. The brochures were still mailed annually to residents and still provided a primer on municipal operations and expenditures. They described the mechanics of municipal government, detailed the work and expenditures of twenty different city departments and facilities, and discussed municipal taxes, licenses, financing public improvements, and some of the engineering challenges facing a growing city. But now the report placed special emphasis on the city's commitment to providing services for its citizens, and it equated citizens with homeowners.

The inaugural issue, a twenty-six-page brochure entitled "Royal Oak—Digest of Municipal Activities, 1948–1949," was prefaced with two messages, the first a letter from Royal Oak's city manager about the importance of furnishing residents with "information required to properly evaluate the [performance of] Municipal Departments." "Good government," he explained, "is dependent upon citizen interest and support." Opposite this was a note from the mayor, addressed to "the Citizens of Royal Oak," which "urge[d] [residents] to not only read this report but also to study it carefully," since it would "answer many questions that may have arisen regarding your city and its administration."[59] Then uniting an otherwise prosaic narrative about municipal departments, service provision, and the budget was a story about public officials' commitment to Royal Oak's homeowners. Tax collection, sanitation, planning, policing: each was designed to sustain comfortable, well-served, and thus economically stable neighborhoods of single-family homes. The Department of Engineering promoted the "arduous, painstaking work by field parties collecting requisite data," the "weeks, months, and sometimes years of work in transferring data to plans on the drawing board," and finally it "supervised construction" to ensure that "work is done according to contract specifications, and that the interests of the City and property owners are fully safeguarded." Royal Oak's City Planning Department, aided by a "full time Planning Technician," was working on "a master land use plan to assure a more orderly development for our City." The city attorney was also looking out for property owners, most recently by "appeal[ing] two cases to the Michigan Supreme Court, Hering versus the City, and the Northwood Properties Association versus the City." (There is no mention that the city attorney undermined the city planner's initial recommendations in both cases.) Even a description of the Department of Parks and Playgrounds reminded residents that Royal Oak had a reputation as "A City of Homes." Local officials were committed to a professional, nonideological approach to city management. "Under 28 years of this form of government," the report concludes, "the City of Royal Oak's affairs have been efficiently, competently, and economically administered, and government itself has been peculiarly free from scandal and inefficiency sometimes associated with older forms of municipal administration."[60]

The report's focus on the single-family dwelling and its celebration of the homeowner-citizen grew more prominent in ensuing years. Each edition was prefaced by letters inviting residents to learn about the mechanics of an "efficient" local government run by dedicated, public-spirited officials. And each catalogued the palpable results—measured in miles of water mains and sewage pipe laid, in miles of streets paved, in numbers of homes and businesses constructed, and in services provided to voters, veterans, and schoolchildren. The report depicted municipal government, service provision, and decisions about land use as technocratic processes designed to best manage local resources for the benefit of homeowners.

Beginning in 1955, the report changed formats again, appearing as a six-page supplement to the *Tribune*. Now it blurred the line between news and municipal advocacy, as the glossy pages and magazine-style layout were replaced with newsprint and a news feature format. Essays about municipal departments were laid out like news articles, below headlines such as "Water, Drains to Open City," "Engineers' Job to Plan Right," or "Specialist Called in for Master Plan." Meanwhile images of the suburban family, a white, nuclear family living in a single-family home, began to appear and occupied an increasingly prominent place in each issue. The cover of the 1955 edition, "City of Royal Oak: Progress Report," invited readers to "Tour our city with the typical family," depicted by drawings of two white, freckled children (presumably a brother and sister), their businessman father, and homemaker mother. The 1956 edition, entitled "Your City . . . Your Home . . . and You," pictured a white family of four, standing in front of their detached, single-family home. They are surrounded, in turn, by photographs of the municipal employees who helped make life so pleasant for Royal Oak's homeowners (see fig. 6.4).[61]

One year later the "annual report" combined images and text that synthesized the lessons of Royal Oak's early postwar battles over planning, development, and local control. The cover was foregrounded by a photograph of a white mother, father, and their four young children. In the distance, behind them, stands their home—a modest bungalow on an open plot of land, surrounded in all directions by green space. (This was a rarity, to be sure, in 1950s Royal Oak.) Then standing between the family and the house, displayed in a semicircle, are a dozen municipal vehicles, including police cars, a fire engine, construction equipment, and a street cleaner, accompanied by sixteen uniform-clad municipal employees. This tableau is entitled "Making Your Home Livable," with a caption that explains the relationship between foreground, background, and middle. "Men and equipment," it explains, "symbolize the behind the scenes, and often invisible services that make your living standard as urban resident one of the highest in the world. Above are only a fraction of the people and things that contribute to the health, welfare, and safety of your family and your home."[62]

For any resident who had participated in or simply followed battles over zoning in Royal Oak, the words "health, welfare, and safety" connoted much more than fire and police protection or snow removal. Since the early 1940s these terms had provided a refrain for an ongoing, contentious local debate about suburban development and homeowners' right to dictate it. In annual reports, council and zoning board sessions, court rulings, the meetings of property improvement associations, and local newspaper reporting, Royal Oak residents learned about the sanctity of their way of life and about the centrality of homeownership, democratic institutions, and citizen vigilance to protecting it. Coverage of zoning controversies consistently introduced the phrase "public health, welfare and safety" into the public record.[63] The 300 residents who attended a workshop on community planning in 1949 learned from a local architect that residents' needed to remain involved in local politics, because it was citizens that designed American cities. Without adequate planning, added an expert from the Cranbrook Institute who spoke at the session, the region's suburban communities ran the risk of the kind of deterioration that had blighted Detroit.[64]

Comparable celebrations of the citizen-homeowner filled the pages of the *Tribune* in regular features on house building, home decorating, and the growth of local institutions. Reporters and editors attributed the spike in suburban homeownership not to federal intervention in the mortgage market, but to the hard work and initiative of the region's homeowners.

6.4 "The City of Royal Oak Annual Report Section," *Daily Tribune,* December 1, 1956. Royal Oak's annual report began appearing as a supplement to the *Daily Tribune* in 1955. The cover often featured photographs of families and homes, juxtaposed to the municipal employees and services that helped make life in the suburb attractive. Reprinted with permission of *The Daily Tribune,* Royal Oak, Michigan. Photographed by Ken Music.

Typical was a profile in January 1949 of a Royal Oak couple, the Molenvelds. The husband was a GM supervisor, his wife was a homemaker, and together they designed and decorated a beautiful new house. "Owners' Vision and Hard Work," the title announced, "Result in a Unique and Comfortable Home." The paper regularly featured photos, sketches, and floor plans of model homes. Even the appearance of new financial institutions, the grand opening of People's State bank in Hazel Park, for example, provided testament that a community could "provide for itself"; the bank was "made possible," an editorial explained, "to a large extent through the capital and effort of men within the city who already are sold on the city and its future." The paper highlighted local efforts to refurbish and maintain homes and to "beautify" neighborhoods, and gave prominent coverage to civic events celebrating the suburb's success and its residents' initiative. In 1953, former mayor and now U.S. senator George Dondero spoke at the dedication of Royal Oak's new city hall, calling the building a "symbol of those guarantees embodied in the American Constitution" and of "the free exercise of personal freedom and effort in pursuit of prosperity and happiness." To Dondero the structure was "a symbol of freedom at the local level" and "a symbol of human responsibility," one that "can serve . . . as an inspiration for better citizenship and a realization of the American dream."[65]

Property owners were constantly exhorted to protect their thriving community by remaining politically engaged. The *Tribune* had always doubled as civic cheerleader, encouraging residents to participate in local elections and community activities. But as late as 1947 it identified both its audience and the suburb's most pressing issues in far more generic terms. That year an editorial on civic duty explained that the paper's political coverage spoke to each reader "as a resident, a parent, a taxpayer, a fan, a neighbor and a clubmember." The region's "citizens" were reminded that they had the right to "exercise [their] franchise privilege: will you, Mr. and Mrs. South Oakland," the editors asked, "be two of them?" But following the Northwood controversy, the *Tribune* began addressing its readership almost exclusively as "homeowners," while describing local government's primary function as the protection of this constituency and its property. In 1954, the *Tribune*'s editor noted correctly that in the South Oakland suburbs "the predominant viewpoint is that of the homeowner." And by then the editorial page was using the privately owned home as a metaphor for suburban community itself. An "editorial in pictures" depicted several rubbish-strewn streets and lots in Royal Oak, describing the scene as "Bad Housekeeping" and reminding readers that "your city is like your home." "You would not tolerate this in your home . . . nor should you in your city."

Even news coverage of suburban growth placed homeowners at its center. The region's expansion was "a sign of progress—of people finding a better place in which to live," Philip Miller wrote in 1954. "It's a process which has been going on in America ever since the Pilgrims first landed here. We have to clear land for houses and streets." The *Tribune* predicted that "more and more people will come here to find the living space denied them in [the city]," encouraging readers to "share with them the treasures and benefits of our type of community." By 1955, it simply addressed readers as "we home owners of South Oakland county," and regularly devoted the editorial page to property owners' concerns—regarding services, ways to protect "valuable assets," or reporting on surveys that reveal "What Home Buyers Want."[66]

Floyd and Philip Miller also devoted considerable attention to the politics of growth and land use, arguing that homeowners could secure the suburb's good fortune and best manage its resources by supporting municipal autonomy and remaining active in local politics. The *Tribune*'s editors were perhaps the region's most vocal supporters of suburban home rule, citing the paper's "conviction," in 1954, "that self-government begins at home." When the residents of Southfield and Madison Heights voted to incorporate as home-rule cities in June 1955, Philip Miller saw "evidence . . . of the desire of the people here to work together under local city governments," and a year later explained that high voter turnout was common in South Oakland County suburbs because "this is an area in which representative government is close to each of us." "We know, or can easily know, the people in our city government. We can find them more approachable and more responsible to our wishes."[67]

———

Royal Oak's conversations about homeownership and its mobilizations to protect the rights of property owners were unique to this suburb, its development history, its local culture, and its personalities. Yet Royal Oak shared with most of the nation's suburbs two important traits that made these discussions and organizing efforts quite similar to those in municipalities around the country. First, most suburban communities, particularly in the North, shared a demographic peculiarity: they were home to thousands of people whose "whiteness" had recently been questioned. In the 1920s, eastern and southern Europeans had been targeted by an explicitly racialist anti-immigration campaign, and as late as the 1930s, they were restricted from neighborhoods deemed "old stock" white. When federal appraisers surveyed Detroit's suburbs in 1939, neighborhoods with a heavy "ethnic" representation ("Hungarians, Greeks, and Italians," for example) were graded C (and even sometimes D) on city survey maps because, as an overview of the region's residential patterns explained, "incompatible social groups prevail."[68] During the 1940s and 1950s, these same people were welcomed in Detroit's suburbs and their ethnic origins gradually became a source of pride. Their access to these suburbs and to homeownership was facilitated by a federally subsidized mortgage market. And their right to remain in these suburbs *because they were white* was often asserted quite forcefully. By 1960, residents who were foreign born or claimed foreign parentage represented 30 percent of the population in Royal Oak, 49.8 percent in Oak Park, 42.5 percent in Dearborn, and 33.9 percent in Ferndale. In some suburbs, including Royal Oak, only a small percentage of the "foreign" population claimed eastern or southern European ancestry. In others this group dominated, accounting for 77 percent of the "foreign stock" in Madison Heights, for example. Like their counterparts in Detroit (32.1 percent of the population in 1960), suburban ethnics were reimagining themselves as part of an American cultural "norm" during these years, further distancing themselves from an immigrant past that had once marked them as unassimilable.[69]

Equally important, this constant celebration of the white, middle-class homeowner and the literal marginalization or exclusion of renters and other "incompatible" neighbors was not unique to Royal Oak or its Oakland County neighbors. Most of the nation's suburbs were fast becoming "cities of homes" and most were almost exclusively white. The mortgage market excluded racial minorities from white suburbs. Suburban zoning practices ensured that apartments and commercial or industrial development were separated from residence A neighborhoods, either by natural or man-made barriers. Realtors, lenders, advertisers, and popular media relentlessly celebrated the white American homeowner and a suburban ideal that pictured the white family at its center. A national network of municipal officers encouraged suburban officials to engage in local public relations campaigns, using annual reports and promotional events to bolster their communities' image.[70] In short, Royal Oak's conversation about suburban growth, homeownership, and the good life was part of a national dialogue, one reproduced in every metropolitan area and reinforced by a housing market that followed strict rules about race and residence.

This fact helps explain why Royal Oak's boosters tried to attract commercial investors to their community in 1954 by portraying it a "city of homes" that was "virtually 100% white." The Chamber of Commerce brochure, "Royal Oak: Michigan's Most Promising Community," celebrated its residents' "strong pride in property ownership" and described the suburb as one "long . . . known for its attractive homes." It attributed the city's "phenomenal growth" to "careful planning by professional city planning engineers, architects and topographers." It described its homeowners as hardworking and well paid. Here the ROCC rehearsed a story about suburban growth and racial privilege long celebrated by both the public and private sectors, in what was fast becoming a nation of homeowners. It revealed that for countless metropolitan whites, "city" and "suburb" were increasingly seen as racially distinct kinds of places.[71]

CHAPTER SEVEN

Saying Race Out Loud: The Politics of Exclusion in Dearborn, 1940–1955

Dearborn residents also worked hard to exclude types of development and types of people seen as threats to their community. Likewise their preferences were not new to this era, a fact demonstrated by an initiative on the ballot in September 1940 in which 57.6 percent of Dearborn's voters rejected a proposal to build federally funded, low-income rental housing in their suburb.[1] Before the privately-owned, single-family home became more accessible and a postwar cultural standard, most Dearborners viewed apartments and low-income residents as some kind of threat.

But it was during and after World War II that exclusion became a guiding principle of local organizing efforts and a defining trope of Dearborn politics. Restriction assumed this new importance when the Detroit region's rapid growth threatened to introduce multiple-unit housing into a community that, like Royal Oak, prided itself as a "city of homes" and threatened to introduce black people into a community that prided itself as white. Again it was suburban homeowners who took the initiative and then sustained the local politics of exclusion. A coalition of Dearborn homeowners quickly took shape in the 1940s, exerted considerable influence on electoral and zoning politics, and guided the suburb toward an ever-more restrictive land-use policy. Homeowners also made the topic of restriction itself, and the suburban exclusivity that it promised to secure, a focal point of local political culture. They did so by embracing the tools, language, and logic of residential exclusion that were shaping suburban development patterns and politics nationwide. Whether organizing to block apartment construction, federally subsidized rental housing, or black occupancy, Dearborn residents defended exclusion as a practical matter, necessary to protect the free market for housing. They insisted that homeowners had the right to exclude any kind of development and any kind of people that threatened the value of their property.

What makes the Dearborn case distinct, and so useful for historians, is that circumstances forced its residents to address the topic of racial exclusion, specifically, and they did so quite directly. Two of the controversies mobilizing Dearborn's homeowners after 1940 involved residential development intended for black occupancy or suspected of being open to it. This forced residents to talk openly about their opposition to racial integration and to organize against it. Their conversations and organizing efforts highlight the subtle but decisive transformation of white racial politics in America's postwar suburbs. The vast majority of Dearborn residents endorsed segregation and treated it as a practical matter, driven solely by market considerations. They openly called for racial exclusion, while insisting that it was not necessarily "about race."

Dearborn residents did not hesitate to disparage and mock black people in other contexts. The local Exchange Club staged minstrel shows, and high school students performed the " 'Slave Dance' . . . and 'Southern Cakewalk' " in productions of *Uncle Tom's Cabin*. Advertisers and locally run comic strips constantly traded on minstrel imagery, and local crime reporting dwelled on the activities of "colored thug[s]" and "dusky robbers." Diagnosing the origins of the Detroit race riot in 1943, Dearborn editorialists concluded that high wartime wages had provided black youth with too much disposable income—presumably they could not handle the responsibility—and predicted that they would be among "the first to appear at the welfare office right after the boom days are over."[2] Yet when Dearborners discussed race in the context of housing or local development issues, they usually talked not about black character but about blacks' relationship to private property. Whites treated race as one of several objective and measurable land-use variables, seldom making distinctions between the threat posed by apartments or overcrowding or even industrial development, on the one hand, and racial integration or "Negro housing," on the other. While Royal Oak's housing activists assumed the importance of racial exclusion but left it largely unspoken, many of their Dearborn counterparts openly discussed the racial assumptions that informed their decision making. Growth politics in Dearborn provides a unique window on the local rearticulation of a national development politics that collapsed racial exclusion into a normative, managerial discourse about markets, property, citizenship, and local control.

The depth of local opposition to rental units in the 1940s is particularly notable given Dearborn's desperate need for well-built, affordable housing,

indeed for housing of any kind. The regional housing shortage hit the suburb especially hard, and the return of servicemen exacerbated the crisis. By
spring 1946, the Veterans Bureau was fielding hundreds of requests from
desperate residents—by one estimate there were 500 homeless veterans and
another 1,500 living in substandard or overcrowded dwellings. When the
Dearborn Press published new rental listings each Thursday, its office was
jammed with men and women, many carrying young children, anxiously
waiting for the paper to come off the press at noon. When a rare new listing
did appear, there was "a mad rush out the door, into cars and a wild drive
to get to the advertised house, flat or apartment, first." That fall, veterans'
groups campaigned for a bond issue to fund construction of a city-run,
500-unit rental project. Their efforts were opposed by local realtors and,
when the bond came to a vote, by 64 percent of the city's electorate.[3] In the
years since the 1940 ballot on rental housing, local opposition to affordable
residential alternatives had only increased.

Why? It is highly unlikely that the percentage of homeowners in Dearborn had grown markedly in six years' time. Since 1940, when 55.3 percent
of Dearborn's dwellings were owner-occupied, housing construction had
come to a virtual standstill, especially in the later years of the war. By 1946
the promise of FHA insurance and now VA mortgage guarantees was clearly
influential, but construction was slow in coming and had not yet provided
enough dwelling units to accommodate aspiring homeowners.

Dearborners' deepening commitment to exclusion is best understood
by examining the emergence of a powerful new homeowners' coalition that
reshaped local development politics in the mid-1940s. The first decisive
contest, a 1944 battle over a proposed "Negro" housing project, raised residents' fears about the threat of "racial invasion," generated considerable
support for racial exclusion, and energized local activists. These activists in
turn waged an aggressive campaign to promote restrictive zoning, adoption
of race-restrictive covenants, and election of a city council committed to
exclusion. After covenants were ruled unenforceable by the Supreme Court
in 1948, homeowners focused their energies on the zoning ordinance and
informal strategies for policing the color line. And throughout these years,
they helped sustain support for Mayor Orville Hubbard, who was more
than willing to play the race card. As in Royal Oak and suburbs nationwide, the spatial and resource pressures created by metropolitan growth and
black migration initiated numerous local contests over land use. Emerging triumphant in most of these communities, and certainly in Dearborn,
were the people who owned their homes and those who counted on soon
joining their ranks. The most concrete product of their activism was restric-

tion itself. Throughout the 1940s and early 1950s, Dearborn residents repeatedly blocked apartment construction, low-income housing, and black occupancy in the city.

The political ascendance of Dearborn's homeowners also helped shift the rhetorical focus of local politics, creating a suburbwide preoccupation with residential restriction, homeowners' rights, and municipal autonomy. Dearborn activists embraced a strategy fast becoming a trademark of suburban politics nationwide: the claim that housing and development issues were best addressed by trusting the unfettered, free market for property, and, by extension, the desires of residents who owned their homes. Dearborners' commitment to protecting property markets and suburban autonomy reveals how residents participated in the creation of a new kind of exclusionary politics during these years. Battles over housing gave rise to a racially coded politics of restriction, unique to the locality but drawing upon national models and national transformations. By war's end, land-use politics in Dearborn was firmly grounded in a racially constructed theory of housing and property.

Many Dearborn residents were far more explicit than their suburban neighbors about the purported links between homeownership, good government, neighborhood stability, and race. But the Dearborn case study, rather than demonstrating how "racist" its residents were, reveals instead how whites throughout the region were learning to see property and neighborhoods through a new kind of racial prism. The difference between land-use politics in Dearborn and other suburbs was not that residents poisoned debates over development, property, taxes, or city services by letting racial preferences influence their decision-making. The difference was that many Dearborn residents explicitly identified black occupancy as the most prominent of the supposedly incompatible land uses that threatened their homes and neighborhoods and against which they saw it as their right as homeowners to organize. Dearborn's development politics reveals that suburban whites were learning to treat the issue of racial exclusion primarily as a land-use issue.

The Dearborn case is valuable for two other reasons. First, Hubbard's prominence and Dearborn's unique (and infamous) history of racial controversy has earned the suburb a symbolic status among historians as a bastion of "working-class racism"; one study describes the community as a "white working class racist utopia." Readers most often encounter postwar Dearborn, regularly coupled with Cicero, Illinois, as a community unique for its intolerance, its blue-collar families under the spell of their outspoken, confrontational, and often bombastic mayor. There are a number of significant problems with this characterization. While Orville Hubbard openly endorsed segregation and served as a lightning rod on racial controversies, he was by no means the ringleader of Dearborn's antiblack mobilizations. Moreover, Dearborn was not entirely working class and its most prominent housing activists were solidly middle class.[4] The cross-class enthusiasm for racial exclusion raises important questions about the role that socioeconomic status played in shaping whites' views about and responses to integration. The cross-class alliances supporting exclusion throughout metropolitan Detroit suggest that working-class and middle-class racism regularly operated in the same terms, relied upon the same strategies, and invoked the same rationales.

The Dearborn case is also revealing because the city's restrictionist forces coalesced quite early, years before a similar coalition took shape in Royal Oak. By the end of World War II, Dearborn's homeowners had already demonstrated their commitment to shaping local land-use patterns. Subsequent zoning and development controversies were seldom over the importance of restriction, on which most residents agreed, but instead provided arenas in which local leaders, businessmen, and residents fought to define the meaning of exclusion and to prove themselves its true champions. The struggles between mayor, council, and homeowners to claim the restrictionist cause as their own reveal that the ideas fueling exclusion were hardly fixed and that arguments for prohibiting apartment construction or black occupancy were not simply about land-use management, *or* race, *or* economics. Instead they were flexible political instruments used to build coalitions, to secure political power, and to control both the nature of new development and the populations that settled there.

Wartime Housing Politics and the FPHA Controversy

When Orville Hubbard was elected mayor in December 1941, Dearborn's local politics focused neither on housing nor on race. The suburb was best known for being the home of a massive Ford Motor assembly plant, for the influence that Ford wielded over the local economy and government, and for municipal corruption. In 1915, Henry Ford bought land at the confluence of the Rouge and Detroit rivers, just southwest of Detroit in what was then Dearborn Township, to build a facility for producing coke, smelt iron, and tractors. Two years later he began construction on a plant that, when completed in 1927, boasted 93 buildings, including a foundry—briefly the world's largest—and facilities for making tires, glass, and engines, 100 miles of railroad track, and its own fire department, police force, and hospital. That year Ford Motor shifted its final assembly line from its Highland Park installation to the new River Rouge complex, making Dearborn the home of a self-contained, 2000-acre industrial city that transformed raw materials into automobiles and soon employed 100,000 workers.

In 1927 Dearborn also became a home-rule municipality and two years later merged with the neighboring Township of Fordson (formerly Springwells). The expanded suburb, which now stretched about seven miles from its eastern border with Detroit to its western border with Dearborn Heights, was widely viewed as a "Ford" town. The Ford Motor Company and related support industries provided most of the jobs, attracted most of the residents, and paid the bulk of the city's taxes. It was Ford's presence that triggered Dearborn's consolidation and remarkable expansion: its population increased from 3,500 to 50,000 during the 1920s. The suburb's first two mayors, Clyde Ford (1929–37) and John Carey (1937–41), were Ford-family surrogates who answered to Harry Bennett, head of Ford security and nationally famous for terrorizing UAW activists at the Rouge facility. Locally, Bennett was equally notorious for running a lucrative gambling and prostitution ring out of Dearborn City Hall, with assistance from two Dearborn police officials, two detectives, and a public safety commissioner.[5]

When Hubbard faced off against the Bennett machine for the first time in 1939, at the age of thirty-six, most voters saw him as little more than a perennial candidate. By then the native of Union City, Michigan, and graduate of Detroit School of Law had waged eight campaigns for city, state, and federal office, registering his best finish in 1938 when he won the GOP nomination for State Senate. (He lost in the general election.) In 1939, his third shot at the mayoralty, he finished a very close second behind Carey. Candidate Hubbard presented a consistent message, promoting municipal public works projects, tax reform, and old-age pensions, proposals that he dismissed years later as "socialistic." Above all else Hubbard cast himself as a self-made man and, especially when running for municipal office, as a reformer. The reformer tag made the difference during his fourth mayoral campaign, in 1941, because Bennett's illicit activities had finally caught up with him. That year a magazine exposé and several grand jury indictments confirmed residents' suspicions about the depth of Dearborn's municipal corruption. Carey wisely chose to retire, making Clarence Doyle, a leading City Council member and long-time political figure, the front-runner to replace him. Doyle was never implicated in any illegal activity, but Hubbard saw an opportunity to highlight his own reform credentials by casting

Doyle as a city-hall insider, thus guilty by association. Hubbard edged past Doyle in the final count to become the third mayor of the young suburb of Dearborn.[6]

While Bennett might have lost his tight grip over city hall, Hubbard took office in a municipality that owed its well-being and its remarkable class and ethnic diversity to the Ford Motor Company. By 1940 the suburb's industries and its proximity to employers on Detroit's west side had attracted almost 64,000 residents; Ford alone provided over one-third of the city's jobs. Ford owned much of the real estate in central Dearborn, practically dividing its eastern and western sections into separate communities. Meanwhile the mammoth Rouge facility in Dearborn's southeast was (and still is) visible from many east-side residential neighborhoods. Yet Dearborn's association with the auto industry and the Rouge plant's iconic status in modern labor history have led most commentators to depict Dearborn, imprecisely, as a working-class suburb. Instead, it was a remarkably heterogeneous place, home not just to industrial workers and secretaries but to professionals, managers, and middle-class housewives. Middle-class households dominated in certain western neighborhoods and blue-collar households were more heavily represented in the east, but at the census-tract level most sections of the city were socioeconomically mixed. The suburb's ethnic divisions broke down a bit more consistently along geographical lines with western Europeans concentrated in the west and other immigrant groups concentrated in the east. The largest white ethnic groups were Polish and Italian, followed by migrants (or their children) from Germany, Syria, Russia, Rumania, Hungary, Austria, Yugoslavia, Czechoslovakia, Ireland, Greece, Lithuania, and Mexico. In 1930, the neighborhood just southeast of the Rouge plant was home to 49 different languages. As late as 1960, over 42 percent of Dearborn's residents were either foreign born or had at least one foreign-born parent.[7]

Hubbard's most loyal political support in his earlier, failed campaigns and then as mayor came from the east side, where working class outnumbered middle class, where self-identified ethnic communities had a much stronger presence, and where suburban residence was more a political and rhetorical distinction than a spatial or aesthetic one. Dearborn's eastern neighborhoods were platted and some partially developed before World War II, simultaneously with identical neighborhoods just across the Detroit border. Dearborn's northeast is a peninsula, surrounded by Detroit on three sides and bordered by Greenfield Road, Tireman Street, and a stretch of industrial property. Dearborn's southeast is largely cut off from the rest of the suburb by the Rouge plant. The neighborhood is closer to Detroit than it is to other residential enclaves in Dearborn, and two cemeteries and a park mark the divide between "city" and "suburb" (see figs. 7.1 and 7.2).[8]

But what sharply distinguished all of Dearborn's neighborhoods from those in Detroit was the absence of black people. Dearborn subdivisions platted in the 1910s and 1920s regularly had race-restrictive language written into their deeds. During the Depression, federal policy provided the next line of defense. By the time Hubbard entered office, nearby Detroit neighborhoods, some separated by nothing more than a city street, had been red-lined by federal appraisers. Then in the early 1940s, subdivisions in northeast Dearborn were being developed by builders who had received advance FNMA commitments on their properties and by local S&Ls "organized and existing under the Home Owners Loan Act of 1933."[9] Dearborn residents further policed the color line, as threats to neighborhood homogeneity gave birth to a powerful new homeowners' coalition. Investment in Dearborn's identity as a suburb and as a community of property owners unified residents across ethnic and class lines and quickly changed the tenor of Dearborn politics. Whites in Detroit neighborhoods just blocks away were equally vigilant during these years about keeping *their* neighborhoods free of black people. But because of the jurisdictional boundary that separated whites in Detroit from their neighbors in Dearborn, the suburban battles over race and residence would have very different implications for homeowners and for their understanding of metropolitan politics.[10]

During Hubbard's first years in office, racial exclusion was simply a given in Dearborn, rather than a prominent topic of discussion. The new mayor and the City Council spent most of their time calling each other names and battling for control over municipal appointments, public services, and the budget. Hubbard's high-handed tactics alienated many of his own constituents, especially city employees. Then in 1944 race and housing quickly became a focal point and unifier, and Dearborn began to gain notoriety as a particularly "racist" suburb.

Ironically, it was the federal government that triggered the controversy. To address the region's desperate housing shortage, and specifically to accommodate blacks who had migrated to Detroit to fill essential war-production jobs, the National Housing Agency instructed the Federal Public Housing Authority (FPHA) to erect 1,000 temporary dwelling units in the metropolitan area. By 1944, 600 units were under construction in Detroit in a black residential enclave at Eight Mile Road and Wyoming Avenue, near the so-called slave market for black day laborers. The FPHA proposed construction of another 400 units to officials in Detroit and in the majority-black Wayne County suburb of Inkster, but both cities refused. So the government

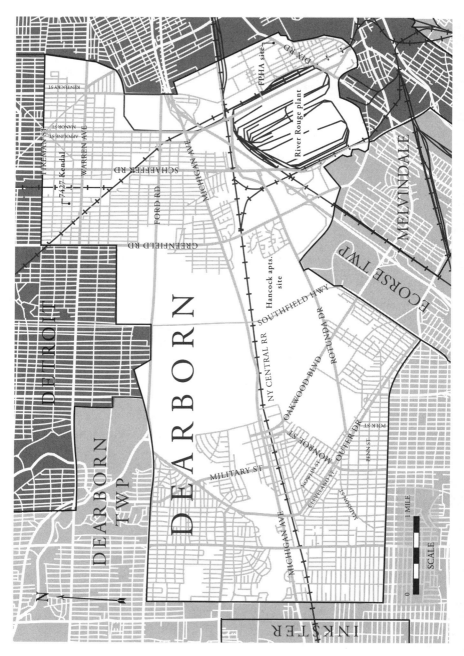

7.1 Dearborn, Michigan, 1955. Much of Dearborn's east side is physically indistinguishable from Detroit's west side. Ford's River Rouge plant dominates the suburb's
southeast. The residential subdivisions in northeastern Dearborn are separated from
Detroit by Tireman Avenue (to the north), Greenfield Road (to west), and a stretch of
industrial land (to the east); just across that industrial tract in the 1940s was one of
Detroit's isolated black residential enclaves. By 1960, blacks lived throughout Detroit's
west side, just north of Dearborn across Tireman Street. Most of the suburb's residential blocks
are lined with the prewar, gridlike subdivisions of small-lot homes characteristic
of the region's first-generation suburbs. Map by Jason Frank.

7.2 Aerial photograph of Dearborn, Michigan, ca. 1959. By the late 1950s, most of
Dearborn had been developed. Shown here is the mostly residential section bounded by
Ford Road (to the south, barely visible in the bottom left corner), Schaefer Road (to
the east), and the railroad (running northwest). Fordson High School is in the foreground.
The undeveloped land was eventually subdivided for single-family, large-lot housing,
sharply distinguishing it from the small, prewar subdivisions that dominate
this neighborhood and eastern Dearborn more generally. Courtesy of Dearborn
Historical Museum, Dearborn, Michigan.

turned to Dearborn, a city whose industries employed 12,000 blacks, the
vast majority at the Rouge facility, but which had not, in the agency's words,
absorbed any of the "publicly financed unrestricted housing for war workers." The proposal was endorsed by the Executive Board of Ford Local
No. 600 (UAW-CIO), whose leadership had for years distinguished itself
by its racial progressivism. In June, they called upon Dearborn's City
Council to provide land for construction of "houses and projects for war
workers regardless of race or creed who are employed in the plants in the
vicinity."[11]

Dearborn officials ignored the UAW-CIO appeal and refused to act
upon the federal request. So the Detroit Housing Commission (DHC) intervened, calling for construction of FPHA housing in Dearborn's southeast, on Dix Road, east of the Ford Rouge plant and just two blocks west
of the Dearborn-Detroit border. At this point Dearborn's homeowners entered the fray, quickly organizing a citywide campaign to block the project.
Meeting at Fordson High School on October 12, members of the Dearborn
Property Owners Protective Association (DPOPA) endorsed a resolution

opposing the FPHA proposal, and urged local congressmen to "use their influence with the Detroit Housing Commission and the responsible officials in Washington." Leading these efforts was DPOPA president and Board of Education member Homer Beadle, who regularly spoke on behalf of homeowners at City Council meetings and formally introduced the DPOPA complaint later that month. Soon joining the protest were several council members, other local homeowners' groups, and Mayor Hubbard, who had never before during his tenure publicly campaigned on racial issues. The mayor and several council members traveled to Washington to present their concerns to the FPHA. By November, sustained protest forced the agency to announce that the project had not yet been approved. A month later, the project for low-cost housing was dead.[12]

The successful campaign highlights three important characteristics of suburban housing politics in the 1940s. Homeowners were willing and able to control local development patterns. The battles themselves—the organizing, meetings, public hearings, and ongoing local debates—were instrumental in shaping whites' understanding of property rights and suburban exclusiveness, including their racial assumptions about both. And the larger, national politics of suburban development—its laws, policies, and public discourses—helped educate whites in this racialized vision of land use. The FPHA controversy reveals how local contests over land use provided a crucial bridge between the prewar and postwar politics of racial exclusion, as homeowners created new organizations and cultivated keen interest in local control by building upon an existing, nationally standardized template for restriction, in the process setting important organizational and ideological precedents that would shape local politics throughout the postwar era.

From the earliest stages of the FPHA controversy, residents collapsed the issue of racial integration into a broader conversation about land-use management, local autonomy, and homeowners' rights. The DPOPA's first public statement attacked the proposal on public safety grounds, noting that the parcel had "always been condemned as a menace to public health because of the smoke and impurities deposited in said area from gigantic blast furnaces and industries." Area residents soon added two more complaints, arguing that the project would infringe upon local government's right to control development and simultaneously create what they called a "racial problem." Few commentators made distinctions among racial change, federal intervention, sound land-use practice, and the proposed rental units themselves. The *Dearborn Independent*'s fall coverage, for example, merged the racial and public health arguments for restriction. When "it was learned . . . that the housing units are to be built exclusively for Negroes," the paper reported in October, the DPOPA asked council to "do what they could to prevent the Housing Commission from carrying out its plans, on the ground that the South End is not the place to locate any low-cost housing project because of the nature of the territory." The editors agreed. "If all the information we have is true, the administration should oppose the project," since Dix Road was "not suitable for human habitation—'no matter how much money is spent on the property'—to put it as Mr. Beadle has stated it. It is not an area where the encouragement of home building should be promoted, at least not by the Federal Government. If this is the best the Federal Government has to offer human beings, then it better get out of the housing business and leave it up to real estate promoters—surely they could do a better job."[13]

This insistence that the parcel was not "suitable for human habitation" if the federal government built the housing previewed a narrative about federal intervention repeated throughout the FPHA controversy. The editors insisted that private developers would "do a better job" than the state because they did not consider the state's involvement in private housing markets to be intervention at all. They drew a sharp distinction between residential development "promoted . . . by the Federal Government," by which they meant public or rent-subsidized housing, and that sponsored by "real estate promoters," despite the latter's reliance on a state-regulated and subsidized mortgage market. This was a common misperception, reinforced nationally by the FHA's Depression-era promotional efforts and by sustained congressional and private-sector opposition to public housing legislation. It was reinforced locally, by a suburban press that uncritically endorsed public-private initiatives to encourage homeownership, that ran countless advertisements for new homes boasting "Lower FHA Down Payments," and that portrayed public housing as an abuse of federal authority and an assault on the private market. Even the suburb's vocal critics of federal intervention, Hubbard among them, did not hesitate to embrace the selective credit programs that were helping Dearborn residents purchase homes. After helping defeat the FPHA project, for example, the mayor invited FHA officials to city hall to discuss strategies for stimulating local housing construction. The meeting saw George Zinky, state director of the FHA, John Neary, of Dearborn's Veterans' Council, and about fifty local contractors join Hubbard in calling upon the federal government to divert building materials to the housing sector. The *Dearborn Press* reprinted their resolution, without editorial comment about federal government's impact on private housing markets. Hubbard also exhorted City Council members to support construction of veterans housing by again embracing public-private collaboration, this time endorsing the Wagner-Ellender-Taft housing bill that was awaiting congressional approval. What made that legislation foresighted, in the mayor's view, was its focus on using private capital to address the housing crisis (by building apartment complexes in urban centers).[14]

The equation of "federal" or "low-income" housing with black occupancy quickly became a prominent refrain in debate over the FPHA project. Hubbard raised the stakes in early November when he called upon the DHC to recommend an alternative location. It dismissed his request. So on November 16, an overflow crowd assembled at the Roulo School, adjacent to the proposed construction site in southeast Dearborn, to hear Hubbard, Beadle, and councilman Norman Edwards rally against the project. Residents were given contact information for federal housing officials in Washington, D.C. Members of Ford Local 600 (UAW-CIO) were urged to press the union's Executive Board to retract its endorsement. Hubbard warned that the apartment complex would "create a racial problem that does not exist here now," because "mixed housing can lead only to more trouble." Repeating this warning the next day to the City Council, Hubbard insisted that countless residents had been contacting him and organizing "vigorous protests and opposition." He added that "Dearborn's attitudes on racial matters are no better and no worse than that of any other Michigan community" and that residents' "resistance and strong feeling" were warranted. "It is expected when something is forced on a community," Hubbard continued, citing the recurring wartime violence at Detroit's federally funded Sojourner Truth homes, where black occupancy was "forced" on a "white neighborhood." If the FPHA project was built, the mayor concluded, "home owners in Dearborn face economic losses."[15]

Versions of this cautionary tale simultaneously about property, local autonomy, race, and rights informed every stage of the ensuing protest. Initially described by journalists and protesters as a "federal housing project," the FPHA proposal soon became the "federal housing project for Negroes" or the "Negro housing project" in most newspaper coverage and public forums. Residents and officials described residential integration as an affront to their freedom of choice and to their rights as homeowners, taxpayers, and responsible community members. A day after the Roulo School meeting, Hubbard called a special session of the City Council to "adopt an appropriate resolution . . . vigorously opposing a Federal Housing project for Negroes in Dearborn" and to take "whatever other action" was necessary to "fully protect the rights, interests and welfare" of Dearborn residents. His draft resolution was reproduced in the *Independent*:

Whereas, [the FPHA's actions] will be a direct interference with, and an invasion of the right of the City of Dearborn as a local governmental unit to determine its housing needs; . . . Whereas, The war is being fought to maintain and continue our American Way of Life and we want to keep Dearborn a desirable place in which to live; . . . Whereas, We have the right and want to choose our own neighbors, friends and associates and resent being forced to accept the dictates of some bureaucrat in Washington that we must accept a Federal Housing project for negroes when we refuse to build a like project for our own race; . . . Now, therefore, be it resolved, That we . . . protest and object to the attitude of the Federal Public Housing Authority.

It was an "attitude," he reiterated, that represented "a direct interference with and challenge to the powers of local governmental units to determine the need for housing with the city."[16]

The council agreed, quickly passing a similar resolution. Other civic groups spoke out as well, although in language far more circumspect about race. A Dearborn Board of Education resolution on the FPHA proposal made no mention of black occupancy, arguing instead that the project would represent "a shocking invasion of the right of local self-government." "The economic well-being and protection of the taxpayers of this district," the board wrote, "demand that local planning, zoning and other regulations be strictly adhered to." Sitting on the board was Homer Beadle, head of the DPOPA and one of the city's most committed segregationists, a clear indication that at least some of its members were focused on keeping black residents out of the city. Meanwhile, most of the calls to protect residents' "economic well-being" sat comfortably with those that warned of a "racial problem," so much so that distinctions between the two strategies escaped the notice of local commentators. The extensive local press coverage regularly conflated the racial and economic arguments for exclusion.[17]

So consuming was the FPHA controversy throughout the fall that local papers devoted comparatively little attention to the November presidential election and Franklin Roosevelt's bid for a fourth term in office. In retrospect, whites' local preoccupations, particularly with development issues, reveal a great deal about the New Deal electoral coalition that Roosevelt had helped to create. Dearborn was a solidly Democratic town. And while it is unlikely that residents drew the connections at the time, local land-use battles were symptomatic of the fortunes of both the Democratic Party and the new activist state that it had fashioned. By the early 1940s, white electoral support for the New Deal had been secured through massive state intervention: relief and employment programs, protections for laborers and consumers, social security, and a fast-growing new market for suburban homeownership. Just weeks after the DHC proposed the FPHA project for Dearborn, Congress passed the GI Bill. With few exceptions, these federal programs had benefited—and continued to benefit—people of European descent while excluding most racial minorities.[18]

Meanwhile, federal involvement in housing markets and zoning politics was helping resegregate metropolitan regions *and* refashion whites' defense of residential segregation. By the 1940s, a narrative about free markets for housing and the market imperative for exclusion was becoming foundational to countless local political battles over development and housing. Dearborn's builders, bankers, realtors, journalists, elected officials, and its FHA representatives rehearsed locally a story about race and property already codified nationwide in court rulings, legislation, economics textbooks, and appraisal manuals. Resolutions opposing the FPHA project defended the "rights of local self-government," the "economic well-being" of homeowners, and a community's right to "choose [its] own neighbors." This was a language inherited from decades of legal, legislative, and planning debates over land use, exclusion, and property markets and inscribed in the statutes and programs fueling suburban growth, metropolitan fragmentation, and new patterns of racial segregation. When Dearborn officials and residents invoked their right to exclude, they were asserting a racially specific concept of economic and political privilege, a concept endorsed and codified by the laws, practices, and programs implemented by Hoover's "associative" state and then, much more extensively, during the New Deal.

Just as federal interventions exhibited a tension between explicit and coded calls for racial exclusion, so too did postwar suburbanites alternate between naming racial integration as a specific threat and collapsing it into an amorphous category of interchangeable hazards or nuisances. Men like Hubbard and Beadle did not hesitate to oppose the FPHA project by discussing race, yet even their appeals, when seen in the context of New Deal–era housing politics, reveal their investment in a new kind of racial politics and a new discourse about racial exclusion. Repeated invocations of the free market and condemnations of the federal government for not building housing "for our own race" betrayed whites' misunderstanding of housing economics in the FHA era. Whites were not building and buying houses by the sheer force of their will and determination. But the story about state support for white homeownership had been erased from public discourse since the earliest days of the New Deal.

It is fitting that in November 1944 two issues dominated local news reporting in Dearborn. The first was the FPHA controversy, described by the *Independent* in a year-end summary of local news as "protests over the pending Negro Housing Project . . . flood[ing] the desk of the mayor from many organizations," forcing the City Council into a special session. The other newsworthy event that month was the presidential election, and the expected outcome: "Roosevelt carries Dearborners." It was a local victory, one of countless such victories nationwide, for what historians would later call the "New Deal coalition."[19]

The Roosevelt administration was listening to whites in suburbs like Dearborn. In late November the FPHA's Detroit-area representative, George Schermer, informed residents that "no conclusion has been reached to build" and that "pending a decision on the present studies, no formal proposal is being submitted to the City Council." The controversy lasted throughout the winter and spring and local residents continued to organize, but the FPHA would never complete the project.[20]

The battle over the FPHA proposal fueled two influential political developments in Dearborn. It provided critical organizational momentum for the city's homeowners' associations. Within weeks of Schermer's announcement, an energized DPOPA opened a new downtown office, from which it continued to fight the FPHA and initiated an aggressive campaign to encourage adoption of race-restrictive covenants in Dearborn's residential subdivisions. The controversy also enabled local activists to popularize a powerful new political narrative about property and race. Building upon decades of public-private efforts and tapping directly into federal resources, Dearborn housing activists insisted that racial restriction was nothing more than a land-use issue, that it had nothing to do with ideology or prejudice. This narrative co-existed, often quite comfortably, with more familiar, traditionally "racist" arguments against integration. Some whites proudly declared their antipathy toward black people. Yet the market-imperative rationale was rapidly gaining currency, in large part because activists and publicists embraced it wholeheartedly and made it central to their organizational efforts. Grassroots organizing and local news coverage of development controversies document the compatibility of—and perhaps the gradual transition between—two complementary white narratives about the need for racial exclusion.

The DPOPA's racial covenant campaign began to take shape in late November, when Homer Beadle scheduled three community meetings at a local high school. Helping spread the word was the *Independent*, which ran a news article announcing the meeting dates and detailing the racial covenants under consideration. Residents from five Dearborn subdivisions—A. P. Ternes, A. P. Ternes No. 1, Galt Park, Horger's Ford Park, and Melrose Gardens—attended the meetings, where the DPOPA collected signatures on a declaration of property restrictions "limiting occupancy to members of the Caucasian race." Two weeks later, the DPOPA invited residents from another eight subdivisions—Ford Chase, Ford Chase 1, Ford Chase 2, Schaefer Heights, Chase Warren, J. M. Welch, Warren Avenue, and Jones Roemer—to a January 4 meeting at Fordson High School, again with the *Independent's* assistance. The "purpose of the association," the paper reported, was "stimulat[ing] interest in property restrictions," specifically to "members of the Caucasian race." At other times the DPOPA campaign was depicted in race-neutral, managerial terms. A December news article announcing the grand opening of the DPOPA's new Michigan Avenue office described it simply as a place "where persons interested in setting up or continuing subdivision restrictions can secure the information they desire." "The association's program," the paper wrote three days later, "is to insure that occupancy restrictions are set up in all subdivisions of the city to insure property values."[21]

Local organizing efforts further blurred the lines between the racial and economic rationale for exclusion. Residents who attended the DPOPA meetings were presented with a "Restriction Agreement," a standardized, ready-to-use covenant that required homeowners only to fill in their names, identify their lots and subdivisions, and sign. Both of the model forms were designed specifically and exclusively to exclude nonwhites, restricting "the use and occupancy [of said premises] to white persons of the Caucasian race." (Employees of white families were excepted.) The restrictions would "run with the land" and were to remain in effect until 75–80 percent of the owners of the subdivision's frontage lots approved their removal (see fig. 7.3). Both forms gave current homeowners considerable power, explaining that all owners "shall be bound" by the agreement "whether or not this agreement or agreement of similar intent shall have been executed" by them. At only one point do the covenants explain why racial restriction was necessary. In signing one model form, homeowners declared simply that they were "desirous of maintaining the general character of the neighborhood," echoing a standardized language used by appraisers, realtors, bankers, and courts nationwide.[22]

The market imperative rationale was repeated even more formulaically in other venues, especially in the DPOPA's membership recruitment drives. Following their victory in the FPHA affair, probably in late 1945 or early

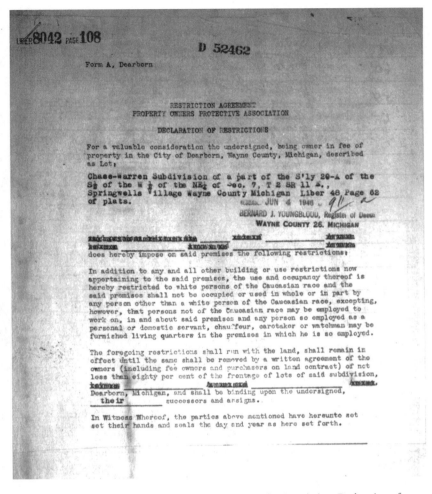

7.3 Restriction Agreement: Property Owners Protective Association, Declaration of Restrictions; completed Form A, for lot in the Chase-Warren Subdivision, Dearborn. At meetings held in 1944 and 1945, the DPOPA encouraged residents to fill out race-restrictive covenants for their properties. Form A restricted "use and occupancy . . . to white persons of the Caucasian race . . . , excepting, however, that persons not of the Caucasian race may be employed to work on, in and about said premises" and "may be furnished living quarters in the premises." Racial exclusion by deed restriction was legally enforceable in the United States until 1948. Courtesy of the Dearborn Historical Museum, Dearborn, Michigan.

1946, the association distributed a pamphlet warning homeowners about the dire threat of racial integration. Equal parts DPOPA advertisement and "how-to" manual in race restriction, the four-page brochure never discusses members' racial views or even the issue of racial compatibility. A prefatory note written by Beadle explains that the pamphlet was distributed to "inform property owners . . . what steps might be taken to preserve the present values of residential property in the city." "A survey of communities," he continues, "reveals that the two factors that most seriously depreciate values of real estate are: first, introduction of Negro housing into white neighborhoods, and second, location of small industry in residential areas." The brochure then follows a question-and-answer format. "Can any provision be placed in the city charter or can any city ordinance restrict a municipality to citizens of the Caucasian race?" The answer is "No"—government authorities were forbidden from restricting municipal residence to "any American citizen" or from "limiting the sale [of property] to members of the Caucasian race." But private "occupancy restrictions" were legal, the text continues, and have "been repeatedly upheld by both the Circuit Court and the Supreme Court of Michigan." After reiterating the important distinction that "you cannot limit sale to any American citizen . . . You can only limit by occupancy and use restriction," the brochure instructs readers on how to add restrictions to a deed.[23]

Next, a detailed discussion of covenant law explains that court rulings on occupancy restrictions "have been clear cut." In cases including "Parmalee vs. Morriss, 218 Mich. 625; Porter vs. Barrett, 233 Mich. 373; Schulte vs. Starke, 238 Mich. 102; [and] Tilletson vs. Gregory, 151 Mich. 128," the pamphlet explains, judges have ruled "that a restriction limited to the occupancy of premises by persons within the purview of the restrictions is valid." Details from a circuit court decision then demonstrate to an average homeowner how these legal abstractions impacted neighborhoods much like their own. "The most recent case [was] in the Circuit Court for the County of Wayne in Chancery, Wagner Saari, et al., Plaintiff, vs. Silas Silvers; Joel Marshall, and Rosa Marshall, his wife, Defendants, #344 548, in which a violation of a restriction which prohibited Negroes from occupying lot No. 487 in the Robert Oakman's 12th-Street Subdivision." The pamphlet quotes a Third Circuit Court ruling by Judge John V. Brennan, from June 25, 1945, which deemed occupancy restrictions against Negroes as "valid and enforceable." "It is common knowledge," wrote Brennan, "that the Courts cannot interfere with the rights of people lawfully to contract. Furthermore, it is well established that the right of restriction, in general, of property, both as to ownership, use, occupancy, condition, etc., is of longstanding, well understood by the buyer, the seller, the owner, the occupant and the public in general." Resuming the question and answer format, the text discusses the status and validity of existing subdivision restrictions in Dearborn. It assures residents that the cost of updating restrictions "would be very nominal" ("if the membership of the subdivision will fully cooperate"). It introduces language to insert in the deed. Finally, it details the procedures for ensuring that the restrictions "comply with the recording laws of the state of Michigan." [24]

Most revealing is the DPOPA's almost exclusive focus on the mechanics, legality, and economics of restriction. It frames a discussion about racial exclusion in the legal and managerial language of land-use science, casting segregation solely as a means to preserve what the authors call "present values." Immediately after introducing sample deed language and procedural instructions, for example, the text asks "what effect . . . an occupancy restriction [has] on the valuation of property in areas such as Dearborn?" The answer: "Within a short time it may become one of the most important factors influencing the sale of property and maintaining property values." A section entitled "Summary" explains that "the surest and quickest way to lower property values in a community is to introduce by-racial [sic] housing." It adds that recent events in Wayne County, clearly referring to the violence of the 1943 race riot in Detroit and whites' attacks on black residents at the Sojourner Truth homes, offer "ample proof that this method of attempting to solve the Negro housing problem has not only failed to advance the Negro cause, but has developed a feeling of intense antagonism . . . that constantly threatens to disrupt the peace and tranquility of the areas where such housing has been attempted." Moving yet further from the organization's focus on excluding black people, the text warns of the "danger of Federal encroachment on the rights of local Government." Only once does the pamphlet betray its authors' struggle to reconcile older racial myths with the new, market imperative argument for exclusion. "Practical idealists," the DPOPA writes, needed to "demand that Congress strip the heads of these Federal bureaus of the power to impose their crackpot theories and personal philosophy in anthropology on communities at the expense of the small home owner whose life savings, in many instances, are at stake." [25]

This is the closest that the organization comes to acknowledging an older, biological narrative about the necessity of racial segregation. The DPOPA never described black people as a threat to whites but focuses instead on black occupancy as categorically destructive to both "small homeowners" and the local institutions that represent them. Indeed it drew a sharp distinction between "personal philosophy" and assorted (unnamed) "crackpot theories," on the one hand, and the hard and fast principles of real estate economics, on the other. The organization never advertised itself as an "anti-Negro" or "pro-Caucasian" group. They called themselves, instead, a "Non Profit Organization" designed—as the pamphlet's header read—"To Establish and Enforce Subdivision Restrictions and promote better Zoning

Ordinances." Further confirmation of their pragmatism comes in the pamphlet's concluding section, which returns to the subject of keeping small industrial plants far from residential neighborhoods so that "slum areas" would not develop. "Public officials who condone this," the text explains, "should be brought to accountability before this practice results in a general breakdown of property values in the areas affected."[26] According to white housing activists, black occupancy was a quantifiable and thus calculable risk, comparable to noxious fumes and traffic congestion.

Whites were learning to campaign for racial exclusion without talking about racial difference or preference. The new homeowners' politics was grounded in a new national land-use politics and practice, both of which codified the myth that property had an intrinsic racial value. To defend their neighborhoods, Dearborn activists studied appraisal guidelines and monitored court rulings on zoning, property rights, and racial restriction. Their lawyers, at the very least, examined relevant case law and presented it to association members, introducing the precedents that defined racial exclusion as a right of property owners, justified as an economic exigency. It is notable that the DPOPA also followed in the footsteps of planners, judges, and federal housing officials, by treating private contract law (concerning restrictive covenants) and public land-use law (concerning zoning) as interchangeable. "Subdivision restriction" and "better zoning," the brochure explains, were complementary tools, designed and implemented solely to ensure efficient and economical land use. These legal and market narratives were presented in DPOPA flyers, debated at association meetings, and presented publicly in its resolutions. Using the courts to validate and further promote racial exclusion, white activists introduced a standardized, social scientific language about homeowners' rights—and about the economic necessity of excluding incompatible development or people—to very particular, local debates over restriction.

The DPOPA campaign highlights the subtle but decisive transformation of white housing politics in the 1940s. Local activists, reluctant to announce their intolerance at a time when whites were publicly embracing the concept of antiracism, found relief in a land-use science and politics codified, paradoxically, during an era that openly sanctioned and rationalized racial inequality. The result was a new, coded land-use politics grounded in the same assumptions about the dangers of integration and drawing upon prewar precedents to justify exclusion but now emphasizing those precedents' supposed ideological neutrality. A new generation of suburban housing activists used the managerial and market language fashioned by an earlier generation of zoning experts and land-use economists. But the post-

1940 campaigns were no longer accompanied by pronouncements about "heaven's first law" and public declarations that "niggers are just different." The DPOPA did not promote restriction after World War II by using ideologically neutral land-use instruments for "racist" purposes. Indeed they did not attempt to distinguish between the "economic" factors that necessitated restrictive zoning and the "racial" factors fueling support for covenants. Rather, white activists promoted restriction by conceiving of real estate economics and land-use politics in specifically racial terms. For whites who advocated residential exclusion in the Detroit region, ideas about property, about homeowners' rights, and about the best means of protecting both were racially constructed.

———

By war's end, the FPHA controversy and DPOPA efforts had combined to make land-use restriction a guiding principle of Dearborn politics. A community that devoted little time to race and housing issues when it elected Orville Hubbard in 1941 was already establishing a regional reputation as a place preoccupied with racial exclusion. Over the next decade, a powerful coalition of homeowners continued to set the terms of debate over development and decisively shape local governance. A prorestriction council was soon voted into office, and its members protected the development vision promoted by Dearborn's homeowners' associations. Most public officials represented themselves as staunch supporters of what was called "responsible" land use. So widespread was electoral support for restriction that Hubbard and council members—who clashed regularly on a range of issues—used the exclusion issue to gain political leverage, seeking to position themselves as the true defenders of the city's homeowners.

In the first municipal elections following the FPHA controversy, Dearborn voters elected a city council firmly committed to residential restriction. In the weeks before the November 1945 ballot, a pro-Hubbard group named the Business and Civic Leaders of Dearborn (BCLD) endorsed seven candidates for council: Dr. Edward F. Fisher, Ray F. Parker, Joseph M. Ford, Howard A. Ternes, Anthony M. Esper, M. O. Nickon, and Harry A. Hoxie. These were men, explained a BCLD flyer, that would "fight" for two things: "a better transportation system" and "to keep Negro housing out of Dearborn." All but Nickon and Hoxie were elected, as was Homer Beadle, a Hubbard-adversary who had demonstrated his restrictionist credentials as DPOPA director.[27]

Homeowners also set the terms of debate over development. The first official to learn this was Fisher, a physician and former state legislator. Upon appointment as council president in January 1946, Fisher spoke publicly about the city's housing crisis and his commitment to helping Dearborn's veterans. To the BCLD's great surprise, Fisher declared that the suburb encouraged "people of every race and nationality" to avail themselves of its "opportunities" and to make "their good contribution to the city's life." Clearly Fisher misjudged the strength of support for racial restriction, or at least mistakenly assumed that he could withstand any backlash against an integrationist stance. Forced to resign days later, he was replaced by Martin Griffith, past president of the Junior Chamber of Commerce, current Rotary Club and Chamber of Commerce member, and District Sales Manager of the Ebling Creamery Company.[28]

The power of the restrictionist bloc was most evident when residents, council, and developers battled over zoning and development. The first contest came in 1946, over the proposal to build low-rent housing for veterans. The ballot initiative asked voters to approve construction of a "City-owned and operated housing project for rental purposes in Dearborn not exceeding 500 units." Residents rejected it by a vote of 10,392 to 5,760. On that same ballot they rejected a proposal for a city-owned trailer camp by a vote of 12,835 to 3,165. These emergency measures were defeated despite an aggressive campaign by nine local veterans groups, joining forces as the Dearborn Veterans Housing Committee, to educate residents and draw them to the polls. The organization pitched pup-tents at thirty Dearborn polling places to dramatize the plight of the city's homeless veterans. The housing crisis could not convince Dearborn residents that rental or "public" housing was suitable for their community.[29]

The emergence of this restrictionist majority did not stifle debate completely. Zoning politics, in particular, remained very contentious in Dearborn throughout the late 1940s and early 1950s, because some builders and residents still saw apartment construction as a viable (and profitable) solution to the housing shortage. They repeatedly pressed the issue, and repeatedly lost. Meanwhile the controversies provided local officials with numerous opportunities to brandish their restrictionist credentials and to express their contempt for other public figures. Hubbard and most council members agreed by 1946 about the need to exclude apartments and low-income housing, but they agreed on little else. Two of the suburb's most vocal proponents of racial exclusion, Hubbard and Beadle, engaged in a very bitter public political rivalry throughout the late 1940s. The contrast with development politics in Royal Oak is instructive. Hubbard and many of his critics in the council, unable to gain leverage by playing the restriction card, worked to position themselves as the true champions of restriction and all that it stood for: local control, property rights, and racial privilege.

The infighting dated back to 1942 and the adoption of a new city charter that considerably enhanced the mayor's power. (A citizen-led petition drive in 1941 created the charter commission in the same election that brought Hubbard to office; the new mayor became the beneficiary of residents' disgust with years of municipal corruption and gridlock.) Throughout 1943 and 1944, the council rejected Hubbard's appointments, accusing him of using municipal jobs and salary increases to "pay . . . political debts." These skirmishes continued throughout the mid- and late 1940s, despite council-mayoral unanimity, for the most part, over housing issues. In the December 1947 elections, with the mayor under fire for pushing through tax cuts that threatened the city's solvency, the anti-Hubbard coalition regained a 4 to 3 council majority. (Councilwoman Marguerite Johnson provided the potential swing vote.) At a lame-duck council meeting later that month, a defiant Hubbard created four new municipal bureaus: Information, Complaint, Public Relations, and Public Service. The new council abolished all four at its first meeting in January. Beadle led the opposition, quickly positioning himself as the mayor's most prominent council critic. A year of jousting followed. When Hubbard proposed massive expenditures for public improvements, the new council replaced them with what they called a more "realistic" plan. Hubbard then introduced legislation to reestablish the Public Relations department and secured Johnson's vote to see it through, only to see that same council abolish it in December by a vote of 6 to 1. Beadle, who had opposed the PR bureau from the outset, called it "nothing more than a political instrument." Councilmen Parker and Ford, who usually supported Hubbard's initiatives, suggested that they would support the bureau if its director was a civil servant instead of a mayoral appointee.[30]

Attempting to distinguish themselves to an ethnically and socioeconomically diverse electorate that shared only European descent and property ownership in common, Hubbard and his opponents maneuvered to portray themselves as the true protectors of Dearborn's homeowner-citizens. This jockeying for popular support was especially evident during the suburb's most famous development controversy: the 1948 battle over a proposal by the John Hancock Life Insurance Company to build a huge multiunit rental project in central Dearborn. Homeowners prevailed again, blocking the Hancock apartments. But the episode deserves careful consideration, because it illustrates residents' preoccupation with land-use issues and racial exclusion. It challenges the common argument that Hubbard spearheaded the anti-Hancock campaign by appealing to residents' "latent" racism.[31] And the controversy reveals how the national and local politics of racial exclusion, together, helped sustain support for suburban restriction while shaping whites' ideas about property, planning, and what it meant to exclude.

Homeowners vs. the John Hancock Apartments

The battle over the Hancock apartments is best understood in the context of local development politics in 1948. The desperate housing shortage was still on residents' minds; as the *Dearborn Guide* commented that fall, "everybody [still] knows some person who needs an apartment." That year two thousand families visited the Housing Bureau to find accommodations or solicit advice for improving rental properties. But Dearborn was also, like its suburban neighbors, in the midst of a construction and tenancy revolution. Federal programs made the difference, as the number and value of mortgage loans supported by the FHA and VA rose exponentially in the late 1940s. In 1946 FHA activity reached its lowest levels in eight years, but the new VA mortgage program began to pick up the slack by guaranteeing $782 million in home loans nationwide. In 1947 that total skyrocketed to well over $3 billion, and 1948 saw another $2.8 billion of activity. By then the liberalization of FHA-insured mortgages, coupled with increased appropriations for FHA operations, had put that agency "fully in" the private market, as Administrator Raymond Foley had hoped at war's end when promoting legislative adjustments to the National Housing Act. In 1948, the FHA insured $2.2 billion worth of loans for home purchases, in addition to its substantial support for home improvement loans. By year's end the FHA and VA combined to support 43 percent of all new housing starts. Local savings and loan institutions, federally chartered by the FHLBB and dependent on the government's reserve system and secondary market purchases, financed much of the remaining construction.[32]

So while many Dearborn families were anxious about finding a place to live, they were also witnessing a flurry of construction that promised to transform their suburb. Renters were daily reminded that their turn for ownership might be next. By 1948, advertisements and news stories constantly announced completion of new residential subdivisions. Typical was the *Independent*'s May 14 news coverage of an open house at the Garling-Lowry Manor subdivision on Greenfield Road, where buyers could choose between seventy-five lots, each between forty-two and fifty-two feet wide, suitable for "bungalows, colonials or ranch type homes convenient to schools, transportation and shopping." Developer Fred Garling Sr. assured prospective buyers that the subdivision was "well restricted and FHA approved." Elsewhere in the paper that day, a half-page advertisement described the Garland subdivision in greater detail.[33]

There were also numerous indicators in 1948 of homeowners' considerable political power. Early that year, the traditionally anti-Hubbard *Independent* emerged as a vocal champion of restriction, endorsing a plan by the city's "property protective" and "improvement" organizations to "form neighborhood civic associations in all sections of the city" and reminding elected officials to remain attentive to these groups' concerns. Officials "can pretty well rely on the judgment of property owners," the editorial continued, "as to what is best for a particular section of the city." When the Dearborn Chamber of Commerce recommended a five-year moratorium on spot zoning and offered to help design a new municipal master plan, the *Independent* encouraged readers to attend the hearings and advised the Planning Department to "have a majority of property owners on its side." "It should be prepared to recommend the purchase by the city of property in purely residential districts which is now zoned for business—that will eventually be the only alternative." In January, the City Council and City Plan Commission debated a proposal offered by Hubbard to restrict all future residential development in Dearborn to single-family and two-family homes. The director of Public Works, Frank Swapka, endorsed the plan by offering a curious piece of evidence; most of the city's existing apartment structures, he noted, were in disrepair. Even the measure's opponents sang the praises of homeownership. Councilman Anthony Smith and city planner Joseph Goldfarb supported apartment construction, but described multiple-unit dwellings as temporary residences, suitable (and necessary) for young couples, traveling salesmen, veterans, and empty-nesters, but not for nuclear families. Clearly many Dearborn residents agreed with the mayor when he announced, during council debate over the plan, that "having people own their own [homes] . . . would provide better citizenry."[34]

Seldom did a week pass in 1948 when homeowners' organizations did not demonstrate their influence over local development. Restrictive spot zonings were regularly approved at council meetings, under intense pressure from the improvement associations. In April, for example, the Aviation Property Owners Association (APOA) convinced the City Plan Commission to recommend rezoning virtually all of the Oakman Aviation Subdivision for single-family homes. The parcel in question, bounded by Tireman, Schaefer, and an industrial tract, covered two-thirds of a square mile in Dearborn's northeast, with Tireman and the industrial land marking the

municipal border with Detroit. Dearborn's city planner agreed with homeowners, according to the *Independent*, that rezoning would "protect and
preserve residences or neighborhood characteristics from the standpoint of
proper zoning and long range planning." A few weeks later, on the other
side of town, the Southwest Dearborn Civic Association (SDCA) successfully
lobbied the City Plan Commission and City Council to block an apartment
project on a large, triangular parcel bounded by Polk Street, Outer Drive,
and Penn Street (see fig. 7.1). (They convinced the city to purchase the lot
for use as a municipal park.) The most visible result of homeowner activism that year, and throughout the decade after World War II, was a sharp
curtailment of apartment construction. In 1948, 1,188 units were built in
Dearborn for owner occupancy compared with 186 for rental purposes.[35]

To what degree was grassroots homeowner activism shaping local development patterns and politics? Federal selective credit programs were clearly
decisive. Only 55 percent of Dearborn's families owned their homes in
1940; by 1950, that number had risen to 75 percent, and 95 percent of those
homeowners lived in detached, single-family units. Meanwhile Hubbard's
outspokenness on the issue of "Negro" housing constantly fanned the
flames of these controversies, occasionally thrusting Dearborn's racial politics into the headlines and heightening homeowners' fears. But the mayor
did not instigate these battles and he rarely led them. When Hubbard ran
for reelection in 1945, the first mayoral contest after the FPHA controversy,
he did not campaign on the race issue. Instead it was his opponent, James
Thompson, who tried to capitalize on whites' racial anxieties, promising
to keep "property restrictions strongly enforced" and to keep Dearborn "as
it is." Thompson lost, badly. In 1947, Hubbard faced former mayor Carey,
again, and beat him, again, by linking his opponent with the corrupt Bennett machine.[36] In the meantime, it was Dearborn's homeowners that kept
the race issue front and center. Their activism sustained the campaign to
exclude apartments and black people from Dearborn throughout the early
postwar years. And it was their activism that set the tone for and helped
established the terms of the fight over the Hancock apartments, when the
project made the headlines in the spring of 1948.

The news involved a Wayne County Circuit Court decision and state legislative action that together cleared the way for the John Hancock Life Insurance Company of Hartford, Connecticut, to build a massive rental housing
project in central Dearborn, on 941 acres of undeveloped Ford Foundation
land. The Ford Motor Company had been in negotiation with Hancock
for over a year to sell the property, which was bounded by Rotunda Drive,
Southfield Road, the New York Central Railroad, and the Ford Foundation

offices. About 25 acres of the site had been platted before World War II as part of the Springwells Park Subdivisions, a portion of which included provision for apartments (see fig. 7.1). Public concern had arisen when Ford filed a friendly suit challenging a state law prohibiting insurance companies from holding land for more than ten years "for a use other than as set forth in its corporate franchise." In late April, the legislature permitted insurance companies to invest in housing projects, and the Hancock proposal quickly became the center of a firestorm in Dearborn. On April 30, under a banner headline announcing "Huge Ford Land Sale Revived," the *Independent* reported on the new insurance bill and confirmed rumors that Hancock hoped to build "huge apartment buildings . . . on the now vacant land in the Ford Foundation district and adjacent to it." The construction, the paper predicted, would "materially solve the housing shortage in Dearborn."[37]

Most homeowners were more preoccupied, however, with protecting Dearborn's status as a "city of homes." A remarkable coincidence added to the urgency, as the Supreme Court issued its ruling in *Shelley v. Kraemer* just three days after the *Independent* reported on the Ford land sale. Homeowners mobilized quickly and found an advocate in Councilman Ray Parker, who submitted "a proposed amendment to the Zoning Ordinance limiting residential construction to single residences in all sections of the city." Far more restrictive than Hubbard's earlier plan, Parker's rezoning called for the elimination of residence B and residence C districts altogether. He felt compelled to act, Parker told the council, to comply "with the wishes of the various Civic Organizations of Dearborn." On July 6 he introduced a resolution to "correct" the existing ordinance. The council adopted it unanimously and referred it to the City Plan Commission for a recommendation. In late September, councilmen Beadle and Parker asked the city clerk to schedule a special council meeting for November 8, just days after the fall election, to act on the rezoning.[38]

Both the Ford Motor and Hancock companies hoped to circumvent the council with a direct mailing to Dearborn residents designed to allay fears about the proposed apartment complex. Meanwhile Lucius T. Hill, director of housing for John Hancock, invited Dearborn's elected officials to Massachusetts to examine a comparable project, the Hancock Village in Brookline, to reassure them that their proposal for Dearborn would not threaten the community's character. Hill forwarded floor plans and a copy of the "Hancock Village Rules," which listed forbidden activities, such as "erect[ing] any device for hanging of laundry" and other so-called "Nuisances," included making "disturbing noises" or in other ways "interfer[ing] with the rights, comforts, or convenience of other tenants." "Overcrowding must be avoided," it instructed, "for health and sanitary reasons."[39]

Hubbard looked into the Brookline project and was not impressed. Further complicating matters, Detroit city officials invited Hancock to build there, instead, and the *Detroit Free Press* endorsed the alternative. Seeing an opportunity to score political points with Dearborn's homeowners, on October 4 Hubbard publicly called upon the council to adopt a resolution "urging John Hancock to immediately accept the invitation of our good friends and neighbors in Detroit . . . where housing projects are so anxiously needed." He later advised Hancock to consider Garden City, Michigan, as well, after its mayor expressed interest. Hubbard reminded council members that "the People of Dearborn, who have twice overwhelmingly rejected housing projects, do not want John Hancock or anyone else to change the character of this community by invading Dearborn with any type of rental housing project." Dearborn was "a home-owners city," he explained, "and the people living here want to keep it that way, so those who may wish to own a home in Dearborn may have a good place to live." Hubbard claimed that "only two of our 85,000 citizens have contacted either my home or the Mayor's office advising that they favor this proposed high-cost housing project," while "officers of 11 property owners' civic associations are vigorously opposed to your changing the zoning."[40]

It took little to persuade the city Zoning Board of Appeals, which on October 6 recommended rezoning the Ford site to residence A. "It was unanimously agreed," the members told the council, "that the question of rezoning this particular area would have repercussions affecting many zoning cases that would appear before this Board," and that the request, if granted, would "establish a precedent incompatible with good zoning for residential development." So urgent was this matter, the board concluded, that Dearborn's City Council should "meet in an emergency session to adopt said rezoning."[41]

But the council was reluctant to hand Hubbard such an easy victory. So throughout October, homeowners' groups and the mayor increased the pressure, demanding an advisory vote on the November ballot. "Give Us a Chance to Vote on the Proposed John Hancock High-Cost Rental Housing Project," read one local petition. "We, your friends and neighbors, who are against the multi-million dollar Boston insurance corporation invading Dearborn and changing the 'character of our fine city' with a huge high-cost rental housing project of thousands and thousands of dwelling units . . . urgently appeal to you as our 'public servants' to give the People of Dearborn a chance to express themselves again on rental housing projects by providing for an 'Advisory Vote' at the General Election on Tuesday, November 2, 1948." On October 15, Hubbard formally requested inclusion of the ballot measure, reiterating that "the People of Dearborn do not want the character of their splendid community changed by the invasion of a huge rental row-housing project." Since residents had opposed similar proposals in the past, the mayor argued, the council was "obligated to give the people a chance to vote."[42]

The same council that supported rezoning the entire city to residence A earlier that summer now refused residents' appeal. At their first October meeting, a "stormy session marked by flaring tempers, harsh accusations and threats to call the police," the council defeated a proposal to include the advisory vote on the November 2 ballot. Council members Marguerite C. Johnson, Joseph M. Ford, Martin C. Griffith, and Ray F. Parker opposed the measure; Patrick J. Doyle, Homer C. Beadle, and Anthony R. Smith supported it. A public hearing was set for October 19. The rezoning had already been approved by the City Plan Commission and all signs suggested that the City Council would support it, making the ballot initiative unnecessary. Then in late October the council changed course and added the measure to the ballot. The decisive factor seems to have been a direct appeal from Henry Ford II. Concerned by the depth of local opposition, the Hancock company had threatened to withdraw its offer for the Ford land. In a last ditch effort to save the deal, Ford put its hopes in support from Dearborn's voters.[43]

As election day approached, homeowners' associations and a handful of Dearborn officials spearheaded a campaign to preserve the Ford land for residence A development. Thousands of flyers distributed to Dearborn residents, most of which appeared to have been prepared by Hubbard's office, criticized the Ford and Hancock companies and warned what an apartment project would bring. Lucius Hill's invitation to Dearborn officials to visit their Brookline complex now played into the hands of Hancock's opponents. In mid-October, Dearborn's city engineer, DeWitt Coburn, its director of Public Works, Frank Swapka, and their wives were in Boston attending the American Public Works Association convention. They took the opportunity to visit the Brookline development. Photographs taken during that visit were then incorporated into a series of anti-Hancock flyers distributed to Dearborn residents. "Look at what the City Engineer saw when he inspected Hancock's model village," read a headline above four photographs, each showing rows of attached, two-story apartment buildings. These "unvarnished pictures of John Hancock's model housing project in Brookline, Mass.," the text continued, "were personally taken . . . by

Dearborn's City Engineer . . . DeWitt M. Coburn," who believes that "this type of mass-rental-housing would invite all types of undesirables and float-ers and change the character of Dearborn." City attorney Dale H. Fillmore was reported to comment that the Hancock buildings "look like warehouses for human storage." A similar flyer pictured Mrs. Coburn and Mrs. Swapka in front of the Brookline project, attributing to Mildred Coburn the claim that "row-housing would ruin Dearborn."[44]

There were two other enclosures, the first reproducing a photograph of two-story apartment houses, taken from the October 9, 1948, issue of *Business Week*, with the warning: "Hancock Village outside Boston, now nearly finished, is made up of . . . Houses Like These." The other began with "A Per-sonal Message from Your Mayor," explaining that "Dearborn home owners do not want nonresidents to invade their splendid community and change its character with huge rental terraces, row-housing or any other type of mass rental housing project." Dearborn was a "home owners city" and residents "want to keep it that way," so they should vote "No" on the advisory vote, in order "to protect the future value of your home and mine." Hubbard added that he had "personally seen the Hancock row-housing in Brookline," com-paring it to "Herman Gardens at Joy Road," a 2,144 unit public housing project built five years earlier on Detroit's Westside, just half a mile from its border with Dearborn at Tireman Street and Greenfield Road.[45]

The envelopes used to distribute these materials named the racial threat that the Hancock project posed. "Wake Up!" and "Open Your Eyes W-i-d-e! . . . John Hancock Gives Housing Double Talk," it read, then equated the threat posed by apartments to the threat of a "Negro" invasion. "With none of the 15,000 Ford Rouge Negro workers living in Dearborn," it con-tinued, "don't be 'lulled into a false sense of security' that John Hancock—with 8,500,000 policyholders of every race, color and creed—can build in Dearborn a multi-million dollar terrace-type rental housing project from its huge insurance funds, *including incomes from Negroes*, and exclude Negro families from living in [its] row-housing project . . . *Keep Dearborn a home-owners city*." A city of homeowners, this campaign made quite clear, was by definition a city of whites. An inset on the envelope instructed residents to "Attend the Meeting—Lindbergh School—Friday, 8 p.m.—October 29, 1948," where they could "hear exposed the multi-million dollar deal of nonresidents to exploit Dearborn home owners."[46]

Even before these materials circulated through Dearborn, local anti-Hancock organizing had clearly struck a chord with the suburb's prop-erty owners. Among them was a postwar arrival, Edward Nebesio, who wrote Hubbard on October 14 to "express [his] heartiest approval" of the mayor's response to the Hancock proposal. Describing himself as a "Dearborn home-owner since May, 1948," and speaking on behalf of his wife as well, Nebesio thanked the mayor for fighting "to eliminate [a] menace to Dearborn." "The proponents of this project claim that the high rental to be charged will bring only 'desirable' elements into Dearborn," he continued, but "obviously these people overlook the fact that there are thousands of colored people able to pay the high rental and they would begin an influx into the City." Nebesio insisted that "pressure groups" were exerting a "powerful force or influence way out of proportion . . . to the people they claim to represent." He also feared that many Dearborn businessmen would welcome the project for the sake of financial gain. It was only the homeowner, he wrote, who "has the long-range interests of the City at heart and wants to keep Dearborn the model community that it is." Opposition to blacks, according to this resident, was simply a matter of protecting property and community prerogatives. His family was "100 per cent behind [Hubbard]," Nebesio signed off, "in [the] fight to keep Dearborn a city of home owners only."[47]

While it is impossible to document how many Dearborn homeowners saw apartment construction as posing a racial threat, the advisory vote results reveal that most opposed the apartments. Voters rejected the rezoning by a margin of 15,948 to 10,562, effectively killing the Hancock project. Hubbard's claim of near unanimous opposition was clearly exaggerated, but his reading of local homeowners' politics, of the property associations' political influence, and of the appeal of a race-baiting campaign proved accurate. On November 8 the council met in special session to adopt a resolution introduced by Parker and Beadle calling for a December 7 public hearing on rezoning the Ford property from "an 'Industrial A' Classification to a 'Residential A' Classification." The resolution paid homage to Dearborn's homeowners; the advisory vote, explained the council, demonstrated residents' opposition to "multiple development . . . in the City." It specifically acknowledged the efforts of the Zoning Board of Appeals, the Southwest Dearborn Civic Association, and "other organizations" that had "recommended that the property in question" be reserved for single-family homes.[48]

On December 7 "interested citizens fill[ed] every available nook and corner of the . . . City Council chambers," where they heard Ford Foundation attorneys announce that the John Hancock company had withdrawn its offer for the parcel. The most prominent political issue of the fall, one that "overshadow[ed] in local importance even the historic presidential election," according to one report, had demonstrated to supporters and opposition alike the centrality of development issues to local governance, the ability of homeowners to shape suburban outcomes, and the contours of a new, postwar discussion about the risks posed by racial integration.[49]

Keeping Dearborn White

The battle over the Hancock apartments exposed important rifts among Dearborn's leaders and residents about the necessity of restriction, the means used to achieve it, and the role that race should play in development politics. Many still believed that housing families should be the city's first priority, a sentiment articulated by councilman Griffith in January 1949, when he accused the mayor of "den[ying] thousands of veterans and good, honest people a decent roof over their heads." Griffith also expressed his disgust with Hubbard's tactics, explaining that he broke with the mayor "when [he] created a phony racial issue in the recent vote on the housing project." Some Dearborners who joined the mayor in blocking the Hancock project nonetheless disagreed with the mayor's strategy, for various reasons. A week after the election, Mildred DeWitt Coburn sued Hubbard and his associates for implicating her (via their campaign flyer) in a campaign of "racial hate and prejudice." Even committed segregationists like Beadle were concerned that Hubbard's outspokenness would attract unwanted scrutiny to the suburb. The mayor's tactics, Beadle feared, would win Dearborn "the enmity of the National Association for the Advancement of the Colored Race and other national organizations."[50]

Political infighting did not slow down Dearborn's housing activists. A surge in housing starts in the late 1940s and early 1950s introduced thousands of new homeowners, providing a steady stream of fresh recruits for an established and fast-growing network of protective associations. The percentage of owner-occupied dwellings nearly doubled between 1940 and 1950, while construction, advertising, and the promise of access made the dream of homeownership appear within reach for most families.[51] By mobilizing Dearborn's homeowners and prospective homeowners, local activists helped determine the kinds of residences built in the suburb and the kind of people who could occupy them. Meanwhile their ascendancy, strategies, goals, tactics, and rhetorical choices helped set the tone of local land-use politics for decades to come.

One indicator of homeowners' influence was the proliferation of property protective groups, alternatively called "homeowners,'" "improvement," and "civic" associations. The available record makes an exhaustive reconstruction of these groups, their memberships, and their activities very difficult, yet there is ample evidence of their growth and sustained influence. In 1940, a survey by a local college student turned up only one organization, the Dearborn Hills Civic Association. By 1949, the Dearborn Federation of Civic Associations (DFCA) *alone* included eight charter members: the APOA, the SDCA, the Dearborn Heights Civic Association, the Frischkorn Club Civic Association, the Fort Dearborn Manor Association, the Golf View Improvement Association, the Northeast Dearborn Property Protective Association, and the Springwells Park Association. In addition to these and other groups, Beadle maintained the Michigan Avenue office of the DPOPA. Together these organizations decisively shaped zoning and development practices—and politics—during the years of the suburb's most vibrant growth.[52]

Activists pursued two complementary strategies. First, they constantly lobbied local government on land-use issues. In September 1949, for example, the DFCA reported to the City Council that its members had been "receiving complaints from home owners to the effect that private homes are being converted to rooming houses in single residence areas." To remedy this, the federation recommended an amendment to Article 3, Paragraph 319 of the Zoning Ordinance, which defined a "family" as "one or two persons or parents with their direct descendants and adopted children . . . together with not more than five persons not so related." By reducing the "number of unrelated persons," the DFCA suggested, "some relief to this undesirable situation would be accomplished." Earlier that year the federation used a campaign against a proposed drive-in theater to lobby for a comprehensive, citywide ban. In other correspondence with the council between 1948 and 1953, it weighed in on a prohibition against metal awnings, endorsed a stricter noise ordinance, and repeated its opposition to "the violation of the Residence zoning" in the city. In February 1950, the DFCA urged the council to reconsider the wording of a proposed Building Code Ordinance (No. 50-514), because the amendment, in its current form, could be interpreted to mean that local hospitals could accept any "ambulatory service" and "indigent out-patients."[53]

Individual associations also lobbied the council directly. The Golf View Improvement Association, the APOA, the SDCA, Fort Dearborn Manor, Dearborn Highlands, the Chase Subdivision Improvement Association, the Miller Homes Subdivision Property Owners Association, these and other groups constantly made their preferences known to the City Council and city clerk. They wrote letters about sewers, bus stops, and weed ordinances. They requested that municipal garbage trucks be fully enclosed, complained about dirty, trash-filled lots and alleys, and identified traffic problem spots.

They supported stricter noise ordinances, opposed the construction of incompatible commercial properties, and called for the prohibition of alcoholic beverages at city parks. Joining this chorus were other civic and professional organizations, including the Dearborn Chamber of Commerce and the Dearborn Board of Realtors. In October 1953, for example, the Real Estate Board wrote Hubbard to "commend" him on his efforts to block the sale of residential property to "non-Caucasians."[54]

Housing activists were especially effective at the regular weekly council meetings, where they called for spot zonings or comprehensive revision of Dearborn's zoning ordinance and building code. At a January 1949 meeting, for example, the DFCA promoted adoption of a Smoke Control Ordinance, while the SDCA called upon the city to retract a permit for a 116-family apartment development at the intersection of Monroe, Madison, and Cleveland. The association presented a petition signed by area residents, arguing that area development patterns made a city park more appropriate for the site. The SDCA cited construction trends again when requesting that a parcel between the Michigan Central Railroad, Elmwood Avenue, and the Ford Foundation be rezoned residence A. Notably, the property in question was not represented by their association. The Dearborn Press predicted, correctly, that the SDCA was on firmer ground with their request for the Monroe site; by a unanimous vote, the council secured the land for use as a public park. Homeowners found ways to circumvent the council if necessary. When officials voted to permit construction of a new drive-in theater, the civic associations convinced Hubbard to overrule them. The mayor declared that licensing should be determined either by the incoming council or by a popular advisory vote, that the project would be "an eyesore," and that it would increase congestion, promote delinquency, and attract "an undesirable element." The net result of homeowner activism, by the mid-1950s, was the disappearance of virtually all residence C and D areas as well as multiple "up-zonings" of residence B districts to residence A. Between 1950 and 1956, alone, Dearborn's ordinance was amended 117 times.[55]

When Dearborn residents mobilized over development they entered a national conversation about suburban land use and invoked its statutory, legal, and social science language. Rarely did homeowners register general complaints about "noise" or "dirt" or "congestion."[56] They examined local statutory powers and land-use laws, identified relevant municipal ordinances, and recommended specific revisions. Activists regularly co-opted the language of zoning statutes, property law, and real estate practice; for example, the SDCA alerted the council in 1953 about the urgency of covering Baby Creek, which marked Dearborn's southeast border with Detroit, by arguing that it posed a "menace to the health and welfare of this community." Likewise homeowners collapsed both apartment construction and nonwhite occupancy into a much broader range of threats to sound development, employing a theory about residential compatibility that had informed zoning practice and mortgage lending for decades. When the Dearborn Real Estate Board wrote Hubbard in 1953 to praise his efforts to exclude "non-Caucasians," for example, it never discussed residents' racial preferences. It simply noted that the mayor was "entirely consistent with the following excerpt from the Realtor's Code of Ethics"—then, tellingly, it cited the *original* code, written by Nathan MacChesney in 1925, rather than the revised version, free of racial language, that replaced it in 1950: "A Realtor should never be instrumental in introducing into a neighborhood a character of property or occupancy, members of any race or nationality, or any individuals whose presence will clearly be detrimental to property values in that neighborhood." Local officials who wrote privately to the mayor warning about land sales to blacks also treated integration as a matter-of-fact land-use issue.[57]

This conflation of the physical, aesthetic, and human threats facing white homeowners was the trademark of activists' other main organizing strategy: mobilizing residents in their neighborhoods. Homeowners' associations constantly drew Dearborn's property owners into local land-use politics, in part by publishing newsletters—such as the *Southwest Dearborn Civic Association News* and the *Springwells Parker*—and distributing them door to door. The monthly *SDCA News* provided updates on zoning board meetings, school and school board news, changes in the city charter, new home construction, local traffic issues, youth programs, commercial development, and even the condition of area sidewalks. A prominent feature was reporting and commentary about specific development controversies and SDCA activities. In the late 1940s and early 1950s, for example, the *News* defended the city's minimum requirements for lot width (50 feet), called upon the city to purchase land in order to preempt construction of a county parkway, denounced a proposed amendment to the weight limits for trucks traveling on residential streets, and debated the merits of the "Proposed Awning Ordinance." The February 1949 issue discussed strategies for shaping industrial zoning patterns (in a piece called "Factories in Our Area?"). In January 1950, the *News* inventoried dozens of home construction plans "reviewed by this Association in the last month," listing them by address, building size (the average house was 30' × 25' × 25'), and often specifying the building materials that would be used. SDCA victories received considerable coverage. "Park Project Won!" announced a banner headline in 1949.

Through "the constant vigilance on the part of members and officers of your Civic association," the article explained, "we have halted the construction of a multiple housing unit in the area bound by Monroe, Madison, and Cleveland. Time was generously given by this organization in petitioning the neighborhood around this project." After a "survey showed the greater majority did not want these apartment buildings near their homes," the SDCA "petitioned the common council to prevent their construction."[58]

Residents' involvement was essential, the *News* explained, because SDCA efforts were driven solely by the needs and interests of homeowners. Updates on local zoning controversies included dates and times of council sessions, public hearings, and SDCA strategy sessions. In February 1949, for example, readers were encouraged to attend an association meeting on the eighth to debate the city's proposed Industrial Zoning Ordinance and then to follow the council's deliberations when it convened the following week. The *News* noted that the Dearborn Federation of Civic Associations ("of which we are members") would be present for the council debate, in order to present "the ideas concerning what we think the home owners of Dearborn desire"; in fact the SDCA's president was chairing the DFCA committee on the ordinance. Homeowners were also assigned more pedestrian tasks. SDCA officials were cooperating with the city on a study of the area's lighting needs, so readers were encouraged to "make it your business to survey your neighborhood for weak or inadequate street lighting." The SDCA also invited volunteers to help distribute its newsletter door to door.[59]

Finally, the *News* provided another primer in the new politics and economics of residential restriction, immersing white homeowners in the legal and social scientific narrative that treated racial homogeneity as a practical requirement rather than ideological preference. SDCA coverage of threats to area homeowners alternated seamlessly between discussions of renters, "unscrupulous" builders, nonwhites, and physical blight. And the organization insisted that its work had nothing to do with politics or ideology. The managerial, free market logic embedded in national mortgage practices and land-use politics served as an organizing principle for activist organizations like the SDCA, both in their efforts to exclude "undesirables" and to educate neighbors about the urgency and the reasonableness of restriction.

The SDCA cast all local debates over land-use restriction, whether lot size minimums or warnings about the incursion of nonwhites, as practical land-use matters. Every issue of the *News* told readers that the misuse or mismanagement of their property would cost them money. Typical was a September 1950 article, "Your Property Dollar," reminding residents that "one of the prime objectives of the Civic Organization is the protection of the home owner's property value." The piece then described the SDCA's successful campaign to establish a city ordinance requiring minimum values of new housing construction. An issue of special concern that year was the future development along Outer Drive, a major throughway bordering the residential enclaves of southwest Dearborn. The frontage of Outer Drive, according to the *News*, would be "a sort of front door for all of us who live in this area," since "people from other sections of town judge the character of the neighborhood by the homes they can see as they motor along the road." Thus "the type of homes built along the Drive will directly affect the property values of all homes in the immediate neighborhood and all of West Dearborn as well." [60]

Efforts to protect this "front door" had begun earlier, when the association blocked apartment construction at Outer Drive, Polk, and Penn in 1948 and Madison, Cleveland, and Monroe in 1949; either project would have been easily visible from Outer Drive. (Cleveland runs parallel to Outer Drive, just a block to the southwest; see fig. 7.1.) Meanwhile the SDCA recommended that residents with lots fronting both Outer Drive and Cleveland should build their homes to face the drive, so that users of Outer Drive saw front doors and lawns, not back doors and garages. But residents on the other side of Cleveland did not want to face the backside of those homes, and local FHA agents took their side, refusing to guarantee mortgages for structures designed to face Outer Drive. The homes were eventually built facing Cleveland, with garages that opened onto Outer Drive. So the SDCA proposed another way to save face, recommending that owners "construct side drives opening onto Cleveland if possible." By "landscap[ing] carefully along Outer Drive where the garages are built," residents could make it a beautiful boulevard "instead of the eyesore it is at present." There was no discussion, not surprisingly, of the FHA's role in facilitating the area's development, nor was that the only form of government largesse quietly assumed as a homeowner's prerogative. "The County could be asked to do [the landscaping on Outer Drive]," the SDCA suggested, "since [it] is a county road." [61]

The SDCA relied on the market-imperative, land-use-management trope to justify all kinds of restriction, from set-back minimums to racial exclusion. The *News* emphasized that three things posed a grave threat to property values: the deterioration of existing structures, the construction of "incompatible" dwelling units (multiple unit dwellings, small or poorly constructed detached homes), and the occupancy of area homes by "nonwhites." Sometimes the racial appeals were direct. "Warning," began a front page *News* article of October 1950 (see fig. 7.4). The association had

SOUTHWEST DEARBORN **SDCA** CIVIC ASSOCIATION

OCTOBER ★ ★ ★ ★ 1950

In Unity . . . There Is Strength

The civic organization is a necessary part of any healthy neighborhood or area setup. Without such organizations, the elected politicians, are handed a blank check as they enter office and can write in what they like so long as there is no united opposition.

Those who give freely of their time and energy to build a strong area group must sometime think of the money which could be theirs if the same effort were put in a gainful occupation.

Perhaps the intangible gains from active community effort is worth a great deal to the individual for he finds as time goes on that his whole outlook on life has broadened and that he has gained dignity and self assurance in his daily contact with other people.

The civic organization is the neighborhood watch-dog, to see that undesirable projects are kept out and to fight for projects which are good for the community.

The Bulletin, which is printed by this organization is our method of keeping the area informed of various problems, and provides a method for alerting the home owners to any development which is against their best interests.

The work connected with running this organization is terrific and the load is carried by a willing few. We are badly in need of people who will consent to act as area leaders in their immediate neighborhood to see that this bulletin is delivered in their block and to help us maintain the present standard of the block and neighborhood in which they reside.

Your home is your gem and as such, requires the bulk of your attention, but like any other gem it requires a beautiful neighborhood for a setting and that setting can only be maintained through united effort of the people.

Next Tuesday a new group of officers will be elected for this association and many of those elected will be chosen from those who volunteered as area leaders last year. They will need a lot of assistance and we hope that the people of this area will volunteer to give it.

Mrs. Edward Birrell, 3837 Williams
Please call at Cox Pharmacy for your Free Gift.

Welcome to New Residents

All new residents are cordially invited to the Whitmore-Bolles School next Tuesday evening for the Civic Association meeting. Introduce yourself and sign a membership card. Dues are one dollar per year per person.

THE VOLUNTEER

The volunteer worker, a whirlwind is she;
The Torch Drive . . . the church . . . P. T. A.
All call for her time, and the lady must be
Up and doing and busy all day.
The world is o'er-run with the forces of Woe,
Everybody must needs do their part.
And millions of agencies vie for her time
As a path through life's troubles they chart.

There's a canvass to do . . . teen-agers to help,
Civic projects . . . Clubs . . . Mom musn't shirk;
Be-jeweled and inspired, our volunteer gal
Gets everything done but housework.
The kids eat cold suppers while Mother departs,
Her hair all elaborately curled.
Then sit home alone or run rampant at will,
While Mama's out fixing the world.

Maybe the world would be just as well off,
And delinquency head for the skids;
If Mom bought an apron—her gladrags she'd doff,
And just stay at home with her kids.

Velma Pamment.

Warning

The Civic Association has received information that certain unscrupulous real estate dealers are attempting to buy up Dearborn property to resell to people of other than the Caucasian race. Exorbitant price offers are one of the indications of this deal.

Anyone contemplating selling his home is asked to get in touch with one of the officers of this Association to check the background of the firm with which he is dealing.

Listing your property with members of the DEARBORN real estate board is one safeguard you can offer your neighbor. Dearborn realtors have been most co-operative in upholding the restrictions here in this city. Patronize your local business men and be sure.

Election of Officers

TAKE NOTICE, the meeting on October 10th is the time — Whitmore-Bolles School is the place, for the election of your officers for the following year.

The Nominating Committee presents for your consideration the following:

President
Albert Ganski, 3839 Madison
Albert Roberts, 2961 Bennett

First Vice-President
Elmer Stitt, 22737 Madison
Paul Joseph, 3229 Gertrude

Second Vice-President
Mrs. Geo. Hummel, 22564 Nona

Secretary
Frank Prosyniuk, 3611 McKinley

Treasurer
Chas. R. Hartline, 21329 Audette

Trustee for Three Years
Elmer Hitt, 22305 Gregory

Oxford P. T. A.

by Mrs. Don Foster

The opening meeting of the combined P.T.A. of Oxford and Nowlin Schools will be held Thursday, October 12th at 8 p.m. in the Oxford auditorium.

"What is a Normal Child?" will be the subject discussed by Dr. Robert S. Drews, a prominent lecturer on Mental Hygiene and Mental Health.

Mrs. Hulme from the Dearborn Public Library will have a selection of adult books on display and a social hour with refreshments will follow the meeting. The public is cordially invited to attend these meetings.

FREE PRIZES!

Is your name listed this month? As an advertising medium, some of the merchants are cooperating with our civic association to give free merchandise or service to you.

Read the Bulletin — your name may be listed.

Prize winners are picked at random from the city directory in this area. No prizes will be less than $1.00 value.

Did You Know . . .

We have an ordinance regulating the size of signs which may be erected on residential lots. Residence A and B (single and double homes) four square feet. Residence C and D (four-family and multiple), six square feet.

If you see a sign that is objectionable, you can notify the complaint department at the City Hall.

Eber L. Squiers, 21368 Audette Please call at F. F. Maxwell, General Insurance, for a Free Prize for your youngster.

Government . . . By the People

By Frank Brown

Today, we are trying to sell our type of government to the people of the world and our boys are fighting to protect the rights of Democratic government everywhere.

"Freedom" is a blessing which we have enjoyed in our country for so long that a great many cannot conceive the hardships those people endure who have lost their right to freedom.

We have grown so used to "government by the people" that those who are best equipped to work as our public servants refuse to be bother with elective office. This leaves the door open for the election of persons who have little or no ability to handle our civic affairs.

There are many who think the political parties are on guard and will refuse to place a candidate who does not qualify. This assumption is false because the parties generally follow a hands-off policy during the primaries. Anyone who can get the required number of signatures and wishes to run for office can enter the race, and if he has the right name can often carry his party's banner in the general election.

If the public is to vote intelligently it must be given a great deal more information than previously. Information about the candidate's educational background for the job should be emphasized.

When our country was born, we were a nation of farmers and small village people who knew each candidate personally. Today, in our cities this is no longer true, and we must find some better method for selecting those who run for office.

We are trying to sell Democracy abroad and save Democracy at home. How can we do this when voters stay away from the polls because of lack of information on the candidates?

Some method should be devised to make it a function of government to give adequate information on the candidates and on the office to be filled. The present system, which gives the "name" candidate all the advantage, is not democratic. It assumes he is endowed with the same leadership qualities as his predecessor and follows the old European custom of "The King is dead—long live the King."

A New Year

Now is the time to let the Association know if your neighborhood is in need of more street lights or other facilities which the city provides.

Let's hear from you on what you think could be done to make ours a better city.

NEXT MEETING OF THE S.D.C.A. WILL BE HELD TUESDAY, OCT. 10th
WHITMORE-BOLLES SCHOOL — Whitmore Near Monroe — 8 P. M.
All Residents of This Area Cordially Invited to Attend!

7.4 *SDCA News* (October 1950). The SDCA newsletter combined neighborhood news, updates on local development issues, articles about the meaning of democracy, community, and freedom ("Government . . . By the People"), and an occasional "Warning" about occupancy threats: "The Civic Association has received information that certain unscrupulous real estate dealers are attempting to buy up Dearborn property to resell to people of other than the Caucasian race." Courtesy of the Dearborn Historical Museum, Dearborn, Michigan.

learned that "certain unscrupulous real estate dealers are attempting to buy up Dearborn property to resell to people of other than the Caucasian race." Residents could avoid problems by working exclusively with qualified real estate professionals or by soliciting the SDCA's help researching the background of brokers operating in the suburb. Better yet: "Listing your property with members of the DEARBORN real estate board is one safeguard you can offer your neighbor. Dearborn realtors have been most co-operative in upholding the restrictions here in this city." [62]

Some calls for racial restriction in the post-*Shelley* era were thinly veiled, such as the October 1949 reminder that many neighborhoods "have covenant restrictions written into their land purchase contracts which they wish enforced so that the present complexion of their neighborhood will not be changed by the construction of undesirable homes." To ensure that subdivisions were held to these standards, an SDCA committee was monitoring new construction in southwest Dearborn and collecting copies of existing restrictive contracts from association members. These contracts would be used, the *News* explained, as guides for designing future covenants. Assuming that homeowners in unrestricted subdivisions "would also like help with the job of seeing that only the better type of homes are built in these areas," the *News* invited "any neighborhood group wish[ing] to maintain the present complexion of their neighborhood" to appoint a representative to the new SDCA committee. [63]

Perhaps most revealing about the SDCA's efforts was these activists' portrayal of their intent. The organization never discussed residents' "racial preferences" or the topic of "racial difference," nor did it even warn about "racial problems." Instead it talked about property values, property owners' rights, and the laws of housing markets. "Your home is your gem," the *News* reminded readers in 1950, so it was incumbent upon them to remain involved and vigilant. Because members had "property rights here which must be protected," civic organizations were a "necessary part of any healthy neighborhood," serving as "neighborhood watch-dog, to see that undesirable projects are kept out and to fight for projects which are good for the community." By the early 1950s, imagining racial exclusion as part of a nonideological campaign to protect property and community had become a trademark of housing activism. [64]

In 1951, the DFCA produced a generic advertisement and membership appeal, calling upon Dearborn residents to "Join Your Civic Association." It appeared in the *SDCA News* in April of that year (see fig. 7.5). The goal of local property protective associations, the promotion explained, was "to obtain through united effort . . . the proper improvements and maintenance

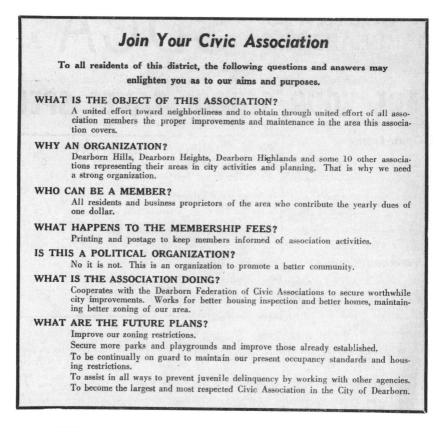

Join Your Civic Association

To all residents of this district, the following questions and answers may enlighten you as to our aims and purposes.

WHAT IS THE OBJECT OF THIS ASSOCIATION?

A united effort toward neighborliness and to obtain through united effort of all association members the proper improvements and maintenance in the area this association covers.

WHY AN ORGANIZATION?

Dearborn Hills, Dearborn Heights, Dearborn Highlands and some 10 other associations representing their areas in city activities and planning. That is why we need a strong organization.

WHO CAN BE A MEMBER?

All residents and business proprietors of the area who contribute the yearly dues of one dollar.

WHAT HAPPENS TO THE MEMBERSHIP FEES?

Printing and postage to keep members informed of association activities.

IS THIS A POLITICAL ORGANIZATION?

No it is not. This is an organization to promote a better community.

WHAT IS THE ASSOCIATION DOING?

Cooperates with the Dearborn Federation of Civic Associations to secure worthwhile city improvements. Works for better housing inspection and better homes, maintaining better zoning of our area.

WHAT ARE THE FUTURE PLANS?

Improve our zoning restrictions.

Secure more parks and playgrounds and improve those already established.

To be continually on guard to maintain our present occupancy standards and housing restrictions.

To assist in all ways to prevent juvenile delinquency by working with other agencies.

To become the largest and most respected Civic Association in the City of Dearborn.

7.5 DPOPA membership appeal, "Join Your Civic Association," from the *SDCA News*, April 1951. Courtesy of the Dearborn Historical Museum, Dearborn, Michigan.

in the area." Then it explained the fundamentals of homeowner activism. What was the local organization doing? It was "cooperat[ing] with the Dearborn Federation of Civic Associations to secure worthwhile city improvements . . . work[ing] for better housing inspection and better homes . . . [and] maintaining better zoning of our area." What were the future plans of the local association? It would focus on improving zoning restrictions, "secur[ing] more parks and playgrounds," remaining "continually on guard to maintain our present occupancy standards and housing restrictions," preventing juvenile delinquency, and becoming the "largest and most respected Civic Association in the City of Dearborn." Further collapsing "occupancy standards" into an inventory of practical land-use concerns, the appeal asked if the local homeowners' association was "a political organization." "No it is not. This is an organization to promote a better community."

Vigilance against incompatible development of any kind was driven not by politics or ideology, argued local activists, but by homeowners' deference to the free market for housing and neighborhoods.[65]

Upon closer scrutiny this claim rings hollow, because the DFCA and its member associations used their political power to defend whites' right to exclude. The rhetorical focus was on responsible land use and the protection of property values, but whites argued, most often implicitly, sometimes explicitly, that only white homeowners could sustain both. Echoing national efforts that had been reshaping land-use politics for over three decades, this market imperative argument defined racial restriction as nonideological by assuming that only a community of property-owning whites was capable of supporting healthy residential neighborhoods and organizing to protect them. The argument's circularity was irresistible, and its contradictions easily ignored. The SDCA defended a homeowner's right to exclude by describing it as a citizenship right. It insisted that homeowners' associations were not political organizations, while claiming that they spoke for and protected the rights of people living in a democratic society. "Without such organizations," the News explained, "the elected politicians . . . are handed a blank check." Articles on zoning controversies, service provision, and racial exclusion shared the pages with brief essays on the meaning of "Freedom," reminding readers that they lived in a country and community where "Government [is] By the People" (see fig. 7.4).[66] Still the association portrayed its members as rising above politics. The SDCA and other homeowners' organizations argued that restriction was necessary not because of political or ideological preferences, but because it was a fundamental tenet of housing and neighborhood economics. They articulated this story, in large measure, by turning to a narrative codified in the laws and policies that had sanctioned and promoted exclusion, in different forms, since the 1910s. Like that national conversation, this local conversation about property and race continually insisted upon its own pragmatism.

For countless white homeowners in Dearborn this contradictory—but still persuasive—story made possible an important rhetorical sleight of hand. When representatives from the SDCA, DFCA, DPOPA, and other property protective associations campaigned for restrictions against black occupancy or warned members about "unscrupulous real estate dealers," they rarely, if ever, argued that local residents preferred not to live near or associate with black people. Instead, they focused on the threat that black occupancy and rental properties posed to homes owned by white people. The distinction is important for understanding a decisive shift in the politics of white housing activism, white racial identity, and white racism in the years after World War II. The organizations that exhorted residents to appear at council meetings, write letters of protest to federal officials, petition and vote for ever more restrictive zoning ordinances, adopt restrictive covenants, and educate themselves about developments in property law, these same groups repeatedly reminded their members that such work was not "political." It was not political, in their view, because it represented an effort to promote responsible land use and protect the market for homes. In debates over development, they insisted, there was simply no room for what the DPOPA had earlier dismissed as "anthropological theory." Protecting homes against black people was simply an act of protecting a natural market so that it could function on its own terms and, as a result, prosper. Foundational to this narrative was the assumption that only white people could sustain private property and the institutions developed to protect it.

———————

The local celebration of free market values in suburbs like Dearborn was deeply indebted to a national political culture that constantly juxtaposed American freedoms to the conditions of life under communist or totalitarian rule. Building upon longstanding popular (and congressional) opposition to public housing legislation, for example, Hubbard and other local leaders regularly invoked the threat of federal meddling in the free market as a foil to combat proposals for low-income and minority housing. These strategies were part and parcel of a national, Cold War–era celebration of free enterprise, the single-family home, and the political principles with which they were so commonly associated.[67]

Occasionally these national and local conversations converged in revealing fashion. In 1950, the *Independent* weighed in on the question of federal intervention, in a report on the threat that socialism posed to free markets and the American way of life. Under the headline "'Socialist Planners' Held Real Enemies," the paper summarized a *Reader's Digest* condensation of John T. Flynn's *The Road Ahead: America's Creeping Revolution.*[68] The paper treated Flynn's argument like a press release, recounting its analysis as a news story. According to Flynn there was an important distinction between American experiments with "National Planning" and the western European model, which included state control of banking, medicine, utilities, and manufacturing. The European initiatives represented a kind of "modern Socialism," he explained, one that meant "State control of the entire economic system." Under this "modern Socialism," advocated domestically, Flynn noted, by groups like the Americans for Democratic Action, the state would "operate the basic functions of credit." And it was these types of proposals that posed the greatest threat to the American people. "Socialist" objectives including "federal invasion of the fields of banking, electric power and medicine" were components of a long-range plan to "liquidate some sector of the private-enterprise system and expand the aim of Socialism."[69]

In Dearborn, at least, most voters supported a version of state planning that was, in their eyes, decidedly market friendly, and worlds apart from the socialist nightmare described in *The Road Ahead*. While homeowners rallied to protect their neighborhoods from the scourge of "federal low income" projects or "Negro housing," they made no complaints about the state interventions that had restructured the market for housing credit and subsidized both suburban development and white homeownership. And for this reason the local politics of property and race, on the one hand, and national electoral politics, on the other, were mutually supportive. Suburban residents' acceptance of federal largesse, their investment in policies that created and secured wealth primarily for whites, their investment in a free market narrative perpetuating the myth that the U.S. government had no control over "the basic functions of credit," together these developments fueled white support both for the local politics of restriction and a national political system reluctant to challenge institutions and structures that for years had systematically discriminated against racial minorities. In the years of the most spectacular growth of suburban housing construction and rates of homeownership in U.S. history, Dearborn residents continued to cast their ballots overwhelmingly for the Democratic Party, the party that had assembled and sustained so many of the programs that contributed to whites' postwar affluence and comfort. So secure was residents' loyalty to the Democrats that just a month after reproducing excerpts from *The Road Ahead*, the editors at the *Independent* quipped about the suburb's political leanings in their weekly "Around Town" column: "The Republicans: Yes, there are such people left in this country and even some in Dearborn, but for 16 years they have been on the short end of the stick."[70]

CHAPTER EIGHT

The National Is Local: Race and Development in an Era of Civil Rights Protest, 1955–1964

By the mid-1950s, whites in metropolitan Detroit were often heard telling one of two complementary stories about their region's remarkable postwar growth and transformation. The first story, a celebration of the fast-growing suburbs, focused on the affluence and independence of these communities and their residents. This narrative described suburban prosperity as a reward for living in a capitalist society. It praised suburbanites for their hard work, civic commitment, pride in homeownership, and respect for private property. And it insisted that autonomous suburban governments were best equipped to secure homeowners' rights and privileges. Typical was a *Tribune* editorial commemorating Labor Day in 1955 that attributed southeast Oakland County's spectacular growth and prosperity to "freedom and enterprise." Its residents had "an average income well above that of the country as a whole," the paper explained, and enjoyed "the type of community living that is attracting more and more people." The suburbs' prosperity provided "definite and material proof," the paper concluded, "that our way of free enterprise and freedom of the individual really works." Elsewhere the editors described the "flight to the suburbs" as a natural response to Detroit's "haphazard growth," even portraying the decision to relocate and residents' attachment to their new homes as part of the "pioneer tradition of America." These new settlers recognized that home-rule suburbs, in particular, offered an "opportunity to create a new type of community," one "that could take advantage of newer concepts of planning" and thus "be free, for a generation at least, of the noise, congestion, and blight of the older cities." In this narrative, the homeowner was simultaneously the motor for suburban growth and its most revered beneficiary. Oakland County's good fortune was "nothing which has been given us," noted the *Tribune* on Labor

Day. "We have had to work hard for—and we will have to keep on working hard to maintain—these happy conditions."[1]

Complementing this vision of the suburban good life was a companion narrative about those "older cities" and their "blight" that painted Detroit as an increasingly run-down, impoverished, and dangerous place. Most often this story attributed the city's decay to residents, especially the poor and minorities, and to local officials who together had rejected the principles ensuring suburban well-being. Suburban papers depicted Detroit's political institutions as hopelessly outdated; suburbanites' "only protection" from the corruption and inefficiency of urban politics, wrote the *Tribune's* Floyd Miller in 1954, "lies at the local level." Journalists accused urban officials of catering to residents unwilling to buy or improve their property, people quick to rely on public housing and other government handouts. The *Tribune* attributed Detroit's physical deterioration, in the final analysis, to the "number of low-income and socially deprived families" residing there.[2] Other white commentators were more direct. In 1956, Dr. H. G. Slagle, of Highland Park, complained to the *Detroit Times'* editor that the city's fine old neighborhoods, once filled with "nice homes" originally "built by White people," had fallen into disrepair since "the negro moved in." Whites responded by moving to the suburbs, Slagle continued, "open[ing] up new subdivisions, buil[ding] more nice homes, [and] organiz[ing] home owners associations," only to hear blacks complain about "discrimination" and "segregation." That year a white Detroiter told Orville Hubbard of his family's desire to move to Dearborn, describing it as a place where "life and property are held at a higher position." "To prove [the] point," he wrote, "drive around Detroit and look at its city parks, housing projects and housing in general . . . [It is] a city where the tax money goes to support city facilities I won't let my wife go to alone." Hubbard received hundreds of similar letters, telegrams, and phone calls from the region's white residents. Many sent photographs of Detroit's residential districts, to "document," as one man wrote, the damage that blacks had done to the city. Suburban correspondents compared run-down sections of Detroit with their well-kept neighborhoods, and then attributed their quality of life to the vigilance of property protective associations and the foresight of local leadership. By defending the principle of residential segregation, explained one Dearborner, Hubbard was speaking for "homeowners."[3]

The prominence of these complementary stories—about suburb and city, growth and decay, white and black—highlights the emergence by the 1950s of a unique political vocabulary about race and property in metropolitan America. Guiding whites' discussions about urban decline and suburban affluence were interwoven assumptions about property ownership, suburban autonomy, and racial compatibility. For countless whites, suburban residence had come to represent a sanctuary from the overcrowding and degradation of city life, from outdated forms of urban planning and government, and from black people. Whites viewed suburban advantages, especially homeownership, municipal autonomy, and racial homogeneity, as inextricably linked. Dearborn was "the outstanding city in the United States," wrote a man from the suburb of Allen Park in 1956, because it was "white" and filled with "choice residence[s]," and he told Hubbard that "it will be kept that way as long as the citizens of Dearborn realize fully that you are protecting their rights and properties." Like most whites who openly endorsed segregation during these years, this man did not discuss black people or character directly, but instead invoked a familiar story about race, property, and places. Many residents took the next step, insisting that their preference for racial exclusion was not driven by racial prejudice. Martha Molian, of Detroit, claimed that her family had originally "accept[ed] [blacks] in good faith," until "we began to learn why they are so objectionable as neighbors." "They've already made slum conditions here," she wrote Hubbard in 1956, "and their homes are deteriorating fast with the crowds of people they insist on retaining on their premises." "Negroes," she insisted, "do not appreciate better housing."[4]

Whites' investment in the affluence and security of the early postwar suburb has long been the subject of critique by academics, journalists, and artists. Since the suburban boom first became a recognizable demographic and cultural phenomenon, most commentators have described life in these places as insular at best and socially debilitating at worst. Until recently, the "1950s" suburb was portrayed almost exclusively in the form of its most familiar incarnation: the racially and socioeconomically homogeneous bedroom community, its residents overly preoccupied with material comforts, immediate gratifications, and visible emblems of status. And commentators have long argued that this environment bred a cultural and political conservatism deeply resistant to change, including racial change.[5] Yet most critics identify a specific *racial* subtext to postwar suburban culture only under specific circumstances: when whites explicitly talk about race, when they refer to nonwhite people, or, in some cases, only when they say openly "racist" things. Writers, especially, usually treat whites' "class" or "status" concerns as conceptually discrete from their "racism" and then explore how class and race sometimes intersect, usually when blacks challenge the residential color line. The implication is that suburban whites forged new ideas about the single-family home, suburban neighborhoods, middle-class status, and middle-class family norms during these years, and then, when driven by circumstance, applied preexisting racial prejudices to this new postwar setting and context.[6]

A careful examination of suburban development politics shows that suburban whites formed their ideas about social status and racial identity simultaneously and did so by building upon lessons learned in their daily lives. They regarded their achievements, lifestyle, and even family arrangements as specifically racial (that is, white), in large measure because they interpreted metropolitan change by employing a mythical narrative about the relationship between race and property. Ignoring the structural transformations and public policies that promoted suburban growth and accelerated urban decline, whites attributed the changing material conditions of suburban and urban life primarily to skin color and, corollary to this, presumed class status. Whites' discomfort with black people was not new to this era, nor were whites' associations of blacks with poverty, political incompetence, and the degradation of homes and neighborhoods. But by the 1950s suburban whites had refashioned older racial narratives, creating a contemporary and geographically specific story about race, property, and politics that enabled them to explain away metropolitan inequality without invoking myths about racial difference. The market imperative argument for exclusion allowed many whites to demand separation while insisting upon their racial progressivism.

Meanwhile this narrative about growth and inequality provided whites with what seemed a commonsensical, nonideological vocabulary for rejecting a newly emerging threat to their status and privileges: the modern civil rights movement. Whites' story about cities, suburbs, property, and race was deeply institutionalized and well rehearsed in northern metropolitan regions by the mid-1950s, when the Supreme Court's ruling in *Brown v. Board of Education* and a new wave of black civil disobedience raised the profile of civil rights activism for northern whites. By then, defenders of neighborhood racial segregation commonly claimed that they were driven solely by practical, economic concerns. Whites tapped into this market imperative argument, in turn, to make sense of and defend against a new wave of civil rights protest and legislative reform in the 1950s and early 1960s. Comparing suburban affluence with urban decay and viewing these changes as the result of fair competition in a free market for housing and employment, many whites concluded that civil rights protest represented blacks' last-ditch effort to achieve through state intervention and other kinds of "coercion" what they could not achieve through initiative. Among the most commonly heard complaints from whites hostile to the protest movement was the charge that civil rights activism represented an assault on *their* rights as white people, in general, and as property owners in particular. Investment in the myth of the free market for residence made it possible for whites to endorse generic calls for civil rights reform and legal equality while still insisting upon the racial segregation of residential neighborhoods. The evidence suggests that most whites held this seemingly contradictory position not because they were self-consciously "hiding" their racism, but because they ignored their investment in a culture and their dependence on institutions that were so deeply racist.

It would be a mistake to interpret every public or private discussion about housing and neighborhoods in this period as an expression of latent or unconscious white racial anxiety. And whites did not monopolize discourses about the "threat" posed by "lower class" or "racially suspect" neighbors.[7] Yet to fully understand the transformation of white racial ideology since World War II and to measure its impact on American political culture, it is important to read whites' conversations about neighborhoods (and neighbors) in light of a decades-long conversation—one deeply embedded in institutions, law, and private practice—that imagined the market for property and neighborhoods as free from government intervention and observing normative, impersonal rules about racial compatibility. This wide-ranging conversation was held in both public and private venues. It was embraced by elected officials and voters, realtors and bankers, newspaper editors and civic association leaders. Its racial assumptions were sometimes outlined formulaically, for example, in appraisal manuals and protective associations' newsletters. At other times they were recast informally, for example, in news editorials and press releases warning about the threat posed by public housing, in municipal publications celebrating the "typical" American homeowner, and in the ongoing local debates over development. Finally, whites continued to talk about race, markets, and property amongst themselves, in conversations that only on occasion have been preserved in the historical record. Some of these more candid discussions are captured in the hundreds and hundreds of letters written by whites to government officials and newspaper editors in metropolitan Detroit in the 1950s and 1960s.

Protecting the single-family home and preserving suburban autonomy were not the only issues shaping whites' response to black people and black protest during these years. But decades of segregated living and segregationist neighborhood politics had presented metropolitan whites with a series of persuasive narratives about their rights and privileges, about the sanctity of property in the free enterprise system, and, ironically, about the "dangers" posed by government interference in private markets or local affairs. Local development politics constantly reminded whites that the U.S. Constitution and the courts protected their right to live with and associate with whomever they chose and that "federal interference" could only distort the natural market mechanisms responsible for the nation's spectacular prosperity. Most important, local politics constantly confirmed the story that a robust free market for homes and neighborhoods could not withstand the burden of "racial mixing." Given the centrality of development politics to early postwar suburban life, it is not surprising that so many whites applied lessons learned locally to their battles, both private and public, against the movement for African American rights.

Race Politics: Defending a Property Owner's Right to Exclude

Dearborn had already earned a regional reputation for intolerance by the spring of 1956, when its racial politics were thrust into the national spotlight. On March 26 the *Montgomery Advertiser* (Alabama) published an interview with Orville Hubbard, in which the mayor declared his support for "complete segregation, one million per cent, on all levels" and acknowledged "an unwritten law against Negroes living in Dearborn." Detroit's black-owned newspaper, the *Michigan Chronicle*, reported on the mayor's remarks, which then stoked a controversy in the metropolitan region and eventually attracted national attention. Many white northerners were outraged. The Dearborn Council of United Church Women announced that they were "not going to let Mayor Hubbard speak for all people of Dearborn." Hubbard publicly dismissed their complaint, prompting Michigan's Episcopal bishop, the Rt. Rev. Richard S. Emrich, to enter the fray. Emrich stated on April 17 that Dearborn's mayor "espouses views which are directly opposed to the teachings of every great section of the Christian Church . . . [and] to the Constitution of the United States." "The logic of his position," the bishop declared, "is the destruction of all law and all rights."[8]

Whites comfortable with racial segregation thought nothing of ignoring the *Michigan Chronicle*, but the public challenge posed by Emrich, a prominent white church leader, precipitated a very contentious, high-profile debate over the politics of housing discrimination in metropolitan Detroit. It also prompted white residents to speak out about racial politics in letters to local officials and newspaper editors. For years Hubbard had received supportive correspondence from area residents. But when the "Emrich affair" raised Hubbard's profile and made him a regional symbol for white intolerance, his office was flooded with letters, telegrams, and phone calls, virtually all of them from white people, the vast majority congratulating him for his "stand" on the "racial situation." The flow of correspondence continued for over a decade, usually surging when a local or regional racial controversy was in the news. After reading press coverage of Emrich's statement, hearing Hubbard's name mentioned "over the radio several times lately," seeing him on television, or reading his "speeches on segregation,"[9] white people from throughout the Detroit region and from states around the country declared their support for residential exclusion. Typical was a postcard from a Dearborn couple, written when the Emrich story broke, "just to let you know we are with you in your stand on segregation" and to express their appreciation "for your fight to keep Dearborn free from undesirables." "We citizens of Dearborn," wrote another couple that week, "back . . . you 100% in your stand on segregation." Hundreds of whites applauded the mayor's "courageous and honest remarks concerning segregation," exhorted him to "keep up the good work!" and wished him "more power . . . in keeping our city white."[10] Many said that their families, friends, and "everyone else with whom [they] talk" agreed with his views, claiming that "most of the people on the east side of Detroit think you are doing a swell job as Mayor," or congratulating him "from myself and one million other Detroiters for your magnificent declaration on segregation." Telegrams poured in from city and suburb alike, many on standard Western Union stationary featuring an illustration of a floral arrangement, with just one word of text: "Congratulations."[11]

Only rarely did these correspondents devote much space to the Emrich affair itself (or, in later years, to the racial controversy of the moment). The few who mentioned Emrich's comments, or what several termed the church's "hypocrisy,"[12] rarely stayed on topic, and most ignored it altogether, instead offering general observations about integration and the region's racial transformation. There were several recurring themes. Correspondents regularly celebrated the promise held out by the new, all-white suburbs. They insisted that blacks had destroyed residential neighborhoods in Detroit and now posed an immediate threat to suburban residents, who needed to prevent a "Negro invasion." And more than any other topic, it was the urgency of protecting white peoples' *homes* that served as a refrain for this running commentary on race relations and racial politics. Even letters that focused on other issues—economic opportunity, crime, civil rights protest, threats to the family, or electoral politics—regularly returned to the topics of property, homeownership, and the suburban institutions designed to protect both. That so many of the region's white residents felt compelled to speak out about race and rights suggests how politically formative their racial anxieties had become by the mid-1950s. The fact that they talked incessantly about homes, neighborhoods, and the rights of property owners reveals how metropolitan growth and local land-use politics had helped to shape their conceptions of their own whiteness. Hubbard's supporters regularly asserted a claim that had long been a touchstone of exclusionary politics in the Detroit suburbs: they openly and wholeheartedly endorsed racial discrimination, while insisting that they were not racist.

They focused instead on the assumption stated succinctly by an Allen Park resident in 1956 that "no matter where the negro has lived the property is hurt." And they insisted that this fact was visible to anyone who just looked around Detroit. "The parks," he explained, "are a good example." "To let colored people settle into a nice vicinity will help no community," wrote a Dearborn woman in 1956. "It will only be destroyed." From Detroit came the claim that there "would be a lot less slums [here] if the colored was kept out," citing the "mess that [the] N. Woodward section" had become and complaining that even the churches had been "taken over." Correspondents depicted racial threats by referencing specific geographical locations and structures and the ways that whites could or could not use them. A Dearborn resident wrote Hubbard a note in the margins of a brochure for Camp Dearborn, a municipally funded facility well-known for barring access to minorities. "We should all keep in mind the *appearance* of [Detroit's] *Belle Isle* and *River Rouge Park* where integration is prevalent," he wrote, since "we don't want the same *in our camp.*" He encouraged suburban officials to "scrutinize every car for *undesirables* which may be guests of the *Dearborn Council of Church Women*" and to do "everything in our power" to "keep our camp peaceful, quiet, clean and respectful." One Detroiter explained that she had "once enjoyed gardening or relaxing on the porch," but that since blacks had moved into her neighborhood "it is a different matter." "With dozens of inhabitants in each house draping themselves all over their front porches and lawns—ogling one—you settle for the privacy of your own living room." This was a common concern, expressed in 1956 by a Dearborn woman convinced that integration would "destroy our freedom of being able to visit our neighbors for coffee and a chat," and by a Detroiter who felt that Dearborn was the only place "where a person may feel free to walk down the street at night without being afraid of being hit on the head or stabbed in the back."[13]

Particularly striking is the frequency with which whites describe racial conflict as a story about property rather than people. Consider the Dearborner who congratulated Hubbard for his comments on residential exclusion (what he referred to as the mayor's "'Equal but Separate' statement") by enclosing photographs that he had taken during a recent visit to Detroit. The pictures, he explained, "show[ed] what the colored people have already done to neighborhoods they have taken over," turning them into "such filthy shambles that visitors from out of State ask to see the 'sights' of the wreckage which was once a fine residential area." But the photos "only partially convey the atmosphere," he continued, because they do not "register the sickening stink of the rubbish filled yards." "The arrogant spokesmen for the colored say that these people do not have enough money to clean up. How much does it cost to rake the rubbish out of a yard; to repair a broken window instead of stuffing it with cardboard? Is a can of paint so expensive?" This man viewed Dearborn as his family's "only haven." Others commented on the fact that similar transformations were being repeated in cities nationwide. One correspondent had witnessed it before, growing up in Chicago, where he "firsthandedly saw the Negro 'block busters' in action," and since then wondered "why minorities such as the colored people will try to force themselves on a community where they're not wanted." Hubbard regularly received clippings from national news magazines. In 1956, for example, a Dearborn resident forwarded an April 13 article from *U.S. News and World Report* on "Chicago's Race Problem." The statistics concerning congestion, crime, and what the magazine called "racial friction" were highlighted, and a handwritten note was added in the margins: "God spare our Dearborn from such a scourge as this . . . Prevent the *above conditions* from being initiated in Dearborn."[14]

What, if anything, was new or distinct about the racial sentiments expressed in this correspondence? By no means does the focus on property and places rather than on people and racial hierarchy indicate that whites' ideas about race had been suddenly transformed. Clearly many of these men and women had long been invested in myths about white superiority. A 40-year-old white suburbanite writing in 1956 had grown up in an age that embraced racial pseudo-science. Meanwhile narratives about blacks' intellectual inferiority or their predisposition to criminality, aggression, and promiscuity were rampant in postwar America.[15] Exposure to the new metropolitan land-use politics did not convert white people overnight into advocates of a purportedly nonracist, market-driven defense for exclusion. Ideological changes occur far more gradually.

But a new language about exclusion was clearly shaping whites' interpretations of regional change and their responses to racial politics and racial conflict. For the one thing uniting most of these men and women—an ethnically, socioeconomically, and geographically very diverse group of self-described white people—was their status as homeowners or aspiring homeowners, and the growing fear that blacks threatened to undermine the suburban communities that were becoming focal points of regional development, wealth accumulation, and status. In such established suburbs as Royal Oak and Dearborn, and in the younger, fast-growing communities surrounding them, thousands of managers, secretaries, autoworkers, business-owners, doctors, and housewives—people with names like Monroe, Schmidt, Luptak, Alessi, Wisniewski, Sraburg, Longmoore, Calcaterra, Kobozny, Baker, Johnson, and Szczisniak—rallied around their shared whiteness. That shared racial identity was now powerfully signified and geographically realized in the region's home-rule suburbs. Suburban whites were surrounded daily by the privileges that they hoped to defend. Urban whites uncomfortable with Detroit's transformation could point across the municipal border, to the promise held out by the region's dynamic suburban "havens." The preoccupation with suburban homeownership saw defenders of racial exclusion treat *white* rights and *property* rights as identical and often use the terms interchangeably. Brief endorsements of racial segregation concluded with generic exhortations to "keep property values in Dearborn at their present high level!" Whites collapsed stories about racial character into stories about property, like the Detroiter who accused blacks of living "high, wide and handsome when they have [money] and then on *Welfare*. They don't scimp and save . . . to buy homes like us. After denying ourselves *all* but necessities for us to buy a home where we want, what do we get? They move next door." Echoing a sentiment registered in scores and scores of notes and phone calls, one Dearborn woman told Hubbard that when he talked about the necessity of racial exclusion, he "spoke for us homeowners."[16]

And the rhetorical emphasis on property and the rights of homeowners was critical, enabling whites to call for segregation while portraying themselves as not racist. They talked far less about black people per se than about the threat that black occupancy posed to white property and places. Correspondents rarely identified themselves as "white," but rather as "homeowners," "citizens," "taxpayers," "longtime residents," "veterans," "parents," or "housewives." Only a handful declared affiliation with supremacist groups. The derogatory language formerly associated with white racism (terms such as "nigger" or "coon") appears very seldom, while demeaning characterizations of blacks' physical or mental capabilities are even rarer. Instead, most of these whites were learning to view racial matters through the prism of property and metropolitan change. They attributed the differences between white and black neighborhoods to preference, custom, or habit. They assessed local politics and defined their rights through descriptions of the region's material and racial geography. They identified themselves, first and foremost, with the place where they lived (or the place they *hoped* soon to call home), and they regularly discussed the current "racial situation" in terms of places, buildings, and ownership. Above all else, they focused on the necessity of protecting white property, white neighborhoods, and the political institutions that secured both. Doing so, they insisted, was not a racist act.

Whites had no qualms describing "white flight" as a response to black people, because they described relocation not as an act of prejudice but practical necessity. Former Detroit residents insisted upon their racial tolerance, explaining that blacks' behaviors had simply "driven every white family out" of their neighborhoods. One Detroiter and self-described "Future Dearborner" explained the racial situation this way: "drive around Detroit and look at its city parks, housing projects and housing in general, then ask the many people who, after Negroes have moved into the house next door, suffered a great depreciation on his house and property." In 1956, Hubbard heard from a Detroit resident of thirty-five years who promised to "purchase [a home in Dearborn] tomorrow" if he could be "sure that Dearborn would hold the [line]." He claimed no ill will toward blacks; they deserved rights too, he argued, but should not "try to horn in on other peoples affairs." According to many correspondents the problem was not race but fairness, and the evidence was visible. Eleanor Varga, of Rochester, an Oakland County suburb, wrote Hubbard in 1956 with an often-heard lament: "My God man, where are my civil rights?" She continued: "I still say [blacks] should stay by themselves. Now, that's where your slums come from. All through Chicago Blvd., Euclid, Seward and all those beautiful homes. They finally got them and once they're in it's slums."[17]

Even the letters that discussed older, more traditional racial preoccupations usually returned to the topics of property and metropolitan locales. When the generations-old bogeyman of the "black rapist" or fears about miscegenation appear in the correspondence, they are threats not only to white women or families but also white-owned property and white-controlled spaces. One Dearborner was certain that blacks did not really want to live among whites, but rather were just trying to "force an issue"; thus it was Hubbard's duty to "keep our Dearborn women safe from the rapist and the murderer." From Highland Park came a warning that "millionaire real estate operators in Detroit" would encourage Hubbard to "flood your modern Dearborn with hundreds of sex hungry negro rapists." A white woman in Dearborn recently relocated from Chicago was "very glad our Mayor is frank and honest about the integration issue," because she wanted "white children and they in turn to have the same, not mongrels." Notably she then turns not to the subject of white superiority or even a discussion of white and black people, but rather to the topic of homes and neighborhoods. "If all those who rant and rave for integration had to live with them they'd change their minds," she continues. "The negroes say they're discriminated against, true and for good reason. They live in slum areas, but slum or not it wouldn't kill them to buy a broom and bucket of paint to at least live in cleanliness; most of them make good money but because they blow it, why cry about it and yell slum. If they want new houses let them have them, far away from us."[18]

It did not require a well publicized housing or civil rights controversy for whites to sound an alarm over transgressions of the color line. They employed a racial calculus about property, neighborhoods, and rights every day—while shopping or running errands, while at work or at home, and on journeys in between. Their reactions to the sight of black people in places deemed "white," be it a single-family home, a residential street, or a shopping mall, suggest that whites did not just think *about* the connection between race, property, and rights at particular moments, but rather that they regularly thought *with* a racialized vocabulary about property and rights.[19] Whites' running commentary on life in the metropolitan region suggests the power and resonance of a new racial vocabulary that assumed links between homeownership, city spaces, and political privilege.

In the fall of 1956, for example, a woman from Dearborn was troubled that black people were patronizing the city's shopping and service facilities. "I went up to pay my [electric and telephone] bills in the vicinity of the Main Library at Mason and Michigan," she wrote, "and in each office while paying my bills there were 4 or 5 negroes in each place paying their bills." "Doesn't it seem to you that they travel quite a distance to pay bills," she asked, since they "surely have closer offices." The woman "was amazed at seeing so many, so as I shopped in Zuiebacks, Winkelmans, Stuarts, Budny Shoe Store, Sanders and several of the other better stores, I counted them and came up with an unbelievable total of 34! I counted this many in just an hour and a half." Suburban whites also viewed public schools as a strictly white domain. Soon after the 1956 school term began, a group identifying themselves as "Parents of Dearborn" wrote the mayor to ask "why a little colored girl is going to Henry Ford School," since they were "sure she isn't a resident of Dearborn." "Even if she is a daughter that's parents are living here is that any reason why their children from generation to generation should keep going to a white school." It was rumored that the girl was "living with her mother on Palmer," but "some of us have followed them and they never go to Palmer address." So they concluded that Hubbard "should look into this as mayor of Dearborn. [A] white town this should remain." That year a former Detroiter told Hubbard that he had moved to Dearborn to prevent his kids from attending integrated schools—that he "had to find a City with your type of surroundings." Yet he still saw cause for concern. "I notice . . . that more and more niggers are beginning to shop in our shopping centers," he wrote, "and I wish there was some way we could stop this."[20]

Whites were watching, sensitive to any visible transgression, any disruption of the local racial order. And in Dearborn, at least, residents interpreted their leaders' public stand on segregation, whether it was Hubbard's pronouncements or the DPOPA's organizing efforts, as license to remain vigilant. In the spring of 1956, at the height of the Emrich controversy, one of Hubbard's neighbors in northeast Dearborn just blocks from the Detroit border reported seeing "a peculiar circumstance in our neighborhood, Thursday morning the 19th while waiting for the bus." "Two colored fellows (well dressed—they did not look like workmen out on a job) drove up to a home on Coleman Avenue (7017 Coleman, to be exact—three houses North from Blesser Avenue, facing East) parked a few minutes—looked around the house—rang the bell, and were admitted without hesitation." The correspondent was "a bit suspicious, so thought perhaps you might be interested in investigating further—in case of a sale of that particular home."[21]

During the 1950s, housing politics in the United States was about much more than just housing. Both financially and geographically, homeownership was fast becoming a foothold for millions of white people, a means of ensuring economic well-being, comfort, and status. Meanwhile the single-family home had taken on an ideological life of its own, as advertisers, politicians, and television programming celebrated homeownership, family togetherness, and the domestic sphere as the locus of a new consumption and indulgence-oriented economy as well as a refuge from a range of subversive forces, both domestic and foreign.[22] For innumerable whites in the Detroit region, protecting neighborhoods from any threats—including black people—had became a potent symbol of their battle to protect a new middle-class lifestyle, the nuclear family, and white privilege itself.

It was in this context that northern whites responded to the early stages of the modern civil rights movement. Many interpreted black protest, particularly in the North, where there was no memory of de jure segregation, as an unwarranted assault on whites' new postwar privileges and lifestyle. These privileges were literally embodied in the region's fast-growing, racially homogeneous suburbs, and so challenges to these havens, especially in the form of open-housing campaigns, triggered considerable hostility. To many, Dearborn held a special status: it was "very much a credit to Michigan," explained one resident in 1956, in a state that "could get along fine with less assailing" by civil rights advocates. Hubbard's supporters viewed national civil rights organizations, prominent civil rights leaders, and even high-profile southern protest activities as evidence of a looming threat for northern whites. They were particularly upset that the NAACP, often referred to as a "pressure group," was lobbying legislators to outlaw FHA and VA support for contractors who "refuse to sell . . . new homes to negroes." "Too many people in public life have not [got] the courage to speak the truth about integration," explained one Dearborn resident. "It seems we are told we must accept integration in all its forms, good and bad, because the N.A.A.C.P. says we must . . . If the N.A.A.C.P. says we must associate with riff-raff, live next to them, marry them, go to school with them, it must be O.K. because they say so. Our choice or preference does not matter." In 1956 a Detroiter wrote Senator James Eastland, of Mississippi, a rabid anticommunist and outspoken critic of the civil rights movement, to complain that influential civil rights organizations were preventing honest discussion about blacks' impact on the city. He enclosed a *Detroit News* article about a young black man accused of murder, "for your information," the correspondent explained, "as to the truth of Northern desegregation and it's affects [sic] on the White Race of People here." Thirty years ago the scene of the crime was "an entirely White respectable law abiding section of the City of Detroit," he added, before it was "infiltrated" by black people.[23]

By the mid-1950s, public figures sympathetic to civil rights reform were already the subject of considerable scorn. From throughout the region came complaints that most urban and suburban officials, unlike Hubbard, could only "squirm" on the issue of racial segregation. "I wish that we had more honest men like [Hubbard] in the north," wrote one Detroiter, so that "Negroes would not be crammed down our throats." Other popular targets included religious leaders, especially Emrich, progressive labor leaders, including UAW president Walter Reuther, and Governor G. Mennen ("Soapy") Williams, who in 1955 signed a controversial Fair Employment Practices bill into law. One of Hubbard's correspondents simply dismissed "all of our politicians in the North" as "hypocrite[s]." He had "spoken to hundreds" of people who "don't want their sons and daughters to intermarry with negroes nor living next door to them." Meanwhile, support for civil rights reform was often lumped into a broad range of seditious, un-American behaviors. An Oak Park resident felt that Hubbard's views on segregation made him a "good American," but feared that such praise "would be considered un-democratic" by Williams, Reuther, Ethel and Julius Rosenberg, and "all of the other filth in this great country of ours." A two-sentence telegram mailed to Hubbard in 1956 suggests the prominence of housing issues in whites' negotiation of a much broader debate over race and rights. The sender explained why he knew far more than the governor about racial politics: "Live in integrated neighborhood. Does Soapy[?]"[24]

Hubbard was clearly a symbol of resistance, and for this reason many viewed him as an expert on civil rights issues. Upon learning in 1957 that the state's Democratic leadership was calling for a legislative commitment to civil rights protections, one Dearborner complained to the mayor that blacks had too many rights already; now officials "want to move them into our Eating and Lodging places." In 1958, correspondents urged Hubbard to block the creation of a state civil rights commission and made general pleas to "do all you can to obstruct any extension of Civil Rights." A man from the Rosedale Park neighborhood of Detroit sent Hubbard a news article from the *Cincinnati Times-Star,* describing a state Supreme Court ruling that an Ohio amusement park (called Coney Island) could not be "forced to admit Negroes." "Substitute 'Dearborn' or 'Rosedale Park' . . . for 'Coney Island,'" he wrote to Hubbard, "and such a decision would be most heartwarming."[25]

Some of the mayor's supporters, in Dearborn particularly, would have preferred him to keep a lower profile. "If we want to lose our fine community," wrote a resident of the suburb's northeast in 1956, "you are using the proper tactics." Hubbard's outspokenness was "the cause of much talk among my neighbors and friends," who fear that "we are headed for trouble with the NAACP if the negro problem and Dearborn's stand on it are talked about so publicly." One resident believed that blacks were shopping in Dearborn only because "the N.A.A.C.P. has read your views on the matter and has sent their people in droves to our beautiful, clean city." But appeals for discretion were far outnumbered by calls for greater vigilance, requests for political counsel, and laments. What could whites do, asked a Dearborn woman in 1956, to "stop the uprising of the negro?" It was "shocking the progress they are making," she continued and wondered if "there are any men in public office who don't crave the colored vote." "Before I vote again," she asked Hubbard "if you can advise me along that line."[26]

This commentary offers a glimpse into an emerging white backlash politics. This politics had taken root in the early postwar battles over suburban (and urban) neighborhoods. Now in the wake of the *Brown* decision and an upsurge in civil rights protest, whites took the lessons learned from their local, neighborhood-focused battles and applied them to a national debate over civil rights reform and racial equality. Long before the heyday of civil rights protest and the radicalization of some movement leaders, long before Kennedy, Johnson, and Congress acted to reassert the government's commitment to protecting blacks' political and civil rights, and long before George Wallace, Barry Goldwater, and other national figures campaigned against the specter of "racial liberalism" to rally white support—long before these better-known flashpoints and supposed triggers of "backlash" politics, whites in metropolitan Detroit had been organizing to check the expansion of black residential neighborhoods and even to block civil rights reform. The people who reached out to Hubbard and other local officials in the mid-1950s were not afraid to declare their support for segregation. Yet with few exceptions, they defended exclusion not by discussing racial difference or even their personal views about black people, but rather by invoking their "rights" simultaneously as homeowners, community members, and white people. They argued, and numerous public and private institutions confirmed for them, that they had a constitutional right to protect their property and maintain their privacy.

Many whites were already contemplating electoral strategies, including the dozens who encouraged Hubbard to "run for [the] governorship." According to a 30-year-old Detroiter employed by Grand Trunk Western Railroad, Hubbard's political prospects were a popular topic of conversation in 1956. "Everyone I've talked with lately has Hubbard on their lips," he wrote, and is "praising you for your stand on colored in Dearborn." "I've asked everyone at work and all other people that I've met how they would vote if you ran for the Governorship, and they all said you would get their vote." A Detroiter who worked for Chrysler and who had heard good things about the mayor from co-workers who lived in Dearborn hoped that Hubbard would become "a big man in politics someday." Personal experience had confirmed his views about segregation. "Colored people come into our shop at Dodge's and abuse every privilege that we had for years," he explained, and "any neighborhood they have moved into has become a run down shambles in 10 years time." He was especially angered by a current proposal to revitalize downtown Detroit, since it would "buil[d] it up again for the Negros" while having "the taxpayers in the suburban districts pay for it."[27]

Men and women regularly volunteered their services, along with those of "countless friends," to help the mayor "uphold . . . the principles of segregation in Detroit and Dearborn." They offered to "go from door to door." They offered financial contributions to publish articles about segregation, or to defray costs of litigation. They suggested fundraising ideas. "If petitions would help," explained the Grand Trunk employee, then he "could get 1000 signatures now or in the future if you ever should decide to run" for governor. Correspondents were particularly enthusiastic about local, grassroots activity. A self-described "housewife" from Detroit had nothing but praise for local housing activists, explaining in 1956 that "the community in which I live is all white thanks to the Greenfield Park Civic Association." One Dearborner enclosed a *Time* magazine article about a recent attack against a black homeowner in Detroit; he was happy to read that the man had been "visited by officers of the neighborhood improvement association" and encouraged Dearborn residents to follow their example. Another resident encouraged his neighbors to organize "through the rank & file, Property owners assn., Real Estate men, golf and bowling alleys," because the governor "wants negroes in F.H.A. financed rentals of 4 units or more, in golf clubs, bowling alleys, hotels, all recreation no matter where." The governor also wanted "to make Real Estate men sell to them no matter where. Nice isn't it?"[28]

The vast majority of these appeals for action were free from declarations of "white supremacy" or "racial incompatibility," but some whites were clearly invested in an explicitly racialist (and implicitly biologist) form of organizing. Correspondents occasionally inquired about white citizens' councils, among them a Dearborner who thought it "unfortunate" that "there is no National Association for the Protection of White People." Notably neither this man, a self-described "home owner," "representative of a home owner ass[ociation]," and "WWII veteran," nor most like-minded whites were necessarily on the margins of electoral politics. Many discussed white citizens' councils and public policy in the same breath, like the Detroiter who asked if "the white group [had] representatives here so I could get in touch with them" before telling Hubbard that "we sure need many more of our official family to take the same stand that you do." Indeed, the evidence suggests that even some committed white supremacists were beginning to adopt the new postwar language and logic of racial exclusion. In 1956, a man from Highland Park encouraged Hubbard to spearhead the formation of a statewide white citizens' council and offered a prospective platform. The first point read: "We hate no one because of his race. We do demand that all politicians who expect our endorsement . . . pledge

themselves to vote against all civil rights measures." Especially revealing is
the apparent confluence between the strategies pursued by self-described
"white" activists and property protective organizations. In the mid-1950s,
for example, the mission statement from a Detroit white citizens' council
used the same generic language adopted by organizations like the DPOPA:
"To promote the development or betterment of communities, municipalities or counties in this state." Those residents who inquired about organizations for "white" people would have no doubt looked upon such a group
with keen interest.[29]

The tension between an older, explicitly racialist defense of exclusion
and the new market-imperative rationale often produced strange juxtaposi-
tions in these letters. Many whites seemed to be struggling to accommodate
familiar understandings of the "racial problem" with the newer, supposedly
nonideological defense of white privilege. The correspondence sometimes
reveals a fair amount of confusion about *how* to defend exclusion, as writers alternate between tirades about racial "mixing," on the one hand, and
dispassionate discussions of property values, the court system, or civil rights
law, on the other. One man from Dearborn accused civil rights activists,
the "writers, politicians, clergy and other critics of segregation," of underestimating the threats posed by integration because they lived in all-white
suburbs, far from the front lines of the battles over housing. "Safe from
encroachment," he wrote in 1956, "these persons . . . feel justified in pro-
nouncing verdicts on the ones of us who have not the money or prestige to
protect the small holdings we possess." He was also amazed by "the sheer
ignorance" of these leaders and commentators "in their views in regards to
the Negro question." They mistakenly interpret the "very natural instinct
of man to association with his own" as "race bigotry," he wrote, while they
interpret "our attempts to procure privacy as 'racial discrimination.'"[30]

In the final analysis, whites' political sensibilities and commitments cannot be gauged solely by documenting their support for elected officials, their
participation in local organizations, or their commentary about national
politics. Even the letters free from references to specific groups, officials, or
controversies were still political pronouncements anchored in race-specific
assumptions about the rights and privileges of property owners. One of the
most forceful political declarations repeated here was also one of the most
common: living in a place "like Dearborn," whites insisted, was a commentary on metropolitan life and racial change. Living there, moving there,
or just expressing a desire to do so, all of these were ways for correspondents to declare their investment—emotional, political, and economic—in
protecting their racial privilege. "As a white Mother of three little children,

I believe in what you stand for," wrote a self-described "Detroit Housewife" in 1956. She was convinced that Hubbard had "higher ideals than the average politician, much higher," and hoped that "as soon as we are financially able we too, will move to Dearborn." Another Detroiter agreed that "the people of Dearborn are indeed fortunate to have [the mayor] defend their rights" and hoped that she and her son "will be privileged to own a home in your City in the very near future." Correspondents frequently reported conversations with others "who are planning to move to Dearborn" or simply declared that "Dearborn must be a nice city in which to live." Meanwhile Dearborn residents celebrated their privileged status, certain that "at least a million other persons would like to live here." One woman concluded a lengthy critique of black political protest by signing off: "Thank goodness I live in Dearborn."[31]

The experience of a Dearborn Township couple illustrates how postwar suburban politics had helped countless whites see residential choice itself as a political act and how homeownership helped draw them into new kinds of political participation and new political commitments. Soon after the Emrich controversy unfolded in April 1956, the couple wrote Hubbard to explain that they were "entirely in accord with you" on the "Negro situation" and suggested that those people "who want to join their negro brethren can . . . move" to "Good old Inkster," a predominantly black suburb just west of Dearborn. "Although we live just inside Dearborn Township now," they continued, the couple was currently "in the process of looking for a home to buy" and "hope[d] to be in Dearborn soon." They were so impressed with the suburb's political leadership that they even "helped campaign for Hubbard at election time." And since then, their commitment had only deepened. "We have never before written to anyone on any issue," they confessed; "however, we believe you can use all the backing and moral support it is possible to give on this subject. If there is anything we can do to help you, will you please let us know."[32]

Local Control: Pursuing the Politics of Exclusion in the Civil Rights Era

To his contemporary critics, and to many subsequent commentators, Orville Hubbard was a demagogue who stoked whites' racial fears to secure political support. While there is much truth to this characterization—Hubbard was often bombastic and he relished controversy—discussions of Dearborn's racial politics ignore the larger grass-roots movement that provided his base and that took the initiative on housing issues throughout his tenure. Hubbard was one of many local officials and business leaders in the Detroit metropolitan region who curried favor with a homeowners' movement very active since the early 1940s. That movement continued to engage in the hard work of racial exclusion throughout the 1950s and 1960s. Equally notable is the fact that while Hubbard was perhaps the most outspoken and visible northern segregationist of the era, he was not strongly associated, in the minds of Dearborn residents at least, with a particular political party. This solidly Democratic suburb was well known for its staunch, often violent opposition to racial integration. Its residents consistently embraced the New Deal state while openly celebrating their whiteness. But because Dearborn's mayoral elections were nonpartisan, residents were generally unaware of Hubbard's party affiliation. Surveyed on the subject in 1956, 36 percent speculated that he was a Democrat and 39 percent said that he was probably a Republican.[33]

The unique combination of Hubbard's notoriety and residents' avid support for the Democratic Party make Dearborn unique among the region's suburbs. But its brand of suburban restrictionist politics was in most ways interchangeable with that practiced by its neighbors. Key to understanding suburban racial politics after 1955, whether in Dearborn, Royal Oak, or the region's other white suburbs, was homeowners' commitment to the mundane work of protecting their neighborhoods from apartment construction, excessive commercial development, and black people. They did so by using most of the strategies and tools employed since the early 1940s: organizing and sponsoring educational campaigns, participating in council and zoning board meetings, challenging zoning reform, and resorting to intimidation and violence. The national political context for homeowner activism had changed, though, as the civil rights struggle received national press coverage and also drew increasing attention to the racial exclusivity of northern residential neighborhoods. After *Brown*, northern civil rights activists grew far more assertive in their attempts to uncover racial discrimination, particularly in the expansive market for suburban housing. And open-housing campaigns obviously threatened suburban whites in ways that earlier protest activities aimed at access to public facilities did not.[34] Suburban whites responded as they always had: by organizing. The tireless efforts of homeowners, businesspeople, and local officials coupled with continued redlining by realtors, mortgage lenders, and federal officials ensured that all-white suburbs remained just that. The black people who lived in suburban Detroit could be found, with few exceptions, in one of three places: Inkster, River Rouge, and Ecorse (in the latter two, they were restricted to subdivisions west of the New York Central Railroad). As late as

1968, there were no homes owned by black people in the following Wayne and Oakland County suburbs: Royal Oak Township, Troy, Dearborn, Hazel Park, Ferndale, Madison Heights, Sterling Heights, Southfield, Redford Township, Westland, Farmington, Allen Park, Melvindale, and Lincoln Park. That year there was a single black family living in Birmingham, another in Livonia, and there were four in Oak Park.[35]

Of equal importance, local organizing efforts continued to shape whites' ideas about metropolitan growth and race. Homeowner activism continued to immerse residents in the politics and law of land-use restriction, its economic rationale, and its assumptions about property owners' rights and privileges. Whites continued to fill council and zoning board meetings, local editorial pages, and the meetings of property protective associations with detailed discussions about the market imperative for exclusion. And whether they won or lost individual battles, suburban whites continued to invoke the statutes, the social science, and the court rulings that articulated a race-coded vision of metropolitan development. Further reinforcing this narrative about race and development were the efforts of municipal officials, publicists, and local boosters to celebrate and promote the suburban ideal. Local publications continued to exalt suburban living and the white nuclear family. And a newer strategy grew increasingly popular: the annual "fix up" campaigns that brought lessons about homeownership, good government, and suburban "cleanliness" to civic groups, churches, and even to elementary school classrooms. When coupled with the day-to-day work of land-use restriction, these new interventions produced a multifaceted local politics—both formal and informal—that constantly shaped whites' responses to debates over race and rights. During the years that saw the civil rights movement ask whites to acknowledge the history of power and privilege that had helped secure their comfortable and stable postwar lives, suburban whites were immersed in a political culture that attributed their affluence and comfort solely to hard work, respect for private property, community involvement, and implicitly to whiteness itself.

Whites in metropolitan Detroit who wanted to imagine that the civil rights movement was a southern phenomenon were caught off guard by the surge of local protest activity in the late 1950s and early 1960s. Organizationally, some of this new activism traced its roots to the Mayor's Interracial Committee (MIC), formed in the wake of the 1943 race riot on Belle Isle. After the *Shelley* ruling, the MIC joined with other local activists to promote fair housing, creating the Coordinating Council on Human Relations

(CCHR) in 1948. Working with a national network of housing activists, the CCHR sponsored educational efforts at churches, schools, and community organizations and distributed literature "extolling the virtues of integrated housing." In the early 1950s, religious leaders often took the initiative in the open housing effort, only to find that most congregants refused to follow. The extent and visibility of housing activism increased in the mid-1950s, and dovetailed, to the chagrin of many white people, with an effective mobilization to promote fair hiring practices. The Detroit Urban League called on the FHA and HOLC to market properties to blacks in white neighborhoods, and housing activists exposed realtors' efforts to maintain segregated markets. By 1959, civil rights groups had forced state legislators to consider two bills that would extend Fair Employment Practices Commission principles to the market for housing sales and rentals. A year later, a highly publicized scandal involving exclusionary real estate practices in the Detroit suburb of Grosse Point helped energize both the local and national open housing movements.[36]

It also encouraged activists to experiment with more aggressive tactics. In 1961, the Congress on Racial Equality (CORE) sent "Freedom Riders" to test public facilities in Dearborn. The NAACP organized demonstrations against residential segregation in Royal Oak, Livonia, Oak Park, Dearborn, and Grosse Pointe, sponsored a fair-housing march in northwest Detroit, and held a rally at the Redford Township Hall to demand passage of an Open Housing Ordinance. Their campaign culminated in 1963, when 200,000 protesters (95 percent of them black) were joined by Dr. Martin Luther King, Detroit mayor Jerome Cavanaugh, and union leader Walter Reuther in a "March for Freedom" along Woodward Avenue.[37] Soon local activists were sending "testers" to identify realtors who were "steering" black customers away from white neighborhoods. The NAACP also put pressure on brokers who openly supported the dual housing market. In May 1963, the NAACP's Housing Committee threatened to publicize the fact that the F. G. Cherry Realty Company was staffing separate offices, one with blacks (at MacDougall and Gratiot) and one with whites (at Mack Avenue and Parker Street). It also contacted the Elsea Realty and Improvement Company of Detroit, asking them to explain why their advertisements listed a separate contact address for inquiries concerning "Colored Property."[38]

The NAACP's campaign helped mobilize the region's small but increasingly assertive white protest community, which joined in a concerted biracial movement to promote fair housing practices. Local religious leaders created the Open Occupancy Conference[39] in 1962, which pressed for opening the Detroit suburbs to middle-class blacks. In September of that year, the Metropolitan Conference on Open Occupancy was cosponsored by the Council of Churches of Metropolitan Detroit, the Jewish Community Council of Metropolitan Detroit, and the Roman Catholic Archdiocese of Detroit. At their two-day meeting in January 1963, Governor Romney delivered the keynote address. In 1962, Dearborn's Christ Episcopal Church sponsored a six-month study of residential segregation, which led, the following spring, to four evening meetings of "parish-wide education on the subject of race, housing, and open-occupancy pledge cards." Dearborn's St. Alphonus church hosted a series of meetings on housing and racial intermarriage.[40]

It was also in the fall of 1963, on Labor Day weekend, that a white mob attacked Giuseppe Stanzione's house on Kendal Street in northwest Dearborn when they suspected that he had sold it to a black couple. Open-housing activists responded by creating the Dearborn Community Council, a coalition dedicated to educating local residents about fair housing practices and "human relations." In late November 1963, the council, headed by an engineer named Fabian Stempian, sponsored a public discussion at the University of Michigan's Dearborn campus, where elected officials, businesspeople, and professors announced their commitment to the civil rights movement. By the following March, the council was setting up committees and planning group functions, including a debate on "Open Occupancy— Is it advantageous for a community?" that attracted about 150 participants, and a "Visitation Day," when white families would "visit negro families at the latter's home." Similar efforts were underway throughout the region. By the spring of 1964, more than twenty-five "human relations" groups were operating or being organized in the Detroit suburbs, including Allen Park, Grosse Pointe, Farmington, Birmingham, Lincoln Park, Southfield, Wyandotte, Dearborn Heights, and Grosse Ile.[41]

The evidence suggests that local activists spoke for a small minority of suburban residents. Many members of Dearborn's St. Alphonus church stormed out of the first three meetings hosted by the Committee for Human Relations, "shout[ing] objections to these affairs," according to one participant. Whites regularly expressed scorn for "pastors" or "clergy" who, as one of Hubbard's correspondents wrote, "stuck their nose in where it does not belong." Ever since Emrich's public challenge to Hubbard in 1956, many whites had been growing "rather bitter," explained one Dearborn woman, "against these churches trying to get into politics."[42] Meanwhile most suburban whites remained invested, both materially and ideologically, in a suburban political culture that defined racial minorities as a threat to property ownership and its privileges. Throughout the late 1950s and early

1960s, whites carefully policed the suburban color line, even, on occasion, with help from white Detroiters. In 1956, whites from the Robson Avenue area of Detroit, after watching the Hays family sell their home to blacks, sent a "delegation" to pay a "special visit to Livonia to warn the Hays' new neighbors that the Hays needed watching because they were just the type who would sell a home to Negroes."[43]

Race-restrictive covenants were ruled unenforceable after 1948, but white realtors still subscribed, along with their customers, to a theory of housing economics that defined racial minorities as a categorical risk to white peoples' property. Realtors and assessors followed nationally standardized appraisal guidelines and discussed the social scientific principles of exclusion at local and regional real estate seminars. Even the suspicion that a broker was marketing properties to nonwhites could destroy their business. In 1962, when the Brokers Realtor Service of Dearborn was accused of showing a home on Dearborn's west side (near Levagood Park) to an "unqualified" buyer, its president, Martin Kosten, sent a form letter to 250 area residents:

> We wish at this writing to set everyone in your fine neighborhood straight and acquaint you with the facts as to the rumor that we tried to sell someone a home located at 1121 N. Denwood, that caused such controversy as to their qualifications. We wish to state at this time that we had no knowledge of this condition . . . We respect our profession . . . and would do anything within the Law to protect and hold the high standards of your neighborhood.

Realtors were sometimes more candid, in private correspondence, about their commitment to racial restriction. In 1961, Detroit realtor Albert Zajac wrote Hubbard to congratulate him for "keeping your City so called 'evil,'" a reference to the comments of a local publicist who had criticized the mayor's support for segregation.[44]

And in Dearborn, at least, local officials provided ample encouragement to residents committed to maintaining the racial status quo. Whites in the Detroit region knew from experience, news coverage, and hearsay that Dearborn and its facilities were intended for use by "whites only." When the Rev. Robert Fehribach of Dearborn's St. Alphonus Parish led the church's annual altar boys' outing at Camp Dearborn in 1956, he "innocently brought a colored fellow," apparently unaware of the facility's prohibition against blacks. "Quite a fuss was made at the park," he wrote in a 1960 letter recalling the incident. By then he had been transferred to Wayne, Michigan, and was planning a joint outing with St. Martha's Parish at the camp.

Hoping to avoid controversy, he requested written permission to bring one of his current parishioners, "a very light-skinned Jamaican." "Really," the Reverend insisted, "one can hardly tell that he is colored."[45] Meanwhile the occasional high-profile controversy continued to reaffirm what whites and blacks alike knew about Dearborn's neighborhoods. Local leaders' endorsement of a "no-Negro" policy and the mayor's encouragement of police harassment against minorities helped spur such white vigilantism as the Labor Day attack on Stanzione's home. Some local residents were outraged by the Kendal Street violence and the city's response, but public officials offered them little solace. Days after the incident, concerned Dearborn residents met to draft a letter of protest to the mayor and council. More than 200 persons attended the next council meeting to hear the city's response, yet neither Hubbard nor the council addressed the issue. Officials' silence was particularly disquieting to one Dearborn couple in attendance that night. The city's handling of the Stanzione affair, they claimed, provided "tacit approval to mob violence," both against black people and whites who would sell them a home.[46]

———

Dearborn's leadership and police practices clearly abetted white vigilantism and helped keep suburban racism in the headlines. Perhaps more important, however, was the quieter white activism that helped maintain the racial status quo. White homeowners continued to work diligently during these years to keep black people out of their neighborhoods. They did so by embracing a land-use politics that claimed to have nothing to do with prejudice. While Hubbard and other local activists felt comfortable warning about possible "racial tension" and "racial conflict," most suburban residents simply supported a property-rights politics that was founded upon racial assumptions but that rarely said race out loud. Homeowners' multifaceted organizing efforts through their property associations, in council and zoning board meetings, and in other venues continually immersed residents in a racially coded conversation about housing, neighborhoods, and the rights of people who owned their homes.

This quieter activism had a measurable impact. It prevented blacks from purchasing suburban homes and either blocked apartment construction or restricted it to supposedly "nonresidential" zones, such as major thoroughfares and commercial districts, which by the late 1950s were often the only remaining undeveloped land in first-generation suburbs. Royal Oak approved construction of nearly 4,500 apartment units between 1960 and 1965, virtually all of them on properties deemed unsuitable for residence A development. Efforts to "down zone" existing single-family districts in first-generation suburbs were regularly denied, often without a hearing. Second-generation suburbs like Troy and Southfield had far more room for multiple unit housing, but they, too, restricted construction almost exclusively to single-family homes. The city of Berkley did not issue a single permit for apartments, Madison Heights excluded them until 1965, and both Clawson and Dearborn reined them in tightly. Meanwhile, suburban residents watched thousands of apartments go up in Detroit. The city issued permits for 5,373 units between 1962 and 1964 alone.[47]

Local development controversies continued to expose residents to the strategies and rhetoric that had guided suburban housing politics since the early 1940s. In May 1957, for example, an Oakland County circuit court ordered a builder to cancel plans for construction of two apartment buildings in Royal Oak, on Crooks north of Vinsetta, pending a public hearing. The injunction was issued at the request of three area residents who accused the builder of undermining a proposed zoning ordinance, expected to be approved in June, that would restrict the neighborhood to single-family residences. Accusing the developer of "opportunistically engaging in a speculative venture of great profit to himself without consideration" of neighboring residents, they charged that the proposed apartments would "overtax an already overtaxed sewage system" and "create obnoxious conditions." In May 1964, the Royal Oak City Commission denied a rezoning that would have split up large residential lots west of Prairie and north of Webster (just east of the Southfield–Royal Oak border) to permit apartment construction in response to homeowners' complaints that multiple-unit housing would pose a threat to nearby "residential" neighborhoods. Defenders of the rezoning again adopted the opposition's language, acknowledging the sharp distinctions between "residential" development and the proposed apartments.[48]

Suburban dwellers' involvement in and exposure to such debates is suggested by the proliferation of legal battles over zoning. The type of high-profile court challenges that preoccupied Royal Oak residents in the late 1940s became far more common in the Detroit suburbs after 1954. Comparatively fewer zoning cases reached the Michigan Supreme Court each year, because of changes in the requirements for appeal. But the frequency of appeals and the percentage of total Michigan cases occurring in the Detroit metropolitan area increased dramatically.[49] The plaintiffs and defendants continued to be homeowners, municipal governments, and commercial builders. They continued to invoke the precedents and legal arguments raised in successful challenges to the Webster Road and Northwood apartment projects. And the courts continued to turn to the same prece-dents and legal arguments: the "presumption of validity"; use of the munici-pal police power to protect "public health, safety, and morals"; and, again most commonly, arguments about "residential" or "neighborhood charac-ter" and property values. Between 1955 and 1967, Michigan courts upheld zoning ordinances as a "valid exercise of the police power" if the stipulated restrictions were "reasonable." They upheld ordinances the sole purpose of which was to protect the "residential character" of an area. They often sim-ply "presumed the validity" of existing ordinances. The decision in *Alderton v. City of Saginaw* (1962) summarized the factors that continued to weigh heavily in legal challenges. "In determining validity of zoning ordinance," the justices wrote, the "court considers character of district, its peculiar suit-ability for particular uses, conservation of property values, general trend and character of building and population development, unsuitability for residential purposes, lack of market for such purpose, and whether land will become nonincome producing land without residential value."[50] Michigan courts did not always uphold restriction, and more and more plaintiffs were *losing* their challenges during these years. But the frequency with which these cases were argued before the courts demonstrates that statutes, professional standards, and legal precedents continued to shape local discussions about the necessity and significance of exclusion.

Equally visible were the urban planners, real estate professionals, and federal housing officials who testified at zoning board meetings, council meetings, and trials. In 1956, when the State Supreme Court heard a chal-lenge to a rezoning proposal that would open up a residential parcel to commercial use in Southfield Township, a real estate agent and a profes-sional city planner explained the factors that affected the "desirability of . . . property . . . for residential purposes" and how to make a property a "sound residential investment." In January 1957, Southfield Township's planner appealed to "everyone connected with planning to look more closely· at the champion who defends their plans, concepts, and ideals on the legal battlefield." It was sound advice. After Southfield gained home-rule status in 1958,[51] the new municipality faced numerous challenges to its first zon-ing ordinance, and residents watched a parade of experts debate the merits of restricting all residential neighborhoods to single-family homes. In the 1962 hearings on *Wenner v. City of Southfield*, a realtor and a contractor testified on the potential value of 284 feet of frontage on Ten Mile Road for residential use, for which it was zoned at the time. In response the plaintiffs, who hoped to rezone the land for a medical clinic, asked four realtors, two builders, an architect, and an FHA appraiser to testify that the land in question would be, as one broker apparently noted, "just about worthless for residential use."[52]

By the late 1950s, land-use controversies were growing especially common in the newer home-rule suburbs such as Lathrup Village, Troy, Madison Heights, and Warren that were now experimenting with comprehensive restriction. As in the first-generation suburbs, incorporation campaigns were followed by debates over municipal zoning ordinances; then battles over revisions and variances continually occupied residents and officials. In 1956, Troy's first City Council proposed a zoning ordinance that would have allowed considerably more commercial development than the township map it would soon replace. At the first two public hearings on the proposal, residents registered general objections. For the third hearing, held at Troy City High School in February 1957, residents of Troy joined with residents from neighboring Bloomfield to challenge specific rezonings. Homeowners asked why an office building had been proposed for an area that they had been "told in the beginning . . . was residential," explaining that if they had known about the commercial rezoning they "would never have buil[t] there." Next the president of the Eastover Farms No. 1 Property Owners Association, from Bloomfield, recited a letter of complaint to the council, formally registered the group's opposition, and warned that the proposed ordinance would "start a downward trend." Residents from neighboring streets also announced their objections; one noted that she had "looked over the planning map and tried to study it carefully." Repeated applause suggests that these speakers were well received by others in attendance. The audience also responded warmly to city manager Norman Barnard's recommendation that the council arrange separate public hearings "in each section of Troy," so that the rezonings could be considered "at smaller meetings when we can hear objections and go into detail."[53]

Land-use politics was hardly an abstraction to suburban homeowners, and local mobilizations against "nonconforming" development were more than reflexive responses to a vague threat of neighborhood change. As they had since the 1940s, property owners studied drafts of proposed zoning ordinances, invoked their court-protected rights as proprietors, and marshaled legal precedents to force the hand of councils, zoning boards, and judges. Those who spoke up at public hearings, at the very least, were well versed in the principles of real estate development and regularly cited case law and land-use studies to defend restriction. When Troy's City Council asked community members to respond to a proposed expressway project in January 1959, area residents complained that the project ignored planning principles. "Seems kind of strange," explained one resident at the public hearing, "to run a highway such as this through a Class B residential area rather than a Class C," since "state reports say the value of property depreciates near [a] highway." When Dearborn resident Dale Libby wrote Hubbard in 1962 to protest a proposed rezoning of residence A property for commercial purposes, he cited at great length a Michigan Supreme Court ruling (*Penning v. Owens*) that condemned "spot zoning." Even those residents who did not reference specific statutes or experts adopted the social scientific and legal terminology that was framing debates over property owners' rights.[54]

The depth of support for restriction kept local officials attentive to the desires of homeowners' and protective associations. When Troy's city attorney spoke at the hearings on the city's first zoning ordinance, he faced an audience skeptical of and often openly hostile to his new, more permissive plan that would accommodate more commercial development. He openly revealed his frustration with the audience but also co-opted the restrictionist, property-rights language that homeowners were embracing. Planners and legal experts, he insisted, argued that the new ordinance would benefit local residents, and the man who designed it, he explained, was "very competent," an "expert" who previously "planned Oak Park." The city attorney predicted that if Troy's homeowners had their way, the suburb would be "a hodge podge," but "if Troy is permitted to develop the way he has planned it I am sure you will see something beautiful." He also assured homeowners that "the supreme court is on your side." "One of the facts is that you are allowed to use your property as you see fit as long as you are not hurting anybody. The supreme court is on the side of the people who want to use the property the way they will." "If the supreme court doesn't know what good zoning is," he concluded, "I don't know how we can tell you."[55]

If the 1957 ordinance represented a compromise to Troy's homeowners, it nonetheless demonstrated their considerable political power. The new zoning map reserved the area north of Big Beaver Road, roughly two-thirds of the suburb's territory, almost exclusively for single-family residential development. The terms and restrictions outlined for various use districts followed national patterns developed since the 1940s, except that Troy, and second-generation suburbs more generally, reserved proportionately far more territory for large-lot residential development. Troy's residential parcels had 60-foot minimum widths, making them considerably larger than the typical single-family property in the first-generation suburbs. For the most part, this compromise measure has governed development in Troy to this day.[56]

The market imperative rationale for restriction continued to guide whites' efforts throughout the region to exclude any type of development or occupancy deemed "incompatible" with their community. By and large the region's white housing activists defended racial exclusion by invoking their rights as property owners. A telling display came in the spring of 1963, when Detroit's Commission on Community Relations (CCR), descendant of the Mayor's Interracial Committee, held a public meeting to discuss its open housing campaign. A group of white residents, representing the Grandvale Civic Association, attended that day to register their objection to the CCR's efforts and denounce the principle of integrated housing. They were ejected from the session. Grandvale member Ralph A. Thompson saw this as censorship and wrote the Detroit Common Council to express his outrage at the organization's treatment. By "castigat[ing]" and "evict[ing]" representatives of a homeowners' association, he wrote, the CCR acted "with absolutely no regard for the wishes, recommendations or opinions of honorable, long-established property owner groups." Thompson insisted that what his organization demanded—the exclusion of minorities from their neighborhood—had nothing to do with ideology or racial prejudice. "Every good, well-preserved community has an improvement association successfully operating," he explained, "and directly responsible for its many assets," including "desirable zoning and businesses, adequate lighting, traffic signs and lights, [and] improved streets and alleys." "These area advantages are further reflected in the City's tax rolls which maintain or even increase property values over a span of several decades." Thus "to deny these people their inherent right to the exclusion of any particular group," he continued, was "un-American." Thompson was "appall[ed]" that the city would "consider the elimination of honorable civic associations that have worked so unselfishly, so conscientiously, over the years, to the City's benefit."[57] To Thompson and like-minded whites, the demand for racial exclusion was not about race or prejudice but about respect for a free market in property, the laws of metropolitan growth, and the rights of people who owned their homes.

Complementing the formal politics of elections, zoning hearings, and neighborhood activism during these years was an even more public conversation about suburban growth and the meaning of homeownership. In a wide range of venues, including newspaper editorials, municipal publications, classroom activities, and even street fairs, whites rehearsed a largely illusory story about the origins of suburban growth and affluence. They described growth as an organic and inexorable process, driven solely by the demands, desires, and abilities of American consumers and businesspeople.

They assumed the superiority of owning over renting, depicting the *desire* for private property as the primary force fueling metropolitan expansion. They portrayed the home-rule suburb as a managerial form of government divorced from "political" considerations because of its singular focus on infrastructural and service needs, that is, the needs of its property owners. And by the 1950s, whites were preoccupied with distinguishing their suburban havens from what they viewed as its urban antithesis, as well as the minority population associated with it. Suburban whites talked constantly about the necessity of preventing "urban blight" and keeping their communities clean.

On one level, whites' fear of physical deterioration and its association with black people was a response to real transformations, taking place before their eyes. While Detroit's black population increased by 223 percent between 1940 and 1960, whites and white-owned businesses were also relocating to the suburbs, encouraged by the new mortgage market, interstate construction, generous federal spending on the military and supporting industries, and anxiety about the city's "racial transformation." The result was a rapid shift in the city's racial balance. In 1940, the 149,119 black Detroiters counted by the U.S. census made up 9 percent of the city's population. By 1960, a population of blacks estimated at 482,223 represented 29 percent of the total. Meanwhile black neighborhoods in Detroit and other cities *were* growing poorer in the 1950s and 1960s, and their housing stock and infrastructure were deteriorating. The federally subsidized mortgage market directed capital for home purchase and repair almost exclusively to whites and primarily to suburban properties. Restrictionist policies and practices kept most African Americans and most poor people in overcrowded sections of the nation's urban centers. Urban renewal and highway programs further undermined existing black neighborhoods, while widespread employment discrimination coupled with plant closings in major industrial centers denied most blacks access to promotions and better paying, stable jobs. So as Detroit's black population continued to expand, more and more of its members found themselves underemployed or unemployed, renting homes or apartments in overcrowded and often structurally compromised neighborhoods. Even the relatively affluent black enclaves in Detroit's north and northwest were capital-poor when compared with most of Detroit's financially stable white neighborhoods or the region's all-white suburbs. If nothing else, most white enclaves were in better material condition and were dominated by owner-occupied dwellings.[58]

But most whites told a story about city and suburb that bore little resemblance to the political and economic processes that were transforming the region. Whites attributed the city's visible poverty and physical decay not to misguided public policy or to discrimination but to the mere presence of black people. Meanwhile, most whites either ignored or were indifferent to the class divisions within black Detroit, regularly insisting that blacks' poverty made racial integration a risk, despite the fact that most vigilantism against "racial invasion" targeted the middle-class black families able to afford and willing to settle in white neighborhoods. Decades of systematic segregation confirmed the myth that black people, because they did not take care of their homes, undermined well-kept neighborhoods. The growth and affluence of all-white suburbs seemed to confirm this story. Driving by yet another new suburban subdivision or a house undergoing renovations and comparing these with the neighborhoods of apartments and weathered prewar homes in Detroit's black enclaves, their streets in disrepair, whites constantly reaffirmed the myths that had helped fuel residential inequality in the first place.

They also drew a conclusion that, while equally misguided, became constitutive of suburban political culture. Whites insisted that blacks' inability to maintain their property had forced the federal government to intervene on their behalf in the housing market. Public housing and housing subsidies, according to this narrative, were symptomatic of black people's failures, not of the failure, let alone the discriminatory intent, of public policy and private practices. Of course, to insist that public housing represented an "unwarranted" government intervention required whites to believe that *their* homes and communities, by contrast, were not beneficiaries of state largesse. And that story was safe, to be sure, in the hands of white officials, publicists, businesspeople, and housing activists. During these years of spectacular metropolitan expansion and prosperity, the state's massive interventions in the market for housing credit and its subsidies for a new "nation of homeowners" were rarely if ever acknowledged in popular conversations about suburban growth, personal wealth, and racial inequality.

A college student from Troy learned one version of the suburban success narrative in 1958, when he prepared a report on his community's development history for a class in Public Finance at Western Michigan University. In interviews with the mayor, treasurer, engineer, and city assessor, he learned that Troy's growth had been fueled by local demand for housing and the ingenuity of local entrepreneurs. Once industry began developing along the township's south side, he was told, "builders and contractors found that the land on the western border . . . made an ideal location for subdivisions and suburbanization." He learned that "great strides have been taken by individual builders to develop certain areas of the city," which in turn "had a great influence in land values on the western borders, especially." A professional planner told a compatible story the following year in a "Community Development Study" prepared for the Big Beaver–Crooks Road area. Troy's rapid growth, he reported, had been spurred by the "expanding network of freeways lacing the area which make it more convenient for new development to take place almost anywhere."[59]

Suburban journalists, officials, and businesspeople attributed the region's growth and prosperity to a combination of demographic pressures, the transport revolution, residents' hard work (coupled with their strong commitment to homeownership and "community"), and the professionals and experts who managed the development process. The suburban press offered this story most consistently—during the years, notably, that saw more and more suburban readers turn to these papers for local news. The *Tribune* published frequent paeans to the "manpower, talent, time, and dedication" that it takes to build a suburban community, in this case a 1964 tribute to Ferndale's Board of Commerce, of which Philip Miller, the *Tribune*'s editor, was a member. Local publicists continued to rely heavily on the real estate industry for its origins stories. A 1961 press release from the Dearborn Board of Realtors celebrated the group's thirty-fifth anniversary by praising its members for "taking the long range view of the best interests of the people"; they had "successfully resisted efforts to compromise the high standards of Dearborn's building and zoning laws, and fought to a standstill all conditions that lead to slum and blight conditions, sometimes against the lure of quick immediate profits." "Cities as beautiful as Dearborn," the article continued, "just don't get that way by accident." The fact that Dearborn had not "become a slum-ridden, low-standard 'factory' town" was a "tribute to the high minded men who wouldn't permit it to happen," especially "the city [administrators] and the realtors, past and present."[60]

The absence of discussion about the state's revolutionary impact on the postwar housing market begs important questions about whites' understanding of the federal government's new stake in the mortgage industry. Clearly for white realtors, officials, and residents, the most comfortable stance on state intervention was to emphasize its compatibility with free market forces. But it would be a mistake to assume that whites consciously downplayed federal involvement because they knew it to be a subsidy. When whites mentioned the FHA and similar programs, they described them in the rhetoric promoted by the New Deal state and its private sector allies since the 1930s as market-friendly, as incentives that helped "stampede" capital "into action," to borrow FHLBB chairman John H. Fahey's memorable characterization. Whites did not hide their enthusiasm for the FHA and VA programs; indeed they were defensive about their access and often offended by suggestions that blacks should be eligible. "In my neighborhood," noted one Detroiter proudly when interviewed in the late 1950s, "a $15,000 house can be bought for $800 down because of Roosevelt." In 1962 an outraged Dearborn resident complained to Hubbard that Kennedy was drafting an executive order that would "require Federal insured banks to make loans to negroes for housing"—"he will allow niggers to go in white suburbs anywhere." The ubiquitous references to FHA financing or to new FHA-approved construction, both in housing advertisements and in press coverage of suburban growth, did not connote subsidy to aspiring homeowners. Instead it confirmed that a house and neighborhood were affordable and "safe" investments—well designed and built, modern, and marketed solely to people like them, people who would be upstanding neighbors.[61]

On the very rare occasion that a local commentator discussed the mundane operations of federal selective credit programs, it was a qualified treatment echoing decades of advocacy for the government's new role. Consider Philip Miller's *Tribune* editorial from 1956 about the slackening market for new home construction and the changes in mortgage lending that had precipitated it. Miller discussed Eisenhower's liberalization of lending terms and down payments on FHA- and VA-eligible loans, as well as his encouragement of the Federal Home Loan Banks to borrow more money from the government. Under the FHA and VA programs, he wrote, "the government assumes the risk for the private lender by promising to pay off most or all of the mortgage if the buyer defaults." Miller portrayed the housing market, however, as responsive solely to consumer demand and private sector initiative. It was NAREB officials, he explained, who were currently meeting in Boston to "search for ways to perk up home building." NAREB members, who were responsible for building 85 percent of all new housing, the editorial notes, were "particularly concerned about the shortage of mortgage money," and so they suggested that "Uncle Sam and others take steps to increase the flow of dollars into housing." Miller even challenged the notion that federal policy directed economic activity. "There is nothing the government can do to force a bank to make the loan," he concluded. Rather federal action was designed to "loosen up the tight money market."[62]

Ubiquitous tributes to local entrepreneurs and the free enterprise system were regularly joined during these years by two complementary stories about suburban development and culture, which together helped frame public and private discussions about land use, local politics, and racial exclusion.

Assuming that most suburban residents were homeowners (which was increasingly true), local commentators and officials argued that what made suburban government unique was its commitment to this homeowning class. Suburban institutions were portrayed as nonpartisan, technocratically minded, and above all responsive to the practical needs of people who owned property. The second narrative followed logically: commentators agreed that residents' pride in ownership coupled with responsible local government meant that what distinguished most suburbs from the central city was that the former were well managed, well maintained, and clean.

By the early 1950s suburban publicists, local advertising, and even public officials increasingly portrayed and addressed residents exclusively as "homeowners." The features in Dearborn's newspapers on homebuilding and decorating, including its weekly "Window Shopping" column on home design, highlighted the "small, one-story ranch type home" that had "proven to be very economical to build." They reminded readers that "home still is where the hearth is," reproducing a national advertising and political narrative about the sanctity of the single-family home and the protection that it afforded to families. In 1955, the *Tribune*'s editor spoke collectively to his readership as "we home owners of South Oakland county," while Royal Oak municipal publications continued to portray the "typical" suburban family as white, nuclear, and living in detached, single-family dwellings. Its annual report continued to feature imitation news articles about local services designed to "Protect . . . a City of Homes" ("Almost every aspect of city government services are geared primarily to the detached home") and to describe local officials as selfless servants, "often working without pay and only working as much as services and land management demands." The importance of responsible land use was reiterated in other municipal publications. "Zoning" was a tool, explained the Royal Oak Plan Commission in its 1958 annual report, used to "guide . . . the growth of a community along orderly lines." Zoning authority was "derive[d] from the police power," so the municipal ordinance "must bear some reasonable relationship to the public health, safety, morals, or general welfare," and any ordinance "which does not have a substantial relation to these objectives is in violation of the 'due process' clauses of state and federal constitutions." The Plan Commission, residents learned, was "semi-autonomous" and therefore "little influenced by political changes," serving the "community without monetary compensation," and assisted by a "technically trained staff."[63]

Further reinforcing this narrative were the officials and publicists who encouraged residents to approve municipal charters, to adopt manager-council governments, and to participate in the local political process. Municipal officials were passing on a message learned from the Michigan Municipal League and its monthly publication, the *Michigan Municipal Review,* which exhorted new home-rule governments to secure and protect their political autonomy, in large part so that they could exercise the zoning power. (The league's central office also collected and distributed municipal ordinances and lobbied the state legislature directly on behalf of municipal governments.) Local suburban publicists endorsed this position consistently. The *Tribune's* Philip and Floyd Miller, perhaps the most vocal champions of home-rule for the unincorporated sections of southeast Oakland County, regularly argued that home-rule governments were "close" to the people and that nonpartisan institutions would govern wisely by rising above "politics." As Madison Heights prepared for a ballot on incorporation in January 1955, Philip Miller portrayed the vote as a choice between politics as usual and a new kind of nonideological local governance, since "townships are run on a political basis" while home-rule municipalities "are nonpartisan by choice." Miller predicted passage, given that "South Oakland residents" had long "shown a fierce pride in self-government," recognizing that "the smaller the community, the more telling is the voice of the individual citizen." Celebrating the measure's approval a week later—the headline announced "9th City for Royal Oak Township"—Miller cast city-building as part of a longstanding suburban tradition, reflecting residents' efforts to build "a strong sense of neighborhood feeling" and their "genuine desire for local autonomy."[64]

The Madison Heights referendum also afforded Miller one of many opportunities to endorse the manager-council form of government, which he believed offered the "best hope for economy and efficiency." This, he added, "has been part of the South Oakland Tradition." Later that year, when Troy and Southfield residents debated upcoming ballots on municipal incorporation, Miller reminded voters that by "follow[ing] the lines of the other South Oakland cities and set[ting] up a city manager-commission form of government, they can remove their local government unit from partisan politics." And he criticized Hazel Park's proposal to abandon its manager-council government in favor of a mayor-council charter. Conceding that manager governments might sometimes seem "aloof," he insisted that "sometimes that is the way it ought to be . . . For the professional municipal manager has goals of efficiency and city-wide service that may outbalance a particular citizen's demand of the moment." Madison Height's adoption of a manager-council government was greeted both with relief and hyperbole; it was a form of governance, wrote

Miller, "better than any system of local self-government yet tried by human experience."[65]

Casting the benefits of suburban autonomy in sharp relief during these years were frequent discussions of Detroit's struggles. In "Why New Cities Are Formed," published in June 1955, the *Tribune* rejected calls by planners, Detroit officials, and community activists to address the inner city's problems by creating a metropolitan government. "We feel that big government nowhere has demonstrated any real efficiency or economy," wrote Miller. Instead suburban residents were opting for home rule, because they had "a very real, even if unexpressed, feeling . . . that they have in the so-called 'new' areas . . . the opportunity to create the new type of community. They want the freedom from congestion and noise, they want quiet where their homes are; and they want a neighborhood stability to protect—in more than just a financial measure—what is usually the family's biggest investment—a home." The desire for homeownership was a "universal desire," Miller added, and local control enabled homeowners to protect their property. "Zoning," he reminded readers, was nothing but "regulation of land use for the public welfare." Proper planning would "insure an orderly and stable growth."[66]

These years saw the increasing prominence of another theme in local conversations about metropolitan life: whites' preoccupation with urban filth and decay and their obsession with suburban cleanliness. Officials, publicists, and residents alike insisted that well managed municipalities were well maintained ones. Good local government kept communities clean. Miller claimed in 1955 that suburban planners looked to the city for a model of what to avoid, "eyeing the blighted areas within Detroit's center, [and then] com[ing] up with a redevelopment scheme that would dead-end streets [and] create open area for rest and play . . . Behind this idea is a growing realization that traffic, noise, [and] maximum use of land contribute as much to the deterioration of neighborhoods as the decay of buildings." "The urban idea," he concluded, "should [suggest] a moral for suburban growth," and it would be a shame if "the 'flight to the suburbs' should be permitted to create the very conditions which brought about the flight in the first place. We would leave a sorry heritage if the slums of the future are in the suburbs."[67]

This preoccupation with order and cleanliness became a prominent fixture of civic culture, as local officials sponsored citywide projects to maintain, and in the process celebrate, the physical suburb. In Clawson, Dearborn, Royal Oak, and other communities, annual "Paint-up, Clean-up, Fix-up" campaigns mobilized adults and schoolchildren to clean yards, paint fences, and refurbish public buildings and parks. Dearborn initiated its campaign in 1952, as part of a national contest sponsored by the "Clean-Up, Fix-Up Bureau," a promotional division of the National Paint and Varnish and Lacquer Association. Alex Pilch, director of the city's new Public Relations Department, envisioned participation as a way to "broaden the picture [nationally] of Dearborn as a nice clean city" and to impress upon residents "that they had such an enviable community." By the mid-1950s, the annual contest had become a major event, in which city officials, civic groups, church leaders, and schoolteachers instructed adults and children about the importance of well-kept properties and warned them against the evils of "blighted" neighborhoods. During the 1957 campaign, for example, the City Beautiful Commission presented an elaborate slide show on the suburb's "Clean-Up" efforts to 5,715 local residents, including students from kindergarten through high school, Cub Scout den mothers, and members of local property owners' associations, the Kiwanis Club, and the Detroit Jaycee Alumni. The presentation was equal parts prescription and boosterism. Against a series of photographs documenting local efforts to paint, clean, clear, and prune, the narrator described residents' commitment to private property and the maintenance of public spaces, while repeatedly highlighting the advantages of living in a city where the government "practices the refreshingly candid policy of 'Good Public Service is the Best Politics.'"[68]

Other annual "Clean-Up" events in the late 1950s and 1960s included "kick off luncheons," initiated in 1955, awards presentations, the Mayor's Beautification Conference, "Clean Your House Day," and annual parades, which featured city officials, marching bands, and an array of municipal service vehicles, from snow plows and weed cutters to a dog wagon and a "dump truck with sprayer." In 1956, at a Dearborn parade for the Ford Motor Company, that year's "Miss Fix-Up" greeted the crowd from a car draped with a banner reading "Salute to Ford Progress." In 1958, the Dearborn Fire Department distributed 1,000 posters advertising both the local and national "Clean-Up" campaigns to businesses on nine major Dearborn thoroughfares, and provided 500 comic books to the City Beautiful Commission for distribution.[69]

Particularly intensive was participation of civic groups, property owners' associations, churches, and schools, which reported on their activities to the City Beautiful Commission. In 1958, the League of Women Voters sent out 200 stickers about beautification with their monthly bulletin, while churches, the Navy and Marine Corps reserve center, AMVETS, and homeowners' associations repaired broken sidewalks, planted flower beds, repainted guns and anchors, and refurbished fences and buildings.[70] Activities for schoolchildren included classroom contests, poetry writing, balloon launchings, poster making, Clean-Up Assemblies, and in-class presentations on clean-up activities. In 1958, the Miller School published a special "Clean-Up" issue of its newspaper, which updated parents about related on-campus events and reprinted award-winning student essays and poems, written in conjunction with the city-wide campaign. Caroline Malizia's poem, "Mr. Lorey," began

> This is a story
> About Mr. Lorey
> His house was so dirty. Yea! Man
> He didn't have a single clean pan.

Dennis Adkins's contribution was called "I Like Dearborn":

> I like Dearborn because of the fishing, the swimming, and the hunting at Camp Dearborn . . . Camp Dearborn is always clean.
> Another reason is that so many new houses are being built in old lots and old houses are being painted with new paint.
> That is why I like Dearborn.

At Ray Adams Junior High School, the Junior Red Cross raised funds by selling trash bags. The Dearborn Junior Chamber of Commerce sold "Litter Baskets" from a parking lot behind Sam's Department Store. And the Junior City Beautiful commissioners visited elementary schools, where they urged younger children to support the local campaign "by refraining from playing on the grass." Students at the Edsel Ford High School filled out questionnaires furnished by the City Beautiful Commission.

Some teachers designed classroom materials to complement these efforts. In Mrs. Elizabeth Gwinnell's classroom at the Miller School, students composed stories and discussed "health in relation to cleanliness and beauty." Mrs. Saunders's kindergarteners discussed "the responsibility of taking care of their own possessions." At the Roulo School, Miss Kennedy's students cleaned up their classroom and "talked about our home and garden [and] yard." They also made up relevant "story problems" for their mathematics lessons, such as:

5 clean yards
+ 5 clean yards
= 10 clean yards

Several teachers used cleanliness pledges for language and penmanship lessons, and held "discussions on . . . [their] purpose of the week" and "what is done in [their] own homes."[71]

Other suburban municipalities held campaigns and awarded prizes to businesses for their commitment to city beautification. In 1954, Ferndale's "Clean Up, Fix Up, Paint Up" program concluded with an industrial landscaping contest, organized by the Chamber of Commerce, with members of the Ferndale Garden Club serving as judges. Beginning in 1952, Royal Oak's Chamber of Commerce cited local businesses that, in the words of its president Ralph Conselyea, "modernized to improve the value and architecture of the business sectors of the city." Hazel Park began its efforts even earlier, in the mid-1940s, with the Junior Chamber of Commerce enthusiastically taking a leadership role. But no suburban campaigns were as extensive or as successful as those staged in Dearborn, which by 1963 had won the national "Clean-Up" contest seven times and had become, for municipal officials nationwide, a model of city pride and beautification. National municipal organizations and popular magazines celebrated Dearborn as a case study in good government, efficiency, and cleanliness, ignoring its well publicized reputation as a "whites only" community. *American City* magazine repeatedly showcased the city's policies, innovations, and achievements, in areas ranging from street maintenance to policing to public recreation. In response to the publicity, municipal officials from around the country contacted Dearborn officials directly for advice on municipal service provision, recreation, and public relations.[72]

Homeowners throughout the region had clearly embraced the "fix-up" ethic, so enthusiastically, in fact, that the *Tribune*'s Philip Miller insisted that the commitment to home improvement had become a defining characteristic of southeast Oakland County. Pointing to the thousands of "amateur carpenters, bricklayers, painters and host of other aspiring 'craftsmen' " visible to anyone who traveled through Detroit's suburbs, Miller speculated about community members' interest in "Do It Yourself." It was probably a result, he wrote in 1955, of "the way in which we live." "Here each of us, by and large, is endeavoring to have his own home on his own plot of ground, as opposed to the apartment life or big-city type of living. In owning our own places we are free to do what we want to improve them or to change them just as the mood strikes us."[73] Echoing years of suburban commentary on regional development, local politics, and local culture, Miller depicted residents' commitment to their property as both the engine of suburban success and its most enduring legacy.

———————

These celebrations of suburban life, politics, and places were seldom "about" race per se. But in the context of residents' expectation that they would live in racially homogeneous communities and their support for land-use politics and practices that achieved the exclusion of black people, the equation of suburban and white was inescapable. Residents saw their homes and neighborhoods as both material and symbolic evidence of their hard work, determination, and community values. Meanwhile, an ethnically quite diverse suburban population saw their new communities as affirmation of their whiteness. In 1951, at a parade commemorating Detroit's 250th anniversary, Dearborn entered a float that literally staged residents' vision of the suburban success story and its racial ideal. On a fifty-foot-long flatbed trailer, four reenactments told the history of Dearborn's development: from Civil War arsenal, to residential settlement (a placard explains that "pioneers clear the land and found a village"), to industrial city, to modern suburban bedroom community (see fig. 8.1). The last two installments are especially telling. In the recreation of pre–World War II Dearborn, a model of Ford's River Rouge plant is surrounded by hard-working European immigrants, each dressed in "old-country," ethnic costume. The final scene, by contrast, depicts a postwar Dearborn family enjoying its leisure, a "white" family of four, relaxing on lawn furniture in front of their detached, single-family home. "All together," the caption explains, "they built Dearborn today."[74]

Discussions about the new suburban ideal rarely addressed the topic of racial segregation explicitly, however, a fact that enabled residents to separate most conversations about zoning or homeownership or cleanliness from the topic of minorities or prejudice. Philip Miller, for example, remained circumspect about the link between black occupancy and urban blight, but his discussions of Detroit's decline strongly suggested it. In 1958 he attributed the "Persistence of Slums" to slum dwellers (presumably both black and white, although he does not specify) and, notably, to federal interference in the housing market. "Formerly good neighborhoods are being engulfed," he wrote, and "some of the new low-cost housing built with federal assistance is already falling into a state of decay." Acknowledging that blight had complex origins, he nonetheless concluded that "the basic

8.1 Dearborn's float for Detroit's 250th Anniversary Parade, July 28, 1951. The text
along the bottom reads: "They Came Seeking a Home and Built a City." Four tableaus
reenact Dearborn's history. The first two scenes (not shown) depict the town's Civil War
arsenal and pioneers who cleared the land and founded a village (they are shown
trading with Indians). The third scene—entitled "1919: A New Industry Brings New
Americans"—shows ethnic European immigrants surrounding the River Rouge
plant. Contemporary Dearborn is depicted by a nuclear family relaxing in front of a
single-family home. The caption reads: "All together they built Dearborn today."
Courtesy of the Dearborn Historical Museum, Dearborn, Michigan.

fact is that in most cities, particularly in the North, the number of low-
income and socially deprived families has been rising at the same time that
the cities have been losing large numbers of their better-off residents to
the suburbs . . . And when housing passes to a lower class of occupancy, it
inevitably declines in quality." Orville Hubbard, by sharp contrast, did not
hesitate to indict black people explicitly. In addition to his notorious pronouncements on race and development, the mayor ran advertisements in
local newspapers calling upon residents to "Open your eyes wide and read
this," then reproduced excerpts from a *U.S. News and World Report* article

describing blacks' living conditions in the mid-nineteenth-century South. In 1964, the Michigan Civil Rights Commission prosecuted Hubbard for using bulletin boards in city hall to display news articles deemed degrading to minorities.[75]

Hubbard was an anomaly, to be sure. Yet it would be a mistake to categorically distinguish his views about race and housing from those of other officials, residents, and local commentators. Philip Miller offers a revealing counterpoint, not simply because he was a careful student of municipal affairs but also because he was an outspoken supporter of the civil rights movement. What makes Miller's running commentary in the pages of the *Tribune* instructive is the publisher's ability to defend the political rights of African Americans while embracing a racialized vision of metropolitan development. His discussions of the "race issue" demonstrate how older myths about inferiority and difference had been written into popular ideas about property, architecture, and city spaces.

Miller used the pages of the *Tribune* to endorse the NAACP, church activism, and the broad black struggle to secure suffrage rights and civil protections.[76] Like so many white northerners, however, he described racism primarily as a southern problem; he referred often to "the tragic cleavage between the races in the South" or the region's "racial restrictions on voting." In 1956, Miller was publicly challenged to address South Oakland County's history of racial exclusion. In the wake of the scandal over Hubbard's published remarks about segregation, the Montgomery, Alabama, *Advertiser* editors accused Detroit's *other* suburbs of hypocrisy for condemning southern whites while "practic[ing] segregation by living in communities 'barred' to the Negro." Miller's response, published in October 1956, sidestepped the *Advertiser*'s accusation and redirected the discussion back to southern racial politics. He underscored the paper's steadfast support for black equality and acknowledged that there were, indeed, prejudiced *individuals* in Oakland County. But he returned immediately to the topic of racist *institutions*, which in his mind existed only in the South. "We would not be so self-righteous," Miller wrote, "as to deny that there are restricted neighborhoods in South Oakland and that many residents here prefer to live in all-white communities. Prejudice and economic fear exist here, too." But what, he continued, does this have to do with school integration? "Do segregated neighborhoods in the North furnish justification for segregated schools in the South?" "What is at stake in the South," Miller wrote, "is the Negro's political and educational opportunity." "If we be hypocrites in the Southern view, then we say there are degrees of hypocrisy. We are less hypocritical than they because Negroes can attend our schools (yes, and vote in our elections)."[77] In Miller's view school desegregation and the franchise were political issues. Residential segregation apparently was not.

Nor did Miller apparently see any contradiction between his civil rights advocacy and his annual participation in the Lion's Club Minstrel Show. By 1964, he and his father had performed in fifteen of the club's eighteen annual performances. Philip had chaired or co-chaired three, served as musical chairman for several years, and had participated in the chorus, in end men skits, and "even as a soloist." In March of that year, he and his wife were once again "rehearsing two nights a week with Club [members] and friends," this time in preparation for the April performances at the Dondero School auditorium.

Some things had changed since the club staged its first show in February 1948. Participation was no longer restricted to club members; by the 1960s they were joined by their "wives, relatives and friends" and by students from a local dance school. More than 100 people were now involved each year, either as performers or backstage. William Spence, of Birmingham, Michigan, stopped directing the productions after 1959, and since 1961, Russell Heckel, the vocal music instructor from Jane Addams Junior High in Royal Oak, had conducted. The shows continued to follow what Miller called a traditional "minstrel" format, with a chorus, skits, solos, and a variety show of musical and dance acts. But since 1960, club members no longer performed in blackface. Miller later expressed some regrets about the change in costume, writing in 1967 that "one advantage [to wearing blackface] as far as the performers were concerned was that no one in the audience could tell who you were . . . and there was a certain feeling of assurance in this anonymity." Still he conceded that there were good reasons to dispense with the practice. "We haven't used this type of makeup for the last seven years and, frankly, we are just as glad we don't have to. It was hard to put on and harder still to get off."[78]

Miller's curious balancing act on racial matters seems less incongruous when viewed in light of the local politics that had created and sustained all-white suburban communities since the 1940s. His defense of blacks' right to political equality and simultaneous participation in minstrel shows; his endorsement of civil rights legislation and acceptance (even defense) of suburban exclusion; his revulsion at southern racism and muted acceptance of its supposedly less virulent northern variant: these positions appear less incompatible when seen in the context of a public conversation about race and property that had suffused public policy, private practices, marketing, and local boosterism since the Great Depression. Miller's description of northern racism as the composite of individual acts and his insistence that only southern racism, by contrast, was deeply institutionalized, re-flected whites' fundamental misunderstanding of the origins of residential segregation in the North. This made it easier for self-described racial liberals like Miller to defend the principle of Negro suffrage, on the one hand, while drawing the line at so-called "forced" racial integration, on the other. Miller's views were in no small part the product of a new politi-cal lexicon about race and rights that insisted that all citizens deserved the right to *choose*, whether it was their elected representatives or where they wanted to live or who their neighbors would be. The only limits placed on such decisions, so the logic went, should be those imposed by the market itself.

Of course, some whites—Hubbard and many of his vocal admirers, for example—made connections between race and property quite explicitly. But Miller and the silent homeowners who supported restriction staked their positions on race and housing, more often than not, without saying "race" or "black" out loud. By insisting that the market required residen-tial restriction, whites supported racial exclusion in fact without supporting it in word. And again Miller's seemingly paradoxical views and behaviors suggest just how complicated and malleable whites' ideas about race had become. On the one hand, his support for civil rights (and eventually even for open housing) is testament to his ability occasionally to see beyond the limits of his own racialist presumptions. But at the same time, his contin-ued and largely uncritical support for FHA subsidies, suburban political autonomy, and restrictive zoning, his denigration of Detroit's "lower class" populations, and his uncritical enthusiasm for blackface minstrelsy demon-strate just how deeply invested he was in his white privilege. His ability to defend suburban exclusion attests to the power of that privilege—operating both structurally and discursively—to blind even its owner to the violence performed by racist caricature.

The suburban stories told by Hubbard and those told by Miller were quite compatible because they shared so many assumptions. Both were grounded in a racially constructed vision of property and place, a vision institutional-ized and popularized for decades by realtors, government officials, bankers, homeowners' associations, and individual property owners. And both were seemingly grounded in physical "proof," thanks to decades of private prac-tices and public policies that had segregated the regions' neighborhoods and its housing capital by race. The fact that these stories shared so much in common would have important implications for the national politics of race and rights throughout the 1960s, and beyond.

The Silent Majority Speaks: Racial Exclusion and the Eclipse of the New Deal Coalition

Many writers argue that during the 1960s, millions of white voters turned against the New Deal's progressive agenda—and against the Democratic Party—in response to the successes and the radicalization of the civil rights movement. Commentators often treat 1964 as a turning point, the beginning of the end for the "New Deal order." That year Congress passed the Civil Rights Act, while Goldwater's and Wallace's presidential campaigns rallied whites nationwide in opposition to black protest politics. Blacks boycotted schools in New York City and Boston, while white and black activists joined forces in Freedom Summer. That summer race riots broke out in New York City, in Paterson, New Jersey, and several other cities. The next four years saw passage of more civil rights legislation, Democratic support for the expansion of social welfare programs, calls by activists for "Black Power," and considerable urban violence. To be sure, these developments convinced many white voters that the civil rights movement represented a destabilizing, even threatening force. But historians' search for turning points and the focus on headline-grabbing incidents, protests, and electoral campaigns has obscured the local origins of backlash politics, its deep roots in the nation's cities and suburbs, and its debt to the policies and politics that had been shaping metropolitan regions for decades. The focus on high-profile controversies obscures the ways that the backlash politics of the 1960s built directly upon a generation of quieter federal interventions and local mobilizations that had helped create and secure white privilege in postwar America.

By 1964, a new politics of race and rights was deeply institutionalized in the lives of metropolitan whites. Consider some of the lesser-known events that engaged the residents of the Detroit suburbs that year. Dearborn sponsored its twelfth annual "Paint-Up, Fix-Up, Clean-Up" campaign. Birmingham, Rochester, Riverview, Wayne, and Plymouth adopted new land-use plans. Royal Oak's city planners and planning commission announced their recommendation to prevent the extension of a "multiple-family zone" near Judson Road into a nearby "residential area." And the Lion's Club of Royal Oak hosted its seventeenth annual minstrel show.[79] Meanwhile federal action continued to undergird the new metropolitan racial order, in these Michigan suburbs and around the nation. In 1964, the FHA and VA combined to facilitate the construction of 263,800 privately owned homes. President Kennedy's executive order requiring nondiscrimination in government housing programs was two years old and having virtually no effect on federal practices. The conventional mortgage market, which facilitated the majority of home purchases, was subsidized by federal programs and still guided by the discriminatory principles written into the original FHA lending guidelines. By the time the Wallace and Goldwater campaigns and calls for "Black Power" helped erode support for the Democratic Party, a federally subsidized and monitored mortgage finance industry, working in concert with a standardized zoning politics, had been segregating American metropolitan areas by race and by wealth for more than thirty years. Meanwhile the men and women who led both the mortgage and zoning revolutions had long insisted that it was free markets, not state policy or white prejudice, that had produced both suburban prosperity and urban decline.

This broader political and economic context helps explain why so many Detroit-area whites had little patience for key demands of the national civil rights movement, particularly the demand for equal access to housing, neighborhoods, and employment. Many whites had "turned" against civil rights protest long before it emerged as a national phenomenon. Since the 1940s, whites had forged ideas about blacks' rights by living in a metropolitan region undergoing dramatic economic and demographic change, by joining in a local politics that helped secure the region's new racial boundaries, and by insisting that both segregation and inequality were natural, market-driven outcomes. By the early 1960s, the region's all-white suburbs had become symbolic and actual havens for whites longing to enjoy a postwar prosperity that was defined as an exclusively white domain. Meanwhile whites throughout the region had been organizing to exclude black people for decades. The history of white mobilizations in suburban Detroit—read in light of important recent work on white resistance in cities and suburbs nationwide—reveals that backlash was not an urban or suburban phenomenon but a metropolitan one, as urban and suburban whites alike viewed the region's "racial changes" as a product of personal choices and group behaviors, not of public policy and systematic white discrimination.[80]

This was the message conveyed in the letters that continued to pour into the offices of Orville Hubbard and other public officials in the early 1960s, letters illustrating that countless whites throughout the Detroit region were making sense of civil rights protest by viewing it through the prism of metropolitan change. Suburban correspondents expressed their relief at having a suburban address, while white Detroiters looked hopefully across the municipal border to those comfortable suburban communities—places attracting more and more of their family and friends, places where they could secure a home mortgage, and places seemingly insulated from the "racial troubles" that they associated with the city. What now distinguished whites' commentary was the frequency with which they linked familiar themes—property owners' rights and the importance of suburban political autonomy—to a narrative about the national politics of race and rights. In a trend first visible in the mid-1950s and quite prominent by the early 1960s, the whites who contacted Hubbard, local journalists, and other elected officials read local racial politics into national racial politics, and they read the national into the local. They fashioned a response to the struggle for African American civil rights in no small part by looking to the racial dynamics of specific, local places and interpreting why those places had developed in particular ways. The geography of metropolitan areas continued to provide them with a cognitive map of race relations and of white racial privilege. Meanwhile local land-use politics continued to teach them important lessons about the origins of that privilege. Together, these local legacies enabled whites to argue that support for residential restriction had nothing to do with racial prejudice.

Portraying urban places as both symptom and symbol of black degradation, whites focused upon Detroit a set of anxieties that were simultaneously about race, property, safety, family, and sex. Familiar antiblack sentiments continued to appear in this correspondence, still framed by a story about city and suburb. "It bothers me to no end," wrote one man from Dearborn in 1964, "when I am in Detroit and see a Negro man 'eyeing' a white woman." Another Dearborn resident predicted that "if we get those colored in here we will soon be going bathing together at Camp Dearborn." Crime, too, was discussed as an urban phenomenon—despite regular press coverage of assaults, public drunkenness, and property crimes in the region's white suburbs. But the topic that dominated these letters was property owners' rights, shorthand for the rights of white people to choose their own neighbors. And the subject continued to be mediated by a narrative about metropolitan change. The consensus position was articulated by the white woman who wrote Hubbard in 1963 to complain that blacks had ruined Detroit, which she called a "once fine city." A former Dearborner (and retired realtor) agreed: "My heart aches when I go back to Detroit for a visit," she wrote in 1961, from her new home in Miami. "It is sickening what they have done to that once beautiful place." Clearly many whites in Detroit shared this view as well. "We all know what will happen if we are integrated in the white sections," explained one resident in 1963, "that our home values will drop up to fifty percent of present values." That year Hubbard heard from a Dearborn woman that she "and the majority of [her] neighbors" were "in complete agreement with you in regards to the 'Negro

Scare' on Kendal Street." "We have all seen what can happen to a good, well kept neighborhood when taken over by negroes. Right now their treatment of property and their behavior is like a slow disease killing off a once healthy neighborhood." For this reason they were very "glad that Dearborn is immune through 'Hubbard' vaccine."[81]

Countless white people had come to equate suburban residence with homeowners and to equate homeownership with whiteness. And the vast majority conveyed those assumptions without talking about inherent racial differences or even about white racial preference. Typical was the Dearborn resident, claiming to speak "for a great majority of voters," who congratulated Hubbard in 1963 "on your wonderful work of keeping Negroes out of Dearborn. This in itself is an act of keeping Dearborn clean. Property values remain high, Dearborn remains clean, and neighborhoods stay together in peace." In a letter to Thomas Poindexter, Detroit's most prominent white housing activist, one woman explained that opposition to the open-housing movement was not racist, but rather an assertion of whites' "constitutional" right to be left alone. As in the past, few correspondents referred to themselves as white, instead self-identifying as "homeowners" or "citizens," particularly in brief notes and post-cards. "Property owners back you all the way and appreciate your efforts," read a typical example. Some articulated the market-imperative argument far more explicitly, by defensively asserting their racial progressivism. In 1963 a woman from Dearborn acknowledged that "the idea of no negroes was a strong factor" in her family's choice to settle there, but insisted that she was not antiblack. Indeed she was deeply offended that the *Detroit News* had recently labeled Dearborn a "sick city." "If living happily with your neighbors, enjoying your city, and being proud of it makes us a sick city," she concluded, "I hope we never get well."[82]

This woman also joined countless others in viewing local battles over neighborhoods as part of a larger, national struggle over race and rights. "The whole Negro situation," she complained, "is getting ridiculous. All I hear about [is] the rights of Negroes. What about our rights."[83] These whites viewed civil rights protest as an unwarranted assault on their communities and hard-earned privileges. Wishing Hubbard "all the luck in the world . . . in keeping Dearborn white and consequently safe for the law abiding citizens," one Detroiter asked why the "sit-ins and demonstrations [had not been] stopped in Detroit? . . . Is there to be a law giving license to the Negro to do anything he wants and the whites rights thereby taken away." Many Detroiters were outraged that a number of Dearborn residents had protested against Hubbard's handling of the Kendal Street incident. "If any of [them] still feel that they are not receiving adequate police protection," wrote one Detroiter, "they are cordially invited to exchange property with the undersigned, provided they are home owners."[84]

These correspondents insisted that the politics of property (i.e., whites' "right" to exclude) deserved equal standing with—if not precedence over—blacks' demands for basic civil protections, a line of thinking symptomatic of the political calculus long informing white housing activism. Whites juxtaposed civil rights protest, which they described as "ideologically" driven, to their defense of property rights, which they believed occupied a realm outside of politics and ideology. Yet in the same breath they demanded that local politicians and homeowners work through political channels to defend white privilege. Many continued to measure officials' integrity or competence by gauging their support for restriction, complaining to Hubbard that "some mayors and other public officials are too wishy-washy to stand up and speak out, afraid that they will get bad publicity." A Detroit couple felt that Hubbard had shown real "heroism . . . in the face of obviously extremely heavy pressure toward integration" and hoped "to see more politicians who are possessed of your foresight." Dearborn was regularly held up as a model for a white "civil rights" politics, which could counter the rising tide of black activism. A couple from Oak Park congratulated Hubbard in 1963 for his "courage" in "upholding the civil rights of the residents of Dearborn" but added regretfully that "we can't say the same about our mayor." From Livonia came word that "95% of [its residents] are behind you" on opposition to the open-housing movement. The writers added that they were "not too fond of their [own] Mayor."[85]

In August 1961, a Dearborn resident of eleven years sat down to write Hubbard for the first time, explaining that "as a property owner and tax payer," he was "confident that you hold my interest above all others in conducting the affairs of government." But "not [too] long ago," he continued, "Freedom Riders came to Dearborn and we can expect they will continue to try to intimidate us into accepting conditions other than those which we as a community desire. This makes me mad to say the least, for I too have rights, one of which is to be left alone, or if you please, maintain the freedom that I fought for not [too] many years ago." This man found Hubbard's "apparent independence . . . and individualism" particularly "refreshing in light of much of the thinking on the National level." Two years later, a self-described "Voter" from Dearborn told the mayor that he was "worried about the forced integration" because "our homes are here and our life's savings" and because "our very lives, time, and effort—as well as our children's—have been spent here." "It is more than money," the letter continues. "We feel we have a constitutional right to private property, private attitudes, and personal privacy. We hope that the Michigan and National government will not take these rights from us because of . . . blackmail [by] . . . a small group." One Dearborn resident encouraged Hubbard to circulate a petition calling for the adoption of legislation, similar to a measure passed in California, that forbade "any law body to enact any more Fair Housing laws."[86]

Most accusations of governmental malfeasance, particularly at the federal level, were focused on race, housing, and neighborhoods. In letters indicting the "integrated Federal Government" and its "discrimination senators [and] congressmen," whites accused officials of helping draw black migrants to Detroit by selling them "properties under F.H.A." and then supporting their stay by providing them with "welfare and . . . [Aid to Dependent Children] within a very few weeks." Federal economic intervention was especially repugnant, yet there was no acknowledgment, and apparently little knowledge, that the federal government had been subsidizing white people for decades. Indeed, one Dearborn resident wrote Governor George Romney in 1963 to register his "disgust" with a proposed tax increase, which he viewed as an unwarranted attempt "to get the state in the loan business."[87] Romney remained a popular target, together with other leaders or activists deemed sympathetic to black protest and, especially, to open housing. The Rockefellers and Kennedys, explained one correspondent in the spring of 1964, can "buy 100 thousands of acres" in order to build their "castle" and have the resources to exclude anyone that they choose, whereas "we—the poor—have just as much pride in our 'little castle' as the rich SOB has in 'his.'" One anonymous correspondent complained to Hubbard about openhousing activist Fabian Stempian, head of the Dearborn Community Council, identifying what must have been, for many whites, the final insult. "It is my understanding," a letter of March 1964 notes, "that this dead beat Stempien [sic] . . . doesn't even own his own home."[88]

There was no one-to-one correspondence in the Detroit region between support for civil rights and support for Democrats or between support for segregation and support for Republicans. Racism did not have a political party in the postwar North because racism did not exist discretely—because it did not simply inflect people's or parties' decisions about economics or politics, but rather was constitutive of so many white people's understandings of both. For these people, choices about candidates and platforms, local and national, were mediated by a powerful politics of property, neighborhood, and local autonomy. It was a politics that operated simultaneously in two arenas: structurally, by allocating most of the nation's housing, employment, and service resources to people of European descent; and ideologically, by assigning specific racial and status signifiers to specific kinds of tenancy and specific metropolitan geographies. As the preceding discussions of policy, private market operations, and local politics demonstrate, these discursive racial politics were integral to producing and reproducing racial inequality in the Detroit region.

It was simultaneously a national politics that shaped metropolitan development patterns and whites' attitudes throughout the country. So it is not surprising that just as many Detroit-area whites saw the national politics of race play out in their region, white people from around the country saw their own experience of racial politics reflected in metropolitan Detroit. For this reason Hubbard heard from white supporters across the United States, beginning with the Emrich affair in 1956. That year a woman from Cicero, Illinois, saw parallels between the racial violence in her hometown (triggered when whites attacked black families settling in their neighborhoods) and similar conflicts in the Detroit region. She approved of Franklin Roosevelt, who "gave us the New Deal" but had little patience for Eleanor, who was supporting the NAACP and "using my property in a conspiracy to carry out the Cicero Race riots." In the late 1950s and early 1960s, letters arrived from Seattle, St. Petersburg, Kalamazoo, Atlanta, and Philadelphia, among others, praising Hubbard's willingness to say "what so many others are afraid to say" and complaining that "pressure . . . organizations" were forcing "our children . . . to integrate in all phases of life." Whites in Chicago who read about Hubbard in the local press complained that "Negroes have taken" the city, congratulated him for his "courage," and encouraged him to "run . . . for President of the U.S.A." A Dearborn resident who was vacationing in Jacksonville, Florida, during the Emrich affair informed the mayor about his widespread popularity. "When I identify myself as a resident of Dearborn, Michigan," he wrote, "everyone to whom I may be talking is aware of the many articles appearing in various publications regarding your views on segregation . . . every person I talk to is in complete agreement with you and compliment me on living in a community that is fortunate to have leadership such as yours."[89]

In March 1963, a woman who had lived in Dearborn since 1949 wrote the mayor to complain about taxes. Margaret von Walthausen explained that it was her family's "misfortune" to have purchased a factory-built home in a notorious subdivision, one "soon labeled 'the future shacktown of Dearborn.'" Still her family was determined to "do all within our means to maintain and upgrade our house and property."

This we have done by adding a dormer to the upstairs bedroom, erecting a garage and fence, maintaining and beautifying an adjoining 35 ft. lot, adding on a 28 ft. family room with fireplace, and seeing to it that our lawn, shrubs, and flowers added much to the community in general. A few months ago we installed a new hot water heating system. Next year when the family room is 'paid off' we would like to enclose our front porch as a vestibule, modernize the exterior front of the house, re-side with aluminum, and have a new roof applied.

"Why have we done all this," she asked, "to a frame home that was of questionable value?" Because "we believe that Dearborn is a wonderful community in which to live," providing "fine schools for our three youngsters," "a place of employment within walking distance for my husband," and "the opportunity to participate wholeheartedly in Cub and Boy Scout activities." She admitted that her enthusiasm for home improvement had recently "been somewhat dampened," though, because the city assessor was increasing tax rates on families who invested in their property. "It hardly seems fair," she continued, "that while we, and many others throughout the city, work diligently to constantly maintain and improve our property, that we should be penalized by additional taxes." It made "much more sense," von Walthausen concluded, "to penalize those who don't keep up and improve their property than it does to slap down those who mortgage their future to help build up a community."[90]

Six months later, James R. Kapple, of Dearborn, wrote Hubbard to praise the mayor for his handling of the Kendal Street affair and other race-related controversies—to "commend" him "for the unique and tactful way you have handled recent occupancy incidents." "An old adage states a man's home is his castle," he wrote, and "if a man's home is his castle, then his community is his kingdom." Kapple wondered if "we [have] come to the time & place in the 'American way of Life' that a man or a community or a city has no righ[t] to build, support & maintain an enterprise in the full rights of our American heritage." He concluded that "instead of paying 'taxes for nothing,'" we should "support our home & our government & [thereby] protect our heritage."[91]

What sort of distinctions can be drawn between these very different discussions of property, taxation, and homeowners' rights? Like so many suburban residents, Kapple collapsed local politics, citizenship, and the rights of property holders into a celebration of white "heritage." Von Walthausen, by contrast, says nothing about race, and since we do not know her ideas about black people or her views on segregation, we cannot assume that she equated property ownership and responsible citizenship with whiteness. Nor can one dismiss the practical challenges facing homeowners and municipal governments during these years. Maintaining properties and managing city streets, public services, and educational facilities, or balancing tax receipts with municipal expenditures, or ensuring that neighborhoods were free from industrial hazards or heavy traffic; these were important considerations for any public official and, of course, for anyone shopping for a home, attending a council or zoning board meeting, or voting on local ballot initiatives.

At the same time, white people had been encouraged to see metropolitan development throughout the postwar period in racial terms. They had been constantly exposed to and often engaged in land-use debates that described black people as threats to their property, their families, and their way of life. Of course in the final analysis, there is no intrinsic relationship between property and racial identity. Meanwhile, whiteness is a quite flexible category that encompassed far more ethnic groups by the 1950s than it had just a few decades earlier. Nonetheless, countless people of European descent were learning to assign specific racial signifiers to private property, city planning, local government, and to city building itself. In the process they came to view homeownership, suburban homeownership especially, as a preserve of "white" people.

This presents the historian with a difficult task. By no means can we assume that whenever a white person spoke at a council meeting or talked with a neighbor about the condition of their neighborhood, or when they expressed concern about property values or Detroit's visible poverty, that they were either assuming or talking about racial differences. Yet the politics of restriction in these suburbs demonstrates that countless white people were applying racial assumptions to their understandings of metropolitan change, private property, and homeowners' rights. What a study of suburban politics demonstrates is that by the mid-1960s, the fact that this racial vocabulary had been embraced so publicly and for so many years, to discuss such a wide range of metropolitan issues, made its underlying logic very convincing to many people. It also made the long history of that logic's invention, a history that began in the decades preceding the nation's spectacular suburban growth, all the more invisible.

CHAPTER NINE

Colored Property and White Backlash

Housing and development politics in postwar America did more than segregate its fast-growing metropolitan regions. It helped give rise to a new kind of racial politics, in which northern whites learned to view inequality—racial inequality, in particular—wholly as a product of free market forces, unaffected by legal constraints, political interventions, or coercive action of any kind. Suburban prosperity and the newly segregated metropolis offered the physical proof. A popular narrative about the free enterprise system and its role in fueling the nation's spectacular postwar growth provided the intellectual rationale.

The power of that narrative was displayed in the summer of 1967, in whites' response to five days of rioting in downtown Detroit. The violence was triggered on July 23 by an early morning police raid on a Twelfth Street saloon patronized by blacks. It quickly devolved into a free-for-all, pitting thousands of black residents against Detroit's police force, the National Guard, and federal troops. Over 7,000 people were arrested, 43 were killed, and 2,509 buildings looted and set afire. In the following weeks, when the Michigan Civil Rights Commission surveyed the region's whites about the violence, 70 percent supported the statement that blacks had been "pushing too fast" for political and economic equality. "We've done so much for them already," explained one white Detroiter. "What more do they want?" Others wrote Mayor Jerome Cavanaugh and Governor George Romney, accusing them of condoning black criminality while ignoring what one correspondent described as "defenseless citizens." "Why should we white people," asked another, "still go on trying to help those people?"

Countless whites in Detroit and its suburbs had indeed felt "defenseless" during those four days in July. Even in neighborhoods untouched by the street violence, some whites armed themselves and distributed weapons to their neighbors. The tension was palpable at a suburban appliance retailer, where arriving customers "walked into a knot of salesmen who piled at the front of the store with anxious expressions on their faces." Suburban police forces worked overtime, and anxious gun vendors removed inventory from their shelves. Many people simply refused to leave their homes. Then on the fourth day of rioting, an all-white organization called Breakthrough printed up posters designed to simulate arrest warrants accusing Cavanaugh and Romney of "Malfeasance, Misfeasance and Nonfeasance" and offering a $1,000 reward for their detention and conviction. In the following weeks, Breakthrough sponsored meetings throughout the metropolitan area, where its leader, Donald Lobsinger, informed large and reportedly enthusiastic audiences with a heavy "ethnic" representation that whites must provide for their own defense. According to Lobsinger the region's public officials were ill prepared to protect residents against attacks by "bands of armed terrorists" from Detroit bent on "murder" and "rape." "If another riot comes," he told one interviewer, "we will protect our property . . . We will protect our homes . . . And we will fire!"[1]

Most local commentary was far less incendiary. Hubbard's constituents, for example, wrote the mayor to thank him for protecting "the residents of Dearborn during the riots." The couple that sent this note lived "on the border of Kentucky and Tireman," at the invisible boundary between northeast Dearborn and the city of Detroit, and were active members of the local property owners' association. "Everytime we looked outside we saw one of your police cars going down the street," they wrote on August 1. "What a thrill it was to know we had a mayor who cared about our safety." Another Dearborn family, residents of thirteen years ("we have enjoyed every minute of it"), was equally thankful and only hoped that "we can keep Dearborn, so that citizens respect persons and property." A twenty-one-year-old woman told Hubbard that it was "a secure feeling to know that there are still influential people who are on the side of peace-loving people. We need more people on the side of the little man."[2]

The civil disorders of the 1960s in Detroit, Newark, and dozens of other cities[3] strengthened the resolve of whites nationwide to exclude black people from their neighborhoods. Elected officials were listening. In early 1968, as the U.S. House of Representatives debated legislation that would outlaw discrimination in housing rental and sales, Republican House leader Gerald R. Ford, of Michigan, stalled negotiations by proposing an exemption for single-family homes. Representative John Anderson, a Republican from

Illinois, was receiving mail indicating that two-thirds of his constituents opposed the fair housing bill. Only after Martin Luther King was assassinated did a number of House Republicans, including Anderson, whose vote was decisive, split with Ford to support passage of what would become the Fair Housing Act of 1968.[4]

Lobsinger was an anomaly, one of a minority of public figures in metropolitan Detroit publicly calling for violent retaliation. Yet what he shared with most opponents of open housing was the conviction that racial integration threatened the hard-earned rights and privileges of white property owners. By the late 1960s, Detroit's suburban residents, realtors, and officials had helped ensure that most neighborhoods remained off-limits to black people.[5] But the politics of residential restriction had come a long way since the 1910s and 1920s, when property owners' associations announced that there was "nothing in the make-up of a Negro, physically or mentally, which should induce anyone to welcome him as a neighbor." In the late 1960s, by contrast, the Kerner Commission reported that only 6 percent of whites living in metropolitan areas thought that "Negroes are just born that way and can't be changed."[6] Instead most whites insisted, and influential urban experts agreed, that neighborhoods and real estate values were racially specific: that property, itself, could be colored.

And during the 1960s, whites in northern cities and suburbs applied this principle to contemporary debates over race and rights. They interpreted civil rights activism, federal intervention on behalf of black people, and urban riots as confirmation that black people posed a threat to their families, their economic well-being, and their "way of life"—all of which were increasingly tied up in whites' status as property owners. By the 1960s, whites could harness a vocabulary and a political practice that enabled them to criticize black people openly and oppose civil rights reform while earnestly claiming that their position was not racist.

Historians and political analysts have traditionally told a different story about northern whites' responses to black people after World War II, asserting three influential arguments about postwar race relations. First, many writers argue that the response of urban, working class, and ethnic whites to the riots of the 1960s and to an insurgent black protest movement represented something new, a backlash politics that set the stage for a generation of white political conservatism and the demise of the New Deal electoral coalition. Corollary to this, many have argued that white flight was central to the process of converting urban white Democrats into suburban Republicans. Finally, scholars in many fields contend that whites' intolerance of minorities in postwar America has been driven by class conflict, especially by concern for protecting property values and autonomous municipal institutions, rather than by racial animus. Racism is still identifiable in the American metropolis, according to this interpretation, but it is fueled less by ideology than by economics.

This study challenges key elements of the dominant narrative about postwar racial politics. It adds to recent work exploring an earlier period of white backlash, during the 1940s, 1950s, and early 1960s, when whites aggressively defended their racial privileges in urban and suburban neighborhoods nationwide. Federal policy abetted the process by denying most nonwhites access to many benefits of postwar prosperity. Decades of local and national politics shaped whites' responses to black protest and to the liberal state itself, and whites' rejection of *certain types* of liberal reform in the 1960s was not new. This study also further complicates the story about suburban political conversion by demonstrating that white suburban Democrats and Republicans alike were active in the politics of racial exclusion throughout the postwar period. Party affiliation did not necessarily correlate with views about racial equality, equal opportunity, or the role of the interventionist state. Finally, this study demonstrates that race and economics are not easily separated, whether in the realm of public policy, in the popular imagination, or in the process of scholarly inquiry.

When northern whites responded to the modern civil rights movement, to Great Society programs, to the "law and order" campaigns of Barry Goldwater and Richard Nixon, and to urban riots, their response was decisively influenced by the policies, metropolitan transformations, and political conversations that had been shaping urban and suburban life for decades. Whites' interpretation of the civil rights revolution was mediated by the material conditions of metropolitan life and a dominant national discourse about urban and suburban racial change. By the 1960s, most whites were property owners, concentrated in all-white communities that were separated from—and in the case of suburbs, viewed as sanctuaries from—urban, minority communities. Most whites were convinced that the spatial and socioeconomic segregation of the metropolis was purely the result of free market forces. Seen in this context, northern white "backlash" against the civil rights movement and a new federal commitment to racial equality hardly seems new. It was a continuation of a well-entrenched political practice and political vision that for decades had defined property, privilege, and the rights of citizens in racially specific terms.

Looking Outward: The Politics of Backlash in an
Age of Metropolitan Growth

Thomas and Mary Edsall have written that, beginning with the presidential campaign of Barry Goldwater in 1964, "race" became "a powerful wedge, breaking up what had been the majoritarian economic interests of the poor, working, and lower-middle classes in the traditional liberal coalition." The collapse of that coalition, they explain, pitted "whites and blacks at the low end of the income distribution against each other." As a result, "the traditional ideological partisan divide—between Democratic liberalism supportive both of domestic-spending initiatives and of an activist federal regulatory apparatus, on the one hand, and Republican conservatism generally opposed to government regulation and in favor of reduced domestic spending, on the other hand—has been infused [since the mid-1960s] with racial and race-coded meanings." In the Detroit area, the Edsalls continue, the "largely white, working-class, once firmly Democratic suburbs" were decisively transformed by the riots of 1967 and a battle over a court-ordered school desegregation plan for the region's urban and suburban schools in 1972. After supporting Democratic presidential candidates in 1960, 1964, and 1968, a majority of Michigan voters selected Nixon in 1972. The Edsalls conclude that the difference was the white working class, especially in the suburbs, whose allegiance to the Democratic Party steadily eroded after 1967. "While Detroit remained firmly Democratic, the busing fight provoked a realignment in the working-class Detroit suburbs that has transformed the presidential politics of the entire state for at least the past five elections."[7]

There is no doubt that the Democratic Party was stigmatized in the 1960s and early 1970s by its new association with "marginalized . . . or historically disenfranchised groups."[8] And the realignment of party support clearly shaped congressional and presidential politics for years to come. Yet there was little that was *new* about the discourse of "race" and "rights" that grew so prominent in national politics during and after the election of 1964. For decades both local and national politics had been infused with "racial and race-coded meanings." The politics of white privilege had a long post–World War II history rooted in neighborhood politics and the federal interventions that structured inequality nationwide. White urban Democrats were hardly champions of racial equality or racial justice between World War II and the election of 1964, their support for "an activist federal regulatory apparatus" notwithstanding. And long before the riots and the controversies over court-ordered busing, white suburbanites, both

Republican and Democrat, had been mobilizing to protect their racial privilege. In short, party affiliation, alone, tells us little about racial attitudes, for whites' support of the New Deal state was partly rooted in their expectations about powerful segments of its "regulatory apparatus"—including its housing programs and their racial protocols—that were *not* viewed, by most white people, as "activist."[9]

One measure of the longevity and continuity of white racial preoccupations can be found in popular responses to civil right politics *after* 1964. In metropolitan Detroit, whites articulated their grievances with a new tide of racial reform by tapping into a well-rehearsed vocabulary about rights, property, and neighborhoods. Again Dearborn's mayor provided impetus for many whites to speak out. On February 2, 1965, CBS News televised a report on a Michigan Civil Rights Commission lawsuit against Hubbard, accusing him of violating blacks' rights by covering municipal bulletin boards with "racially insensitive" flyers and newspaper clippings. Then throughout the spring and summer, the press covered a federal trial initiated by the Dearborn Community Council charging Hubbard and two Dearborn police commissioners with denying Giuseppe Stanzione's civil rights in the Kendal Street affair.[10] Immediately after the CBS broadcast, not only Hubbard but Cavanaugh, Romney, local newspaper editors, and even President Johnson heard from whites in metropolitan Detroit about the "persecution" of Dearborn's mayor. And from Madison, Wisconsin; Eugene, Oregon; St. Louis; Nashville; San Francisco; New York City; Washington, D.C.; and other cities came letters celebrating the "rights of the individual," decrying the "Communistic N.A.A.C.P." and informing Hubbard that people "would welcome the opportunity to vote for you for President of the United States." Media coverage of the civil rights suit was especially heavy during the winter, spring, and summer of 1965, and so too was the flow of correspondence. Clearly many people were following the case closely and, like the Szczesniaks, of Dearborn, expressed their "interest, amusement, and disgust" with Hubbard's "harassment by the newspapers." Fay Haines, of Detroit, wrote the editors of the *News* to condemn their criticism of Hubbard and to cancel her subscription.[11]

When these men and women talked about racial politics in 1965 they told a familiar story, juxtaposing what they described as the "rights" of "citizens" and "homeowners" and the sanctity of local institutions against the "demands" and "interventions" of blacks, civil rights organizations, and state and federal governments. "As an elected official," James and Bettie Chappelle told Hubbard days after the CBS program aired, "you must answer to the people of Dearborn and not the State Civil Rights Commission."

Many correspondents agreed with the man who wished that there were "more people in public life with the courage you have shown." From Houston came word that not "all Texans" were like Lyndon Johnson, who was "mis-lead[ing] the American people." ("Instead of being all the way with LBJ," wrote W. A. Settle, "we are all the way with Mayor Hubbard.") Johnson heard directly from a Dearborn resident upset about "the unfair treatment our Mayor Hubbard is getting," in a letter that detailed the "many good things" he had done for the community. "We have a beautiful clean city, good clean government, and good law abiding citizens. Can you blame us for being proud not only of our city but also of our Mayor." The note concluded with a question for the president: "What has happened to freedom? . . . Why is it possible for some groups to inte[r]fere with law abiding citizens? Why is it possible for some groups to cause unrest and persecution?"[12]

This narrative about property, community, race, and rights helped whites negotiate the ongoing national debate over protest and reform. Ten days after the March 8, 1965, attack by Alabama state troopers against civil rights demonstrators in Selma, a municipal employee from Detroit wrote Orville Hubbard to comment on the black protest movement. He began, as did so many correspondents, by talking about where he lived, announcing his wish not to be "restricted to residing in integrated Detroit." His preference was to "reside in a clean, crime free, well managed city like Dearborn!" Then he turned to the topic of civil rights, asking Hubbard if he had "observed on television and in the newspapers . . . the spectacle Mayor Cavanaugh, Gov. Romney and the various churches made on Woodward Ave. in the protest march [like the one] in Selma, Ala." All this, he continued, while black people, whom he derisively described as the " 'good' citizens" of Detroit, were "robbing, raping, and stabbing the white people here!" Another Detroiter thought that Hubbard's actions showed that "Selma Was Not Necessary" and reminded the mayor that "not nearly all your admirers are in Dearborn."[13]

Commitment to the defense of neighborhoods and property continued to draw whites into political activism. One Dearborn resident asked Congressman John Dingell to request a Department of Justice investigation into the federal indictment of Hubbard. Many offered tactical or financial support to the mayor's legal defense fund. In 1965, hundreds of whites, mostly from Dearborn but also from Detroit, Oak Park, Livonia, Warren, Allen Park, Southfield, Birmingham, and elsewhere, donated money to cover Hubbard's legal expenses. Irene Nagy announced that she and other Dearborn women were "standing by ready to help out in any way they can, i.e., circulate petitions, organize cit[i]zens committee." Gregory M. Pillon, of Detroit, offered "to represent you in your Federal Court trial, free of any charge." From the northern Chicago suburb of Wilmette came the query: "Do you need money? Let the people know—we will help." Whites kept a careful eye on ballot initiatives, especially regarding housing issues, and linked them to Hubbard's fight against the Civil Rights Commission. "Stay with it Mayor," wrote a man from New York City the night that CBS aired its profile. "The recent California and Detroit referendums prove you're right. Two public housing amendments were defeated in this [state] also." Others mobilized more quietly, like the self-identified "little Dearborn housewife and mother" who told Hubbard in 1965 that "there is nothing I can do but continue to vote for you and talk this way around our still safe community." A Detroit woman, whose husband worked in Dearborn, revealed her political investment in segregation by simply congratulating Hubbard for his efforts and signing off: "an interested citizen."[14]

The politics of backlash in the 1960s was far more than a reaction to black protest, urban violence, and federal reform. Countless whites living in the nation's growing metropolitan regions responded to civil rights protest by tapping into a familiar political vocabulary and political practice, both of which equated whiteness with homeownership and citizenship, both of which interpreted civil rights politics as part of a battle between "localism" and "federal intervention," and both of which were well rehearsed and deeply institutionalized long before the presidential contest of 1964, passage of the Civil Rights Act, and another wave of urban riots.

Neither Race nor Economics

There is a long tradition of scholarship and commentary arguing that suburban development in the modern United States, along with its demographic and economic peculiarities, have been natural processes wholly unaffected by decades of federal pump-priming and systematic discrimination in both the public and private sectors. Most often this argument assumes a market or at least a demographic teleology, as in Robert Wood's conclusion that suburban homogeneity was not a "conscious, deliberate act of public policy." The "results of public action at the Regional level are unpremeditated," he concluded, "the products of accident." Robert Bruegmann dismisses the claim that Depression-era and postwar policy decisively shaped suburban growth or structured its particular form. He argues that since the general phenomenon of sprawl predates federal intervention and because several of the unique motors fueling its postwar variant had pre-Depression precedents (mortgage lending and highway construction, for example), there is no reason to believe that the New Deal altered postwar development patterns, consumer decision making, or opportunities. David Brooks compares the newest wave of sprawl to an act of divine intervention: "It's as if Zeus came down and started plopping vast towns in the middle of the farmland and the desert overnight. Boom! A Master planned community! Boom! A big-box mall! A rec center, pool, and four thousand soccer fields! The food courts come first, and the people follow."[15]

Far more common in academic studies is an acknowledgment that institutions, both public and private, have been foundational to making the modern metropolis possible, creating its particular geographic and architectural forms, and segregating it by race and class. These studies often debate the relative importance of racial (or ideological) and class (or economic) variables in promoting patterns of "uneven development." Many conclude, as Kenneth Mladenka did in an essay on public service distribution patterns, that "class has replaced race as the primary determinant" of development decisions, while others argue that whites' racial attitudes have remained decisive.[16] But both camps tend to treat economic and ideological variables as conceptually separate and suggest that we can measure their relative importance when both are deemed causative. For example, Douglas Massey and Nancy Denton argue that past federal discrimination and subsequent failures to rectify its impact are the product of two complementary, yet distinct, forces. Fair housing legislation has not been enforced, they argue, because politicians, especially southern Democrats and "liberal northern legislators," have "feared the wrath of ethnic, blue-collar constituents" *and* because "conservative Republicans, apart from any racist feelings they might have had, objected to governmental interference in housing markets on ideological grounds." "The issue," they conclude, "is not whether race *or* class perpetuates the urban underclass, but how race *and* class *interact* to undermine the social and economic well-being of black Americans."[17]

This separation of economic and racial variables does not adequately describe most white northerners' experience of housing and development politics during the decades that saw the simultaneous emergence of a metropolitan America, a home-owning America, and a zoned America. On the subjects of exclusion, homeowners' rights, and neighborhood integrity, most white people, whether average residents, government officials, realtors, builders, or publicists, did not make sharp distinctions between racial and economic variables. The question is not whether "race" *or* "economics" fueled segregation and segregationist politics or even how "race *and* class interact" to do so. The question is how and why people of European descent became so deeply invested, both materially and ideologically, in a new market for residence that was racially constructed. After World War II, most whites assumed that black occupancy posed a categorical threat to white-owned property. They equated whiteness with homeownership and citizenship, and they understood residential segregation not primarily as a matter of "ideology" or prejudice but rather as a matter of development economics. By the 1960s, countless whites had determined that private property, neighborhoods, and local government institutions had economic values that were racially specific.

Whites' conflation of the racial and economic was readily visible in the activities of Dearborn's homeowners' associations. During the 1960s these groups—fifteen of them either members or "associates" of the DFCA—continued to meet regularly, recruit new members, and attend to matters deemed crucial to homeowners: "maintenance of property values," "good property appearance," "safe traffic conditions," "care of streets, parkways and parks," "improved lighting," and "compliance with zoning and building restrictions." The Aviation Property Owners Association (APOA), representing a section of northeastern Dearborn home to about 1800 people,[18] increased its membership throughout the decade. (Only property owners were permitted to join.)[19] In a message to members, the Board of Directors promised to "keep in touch with problems that may have an effect on your property values, and on anything that may tend to undermine the high quality of your neighborhood." Monthly meetings were held at the cafeteria of the McDonald School, at Freda and Diversey. Members heard talks on "care of lawns, shrubbery and trees" and presentations by local legislators (in 1965 a discussion of the Michigan Homestead Exemption Act, for example). They discussed schools and reapportionment, local development controversies, and the condition of neighborhood streets and sidewalks. They viewed slide shows, planned social events, and held award presentations for the annual "Clean-Up" and Christmas home-decoration contests.[20]

Monitoring land use and occupancy remained a primary focus of the APOA's efforts. Residents appealed to the organization for action on public nuisances such as garbage accumulating in empty lots or teenagers playing cards at night in a local schoolyard, and APOA members, in turn, "actively participated" in the DFCA and served on its board. APOA officers wrote to and appeared before Dearborn's City Council and Zoning Board of Appeals to enforce the suburb's ordinance and register objections to proposed variances. Early in 1964, for example, the association opposed construction of a cocktail lounge on the corner of Hartwell and Warren, arguing that it threatened homeowners with late-night noise, increased traffic, and "a substantial loss in the value of their property." Meanwhile handwritten notes and phone calls warned APOA officials about specific occupancy threats. "Home at 7840 Normile . . . is now vacant and for sale again," reported one member. "Neighbors noticed colored being shown this by [real estate] salesmen. [I] advised her to keep me advised of any further developments." An update, two weeks later, noted that the "house is still vacant and for sale . . . Neighbors talked to [real estate] man, who stated that he had inquiries from colored, who were told that he has a deposit." Other members had more sweeping suggestions for preventing racial invasion. "Will you kindly tell me why you do not get petitions signed against this Civil Rights Bill?" asked member Bessie M. Blaska in a note to APOA president William Hoeck in March 1964. "These are pressure groups or monopolies trying to put this over. Monopolies destroy our Constitution." One area resident encouraged the association to "stir up Detroit Property Owners [Associations] to get out the vote, so open housing will not pass in Detroit." "That will help Dearborn."[21]

Following the riots in July 1967, the APOA encouraged residents to "install lawn lights as a crime prevention measure," dubbing the initiative "Operation Porch Light," and held sessions "on the subject of safety action in the event of civil disturbances." It considered petitioning the city to abandon a planned conversion of a local park bounded by Tireman, Appoline, Patton, and Manor avenues into a fenced-in playground. "The location of this playfield, being at the City Limits," the APOA wrote, "would invite attendance of other than our property owners and their children; it could easily precipitate a situation we have been jealously guarding against." By the fall of 1968, the association reported a paid membership of 645, "the highest number" in its history. Nearly half of the families in northeastern Dearborn, east of Schaeffer Road, were now actively participating.[22]

Homeowners' associations represented local, organized advocacy for a theory of metropolitan development that by the 1960s had become constitutive of white suburban political culture and the national market for housing. It was a politics that viewed postwar growth, property ownership, and their unique racial geography as the products of unrestricted free market activity. And it was this free market narrative that mediated whites' responses to black activism and urban violence. Geography loomed large both in whites' complaints about civil rights protest and in their defense of racial exclusion. In March 1965, one recent newcomer to Dearborn told Hubbard that the origins of current racial conflicts were readily visible, specifically where black people lived or socialized. To understand the "current controversy" and the problems facing "citizens," wrote Arthur Durham, "all one needs to do is visit Elizabeth Park on Belle Isle on a warm Sunday during the summer!"[23] Whites commented on civil rights controversies by comparing the physical condition and amenities of white and black neighborhoods. After watching the CBS profile on Hubbard, one Detroit woman wrote several local officials, religious leaders, and journalists to ask why Dearborn's mayor was "being persecuted."

> Is it because he believes in good clean government?
> Is it because he believes in excellent schools? . . .
> Is it because the people of Dearborn . . . feel safe and secure? . . .
> Is it because he has established many beautiful parks . . . ?

Hubbard's critics ought to "follow . . . [his] example . . . in developing their own communities like Dearborn," she concluded, instead of "trying to knock Dearborn down into their own level." Another Detroiter, anxious to find a home in Dearborn, blamed "the Supreme Ct. for all the racial troubles." "The President," he noted dismissively, "can divide his property into 30 ft. lots" if he wants to and "fill the whole thing" with black people.[24]

The hundreds of letters, telegrams, and phone messages received by Hubbard in the mid-1960s built upon a local narrative about race and metropolitan geography that had been tested and refined since the early 1940s.[25] A flood of correspondence arrived in response to the "billboard" case and the federal civil rights case. These well publicized trials provided fodder for area residents who, like Chester Witkowski, were disgusted by "bureaucrats" and the "power hungry central government." "It is regrettable," wrote F. J. Hildebrandt, "that the federal government meddles in strictly local affairs when there is so much to accomplish on a national basis, to say nothing of the serious international problems." From Detroit and its suburbs came wishes that more people would join Hubbard in preserving the "civil rights of white people"; "we don't need any outside interference," this note explained, adding that federal meddling in Detroit led to integration, "and look at all the trouble they got."[26] Others in the city appealed to Hubbard to "come to Detroit and Clean it up, Be our mayor." Dearborners thanked him for maintaining a "clean place to raise a family." It takes "people like you," wrote another satisfied resident, "to be able to understand and prove the true meaning of Democracy."[27]

Notably, most correspondents invoked their racial privilege without calling it "white"; instead they thanked Hubbard for defending the rights of "citizens" and "property owners." One couple that had recently moved to Dearborn often found themselves boasting to their friends about life in the suburb. "Of course we had only the highest praise for the schools, recreation and the Mayor." Thus, they felt it was important to help Hubbard with his legal fees, because he was a man "who will stand up and fight for . . . the rights of the people he serves."[28] Some people were more inclusive, but certainly not of minorities: "I feel that every property owner, as well as each resident of Dearborn," wrote Lawrence Williams in 1965, "should rally around the Mayor and give him their wholehearted support."[29] Phone calls poured into city hall from Detroit, Livonia, Grosse Pointe, Birmingham, Redford, Allen Park, and elsewhere, from blue-collar workers and engineers, physicians and housewives, declaring that blacks threatened to overrun Dearborn—"The way they did Detroit," as one caller noted. "Property owner has no more rights."[30]

Three pieces of commentary from 1965 suggest the power of a new white racial politics that proclaimed the sanctity of suburban communities by erasing the policy history that was foundational to creating the postwar metropolis. In February, after the CBS profile aired, a self-appointed "Friends of Hubbard" group from central Michigan (Gratiot, Isabella, and Montacalm counties) described the Michigan Civil Rights Commission as an "unnecessary interference with their private lives. Perhaps there would have been justification for a commission of this type in some states of the union," they explained, "but . . . Michigan has certainly been foremost in the equal treatment of its citizens." For this reason they resented "the government interference in a private aspect of *our* civil rights." In July a Dearborn resident wrote *Newsweek* magazine to condemn its coverage of the federal suit against Hubbard and Dearborn's police. The magazine was incorrect, wrote Jerome T. Smutek on July 6, that Hubbard's support stemmed from his promise to "keep Dearborn white." "Many of this nation's suburbs are virtually all white," he continued, "not because of any mayor, but rather for a number of complex social and economic reasons. Dearborn is no different, and most people here know it. Mayor Hubbard draws his voter strength from the fact that the Dearborn residents are provided with one of the finest school systems in the country, a clean, progressive, efficiently-run city, and services and recreational facilities surpassed by none."[31]

Finally the CBS broadcast inspired a group of whites from Dearborn and the "surrounding area" to declare that they, too, were "proud of the city of Dearborn and especially of its Mayor." We "believe in freedom for all," they wrote, "including the freedom to choose with whom we will be associated and the freedom to maintain or dispose of our possessions according to our discretion." They were relieved that Hubbard had "the courage to speak up for his convictions in a time when most people seem to have a backbone in need of a little starch." Among the signers was a resident of the 7000 block of Kendal Street, scene of the 1963 attack on Giuseppe Stanzione's home.[32]

The politics of race and racism in postwar America regularly returns to places like Kendal Street, both literally and in the political imaginations of white metropolitan residents. It was largely in their neighborhoods that white people daily found their lessons about the relationship between property, racial privilege, and political rights. It was in the meetings of zoning boards or city councils or property improvement associations. It was in mobilizations to terrorize blacks or "unscrupulous" white realtors. It was in the daily commute between a job in Detroit and a new, all-white suburban subdivision that afforded another opportunity to marvel at "the new four-story Michigan Life Insurance Building on Woodward, the new Thirteen Mile and Woodward Shopping Center, the new shopping area in Oak Park and other such evidence of progress and improvement in [the] community."[33] And it was in countless everyday conversations—with friends, in property protective association newsletters, and in the suburban press—about neighborhood change, "sound development," and the "threat" of a black "invasion." It was in these local places and venues that two important political processes took shape during these decades. First, millions of people of European descent benefited materially from their whiteness. And second, *any* person of European descent was encouraged to develop a new vocabulary about white privilege and its relationship to economic growth, property, responsible government, and the rights of homeowners.

The "long" postwar history of suburban politics—a story that includes federal policy, local political engagement, and popular interpretations of metropolitan change—is central to helping us understand whites' responses to black protest and civil rights reform in the 1960s and beyond. It helps explain why Arnold S. Wiwigacz, of Dearborn, angered by the Michigan Civil Rights Commission's treatment of his mayor, sat down to write Hubbard in February 1965. His lengthy letter was devoted—remarkably—only to the incident, a year and half earlier, at 7427 Kendal Street. Spurred by Hubbard's trial to speak out about the era's civil rights challenges, this resident recalled a moment when Dearborners responded en masse to defend their homes, neighborhoods, and local prerogatives against a "racial invasion." Wiwigacz blamed Stanzione for disrupting the lives of nearby homeowners. He defended the city's response to the incident and applauded the administration's stance on integration. He concluded by telling the mayor that "we have a clean and proud city here in Dearborn and we owe it all to you and your aids. If I can help you in any way, financially or otherwise, don't hesitate to call on my support."[34]

Looking Forward: Race, Markets, and the Federal Response to Metropolitan Inequality

In their 1947 study of race-restrictive covenants, Charles Johnson and Herman Long explored the links among the real estate industry, local politics, federal policy, court decisions, and white people's ideas about race and property; "Where the factor of decline in property values can be directly linked to Negro occupancy or threatened 'invasion,' it is evident that the phenomenon is a psychological one existing in the minds of white people rather than attributable to the Negroes themselves." The authors explained that it was the widespread use of restrictive covenants, the vigilance of white neighborhood improvement associations, and the complicity of both private interests and public officials that translated whites' fears into policy, legal precedents, residential subdivisions, and housing equity.[35] Their analysis was part of an important contemporary critique by scholars, government officials, and activists focused on the discriminatory impacts of U.S. policy and the inextricable connections between race, wealth, political rights, and political power.[36] But theirs was a minority voice, barely acknowledged in the early postwar debates over housing and development. Instead, most federal officials, businesspeople, and urban experts told a story about the inexorable market forces that fueled suburban affluence for some while unfortunately leaving others behind.

Beginning in the late 1960s, sustained civil rights protest and high-profile urban violence spurred federal commissions and academics to examine the origins of residential inequality and racial conflict. With the notable exception of the Kerner Report, however, most of their studies ignored or masked the state's role in subsidizing and segregating the American metropolis. The Kerner Commission offered a scathing historical assessment of unequal development, indicting public agencies and the private sector for fueling residential apartheid. Far more typical, though, was the National Commission on Urban Problems' exoneration of the FHA in its 1968 report, *Building the American City*. The authors did concede that the "chief beneficiaries of FHA" were suburban communities, developers, and "middle-income home buyers" and acknowledged that the agency had operated "with the conventional racial prejudice characteristic of many middle class real estate men." Its "segregation position cannot be defended by any current standard of what is right for the home, the neighborhood, the city, or the nation," the report concludes. Still the commission denied government culpability for the racial segregation of the American metropolis. "The FHA had a strong case for its economic conservatism which, in all fairness, needs to be stated and understood," the authors explained, later adding that FHA officials and congressmen had been torn between pursuing "social" and "business" goals. Most remarkable, the section entitled "Segregation in Housing" did not discuss the impact of FHA underwriting standards, but rather federal urban renewal policy, the FHA's reserve structure, and "defaults by home-owners on mortgage obligations." And the legacy of federal appraisal and insurance practices disappeared entirely in the general conclusions about se-lective credit programs. The FHA, the report explains, "has performed well," enabling "millions of young families [to enjoy] homeownership at a much earlier age" and to "bring their children up in what we like to think of as the conventional American manner." "It is difficult to see how any institu-tion could have served the emerging middle class more effectively than has the FHA and its counterpart, the Federal home loan bank systems [*sic*]."[37]

A year later the President's Committee on Urban Housing described postwar metropolitan growth as a natural, market-driven process. "Ameri-can private enterprise," explained the authors of *A Decent Home*, "has built an impressive, world-leading housing inventory, and can build housing ef-ficiently and at the highest standards, when there is effective demand for it." The authors noted that "private enterprise alone cannot provide for the poorest Americans," who were hampered by the lack of educational and employment opportunities as well as "social disorganization" that was "collected and then compounded in particular sections of cities." But they reiterated the belief that the " 'squalor' of slum housing is not the result of any essential defect in America's 'productive power'. That productive power (private enterprise, sometimes joined with collaborative public policy) has shown not only that it can 'master space and provide unmatched abun-dance in the marketplace' but also that it can produce housing." By the early 1970s, most influential urban experts were simply erasing the history of federal intervention from the story of metropolitan change, while draw-ing sharp lines between the economic and racial origins of residential dis-crimination. In 1974, the President's Task Force on Suburban Problems, a group of businessmen, planners, educators, and scholars, lamented that "to millions of black Americans and others, the metropolitan frontier has been closed." It claimed that "part of [the cause was] economic but too large a part is due to prejudice." Then the report's recommendations for address-ing the problem reveal the way urban experts blurred the lines between racial and economic values: the authors proposed a federal program "to insure homeowners against loss due to racial integration." The remedy was directed to *white* people (the report regularly implies that homeowners are white), in the form of a program recommended elsewhere, in modified form, as a means to compensate homeowners for losses incurred because of aircraft noise.[38]

The Task Force's discussion of racial discrimination in housing markets does not mention federal mortgage programs, while its celebration of the postwar suburban miracle has nothing but praise for the FHA. In the final analysis the report described individual homeowners as the force determining the success—or alternatively the failure—of the suburban experiment. "Most problems of the suburbs," the authors explained, "derive from rapid, unregulated, confusing growth." "The millions of American families that have moved to the suburbs have gone there in search of space, quiet, decency and comfort. They have gone there for a modern counterpart of the New England village, a model of prosperity and order, small enough to be understood and managed by its citizens, cherished for its beauty and its friendliness." Unfortunately, however, "blight and decay" had "begun to set in," even in suburban America. This happens, the Task Force concluded, "in any community that has lost the love of its inhabitants."[39]

A close examination of suburban development politics, at both the local and national levels, helps us understand how ideas about difference are written into the political and economic institutions that create, distribute, and police material resources in metropolitan America, whether utilities and well-maintained roads, fire and police protection, money for education or healthcare, or credit to buy and maintain a house. The public officials and private entrepreneurs who constructed the nation's land-use and development tools rarely made sharp distinctions between the economic and the racial. Beginning in the 1910s, white municipal officials and businesspeople designed land-use and real estate instruments that assumed racial differentials. Beginning in the 1930s, these principles were systematically written into a revolutionary new mortgage market that was fashioned, subsidized, and regulated by the federal government. Well into the 1960s, federal officials encouraged private operators to invoke these principles when developing, selling, and managing residential resources. The discriminatory practices that stem from these principles have endured in countless communities, unofficially, to this day. Meanwhile, this theory of race and property value became a part of everyday political conversation and political practice among metropolitan whites. In a series of formal and informal mobilizations, countless people of European descent grew deeply invested, both materially and ideologically, in the idea that property, neighborhoods, and government institutions had specific racial values.

Critics have documented the fact that public policy has structured access to housing and neighborhoods and, therefore, to wealth, employment, healthful environments, and physical safety along racial lines. They have demonstrated that the history of metropolitan change and racial privilege cannot be reduced to a calculus about "race" *or* "economics." Yet most of this work stops short of exploring the gray area between the racial and the economic. Thus, many scholars argue, in the case of housing in particular, that racial minorities have historically been "denied full access to a crucial market."[40] To make this claim assumes a model of analysis in which a pure, discrete market for housing exists, a market that operates outside of people's assumptions about color and property. It assumes that a market for housing exists outside of the institutions, political discourses, and local efforts that continue to separate racial groups by place throughout the United States.

National Archives II, College Park, Maryland

RG 31	Record Group 31, Records of the Federal Housing Administration, 1930–1965
CFH	Case Files for Homes, 1934–1938
CCSF	Commissioner's Correspondence and Subject File, 1938–1958
HMD	Housing Market Data, 1938–1952
IOPM	Interoffice Policy Memos, 1945 ff.
PCACO	Program Correspondence of the Assistant Commissioner for Operations, 1936–1956
RRFM	Records Relating to First Mortgages
RRHMA	Records Relating to Housing Market Analysis, 1935–1942
RHMA	Reports of Housing Market Analysts, 1937–1963
SP	Speeches
RG 195	Record Group 195, Records of the Federal Home Loan Bank Board
FHLBB/CSF	Records of the Federal Home Loan Bank Board, Records Relating to the City Survey File, 1935–1940
RG 207	Record Group 207, General Records of the Department of Housing and Urban Development, 1931–1995

Michigan Collections

ALUA	Archvives of Labor and Urban Affairs, Walter P. Reuther Library, Wayne State University, Detroit, Michigan

DHM	Dearborn Historical Museum and Archive, Dearborn, Michigan
Hancock	City, Departments, Housing, "John Hancock Rental Housing Project, 1948"
OHP	Orville Hubbard Papers
CR/1956	Civil Rights, "1956: Emrich"
CR/1957	Civil Rights, "1957: Correspondence"
CR/1957–61	Civil Rights, "Correspondence, 1957–61"
CR/1958	Civil Rights, "1958: Correspondence"
CR/1962–3	Civil Rights, "Correspondence, 1962–3"
CR/1964	Civil Rights, "Correspondence, general, 1964"
CR/1967	Civil Rights, "1967"
CR/1967, riots	Civil Rights, "1967, Riots, U.S."
CR/AD, 6–27	Civil Rights, "Advertiser—Detroit, April 6–27" (1956)
CR/AD, 28–31	Civil Rights, "Advertiser—Detroit, April 28–31" (1956)
CR/ADb	Civil Rights, "Advertiser—Dearborn" (1956)
CR/ADb, 1956	Civil Rights, "Civil Rights, corr., Advertiser Interview, Dearborn, 1956"
CR/AN, 1956	Civil Rights, "Advertiser, Northern, 1956"
CR/BB	Civil Rights, "Civil Rights Commission, Bulletin Board, supporting" (1965)
CR/CNS, 1–24	Civil Rights, "Case not specified, supporting, Feb. 1–24" (1965)
CR/CNS, 1–13	Civil Rights, "Case not specified, supporting, March 1–May 13" (1965)
CR/CNS, J–S	Civil Rights, "Case not specified, supporting, July–Sept." (1965)
CR/DF, 20	Civil Rights, "Defense Fund, Under $20"
CR/DF, 24–30	Civil Rights, "Defense Fund, Feb. 24–30, 1965"
CR/DF, F–M	Civil Rights, "Defense Fund, Feb.–March 15, 1965"
CR/DF, M–J	Civil Rights, "Defense Fund, March 16–June, 1965"
CR/Stanz	Civil Rights, "Stanzione Case, general"
CR/Stanz, 1963	Civil Rights, "Correspondence, Stanzione, supporting, 1963"
CR/Stanz, 1964	Civil Rights, "Correspondence, Stanzione case" (1964)
CR/Stanz, 1965	Civil Rights, "Stanzione Case, Correspondence Supporting Hubbard, July" (1965)

CR/Stanz, DCC	Civil Rights, "Stanzione Case, Dearborn Community Council, 1964"
CR/Stanz, J–J	Civil Rights, "Stanzione Case, Correspondence Supporting Hubbard, Jan.–June 23" (1965)
CR/Stanz, 24–30	Civil Rights, "Stanzione Case, Correspondence Supporting, June 24–30" (1965)
HP	Hazel Park City Hall, City Clerk's office
MHC	Michigan Historical Collection, Bentley Historical Library, Ann Arbor, Michigan
MML	Michigan Municipal League, Ann Arbor, Michigan
OCPC	Oakland County Planning Commission, Pontiac, Michigan
ROHC	Historical Collection, Royal Oak Public Library
THM	Troy Historical Museum, Troy, Michigan

Newspapers, Periodicals, and Reports

CC	*County/City Data Book* (USBC)
DC	*Detroit Courier*
DFP	*Detroit Free Press*
DI	*Dearborn Independent*
DG	*Dearborn Guide*
DN	*Detroit News*
DP	*Dearborn Press*
DT	Oakland County *Daily Tribune* (Royal Oak)
PODU	*Population and Occupied Dwelling Units* (DMARPC)

Government Agencies, Federal Legislation, and Private Organizations

AIREA	American Institute of Real Estate Appraisers
APOA	Aviation Property Owners Association (Dearborn)
ASPO	American Society of Planning Officials
BCLD	Business and Civic Leaders of Dearborn
CCHR	Coordinating Council on Human Relations
DFCA	Dearborn Federation of Civic Associations
DHC	Detroit Housing Commission
DMARPC	Detroit Metropolitan Area Regional Planning Commission

DPOPA	Dearborn Property Owners Protective Association
FHA	Federal Housing Administration
FHLB	Federal Home Loan Bank system
FHLBB	Federal Home Loan Bank Board
FNMA	Federal National Mortgage Association
FPHA	Federal Public Housing Authority
FSLIC	Federal Savings and Loan Insurance Corporation
GPO	Government Printing Office
HHFA	Housing and Home Finance Agency
HOLC	Home Owners Loan Corporation
MIC	Mayor's Interracial Committee
NAACP	National Association for the Advancement of Colored People
NAHB	National Association of Home Builders
NAREB	National Association of Real Estate Brokers
NCCP	National Conference on City Planning
NHA	National Housing Act (1934)
RFC	Reconstruction Finance Corporation
SEMCOG	Southeast Michigan Council of Governments
SDCA	Southwest Dearborn Civic Association (Dearborn)
USBC	U.S. Department of Commerce, Bureau of the Census
USSLL	United States Savings and Loan League
VA	Veterans Administration

NOTES

CHAPTER ONE

1. David Allan Levine, *Internal Combustion: The Races in Detroit, 1915–1926* (Westport, Conn.: Greenwood Press, 1976), 161. See also Kevin Boyle's detailed account in *Arc of Justice: A Saga of Race, Civil Rights and Murder in the Jazz Age* (New York: Henry Holt, 2004), chaps. 1 and 5. Three other family friends had joined the Sweets that evening by the time the assault began.

2. *DFP*, November 19–22, 1925 (paraphrasing Gill's testimony); Levine, *Internal Combustion*, 162–63; David E. Lilienthal, "Has the Negro the Right to Self-Defense?" *The Nation*, December 23, 1925, 724–25.

3. Levine, *Internal Combustion*, 175, 202–3; *DFP*, November 26 and 28, 1925; Boyle, *Arc of Justice*, 273–79, chap. 10.

4. Eyewitness accounts reported in "Citizens of Dearborn" (Bailey, Ciesniewski, Granger, Morey, and Willaughty) to Orville Hubbard (hereafter "OH") and City Council, ca. September 11, CR/1962-3; "Officials and Police at 7427 Kendal on September 2 and September 3, 1963," typescript, CR/Stanz; extensive local news coverage, from September 8 until September 21, in *Detroit News, Michigan Chronicle, Detroit Free Press,* and *Detroit Courier.* See also *DFP*, June 19, 1965.

5. *DFP*, August 15, 1963; letters to Hubbard (hereafter "letters") from Mr. and Mrs. Hutchins, ca. September 16, and Mrs. Frances Szczisniak, September 17, CR/Stanz, 1963; H. Bianchi, January 29, 1965, CR/BB.

6. Charles Abrams, *Forbidden Neighbors: A Study of Prejudice in Housing* (Port Washington, N.Y.: Kennikat Press, 1971); St. Clair Drake and Horace R. Cayton, *Black Metropolis: A Study of Negro Life in a Northern City,* rev. ed. (Chicago: University of Chicago Press, 1993); Arnold R. Hirsch, *Making the Second Ghetto: Race and Housing in Chicago, 1940–1960* (New York: Cambridge University Press, 1983); Thomas J. Sugrue, *The Origins of the Urban Crisis: Race and Inequality in Postwar Detroit* (Princeton: Princeton University Press, 1996); Becky M. Nicolaides, *My Blue Heaven: Life and Politics in the Working-Class Suburbs of Los Angeles, 1920–1965* (Chicago: University of Chicago Press, 2002); Wendell Pritchett, *Brownsville, Brooklyn: Blacks, Jews, and the Changing Face of the Ghetto* (Chicago: University of Chicago Press, 2002); Robert O. Self, *American Babylon: Race and the Struggle for Postwar Oakland* (Princeton: Princeton University Press, 2003); Amanda I. Seligman, *Block by Block: Neighborhoods and Public Policy on Chicago's West Side* (Chicago: University of Chicago Press, 2005).

7. By 1950, the nation's suburban population was expanding at ten times the rate of its urban population. Between 1950 and 1970, Chicago's suburban population increased by 117 percent, New York's by 195 percent, and Detroit's by 206 percent, while all three cities lost inhabitants. Even in the southwest, where urban populations continued to grow (often through annexation), suburban populations still grew more rapidly. See Howard P. Chudacoff and Judith E. Smith, *The Evolution of American Urban Society*, 4th ed. (Englewood Cliffs, NJ: Prentice-Hall, 1994), 260–61. By the late 1960s, a plurality of Americans lived in suburban regions for the first time.

8. Abrams, *Forbidden Neighbors*; Henry J. Aaron Jr., *Shelter and Subsidies: Who Benefits from Federal Housing Policies?* (Washington, D.C.: Brookings Institution, 1972); Mark I. Gelfand, *A Nation of Cities: The Federal Government and Urban America, 1933–1965* (New York: Oxford University Press, 1975); Kenneth Jackson, *Crabgrass Frontier: The Suburbanization of the United States* (New York: Oxford University Press, 1985); Douglas S. Massey and Nancy A. Denton, *American Apartheid: Segregation and the Making of the Underclass* (Cambridge, Mass.: Harvard University Press, 1993); Melvin L. Oliver and Thomas M. Shapiro, *Black Wealth, White Wealth: A New Perspective on Racial Inequality* (New York: Routledge, 1997); Arnold R. Hirsch, "'Containment' on the Home Front: Race and Federal Housing Policy from the New Deal to the Cold War," *Journal of Urban History* 26, no. 2 (January 2000): 158–80.

9. See Adolph Reed Jr., "Race and the Disruption of the New Deal Coalition," *Urban Affairs Quarterly* 27, no. 2 (1991): 326–33; Arnold R. Hirsch, "Massive Resistance in the Urban North: Trumball Park, Chicago, 1953–1966," *Journal of American History* 82 (1995): 522–50; Thomas J. Sugrue, "Crabgrass-Roots Politics: Race, Rights, and the Reaction against Liberalism in the Urban North, 1940–1964," *Journal of American History* 82 (1995): 551–78; Hirsch, *Making the Second Ghetto*; Sugrue, *Origins of the Urban Crisis*; Nicolaides, *My Blue Heaven*; Self, *American Babylon*. On urban flight and suburban politics in the American South, see Kevin M. Kruse, *White Flight: Atlanta and the Making of Modern Conservatism* (Princeton: Princeton University Press, 2005) and Matthew D. Lassiter, *The Silent Majority: Suburban Politics in the Sunbelt South* (Princeton: Princeton University Press, 2006).

10. Few scholars totally dismiss the influence of whites' racial attitudes, but an enormous body of work—especially in the social sciences—identifies presumably discrete "economic," "ecological," "political," and other variables as equally important or, quite often, as primary. Some prominent examples include Karl E. Taeuber and Alma F. Taeuber, *Negroes in Cities: Residential Segregation and Neighborhood Change* (New York: Atheneum, 1969); William H. Frey, "Central City White Flight: Racial and Nonracial Causes," *American Sociological Review* 44 (June 1979): 425–48; Lawrence Bobo, "Whites' Opposition to Busing: Symbolic Racism or Realistic Group Conflict?" *Journal of Personality and Social Psychology* 45 (1983): 1196–1210. A complicated variation of this tradition is Kenneth D. Durr, *Behind the Backlash: White Working-Class Politics in Baltimore, 1940–1980* (Chapel Hill: University of North Carolina Press, 2003). See Wendell Pritchett's important discussion of this scholarship in *Brownsville, Brooklyn*, chap. 5. Social scientific work on employment, workplace discrimination, and labor organizing generally makes similar distinctions. The most influential statement is William Julius Wilson, *The Declining Significance of Race: Blacks and Changing American Institutions* (Chicago: University of Chicago Press, 1978).

11. Prominent examples include Abrams, *Forbidden Neighbors*; Clement E. Vose, *Caucasians Only: The Supreme Court, the NAACP, and the Restrictive Covenant Cases* (Berkeley:

University of California Press, 1959); Davis McEntire, *Residence and Race: Final and Comprehensive Report to the Commission on Race and Housing* (Berkeley: University of California Press, 1960); Kenneth Clark, *Dark Ghetto: Dilemmas of Social Power* (Hanover, N.H.: University Press of New England, 1965); Mike Davis, *City of Quartz: Excavating the Future in Los Angeles* (London: Verso, 1990); Thomas Byrne Edsall and Mary D. Edsall, *Chain Reaction: The Impact of Race, Rights, and Taxes on American Politics* (New York: W. W. Norton, 1991); Jill Quadagno, *The Color of Welfare: How Racism Undermined the War on Poverty* (New York: Oxford University Press, 1994); Sugrue, *Origins of the Urban Crisis*; George Lipsitz, *The Possessive Investment in Whiteness: How White People Profit from Identity Politics* (Philadelphia: Temple University Press, 1998); Michael K. Brown, *Race, Money, and the American Welfare State* (Ithaca: Cornell University Press, 1999); Nicolaides, *My Blue Heaven*; Self, *American Babylon*; Lizabeth Cohen, *A Consumers' Republic: The Politics of Mass Consumption in Postwar America* (New York: Knopf, 2003); Ira Katznelson, *When Affirmative Action Was White: An Untold History of Racial Inequality in Twentieth-Century America* (New York: W. W. Norton, 2005).

12. See especially Sugrue, *Origins of the Urban Crisis*, Cohen, *Consumers' Republic*, Self, *American Babylon*, and Lassiter, *Silent Majority*.

13. The multidisciplinary scholarship on racial identity, racial conflict, and racism is enormous. Different fields have adopted unique languages and engage in discipline-specific debates over both method and terminology. (Psychologists, for example, have identified "five different ways of conceptualizing and operationalizing racial attitudes.") My critique cannot address the specifics of these debates but rather addresses the common tendency to compartmentalize "racial" variables and measure them in relation to presumably discrete, "nonracial" variables. Most work on racial conflict weighs the relative importance of racial, ethnic, economic, spatial, political, and other factors in whites' decisionmaking. In a representative formulation, Ronald Formisano argues that "racism added an ugly, frenetic charge of ferocity and violence" to white antibusing protests in 1970s Boston but that "as powerful as racism was, it formed only part of the story"; *Boston against Busing: Race, Class, and Ethnicity in the 1960s and 1970s* (Chapel Hill: University of North Carolina Press, 1991), 8. For introductions to debates in the social sciences, see David O. Sears et al., "Is It Really Racism? The Origins of White Americans' Opposition to Race-Targeted Policies," *Public Opinion Quarterly* 61, no. 1 (spring 1997): 16–53 (quoted on 19), and Howard Schuman, Charlotte Steeh, and Lawrence Bobo, *Racial Attitudes in America: Trends and Interpretations* (Cambridge, Mass.: Harvard University Press, 1985).

14. For example, Gelfand, *A Nation of Cities*, chap. 6, and Jackson, *Crabgrass Frontier*, chaps. 11 and 12. A notable exception is Kevin Fox Gotham, *Race, Real Estate, and Uneven Development: The Kansas City Experience, 1900–2000* (Albany: State University of New York Press, 2002).

15. See, for example, Joseph T. Howell, *Hard Living on Clay Street: Portraits of Blue Collar Families* (Garden City, N.Y.: Doubleday Anchor, 1973); Lewis M. Killian, *White Southerners* (New York: Random House, 1970); Todd Gitlin and Nanci Hollander, *Uptown: Poor Whites in Chicago* (New York: Harper & Row, 1970); Domenic J. Capeci, *Race Relations in Wartime Detroit: The Sojourner Truth Housing Controversy of 1942* (Philadelphia: Temple University Press, 1984). Stephen Grant Meyer defines racism as "an innate form of xenophobia" and argues that it is the persistence of white racism— not government policy or institutions—that best explains the endurance of residential segregation in the U.S. With time, he writes, "racial prejudice can diminish";

Meyer, *As Long As They Don't Move Next Door: Segregation and Racial Conflict in American Neighborhoods* (Lanham, Md.: Rowman & Littlefield Publishers, 2001), quoting 5.

16. The history of the white racial imagination in the U.S.—the story of how people of European descent came to define themselves and others as racial subjects—is explored in generations of work on the politics and ideology of race, slavery, immigration, science, and "whiteness." For an introduction, see the writings of Ida B. Wells, Ralph Ellison, Winthrop Jordon, Joel Kovel, George Frederickson, Alexander Saxton, Edmund Sears Morgan, Reginald Horsman, Derrick Bell, Stuart Hall, Paul Gilroy, Stephen J. Gould, James Baldwin, Michael Omi, Howard Winant, Cheryl Harris, Toni Morrison, David Roediger, David Goldberg, Ruth Frankenberg, Ian Haney Lopez, and Matthew Frye Jacobson. Good starting points include Alden T. Vaughan, "The Origins Debate: Slavery and Racism in Seventeenth-Century Virginia," in Vaughan, ed., *Roots of American Racism: Essays on the Colonial Experience* (New York: Oxford University Press, 1995): 136–75; David Eltis, "Europeans and the Rise and Fall of African Slavery in the Americas: An Interpretation," *The American Historical Review*, vol. 98, no. 5 (Dec. 1993), 1399–1423; David R. Roediger, ed., *Black on White: Black Writers on What It Means to Be White* (New York: Schocken, 1998); Michael Omi and Howard Winant, *Racial Formation in the United States from the 1960s to the 1990s*, 2nd ed. (New York and London: Routledge, 1994); and David Theo Goldberg, *Racist Culture: Philosophy and the Politics of Meaning* (Cambridge, Mass.: Blackwell Publishers, 1993). My thinking on racial formation—and its relationship to structural and institutional change—has been shaped by many writers who had little if anything to say about race, especially Pierre Bourdieu, Henri Lefebvre, Karl Marx, and Raymond Williams.

17. The Tay-Sachs "race" would be dominated by Jews of Ashkenazi origins, French Canadians living near the St. Lawrence River, and members of Louisiana's Cajun community but would still include people of all modern "racial groups." The blood-type and foot-size groups would be similarly "multiracial" by contemporary standards. Excellent introductions include Stephen J. Gould, *The Mismeasure of Man*, rev. ed. (New York: W. W. Norton, 1996); Audrey Smedley, *Race in North America: Origin and Evolution of a Worldview*, 2nd ed. (Boulder, Co.: Westview Press, 1999); and Jonathan Marks, *Human Biodiversity: Genes, Race, and History* (New York: Aldine de Gruyter, 1995).

18. For an excellent introduction, see the documentary (and companion Web site), *Race: The Power of an Illusion* (San Francisco: California Newsreel, 2003).

19. See David R. Roediger, *The Wages of Whiteness: Race and the Making of the American Working Class* (London: Verso, 1991) and *Working toward Whiteness: How America's Immigrants Became White* (New York: Basic Books, 2005); Cheryl L. Harris, "Whiteness as Property," *Harvard Law Review* 101 (June 1993): 1707; and Lipsitz, *Possessive Investment*. My own study explores one chapter in a long history of what Cheryl Harris calls a "racialized concept of property implemented by force and ratified by law"; "Whiteness as Property," 277. Whereas Harris is most interested in the commodification of humans—in white identity, itself, as a "property interest"—I focus on the racialized commodification of places, the ways in which specific kinds of property, places, and built environments are viewed as "white" or "nonwhite." Rather than a study of "whiteness as property," the focus here is on property that is viewed as racially white.

20. Thomas Lee Philpott, *The Slum and the Ghetto: Immigrants, Blacks, and Reformers in*

Chicago, 1880–1930, 2nd ed. (Belmont, Calif.: Wadsworth, 1991), 163, 165, 167–68, 201, 217 (quoting the *Defender* and *Property Owner's Journal*); James Grossman, *Land of Hope: Chicago, Black Southerners, and the Great Migration* (Chicago: University of Chicago Press, 1989), 169, 174–75 (quoting the *Chicago Tribune*); Drake and Cayton, *Black Metropolis*, 116; Chicago Commission on Race Relations, *The Negro in Chicago: A Study of Race Relations and a Race Riot in 1919* (New York: Arno Press, 1968), 118–29, 453 (citing *Property Owner's Journal* and speakers), chap. 9 (citing interviews on 460–75); Allan H. Spear, *Black Chicago: The Making of a Negro Ghetto, 1890–1920* (Chicago: University of Chicago Press, 1967), 211–12, 216–17. The CCRR report provides the best introduction to northern whites' views on blacks in the years following World War I. The vast majority of white respondents insisted in their interviews that "Negroes possess distinguishing traits of both mentality and character" and that blacks were "characterized by distinctly inferior mentality, deficient moral sense, shiftlessness, good nature, and a happy disposition." Whites' prejudice, explained one interviewee, was "based on the relative inferiority of the Negro race." "I would feel more hopeful of the overcoming of the prejudice through more intimate contact with Negroes," the speaker continued, "if the difference between Negroes and white men were not so fundamental." A small number of whites insisted upon blacks' fundamental equality, but the far more common progressive stance held that black difference and backwardness was the product of past mistreatment, or what one respondent called their "hinderment."

For an excellent exploration of turn-of-the century white neighborhood organizing, see Margaret Garb, *City of American Dreams: A History of Home Ownership and Housing Reform in Chicago, 1871–1919* (Chicago: University of Chicago Press, 2005), chap. 7. On the white-owned media's depiction of blacks, see *Negro in Chicago*, chap. 10. In Kenwood and Hyde Park alone, there were 58 bombings against blacks and sympathetic whites between July 1917 and March 1921.

21. *DFP*, November 19, 20, 22, and 25, 1925; Levine, *Internal Combustion*, 153–57, 159–60, 183–84; Lilienthal, "Has the Negro the Right to Self-Defense?" 724–25; Boyle, *Arc of Justice*, 106–7, 151, 333 (quoting Darrow). In his closing argument, Darrow stated that members of the Waterworks Improvement Association "honestly believe that the blacks are an inferior race." Meanwhile, the *Free Press* trial coverage appeared adjacent to articles about the infamous "Rhinelander" case in New York, in which a white man sought annulment from his wife after learning that she had "mixed" blood. On the Rhinelander trial, see Earl Lewis and Heidi Ardizzone, *Love on Trial: An American Scandal in Black and White* (New York: W. W. Norton, 2002). Vollington Bristol had owned the Detroit property for some time but was forced to move in that summer because white renters were consistently delinquent with monthly payments. He could not afford to leave the property vacant.

Excellent introductions to the history of white racial violence in the late nineteenth and early twentieth centuries include Ida B. Wells-Barnett, *On Lynchings: Southern Horrors, A Red Record, Mob Rule in New Orleans* (New York: Arno Press, 1969); Walter Francis White, *Rope and Faggot: A Biography of Judge Lynch* (New York: Arno Press, 1969); Chicago Commission on Race Relations, *Negro in Chicago*; Elliott M. Rudwick, *Race Riot at East St. Louis, July 2, 1917* (Carbondale: Southern Illinois University Press, 1964); William M. Tuttle Jr., *Race Riot: Chicago in the Red Summer of 1919* (New York: Atheneum, 1970); and Herbert Shapiro, *White Violence and Black Response: From Reconstruction to Montgomery* (Amherst: University of Massachusetts Press, 1988).

22. Rose Helper, *Racial Policies and Practices of Real Estate Brokers* (Minneapolis: University of Minnesota Press, 1969), 201; Philpott, *The Slum and the Ghetto*, 160, 165, 185, 191–92, 212, and Appendix A. See also Garb, *City of American Dreams*, chap. 7 and Jeffrey M. Hornstein, *A Nation of Realtors: A Cultural History of the Twentieth-Century American Middle Class* (Durham: Duke University Press, 2005), chap. 3.

23. CCRR, *Negro in Chicago*, 121–22 (citing *Property Owners' Journal*); Philpott, *The Slum and the Ghetto*, 193 (quoting CREB); Spear, *Black Chicago*, 220; Harold Black, "Restrictive Covenants in Relation to Segregated Negro Housing in Detroit" (master's thesis, Wayne State University, 1947), 29 (quoting Warner Subdivision Agreement); Richard T. Ely, *Outlines of Economics* (New York: Macmillan, 1914), 61–62. Elsewhere Ely described agricultural tenancy as best suited for "the lower strata" groups "somewhat deficient in economic qualities. The Negroes of the South furnish an illustration"; Richard T. Ely and Charles J. Galpin, "Tenancy in an Ideal System of Land-ownership," *American Economic Review* 9, no. 1, Supplement (March 1919): 180–212 (citing 182–83).

   Some homeowners were already adopting the "economist" argument, but the evidence suggests that it was less tenable, and far less coherent, at a time when racial science defined blacks as unassimilable. For example, compare Philpott, *The Slum and the Ghetto*, 169–70, 196 with the interview of L. M. Smith, cited in Carl Sandburg, *The Chicago Race Riots, July 1919* (New York: Harcourt, Brace, & World, 1969), 14.

24. Letters from Mrs. Edna Flannery, February 23, CR/CNS, 1–24; Martin Kosten, May 12, 1962, with form letter enclosed, CR/1962–3; George Buckenhizer, September 18, CR/Stanz, 1963.

25. When John Bileck of Detroit learned that some Dearborn residents were critical of Hubbard, he invited them "to exchange property with the undersigned, provided they are home owners." Letters from Mr. and Mrs. Hutchins, ca. September 16, 1963, George Buckenhizer, September 18, anonymous, September 20, and John G. Bileck, October 23, CR/Stanz, 1963; John J. Richards, n.d., and "A St. Claire Shore Citizen," January 30, 1965, CR/BB; Jeff Brescoe, September 17, CR/1964; "Proud Citizen of Dearborn" to "editor" (cc OH), February 17, CR/CNS, 1–24.

26. Virginia Fox to Thomas Poindexter (cc OH), April 18, CR/Stanz, 1964.

27. Letters from "A New York State Resident," February 2, CR/CNS, 1–24; Ralph A. Thompson, for Grandvale Civic Association, to Detroit Common Council, April 1, 1963, CR/1962–3; Thomas Poindexter quoted in summary/transcript of Dearborn Community Council meeting, typescript, April 17, 1964, CR/Stanz, DCC.

28. Contemporary commentators first popularized this image of the "typical" suburb. William H. Whyte described the "great package suburbs" and "curving superblocks" that represented "the end of a long road from the city wards to middle-class respectability"; *The Organization Man* (New York: Simon & Schuster, 1956), 295. To Herbert J. Gans, the Levittowns were "undoubtedly the prototype" and their residents were "typical of America"; *The Levittowners: Ways of Life and Politics in a New Suburban Community* (New York: Pantheon Books, 1967), v–vii.

29. Most writers argue "for" or "against" suburbia by starting with assumptions about the size and design of its neighborhoods and homes, then presenting a dichotomy, often simplistic, between urban and suburban settings and lifestyles—between the supposedly heterogeneous city center and what William Sharpe and Leonard Wallock refer to as the "typical commuter suburbs of the 1950's"; "Bold New City or Built-Up 'Burb? Redefining Contemporary Suburbia," *American Quarterly* 46, no. 1 (March 1994):

1–2. Writers often attribute the formation of "suburban" political attitudes and dispositions to a material suburbia assumed to be quite homogeneous. The classic statements are Louis Harris, *Is There a Republican Majority? Political Trends, 1952–1956* (New York: Harper, 1954), and Whyte, *Organization Man*. In his celebrated 1958 study of "suburban political ideology," Robert C. Wood argues that suburban residents were unwilling to abandon their "pre-modern" political arrangements—in other words, their defense of local autonomy—because of their misguided celebration of "provincial" life. Suburbia, he writes, is the result of a "theory of community and a theory of local government . . . There is no economic reason for its existence and there is no technological basis for its support. There is only the stubborn conviction of the majority of suburbanites that it ought to exist"; *Suburbia: Its People and Their Politics* (Boston: Houghton Mifflin, 1958), v, 9–12, 18–19, 54–55. See also Scott A. Greer, *Governing the Metropolis* (New York: Wiley, 1962), 85; Stephanie Coontz, *The Way We Never Were: American Families and the Nostalgia Trap* (New York: Basic Books, 1992), 24, 28; Clifford E. Clark, *The American Family Home: 1800–1960* (Chapel Hill: University of North Carolina Press, 1986), esp. chap. 7; idem, "Ranch House Suburbia: Ideals and Realities," in Lary May, ed., *Recasting America: Culture and Politics in the Age of Cold War* (Chicago: University of Chicago Press, 1989), 171–91. Essential reading is Frederick M. Wirt et al., *On the City's Rim: Politics and Policy in Suburbia* (Lexington, Mass.: Heath, 1972). See also Howard Pack and Janet Rothenberg Pack, "Metropolitan Fragmentation and Suburban Homogeneity," *Urban Studies* 14 (1977): 191–201.

30. See especially William Dobriner, *Class in Suburbia* (Englewood Cliffs, N.J.: Prentice-Hall, 1963), 13–15, 23–24 (the line between city and suburb, noted Dobriner, was sometimes "more visible on a map than to the eye."); Bennett Berger, *Working-Class Suburb: A Study of Auto Workers in Suburbia* (Berkeley: University of California Press, 1960); Louis H. Masotti and Jeffrey K. Hadden, eds., *The Urbanization of the Suburbs* (Beverly Hills, Calif.: Sage Publications, 1973). Important recent studies include Richard Harris, "Chicago's Other Suburbs," *Geographical Review* 84 (1994): 394–410; Richard Harris and Robert Lewis, "Constructing a Fault(y) Zone: Misrepresentations of American Cities and Suburbs, 1900–1950," *Annals of the Association of American Geographers* 88 (1998): 622–39; Nicolaides, *My Blue Heaven*; and Self, *American Babylon*.

31. Of course many suburbs *were* geographically isolated and architecturally quite distinct, but this was far from universal, especially in the early postwar years. Even authors well aware of the variety of suburban forms occasionally portray whites' investment in the physical suburb without differentiation. See, for example, Davis, *City of Quartz*, chap. 3; Jackson, *Crabgrass Frontier*, chap. 13, and 289–90; and Jonathan Rieder, *Canarsie: The Jews and Italians of Brooklyn against Liberalism* (Cambridge, Mass.: Harvard University Press, 1985), chap. 1.

32. Sidney Fine, *Sit Down: The General Motors Strike of 1936–1937* (Ann Arbor: University of Michigan Press, 1969); Dan Georgakas and Marvin Surkin, *Detroit, I Do Mind Dying: A Study in Urban Revolution* (New York: St. Martin's Press, 1975); August Meier and Elliot Rudwick, *Black Detroit and the Rise of the UAW* (New York: Oxford University Press, 1979); Richard W. Thomas, *Life for Us Is What We Make It: Building Black Community in Detroit, 1915–1945* (Bloomington: Indiana University Press, 1992); Kevin Boyle, *The UAW and the Heyday of American Liberalism, 1945–1968* (Ithaca: Cornell University Press, 1995); Sugrue, *Origins of the Urban Crisis*, 23, table 1.1; Nelson Lichtenstein, *Walter Reuther: The Most Dangerous Man in Detroit* (Urbana: University

of Illinois Press, 1997); Victoria W. Wolcott, *Remaking Respectability: African American Women in Interwar Detroit* (Chapel Hill: University of North Carolina Press, 2001); Heather Ann Thompson, *Whose Detroit? Politics, Labor, and Race in a Modern American City* (Ithaca: Cornell University Press, 2004).

33. Joe T. Darden et al., *Detroit: Race and Uneven Development* (Philadelphia: Temple University Press, 1987), 22–26 (table 2.3), 69; Barry Bluestone and Bennett Harrison, *The Deindustrialization of America: Plant Closings, Community Abandonment, and the Dismantling of Basic Industry* (New York: Basic Books, 1982), chap. 5; Sugrue, *Origins of the Urban Crisis*, esp. 17–18, 24–28, 95–105, 126, 128–33, 140–41; Roger W. Lotchin, *Fortress California, 1910–1961: From Warfare to Welfare* (New York: Oxford University Press, 1992); on income differentials between Detroit and its near suburbs, see *Emergence and Growth of an Urban Region: The Developing Urban Detroit Area*, vol. 1: *Analysis* (Detroit: Detroit Edison, 1966), 225.

34. Fifty-three percent of the Dearborn homes standing in 1960 had been built since 1940, the vast majority after World War II. See *CC*, 1962, table 6; *PODU*, 1956, 2, 4 and 1962, 3–4 (copies in MHC); *CC*, 1949, table A-2; USBC, *Sixteenth Census of the United States: 1940, Housing*, vol. 2, *General Characteristics*, pt. 3, *Iowa-Montana* (Washington, D.C.: GPO, 1943), table 5; USBC, *Seventeenth Decennial Census of the United States: Census of Housing: 1950*, vol. 1, *General Characteristics*, pt. 4, *Michigan–New York* (Washington, D.C.: GPO, 1953), table 17; *CC*, 1952, table 4; USBC, *United States Censuses of Population and Housing: 1960 (Census Tracts: Detroit, Mich. Standard Metropolitan Statistical Area)* (Washington, D.C.: GPO, 1961), table H-1. Compare the conclusions in City Plan Commission, "The Population Base of Dearborn" (unpublished report), 1950, 10, DHM, City, Departments, "City Plan."

It is difficult to gauge construction in the Royal Oak Township municipalities with the precision of figures for Dearborn because several cities within the township incorporated between 1940 and 1960 (and because data on demolitions is unavailable). Figures cited here are based on a comparison of decennial data, annual construction estimates, and 1960 measures of housing built "by period." All construction figures for Royal Oak City are estimates and are rounded off.

35. Of the 25,556 single-family homes standing in Dearborn in 1959, almost 70 percent had been built since 1940. See USBC, *1940, Housing*, vol.2, pt.3, tables 5, 22, 23, 27; USBC, *1950, Housing*, vol. 1, pt. 4, tables 17, 24; *CC*, 1962, table 6; USBC, *U.S. Census of Housing: 1960, City Blocks: Dearborn, Mich.* (Washington, D.C.: GPO, 1961), table 1; USBC, *Population and Housing, 1960, Detroit SMSA*, table H-1; "Tabulation of Structures on Subdivided Property—City of Dearborn," March 1958, and "Tabulation . . .," March 1959 (Office of the City Plan Commission, mimeos) and "Period of Construction," 1972, DHM, City, Departments, "City Plan"; USBC, *Construction Statistics, 1915–1964* (Washington, D.C.: GPO, 1966), 16, table 5; Harry Harold, CBS interview with Orville Hubbard, March 1965, transcript in OHP, "Civil Rights Commission." On national patterns of residential segregation, see Taeuber and Taeuber, *Negroes in Cities*, and Massey and Denton, *American Apartheid*.

36. Among those sixteen communities were Royal Oak Township, Troy, Grosse Pointe, Dearborn, Hazel Park, Ferndale, Madison Heights, Southfield, Redford Township, and Allen Park. In 1970, Warren's workforce was 30 percent black, but its homeowners only 1 percent. The rate of black suburbanization grew slightly during the postwar decades in northern metropolitan regions but took place almost exclusively in municipalities that were traditionally black and highly segregated. See Darden et al., *Detroit*, 140–42; Andrew Wiese, *Places of Their Own: African American Sub-*

urbanization in the Twentieth Century (Chicago: University of Chicago Press, 2004), chaps. 5–6.

37. Homeownership rates for suburban blacks were much higher. Massey and Denton, *American Apartheid,* 53; Gertrude Sipperly Fish, "Housing Policy during the Great Depression," in Fish, ed., *The Story of Housing* (New York: Macmillan, 1979), 226; Wiese, *Places of Their Own.*

38. At the same time, numerous forces were easing immigrants' acceptance in "white" organizations and, some evidence suggests, neighborhoods. See the excellent discussions in Roediger, *Working toward Whiteness,* esp. 145–56, 170–71, and Abrams, *Forbidden Neighbors,* 158ff. For a remarkable first-hand account, see Alfred Kazin, *A Walker in the City* (New York: MJF Books, 1997).

39. HOLC/FHLBB Security Map, Greater Detroit Michigan (1939); "Summary of Economic, Real Estate and Mortgage Survey and Security Area Descriptions of Greater Detroit, Michigan" (March 1, 1939); Area Description forms for C-118, C-107, and D-39: all in RG 195, FHLBB/CSF, Box 18, "Greater Detroit Michigan Security Maps and Area Descriptions."

40. Percentage foreign stock in other municipalities: Madison Heights, 24.7; Southfield, 36.1; Hazel Park, 26.6; Detroit, 32.1. Many of these immigrants were first generation; for example, the 1950 census counted 2,238 Polish-born, 2,962 Canadian-born, and 1,847 Italian-born residents in Dearborn. See USBC, *Population and Housing, 1960, Detroit SMSA,* table P-1; USBC, *United States Census of Population: 1950* (Washington, D.C.: GPO, 1952), vol. 3, chap. 17, table 1; Albert M. Ammerman, "A Sociological Survey of Dearborn" (master's thesis, School of Education, University of Michigan, 1940), 20, 22. A 1948 study by the Dearborn Plan Commission reported that 52.9 percent of the residents in southeast Dearborn and 29.6 percent in the northeast were immigrants, compared with 15 percent in the western tracts. Polish immigrants congregated in the east end, 80 percent of the Italians and half of the Canadians lived in the northeast, and 88.2 percent of the Syrian-born, 56.2 percent of the Rumanian-born, and most of the Greek, Asian, and Mexican-born lived in Dearborn's south; Ralph E. Eccles, "The Community of Dearborn," typescript (May 9, 1961), 34–40 (copy in DHM).

41. Important recent exceptions are Nicolaides, *My Blue Heaven* and Self, *American Babylon.*

42. Prior to 1960, about 80 percent of the residential construction in the tricounty suburbs took place in Oakland County (excluding Pontiac) and "out-Wayne" County (here, all Wayne County territory excluding Detroit, Hamtramck, and Highland Park), and within these counties it was heavily concentrated in the 'first generation" suburbs. During the 1940s, about four housing units were built in the first-generation suburbs for every one built in second-generation communities such as Livonia, Southfield, and Troy. In the 1950s, the suburbs within the original Royal Oak Township boundary saw construction of 34.3 percent of Oakland County's new homes, compared with 9.3 percent in Troy and Southfield combined. See USBC, *Population and Housing, 1960, Detroit SMSA,* table H-1; USBC, *United States Census of Housing: 1960, City Blocks: Troy, Mich.* (Washington, D.C.: GPO, 1961), table 1; *CC,* 1962, table 6.

43. Michigan Planning Commission, *A Study of Subdivision Development in the Detroit Metropolitan Area* (Lansing, Michigan, June 1939), secs. 2, 3, tables 5, 6, 8; Harold W. Lautner, *Subdivision Regulations: An Analysis of Land Subdivision Control Practices* (Chicago: Public Administration Service, 1941), esp. 56–63, 155–71; real estate advertise-

ments ("Going Over the Top! Dearborn-Warren Subdivision No. 2," "A Beautiful New Homeland Unfolds: Our Greater Woodward," "Buy in the Path of Detroit's Greatest Growth: Eastwood Gardens," and "Wayne Watch: Increasing Valuations") in *DFP*, November 22, 1925; Dearborn subdivision brochures, DHM; Ammerman, "Sociological Survey," 107–8; Nicolaides, *My Blue Heaven*, chap. 1. See also Alexander James Field, "Uncontrolled Land Development and the Duration of the Depression in the United States," *Journal of Economic History* 52, no. 4 (December 1992): 785–805. Of the lots platted in out-Wayne County and Oakland County in the 100 years prior to 1937, over 86 percent and 82.7 percent, respectively, were recorded during this twelve-year speculative frenzy. As late as 1925, the *Detroit Free Press* instructed "people who are planning to make money in . . . real estate" to "look toward the outlying sections of the city"; "Suburbs Held City's Future," *DFP*, November 22, 1925.

44. Michigan Planning Commission, *Subdivision Development*, 11, 15; J. Carlton Starbuck, "Oakland County, Michigan: A Statistical History of a Detroit Suburban County," unpublished report, Oakland County Planning Commission, 1967, p. 242 (copy at OCPC); "City Survey, Metropolitan Detroit, Michigan . . . June 30, 1939," RG 195, FHLBB/CSF, Box 17, "Greater Detroit Michigan—Re Survey Report," 31. See also Greg Hise, *Magnetic Los Angeles: Planning the Twentieth-Century Metropolis* (Baltimore: John Hopkins University Press, 1997), 26–30.

45. For an excellent description of residential patterns in Detroit, see Sugrue, *Origins of the Urban Crisis*, 20–23. On the region's geography, see *Emergence and Growth*, vol. 1, pt. 4.

46. Berkley incorporated (from Royal Oak Township) in 1932. Each "section" is one square mile, or 640 acres. Based on comparison of original plat maps, real estate maps (1956), and cadastral maps (1960); for section 18, see plat maps in Real Estate Data, *Real Estate Atlas of Oakland County, Michigan* (1956), 36, 30-10, 35-10, 15-8, 16-5, 15-35, Assessors Plat 49-18, 28-18, 24-10, and 29-19 (copy at MHC); "Southeast Oakland County, 1960" (cadastral map, copy at OCPC). For Dearborn, see DHM, "Dearborn Subdivisions: Abstracts"; plat maps and aerial photographs in DHM, maps, "Dearborn-Springwells, 1910–1919," "Dearborn, Village of, Insurance Maps," 1921 and 1924, and "Dearborn, City of, 1940–1949," "Dearborn, City of, 1950–1959"; Sanborn Maps and "Plat Maps of the City of Dearborn" (1938), DHM, "Dearborn Subdivisions." Gwendolyn Wright, *Building the Dream: A Social History of Housing in America* (Cambridge, Mass.: MIT Press, 1981), 203–4; Clark, *American Family Home*, 228; Sugrue, *Origins of the Urban Crisis*, 20–23, 266.

47. The earlier wave of speculation had a limited impact on these outer suburban regions. Michigan Planning Commission, *Subdivision Development*, 16, table 5; Oakland County 4-H Leaders Association, *Farm Plat Book: Oakland County, Michigan* (Rockford, Ill.: Rockford Map Publishers, 1956); Real Estate Data, *Real Estate Atlas* (1956); Oakland County Cooperative Extension Service, *Triennial Atlas and Plat Book, Oakland County, Michigan* (Rockford, Ill.: Rockford Map Publishers, 1970); Real Estate Data, *Real Estate Atlas of Oakland County, Michigan* (1977); "Southeast Oakland County, 1960" (baseline map, copy at OCPC).

48. "When Old Landmarks Go . . . ," *DT*, October 29, 1954.

49. "Hazel Park: A Suburban City That Is Growing Up," *Inside Michigan*, March 1953, 35–38; sewage work depicted in advertisement for Concrete Pipe Association of Michigan, *Michigan Municipal Review*, May 1951 (back cover); aerial photographs of Dearborn from 1940s and 1950s by Aerial Surveys, Cleveland Ohio, in DHM, photo files, Dearborn, "Aerial Views."

50. *DT,* February 4 and 18, 1949, September 10, 1948. The developments were a half-mile south of the city's border with Birmingham.

51. FHA, *Underwriting Manual: Underwriting and Valuation Procedure under Title II of the National Housing Act* (Washington, D.C.: GPO, 1936), pt. 2, secs. 229 and 233. See also sec. 266 (on keeping "incompatible racial element[s]" out of the schools) and sec. 284(3)(g–h). If a floor plan for new construction met FHA approval, an agency stamp indicated that structures "shall be located on the plot so as to comply with all restrictions" and all "F.H.A. property standards." Examples in RG 31, CFH, 1934–38, Box 8. The best introductions to FHA policy and its long-range impacts are Jackson, *Crabgrass Frontier,* chap. 11; Massey and Denton, *American Apartheid;* Oliver and Shapiro, *Black Wealth, White Wealth.* For a detailed discussion of the debate over federal subsidy and the impact of federal intervention on postwar sprawl see chap. 3 of this study.

52. Quote is from Jackson, *Crabgrass Frontier,* 213.

53. Hirsch, *Making the Second Ghetto;* Sugrue, *Origins of the Urban Crisis;* Pritchett, *Brownsville;* Seligman, *Block by Block;* Kruse, *White Flight.*

54. Nicolaides, *My Blue Heaven;* Self, *American Babylon;* Lassiter, *The Silent Majority.*

55. Royal Oak and Troy Townships were two of the six Oakland County areas that provided upwards of 75 percent of Oakland County's Democratic vote between 1940 and 1964. Dearborn consistently voted Democratic throughout these years. Overall, residents of Oakland and out-Wayne suburbs split their vote between Democratic and Republican candidates between 1940 and 1964. Districts that tended to favor Democrats were Warren, Dearborn, Dearborn Township, Clawson, Ferndale, and Royal Oak Township. Districts leaning Republican were Royal Oak and Southfield. See *Michigan Manual,* 1940–64.

CHAPTER TWO

1. Michael N. Danielson, *The Politics of Exclusion* (New York: Columbia University Press, 1976), 15; Jon C. Teaford, *City and Suburb: The Political Fragmentation of Metropolitan America, 1850–1970* (Baltimore: John Hopkins University Press, 1976), chaps. 2 and 3; National Municipal League, Committee on Metropolitan Government, *The Government of Metropolitan Areas in the United States* (1930; reprint, New York: Arno Press, 1974), 68, and table VI.

2. Rodney L. Mott, *Home Rule for America's Cities* (Chicago: American Municipal Association, 1949), appendix 1, 58–59, 63–68; Ferris Lewis, *State and Local Government in Michigan,* 3rd ed., 2nd rev. ed. (Hillsdale, Mich.: Hillsdale Educational Publishers, 1964), 160–61; State of Michigan, *Laws Relating to the Incorporation of Cities* (Lansing, Mich.: Wynkoop Hallenbeck Crawford, 1909); Act 279, P.A. 1909, sec. 117.3 ff., in State of Michigan, *Laws Relating to the Incorporation and General Powers of Cities* (Lansing, Mich.: Wynkoop Hallenbeck Crawford, 1956), 115–53; Teaford, *City and Suburb,* 6–7; J. A. Chandler, "The United States of America," in J. A. Chandler, ed., *Local Government in Liberal Societies: An Introductory Survey* (London: Routledge, 1993), quoted on 140.

3. Teaford, *City and Suburb,* chap. 5; Danielson, *Politics of Exclusion,* 17; Kenneth Jackson, *Crabgrass Frontier: The Suburbanization of the United States* (New York: Oxford University Press, 1985), chap. 8 and 172–86. On public support for incorporation as a cost-saving measure, see Stephen Hoffman, "'A Plan of Quality': The Development of Mt. Lebanon, a 1920's Automobile Suburb," *Journal of Urban History* 18, no. 2 (1992), esp. 144–48.

4. Danielson, *Politics of Exclusion*, 16–17; National Municipal League, *Government of Metropolitan Areas*, 8 (table I), 18 (table II); State of Michigan, "Incorporated Cities in Michigan," *Michigan Manual* (1967/68), 335–55; Richard Stauber, *New Cities in America: A Census of Municipal Incorporations in the United States, 1950–1960* (Lawrence, Kan.: Governmental Research Center, University of Kansas, 1965); James M. Leonard and Lent D. Upson, *The Government of the Detroit Metropolitan Area*, Michigan Commission of Inquiry into County, Township and School District Government (Michigan Local Government Series, May 1, 1934), 12–13; State of Michigan, *Laws Relating to Incorporation and General Powers of Villages* (Lansing, Mich.: Robert Smith Co, 1925). For good introductions, see Claude Tharp, *Michigan Cities and Villages: Organization and Administration*, Michigan Pamphlets, no. 23 (Ann Arbor: University of Michigan Press, 1951); and idem, *A Manual of Village Government in Michigan*, rev. ed. (Ann Arbor: Bureau of Government, 1957).

5. Lawrence Veiller, *Housing Reform: A Hand-Book for Practical Use in American Cities* (New York: Charities Publication Committee, 1910); Frank M. Stewart, *A Half Century of Municipal Reform: The History of the National Municipal League* (Los Angeles: University of California Press, 1950); Harvey A. Kantor, "Benjamin C. Marsh and the Fight over Population Congestion," *Journal of the American Institute of Planners* 40, no. 6 (1974), 423. On early CCP promotional efforts, see Daniel T. Rodgers, *Atlantic Crossings: Social Politics in a Progressive Age* (Cambridge, Mass.: Belknap Press of Harvard University, 1998), 181–82.

6. Marc A. Weiss, *The Rise of the Community Builders: The American Real Estate Industry and Urban Land Planning* (New York: Columbia University Press, 1987), 9–10, 13, 80–86; Richard E. Fogelsong, *Planning the Capitalist City: The Colonial Era to the 1920's* (Princeton: Princeton University Press, 1986), chaps. 3–6; Mel Scott, *American City Planning Since 1890* (Berkeley: University of California Press, 1969), chaps. 1 and 2, esp. pp. 74–76; John L. Hancock, "Planners in the Changing American City, 1900–1940," *Journal of the American Institute of Planners* 33, no. 5 (September 1967), 290–304; Robert B. Fairbanks, "From Better Dwellings to Better Neighborhoods: The Rise and Fall of the First National Housing Movement," in John F. Bauman, Roger Biles, and Kristin Szylvian, eds., *From Tenements to Taylor Homes: In Search of an Urban Housing Policy in Twentieth-Century America* (University Park: Pennsylvania State University Press, 2000), 21–42; Kenneth Baar, "The National Movement to Halt the Spread of Multifamily Housing, 1890–1926," *Journal of the American Planning Association* 58, no. 1 (winter 1992), 39–40 (citing Bender and Ward); Benjamin C. Marsh, *An Introduction to City Planning: Democracy's Challenge to the American City* (1909; reprint, New York: Arno Press, 1974), esp. 28–30 (quoting 28), 146–48 (reproducing Wisconsin legislation); Kantor, "Benjamin C. Marsh," 422–23; Clinton Rogers Woodruff, "Introduction," in John Nolen, ed., *City Planning: A Series of Papers Presenting the Essential Elements of a City Plan*, 2nd ed. (New York: D. Appleton, 1929), xi–xii. Much of the energy for planning was generated locally, by concerned citizens and realtors. See Dolores Hayden, *Building Suburbia, 1820–2000* (New York: Pantheon Books, 2003), 120; Alison Isenberg, *Downtown America: A History of the Place and People Who Made It* (Chicago: University of Chicago Press, 2004), chap. 2; and Jeffrey M. Hornstein, *A Nation of Realtors: A Cultural History of the Twentieth-Century American Middle Class* (Durham, N.C.: Duke University Press, 2005), chaps. 1 and 2.

7. Kantor, "Benjamin C. Marsh," 422–24, 427 (citing Marsh); Scott, *American City Planning*, 76, 427; Fogelsong, *Planning the Capitalist City*, 3, 201, 207–8, 217–18; Seymour I. Toll, *Zoned America* (New York: Grossman Publishers, 1969), 120–26;

Garrett Power, "The Advent of Zoning," *Planning Perspectives* 4, no. 1 (1989): 1–13. On the impact of the German zoning model on the NCCP, see Frank Backus Williams "Public Control of Private Real Estate: Eminent Domain and Police Power," in John Nolen, ed., *City Planning: A Series of Papers Presenting the Essential Elements of a City Plan* (New York: D. Appleton & Co., 1915), 48–87.

8.   George B. Ford, "The City Scientific,' *Proceedings of the Fifth National Conference on City Planning* (Cambridge, Mass.: University Press, 1913), 31–41; Nolen, ed., *City Planning* (1915), xx–xxi; Marsh, *Introduction to City Planning*, 123–36; Keith D. Revell, "The Road to *Euclid v. Ambler*: City Planning, State-Building, and the Changing Scope of the Police Power," *Studies in American Political Development* 13, no. 1 (spring 1999), 74. Olmsted's response to Ford reveals the tensions between the late nineteenth- and early twentieth-century visions of city planning (*Proceedings*, 41–42). See also Isenberg, *Downtown America*, chap. 2.

9.   Robert Walker, *The Planning Function in Urban Government* (Chicago: University of Chicago Press, 1950), 22; Scott, *American City Planning*, 97–100, 123–24; *Proceedings of the Second National Conference on City Planning* (Cambridge, Mass.: University Press, 1910), 67–91; *Proceedings of the Fourth National Conference on City Planning* (Boston: The Conference, 1912), 173–88; *Proceedings of the Sixth National Conference on City Planning* (Cambridge, Mass.: University Press, 1914), 92–111; *Proceedings of the Eighth National Conference on City Planning* (New York, 1916), 119–58; *Proceedings of the Ninth National Conference on City Planning* (New York, 1917), 168–214.

10.   Weiss, *Community Builders*, chaps. 2–3, pp. 57–58; Hornstein, *Nation of Realtors*, chap. 2. On Marsh's decision to leave the NCCP, see Kantor, "Benjamin C. Marsh." On the local growth machines that helped give rise to NAREB, see Hayden, *Building Suburbia*, 94–96.

11.   *Proceedings* (1910), vii; *Proceedings* (1913), 266; Weiss, *Community Builders*, 54–58, 66, 180 n. 5. On the importance of government intervention, see Flavel Shurtleff, Esq., "Six Years of City Planning in the United States," and Robert H. Whitten, "Constitution and Powers of a City Planning Authority," in *Proceedings of the Seventh National Conference on City Planning* (Cambridge, Mass.: University Press, 1915), 33–41, 135–43.

12.   *Proceedings* (1915), 71–106.

13.   *Proceedings* (1910). vi; "Popularizing the City Planning Principle," *Proceedings* (1912), 168–72; *Proceedings* (1916), 273–75; J. C. Nichols, "Financial Effect of Good Planning in Land Subdivision," *Proceedings* (1916), 91–106; Weiss, *Community Builders*, 56–66; Kantor, "Benjamin C. Marsh," 428; Thomas S. Ingersoll, "How the Real Estate Man Can Help," *Proceedings* (1917), 139–40. Ingersoll identified himself as the "personal representative of [NAREB president] Haas." See also Hancock, "Planners in the Changing American City," 290–303. Compare the discussion in Pearl Janet Davies, *Real Estate in American History* (Washington, D.C.: Public Affairs Press, 1958), 65, 73–74.

14.   J. C. Nichols, "Financial Effect"; Weiss, *Community Builders*, 64–66. Nichols greatly simplified Nolen's argument about planning and land values. See Nolen's discussions of land subdivision, profit, and the public good; *City Planning* (1915), 35–44.

   For good introductions to the discriminatory mechanisms of early zoning ordinances, see R. Babcock and F. P. Bosselman, *Exclusionary Zoning: Land Use Regulation in the 1970s* (New York: Praeger, 1973); Michelle J. White, "Fiscal Zoning in Fragmented Metropolitan Areas," in Edwin S. Mills and Wallace Oates, eds., *Fiscal Zoning and Land Use Controls: The Economic Issues* (Lexington, Mass.: D. C. Heath, 1975),

31–100; Ann Markusen, "Class and Urban Social Expenditure: A Marxist Theory of Metropolitan Government," in William K. Tabb and Larry Sawers, eds., *Marxism and the Metropolis* (New York: Oxford University Press, 1984).

15. Hon. Lawson Purdy, "Districting and Zoning of Cities," *Proceedings* (1917), 170–71; Walker, *Planning Function*, 22–23.

16. See Richard H. Chused, "*Euclid*'s Historical Imagery," *Case Western Reserve Law Review* 51, no. 4 (summer 2001): 597–617; Power, "Advent of Zoning"; Christopher Silver, *Twentieth-Century Richmond: Planning, Politics, and Race* (Knoxville: University of Tennessee Press, 1984); Garrett Power, "Advocates at Cross Purposes: The Briefs on Behalf of Zoning in the Supreme Court," *Journal of Supreme Court History* 2 (1997): 79–87; and Raphael Fischler, "The Metropolitan Dimension of Early Zoning: Revisiting the 1916 New York City Ordinance." *Journal of the American Planning Association* 64 (spring 1998), 170–88. For biographies of major contributors to early zoning, see William M. Randle, "Professors, Reformers, Bureaucrats, and Cronies: The Players in *Euclid* v. *Ambler*," in Charles M. Haar and Jerold S. Kayden, eds., *Zoning and the American Dream: Promises Still to Keep* (Chicago: American Planning Association, 1989), 31–69.

17. An excellent introduction to nineteenth-century racial science and its centrality to politics and popular culture is Reginald Horsman, *Race and Manifest Destiny: The Origins of American Racial Anglo-Saxonism* (Cambridge, Mass.: Harvard University Press, 1981).

18. For an excellent introduction to the politics and culture of white racial identity in the early twentieth century, see Ian Haney-Lopez, *White by Law: The Legal Construction of Race* (New York: New York University Press, 1996); Matthew Frye Jacobson, *Whiteness of a Different Color: European Immigrants and the Alchemy of Race* (Cambridge, Mass.: Harvard University Press, 1998); Mai M. Ngai, *Impossible Subjects: Illegal Aliens and the Making of Modern America* (Princeton: Princeton University Press, 2004), especially chap. 2; and David R. Roediger, *Working toward Whiteness: How America's Immigrants Became White* (New York: Basic Books, 2005), citing congressional hearing on 67. Roediger documents the considerable confusion among immigrants and self-described "whites" regarding the racial identity of those people deemed "inbetween." The racial status of new European immigrants "was constantly under review" (*Working toward Whiteness*, 13).

19. Jacobson, *Whiteness*, 68–69, 77–78 (quoting the Dillingham Commission), 80–81; Daniel J. Kevles, *In the Name of Eugenics: Genetics and the Uses of Human Heredity* (New York: Knopf, 1985), 45–46; Roediger, *Working toward Whiteness*, 133 (citing Fairchild). See also John Highham, *Strangers in the Land: Patterns of American Nativism, 1860–1925* (New York: Atheneum, 1963) and Desmond S. King, *Making Americans: Immigration, Race, and the Origins of the Diverse Democracy* (Cambridge, Mass.: Harvard University Press, 2000).

20. Kenneth L. Roberts, "Ports of Embarkation," *Saturday Evening Post*, May 7, 1921, 72 (and "Plain Remarks on Immigration for Plain Americans," *Saturday Evening Post*, February 12, 1921); Jacobson, *Whiteness*, 80, 83, 89–90; "Immigration and Labor," *Hearings before the Committee on Immigration and Naturalization*, HR, 67th Congress, January 1923 (Washington, D.C.: GPO, 1923); Ngai, *Impossible Subjects*, 21–25; Dorothy Ross, *The Origins of American Social Science* (New York: Cambridge University Press, 1991), 146–47; Roediger, *Working toward Whiteness*, 139, 141 (citing Coolidge and Yerkes). R. M. Bradley presented Clearwater's speech at the *Hearings before the Committee on Immigration and Naturalization*. See also Roy L. Garis, "American Im-

migration Policy," *North American Review* 220 (1924), and *Immigration Restriction* (New York: Macmillan, 1927). Few professional historians questioned Garis's racial assumptions; see *Mississippi Valley Historical Review* 15 (1928–29): 139–40.

21. Fairbanks, "From Better Dwellings," 24–25; Marsh, *Introduction to City Planning*, 9; William S. Bennet, "Immigration and Congestion of Population" and Lawrence Veiller, "The Safe Load of Population on Land," *Proceedings* (1910), 40–41, 72–74; Fogelsong, *Planning the Capitalist City*, 3, 201–7, 217–18; Toll, *Zoned America*, 122–24; Randle, "Professors, Reformers, Bureaucrats, and Cronies," 42–43; Baar, "National Movement," 43; Richard T. Ely, *Outlines of Economics* (New York: Macmillan, 1914), 62–66, quoting Francis Amasa Walker, *Discussions in Economics and Statistics* (1899). Marsh's treatment of race is quite ambiguous but is among the discussions that reveal planners' uncertainty about the "new immigrants' " racial status. See also James Ford, "Residential and Industrial Decentralization," in Nolen, ed., *City Planning* (1915), 335–36.

22. Christopher Silver, "The Racial Origins of Zoning: Southern Cities from 1910–1940," *Planning Perspectives* 6 (1991): 189–205; Robert B. Fairbanks, "Rethinking Urban Problems: Planning, Zoning, and City Government in Dallas, 1900–1930," *Journal of Urban History* 25, no. 6 (1999): 817–18; Ronald Bayor, *Race and the Shaping of Twentieth-Century Atlanta* (Chapel Hill: University of North Carolina Press, 1996); Silver, *Twentieth-Century Richmond*, 190–91; Keith Revell, *Building Gotham: Civic Culture and Public Policy in New York City, 1898–1938* (Baltimore: Johns Hopkins University Press, 2003), 192–93; Garrett Power, "Apartheid Baltimore Style: The Residential Segregation Ordinances of 1910–1913," *Md.L.Rev.* 42 (1983): 289–328; Florence Wagman Roisman, "Opening the Suburbs to Racial Integration: Lessons for the Twenty-first Century," *W. New England L. Rev.* 23 (2001–2002): 65–114. Thomas Lee Philpott cites the NHA's article "Racial Zoning" from its December 1928 issue in *The Slum and the Ghetto: Immigrants, Blacks, and Reformers in Chicago, 1880–1930*, 2nd ed. (Belmont, Calif.: Wadsworth, 1991), 96. Both Richmond's racial ordinance (1911) and New York City's comprehensive zoning ordinance (1916), the first of its kind, cited as a precedent Richmond's *original restrictions on heights and buildings*, passed in 1908 and upheld by the courts in 1910; see Silver, "Racial Origins," n. 11. See also the important discussions in Weiss, *Community Builders*, 83–84, and Garrett Power, "The Unwisdom of Allowing City Growth to Work Out Its Own Destiny," 47 *Md. L. Rev.* (1988): 626–74. The first race-specific exclusionary land-use ordinance was San Francisco's "Bingham Ordinance," struck down by a circuit court in 1890. See *In re Lee Sing et al.*, 43 F. 359 (N.D. Cal 1890).

23. Weiss, *Community Builders*, 57–58; Scott, *American City Planning*, 152. For a detailed account of early collaborative efforts. see Davies, *Real Estate*, chaps. 3 and 4. See also Fukuo Akimoto, "Charles H. Cheney of California," *Planning Perspectives* 18 (July 2003), 253–75. The ACPI was later renamed the American Institute of Planners.

24. *Proceedings* (1914), 111–14; Revell, *Building Gotham*, 196 (citing Veiller's 1914 talk, "Protecting Residential Districts"); Baar, "National Movement," 43–44 (citing Veiller at the NHA and NCCP); Revell, "Road to Euclid," 63–67; Scott, *American City Planning*, 152 (citing Bettman). On Bettman's earlier reform career, see Charles Ascher, "City Planning, Administration—and Politics," *Land Economics* 30, no. 4 (November 1954): 320. By 1900 the concepts of "health" and "public welfare" appeared with increasing frequency in the work of neoclassical economists, as they replaced a defense of capitalist markets rooted in moral principles with one grounded in science. See Ross, *Origins*, chap. 6, esp. 181.

25. S. K. Makielski Jr., *The Politics of Zoning: The New York Experience* (New York: Columbia University Press, 1966), chaps. 1–4; Toll, *Zoned America*, chap. 3; M. Christine Boyer, *Dreaming the Rational City: The Myth of American City Planning* (Cambridge, Mass.: MIT Press, 1983), 90–95; Chused, "*Euclid's* Historical Imagery"; Silver, *Twentieth-Century Richmond*; Fischler, "Metropolitan Dimension."

26. Toll, *Zoned America*, 74–116, 122–24, 143–45 (citing a contemporary description of an earlier flight, south of Fourteenth St.); Boyer, *Dreaming the Rational City*, 91–95; Makielski, *Politics of Zoning*, chap. 1. Rodgers discusses a range of concerns animating supporters of the New York City ordinances in *Atlantic Crossings*, 184–87. McAneny participated in the inaugural NCCP.

27. Revell, "Road to Euclid"; Randle, "Professors, Reformers, Bureaucrats, and Cronies," 37–38; Makielski, *Politics of Zoning*, chap. 1; Toll, *Zoned America*, chap. 5, esp. 150–65. The HBC was "dominated by the ideas of Robert H. Whitten and Edward M. Bassett"; Randle, 37.

28. "Shall we save New York?" (advertisement), *New York Times*, March 5, 1916; Fischler, "Metropolitan Dimension," 683–85 (citing the *Times* and McAneny); Toll, *Zoned America*, 150–51, 158. See also Fogelsong *Planning the Capitalist City*, 221, and "The New York Zone Plan," *New York Times*, April 11, 1916.

29. Toll, *Zoned America*, 116. In other venues, the supposed racial nature of the immigrant threat was described in no uncertain terms. In 1922, the Regional Plan of New York attributed "much that is chaotic in the clothing industries . . . to the psychological peculiarities of the predominant racial group which has provided both wage-earners and manufacturers"—specifically, "the influx of immigrants from Russia and Italy"; Fischler, "Metropolitan Dimensions," 676 (quoting Regional Plan report). Still Fischler (p. 689) concludes that race was ultimately secondary to early zoning's "emphasis on class-based differentiation."

30. On the committee's membership, see Fischler, "Metropolitan Dimensions" and Revell, "Road to Euclid." Fischler refers to the Committee on City Planning as the Commission on Building Districts and Restrictions and describes it as the successor agency to Heights and Buildings.

31. McAneny served from 1914 to 1916; Bassett served in 1914 and 1916. *Proceedings* (1914), 352; *Proceedings* (1915), 243; *Proceedings* (1916), 274.

32. New York zoning politics would be dominated by local interests for decades to come. See Makielski, *Politics of Zoning*, 7–106.

33. He cited with approval a dissenting opinion in a Minnesota Supreme Court ruling in which a judge invoked the "health and welfare" justification for residential restriction and suggested that the NCCP "should popularize that idea, so that the courts will be ready to follow the good example of that judge in Minnesota"; *Proceedings* (1918), 41–42. See also Randle, "Professors, Reformers, Bureaucrats, and Cronies," 37.

34. Comments of W. J. Donald, Bassett, Louis Lott, and Olmsted, *Proceedings* (1918), 43–45. Notably, Purdy would later be very active in the eugenics movement.

35. American Institute of Architects, Committee on Town Planning, George B. Ford, ed., *City Planning Progress in the United States* (Washington, D.C.: Journal of the American Institute of Architects, 1917); Scott, *American City Planning*, 168–69; Weiss, *Community Builders*, 54; U.S. Department of Commerce (hereafter "Commerce"), Advisory Committee on City Planning and Zoning, *A Zoning Primer* (Washington, D.C.: GPO, 1922), 6–7; Davies, *Real Estate*, 78.

36. Lasker and Whitten cited in Randle, "Professors, Reformers, Bureaucrats, and Cronies," 42–43. See also Bayor, *Twentieth-Century Atlanta*.

37. Harlean James served simultaneously as an NCCP executive and executive secretary of NAREB's Town Planning Division. The Division's standards, published in March 1918, were primarily authored by Lawrence Veiller. Weiss, *Community Builders*, 59; Davies, *Real Estate*, 136–37.

38. The courts established the distinction between "public" and "private" nuisances in the early nineteenth century. The theory of public nuisance was first applied to land-use restriction in state and federal supreme court rulings on challenges to San Francisco's exclusion of laundries from residential areas. See *In the Matter of Yick Wo*, 68 Cal. 294, 9 P. 139 (1885); *Soon Hing v. Crowley*, 113 U.S. 703 (1885); and *Barbier v. Connelley*. 113 U.S. 27 (1885). Courts subsequently invoked the "nuisance" argument in *City of Rochester v. West*, 164 N.Y. 510, 58 N.E. 673 (1900); *Ex parte Quong Wo*, 161 Cal. 220, 118 P. 714 (1911); *Matter of Montgomery*, 163 Cal. 457, 125 P. 1070 (1912); *Hadacheck v. City of Los Angeles*, 239 U.S. 394 (1915). and *Cusack Co. v. City of Chicago*, 242 U.S. 526 (1917). See Walker, *Planning Function*, 54–59; Beverly J. Pooley, *Planning and Zoning in the United States* (Ann Arbor: University of Michigan Law School, 1961), 40 ff.; Jesse Dukeminier and James E. Krier, *Property*, 6th ed. (New York: Aspen Publishers, 2006), chap. 8; and Weiss, *Community Builders*, chap. 4.

39. *Welch v. Swasey*, 214 U.S. 91 (1909). See also *Cusack Co. v. City of Chicago*. See Pooley's excellent discussion in *Planning and Zoning*, 42. On the importance of *Hadacheck*, see Commerce, *Zoning Primer* (1922), 4, and below. Walker distinguishes between court decisions grounded in the nuisance doctrine, on the one hand, and those that defined a distinct "planning" function of land-use control, on the other. Yet rulings on height restrictions, and *Euclid v. Ambler*, suggest that the mature legal doctrines in support of municipal zoning powers were shaped directly by the "prezoning" principle of nuisance abatement. See Walker, *Planning Function*, 56–60. 68.

40. Commerce, *Zoning Primer* (1922), 4; Walker, *Planning Function*, 66–67; Toll, *Zoned America*, 201–2; Scott, *American City Planning*, 193–95 and 237–48. On Basset and Bettman's involvement, see Randle, "Professors, Reformers, Bureaucrats, and Cronies," 47–49; Chused, "*Euclid*'s Historical Imagery," 604.

41. The New York court does not discuss nuisances but bases its ruling on a long list of rulings grounded in the nuisance doctrine. *In re Opinion of the Justices*, 234 Mass. 597, 127 N.E. 525 (1920); *Lincoln Trust Co. v. Williams Building Corp.*, 229 N.Y. 313, 128 N.E. 209 (1920); Pooley, *Planning and Zoning*, 42; Walker, *Planning Function*, 69–70.

42. Quote is from *State ex rel. Carter v. Harper*, 182 Wis. 148, 196 N.W. 451 (1923). See also *Calvo v. City of New Orleans*, 154 La. 283, 97 So. 440 (1923), and Walker, *Planning Function*, 70–72.

43. Act 207 of 1921, "Establishment of Zones" and Act 5, 2nd ex. sess., of 1921, amending Act 279 of 1909, "Permissive charter provisions: (x)," State of Michigan, *Laws Relating to the Incorporation and General Powers of Cities* (Supplement to Pamphlet Compilation of 1919), (Lansing, Mich., 1922).

44. Michigan, *Incorporation of Cities*, 1909, pt. II, chap. XI, 152 (3107), sec. 1 and chap. XI, 419 (3366); State of Michigan, *Laws Relating to the Incorporation of Cities* (Fort Wayne, Ind.: Fort Wayne Publishing, 1919), 147 (3021), sec. 1 (on nuisances). The statutory provisions defining municipal powers in these areas remained unchanged

in subsequent amendments. See Michigan, *Incorporation of Cities*, 1919, 147 (3021). There is little evidence that townships and charter cities, both of which had the power to reject plats, did so to control development patterns in the Detroit Metropolitan region before World War II.

45. "Miscellaneous Provisions," Act 207 of 1921, sec. 7, and Act 5, 2nd ex. sess., 1921, amending Act 279 of 1909, Michigan, *Incorporation and General Powers of Cities*, 1922.

46. For a good introduction to Hoover's career at Commerce, see Ellis W. Hawley, "Herbert Hoover, the Commerce Secretariat, and the Vision of the 'Associative State,'" *Journal of American History* 61 (June 1974): 116–40, and William R. Tanner, "Herbert Hoover's War on Waste, 1921–28," in Carl E. Krog and William R. Tanner, eds., *Herbert Hoover and the Republican Era: A Reconsideration* (Lanham, Md.: University Press of America, 1984), 1–35.

47. Davies, *Real Estate*, 129–36, citing letter from NAREB president William May Garland on 129.

48. Ibid., chap. 5, esp. 129–36; Walker, *Planning Function*, 66–67. On debates among realtors over strategy, the meaning of federal subsidy, and legislative proposals, see Hornstein, *Nation of Realtors*, 134–36.

49. Hayden, *Building Suburbia*, 121. The NAREB–Department of Labor collaboration was short lived, lasting from 1918 to 1919.

50. Davies, *Real Estate*, 137–38, 172–88; Hayden, *Building Suburbia*, 117–18, 121–23; Hawley, "Herbert Hoover," 133–34; Gwendolyn Wright, *Building the Dream: A Social History of Housing in America* (Cambridge, Mass.: MIT Press, 1981), 196–98; Janet Hutchinson, "Building for Babbitt: The State and the Suburban Home Ideal," *Journal of Policy History* 9, no. 2 (1997): 184–210; Greg Hise, *Magnetic Los Angeles: Planning the Twentieth-Century Metropolis* (Baltimore: John Hopkins University Press, 1997), 38–40 (quoting Commerce publication). See Hornstein's discussion of the collaborative efforts and their gender dynamics in *Nation of Realtors*, 120–44. The homeowner, according to Commerce's *How to Own Your Own Home: A Handbook for Prospective Home Owners* (Washington, D.C.: GPO, 1923), was a "he" who was "master of his dwelling."

51. Ely's *Outlines of Economics*, first published in 1889, was a standard college text, in its 6th edition in the 1930s. Among his most celebrated students were Woodrow Wilson, John R. Commons, and Frederick Jackson Turner. Early in his career, Ely was criticized for his "socialist" leanings; see Ross, *Origins*, 109–17.

52. Davies, *Real Estate*, 124–27; Hornstein, *Nation of Realtors*, 85–104, citing Nichols on 110. Ross discusses the professionalization of the social sciences and the influence of marginalist (neoclassical) economics on Ely's work, *Origins*, chaps. 5 and 6. For more on the growth of a professional credential system for the real estate industry and the institute's formative role, see the important discussion in Randle, "Professors, Reformers, Bureaucrats, and Cronies," 46.

53. Roy Lubove, *Community Planning in the 1920's: The Contribution of the Regional Planning Association of America* (Pittsburgh: University of Pittsburgh Press, 1963), 17; Weiss, *Community Builders*, 58–59, 67–68; Walker, *Planning Function*, 66–67; Commerce, *Zoning Primer* (1922), 7; Fairbanks, "Better Dwellings," 35, and "Rethinking Urban Problems," 815–16. Congressional appropriations for the Division of Building and Housing were to be used "to collect and disseminate such scientific, practical, and statistical information" regarding methods in building, planning, construction, and codes.

54. Commerce, Advisory Committee on Zoning, *A Standard State Zoning Enabling Act: Under Which Municipalities May Adopt Zoning Regulations* (Washington, D.C.: GPO, 1924), Introduction and Secs. 1–2, 4–9. See Herbert Hoover's, "Forward," iii–iv.

55. Commerce, *Zoning Primer* (1922), 1–2, 5 (emphasis in original).

56. Ibid., 1–4; Commerce, Advisory Committee on City Planning and Zoning, *A Zoning Primer* (Washington, D.C.: GPO, 1926), 4. The authors do not depict all apartment houses as menaces. Proper restriction can prevent "an apartment house from becoming a giant airless hive, housing human beings like crowded bees"; *Zoning Primer*, 1922, 2. The creation of multiple residential use districts would be commonplace after World War II. See chap. 5.

57. Commerce, *Standard Act* (1924), introduction, iii–iv, and secs. 1–2, 4–9; Commerce, *A Standard State Zoning Enabling Act: Under Which Municipalities May Adopt Zoning Regulations* (Washington, D.C.: GPO, 1926), 1–2. On Basset and Bettman's influence, see Ascher, "City Planning," 310; Chused, "*Euclid*'s Historical Imagery," 603, n. 33; Power, "Advent of Zoning," 6.

58. Commerce clearly differentiates sec. 3 from the "statement of purpose (under the police power)" in sec. 1. "*That* defined and limited the powers created by the legislature to the municipality under the police power. *This* section contains practically a direction from the legislative body as to the purposes in view in establishing a zoning ordinance and the manner in which the work of preparing such an ordinance shall be done. It may be said, in brief, to constitute the 'atmosphere' under which the zoning is to be done"; Commerce, *Standard Act* (1924), 6, sec. 3 and n. 21.

59. Commerce, *Standard Act* (1924), 6, nn. 24, 25. While the notes define numerous terms, the text instructs state officials not to include definitions in their enabling legislation. "The terms used in the act are so commonly understood that definitions are unnecessary. Definitions are generally a source of danger. They give to words a restricted meaning"; see "Explanatory Notes."

60. Commerce, *Zoning Primer* (1922), 6–7; Commerce, *Zoning Primer* (1926), 4, 7; Commerce, *Standard Act* (1924), ii, iv; Commerce, *Standard Act* (1926) 3, 6, 7, and p. III, nn. 1, 2; James G. Coke and John J. Gargan, for the National Commission on Urban Problems, *Fragmentation in Land-Use Planning and Control*, Research Report no. 18 (Washington, D.C.: GPO, 1969), 5; American Society of Planning Officials, "Problems of Zoning and Land-Use Regulation," Research Report no. 2 (Washington, D.C.: GPO, 1968), 28; Pooley, *Planning and Zoning*, 8; Walker, *Planning Function*, 65–67. See also Boyer, *Dreaming the Rational City*, chap. 7. On states' use of standard act language, see HHFA, *Comparative Digest of Municipal and County Zoning Enabling Statutes* (HHFA, Office of the Administrator, Division of Law, 1953).

61. The Department of Commerce's Committee on Social Trends applauded the Johnson-Reed Act for giving preference to "a physical type which closely resembles the prevailing stock in out country"; quoted in Jacobson, *Whiteness*, 88.

62. Helen C. Monchow predicted that the courts were heading toward the acceptance of racial restriction as a "right of contract," yet warned developers to familiarize themselves with the laws in their state; Monchow, *The Use of Deed Restrictions in Subdivision Development* (Chicago: Institute for Research in Land Economics and Public Utilities, 1928), esp. 47–53; *Urban Land Economics* (New York: Macmillan, 1928). On the NAREB Code of Ethics, see Davies, *Real Estate*, chap. 8.

63. For early explorations of this point, see Richard F. Babcock, *The Zoning Game: Municipal Practices and Policies* (Madison: University of Wisconsin Press, 1966); Danielson, *Politics of Exclusion*; and White, "Fiscal Zoning."

64. *Ambler Realty Co. v. Village of Euclid,* 297 F. 307, 316 (N.D. Ohio 1924); Toll, *Zoned America,* 214–17; Power, "Advent of Zoning," 4. Metzenbaum modeled the Euclid ordinance directly on New York City's comprehensive ordinance of 1916 and designed his defense by turning to Whitten's work in other Cleveland suburbs; Randle, "Professors, Reformers, Bureaucrats, and Cronies," 39–40. Randle provides the best discussion of several key actors in the early zoning movement and their complicated motivations.

65. The court did acknowledge the ordinance's "esthetic" purpose but distinguished this from what it considered the plan's interest in "furthering . . . class tendencies." On Westenhaver, see Randle, "Professors, Reformers, Bureaucrats, and Cronies," 41. See also Chused, "*Euclid's* Historical Imagery," 605–9.

66. *Village of Euclid, Ohio v. Ambler Realty Co.,* 272 U.S. 365 (1926). For good introductions to *Euclid's* police-power precedent see White, "Fiscal Zoning"; Pooley, *Planning and Zoning,* 10.

67. Chused makes a similar argument in "*Euclid's* Historical Imagery," esp. 609–14. See also Randle, "Professors, Reformers, Bureaucrats, and Cronies," 40–43.

68. *Euclid v. Ambler.* See also Walker, *Planning Function,* 63.

69. *Euclid v. Ambler.*

70. In prefatory remarks the court includes apartments in the category of "business and trade"; *Euclid v. Ambler.* See discussions in White, "Fiscal Zoning," 34, and Danielson, *Politics of Exclusion,* 52–53. Lower courts began to articulate this opinion years earlier. In *Morris v. East Cleveland* (1920), for example, an Ohio court described "an apartment house, or tenement, in a section of private residences, [as] a nuisance to those in the immediate vicinity," because of the "smoke and soot," "noise," "fire hazard," and the "number of people passing in and out" who "render immoral practices therein." Cited in Baar, "National Movement," 44–45.

71. *Euclid v. Ambler.* See also White, "Fiscal Zoning," 34.

72. Walker, *Planning Function,* 78–79; Randle, "Professors, Reformers, Bureaucrats, and Cronies," 32, 48–49; Power, "Advocates," 8–9.

73. Indeed, even Ernst Freund, author of the influential *Police Power* (1904) and advocate of *not* using zoning to discriminate against specific populations, altered his views by the 1920s in response to the "coming of colored people" to his South Side Chicago neighborhood; cited in Power, "Advocates," 85.

74. See, for example, *Marblehead Land Co. v. City of Los Angeles,* 47 F.2d 528, 532 (9th Cir. 1931), citing *Zahn v. Board of Public Works,* 274 U.S. 325 (1927), and Pooley's discussion in *Planning and Zoning,* 10–11.

75. For an introduction to prewar working-class suburbs, see Richard Harris and Robert Lewis, "Constructing a Fault(y) Zone: Misrepresentations of American Cities and Suburbs, 1900–1950," *Annals of the Association of American Geographers* 88 (1998): 622–39, and Nicolaides, *My Blue Heaven.* On the early automobile suburbs, see Jackson, *Crabgrass Frontier,* chaps. 9–10.

76. Weiss, *Community Builders,* 44, 73–74, and 186, n. 41 (Weiss quote on 73; Weiss quotes Shuler on 74).

77. Commerce, Advisory Committee on City Planning and Zoning, *A Standard City Planning Enabling Act* (Washington, D.C.: GPO, 1928); Weiss, *Community Builders,* 75, 77–78 (reprinting *Statement*); Commerce, *Standard Act* (1924); Commerce, *Standard Act* (1926); "Standard City Planning Enabling Act" (draft mimeo), February 1927, 38, n. 68. The committee conceded that its recommendations on subdivision control

were still in the "trail and error stage." On the influence of the New York City and other metropolitan ordinances, see discussion of eminent domain in the February 1927 draft (48–49, n. 93, 61–64, n. 119).

78. Compare discussions in Dukeminier and Krier, *Property;* Coke and Gargan, *Fragmentation;* and Weiss, *Community Builders.*

79. Commerce, *Standard State Zoning Enabling Act,* 1926, p. III, nn. 1, 2; Coke and Gargan, *Fragmentation,* 5; Commerce, *Zoning Primer* (1926), 6–7; Scott, *American City Planning,* 248–49. See also Ascher, "City Planning," 310.

80. John Hancock, "The New Deal and American Planning: The 1930s," in Daniel Schaffer, ed., *Two Centuries of American Planning* (Baltimore: Johns Hopkins University Press, 1988), 200–202, 219–20 (quoted on 198); Marion Clawson, *New Deal Planning: The National Resources Planning Board* (Baltimore: Johns Hopkins University Press for Resources for the Future, 1981). See also Weiss, *Community Builders,* 5, 183, n. 29, and Walker, *Planning Function,* 58. The "Zoning Progress" report was distributed in mimeographed form by the Division of Building and Housing. Clawson argues that the NRPB reports were little used. Weiss calculates the number of city and county ordinances at 1,360, while Walker uses the NRC figures.

81. He continued: "to enhance the plans of living; to promote a balanced social economy with a better distribution of wealth; and to conserve natural resources." Cited in Hancock, "The New Deal and American Planning," 200–201.

82. During the intervening years, the only modification to the Michigan enabling act was a 1925 prohibition against the construction of gas stations or garages in residential neighborhoods; Michigan, *Laws Relating to the Incorporation and General Powers of Cities* (Lansing, Mich.: Robert Smith, 1926).

83. *DT,* November 8, 1951, March 4, 1952, and January 23, 1972. On early planning commissions, see county surveys reproduced in State of Michigan, Office of Intergovernmental Relations, *Michigan Planning and Zoning Survey: Region 1* (January 1978).

84. Royal Oak, "Zoning Ordinance and Map No. 254," Article I, 3, 7–8; Article I, Sec. 122; Article II: Boundaries and Regulations, ROHC, "Zoning."

85. *DT,* January 23, 1972. In 1930, Jones and his colleagues believed that Royal Oak would remain, for the most part, a residential community, "a natural residential area for Detroit's excess population."

86. Studies of restrictive zoning usually ignore race-restrictive covenants or at best treat them as compatible instruments that often reinforced patterns achieved through municipal restriction. Many note, correctly, that the use of racial covenants increased after *Buchanan.* And comprehensive zoning, in turn, is described as "replacing" racial covenants after *Shelley.* Compare, for example, the discussions in Walker, *Planning Function,* chap. 3; Evan McKenzie, *Privatopia: Homeowner Associations and the Rise of Residential Private Government* (New Haven: Yale University Press, 1994), 68–74; Norman J. Williams, "Planning Law and Democratic Living," *Law and Contemporary Problems* 20, no. 2 (1955): 317–50, esp. 335–38; Clement E. Vose, *Caucasians Only: The Supreme Court, the NAACP, and the Restrictive Covenant Cases* (Berkeley: University of California Press, 1959), chap. 1; Power, "Advent of Zoning"; Wagman Roisman, "Opening the Suburbs"; Charles Johnson, *Negro Housing* (President's Conference on Home Building and Home Ownership, Report of the Committee on Negro Housing), edited by John M. Gries and James Ford (1931; reprint New York: Negro Universities Press, 1969), 35–40. Weiss argues that covenants "served as both the physical and political model for zoning laws and subdivision regulations"; *Community Builders,* 3–4.

87. McKenzie, *Privatopia*, 8–9, 31–51. See McKenzie's excellent treatment of homeowner association politics and the "Radburn" idea. Homeowner associations, he writes, served as council-manager governments, a synthesis of the "community builder experience and Progressive Era political science." See also Robert Fogelson's discussion of covenant use in late nineteenth- and early twentieth-century America, *Bourgeois Nightmares: Suburbia, 1870–1930* (New Haven: Yale University Press, 2005).

88. See Vose, *Caucasians Only*, 7–8 and Margaret Garb's important discussion of property owners' early role in ascribing racial values to real estate; *City of American Dreams: A History of Home Ownership and Housing Reform in Chicago, 1871–1919* (Chicago: University of Chicago Press, 2005), chap. 7.

89. Despite the new immigrants' "in between" racial status, they joined in barring "non-Caucasians" from their neighborhoods. See David Roediger's superb discussion in *Working toward Whiteness*, chap. 6.

90. Monchow, *Deed Restrictions*, chap. 5. esp. 46–52; McKenzie, *Privatopia*, 43–44; Harold Black, "Restrictive Covenants in Relation to Segregated Negro Housing in Detroit" (master's thesis, Wayne State University, 1947), 24–28; John P. Dean, "Only Caucasian: A Study of Race Covenants," *Journal of Land and Public Utility Economics* 23, no. 4 (November 1947): 428–32, tables I and II; Michigan Planning Commission, *A Study of Subdivision Development in the Detroit Metropolitan Area* (Lansing, Michigan, June 1939), 20. On the Detroit area's real estate bubble, see chap. 1. In 1947, Harold Black confirmed that restricting property to "Caucasians" or the "white race" was a concept "recent among subdividers, and has been used with increasing frequency since the 1920's."

   On the national history of racial zoning, covenants, and legal precedents for both, see Johnson, *Negro Housing*, 35–46; Herman H. Long and Charles S. Johnson, *People vs. Property: Race Restrictive Covenants in Housing* (Nashville: Fisk University Press, 1947); Robert Weaver, *The Negro Ghetto* (New York: Russell & Russell, 1948), esp. 38–40, 211–56; Abrams, *Forbidden Neighbors*; Williams, "Planning Law"; Vose, *Caucasians Only*, chap. 1.

91. Black, "Restrictive Covenants," 27–29; Monchow, *Deed Restrictions*, chap. 5; Dean, "Only Caucasian," table I; McKenzie, *Privatopia*, 43–45; Vose, *Caucasians Only*, chap. 1; *Schulte v. Starks*, 238 Mich. 102, 104, 213 N.W. 102 (1927); Abstract and Title for Lot 732, Firschkorn's Columbus Park No. 1, Dearborn, Michigan (Jan. 28, 1925), DHM, "Dearborn Subdivisions: Abstracts." Dean's statistics for New York refer to projects with 75 or more units. In Detroit, the earliest deed restrictions were found for 1910; their use increased dramatically during the 1920s.

92. Black, "Restrictive Covenants," 29–30 (citing Bonaparte Heights covenant).

93. In *Parmalee v. Morris*, 218 Mich. 625, 188 N.W. 330 (1922), the Michigan Supreme Court found a race-restrictive covenant to be enforceable, and over the next eight years another seven states upheld restrictions against either sale to or occupancy by blacks. The nuisance doctrine is occasionally raised explicitly, but more often through example. In 1938, for example, a Maryland court compared neighborhood conditions created by black occupancy to the construction of an elevated railway and commercial development (and its relevance for a New York state ruling); *Meade v. Dennistone*, 173 Md. 295, 301, 196 A. 330 (1938). See Vose, *Caucasians Only*, 22–23; Black, "Restrictive Covenants," 16, 28; Johnson, *Negro Housing*, 41; D. O. McGovney, "Racial Residential Segregation by State Court Enforcement of Restrictive Agreements, Covenants, or Conditions in Deeds Is Unconstitutional," *California Law Review* 33,

no. 1 (March 1945): 5–39, citing court rulings, including list of objectionable uses in *Cowell v. Springs Co.*, 1879. See also Vose's important discussion of the "changed conditions" doctrine cases, in which neighborhood conditions were deemed *not* acceptable for upholding racial restrictions, specifically *because black people already lived in the neighborhood.* Or as a D.C. circuit court ruled in 1942, "when the neighborhood in question has so changed in its character and environment and in the uses to which property therein may be put that purpose of the covenant cannot be carried out"; Vose, 25–28, citing *Hundley v. Gorewitz*, 132 F.2d 23, 24 (D.C. Cir. 1942).

94. *Sanborn v. McLean*, 233 Mich. 227, 206 N.W. 496 (1925). The covenant also set minimum cost requirements for any residential construction.

95. *Sanborn v. McLean.* Compare McKenzie's discussion in *Privatopia*, 51–55. Notably, the plaintiffs argued that the gas station would be a "nuisance per se," a charge denied by the defendants. The courts found "no occasion to pass upon the question of nuisance, as the case can be decided under the rule of reciprocal negative easement."

96. In *Snow v. Van Dam*, 291 Mass. 477, 197 N.E. 224 (1935); *Neponsit Property Owners Association, Inc. v. Emigrant Industrial Savings Bank*, 278 N.Y. 248, 15 N.E.2d 793 (1938). The New York court argued that the property owners' association could stand in for the plaintiff and that in subsequent cases judges might "look behind the corporate form of the plaintiff."

97. Quote is from *Neponsit Property Owners Association, Inc., v. Emigrant Industrial Savings Bank.* A comparison between zoning law and racial zoning ordinances in the South would be very revealing. An exclusionary zoning ordinance in Richmond, Virginia was, as Charles Johnson wrote, "clothed in expressions of solicitude for the public welfare" ("to preserve the general welfare, peace, racial integrity, morals and social good order of the city . . ."); *Negro Housing*, 38. The Supreme Court ruled that the police power did not justify it.

98. Numbers 4–6 specify floor space minimums for other lots. "Restrictions" (July 29, 1947), Liber 2129, Page 326, reproduced in "'Golf Estates': A Subdivision of a Part of the SE 1/4 of Sec. 3 T.2.N.R.11E, Troy Twp., Oakland County, Mich.," "Abstract of Title, Section 3, Kemp, Niles, 1819–1947," THM, Box 9: "Land Records: Abstracts of Title, Supervisors Plats and Sections 2–16." The land was originally awarded by the U.S. government in 1819 to Michel Kemp, and passed between the Kemp, Niles, and Skillman families until purchased by Lewis and Lola Erb. The Erb family incorporated as "Golf Estates" in 1947. For comparable texts in Dearborn, see covenants collected in DHM, "Dearborn, Housing." For a statistical breakdown of race restrictions in four Wayne County townships, see Michigan Planning Commission, *Subdivision Development*, 20.

CHAPTER THREE

1. For an introduction, see Charles M. Haar, *Federal Credit and Private Housing* (New York: McGraw-Hill, 1960), and U.S. Committee on Banking and Currency, *Federal Housing Programs: Chronology and Description*, 80th Cong., 2d Sess., 1948. Prior to 1932, the federal government made sporadic and very limited forays into private housing markets, usually to accommodate migrant labor forces for wartime production.

2. For excellent discussions of FHA activity and its relationship to broader trends in federal housing policy and residential discrimination, see Robert Weaver, *The Negro Ghetto* (New York: Russell & Russell, 1948); Charles Abrams, *Forbidden Neighbors: A Study of Prejudice in Housing* (Port Washington, N.Y.: Kennikat Press, 1971); Chester

W. Hartman, *Housing and Social Policy* (Englewood Cliffs, N.J.: Prentice-Hall, 1975); Mark I. Gelfand, *A Nation of Cities: The Federal Government and Urban America, 1933–1965* (New York: Oxford University Press, 1975); Kenneth Jackson, *Crabgrass Frontier: The Suburbanization of the United States* (New York: Oxford University Press, 1985); Arnold R. Hirsch, "With or Without Jim Crow: Black Residential Segregation in the United States," in Arnold R. Hirsch and Raymond A. Mohl, eds., *Urban Policy in Twentieth-Century America* (New Brunswick, N.J.: Rutgers University Press, 1993), 65–99; Douglas S. Massey and Nancy A. Denton, *American Apartheid: Segregation and the Making of the Underclass* (Cambridge, Mass.: Harvard University Press, 1993); Joe R. Feagin, "A House Is Not a Home: White Racism and U.S. Housing Practices," in Robert D. Bullard, J. Eugene Grigsby, III, and Charles Lee, eds., *Residential Apartheid: The American Legacy,* CAAS Urban Policy Series, vol. 2 (Los Angeles: CAAS Publications, Center for Afro-American Studies, University of California, 1994), 17–48; Melvin L. Oliver and Thomas M. Shapiro, *Black Wealth, White Wealth: A New Perspective on Racial Inequality* (New York: Routledge, 1997); essays in part I of John Goering and Ron Wienk, eds., *Mortgage Lending, Racial Discrimination, and Federal Policy* (Washington, D.C.: Urban Institute Press, 1996), 29–73.

Several studies have begun to explore the connections between pre-Depression housing politics and New Deal policy. See Marc A. Weiss, "Richard T. Ely and the Contribution of Economic Research to National Housing Policy, 1920–1940," *Urban Studies* 26 (1989): 115–26; Gail Radford, *Modern Housing for America: Policy Struggles in the New Deal Era* (Chicago: University of Chicago Press, 1996); Adam Rome, *The Bulldozer in the Countryside: Suburban Sprawl and the Rise of American Environmentalism* (New York: Cambridge University Press, 2001), chap. 1; Kevin Fox Gotham, *Race, Real Estate, and Uneven Development: The Kansas City Experience, 1900–2000* (Albany: State University of New York Press, 2002); Jeffrey M. Hornstein, *A Nation of Realtors: A Cultural History of the Twentieth-Century American Middle Class* (Durham, N.C.: Duke University Press, 2005); Margaret Garb, *City of American Dreams: A History of Home Ownership and Housing Reform in Chicago, 1871–1919* (Chicago: University of Chicago Press, 2005). Many general studies of federal housing and credit policies do not discuss their racial protocols, yet still provide crucial context for understanding federal decision-making. See especially Roger Starr, *Housing and the Money Market* (New York: Basic Books, 1975).

3. Important exceptions are Weiss, "Richard T. Ely"; Janet Hutchinson, "Building for Babbitt: The State and the Suburban Home Ideal," *Journal of Policy History* 9, no. 2 (1997): 184–210; Mark A. Weiss, *The Rise of the Community Builders: The American Real Estate Industry and Urban Land Planning* (New York: Columbia University Press, 1987), chap. 6; and Gotham, *Race, Real Estate and Uneven Development.*

4. Compare, for example, the discussions in Jackson, *Crabgrass Frontier,* and Lizabeth Cohen, *A Consumers' Republic: The Politics of Mass Consumption in Postwar America* (New York: Knopf, 2003). Many commentators dismiss the notion that federal intervention decisively shaped suburban sprawl. For further discussion of historians' treatments of state building and postwar economic growth, see David M. P. Freund, "Marketing the Free Market: State Intervention and the Politics of Prosperity in Metropolitan America," in Kevin M. Kruse and Thomas J. Sugrue, eds., *The New Suburban History* (Chicago: University of Chicago Press, 2006).

5. For an introduction to the mortgage crisis, see J. Paul Mitchell, "The Historical Context for Housing Policy," in J. Paul Mitchell, ed., *Federal Housing Policy and Programs:*

Past and Present (New Brunswick, N.J.: Rutgers University, Center for Urban Policy Research, 1985), 3–8, and Jackson, *Crabgrass Frontier,* 193.

6.   James Ford, "The President's Conference on Home Building and Home Ownership," *Journal of Home Economics,* October 1931, 924–25.

7.   John M. Gries and James Ford, eds., *Planning for Residential Districts,* President's Conference on Home Building and Homeownership, vol. 1 (Washington, D.C.: National Capital Press, 1932); John M. Gries and James Ford, eds., *Slums, Large-Scale Housing and Decentralization,* President's Conference, vol. 3 (Washington, D.C.: National Capital Press, 1932), iii–iv, vii–x. On NAREB's role and the background of individual committee members, see Weiss, *Community Builders,* 143–45, 213–14 (n. 3).

8.   Henry J. Aaron Jr., *Shelter and Subsidies: Who Benefits from Federal Housing Policies?* (Washington, D.C.: Brookings Institution, 1972), 76; Leo Grebler, David M. Blank, and Louis Winnick, *Capital Formation in Residential Real Estate: Trends and Prospects* (Princeton: Princeton University Press, 1956). For a more generous interpretation, see Michael S. Carliner, "Development of Federal Homeownership 'Policy,'" *Housing Policy Debate* 9, no. 2 (1998): 3–5. Before the Depression, S&Ls held about half of the nation's outstanding mortgage debt.

9.   On the pre-Depression transformation of mortgage lending practices, see Weiss, *Community Builders,* 31–36, and Gwendolyn Wright, *Building the Dream: A Social History of Housing in America* (Cambridge, Mass.: MIT Press, 1981), 100–101, 199. Weiss correctly notes that the "revolutionary rise in higher loan-to-value debt financing for residential realty, often ascribed to the post–World War II era, clearly began in the early decades of this century" (p. 32). However, New Deal–era programs dramatically altered the structure, stability, accessibility, and growth potential of this market for home finance.

10.   Weiss, "Richard T. Ely," quoted on 116; Radford, *Modern Housing,* 44, 47–48; Pearl Janet Davies, *Real Estate in American History* (Washington, D.C.: Public Affairs Press, 1958), chap. 5, esp. 140–43; Oliver Jones and Leo Grebler, *The Secondary Mortgage Market: Its Purpose, Performance, and Potential* (Los Angeles: Real Estate Research Program, Graduate School of Business Administration, University of California, 1961), 111–15. See also William M. Randle's discussion of Ely's collaboration with the private sector and its implications for the institute's research; "Professors, Reformers, Bureaucrats, and Cronies: The Players in *Euclid v. Ambler,*" in Charles M. Haar and Jerold S. Kayden, eds., *Zoning and the American Dream: Promises Still to Keep* (Chicago: American Planning Association, 1989), 46–47.

11.   Weiss, "Richard T. Ely"; Davies, *Real Estate;* USBC, *Mortgages on Homes* (Washington, D.C.: GPO, 1923); Ernest McKinley Fisher, *Principles of Real Estate Practice* (New York: Macmillan, 1923); Adrian Daniel Theobald, *Financial Aspects of Subdivision Development* (Chicago: Institute for Economic Research, 1930). On 1920s practices, see Hornstein, *Nation of Realtors,* esp. 67–75; Richard T. Ely, "Economic Factors underlying Housing, and Experience of Limited Dividend Companies," in Gries and Ford, eds., *Slums,* 151–69.

12.   Weiss, "Richard T. Ely," 122; Frederick M. Babcock, *The Appraisal of Real Estate* (New York: Macmillan, 1924); Horace F. Clark, *Appraising the Home: A Discussion of One of the Most Fascinating Subjects in the Field of Real Estate* (New York: Prentice-Hall, 1930); FHA, *The FHA Story in Summary* (Washington D.C.: GPO, 1960), 11.

13.   An excellent introduction is Radford, *Modern Housing.*

14.   Gries and Ford, eds., *Slums,* 149.

15. Weiss, "Richard T. Ely," 122; Davies, *Real Estate,* 173–76. See also David L. Mason, *From Building and Loans to Bail-Outs: A History of the American Savings and Loan Industry, 1831–1995* (New York: Cambridge University Press, 2004).

16. The claim is technically correct, but misleading. The FHLB was designed to lend federal funds to private institutions, so that *they,* in turn, could originate mortgages for consumers.

17. "A Statement on the Proposed Mortgage Discount Bank," Gries and Ford, eds., *Slums,* app. III; Haar, *Federal Credit,* 2, n. 2. Miles Colean discusses the conference's legacy for urban policy in *The Impact of Government on Real Estate Finance in the United States,* Studies in Urban Mortgage Financing (New York: National Bureau of Economic Research, 1950), 92, n. 22.

18. Thomas B. Marvell, *The Federal Home Loan Bank Board* (New York: Praeger, 1969), 4–5, 19–24, 218; Sherman J. Maisel, *Financing Real Estate: Principles and Practices* (New York: McGraw-Hill, 1965), 89–90; Milton Semer et al., "Evolution of Federal Legislative Policy in Housing: Housing Credits," in Mitchell, ed., *Federal Housing Policy,* 73; U.S. Federal Home Loan Bank Board, *The Federal Home Loan Bank System, 1932–1952* (Washington, D.C.: FHLB, 1952), 38–39. The FHLB act made some provisions for direct mortgage loans, which were rarely used.

19. J. Paul Mitchell, "Historical Overview of Federal Policy: Encouraging Homeownership," in Mitchell, ed., *Federal Housing Policy,* 6–7, 41–42 (quoted on 42); Semer et al., "Evolution," 73; Marvell, *Bank Board,* 19 and 193. On the technical and structural changes in the mortgage market during and after the Depression, see Raymond Goldsmith, *The Flow of Capital Funds in the Postwar Economy* (New York: National Bureau of Economic Research, 1965), 300–307.

20. J. Carlton Starbuck, "Oakland Michigan: A Statistical History of a Detroit Suburban Community" (unpublished report, Oakland County Planning Commission, 1967), 233, 238, and table 73 (p. 235); Nelson J. Young, "A Study of the Problems of the Distressed Home Owner of Detroit as Revealed by Applications to the Home Owners' Loan Corporation" (Report to the Earhart Foundation, June 8, 1934), 1; Robert Gordon Rodkey, *State Bank Failures in Michigan,* Michigan Business Studies, 7, no. 2 (Ann Arbor: University of Michigan Bureau of Business Research, 1935), 9–10; Michigan Planning Commission, *Subdivision Development,* 29, 30 (table 13), 31 (table 15), 126, 127 (table 10). The "group" banks were holding companies established in 1928 and 1930 to sidestep state prohibitions against branch banking outside of an institution's home city.

21. Davies, *Real Estate,* 176–77. Compare discussion in C. Lowell Harriss, *History and Policies of the Home Owners' Loan Corporation* (New York: National Bureau of Economic Research, 1951). NAREB lobbied for direct federal lending immediately after passage of the FHLB act.

22. William F. Stevenson, "The Home Owners' Loan Corporation" ("Statement Relative to the Method and Procedure of Procuring Loans from the Federal Home Owners' Loan Corporation"), Senate Document No. 74, in *Senate Documents,* 73rd Congress, 1st session (March 9–June 16, 1933), "Miscellaneous" (Washington, D.C.: GPO, 1934); Carl F. Behrens, *Commercial Bank Activities in Urban Mortgage Financing,* Studies in Urban Mortgage Financing (New York: National Bureau of Economic Research, 1952), 20; Harriss, *History and Policies,* 11–12, 25, 152–53; Marvell, *Bank Board,* 19, 24–25; Semer et al., "Evolution," 73; Davies, *Real Estate,* 177–78; FHLB, *Second Annual Report* (December 31, 1934).

23. Harriss, *History and Policies*, 17 (table 1), 18–19, 21–22 (table 2), 31, 35, 50; Jackson, *Crabgrass Frontier*, 196; *Business Week*, September 1, 1934, 14–15; Davies, *Real Estate*, 177; Young, "Problems of the Distressed Home Owner," esp. 7–8. The Detroit office of the HOLC, established in April 1933, received 67,394 applications in its first year from Wayne, Oakland, Macomb, and Monroe counties, 90 percent of which were from the Detroit metropolitan area. Harriss identifies considerable regional variation in the reasons for default. On the program's benefits for lenders and variations in lending activity by state, see Harriss, 16–22, 25–26.

24. Harris, *History and Policies*, 9 (paraphrasing Roosevelt's April 13, 1933 appeal to Congress); Jackson, *Crabgrass Frontier*, 195–96.

25. Jackson, *Crabgrass Frontier*, 199–200.

26. Abrams, *Forbidden Neighbors*, 229, 237–38; Jackson, *Crabgrass Frontier*, 196–203 (citing a housing official writing, presumably, in 1940); Harriss, *History and Policies*, 45–48; Detroit quotes from "Area Description" reports for D-53 and D-39, in RG 195, FHLBB/CSF, Box 18 and "City Survey Metropolitan Detroit, Michigan . . . June 30, 1930," 3, in RG 195, FHLBB/CSF, Box 17, "Greater Detroit Michigan Re Survey Report."

27. Jackson, *Crabgrass Frontier*, 213.

28. Ibid.

29. The agency appointed full-time appraisers in larger cities and part-time ones in smaller cities, but in either case all individual appraisal reports were reviewed, sometimes twice, by HOLC staff. See Davies, *Real Estate*, 177–78; Timothy L. McDonnell, *The Wagner Housing Act: A Case Study of the Legislative Process* (Chicago: Loyola University Press, 1957), 60–61; Harriss, *History and Policies*, 42–48; FHLB, *First Annual Report* (December 31, 1933), 48. Amy Hillier argues that because HOLC maps were not produced until the FHA had begun its operations, because the maps were not widely distributed, and because there were numerous other sources of information about the "need" to segregate neighborhoods by race, that the HOLC had minimal influence on federal lending decisions. What she ignores is the fact that the HOLC was inextricably linked to the extensive institutional networks that created and disseminated appraisal practices in both the private and public sectors throughout the 1920s and 1930s. Amy E. Hillier, "Redlining and the Home Owners' Loan Corporation," *Journal of Urban History* 29, no. 4 (May 2003): 394–420. Meanwhile, long before the Residential Security Maps were produced, the HOLC's elaborate mortgage application process included questions about applicants' "color" as well as confirmation about racial identity from the applicants' credit reports. See Harriss, *History and Policies*, 47 and app. A.

30. The best discussions are Kenneth Jackson, "Race, Ethnicity, and Real Estate Appraisal: The Home Owners Loan Corporation and the Federal Housing Administration," *Journal of Urban History* 6, no. 4 (1980): 419–52; Jackson, *Crabgrass Frontier*, 195–203.

31. On restrictive covenants and their relationship to zoning, see chap. 2.

32. Haar, *Federal Credit*, 2, n. 3; Semer et al., "Evolution," 73–74; Marvell, *Bank Board*, 112–14; Abrams, *Forbidden Neighbors*, chaps. 1, 9, and 11; Jackson, *Crabgrass Frontier*, 202–3. Federal associations automatically became members of the regional reserve bank, while state-chartered associations were encouraged to apply.

33. The HOLC stopped operations in late 1951, after recording net earnings of over $14 million. Jackson, *Crabgrass Frontier*, 202–3; Weaver, *Negro Ghetto*, 69–70; Mar-

vell, *Bank Board*, 24–25, 38. See Weaver's useful discussion of the forces limiting blacks' access to HOLC financing.

34. Jackson, *Crabgrass Frontier*, 207. See also Allen R. Hays, *The Federal Government and Urban Housing: Ideology and Change in Public Policy*, 2nd ed. (Albany: State University of New York Press, 1995), 85–87; Arnold R. Hirsch, "'Containment' on the Home Front: Race and Federal Housing Policy from the New Deal to the Cold War," *Journal of Urban History* 26, no. 2 (January 2000): 159; and Semer et al., "Evolution," 73. On the HOLC's lending record, see Hillier, "Redlining."

35. "Address by Abner H. Ferguson before the American Title Association Convention, Memphis, Tennessee," October 14, 1935, RG 31, SP, "Speeches, 1935–1939." FDR cited in press release of November 1, 1934, RG 31, Correspondence between State Governors and President Franklin Roosevelt concerning FHA legislation, 1934–5, Box 1.

36. Davies, *Real Estate*, 178–79; Maisel, *Financing Real Estate*, 100; McDonnell, *Wagner Housing Act*, 60; Weiss, *Community Builders*, chap. 6, esp. 146. See also Barry Checkoway, "Large Builders, Federal Housing Programs, and Postwar Suburbanization," *International Journal of Urban and Regional Research* 4, no. 1 (March 1980): 21–45; and Gertrude S. Fish's discussion of the negotiations that led to creation of the FHA in "Housing Policy During the Great Depression," in Gertrude Sipperly Fish, ed., *The Story of Housing* (New York: Macmillan, 1979), 200–203. NAREB's president Hugh Potter also lobbied aggressively for the act.

37. FHA, *FHA Story*, 11; Weiss, "Richard T. Ely," 122–26. Ely and NAREB collaborated to create a "standard course" in real estate in the 1920s; before then, training was a local, largely informal affair; Hornstein, *Nation of Realtors*, chap. 4.

38. Checkoway, "Large Builders," 29–34; Wright, *Building the Dream*, 241–42; Jackson, *Crabgrass Frontier*, 203–18; Maisel, *Financing Real Estate*, 97–124; Marion Clawson, *Suburban Land Conversion in the United States: An Economic and Governmental Process* (Baltimore: Resources for the Future, 1971), 101–9, 137–38; Leo Grebler, *The Role of Federal Credit Aids in Residential Construction* (New York: National Bureau of Economic Research, 1953), chap. 2.

39. Tom Martinson, *American Dreamscape: The Pursuit of Happiness in Postwar Suburbia* (New York: Carroll & Graf, 2000), 134–35, 261, nn. 14 and 15. Several scholars have challenged the claim that federal policy fueled suburban sprawl at all. Robert Beauregard describes the evidence of government influence as "circumstantial." For example, he argues that the "timing" of suburban growth and urban decline suggest that selective credit programs were not necessarily influential because passage of the NHA "precede[d] the postwar shedding of residents by central cities" by "at least 10 to 12 years"; Robert A. Beauregard, "Federal Policy and Postwar Urban Decline: A Case of Government Complicity," *Housing Policy Debate* 17, no. 1 (2001): 129–51 (quoting 138–39). Robert Bruegmann's challenge to the "government culpability" argument is even less convincing. Since the long-term, amortized mortgage and racial discrimination existed before the New Deal, he argues, federal interventions were not decisive. Noting the long history of informal redlining, he concludes that "neither the government nor the banks were doing anything either new or necessarily prejudicial to urban neighborhoods"; Robert Bruegmann, *Sprawl: A Compact History* (Chicago: University of Chicago Press, 2005), 102. Both authors ignore the fundamental changes in the structure of mortgage markets, changes created by New Deal programs, as well as the systematic racial separation, both geographical and financial, accelerated by federal mortgage insurance.

40. Like the "Manchesterian liberals," writes Wood, the FHA and VA "defin[ed] their public in terms of the individual buyer and striving to give the buyer what he wants." "By increasing the credit capacity of individual home-buyers," he explained, the federal programs "work through private banking and lending institutions to support the marketplace"; Robert C. Wood, *1400 Governments: The Political Economy of the New York Metropolitan Region* (Cambridge, Mass.: Harvard University Press, 1961), 156–57, 172.

41. Cohen, *Consumer's Republic*, 122, 197, 404. Kenneth Jackson describes FHA programs as a "subsidy" but argues that the process of suburbanization was inexorable. "It is hazardous to condemn a government for adopting policies in accord with the preference of a majority of citizens," he writes, noting that "suburbanization was not willed on an innocent peasantry." Jackson argues that "federal housing policies were not the *sine qua non* in the mushrooming of the suburbs, . . . [since] the dominant residential drift in American cities had been toward the periphery for at least a century before the New Deal." Thus "there is no reason to assume that the suburban trend would not have continued in the absence of direct federal assistance"; *Crabgrass Frontier*, 216–17.

It is impossible to predict what shape American metropolitan areas would have taken without federal intervention. But the record of federal programs—for the mortgage market, urban redevelopment, and other efforts that fueled the decentralization of both residence and industry nationwide—makes it difficult to imagine how suburbanization, private homeownership, and large-lot housing would have otherwise become *mass* phenomena and, closely related, constitutive elements of postwar economic growth. As the discussions here and in chap. 5 demonstrate, federal programs created the institutions that enabled a majority of Americans, for the first time, to become homeowners (and that eventually encouraged and enabled borrowers to buy larger and larger homes). These programs made suburban relocation necessary to qualify for most state-subsidized mortgage loans. Finally they made suburban homeownership a motor of the postwar consumption economy and, with it, postwar economic growth. Without the new federal presence, there is no reason to assume that the far more limited prewar market for mortgage credit—*if* it had even recovered, without federal support, from its precipitous collapse—would have produced and sustained comparable postwar activity, regardless of increased demand and technological and managerial innovations in the housing industry.

Many studies downplay or simply ignore the ways that New Deal reform revolutionized and subsidized housing markets and suburban growth. David M. Kennedy captures a common formulation, writing that selective credit programs "arranged an institutional landscape in which unprecedented amounts of private capital could flow into the home construction industry." The programs "proved not to have checked or intimidated capital," he concludes, "so much as to have liberated it." Even Henry Aaron's study of federal housing subsidies argues that most FHA programs did *not* provide subsidies. Marc Weiss and Michael Carliner are among the commentators who describe the modern mortgage market primarily as the product of early twentieth-century private-sector innovation; they argue for much more continuity between the pre-Depression experiments with the long-term mortgage and its New Deal–era reconfiguration. Most contemporary economists portray federal mortgage programs as "stabilizing" measures, while most general economics textbooks, for example, Atack and Passel's volume, do not count housing programs as part of U.S. economic history. David Kennedy, *Freedom from Fear: The American People in Depression and War, 1929–1945* (New York: Oxford University Press, 2001), 369–70; Aaron, *Shelter and Subsidies,* appendix A (compare his discussion of loss risk, 74–76); Weiss, *Community Builders,* e.g., 31–36; Weiss, "Richard T. Ely"; Carliner, "Development"; Jeremy Atack and Peter Passel, *A New Economic View of American History,* 2nd ed. (New York: W. W. Norton, 1994). See also George D. Green, "The Ideological Origins of the Revolution in American Financial Policies," in Karl Brunner, ed., *The Great Depression Revisited* (Boston: Martinus Nijhoff, 1981), 220–52.

42. Goldsmith, *Capital Funds,* 277–79, 303, 446.

43. For an introduction to housing finance strategies in the late nineteenth and early twentieth centuries, see Dolores Hayden, *Building Suburbia, 1820–2000* (New York: Pantheon Books, 2003), chap. 5; Mason, *From Building and Loans;* Garb, *City of American Dreams;* and Becky M. Nicolaides, *My Blue Heaven: Life and Politics in the Working-Class Suburbs of Los Angeles, 1920–1965* (Chicago: University of Chicago Press, 2002).

44. For an excellent introduction to the mechanics of FHA insurance and its ability to increase capital gains in real estate assets by creating new demand, see George F. Break, *The Economic Impact of Federal Loan Insurance* (Washington, D.C.: National Planning Association, 1961), 55. Quote is from a study of Title I activity in the New York metropolitan region, Sidney M. Robbins and Nestor E. Terleckyj, *Money Metropolis: A Locational Study of Financial Activities in the New York Region* (Cambridge, Mass.: Harvard University Press, 1960), 55. On the role of FHA advance commitments in helping merchant builders secure capital, see Jones and Grebler, *Secondary Mortgage Market,* 42–44.

45. The mortgage insurance program did not totally insulate private lenders from risk, yet it did pool that risk in a way that made mortgage lending less dangerous and, potentially, far more lucrative. For each home loan granted with FHA approval, the mutual mortgage insurance fund issued negotiable debentures to the lending institution, the interest and principle of which were guaranteed by the U.S. government. These debentures, in turn, could be used to make regular payments back to the fund. For good summaries of these impacts, see Jackson, *Crabgrass Frontier,* 204; Maisel, *Financing Real Estate,* 100–101, 104–5 (especially his discussion of the risk environment).

46. Between 1932 and 1935, the state began to regulate and provide capital for private banks and the savings and loan industry, transformed the Federal Reserve from a central bank into a federal regulatory body, and assumed control of discount rates and interest rates. By 1935, it had abolished the gold standard, was insuring a host of private lenders against loss, had expanded its ability to buy and sell Treasury securities as a means to supplement private bank reserves, and had greatly expanded its powers to provide emergency loans to institutional lenders. In short, by the mid-1930s the federal government set up the mechanisms to promote a new kind of national economic growth by creating and sustaining a very safe and flexible market for consumer credit. The new system gave the state considerable control over both money creation and credit cycles, so it could strategically target chosen industries and consumer markets for subsidy. Perhaps most important, the state's credit had now become the linchpin for both stabilizing the economy and fueling a debt-driven economic growth. The U.S. government essentially socialized debt. The best intro-

duction is Robert Guttman, *How Credit Money Shapes the Economy: The United States in a Global System* (Armonk, N.Y.: M. E. Sharpe, 1994).

This study contributes to an ongoing reassessment of New Deal policy, the rise of the liberal state, and its implications for racial politics in modern America. Most standard works on New Deal reform pay little, if any, attention to the impact and legacy of selective credit programs, monetary policy, and banking reform. Careful examination of New Deal policy and politics suggests that the state did not communicate an "ambivalent message on matters of race," as Sugrue writes, but rather a quite resolute—if sometimes muted—message about the necessity of racial segregation and exclusion; Thomas J. Sugrue, *The Origins of the Urban Crisis: Race and Inequality in Postwar Detroit* (Princeton: Princeton University Press, 1996), 10. See the important critiques of the state-building literature in Michael Brown, "State Capacity and Political Choice: Interpreting the Failure of the New Deal," *Studies in American Political Development* 9, no. 1 (spring 1995): 187–212, Julian E. Zelizer, *Taxing America: Wilbur D. Mills, Congress, and the State, 1945–1975* (Princeton, N.J.: Princeton University Press, 2003), and David Roediger's important discussion of New Deal policy and white privilege/identity, in *Working toward Whiteness: How America's Immigrants Became White* (New York: Basic Books, 2005), esp. 224–34. For a further discussion, see Freund, "Marketing the Free Market" and Robert Self's discussion of postwar growth liberalism in *American Babylon: Race and the Struggle for Postwar Oakland* (Princeton: Princeton University Press, 2003).

47. Colean, *Impact of Government,* 107, and chap. 7 for a summary. Colean does not specifically refer to selective credit policy as a subsidy, instead describing a federally monitored and "directed" market for housing credit. In a policy brief prepared for Eisenhower's 1952 presidential campaign, however, the economist was very critical of previous administrations' attempts to "directly . . . influence the volume of new building and the types of houses erected." Federal policy "should not . . . exercise . . . direct and detailed influence on the building market," Colean wrote, or "enter . . . the lending market directly or indirectly with government funds" or "attempt . . . to regulate the rate of interest by arbitrary devices"; Miles L. Colean, "A National Policy on Federal Intervention in Mortgage Finance and Community Development," memorandum prepared for Aksel Nielsen, consultant to Eisenhower, reprinted in Fish, ed., *Story of Housing,* 268–76, quoting 270, 272.

48. Goldsmith, *Flow of Capital Funds,* 277–79, 303, 446; James Gillies, "Federal Credit Programs in the Housing Sector of the Economy: An Aggregate Analysis," in Stewart Johnson et al., eds., *Federal Credit Programs* (Englewood Cliffs, N.J.: Prentice-Hall, for the Commission on Money and Credit, 1963), 427, 434, 457–60; Frederick E. Balderston, *Thrifts in Crisis: Structural Transformation of the Savings and Loan Industry* (Cambridge, Mass.: Ballinger, 1985), 21; Raymond J. Saulnier, *Constructive Years: The U.S. Economy under Eisenhower* (Lanham, Md.: University Press of America, 1991), 42; Raymond J. Saulnier, "Introduction" to J. E. Morton, *Urban Mortgage Lending: Comparative Markets and Experience* (Princeton: Princeton University Press, 1956), 5, 70; William E. Dunkman, *Money, Credit, and Banking* (New York: Random House, 1970), 394; George F. Break, *The Economic Impact of Federal Loan Insurance* (Washington, D.C.: National Planning Association, 1961), 45; William L. Silber, "Selective Credit Policies: A Survey" and Jack M. Guttentag, "Selective Credit Controls," in Ira Kaminow and James M. O'Brien, *Studies in Selective Credit Policies* (Philadelphia: Federal Reserve Bank of Philadelphia, 1975), 35–40, 95–121, 116–18; Jones and Grebler,

Secondary Mortgage Market, 30–33, 174; Warren A. Law, "The Aggregate Impact of Federal Credit Programs on the Economy," in Johnson et al., eds., *Federal Credit Programs,* 290–99. See also Guttman, *Credit-Money,* chaps. 4 and 5.

In 1961, Break estimated that FHA and VA operations had already "provided an important stimulus to the residential construction industry" worth "between $2 billion and $4 billion a year." "Income transfers" from taxpayers to recipients, wrote Silber in 1975, "occur in all selective credit policies, only in some cases they occur within the budget and in other cases outside the budget." Jones and Grebler complained that selective credit activity distorted interest rates; those rates, they argued, should "be market determined." Attempting to sort out the ambiguity surrounding the influence of federal interventions, Warren Law explained that "almost all federal credit programs involve some degree of subsidy but, as is so often the case . . . the degree is immeasurable. This stems from the fundamental difficulty in defining 'subsidy.'"

Economists were not the only ones making this claim. During the 1950s and 1960s, many mainstream social scientists called selective credit programs state subsidies, without apology. Examples include Edward C. Banfield and James Q. Wilson, *City Politics* (Cambridge, Mass.: Harvard University Press 1963), 10; Andrew J. Glass, "The Urban Dilemma," in Robert A. Gordon, ed., *A Nation of Cities: Essays on America's Urban Problems* (Chicago: Rand McNally, 1966), 37–46; and James Q. Wilson, "The War on Cities," in Gordon, ed., *Nation of Cities,* 17–36.

49. "Address by Stewart McDonald, Federal Housing Administrator, before the Ohio Building Association League Convention, Columbus, Ohio," October 21, 1937, RG 31, SP, Box 3, "1937—Speeches"; "Address by Abner H. Ferguson before the American Title Association Convention, Memphis, Tennessee," October 14, 1935, RG 31, SP, Box 29, "Speeches—1935–1939"; Harris, *History and Policies,* esp. chap. 9; Marvell, *Bank Board,* 217–223. For examples of industrial lobbying efforts, see untitled memos, "Statement by Stewart McDonald, Federal Housing Administrator" (March 15, 1939), and "Milton W. Morris, Association of Home Builders of San Francisco, Inc.—Statement to: Members of the House Banking and Currency Committee, Members of the Senate Banking and Currency Committee" (n.d.), in RG 31, CCSF, "Existing Construction, 1936–40." Suggestions and complaints from individuals and organizations received between 1935 and 1940 are summarized in "Excerpts from Letters Protesting Discrimination against Existing Construction" (internal document), RG 31, CCSF, "Existing Construction, 1941–46."

Collaboration produced an extensive paper record on municipalities nationwide concerning local housing demand, assessed valuations, income tax returns, sales volume, workers by industry, employment and payrolls, housing by tenure, and financial resources of local lending institutions. The data on the Detroit region is collected in RG 31, HMD, Boxes 11–13; RG 31, RRHMA, Box 6; and RG 31, RHMA, Boxes 9–10.

50. Babcock to McDonald, December 30, 1936, and untitled internal memo regarding debate over "pending bill," March 9, 1939, in RG31, Box 3, "Existing Construction, 1936–40"; Davies, *Real Estate,* 179; Weiss, *Community Builders,* 148–49. Individual companies contacted the FHA to request maps, materials, and contact information for regional zone commissioners (see RG 31, PCACO, Boxes 2–3). The FHA provided free consulting services to large-scale subdividers during the 1930s to ensure that their projects met FHA construction requirements, and its Land Planning Unit published guidebooks on topics including *Subdivision Development* (1935) and *Planning Profitable Neighborhoods* (1938).

51. Stewart McDonald to Franklin D. Roosevelt, November 26, 1937; statement of

T. D. Webb (FHLBB); and memos between McDonald, Ferguson, Babcock, Green, and Mack, all in RG 31, CCSF, Box 3, "Existing Construction, 1936–40"; Senator W. Warren Barbour (N.J.) to Ferguson, March 20, 1941, enclosing letter from James Forsyth, vice president, Asbury Park National Bank and Trust Company (N.J.), March 19, 1941; Ferguson to Barbour, n.d.; H. Edward Fry to Ferguson, February 21, 1941; Fry to President Franklin D. Roosevelt, February 19, 1941; Nelson to Ferguson, February 10 and March 17, 1941; Ferguson to Nelson, February 13 and March 19, 1941: all in RG 31, CCSF, Box 3, "Existing Construction, 1941–46." NAREB had been hearing from real estate boards nationwide about their concern. "I have assured them," Nelson wrote to Ferguson, that the administration would submit the amendments soon—"it is what we planned to do and the line of action that we had mutually agreed upon"; Nelson to Ferguson, March 17.

52. "Address delivered by Mr. James A. Moffett [to the] Advertising Club of New York," December 13, 1934, RG 31, SP, Box 29, "Early Moffett Speeches"; "Address by Stewart McDonald . . . Before the Ohio Building Association League Convention," October 21, 1937 (in folder labeled: "1937—Speeches"), RG 31, SP, Box 29, "Speeches—1935–1939." Members of the Oklahoma Chamber of Commerce learned that the FHA was "undertaking nothing less than the development of a new nation-wide home mortgage system," by "coordinat[ing] and standardiz[ing]" the practices of private lenders and "supplement[ing] them by the establishment of certain new institutions"; "Address of Federal Housing Administrator James A. Moffett at Oklahoma City . . Before the Chamber of Commerce," March 1, 1935, RG 31, SP, Box 29, "Early Moffett Speeches." See also Weiss's discussion of FHA "volunteerism" in *Community Builders*, 152–54.

53. "Statement by Stewart McDonald," March 15, 1939; Babcock to McDonald, December 30, 1936; untitled memo, March 9, 1939: all in RG 31, CCSF, Box 3, "Existing Construction, 1936–40."

54. FHA, *The Structure and Growth of Residential Neighborhoods in American Cities* (Washington, D.C.: GPO, 1939), 28; see also 42–48 and chap. 5 on the correlation between renting, overcrowding, dilapidated structures, and nonwhite occupancy.

55. First quote is from FHA, *Underwriting Manual: Underwriting and Valuation Procedure under Title II of the National Housing Act*, with revisions to February 1938 (Washington D.C.: GPO, 1938). The 1936 edition was less self-conscious but makes the same points in "Objectives," pt. 1, sec. 1, 101–3; FHA, *Underwriting Manual: Underwriting and Valuation Procedure under Title II of the National Housing Act*, with revisions to April 1, 1936 (Washington, D.C.: GPO, 1936). See also FHA, *FHA Underwriting Manual* (Washington, D.C.: GPO, 1947), 1. The 1936 edition indicates that FHA staff and consultants are "furnished with loose-leaf Underwriting Manuals," to which revisions would be made by "supplying new or substitute pages." Individuals and institutions were issued bound copies. Compare Jackson, *Crabgrass Frontier*, 364–65, n. 51.

56. FHA, *Underwriting Manual* (1936), pt. 2, secs. 229 and 233 (also sec. 266 and sec. 284(3)(g–h)); see also FHA, *Underwriting Manual* (1938), pt. 3, sec. 13:1412.

57. Agents filed these forms in ring binders at local agency offices, where they could consult the Economic Background Data Files and other collections for further information on area neighborhoods. FHA, *Underwriting Manual* (1938), pt. 5, sec. 1805, 1845–50.

58. Report of Valuator, and Exhibit C—Description of Real Estate, re 239 East Howell Avenue, Alexandria, VA, December 10, 1934, in RG 31, RRFM, Box 1, "Amos

Herbert—Alexandria National Bank." By 1938, the valuator's form asked if there was a "change in class of occupancy" but also left space to "name existing or threatening adverse influences," while the accompanying Standardized Factual Data Form asked about the "racial descent" of the applicant; copies in RG 31, PCACO, Box 9, "Mortgage Conference—Suggestions for Conducting."

59. Kramer to FDR, July 14, 1941, RG 31, CCSF, Box 6, "Racial Restrictive Covenants, 1938–1948." See the extensive correspondence regarding the Kramer complaint. Other than examining the geographic patterns of FHA activity and anecdotal evidence, the best source for information on the agency's insurance practices is the record of decades of opposition to its requirements for racial restriction. An incredibly rich resource is the correspondence between the NAACP and FHA in RG 31, CCSF, Box 6, "Racial Restrictive Covenants, 1938–1948" and "Racial Restrictive Covenants, 1949." See also contemporary critiques by black journalists, activists, and scholars, for example, "Reveal Rigid Policy of Segregation in FHA," New York *Amsterdam News*, December 31, 1938, Weaver, *Negro Ghetto*, 70–73, 92–93, 148–53, 219–22, and Hirsch's discussion in "Searching for a 'Sound Negro Policy': A Racial Agenda for the Housing Acts of 1949 and 1954," *Housing Policy Debate* 11, no. 2 (2000): 393–441.

60. Totals exclude project units financed under Section 207 (which accounted for a small percentage of FHA insurance activity) and Class-3 Title I loans insured between 1938 and 1940. U.S. Housing and Home Finance Agency (HHFA), *First Annual Report, 1947* (Washington, D.C.: GPO, 1948), III-9, III-12; U.S. HHFA, *Twelfth Annual Report* (Washington D.C.: GPO, 1958), 62; Commerce, *Construction Statistics, 1915–1964* (a supplement to *Construction Review*) (Washington, D.C.: GPO, 1966), 16, tables 5 and 6; Davies, *Real Estate*, 179; FHA, *FHA Story*, 9–11. City Survey maps, area reports, and surveys for most metropolitan areas are held in RG 195, FHLBB/CSF.

61. By comparison, only 2.6 percent of the homes in metropolitan Chicago carried FHA mortgage insurance during this period, and 4.2 percent in metropolitan Cleveland.

62. For two thirds of the region's new home buyers, the average down payment probably ranged between $400 and $1,140. This average represents the range between a 10 percent down payment on a $4,000 home and a 19 percent down payment on a $6,000 home. In the tricounty area, 62.3 percent of the new homes that received FHA insurance were valued by the agency between $4,000 and $6,000, while 9.1 percent of the new homes were valued between $3,000 and 4,000 and 24.8 percent were valued between $6,000 and $8,000. Nationwide in 1940, the average price for a one-family house was about $4,400.

63. In many neighborhoods, however, they would pay between $40 to $60 or even more. The lower figure represents the average rent for "tenant-occupied units by contract or estimated monthly rent" for "white" renters in Detroit. "Nonwhite" renters paid an average of $25.84 per month. The higher figures are estimates drawn from block statistics; average monthly costs vary widely throughout the city.

64. FHA, *FHA Homes in Metropolitan Districts: Characteristics of Mortgages, Homes, Borrowers under the FHA Plan, 1934–1940* (Washington, D.C.: GPO, 1942), 104, 106, 127; Maisel, *Financing Real Estate*, 310; USBC, *Sixteenth Census of the United States: 1940, Housing*, vol. 2, *General Characteristics*, pt. 3, *Iowa-Montana* (Washington, D.C.: GPO, 1943), 592; and USBC, *Housing: Supplement to the First Series Housing Bulletin for Michigan: Detroit (Block Statistics)* (Washington, D.C.: GPO, 1942), 5–9.

65. RG 195, FHLBB/CSF, Box 18, "Greater Detroit Michigan, Security Maps and Area Descriptions," quoting Area Description for D-39 (the neighborhood in question was

20 percent black and 70 percent southern and eastern European); FHA, *FHA Homes in Metropolitan Districts*, 127.

66. Marvell, *Bank Board*, 19, 27–29, 31; Semer et al., "Evolution," 74; Balderston, *Thrifts in Crisis*, chaps. 1–2. The Reconstruction Finance Corporation (RFC) lent more than $100 million to the national S&Ls before the FHLBB assumed this function.

67. The best introduction to the secondary market is Jones and Grebler, *Secondary Mortgage Market*, chaps. 3, 7–9.

68. Ibid., 115–18, quoted on 117.

69. The $80 million included $34 million in mortgages transferred from the RFC Mortgage Company, which directly purchased FHA-insured mortgages in its early years and continued to do so after creation of FNMA (with RFC targeting existing construction, and FNMA new construction); Jones and Grebler, *Secondary Mortgage Market*, chap. 8. FNMA was chartered as the National Mortgage Association of Washington and renamed the Federal National Mortgage Association on April 5.

70. An excellent introduction is Jess Lederman, ed., *The Secondary Mortgage Market: Strategies for Surviving and Thriving in Today's Challenging Markets*, rev. ed. (Chicago: Probus, 1992).

71. Meanwhile Federal Reserve policy increasingly complemented the efforts of the FHA. See Carl E. Parry, "Selective Instruments of National Credit Policy," in Karl R. Bopp et al., *Federal Reserve Policy*, Postwar Economic Studies, no. 8 (Washington, D.C.: Board of Governors of the Federal Reserve System, 1947), 73–74. On HOLC support for S&Ls, see Balderston, *Thrifts in Crisis*, 12; Jones and Grebler, *Secondary Mortgage Market*, 119, 121. Passed on June 7, 1939, Reorganization Plan No. 1 created a Federal Loan Agency to coordinate the efforts of the RFC Mortgage Co., the FNMA, the FHLB, the HOLC, the FSLIC, and the FHA.

72. For discussion of national impact, see Parry, "Selective Instruments," 74; FHA, *FHA Homes in Metropolitan Districts*, 127.

CHAPTER FOUR

1. For an introduction to debates over New Deal experimentation, see William E. Leuchtenberg, *Franklin D. Roosevelt and the New Deal, 1932–40* (New York: Harper & Row, 1963); Anthony J. Badger, *The New Deal: The Depression Years, 1933–1940* (Chicago: Ivan R. Dee, 2002). On housing and urban development initiatives, see Mark I. Gelfand, *A Nation of Cities: The Federal Government and Urban America, 1933–1965* (New York: Oxford University Press, 1975); Timothy L. McDonnell, *The Wagner Housing Act: A Case Study of the Legislative Process* (Chicago: Loyola University Press, 1957); Rachel G. Bratt, "Public Housing: The Controversy and Contribution," in Chester Hartman et al., eds., *Critical Perspectives on Housing* (Philadelphia: Temple University Press, 1986), esp. 336–38; and Gail Radford, *Modern Housing for America: Policy Struggles in the New Deal Era* (Chicago: University of Chicago Press, 1996).

2. Government credit would "not interfere with the work of private builders," explained Wood, "who would continue to cater to the only section of the population which they have ever supplied," i.e., the upper income group; Edith Elmer Wood, "Is Government Aid Necessary in the Financing of Low-Cost Housing?" *American City*, March 1929, 99–100 (emphasis in original). Wood was a legendary reformer, long involved in the zoning movement and a vocal advocate for the promotion of noncommercial housing alternatives.

3. Harold Buttenheim, "Private Effort and Public Action Must Unite for Effective Slum Improvement," *American City*, March 1929, 99–100.

4. James Ford, "The President's Conference on Home Building and Home Ownership," *Journal of Home Economics*, October 1931, 928, 924. A professor of social ethics at Harvard, Ford specialized in housing reform and worked with numerous local and regional planning commissions. On his earlier work with Hoover, see chap. 2.

5. More families would buy homes, they noted, if homes were modern ("in arrangement and equipment"), conveniently located, and affordable; John M. Gries and James Ford, eds., *Home Ownership, Income and Types of Dwellings*, President's Conference on Home Building and Home Ownership, vol. 4 (Washington, D.C.: National Capital Press, 1932), 197–201.

6. Ibid., 76–77, 98–101, tables XVIII and XIX. The language and logic of early zoning debates suffuses these reports. The Committee on Home Finance and Taxation explained that zoning was necessary to eliminate "nuisances" from residential enclaves and called for the "improvement and wider adoption" of deed restrictions, describing them as the best tool for eliminating "incompatible ownership occupancy"; John M. Gries and James Ford, eds., *Home Finance and Taxation*, President's Conference on Home Building and Home Ownership, vol. 2 (Washington, D.C.: National Capital Press, 1932), 44–46.

For a broader perspective on homeownership desire in the twentieth century, see Jim Kemeny, *The Myth of Home-Ownership: Private versus Public Choices in Housing Tenure* (London: Routledge & Kegan Paul, 1981), and Joe R. Feagin and Robert Parker, *Building American Cities: The Urban Real Estate Game*, 2nd ed. (Englewood Cliffs, N.J.: Prentice-Hall, 1990), esp. 231–43. As late as 1940, homeownership rates were *higher* among the foreign-born in many American cities. See Olivier Zunz, *The Changing Face of Inequality: Urbanization, Industrial Development, and Immigrants in Detroit, 1880–1920* (Chicago: University of Chicago Press, 1982), and David Roediger's discussion in *Working toward Whiteness: How America's Immigrants Became White* (New York: Basic Books, 2005),158–59.

7. Gries and Ford, eds., *Home Ownership*, 8–9.

8. John M. Gries and James Ford, eds., *Slums, Large-Scale Housing and Decentralization*, President's Conference, vol. 3 (Washington, D.C.: National Capital Press, 1932), xiv–xv; see also 66–95, "Large Scale Operations."

9. Ibid., 85, 149.

10. William F. Stevenson, "The Home Owners' Loan Corporation" ("Statement Relative to the Method and Procedure of Procuring Loans from the Federal Home Owners' Loan Corporation"), Senate Document No. 74, in *Senate Documents*, 73rd Congress, 1st session (March 9–June 16, 1933), "Miscellaneous" (Washington, D.C.: GPO, 1934), 5.

11. Hill thought that the "the greatest benefit" would be "to steady the nerves of people who are owners of small homes, and to provide proper banking facilities"; U.S. Congress, Senate, "Creation of a System of Federal Home Loan Banks," *Hearings before a Subcommittee of the Committee on Banking and Currency*, 72nd Congress, pt. I, January 1932, 43–53. At hearings on the HOLC, Baltimore realtor Harry E. Karr described savings and loans institutions as "nonprofit" institutions. See also testimony by H. S. Kissell, Morton Bodfish, and G. Eidt, U.S. Congress, Senate, "Home Owners' Loan and National Housing Act," *Hearings before the Subcommittee on Banking and Currency*, March 1935.

12. Statement of Harry Hopkins, U.S. Congress, House of Representatives (HR), "National Housing Act," *Hearings before the Committee on Banking and Currency, House of Representatives*, 73rd Congress, May–June 1934, 2.

13. Statement of Winfield W. Riefler, in HR, "National Housing Act," 3–6. Riefler was the primary author of Title II; see Gertrude Sipperly Fish, ed., *The Story of Housing* (New York: Macmillan, 1979), 201.

14. The program would cause "that money to go where it will go to work," by encouraging "that type of saver to put his money into an institution that will use it"; statement of John H. Fahey, in HR, "National Housing Act," 12–14, 21.

15. Statement of Marriner C. Eccles, HR, "National Housing Act," 6–8. "There is hardly a section of this country," continued Eccles, "but what there are excess funds not working—not working, first, because banks won't take the risks involved and, secondly, because there is no adequate form of credit available on a sufficiently attractive basis over a period of time to induce borrowers to use that credit." See also statement of Winfield W. Riefler, HR, "National Housing Act," 3–6, and Leuchtenberg *Franklin D. Roosevelt*, 158–59.

16. Statements of Henry Harriman, Hugh Potter, and John Fahey, HR, "National Housing Act," 12–14, 21, 123, 226–27, 232. See also Fahey's discussion of consumer confidence and institutional functionality.

17. "Under our present form of production and distribution," Perkins explained, "I think that we have got to regard debt as indefinitely more of an asset than we used to regard it"; statement of Frances Perkins, HR, "National Housing Act," 73–74. See also Hopkins' debate with Luce (77) and Albert Deane's discussion of the government's limited role (11).

18. Statement of Harry Hopkins, HR, "National Housing Act," 105–8.

19. Ibid.; Statements of H. S. Kissel and John Sprunt Hill, in Senate, "Creation of a System of Federal Home Loan Banks" (a), 76, 48–49; Statement of Hugh Potter, HR, "National Housing Act," 232. On the importance of "character" in lending and borrowing, see Harry E. Karr's comments at the 1932 FHLB hearings and Horace Russell, HOLC general counsel, on credit reports in C. Lowell Harriss, *History and Policies of the Home Owners' Loan Corporation* (New York: National Bureau of Economic Research, 1951), 47–48, n. 16.

20. Statement of Harry Hopkins, HR, "National Housing Act," 105–8.

21. Ibid., 107.

22. For an introduction, see Charles Johnson's Depression-era commentary in the NAACP's magazine *The Crisis*; Radford, *Modern Housing*; Arnold R. Hirsch, "'Containment' on the Home Front: Race and Federal Housing Policy from the New Deal to the Cold War," *Journal of Urban History* 26, no. 2 (January 2000): 158–80; and Robert Weaver, *The Negro Ghetto* (New York: Russell & Russell, 1948), chap. 5.

23. "Better Homes—Better Business," *Business Week*, June 30, 1934, 15–16; "Housing Campaign," *Business Week*, July 21, 1934, 9. See also *Business Week* articles "Auditing the New Deal" (July 28 and August 25, 1934) and warnings of possible federal overreach in "Politics and Banking" (November 3, 1934) and "Socialism and Banking" (October 13, 1934).

24. Wayne W. Parrish, "New Deal's Far-Reaching Housing Program" and "A Real New Deal for the Home Owner," *Literary Digest*, July 14 and 21, 1934. Publications quoted in Parrish, "Housing Campaign Moves into High Gear," *Literary Digest*, July 18, 1934, 8.

25. Insistence upon the "market-friendly" nature of New Deal programs was crucial to garnering congressional, business, and electoral support for some of the administration's most radical innovations. See, for example, Henry Wallace's endorsement of the Agricultural Adjustment Act as a means for getting agriculture

"back on a business footing"; Henry A. Wallace, *Report of the Secretary of Agricul-
ture, 1938* (Washington D.C.: GPO, 1938), 11–33; Leuchtenberg's discussion of the
AAA and the Commodity Credit Corporation, in *Franklin D. Roosevelt,* 72–78; and
Dean L. May's discussion of Federal Reserve policy, in *From New Deal Economics to
New Economics: The American Liberal Response to the Recession of 1937* (New York:
Garland, 1981), esp. 38.

26. James Moffett, "Back to Prosperity with Housing," *Scientific American* 152, no. 5 (May
1935): 234–35.

27. Charles Abrams, *Forbidden Neighbors: A Study of Prejudice in Housing* (Port Washington, N.Y.: Kennikat Press, 1971), 229–37, quoting 229.

28. Ford, "President's Conference on Home Building," 926–27; Charles Johnson, *Negro
Housing* (President's Conference on Home Building and Home Ownership, Report of
the Committee on Negro Housing), edited by John M. Gries and James Ford (1931;
reprint New York: Negro Universities Press, 1969), viii (Lamont's introduction),
48–51. Lamont continues: "Racial factors and the primitive housing conditions to
which he has been accustomed, and which necessitate a more drastic readjustment
than for other groups, contribute to make the Negro the worst sufferer." Compare
the volume's analysis of "Property Depreciation and Negro Residence."

29. Early real estate texts and HOLC Residential Security Maps also considered eastern
and southern European immigrants to constitute a racial threat, at least in the short
run. Yet by the 1930s, more and more of these populations were being included in
campaigns to restrict neighborhoods to "whites" only. See Roediger's excellent treatment in *Working toward Whiteness,* 171–73.

30. FHA, *Underwriting Manual: Underwriting and Valuation Procedure under Title II of
the National Housing Act,* with revisions to February 1938 (Washington D.C.: GPO,
1938), preface.

31. FHA, *Underwriting Manual* (1936), pt. 2, secs. 227–32; FHA, *Underwriting Manual*
(1938), pt. 2, sec. 8, and secs. 904–9; see also "Summary of Significant Considerations" for the "Rating of Location," sec. 987. The interchangeability of material
and racial variables is characteristic of FHA publications about residential markets.
Homer Hoyt discusses the usefulness of aggregate block data, for example, to assess
the important "characteristics" of specific residential enclaves. "When expressed as a
percentage," he wrote in 1939, "the relative condition of the entire block with respect
to that factor is clearly brought out. The same is true of the number of dwelling units
lacking private baths or the number of persons of a race other than white in a given
block . . . It is the predominant condition of the block with respect to these factors
that is important in determining its character. The existence of a certain proportion
of buildings in a block requiring major repairs influences the value of other structures that are in good condition. The presence of a certain proportion of members
of an inharmonious race in a block affects the characteristics of the entire block";
FHA, *Structure and Growth,* 31. Compare Kenneth Jackson's discussion of the *Manual's* treatment of race-restrictive covenants in *Crabgrass Frontier: The Suburbanization
of the United States* (New York: Oxford University Press, 1985), 365, n. 54. The 1936
edition of the *Underwriting Manual* lists examples of "nuisances": "billboards, undesirable domestic animals, . . . liquor dispensing establishments, rooming houses, . . .
industrial establishments, . . . offensive noises and odors, and poorly-kept, unsightly
properties."

32. "A change in social or racial occupancy generally leads to instability and a reduction
in values. The protection offered against adverse changes should be found adequate

before a high rating is given to this feature. Once the character of a neighborhood has been established it is usually impossible to induce a higher social class than those already in the neighborhood to purchase and occupy properties in its various locations."

33. FHA, *Underwriting Manual* (1936), pt. 2, secs. 227–28, 251–53, 266. See also secs. 280–89, esp. 284(3)(g–h). Sec. 257 notes that residents' expectations for service provision, such as police and fire protection, water supply, sewerage and street lighting, "will vary with differences in the social and financial class of people occupying the area." Sec. 266 suggests a solution for racially mixed neighborhoods. "In such an instance it might well be that for the payment of a fee children of this area could attend another school with pupils of their same social class. The question for the Valuator to determine is the effect created by the necessity for making this payment upon the occupants of the location."

34. FHA, *Underwriting Manual* (1938), pt. 2, secs. 929, 1011–14, and 1380 (2–3); "Report of Mortgage Risk Examiner," "Report of Valuator," "Exhibit A—Personal History," and "Exhibit C—Description of Real Estate," re 239 East Howell Avenue, Alexandria, VA, December 10, 1934, in RG 31, RRFM, Box 1, "Amos Herbert—Alexandria National Bank." If appraisers answered that were *was* a "danger of infiltration," they were instructed to explain "when?" Appraisers were expected to do a fairly thorough background check of applicants, or at least be familiar with their "associates." "The highest rating could hardly be ascribed in cases where the borrower's chosen associates are other than substantial, law abiding, sober-acting, sane-thinking people of acceptable ethical standards."

35. FHA, *Underwriting Manual* (1938), sec. 1380; FHA, "Standardized Factual Data Report," sample attached to "Suggestions for Conducting a Mortgage Conference," in RG 31, PCACO, Box 9, "Mortgage Conference—Suggestions for Conducting." In the completed sample form distributed to appraisers at a regional FHA conference the space next to "racial descent" had been filled in: "Anglo-Saxon." Under general remarks, the sample read: "associates with a good class of people." This form, dated 1938, was subsequently distributed after World War II. See chap. 5.

36. FHA, *Underwriting Manual* (1938), pt. 3, sec. 1412 (1–3).

37. Ibid., sec. 1412 (3), 1413.

38. Ibid., sec. 1850, b.

39. Ferguson to Draper, with attached clipping, April 3, 1941, and Baxter to Ferguson April 7, 1941, RG 31, SP, Box 29, "Speeches—1939–1941." Ferguson's assistant reminded him not to "forget" that "I have you tied up" on April 18 "to make a speech to the Negro Business Conference" but assured him that he would "not have to speak more than five or ten minutes." The sample language came from the Grand Rapids *Herald*. Ferguson replaced Stewart McDonald as FHA administrator on November 29, 1940. Four months earlier, the FHA became financially self-sustaining. Two years later, Ferguson objected to the inclusion of a nondiscrimination clause in a proposed amendment to the NHA.

40. Ferguson, "Talk before Negro Business Conference, April 18, 1941," RG 31, SP, Box 29, "Speeches—1939–1941" (emphasis in original). In the typescript, "the barometers of" is handwritten, replacing "responsible for."

41. Lancaster to Ferguson, April 28, 1941, and Ferguson to Lancaster, April 29, 1941, RG 31, SP, Box 29, "Speeches—1939–1941."

42. "Address of . . . James A. Moffett at Oklahoma City . . . before the Chamber of Commerce," March 1, 1935, RG 31, SP, Box 29, "Early Moffett Speeches." Agency

historians would later compare their early promotional efforts to "a Government war bond drive"; FHA, *The FHA Story in Summary* (Washington D.C.: GPO, 1960), 9.

43. Ibid. On public-private collaboration, see chap. 3.

44. Ibid.

45. FHA, *Insured Mortgage Portfolio*, vol. 1, no. 6 (December 1936), Babcock and Grove essays on 11–13, 15–17, 24 (copy in RG 31, RRFM, Box 1, "Amos Herbert—Alexandria National Bank"). Nonqualified lenders could subscribe to the *Portfolio* for $1.25 per year. For other promotional materials, see Fish, ed., *Story of Housing*, 204–5.

46. "Better Housing News Flash," nos. 1–4 (1935), RG 31, Motion Picture, Sound and Video Records.

47. "Better Housing News Flash," nos. 6–8 (1936), RG 31, Motion Picture, Sound and Video Records.

48. FHA, *FHA Story*, 9; Moffett speaking over a CBS hookup, under auspices of the U.S. Building and Loan League, September 28, 1934, RG 31, SP, Box 29, "Early Moffett Speeches"; Mathew F. Bokovoy, "The FHA and the 'Culture of Abundance' at the 1935 San Diego World's Fair," *Journal of the American Planning Association* 68, no. 4 (autumn 2002): 371–86, citing FHA promotional materials and Moffett's comments. For film footage of "Modernization Magic" display, see "Better Housing News Flash" no. 6. The FHA told San Diego realtors that it wanted to "see realty firms throughout California join hands in building up [a] nation-wide business recovery."

49. Moffett, "New U.S. Housing Plan," (August 15, 1934), RG 31, SP, Box 29, "Early Moffett Speeches." A pamphlet version of the presentation was published and distributed (at no cost) by two District of Columbia papers, the *Evening Star* and *Sunday Star*.

50. Moffett speaking over a CBS and NBC hookup, September 19, 1934, transcript; Moffett speaking over a CBS hookup, September 28, 1934, transcript; Moffett, "New U.S. Housing Plan," August 15, 1934, transcript, RG 31, SP, Box 29, "Early Moffett Speeches"; Abner H. Ferguson, "Address over Station WCFL, Chicago," March 16, 1938, transcript, RG 31, SP, Box 29, "Speeches, 1935–1939." Ferguson received requests from around the country for copies of his talk.

51. Speeches collected in RG 31, SP, Box 29, "Early Moffett Speeches" and "Speeches, 1935–1939." Talks before business groups were occasionally broadcast to the public; see, for example, Moffett to Construction League and the Construction Code Authority at hotel in Knoxville, Tenn., December 6, 1934.

52. Moffett to Oklahoma City Chamber of Commerce, March 1, 1935; Moffett to National Retail Lumber Dealer's Association, April 17, 1935; Moffett to Advertising Club of New York, December 13, 1934, RG 31, SP, Box 29, "Early Moffett Speeches"; "Address by Abner H. Ferguson before the American Title Association Convention, Memphis, Tennessee," October 14, 1935, RG 31, SP, 29, "Speeches, 1935–1939."

53. Moffett to Oklahoma City Chamber of Commerce, March 1, 1935, RG 31, SP, Box 29, "Early Moffett Speeches"; Ferguson to American Title Association, October 14, 1935, RG 31, SP, Box 29, "Speeches, 1935–1939."

54. Ferguson, "Talk before Negro Business Conference," April 18, 1941, RG 31, SP, Box 29, "Speeches—1939–1941."

55. Babock to McDonald, January 6, 1939 and M. R. Young to Wilkins (draft, with notations), October 14, 1938, RG 31, CCSF, Box 6, "Racial Restrictive Covenants, 1938–1948." The heavily edited draft to Wilkins shows housing officials literally sorting out the terms of the market imperative defense. Original text is crossed out

and replaced—for example, "We do not operate with, as you say, tax payers money" becomes "We have no money to lend or grant for any purpose." The claim that the FHA only insures mortgages "in accordance with our rules and regulations" becomes "in accordance with the requirements in the law that they be economically sound."

56. M. R. Young to Thurgood Marshall, July 26, 1940, RG 31, CCSF, Box 6, "Racial Restrictive Covenants, 1938–1948." Later that fall, the FHA corrected itself and informed Marshall that it had "deleted the racial occupancy clause from its form of suggested minimum covenants" but then reiterated its defense of covenants as a "favorable element in the determination of economic soundness." The agency was not empowered to "reject protective covenants except those that may adversely affect the economic soundness of an insured mortgage"; Young to Marshall, November 12, 1940.

CHAPTER FIVE

1. Beth J. Lief and Susan Goering, "The Implementation of the Federal Mandate for Fair Housing," in Gary A. Tobin, ed., *Divided Neighborhoods: Changing Patterns of Racial Segregation* (Newbury Park, Calif.: Sage Publications, 1987); Arnold R. Hirsch, "'Containment' on the Home Front: Race and Federal Housing Policy from the New Deal to the Cold War," *Journal of Urban History* 26, no. 2 (January 2000): 158–80; idem, "Choosing Segregation: Federal Housing Policy between *Shelley* and *Brown*," in John F. Bauman, Roger Biles, and Kristin Szylvian, eds., *From Tenements to Taylor Homes: In Search of an Urban Housing Policy in Twentieth-Century America* (University Park: Pennsylvania State University Press, 2000); David M. P. Freund, "'Democracy's Unfinished Business': Federal Policy and the Search for Fair Housing, 1961–1968," in Chester Hartman, ed., *Poverty and Race in America: The Emerging Agendas* (Lanham, Md.: Lexington Books, 2006), 173–77.

2. Miles Colean, *The Impact of Government on Real Estate Finance in the United States*, Studies in Urban Mortgage Financing (New York: National Bureau of Economic Research, 1950), 102–5; HHFA, *First Annual Report, 1947* (Washington, D.C.: GPO, 1948), III-60 ff.; Pearl Janet Davies, *Real Estate in American History* (Washington, D.C.: Public Affairs Press, 1958), chap. 8. By December 1941, the U.S. was spending almost $75 million a day on "military preparedness"; William H. Chafe, *The Unfinished Journey: American Since World War II* (New York: Oxford University Press, 1986), 7. The best introductions to wartime migration are Jacqueline Jones, *The Dispossessed: America's Underclass from the Civil War to the Present* (New York: Basic Books, 1992), chaps. 7–8, and James N. Gregory, *The Southern Diaspora: How the Great Migrations of Black and White Southerners Transformed America* (Chapel Hill: University of North Carolina Press, 2005).

3. HHFA, *Twelfth Annual Report* (Washington D.C.: GPO, 1958), 62, table III-4; HHFA, *First Annual Report, 1947*, III-60, table 43; Colean, *Impact of Government*, 102–3; 55 Stat 55, March 28, 1941; Barry G. Jacobs et al., *Guide to Federal Housing Programs*, 2nd ed. (Washington, D.C.: Bureau of National Affairs, 1982), 9–11. On builders' long-standing opposition to public housing legislation, see Timothy L. McDonnell, *The Wagner Housing Act: A Case Study of the Legislative Process* (Chicago: Loyola University Press, 1957), and Gail Radford, *Modern Housing for America: Policy Struggles in the New Deal Era* (Chicago: University of Chicago Press, 1996).

4. *Servicemen's Readjustment Act.* Public Law 78-346, U.S. Statutes at Large 58 (1944): 291–92. For a summary of VA lending terms, see Colean, *Impact of Government*, 107–8 (note that he misstates the original amortization period).

5. Colean, *Impact of Government*, 107–8; George F. Break, *The Economic Impact of Federal Loan Insurance* (Washington, D.C.: National Planning Association, 1961), 48–49; Henry J. Aaron Jr., *Shelter and Subsidies: Who Benefits from Federal Housing Policies?* (Washington, D.C.: Brookings Institution, 1972), 80; Executive Office of the President, Bureau of the Budget, "Special Analysis of Federal Credit Programs in the 1961 Budget," derived from the Budget of the United States Government for the Fiscal Year Ending June 30, 1961 (Washington, D.C.: Executive Office of the President, Bureau of the Budget, January 1960), 10–11. On early alterations to VA operations, see William B. Thompson, "The Federal Housing Administration—Its Functions and Operations," in Robert H. Pease and Lewis O. Kerwood, eds., *Mortgage Banking*, 2nd ed. (New York: McGraw-Hill, 1965), 47, 55. Like many commentators, Aaron distinguishes between VA and FHA operations, describing the former, only, as a "subsidy." See also J. Paul Mitchell, "Historical Overview of Federal Policy: Encouraging Homeownership," in Mitchell, ed., *Federal Housing Policy and Programs: Past and Present* (New Brunswick, N.J.: Rutgers University, Center for Urban Policy Research, 1985), 9. Mortgage textbooks generally avoid the term when discussing the VA program: the "government absorbs the cost of the mortgage guarantee," writes Marshall W. Dennis in *Residential Mortgage Lending*, 2nd ed. (Englewood Cliffs, N.J.: Prentice-Hall, 1989), 12.

6. *Servicemen's Readjustment Act*. Public Law 78-346, U.S. Statutes at Large 58 (1944): 292; H.R. 3749. Public Law 79-268, U.S. Statutes at Large (1945): 627–28; Break, *Economic Impact*, 47–49; Lizabeth Cohen, *A Consumers' Republic: The Politics of Mass Consumption in Postwar America* (New York: Knopf, 2003), 170–72; Andrew Wiese, *Places of Their Own: African American Suburbanization in the Twentieth Century* (Chicago: University of Chicago Press, 2004), 188–89. In 1955, one VA official estimated that no more than 30,000 black GIs had benefited from its mortgage guarantee program. See Cohen's important discussion of the forces limiting black veterans' access to postwar GI benefits in *Consumer's Republic*, 167–73.

7. Before World War II, one-third of all homes were built by their owner, and one-third by small contractors. By the late 1950s, about two-thirds of all homes were built by large developers. For good introductions to construction innovations, cost-cutting measures, and the scale of postwar housing production, see Clifford E. Clark, *The American Family Home: 1800–1960* (Chapel Hill: University of North Carolina Press, 1986), chap. 7; Barry Checkoway, "Large Builders, Federal Housing Programs, and Postwar Suburbanization," *International Journal of Urban and Regional Research* 4, no. 1 (March 1980); Dolores Hayden, *Building Suburbia, 1820–2000* (New York: Pantheon Books, 2003), chap. 7; Kenneth Jackson, *Crabgrass Frontier: The Suburbanization of the United States* (New York: Oxford University Press, 1985), chap. 13.

8. David M. P. Freund, "Marketing the Free Market: State Intervention and the Politics of Prosperity in Metropolitan America," in Kevin M. Kruse and Thomas J. Sugrue, eds., *The New Suburban History* (Chicago: University of Chicago Press, 2006).

9. Foley to Greene, August 14, 1945; Greene to Foley, August 18, 1945; Greene to Franklin D. Richards, August 18, 1945; Greene to Ernest P. Jones, August 18, 1945; Greene to Kent R. Mullikan, August 18, 1945; Greene to Foley, September 6, 1945; see also Planning Committee (Greene) to Foley, November 2, 1945 ("Report No. 23—Veterans"): all in RG 31, CCSF, Box 1, "Committee-Planning, 1945–1946"; Fisher to Foley, October 6, 1945, RG 31, CCSF, Box 4, "Meetings—Outside Committee on Planning." Jones was chairman of the Rehabilitation of Existing Housing and Promotional and Educational Campaigns.

Foley met with dozens of executives representing banks, trust companies, S&Ls, insurance companies, and mortgage banks, as well as real estate agents. economists, and builders, among them a number of NAHB officers. The Operating Committee recommended separate meetings with the insurance companies, "because they largely represent the secondary financing field." For dates of meetings, lists of participating institutions, and meeting agendas, see typescript invitation inventories and memos in RG 31, CCSF, Box 4, "Meetings—Outside Committee on Planning." See also RG 31, CCSF, Box 3, "Economy Housing, Corr." (1945–49), and the extensive correspondence from realtors, trade groups, banks, title companies, and real estate boards supporting extension of Title II insurance for existing housing, in RG 31, CCSF, Box 3, "Existing Construction, 1941–46."

10. Truman quoted in Congressional Quarterly Service, *Congress and the Nation, 1945–1964* (Washington, D.C.: Congressional Quarterly, 1965), 475. See also Gwendolyn Wright, *Building the Dream: A Social History of Housing in America* (Cambridge, Mass.: MIT Press, 1981), 242.

11. Rosalyn Baxandall and Elizabeth Ewen, *Picture Windows: How the Suburbs Happened* (New York: Basic Books, 2000), 93–96, 104. Perhaps the most famous critic of public housing was builder William Levitt, who claimed in a 1948 *Harper's* article that "No man who has a house and a lot can be a Communist" because he has "too much to do"; cited in Hayden, *Building Suburbia*, 135. See also Congressional Quarterly Service, *Congress and the Nation*, 477–80.

12. For an introduction, see correspondence regarding the GI Bill, the Taft-Ellender bill, and extension of Title VI mortgages in RG 31, IOPM, Box 41, "Raymond Foley—Commissioner—FHA, July 1945–December 31, 1946" and Box 43, "Telegrams to Blandford Urging Legislation." For an introduction to coordination with the FHLBB, see correspondence regarding pending legislation and copies of FHLBB speeches in RG 31, CCSF, Box 8, "Federal Home Loan Bank Board."

13. RG 31, CCSF, Box 5, "Outside Activities: Actions Taken by the Committee, 1949 through 1953." On calculating business volume, see RG 31, CCSF, Box 1, "Classification of Field Offices, 1947–1950." On postwar promotional campaigns and collaboration with private operatives, see RG 31, CCSF, Box 1, "Committee—Planning, 1945–1946" and "Committee—Special Field, 1947–1948"; zone meeting collections in RG 31, PCACO, Box 9; and RG 31, CCSF, Box 2, "Coordination FHA-VA Technical Functions, 1954–1956." On city-by-city meetings with construction and finance representatives, see RG 31, CCSF, Box 3, "Economy Housing, Corr." FHA administrators forwarded copies of their congressional testimony to leaders of the banking, S&L, mortgage banking, trust company, and building industries. See, for example, copy of Foley's testimony at hearings on the Wagner-Ellender-Taft bill, with attached mailing list, RG 31, CCSF, Box 4, "Meetings—Outside Committee on Planning."

14. The NAHB provided copies of the amendments to Section 203 for distribution to local membership and urged officers to invite local builders and lenders—even those not affiliated with the NAHB because this would be a good way to recruit them. Zone Commissioner form letter, "September Meetings with Industry," August 31, 1948; Lockwood to Directors of All Field Offices, "Meetings with Industry," August 19, 1948; Frank W. Cortright (NAHB) to Officers, Directors and Alternative Directors of NAHB, August 25, 1948; John W. Dickerman (NAHB), to Officers and Directors of NAHB and Presidents and Secretaries of Affiliated Associations, August 20, 1948; Richards to Foley, October 13, 1948; zone commissioner form letter, September 8,

1948, and "Summary of the Housing Act of 1948 for September Meetings with Industry." For a detailed description of presentations and panel discussions, see "Combined Home Builders and FHA Conference," Fort Pitt Hotel, September 22, 1948 (Home Builders' Association of Allegheny Co.). For a description of meetings in Baltimore, see E. Lester Muller, FHA state director, Baltimore, Md., to W. Stanley Newlin, zone commissioner, October 15, 1948. On meetings in Ohio, see J. L. Wadsworth, district director, FHA, to Zone Commissioner George A. Bremer, October 11, 1948 (about 550 builders and lenders attended meetings in Canton, Akron, Cleveland, Youngstown, and Toledo). See also Richards to Builders and Lenders, Greensboro, North Carolina, March 14, 1949. All in RG 31, CCSF, Box 4, "Meetings—Industry, 1948." See also Davies, *Real Estate,* 196–205.

Public interest groups did not receive the same consideration. The FHA scheduled regular meetings with labor, civil rights, and other "public interest groups" but never granted them a comparable advisory role in the policymaking process. In January 1953, an internal agency memo described these meetings' goals: to keep public interest groups "informed regarding developments in housing programs and policies," to give them a forum in which to discuss "local problems, reactions and developments regarding housing programs," and to enable them to "identify key issues and problems that arise." The agency initially balked at the idea of inviting the U.S. Conference of Mayors or the American Municipal Association, because these were not seen as "public interest" organizations. See "Comments on Economic and Housing Situation, July 1950" ("for administrative use"); agendas for and memos regarding "Regular Meetings of Representatives of National Public Interest Organizations and Housing Agency Officials," held in 1952, 1953, and 1955; "Statement of Purpose: Regular Meetings of Representatives of National Public Interest Organizations," January 16, 1953: all in RG 31, CCSF, Box 4, "Meetings—Public Interest Groups."

15. Quotes from C. N. Nichols, National Established Roofing, Siding and Insulating Contractors Association, Inc., to Hollyday, March 8, 1954, RG 31, SP, Box 34, "NERSICA, NYC, March 23, 1954." Appearances by FHA officials were heavily publicized in trade publications. See, for example, *Planner* (Home Builders Institute, Inc.), 2, no. 3, March 1, 1954, RG 31, SP, Box 34, "L.A., San Diego, Salt Lake City, March 3–March 6, 1954" (file: "Los Angeles, Cal., March 3, 1954"). Just keeping local FHA operatives up to date on changes to the NHA was an arduous task; see RG 31, PCACO, Box 9, "Meetings: Zone Conferences, 1952." The FHA constantly heard from individual businessmen, but mostly from professional associations of builders, realtors, retailers, and building supply manufacturers. For an introduction to the extensive correspondence after 1945, see RG 31, IOPM, Box 43, "Telegrams to Blandford Urging Legislation."

16. H.R. 3749. Public Law 79-268, U.S. Statutes at Large (1945): 627–28. Congressional actions extended the FHA mandate, increased its insurance fund, and/or liberalized the terms of insured loans in the following years: 1949, 1950, 1951, 1952, 1955, 1956, 1957, 1958, and 1959. See also George F. Break, ed., *Federal Credit Agencies: A Series of Studies Prepared for the Commission on Money and Credit* (Englewood Cliffs, N.J.: Prentice-Hall, 1963), 5, table I-1, I-3.

17. Mitchell, "Historical Overview," 10–11; Colean, *Impact of Government,* 104. See also Hirsch, "'Containment' on the Home Front," 170–78. Largely as a result of FHA policy, writes Mark Gelfand, "new rental units as a percentage of total new starts fell from 43.9 per cent in 1927 to 8.3 per cent in 1956"; *A Nation of Cities: The Federal Government and Urban America, 1933–1965* (New York: Oxford University Press,

1975), 217. After World War II the supply of rental housing was further reduced as units were transferred from a controlled rental market to an uncontrolled sales market.

18. Between 1945 and 1960, less than 2 percent of all homes constructed with FHA assistance and 3 percent of VA-guaranteed properties were occupied by nonwhites. Wiese calculates that the agencies helped blacks purchase or occupy (as renters) about 300,000 units, almost exclusively in all-black neighborhoods and disproportionately in southern states; Wiese, *Places of Their Own,* 138–40, chap. 7; U.S. Commission on Civil Rights, *Report, 1959* (Washington D.C.: GPO, 1959), 462–65; Robert Weaver, *The Negro Ghetto* (New York: Russell & Russell, 1948), 143–48, 219–22.

19. Arnold Hirsch has reconstructed the work of the RRS and documented the depth of HHFA resistance to its efforts in "'Containment' on the Home Front," "Choosing Segregation," and "'The Last and Most Difficult Barrier': Segregation and Federal Housing Policy in the Eisenhower Administration, 1953–1960" (report submitted to the Poverty and Race Research Action Council, July 8, 2002). For further discussion of the RRS and its descendant, the Intergroup Relations Service, during the Weaver era, see Wiese, *Places of Their Own,* 138–40, and Freund, "Democracy's Unfinished Business."

20. Blumberg to Hubbard, April 2, 1952; Blumberg to Kadow, April 10, 1952; Blumberg to Hubbard, September 19, 1952; "An Analysis of the Redevelopment Potentialities of the Gratiot-Orleans Area, Detroit, Michigan, March 1955" ("For Administrative Use Only: Not for Publication or Release"): all in RG 31, RHMA, Box 9, "Detroit, Michigan—Market Analyst's Report on Housing."

21. W. S. Newlin to Snowden, March 29, 1954, with draft of "Racial Relations Handbook," RG 31, PCACO, Box 3, "Race Relations Handbook." Richards quoted in "Address . . . at Opening of Vandalia Homes, Memphis, Tenn., June 9, 1949," RG 31, SP, Box 31. See also the detailed 1954 report, "The Federal Housing Administration and Minority Groups," which outlined "necessary adjustments to meet the expanding housing requirements of the minority group segment of the effective market." Presumably without irony, the report calls upon the FHA to "undertake market and other fact-finding studies, pin pointing in each locality the factors inhibiting the development of housing available to minority groups"; unpublished report, RG 31, PCACO, Box 3 (reference to "problem areas" on p. 1). For an excellent introduction to the agency's rhetoric about meeting the needs of "lower income populations and minorities," see administrators' presentations to industry groups in the late 1940s and early 1950s, RG, 31, SP, Box 32.

22. Congressional Quarterly Service, *Congress and the Nation,* 478–81; Baxandall and Ewen, *Picture Windows,* chap. 8; HHFA, *Twelfth Annual Report,* 62, table III-4. On Sec. 608, a program further undermined by scandal and abuse, see Albert M. Cole, "Federal Housing Programs: 1950–1960," in Gertrude Sipperly Fish, ed., *The Story of Housing* (New York: Macmillan, 1979), 296 and Wright, *Building the Dream,* 246–47.

23. Break, *Economic Impact,* 65–76; USBC, *Historical Statistics of the United States: Colonial Times to 1970* (Washington, D.C.: GPO, 1975), 641, Series N 180–85. On the impact of FHA size and design requirements on construction trends, see Greg Hise, *Magnetic Los Angeles: Planning the Twentieth-Century Metropolis* (Baltimore: John Hopkins University Press, 1997), chap. 2.

24. HHFA, *Twelfth Annual Report,* tables III-4, III-5, and III-7; USBC, *Statistical Abstract of the United States, 1965* (Washington, D.C.: GPO, 1965), 752, 766, 767; Leo Grebler,

The Role of Federal Credit Aids in Residential Construction (New York: National Bureau of Economic Research, 1953), 16, 18, 30, 32; Sherman J. Maisel, *Financing Real Estate: Principles and Practices* (New York: McGraw-Hill, 1965), 99–100, 111; Jackson, *Crabgrass Frontier,* 215; HHFA, *Housing Statistics,* Historical Supplement (Washington, D.C.: HHFA, 1958), 17–18, 160–61, (and 1959), 17; Commerce, *Statistical Abstract, 1965;* Raymond Goldsmith, *The Flow of Capital Funds in the Postwar Economy* (New York: National Bureau of Economic Research, 1965), 279, 286, 303; Executive Office of the President, "Special Analysis of Federal Credit Programs," 10–11; Break, *Economic Impact,* 45, 70 (table 21). The figures for FHA and VA support for new construction slightly overstate the impact of FHA financing and slightly understate the impact of VA guarantees; see discussion in Grebler, *Role of Federal Credit,* 16 n. 1, 18, 30. Also see Cohen's important discussion of the distribution of GI benefits and postwar class politics in *Consumers' Republic,* 156–60.

In 1945 and 1946, the FHA and VA supported just under a quarter of the nation's housing starts. Over the next five years federally secured loans paid for the purchase of about half of all new homes. Between 1945 and 1950, 57.5 percent of the mortgages backed by the FHA and VA were for new construction, and between 1934–51, the FHA and VA financed about 45 percent of the "total estimated flow of mortgage funds into new construction." Federal insurance commitments fluctuated, yet continued at comparable rates, through the late 1950s and early 1960s. In most years veterans received more than half of all mortgages; in 1955, for example, 30 percent of the nation's mortgages on single-family homes were secured by the VA and 21 percent were insured by the FHA. Single-family construction remained the focus. In all but one of the years between 1951 and 1958, the agencies helped finance the construction of single-family homes at a rate even higher than that at which they supported overall housing starts. Of the 5.6 million loans guaranteed by the VA through June 30, 1959, nearly 95 percent were for homes. Between 1950 and 1960, 40 percent of all residential mortgage debt had been underwritten by the federal government.

25. Grebler, *Role of Federal Credit,* 42–44; Oliver Jones and Leo Grebler, *The Secondary Mortgage Market: Its Purpose, Performance, and Potential* (Los Angeles: Real Estate Research Program, Graduate School of Business Administration, University of California, 1961), chap. 3.

26. Carl F. Behrens, *Commercial Bank Activities in Urban Mortgage Financing,* Studies in Urban Mortgage Financing (New York: National Bureau of Economic Research, 1952), 3, 14–25, 33 (table 4), 45 (table 11); Grebler, *Role of Federal Credit,* 39–40, 43; R. J. Saulnier, *Urban Mortgage Lending by Life Insurance Companies,* Studies in Urban Mortgage Financing (New York: National Bureau of Economic Research, 1950), 4 (table 2), 10; Haar, *Federal Credit,* 11; Jones and Grebler, *Secondary Mortgage Market,* chap. 3. Behrens's figures are for 1929 and 1949. For an excellent summary of the government's influence, see Goldsmith, *Capital Funds,* chap. 10.

27. Break, *Economic Impact,* esp. chap. 5; Aaron, *Shelter and Subsidies,* 92; Haar, *Federal Credit,* 86; Jones and Grebler, *Secondary Mortgage Market,* 123–27.

28. Maisel, *Financing Real Estate,* 91–94; Mitchell, "Historical Overview," 42–43; Grebler, *Role of Federal Credit,* 45–46, 47 (table 7); HHFA, *Eighth Annual Report* (Washington, D.C.: GPO), 424; Haar, *Federal Credit,* 113–25; Break, *Economic Impact,* 52 (table 14); Jones and Grebler, *Secondary Mortgage Market,* 33–37 (quoting 34), 128–31; Goldsmith, *Capital Funds,* 277; Aaron, *Shelter and Subsidies,* 92–94, 96.

29. Haar, *Federal Credit,* 86, 113–25; Aaron, *Shelter and Subsidies,* 92, 95–96; Jones and

Grebler, *Secondary Mortgage Market*, 34, 86–87, 152–53; Maisel, *Financing Real Estate*, 92–94; Goldsmith. *Capital Funds*, 277.

30. Thomas B. Marvell, *The Federal Home Loan Bank Board* (New York: Praeger, 1969), 4–5, 19–25, 29–32, 39–40, 112–13, 259, 261; PL 91-151; Semer et al., "Evolution," 77, 75; Maisel, *Financing Real Estate*, 89–91; HHFA, *Eighth Annual Report*, 52–54; Jones and Grebler, *Secondary Mortgage Market*, 37–39. Originally an independent agency, the FHLB was moved to the Housing and Home Finance Agency in 1947 and finally, in 1955, resumed its independent status. PL 81-576 (June 27, 1950) authorized the FSLIC to insure accounts in S&Ls up to $10,000 (up from $5,000). In 1966 the limit was raised to $15,000.

31. HHFA, *Eighth Annual Report*, 61 (table 11); Marvell, *Bank Board*, 8–9; Haar, *Federal Credit*, 13 (fig. 2), 14 (fig. 3), 15 (fig. 4), 17 (table 2); Grebler, *Role of Federal Credit*, 36–42; Aaron, *Shelter and Subsidies*, 98, 103. For figures on S&L assets in the conventional mortgage market, see Goldsmith, *Capital Funds*, 282 and 283 (table 98). See also Checkoway, "Large Builders" and Aaron's discussion of the FHLB bail-out of its members in 1969–70 (103). Aaron describes the postwar FHLB as "a member-owned instrument for regulating and aiding its membership."

32. Aaron, *Shelter and Subsidies*, 53–73 (quoting 53), 81–85, 94–95; Mitchell, "Historical Overview," 42; Wright, *Building the Dream*, 260; Gelfand, *Nation of Cities*, 217–18, 426, n. 52. See Lizabeth Cohen's excellent discussion of the postwar tax system and its reward structure in *Consumer's Republic*, 143–47. The $7 billion figure is Aaron's and represents the taxes that homeowners would have to pay if they had been governed by the rules applicable to investors in other assets. Aaron argues—and I disagree—that while the mortgage market helps explain the growth of homeownership, the "most important factor . . . is undoubtedly the personal income tax system"; Aaron, 62.

33. Between 1940 and 1970, the black suburban population *outside of the South* grew by only 700,000. While the rate of homeownership among blacks increased from 24 percent to 39 percent between 1940 and 1960, among suburban blacks it increased from 32 percent to 51 percent. Wiese, *Places of Their Own*, esp. chaps. 4 and 5.

34. "Since World War II," wrote Jackson in 1985, "the largest private contractors have built all their new houses to meet FHA standards, even though financing has often been arranged without FHA aid," because "many potential purchasers will not consider a house that cannot earn FHA approval"; *Crabgrass Frontier*, 205.

35. FHA, *Successful Subdivisions: Principles of Planning For Economy and Protection Against Neighborhood Blight* (Land Use Planning Bulletin no. 1) (Washington, D.C.: GPO, [n.d., ca. 1940]), frontispiece, 9–10; Urban Land Institute, Community Builders' Council, *Community Builders' Handbook* (Washington, D.C.: Urban Land Institute, 1947), 2–4, and see 30, 35, 56–57, model plat, and sample covenant in Appendix A. The ULI updated the *Handbook* in 1948, 1950, 1954, 1956, 1960, and 1968. The passages cited here from the 1947 edition were reproduced in subsequent volumes.

36. William B. Thompson, "Federal Housing Administration," 46; AIREA, *The Appraisal of Real Estate* (Chicago: AIREA, 1960), 456. The AIREA manual first appeared in 1951.

37. HHFA, *Twelfth Annual Report*, 230, 233, table III-13, and table III-16; United States Savings and Loan League, *Savings and Loan Annals* (Chicago, 1948–58), esp. 1948, 112, and 1958, 262; idem, *Savings and Loan Annals* (Chicago, 1944/45), D74–D75, (1951/52), D79–D80. The League stopped publishing local directories after 1951.

38. Minutes of the Hazel Park City Council, September 8, 1942, May 24, 1948, and May 26, 1947, HP.

39. See Thomas Sugrue's important discussion of this point in *Origins of the Urban Crisis: Race and Inequality in Postwar Detroit* (Princeton: Princeton University Press, 1996), esp. chap. 8.

40. "Suggestions for Conducting a Mortgagee Conference," including sample "Program," typescript, n.d., RG 31, PCACO, Box 9, "Mortgagee Conference—Suggestions for Conducting."

41. Ibid.; radio scripts "To be delivered by Realtor" and "To be Delivered by Mortgagee," RG 31, PCACO, Box 9, "Meetings, Zone Meeting in Field, 1944–5." Layouts, mats, and sample texts collected in RG 31, PCACO, Box 9, "Meetings—Zone Meetings in Field, 1944–1945." Quotes from texts for "Points on Buying a Home" (Layout FHA 471-2) and "The Sensible Way to Buy a Home Today" (Layout FHA 471-4). FHA regional directors were also furnished with news releases that detailed the terms of government-insured loans and reported on local enthusiasm for the program. They were instructed to distribute these to all newspapers in cities and towns with 4,000 or more residents.

42. Greene to Foley, August 18, 1945; Greene to Richards, August 18, 1945; Greene to Jones, August 18, 1945; Greene to Mullikan, August 18, 1945; Green (for Planning Committee) to Foley September 17, 1945; Richards to Foley, January 25, 1946; "Outline of Proposed FHA Promotional Activities," September 10, 1945: all in RG 31, CCSF, Box 1, "Committee-Planning, 1945–1946"; "Zone Commissioners, Notes for Zone Meetings," RG 31, PCACO, Box 9, "Meetings—Zone Meeting in Field, 1944–5." At war's end, FHA zone commissioners were reporting that "the mortgage educational program is being neglected in many field offices." Meanwhile the subcommittee acknowledged that "without these activities, it is doubtful whether, during the past decade, the Federal Housing Administration could have performed the public service now commonly accredited to it."

43. It is impossible to calculate the total number of presentations or participants. The agency prepared at least 130 different speeches between 1945 and 1953, many of which were given to multiple audiences (for example, "Speech made on West Coast trip"). Most audiences were at trade conventions, but many were listed as "General Industry Group," making it difficult to measure the reach of this campaign. But agency reports suggest that it was dramatic. For example, in just the first two months of the 1949 Economy Housing Campaign, designed to encourage lending under Sec. 203D, FHA officials held over 300 meetings, attended by more than 40,000 people. See Richards to "Detroit Mortgage Bankers Association Clinic," Detroit, April 26, 1949, RG 31, SP, Box 31. The last speech in the National Archives collection is dated March 30, 1954.

44. Officials regularly assured businessmen that they did "not foresee any change in FHA maximum interest rates during the present calendar year" or that "no changes in basic policy are contemplated."

45. Greene to "Philadelphia Mortgage Bankers Association," May 5, 1950 (for details on the Sec. 203D program); Richards to the NAHB, Chicago, January 24, 1951; Richards to Texas Mortgage Bankers Association, Fort Worth, Texas, April 12, 1951; Richards to Mortgage Bankers Association, Drake Hotel, Chicago, January 25, 1951; Greene to "Michigan Association of Approved Mortgagees," December 5, 1952; Greene to "Mortgage Bankers Association Convention," Chicago, October 2, 1952; and Greene to "Manufacturers, Builders, Lenders and Dealers," Seattle, September 9,

1953: all in RG 31, SP, Box 32; Oscar R. Kruetz (NSSL) to Richards, February 18, 1949, RG 31, SP, Box 33, "Sixth Annual Convention, National Savings and Loan League, Mackinac Island, Michigan, June 18, 1949."

46. For an excellent introduction to the broader national conversation about free markets and consumption, see Cohen, *Consumers' Republic*, esp. chap. 3.

47. Foley to "a committee of financial and building interests, hotel Waldorf-Astoria, New York, New York," September 12, 1945; Richards to "the National Association of Home Builders, Chicago, Ill., Stevens Hotel," February 24, 1948; Richards to Regional Meetings of Oklahoma and Texas Home Builders, Fort Worth, Texas, June 25, 1948; Richards' "West Coast" speech, delivered in Los Angeles, July 1948 to an unspecified audience of home builders and financiers; Richards to Wisconsin Builders Association, Madison, Wisconsin, May 26, 1948; Richards to Annual Mortgage Bankers Convention, Hotel Commodore, NYC, September 23, 1948; Richards to Builders and Lenders, Greensboro, North Carolina, March 14, 1949; Richards to American Bankers Association, Western Savings and Mortgage Conference, San Francisco, April 4, 1949: all in RG 31, SP, Box 31; Richards to Washington Conference for Men under 35, Sponsored by Mortgage Bankers Association of America, Mayflower Hotel, Washington, D.C., January 15, 1952; Richards to the Georgia Association of Real Estate Boards, Atlanta, October 19, 1951; Richards to NAHB, Low Cost Rental Housing Conference, Memphis, Tennessee, May 4, 1951: all in RG 31, SP, Box 32. In 1950, Richards scolded the Advertising Club of Baltimore for not doing a "better job" of popularizing "the lower cost housing insurance plan (Section 203D of the National Housing Act)," which has "not been utilized in this area to the extent that it has in the country as a whole." "In the year 1950," he concluded, "good merchandizing is going to count more than ever"; Richards to "Advertising Club of Baltimore City," March 1, 1950.

48. "Prepared Talks Given at FHA Director Meetings, Washington, D.C., August 16–17, 1954" ("Talk by Herbert Welch," 8–10), RG 31, PCACO, Box 9, "Meetings, Directors Meeting in Washington."

49. "Statement of Franklin D. Richards . . . Before the Subcommittee of the House Banking and Currency Committee," February 5, 1952, in RG 31, SP, Box 32; FHA, *The FHA Story in Summary* (Washington D.C.: GPO, 1960), 22; Elaine Tyler May, *Homeward Bound: American Families in the Cold War Era* (New York: Basic Books, 1988); Clifford E. Clark, "Ranch House Suburbia: Ideals and Realities," in Lary May, ed., *Recasting America: Culture and Politics in the Age of Cold War* (Chicago: University of Chicago Press, 1989); Hayden, *Building Suburbia*, 146–51. For a sample of local press coverage, see *DN*, April 29, 1949. Perhaps most famously it was in 1959, in the "kitchen debate" between Vice President Richard Nixon and Soviet Premier Nikita Khrushchev, that the former touted the importance of American consumer goods and described the American consumer as someone unwilling "to have decisions made at the top by government officials who say that all homes should be built in the same way"; *New York Times*, July 25, 1959.

50. Stanley L. McMichael and Paul T. O'Keefe, *How to Finance Real Estate*, 3rd ed. (Englewood Cliffs, N.J., Prentice-Hall, 1967), chaps. 12, 13; Thompson, "Federal Housing Administration," 46–47; Preston Martin, *Real Estate Principles and Practices* (New York: Macmillan, 1959), 31–32, 311–12, 323. McMichael and O'Keefe praise FHA programs while decrying "the growing tendency toward governmental paternalism," which had been "clearly demonstrated in the over-promotion of rental housing during the early post-war period." This distinction is repeated in contemporary

volumes on mortgage lending; see, for example, Dennis, *Residential Mortgage Lending,* esp. 312–53, and chap. 11 (on the secondary mortgage market). According to Janet Davies, in 1950 NAREB president Robert P. Gerholz said that an American GI offered a "moral equity which is real, if not tangible"; Davies, *Real Estate,* 213.

51. For a discussion of opposition to the FHA's racial policies and the response of administration officials, see Hirsch, "'Containment' on the Home Front," esp. 162–65; Freund, "Democracy's Unfinished Business."

52. FHA, "Standardized Factual Data Report" and "Suggested Topics Which the Representative of the Underwriting Division Should be Sure to Mention," both in "Suggestions for Conducting a Mortgage Conference," RG 31, PCACO, Box 9, "Mortgage Conference—Suggestions for Conducting."

53. On the importance of "record[ing] suitable protective covenants," see FHA, *Successful Subdivisions,* 2–11, 28. See also FHA, *Better Housing* (Washington, D.C.: GPO, 1938) and *Principles of Planning Small Homes* (Washington, D.C.: GPO, 1940).

54. For a discussion of early *Underwriting Manual* language, see chap. 4, and Rose Helper, *Racial Policies and Practices of Real Estate Brokers* (Minneapolis: University of Minnesota Press, 1969). In 1947, a year before the *Shelley* ruling, the ULI's handbook discussed strategies for distancing subdivisions from "nonconforming uses," noting that developments should be "safeguarded by recorded protective covenants [and] the establishment and enforcement of a zoning ordinance." During World War II, NAREB publications lumped together blacks, gangsters, bootleggers, and prostitutes; ULI, *Community Builders' Handbook,* 10, 17, 43, 57, 85–93; Herman H. Long and Charles S. Johnson, *People vs. Property: Race Restrictive Covenants in Housing* (Nashville: Fisk University Press, 1947), 56–70. For a glimpse of the impact of national standards on local marketing practices, see proceedings from the April 1950 Real Estate Clinic in Ann Arbor, Michigan, especially Arthur Early ("Listing the Property") and J. Philip Wernette ("The Future of the Private Enterprise System"), in School of Business Administration, University of Michigan, *Lectures and Papers of the Annual Real Estate Clinic at the University of Michigan, Ann Arbor* (April 11–12, 1950), 28, 1–15, 111–23, and 39–43.

55. For an introduction, see correspondence and NAACP memoranda in RG 31, CCSF, Box 6, "Racial Restrictive Covenants, 1938–1948."

56. Mack to Draper, re NAACP memo, November 23, 1944 and Lockwood to Konvitz, March 2, 1944, RG 31, CCSF, Box 6, "Racial Restrictive Covenants, 1938–1948."

57. Ibid. See also Arnold Hirsch's discussion of these documents and the FHA's response to the NAACP and *Shelley* in "'Containment' on the Home Front," 162–65.

58. FHA, *Underwriting Manual* (1952), secs. 1016(5), 1013(5), 1104(b). See also "Analysis of Location," 1104 (a–b), and Helper, *Racial Policies,* 202–3. On the FHA's negotiation of *Shelley,* see Hirsch, "'Containment' on the Home Front," 165 (quoting minutes of an FHA executive board meeting from 1949).

59. Helper, *Racial Policies,* chap. 7, esp. 201.

60. Hirsch, "'Containment' on the Home Front," esp. 161–65, 170–78 (quoting Cole), 182; idem, "Choosing Segregation"; Lockwood to Herman Will Jr., November 19, 1948, Franklin D. Richards to Scott W. Lucas, November 19, 1948, and 1948 memo re court challenges, RG 31, CCSF, Box 6, "Racial Restrictive Covenants, 1938–1948"; Flora Y. Hatcher, "Overall Summary Report of Housing Hearing of Commission on Civil Rights, Feb. 2–3, 1959, NYC," RG 207, Box 25, "Race Relations, Intergroup Relations"; "Material prepared for Harold Tyler . . . [re] executive order," October 4, 1960, RG 207, Box 40, "Intergroup (Snowden policy memos), 1960"; National Commit-

tee Against Discrimination in Housing, "Needed: 'A Stroke of the Pen,'" RG 207, Box 64, "Intergroup, Exec. Order, 1961"; Norman P. Mason address to "the Annual Convention of the National Association of Real Estate Boards," November 11, 1959, RG 207, Box 49, "NAREB, Royal York Hotel, Toronto, November 11, 1959"; Freund, "Democracy's Unfinished Business." When asked by the Justice Department in 1960 about the potential impact of Kennedy's proposed executive order, the HHFA predicted that insertion of a nondiscrimination clause in the FHA's insurance agreement would "have the practical effect of destroying the FHA mortgage insurance program." Meanwhile in other settings FHA administrators assured realtors that the HHFA distinguished between "Mr. Average Citizen" and the "unfortunate citizen[s] who may have to be supported with subsidy."

61. "It may shock you to learn," wrote Herman Will Jr., and Francis J. de Neveu to President Harry Truman in 1948, "that FHA has, as we have been informed in face to face talks with its officials, a policy of refusing to approve a loan to any subdivision or project, regardless of its other features, if its occupants are to be of more than one race"; Will and de Neveu to Truman, ca. November 1, 1948, RG 31, CCSF, Box 6, "Racial Restrictive Covenants, 1938–1948."

62. Helper, *Racial Policies*, 203–5; *Jones v. Mayer*, 392 U.S. 409 (1968).

63. Helper, *Racial Policies*, 203–17, citing Stanley L. McMichael's *Real Estate Subdivisions* (New York: Prentice-Hall, 1949).

64. AIREA, *Appraisal of Real Estate*, 100–101, 97. The 1952 edition was less circumspect, citing the threat posed by a "clash" of "people of different race, color, nationality, and culture." Helper discusses the 1952 volume in *Racial Policies*, 201.

65. AIREA, *Handbook for Appraisers* (Chicago: AIREA, 1948), 32, 46, 57, 70. The *Handbook* defines 38 different kinds of "value"—including "subjective value" (otherwise known as "personal value"). The *Handbook* was revised in 1950; definitions cited here, all from 1948, were unchanged.

66. AIREA, *Appraisal of Real Estate*, 97, 100, 456. See also ULI, *Community Builders' Handbook* (1947) 2–4, 30, 35, 56–57. These passages are reproduced in the 1954 and 1960 editions.

67. For excellent introductions, see Michael Danielson, *The Politics of Exclusion* (New York: Columbia University Press, 1976); Gregory R. Weiher, *Fractured Metropolis: Political Fragmentation and Metropolitan Segregation* (Albany: State University of New York Press, 1991); John R. Logan and Harvey Molotch, *Urban Fortunes: The Political Economy of Place* (Berkeley: University of California Press, 1987), chap. 4; David L. Kirp et al., *Our Town: Race, Housing and the Soul of Suburbia* (New Brunswick, N.J.: Rutgers University Press, 1995); and Wiese, *Places of Their Own*, 101–4.

68. For example, see Sugrue, *Origins of the Urban Crisis*, 205–6; Wiese, *Places of Their Own*, 159–63.

69. *American City*, December 1950, 131; "Royal Oak—Digest of Municipal Activities, 1948–9," in ROHC, "Annual Reports"; "Royal Oak Home Building Sets All Time Record," *DT*, May 18, 1949; "Building Boom Results in Lot of Work in Little Room," *DT*, December 20, 1949; Allen Fonoroff, "The Relationship of Zoning to Traffic-Generators," *Law and Contemporary Problems* 20, no. 2 (spring 1955): 238; "Woodward–Eight Mile Jam Backs Up to Nine-Mile Road," *DT*, April 6, 1951; "Woodward Ave. Corridor Project," *Woodward Avenue Corridor Study Background Report*, 1995, especially II-5, II-13–19, and II-22, in OCPC. Special thanks to the staff of the Oakland County Planning Department for providing a copy of the Woodward study.

For an introduction to the challenges posed by service provision in other Detroit-area suburbs, see "Township of Troy: Board Meeting with petition, report 1949," July 6 and August 3, 1949, THM, Box 6; "City of Troy: Board of Review, Reassessment Program Report, 1958," "City of Troy, Chrysler Expressway Meeting Minutes, January 1959," and Harold Black, "City of Troy, Community Development Study, Big Beaver/Crooks Rd. Site, 1966," THM, Box 14; Bureau of Business Research, School of Business Administration, University of Michigan (in cooperation with Dearborn Chamber of Commerce), *Better Service Survey: Dearborn, Michigan, 1957*, esp. 7–37 (copy in DHM); "History of Retail Projects in Oakland County" (copy in OCPC); and DMARPC and SEMCOG reports on commuter patterns and shopping preferences in ALUA and MHC. Annual "Tax" and "Service" pamphlets detail suburban governments' expenditures on infrastructure, services, and education. See, for example, "City of Troy" for the 1950s and 1960s in THM, Box 14; Royal Oak annual reports and tax pamphlets (various titles) in ROHC; and Dearborn's extensive promotional literature on taxes, services, and improvements in DHM, "Alex Pilch," "City Beautiful," and "Public Relations."

70. Robert C. Wood, *1400 Governments: The Political Economy of the New York Metropolitan Region* (Cambridge, Mass.: Harvard University Press, 1961), 14–15; John Delafons, *Land Use Controls in the United States* (Cambridge, Mass.: Joint Center for Urban Studies MIT-Harvard, 1962), esp. 41–89, 160–62; P. J. Adang, "Snob Zoning: A Look at the Economic and Social Impact of Low Density Zoning," *Syracuse Law Review* 15 (1964): 507–11; National Municipal League, Committee on Metropolitan Government, *The Government of Metropolitan Areas in the United States* (1930; reprint, New York: Arno Press, 1974); R. Babcock and F. P. Bosselman, *Exclusionary Zoning: Land Use Regulation in the 1970s* (New York: Praeger, 1973), chap. 1. Essential reading on intraregional competition is Weiher, *Fractured Metropolis*, and Robert O. Self, *American Babylon: Race and the Struggle for Postwar Oakland* (Princeton: Princeton University Press, 2003).

71. James G. Coke and John J. Gargan, for the National Commission on Urban Problems, *Fragmentation in Land-Use Planning and Control*, Research Report No. 18 (Washington, D.C.: GPO, 1969), 12–14; Adang, "Snob Zoning"; Seymour Sacks and Alan Campbell, "The Fiscal Zoning Game," *Municipal Finance* 35, no. 4 (1964): 140–49; Michelle J. White, "Fiscal Zoning in Fragmented Metropolitan Areas," in Edwin S. Mills and Wallace Oates, eds., *Fiscal Zoning and Land Use Controls: The Economic Issues* (Lexington, Mass.: D. C. Heath & Co.); and Duane Windsor, *Fiscal Zoning in Suburban Communities* (Lexington, Mass.: D. C. Heath, 1979).

72. Coke and Gargan, *Fragmentation*, 12–14; Adang, "Snob Zoning"; Sacks and Campbell, "Fiscal Zoning Game"; White, "Fiscal Zoning"; Richard Stauber, *New Cities in America: A Census of Municipal Incorporations in the United States, 1950–1960* (Lawrence, Kan.: Governmental Research Center, University of Kansas, 1965), 1–3, 5, 10–13, 15–16, 35; Windsor, *Fiscal Zoning*; Harry Schmandt, "The Municipal Incorporation Trend, 1950–1960" (Madison: Bureau of Government, University Extension Division, University of Wisconsin, 1961). It is likely that the Stauber and Schmandt studies, based on a data set covering the period between April 1, 1950 and March 31, 1960, provide conservative estimates of total incorporation activity. Stauber does not include the 4 incorporations in Macomb County, including Warren and St. Claire Shores (which had a combined population of 165,903 in 1960).

73. Calculated from Michigan, "Incorporated Cities in Michigan," 335–55; Stauber, *New Cities*; DMARPC, *Regional Reporter*, January 1965, 2 (copies in MHC, "SEMCOG: pub-

lications"); Lewis, *State and Local Government*, 161. By 1964, there were 190 home-rule cities in Michigan.

74. Schmandt, "Municipal Incorporation," 14 (table IX); Stauber, *New Cities*, 32 (fig. 3); Allen D. Manvel, "Metropolitan Growth and Governmental Fragmentation," in A. E. Kier Nash, ed., *Governance and Population: The Governmental Implications of Population Change*, vol. 4, Research Reports, U.S. Commission on Population Growth and the American Future (Washington, D.C.: GPO, 1972), 181. The 2.5 million figure is conservative, since it was calculated from 1960 census statistics. Of the ten cities created in 1954 and 1955, only Northville and Warren were home-rule versions of preexisting villages.

75. Leo F. Schnore, "Municipal Annexations and the Growth of Metropolitan Suburbs, 1950–60," *American Journal of Sociology* 67 (1962): 315–28; *DT*, May 27, 1954; Silla G. Tomasi, "Incorporations and Annexations in the Detroit Region," DMARPC, *Regional Reporter*, January 1962, 7–9; "Planning Facts and Figures no. 14: Incorporations and Annexations in the Detroit Region," *Regional Reporter*, October 1966, 7–8. Clawson later took territory from Troy and Bloomfield Township.

76. *DT*, July 7, 1954; Tomasi "Incorporations and Annexations," 7–9; Stauber, *New Cities*, 14–15, 33–35; Schmandt, "Municipal Incorporation Trend," 16.

77. *DT*, August 22, 1952. See also "Hazel Park: A Suburban City That Is Growing Up," *Inside Michigan*, March 1953, 35–38.

78. Sacks and Campbell, "Fiscal Zoning Game," 145. On average in 1962, property taxes accounted for 84 percent of local tax revenues.

79. Coke and Gargan, *Fragmentation*, 5–6, 18 (table 2), and 19; Danielson, *Politics of Exclusion*, 50; U.S. National Commission on Urban Problems, *Building the American City* (Washington, D.C.: GPO, 1968), 208–9; Allen D. Manvel, *Local Land and Building Regulation: How Many Agencies? What Practices? How Much Personnel?* (Washington, D.C.: GPO, 1968), 31 (table 9). Figures for metropolitan municipalities do not include cities with populations under 1,000 or New England–type townships.

80. Coke and Gargan, *Fragmentation*, 19 (table 3); Manvel, *Land and Building Regulation*, 9–10 (table 9), 28 (table 6), 31, 33; Francine Rabinovitz, *Politics and Planning* (New York: Atherton Press, 1969), 3. In 1968 almost half of the extant zoning ordinances in the smaller SMSA cities had been updated or comprehensively revised in the previous three years alone. Of the metropolitan area cities with 5,000 or more residents in 1968, 97.3 percent had adopted zoning ordinances, and 90.5 percent had adopted subdivision regulations.

81. Michigan Department of Economic Expansion, Research Division, *Local Planning and Zoning Agencies in Michigan* (March 1965), pt. 2, pp. 2–3, 54, 67–68; DMARPC, *Regional Reporter*, January 1965, 3; Wood, *1400 Governments*, 94, 105. Compare Louis Wolfganger, *Your Community and Township Zoning*, Circular Bulletin 194 (East Lansing: Michigan State College, Agricultural Experiment Station, February 1945).

82. The classic statement of this argument by Charles Tiebout has had enormous influence on urban scholarship; see Tiebout, "A Pure Theory of Local Expenditure," *Journal of Political Economy* 64 (1956): 416–24. See, for example, R. Warren, "A Municipal Services Market Model of Metropolitan Organization," *Journal of the American Institute of Planners* 30 (1964): 193–204; O. Williams, "Lifestyle Values and Political Decentralization," in T. Clarke, ed., *Community Structure and Decision Making: Comparative Analyses* (San Francisco: Chandler, 1968); M. Baldassare and W. Protash, "Growth Controls, Population Growth and Community Satisfaction," *American Sociological Review* 47 (1982): 339–46; and William Wheaton, "Land Capitalization, Tiebout

Mobility, and the Role of Zoning Regulations," *Journal of Urban Economics* 34 (1993): 102–17. For a discussion of other possible suburban "outcomes," see David Rusk, *Cities without Suburbs* (Washington, D.C.: Woodrow Wilson Center Press, 1993); Institute for Policy Studies Working Group on Housing, *The Right to Housing: A Blueprint for Housing the Nation* (Washington, D.C.: Institute for Policy Studies, 1989); and Rachel Bratt, Michael Stone, and Chester Hartman, eds., *A Right to Housing: Foundation for a New Social Agenda* (Philadelphia: Temple University Press, 2006).

83. Wood, *1400 Governments*, 158; Coke and Gargan, *Fragmentation*, 8–9; Advisory Commission on Intergovernmental Relations, *Impact of Federal Urban Development Programs on Local Government Organization and Planning* (Washington, D.C.: GPO, 1964), 16–19; Michigan Department of Economic Expansion, *Local Planning and Zoning*, 54, 67–68, 90–91; W. P. Edmonson, "Within Our Region," DMARPC, *Regional Reporter*, July 1961, 7, and October 1961, 7; Rabinovitz, *Politics and Planning*, 3–4 (quoting page 3); ASPO, "Problems of Zoning and Land-Use Regulation," Research Report no. 2 (Washington, D.C.: GPO, 1968), quoting 30.

84. Rabinovitz, *Politics and Planning*, 180, nn. 26 and 27. Eight universities introduced planning curricula between 1958 and 1964 alone.

85. ASPO, "Problems of Zoning," 30–31; Marion Clawson and Peter Hall, *Planning and Urban Growth: An Anglo-American Comparison* (Baltimore: Johns Hopkins University Press, for Resources for the Future, 1973), 196; Coke and Gargan, *Fragmentation*, 8. The Highway Act of 1962 required SMSAs to have comprehensive transportation plans in place in order to qualify for federal highway aid.

86. Clawson, *Suburban Land Conversion*, 63–67; Richard F. Babcock, *The Zoning Game: Municipal Practices and Policies* (Madison: University of Wisconsin Press, 1966), 40; Beverly J. Pooley, *Planning and Zoning in the United States* (Ann Arbor: University of Michigan Law School, 1961), 4–7, 12–13 (especially her discussion of *Mansfield and Swett, Inc. v. Town of West Orange*); Charles M. Haar, "In Accordance with the Comprehensive Plan," *Harvard Law Review* 68, no. 7 (1955): 1154–75; Coke and Gargan, *Fragmentation*, 10, 15. In suburban Detroit, city councilmen felt compelled to condemn their own planners publicly for unprofessional conduct, such as unexcused absences; see, for example, minutes of Hazel Park City Council, March 23, 1942, HP.

87. Delafons, *Land Use Controls*, 42; Coke and Gargan, *Fragmentation*, 8; Rabinovitz, *Politics and Planning*, 10, 12–14; Robert Walker, *The Planning Function in Urban Government* (Chicago: University of Chicago Press, 1950); Ascher, "City Planning"; T. J. Kent, *The Urban General Plan* (San Francisco: Chandler, 1964), 53–59. See also Alan A. Altshuler, *The City Planning Process: A Political Analysis* (Ithaca: Cornell University Press, 1965). When the Department of Commerce published model planning legislation in 1928, it urged municipalities to create independent planning commissions. By contrast the Model City Charter, drafted in 1964, calls upon city managers to establish municipal planning departments and to appoint their directors.

Given the fragmentation of local and regional planning efforts and planners' increasing deference to property owners after World War II, it is fitting that Charles Haar, writing in 1955, cited the Supreme Court's decision in *Euclid v. Ambler* as a formative event in the history of city planning; Haar, "In Accordance with the Comprehensive Plan."

88. Coke and Gargan, *Fragmentation*, 9, 16–17. Meanwhile reapportionment in the 1960s further enhanced suburban political power in state legislatures.

89. DMARPC, *Regional Reporter*, July 1955, and January 1965; DMARPC, *Annual Report*

(1949), 5, 9, 11, (1950), 16–17, and (1951), 18: all in MHC, "SEMCOG: publications." About 150 local officials were "actively cooperating" with the commission by the end of its first full year of operation.

90. DMARPC, *Annual Report* (1950), 3, 8, 12–13, and 1949, 11.

91. "Project Completion Report: Part I," "Part II," 10, and "Part III," 11–12, MHC, SEMCOG I, Box 9, Folder 6; W. P. Edmonson, "Within Our Region," DMARPC *Regional Reporter,* July 1961, 7, MHC, SEMCOG publications; "Digest of Existing and Proposed State and Federal Laws Relating to Planning in Southeast Michigan" (November 16, 1966), MHC, SEMCOG publications, "Publications 1966–1968." DMARPC and SEMCOG reports covered topics including development patterns, industrial decentralization, residential patterns of industrial workers, industrial sites, existing planning law, population growth projections, residential construction, and general employment projections. Originals of DMARPC land-use maps (at a scale of 2 inches to 1 mile) were available for use by local governments, nongovernmental groups and "private interests." Collected in MHC, SEMCOG.

92. *Annual Report* (1949), 7, 9; DMARPC, "Planning Thoughts No. 2: Regional and Local Planning" mimeo, October 21, 1949; DMARPC, "Planning Thoughts No. 1: The Planning Board's Job," mimeo, June 6, 1949, 3–4: all in MHC, "SEMCOG: publications." Emphasis in original.

93. Danielson, *Politics of Exclusion,* 1.

94. Pooley, *Planning and Zoning,* 74–81; Babcock and Bosselman, *Exclusionary Zoning,* 13–14. In some cases, other municipal departments were responsible for granting variances.

95. Pooley, *Planning and Zoning,* 8–12; Wood, *1400 Governments,* 77–78; Babcock and Bosselman, *Exclusionary Zoning,* 8–10; Daniel R. Mandelker, *The Zoning Dilemma: A Legal Strategy for Urban Change* (Indianapolis: Bobbs-Merrill, 1970), 63–68; Manvel, *Land and Building Regulation,* 10, 32 (table 9); Danielson, *Exclusionary Zoning,* 10; Coke and Gargan, *Fragmentation,* 12–14. Where local party structures were particularly weak, suburban officials often relied on developers for political support. For an excellent examination of the quid pro quo politics of suburban land use, see Mark Gottdiener, *Planned Sprawl: Private and Public Interests in Suburbia* (Beverly Hills, Calif.: Sage, 1977). In the late 1960s, almost half of the nation's metropolitan township governments forbade the creation of lots smaller than a quarter acre, and another 25 percent included at least some restrictive areas.

96. Delafons, *Land Use Controls,* 45–46, 61–64; Babcock and Bosselman, *Exclusionary Zoning,* 6–7, 10–11; Adang, "Snob Zoning," 511–13; National Commission on Urban Problems, *Building the American City,* 215, 254–307. The Douglas Commission estimated that many building requirements far exceeded even FHA standards and added $1,838 to the cost of an average unit.

97. Wood, *1400 Governments,* 94; Danielson, *Politics of Exclusion,* 52–53, 55 (table 3.3). By 1970 there were 17,793,000 single-family homes and 5,244,000 units in multiple-unit structures nationwide.

98. Danielson, *Politics of Exclusion,* 53; Adang, "Snob Zoning," 509; Babcock and Bosselman, *Exclusionary Zoning,* 10; Pooley, *Planning and Zoning,* 50, n. 144. Duane Windsor argues that restrictive zoning is often a fiscally *unsound* practice; *Fiscal Zoning,* 76–77, 146. See also R. Cutler, "Legal and Illegal Methods for Controlling Community Growth on the Urban Fringe," *Wisconsin Law Review* 370, 380 (1961). Compare studies in the "consumer choice" tradition, such as D. Schoenbrod, "Large Lot Zoning," *Yale Law Review* 78 (1969): 1418–41, and Wheaton, "Land Capitalization."

99. Adang, "Snob Zoning," 509, 512–13; Pooley, *Planning and Zoning,* 93–97. See also ASPO, "Problems of Zoning," 28–31.

100. White, "Fiscal Zoning," 34; Manvel, *Land and Building Regulation,* 200–217. On the nuisance doctrine, see chap. 2.

101. "Charter of the City of Dearborn," November 3, 1942, "Charter of the City of Dearborn," January 1, 1957, and "Charter: City of Troy, Michigan," December 14, 1955, MHC, "City Charters"; *Michigan Municipal Review,* January 1941, 11; interview with Larry Kiesling, Troy City Planning, August 12, 1996; W. P. Edmonson, "Within Our Region," January 1958, 3; DMARPC, *Regional Reporter,* January 1965, 3.

102. *DP,* January 20, 1949, February 10, 1949; "Our Zoning Headache," *DI,* March 5, 1948; *DT,* August 13, 1947; Edmonson, "Within Our Region," January 1957, 4–5, October 1961, 6–8, and Jan 1962, 3–4, 6. For an introduction to upzonings, residents' concerns about "rumored" apartment construction, and improvement associations' influence on land-use decisions in Hazel Park, see "Regular Meeting Hazel Park City Council," January 27, 1947, August 11, 1947, October 13, 1947, and May 24, 1948, HP.

103. By 1956, Dearborn had approved hundreds of spot zoning changes to its ordinance, removing most of the business corridors in the northeast, removing virtually all of the city's residential D districts, and replacing most residence B districts with residence A. *DT,* September 9, 1942, June 7, 1946, April 4, 1952, and February 20, 1975; City of Royal Oak, "Zoning Ordinance and Map No. 254" (adopted April 20, 1931, as amended to January 1, 1949), ROHC, "Zoning"; "Zoning Ordinance . . . October 1, 1937," "Zoning Ordinance No. 33 . . . May 1, 1950," with attachments, and "Zoning Map . . . Sept. 25, 1956," DHM, Dearborn, City, Departments, "Zoning Ordinances, 1933–1973."

104. The Oak Park map and ordinance were published in the *Daily Tribune* in March 1952. *DT,* October 10 and July 25, 1950, March 15, 1949, March 4, March 8, and January 29, 1952; *Michigan Municipal Review* (November 1950), 171; "Regular Minutes of the Hazel Park City Council," September 8, 1942, and May 24, 1948, HP. In 1949, Dearborn increased the lot size minimum for residence A homes from 5,000 to 6,000 square feet, with a width minimum of 50 feet. See amendment of April 19, 1940 in DHM, Dearborn, Departments, "Zoning Ordinances, 1933–1973."

105. Act 222, P.A. 1943, State of Michigan, *Laws Relating to the Incorporation and General Powers of Cities* (Lansing, Mich.: Franklin Dekleine, 1950); Michigan Statutes Annotated, vol. 4A (1949 revision), including 1951 Supplement and 1952 Session Laws, Title 5, chap. 54, in HHFA, *Comparative Digest of Municipal and County Zoning Enabling Statutes* (HHFA, Office of the Administrator, Division of Law, 1953), 33.

106. DMARPC, *Regional Reporter,* January 1965, 3.

107. *DT,* July 3 and August 8, 1951, June 8 and December 28, 1954; Southfield Planning Commission, *Economic Base Study of Southfield: A Master Plan Study* (Southfield, 1960). Similar planning language (and assumptions about residential neighborhoods) were repeated in local news reporting on land-use controversies. See, for example, *DT,* March 18, 1955 and May 27, 1964.

108. Royal Oak Chamber of Commerce, "Royal Oak: Michigan's Most Promising Community," 8–9, 12, 16, inside of back cover, and back cover, ROHC, "Royal Oak." Already by 1951 the Royal Oak Chamber of Commerce stressed the importance of marketing the city, describing it as "a good place to sell to potential retailers and manufacturers"; *DT,* July 3, 1951.

109. Babcock, *Zoning Game,* 31; ASPO, "Problems of Zoning," 36–37. For early explora-

tions of the social construction of property values, see Charles Abrams, *Forbidden Neighbors: A Study of Prejudice in Housing* (Port Washington, N.Y.: Kennikat Press, 1971), 138; Abrams, *The City Is the Frontier* (New York: Harper & Row, 1965), chap. 2 (on "vested errors" and "vested fictions"); and Drake and Cayton, *Black Metropolis*, rev. ed. (Chicago: University of Chicago Press, 1993), chap. 8. The purchase of a house, wrote Abrams, is "also an emotional experience."

CHAPTER SIX

1. For a comparison, see Arnold R. Hirsch, *Making the Second Ghetto: Race and Housing in Chicago, 1940–1960* (New York: Cambridge University Press, 1983); idem, "Massive Resistance in the Urban North: Trumball Park, Chicago, 1953–1966," *Journal of American History* 82 (1995): 522–50; Thomas J. Sugrue, *The Origins of the Urban Crisis: Race and Inequality in Postwar Detroit* (Princeton: Princeton University Press, 1996); Domenic J. Capeci Jr., *Race Relations in Wartime Detroit: The Sojourner Truth Controversy of 1942* (Philadelphia: Temple University Press, 1984); David R. Riddle, "Race and Reaction in Warren, Michigan, 1971–1974: *Bradley v. Milliken* and the Cross-District Busing Controversy," *Michigan Historical Review* 26, no. 2 (2000): 1–49; and chap. 7 of this study. On government support for black housing in the Detroit suburbs, see Andrew Wiese, *Places of Their Own: African American Suburbanization in the Twentieth Century* (Chicago: University of Chicago Press, 2004), 135–37.

2. USBC, *Sixteenth Census of the United States: 1940, Housing,* vol. 2, *General Characteristics,* pt. 3, *Iowa-Montana* (Washington, D.C.: GPO, 1943), table 22; USBC, *Seventeenth Decennial Census of the United States: Census of Housing: 1950,* vol. 1, *General Characteristics,* pt. 4, *Michigan-New York* (Washington, D.C.: GPO, 1953), table 17; Sugrue, *Origins of the Urban Crisis,* 119–21; Wiese, *Places of Their Own,* 135–37; Joe T. Darden et al., *Detroit: Race and Uneven Development* (Philadelphia: Temple University Press, 1987), 79 (table 3.2). In 1940, there were four black households in Royal Oak.

3. Harold Black, "Restrictive Covenants in Relation to Segregated Negro Housing in Detroit" (master's thesis, Wayne State University, 1947), 4; Sugrue, *Origins of the Urban Crisis,* chap. 8; Capeci, *Race Relations;* Darden et al., *Detroit,* 67–71.

4. "Need We Be Hypocrites and Fools?" *DT,* October 22, 1956; *U.S. News and World Report,* May 11, 1956, 38. See also Wiese, *Places of Their Own,* 44–50. Even well intentioned efforts to address these changes reveal whites' anxieties. In 1944, the Ferndale–Pleasant Ridge Community Council proposed a program of "interracial co-operation" in response to the "present and future problem created by the government-sponsored influx of Negroes to the West Eight-Mile community"; *DT,* November 20, 1944. The growth of Detroit's black population was no doubt a concern to any long-time Royal Oak residents who had been active in the city's large Ku Klux Klan chapter during the 1920s and 1930s. On KKK activity in Royal Oak and the Detroit region, see Kenneth Jackson, *The Ku Klux Klan in the City, 1915–1930* (New York: Oxford University Press, 1967), chap. 9, and Alan Brinkley, *Voices of Protest: Huey Long, Father Coughlin, and the Great Depression* (New York: Vintage Books, 1982), 89–91.

5. For good introductions, see Joseph Boskin, *Sambo: The Rise and Demise of an American Jester* (New York: Oxford University Press, 1986); Donald Bogle, *Toms, Coons, Mulattoes, Mammies, and Bucks: An Interpretive History of Blacks in American Films,* 4th ed. (New York: Continuum, 2001); *Ethnic Notions,* written and directed by Marlon Riggs (1987); Melvin Patrick Ely, *The Adventures of Amos 'n' Andy: A Social History of an American Phenomenon* (New York: Free Press, 1991). See also Sugrue, *Origins of*

the Urban Crisis, 8–9. The USO's comedy division, which supplied entertainment materials for enlisted men during World War II, was run by Mort Lewis, a former scriptwriter for the *Amos 'n' Andy* show. It produced hundreds of individual scripts for minstrel shows to military bases worldwide, recommending the use of blackface (at least for the end men) "to give the traditional atmosphere of the minstrel show"; Boskin, 88–90, quoting the introductory materials.

6. For a sample of the extensive newspaper coverage, see "Businessmen-Turned Minstrels Plan 'Roaring' Show," *DT,* March 23, 1951, and "Black-Faced Royal Oak Lions Club Ready for Minstrel Show, Benefit for Blind," *DT,* April 16, 1954. See also related materials in ROHC, "Lion's Club." The minstrel show and local minstrel troupes were quite common in suburban and rural communities in the decades after World War II, often well into the 1970s. See Boskin, *Sambo,* chap. 4.

7. Charles Abrams, *Forbidden Neighbors: A Study of Prejudice in Housing* (Port Washington, N.Y.: Kennikat Press, 1971), chaps. 8–10; Hirsch, *Making the Second Ghetto;* Kathy Cosseboom, *Grosse Pointe, Michigan: Race against Race* (East Lansing: Michigan State University Press, 1972); Mike Davis, *City of Quartz: Excavating the Future in Los Angeles* (London: Verso, 1990), 160–73. See also James W. Loewen, *Sundown Towns: A Hidden Dimension of American Racism* (New York: New Press, 2005), chap. 4.

8. Few scholars deny that some whites might also have been driven by "prejudice." Likewise, most studies acknowledge that efforts to exclude rentals and modest private homes had the *effect* of excluding racial minorities. But many scholars still insist that white peoples' goals were primarily material and calculable, and thus separable from ideological considerations.

9. *DT,* April 13, 1926, April 6, 1923, December 16, 1921, January 23, 1971; *CC,* 1949, table A-2.

10. *CC,* 1949, table A-2; DMARPC, "Population and Occupied Dwelling Units," 1956, 2; USBC, *Census, 1940, Housing,* vol. 2, pt. 3, tables 22, 23; USBC, *Sixteenth Census of the United States, Population and Housing, 1940* (Statistics for census tracts, Detroit, Mich., and adjacent area) (Washington, D.C.: GPO, 1942), table 4; Sugrue, *Origins of the Urban Crisis.* The rate of homeownership was on average much higher in northern Royal Oak.

11. *DT,* February 3, 1948, October 14, 1947; Real Estate Data, *Real Estate Atlas of Oakland County, Michigan* (1956), copy in MHC.

12. *DT,* February 3, 1948, October 14, 1947, February 17, 1948, October 13, 1947, October 17, 1947. One commissioner later reported that the crowd assembled at Shrine School was "prejudiced against Clawson [and] against renters."

13. *DT,* October 10, 1948, and "Zoning, Bulwark or Obstacle," *DT,* January 21, 1947.

14. *DT,* February 18, 1947. Clawson participated in the commission debates.

15. "Southeast Oakland County, 1960" (cadastral map, in OCPC); *DT,* October 20, 1949, February 18, 1947.

16. *DT,* December 4, 1945; see also "16 Answer Rental Plea."

17. Classified ads illustrate the demand for suburban homes. "List your homes with us for quick sale," advertised one Ferndale Broker, "Buyers waiting." A Detroit realtor had "all cash buyers waiting who want to locate in Oakland County for five room bungalows, nine room singles and income property"; *DT,* September 15, 1947. On the national crisis, see Gwendolyn Wright, *Building the Dream: A Social History of Housing in America* (Cambridge, Mass.: MIT Press, 1981), 242. On Hazel Park's response to the regional crisis, see "Regular Meeting, Hazel Park City Council," August 11, 1947 and January 26, 1948, HP.

18. Sparks concluded that a "law that tells people what they can build and where they must build it, the size it must be and how much they must pay for it and what it can be used for, must have been conceived by a dictator or was originated in Russia"; *DT,* August 13, 1947, September 15, 1947.

19. The parcel was zoned residence A in the city's original ordinance, drafted in 1931, then changed to residence C in the late 1930s. Ownership was divided between Northwood (11.3 acres), the Rev. Fr. Charles E. Coughlin (7.81 acres), the Grand Trunk railway, and the city; *DT,* September 9, 1949, October 7, 9, 13 and 14, 1947, May 28, 1948, September 9, 1948, February 3, 1948, March 2, 1948. Estimates for the number of units ranged from 250 to 350.

20. Ibid. Christie quoted in October 9, 1947.

21. The names of the participating homeowners' associations are represented differently throughout the controversy, reflecting perhaps their lack of coherent organizational structure. *DT,* October 7, 9, 11 and 13, 1947. Christie was the only commission member *not* seeking re-election.

22. *DT,* October 14, 1947.

23. Ibid.

24. *DT,* May 18, 1949; Royal Oak Chamber of Commerce, "Royal Oak: Michigan's Most Promising Community," ROHC, "Chamber of Commerce"; *CC,* 1949, table 5. By 1950, half of the households in Royal Oak lived in dwellings built since 1940.

25. *DT,* October 17 and 22, 1947. "Decision on this issue has vast implications for Royal Oak," the editorial concluded. "Far in debt and in pressing need of more revenue, its thousands of vacant lots are its greatest potential asset."

26. *DT,* December 2, 1947, November 5, 1947, September 24, 1948, February 2, 1948.

27. Sparks concluded by praising city employees as "capable, reliable, trustworthy and underpaid servants"; *DT,* December 2, 1947.

28. *DT,* November 11, 1947, February 3 and 17, 1948, September 24, 1948.

29. *DT,* February 5, 1948. The suit also charged the city with taking property for public use without compensating its owners.

30. *DT,* February 17, 23–24, and 27, 1948, February 24, 1947.

31. *DT,* March 2 and 6, 1948. See also "Zoning Suits against Royal Oak Offer Study in Apparent Paradoxes," *DT,* March 5, 1948.

32. *DT,* March 17, 1948. Notably, the homeowners' petition cited the *Tribune's* reporting on Horne and Laidlaw's support for the apartments.

33. *DT,* March 2, 7, and 22, 1948.

34. *DT,* April 6–7, 1948.

35. *DT,* September 24, 1948, April 7, 1948.

36. *DT,* May 1 and 12, 1948. Northwood's attorneys challenged arguments that had been used to justify exclusionary zoning for decades. "It is hard to conceive," their brief argued, "how a multiple housing unit can have any different effect on the public health, safety or general welfare than a hospital, school, boarding house, club or the like would have." The latter were permitted in residence A zones. For a discussion of *Euclid, Sanborn,* the relationship between zoning and covenant law, and the centrality of the *prima facie* defense, see chaps. 2 and 5.

37. *DT,* September 24, 1948.

38. Quote is from Laidlaw. *DT,* May 28, 1948, October 2 and 5, 1948. The *Tribune's* editors clearly recognized the shifting tide in favor of restriction. See "Sketches of Apartments Judge Rules May be Built in Northwood," *DT,* September 24, 1948.

39. *DT,* October 6 and 12, 1948. On the "presumption of validity," see chaps. 2 and 5.

40. *DT,* October 18, 27, and 29, 1948.

41. *DT,* November 2, 1948, and January 6, June 7, and September 8, 1949.

42. *Northwood Properties Company v. Royal Oak City Inspector,* 325 Mich. 419, 39 N.W.2d 25 (1949).

43. *Austin v. Older,* 283 Mich. 667, 278 N.W. 727 (1938) cited *Euclid* as precedent.

44. *Northwood Properties Company v. Royal Oak City Inspector;* specifically, the court referred to *City of Pleasant Ridge v. Cooper,* 267 Mich. 603, 255 N.W. 371 (1934).

45. Compare Sugrue, *Origins of the Urban Crisis,* 211–29, and Capeci, *Race Relations,* 64.

46. "Royal Oak Home Building Sets All Time Record, 157 in April," *DT,* May 18, 1949. On the Homebuilders' Association development, see chap. 1.

47. *DT,* September 9, 1949.

48. *Michigan Digest,* vol. 14B (St. Paul, Minn.: West, 1963), 450–509; Louis C. Andrews, for the Michigan Municipal League, "Michigan Zoning Cases—1949 through 1986," unpublished report, ca. 1986, 1 (in MML). Special thanks to Lois Thibault, associate director of the Michigan Municipal League, for providing a copy of this study.

    Illustrative examples include *Fass v. City of Highland Park,* 321 Mich. 156, 32 N.W.2d 375 (1948), in which the court noted that "a city, in exercise of its police power, has authority to enact a zoning ordinance reasonably necessary for preservation of public health, morals or safety"; *Frischkorn Constr. Co. v. Redford Township Building Inspector,* 315 Mich. 556, 24 N.W.2d 209 (1946), and *Hitchman v. Oakland Twp.,* 329 Mich. 331, 45 N.W.2d 306 (1951), which saw the courts rule that "aesthetics" may be considered in determining the validity of building regulations and zoning ordinances; *Connor v. West Bloomfield Twp.,* 207 F.2d 482 (6th Cir. 1953), on the restriction of trailer homes; *Ritenour v. Dearborn Twp.,* 326 Mich. 242, 40 N.W.2d 137 (1949), where the court ruled that "depreciation in value" should be given consideration in determining the "reasonableness of a zoning ordinance." Cases involving the "presumption of validity" argument were increasingly common after 1955; see chap. 8.

49. *DT,* September 9, 1949.

50. Ibid., and October 20, 1949. Hayward remembered the events of winter 1947 quite differently, claiming that Commissioner Price reversed himself on the small homes project.

51. *DT,* February 28, 1950. For examples of updates on construction and building permits, see May 19, 1949, July 22, 1949.

52. Complicating matters further, both the FHA and many leading housing experts had been encouraging builders to construct *smaller* homes throughout much of the 1940s. Nationwide, average house size actually decreased in the late 1940s, prior to the liberalization of the mortgage market. In 1950, the median house was 983 square feet (down 12 percent from a decade earlier). By contrast in 1955, the median was 1,100 square feet; Clifford E. Clark, *The American Family Home: 1800–1960* (Chapel Hill: University of North Carolina Press, 1986), 219, 228–31. See also Greg Hise, *Magnetic Los Angeles: Planning the Twentieth-Century Metropolis* (Baltimore: John Hopkins University Press, 1997), 66–71. On FHA, VA, and secondary market activity, see chap. 5.

53. Royal Oak CC, "Royal Oak: Michigan's Most Promising Community," ca. 1954, ROHC, "Chamber of Commerce"; *DT,* August 8, 1949, May 21, 1949.

54. The Federation of Hazel Park Improvement Associations, as well as individual homeowners, fought similar battles, in part by submitting recommendations on rezonings

at the regular council meetings. See "Council Minutes, vol. 3," September 22, 1942, August 12, 1946, September 23, 1946, May 24, 1948, January 27, 1947, and the fall 1947 debate over rezoning for the Stephenson highway, HP.

55. "Residents' Pressure Kills Business Plan," *DT,* May 5, 1951.

56. *DT,* April 4, 1952, March 3, 1952, June 8, 1954, August 22, 1952, July 2, 1953, April 13, 1955. See also May 18, 1957, June 11, 1959.

57. City of Royal Oak, "How Will We Get It?" (1947–48), in ROHC, "Annual Reports"; *DT,* June 8, 1954. See also "Put Building Curbs on NE RO Section," *DT,* December 28, 1954.

58. *DT,* July 3, 1951, August 21, 1951; see also March 24, 1948.

59. "Royal Oak—Digest of Municipal Activities, 1948–1949," ROHC, "Annual Reports."

60. Ibid.

61. "City of Royal Oak: 1954–1955—Progress Report," *DT,* October 8, 1955 (Royal Oak City section); "City of Royal Oak Annual Report Section," *DT,* December 1, 1956. Mayor V. E. Horn prefaced one report by acknowledging that readers, as "taxpayers," would "of course . . . want to know how [their] money has been spent and how efficiently [their] municipal services are being administered"; "1952 Annual Report: City of Royal Oak, Michigan," ROHC, "Annual Reports."

62. "Annual Report: City of Royal Oak," *DT,* August 17, 1957. This language appeared frequently. "In short, zoning . . . is related to the public health, welfare and safety of the entire community. That in Michigan is the legal requirement for zoning"; "Annual Report: City of Royal Oak," *DT,* December 1, 1956.

63. For one example, see "RO Planners Reject Northwood Apartments," *DT,* April 13, 1955.

64. *DT,* January 28, 1949.

65. *DT,* January 7, 1949, November 2, 1946, and April 28, 1953. A 1947 editorial applauded the residents of the 600 block of Walnut Avenue for helping the Royal Oak City government to plant trees on city streets. "Both will gain," the piece concluded, "by this plan to make Royal Oak a better and more beautiful place"; *DT,* May 1. The local press constantly blurred the line between news reporting on residential development and advertising for homebuilders. See, for example, "Small Cottage Has Three Bedrooms," part of its "weekly house plan" series; *DT,* May 13, 1949.

66. *DT,* April 2, 1947 ("It's Your Government, Vote"), October 9, 1947 ("It's Your Newspaper"), October 29, 1954, December 4, 1952, November 30, 1954, December 1 and 13, 1954. Floyd Miller published the *Tribune* and served as chief editorialist until his death in September 1954, when his son Philip assumed both roles. See also Southfield Planning Commission, *Economic Base Study of Southfield: A Master Plan Study* (Southfield, 1960), 17, and Philip Miller's commentary on the role of the home in preventing juvenile delinquency, *DT,* November 9, 1956, February 14, 1955. The *Tribune*'s boosterism was no doubt influenced by its dependence on local businesses for advertising revenue. Meanwhile Floyd Miller served as vice president of People's Federal Savings and Loan and director of the Royal Oak Credit Bureau. See Floyd Josiah Miller, "Diary, 1932–1954," entries for December 27, 1941 and July 26, 1943, MHC, F. J. Miller Papers, 1907–1954, Box 2, and *DT,* June 13, 1941.

67. *DT,* April 2, 1947, October 9, 1947, June 1, 1955, October 5, 1956, December 15, 1954.

68. Most of the neighborhoods appraised by the FHLBB in Dearborn, Royal Oak, and neighboring suburbs received a C rating—several received a D; "City Survey,

Metropolitan Detroit, Michigan . . . June 30, 1939," RG 195, FHLBB/CSF, Box 17, "Greater Detroit Michigan—Re Survey Report," 3; Security Map, June 1, 1939 and Area Descriptions, RG 195, FHLBB/CSF, Box 18, "Greater Detroit Michigan, Security Maps and Area Descriptions."

69. Capeci, *Race Relations*, 101–2; B. J. Widick, *Detroit: City of Race and Class Violence*, rev. ed. (Detroit: Wayne State University Press, 1989), 28; Sugrue, *Origins of the Urban Crisis*, 21–22. In New York City, an Italian American man remembered joining his friends during World War II for trips to Harlem, where they would "beat up some niggers." "It was wonderful," he explained, "it was new. The Italo-American stopped being Italo and started becoming American"; cited in David R. Roediger, *Working toward Whiteness: How America's Immigrants Became White* (New York: Basic Books, 2005), 137.

70. Television sitcoms even traced the experience of "ethnic" whites relocating to their new suburban communities; George Lipsitz, "The Meaning of Memory: Family, Class, and Ethnicity in Early Network Television," in *Time Passages: Collective Memory and American Popular Culture* (Minneapolis: University of Minnesota Press, 1990), 39–76. A rich source for study of the links between municipal governments and their state and national organizations is the Alex Pilch papers in DHM.

71. Royal Oak Chamber of Commerce, "Royal Oak: Michigan's Most Promising Community," c. 1954, 16, ROHC.

CHAPTER SEVEN

1. The initiative would have authorized the city's Housing Commission to go under contract with the U.S. Housing Authority "for the purpose of erecting a Low Rent Housing Project"; *DP*, October 17, 1946; quotes from sample ballots (1940 and 1946) and vote totals from memo by Office of City Clerk, September 27, 1948, DHM, Hancock.

2. "Talented Children Act in 'Uncle Tom's Cabin,'" *DI*, April 2, 1948; "Young Negroes Rob Two Gas Stations," March 27, 1942; "Minstrel Show Benefit of Men in Service Here," February 23, 1945; advertisement for "Exchange Minstrels," April 20, 1945; and the promotional materials, programs, and photographs in DHM, "Exchange Minstrels." For other examples of public minstrelsy and racial caricature, see advertisement for pancake promotion ("Aunt Jemima to Visit Dearborn," *DI*, February 3, 1950); Ray Adams's discussion of the "Jolly Nigger" mechanical bank in his weekly talk show (July 1947, typescript, DHM, Adams, 4); and the comic strips "Nappy" and "Jackie" (the latter loosely based on Bud Fisher and Al Smith's "Mutt and Jeff," but with minstrel characters) featured in the *Independent* during the 1940s and early 1950s.

3. *Detroit Times*, November 5, 1946; Albert M. Ammerman, "Sociological Survey of Dearborn," (master's thesis, School of Education, University of Michigan, 1940), 56–58; *DP*, October 17, 1946. For examples of daily coverage, editorials, advertisements, and letters from residents, see *DI*, February 20, 1942 and March 6, 1942.

4. Joe T. Darden et al., *Detroit: Race and Uneven Development* (Philadelphia: Temple University Press, 1987), 119–25. Immigrants flocked to Dearborn, the authors write, because of the "mass racial hysteria of the white working class that black movement into their neighborhoods would depress property values." Despite acknowledging that Hubbard had support from other constituencies, they still describe the city's racist political culture as a "working class" one ("Hubbard had created a white working-class utopia that many white liberals also found satisfying.") Social scientists

have accepted historians' depictions of Dearborn's class composition (and the comparison with Cicero) at face value, subsequently writing this narrative into quantitative studies of land use discrimination. See Reynolds Farley, "Suburban Persistence," *American Sociological Review* 29, no. 1 (1964): 38–47; Max Neiman, "Zoning Policy, Income Clustering, and Suburban Change," *Social Science Quarterly* 61, nos. 3–4 (December 1980), 674. "[A] Dearborn, Michigan, or Cicero, Illinois," writes Neiman, "can remain almost entirely white working class, regardless of their zoning ordinance and despite their economic and geographic accessibility to minorities." Meanwhile even national press corps described Dearborn's antiblack mobilizations as orchestrated by Hubbard (e.g., New York *Herald Tribune,* June 27, 1965).

5. League of Women Voters, *Dearborn,* 4th ed. (Dearborn, Mich.: League of Women Voters, 1976), 19–20; Ammerman, "Sociological Survey," 11–14, 30–33; David L. Good, *Orvie, the Dictator of Dearborn: The Rise and Reign of Orville L. Hubbard* (Detroit: Wayne State University Press, 1989). Major employers in the early 1940s included the Graham-Paige Motor Co., Detroit Seamless Steel Tube Co., Universal Products, Co., Dearborn Stamping Co., United States Tool Co., and Bopp Steel Co.

6. Good, *Orvie,* chap. 14; Darden et al., *Detroit,* 119–20.

7. Darden et al., *Detroit,* 119–25; Ammerman, "Sociological Survey"; USBC, *Census, 1950, Population,* table 2; Ralph E. Eccles, "The Community of Dearborn," typescript (May 9, 1961), 126, copy in DHM; League of Women Voters, *Dearborn,* 20–21. Of the employed men and women in tract 828 (on Dearborn's west side), nearly 40 percent were counted as "professionals," "technical" workers, "managers," "officials," or "proprietors," compared with 25 percent in tract 835 and 21 percent in tract 837, both on the east side. Residents traditionally counted as "working class," that is, laborers and industrial workers, including craftsmen, foremen, and operatives, made up only 30 percent of the workforce in the western tract, compared with 41 percent and 53 percent, respectively, in the eastern tracts.

8. See plat maps and abstracts of title in DHM, Dearborn Subdivisions, Abstracts (folders: "Dearborn Golf Park Association," "Frischkorn's Columbus Park No. 1," "Albert P. Ternes Subdivision," and unlabelled folder for Aviation Field Subdivision No. 2).

9. "Abstract of Title" (recorded July 14, 1923, purchased January 14, 1942), in "Dearborn Golf Park Subdivision" and (quoting) "Abstract of Title," Lot 1246, Aviation Field Subdivision No. 2, both in DHM, Dearborn Subdivisions, Abstracts; Residential Security Map, June 1, 1939, RG 195, FHLBB/CSF, Box 18, "Greater Detroit Michigan Security Maps and Area Descriptions." The local FNMA agent who purchased the Golf Park deed from a Detroit investment company then passed it to the Michigan National Bank, which in turn resold it to the original owners.

10. Dearborn was among the "Downriver" suburbs that had a tradition of excluding or sharply segregating blacks. See discussions of River Rouge, Wyandotte, and Ecorse in Andrew Wiese, *Places of Their Own: African American Suburbanization in the Twentieth Century* (Chicago: University of Chicago Press, 2004), 43–50. On neighborhood mobilizations in Detroit, see Thomas J. Sugrue, *The Origins of the Urban Crisis: Race and Inequality in Postwar Detroit* (Princeton: Princeton University Press, 1996).

11. FPHA statement reprinted in *DI,* November 24, 1944; Shelton Tappes, Local 600, to Dearborn City Council, June 12, 1944, reprinted in *DI,* November 17, 1944. On African American settlement patterns in wartime Detroit, see Sugrue, *Origins of the Urban Crisis,* 36–41. On Local 600, see Kevin Boyle, *The UAW and the Heyday of American Liberalism, 1945–1968* (Ithaca: Cornell University Press, 1995). Hubbard

did not take a public stance on racial issues during his first years in office, until the FPHA controversy.

12. *DI*, November 24, 1944; Ammerman, "Sociological Survey," 58; Sugrue, *Origins of the Urban Crisis*, 76–77; Good, *Orvie*, 140–42. At one point, the proposal called for a $1,750,000 project of 250 units, including one-story twin houses, two-story homes, and 12-family structures. It would have accommodated families earning less than $1,000 a year as well as welfare recipients.

13. *DI*, October 20, 1944.

14. *DI*, April 3, 1942, quoting advertisement by Malpeli Construction Company; "Housing Demand Now Reaches Acute Stage," *DI*, February 27, 1942 (reproducing a NAREB press release); *DI*, December 28, 1945, October 27, 1946, and September 27, 1946; *DP*, January 3, 1946 and April 11, 1946. In April 1946, Hubbard appointed a new housing expediter, who was instructed to "maintain connection with all existing Federal, State and local officials and agencies which are in position to assist in any way in alleviating the present housing shortage." See also Mark Gottdiener, *The Decline of Urban Politics: Political Theory and the Crisis of the Local State* (Newbury Park, Calif.: Sage Publications, 1987), esp. 92.

15. *DI*, November 17, 1944. On the Sojourner Truth incident, see Domenic Capeci, *Race Relations in Wartime Detroit: The Sojourner Truth Housing Controversy of 1942* (Philadelphia: Temple University Press, 1984). The Roulo School, located at the intersection of Dix Road and Roulo Avenue, was torn down in 1979. Thanks to William K. McElhone of the Dearborn Historical Museum for finding it.

16. Mayor to City Clerk; reprinted in *DI*, November 17, 1944. For a sample of local press coverage, see "Review of the News," *DI*, December 29, 1944.

17. The paper reprinted the board's statement under the headline: "Board of Education Joins Fight against Federal Housing Project: Passes Resolution Protesting Location of Housing Project against Wishes of Citizens"; Board of Education, "Resolution," reprinted in *DI*, November 24, 1944; Good, *Orvie*, 141.

18. For good introductions, see Michael K. Brown, *Race, Money, and the American Welfare State* (Ithaca: Cornell University Press, 1999), and Ira Katznelson, *When Affirmative Action Was White: An Untold History of Racial Inequality in Twentieth-Century America* (New York: W. W. Norton, 2005).

19. *DI*, December 29, 1944 ("Review of the News").

20. *DI*, November 24, 1944 (reprinting Shermer's statement); Good, *Orvie*, 140–42; Sugrue, *Origins of the Urban Crisis*, 76–77. The following May, the FPHA began condemning 170 acres of Ford land to build 1,410 temporary houses, but the armistice stopped the project and forestalled any controversy.

21. "Property Protective Association Urges New Restrictions," *DI*, December 1, 1944; and see December 15, 1944, December 18, 1944. See also "Property Protective Association Plans Meeting at Fordson," *DI*, December 29, 1944. In some cases the DPOPA used meetings originally called to oppose the FPHA (for example a meeting of the Dearborn Highlands Improvement Association) to promote its covenant campaign.

22. "Restriction Agreement: Property Owners Protective Association—Declaration of Restrictions," "Form A" (for Galt Park Subdivision) and "Form B" (for Ternes, Galt Park, and Ford-Chase subdivisions), DHM, OHP, Organizations, "Property Owners Protective Association." The group used three names—the Dearborn Property Protective Association, the Property Owners Protective Association, and the Dearborn Property Owners Protective Association.

23. DPOPA, "Dearborn Property Protective Association," pamphlet, n.d., DHM, "DPOPA." It was produced after June 1945 and before the Supreme Court's ruling in *Shelley v. Kraemer*. Residents were instructed to read it carefully and then "pass it on to one of your neighbors."

24. Ibid.

25. Ibid.

26. Ibid.

27. Ford biography (mimeo), February 15, 1953, DHM, Council; *DN*, January 9, 1946; *DP*, January 3, January 9, and March 28, 1946. The election flyer was used as scratch paper for a memo written to Hubbard on March 25, 1946, which was subsequently attached to a letter from Giovanni Briglio. Briglio to OH, March 25, 1946, DHM, OHP, "Organizations."

28. *DN*, January 9, 1946; *DP*, January 3 and 17, 1946.

29. *DP*, October 17, 1946. Quotes are from sample ballots, and vote totals from memo by Office of City Clerk, DHM, Hancock.

30. Hubbard vetoed the council's decision, and the council overrode his veto. *Detroit Times*, January 21, 1948, December 4, 1948; *DN*, December 21, 1947; *DP*, April 6, 1944, June 10, 1943, and May 20, 1948; *DFP*, January 7, 1948, February 1 and February 2, 1948, December 6, 1948; Good, *Orvie*, chaps. 17–18.

31. Darden et al., for example, write that "Hubbard went into action as the suburban white knight protecting Dearborn's white citizens from Detroit's 'black hordes' . . . He organized meetings to attack the project, which once again evoked the latent mass racial hysteria." They also contend that Hubbard lead opposition to the FPHA project in 1944. Darden et al., *Detroit*, 120.

32. George F. Break, *The Economic Impact of Federal Loan Insurance* (Washington, D.C.: National Planning Association, 1961), 54 (table 15) and 70 (table 21). For a detailed treatment, see chap. 5.

33. *DG*, October 14, 1948; Peter Karapetian (for the Housing Bureau) to Mayor and City Council, January 14, 1949, DHM, OHP, Departments, "Housing Department Business, 1949–64"; *DI*, May 14, 1948.

34. *DI*, January 2 and 30, 1948, and "Our Zoning Headache," March 5, 1948. On the *Independent*'s politics (anti-Hubbard) and readership (east side), see Oliver Moles Jr., "Voter Characteristics and the Mayor of Dearborn, Michigan," May 4, 1956, 55–57, copy in DHM. The *Press* was viewed as a "pro-Hubbard" paper.

35. *DI*, April 30, 1948; *DP*, May 20, 1948; Peter Karapetian (for the Housing Bureau) to OH and Council, January 14, 1949, DHM, OHP, Departments, "Housing Department Business, 1949–64." For sample announcements of spot zonings, see *DI*, January 30, 1948 regarding Ordinance No. 48-383 (rezoning Outer Drive).

36. USBC, *Housing 1940*, vol. 2, pt. 3, table 22; USBC, *Population and Housing 1940* (Detroit), table 4; USBC, *Seventeenth Decennial Census of the United States: Census of Housing: 1950*, vol. 1, *General Characteristics*, pt. 4, *Michigan-New York* (Washington, D.C.: GPO, 1953), table 17; CC, 1962, table 6; Good, *Orvie*, 145–46, 153–55.

37. "Information Relative to Land Area Involved in Proposed Land Purchase of Ford Foundation Property by John Hancock Life Insurance Company," D. M. Coburn, City Engineer, internal memo, October 12, 1948, DHM, Hancock; *DI*, April 30, 1948.

38. Ray Parker to the Honorable City Council, June 28, 1948, with attachment ("Proposed Amendments to the Following Sections of Ordinance No. 33, Zoning Ordinance"); Minutes, "Regular Meeting of the Council of the City of Dearborn," July 6,

1948; Beadle and Parker to the City Clerk, September 20, 1948, reprinted in minutes of "Special Meeting of the Council of the City of Dearborn," November 8, 1948: all in DHM, Hancock.

39. Hancock Village Management, "Use of Property Rules" and Lucius T. Hill to Chairman, City Council, Dearborn, Michigan, October 1, 1948, DHM, Hancock. See also John Booth to OH, October 5, 1948 regarding Hubbard's request for additional materials.

40. OH to City Council, October 4, 1948 and October 10, 1948, and E. W. Schaller to OH, October 8, 1948, DHM, Hancock.

41. Robert Young, for the Zoning Board of Appeals, to City Council, October 7, 1948 and "Resolution," DHM, Hancock.

42. "Give Us a Chance to Vote on the Proposed John Hancock High-Cost Rental Housing Project" (mimeo) and OH to City Council (mimeo), October 15, 1948, DHM, Hancock.

43. DP, October 7, 1948; DG, October 21, 1948; Hill to Henry Ford II, October 16, 1948 and Henry Ford II (for the Ford Foundation) to Common Council, October 18, 1948, DHM, Hancock.

44. DG, October 21, 1948, November 5, 1948; "Look at what the City Engineer . . ." (mimeo, n.d.), DHM, Hancock. On the breadth of its distribution, see "Declaration," *Mildred Coburn v. Orville Hubbard, Frank Swapka, Harold DeWyk, and Norbert Schlaff,* DHM, Hancock.

45. "A Personal Message from Your Mayor," mimeo, n.d. and "Insurance Company Builds Homes . . ." mimeo, n.d., DHM, Hancock.

46. "Wake Up, Dearborn," envelope, DHM, Hancock (emphasis in the original).

47. In the week before the election, Hubbard shared Nebesio's views with Dearborners in another campaign flyer, juxtaposing the letter to a telegram from UAW 600 leaders (inquiring if blacks would be permitted to occupy the Hancock project) and coverage of the controversy by Detroit's black press. Flyer with reproductions, DHM, Hancock.

48. DG, November 4, 1948; DP, January 29, 1949; City Planner to OH, November 3, 1948, DHM, Hancock. The ballot, by contrast, read: "Do you favor the John Hancock Mutual Life Insurance Company enlarging and developing the Springwells Park area?" On the day after the vote, Dearborn's city planner, Joseph Goldfarb, called a special meeting of the plan commission to "discuss wholesale rezoning by neighborhoods." David Good argues that Hubbard orchestrated the anti-Hancock campaign, frustrating the wishes of most Dearborn residents and civic organizations; *Orvie,* chap. 19.

49. "Democrats Sweep City in Big Vote," DG, November 4, 1948 and December 8, 1948.

50. DI, January 14, 1949; DG, December 8, 1948 and December 21, 1948 (presumably paraphrasing Beadle); "Declaration," *Mildred Coburn v. Orville Hubbard et al.,* DHM, Hancock. Parker was also reportedly upset with Hubbard for playing the race card; see Good, *Orvie,* 157–58.

51. See, for example, "Home Builders Look Forward to Record Year in 1950," DI, January 27, 1950, "Grant 113 Permits For Single Homes During January," DI, February 3, 1950, and "Nearly $7 million in building permits issued in February," DI, February 10, 1950. By 1950 local papers constantly carried advertisements for home upgrades and improvements, a market spurred by FHA Title I activity. See, for example, announcement for Detroit Builders Show and "Cost of Modernizing Average 30-Year House is $4,000," DI, February 3, 1950.

52. DFCA letterhead (1949), DHM, Organizations, Civic Associations, "Dearborn Federation of Civic Associations"; DPOPA, informational brochure (ca. 1946), DHM, OHP, "Assessors"; Ammerman, "Sociological Survey," 71. By the early 1950s, applicants for positions in city government were touting their status as "homeowners," and even some municipal employment forms asked if "you are a homeowner." John Baja to OH, DHM, Departments, "Housing Department Business, 1949–1964"; "City Commissioner Personal Data" form, DHM, Commissions and Boards, City Beautiful.

53. Lucille McCollough (for DFCA) to City Council, September 6, 1949; McCollough to City Council, June 3, 1949; Clyde Halle and Harry Hoxie, for DFCA to Common Council, February 4, 1950: all in DHM, "Dearborn Federation of Civic Associations." See other DFCA correspondence in DHM, OHP, Organizations, "Civic Associations, General."

    Both Hubbard and the council arranged meetings with local builders and instructed them to respond to residents' preference for detached, single-family dwellings. See, for example, Dearborn Department of Research and Development, press release, February 1950, DHM, Business and Industry: Buildings and Construction.

54. Letters collected in DHM, Civic Associations (see: "general," "Aviation," "Fort Dearborn Manor," "Golf View," "Southeast Dearborn Civic Association," and "Dearborn Highlands"); Keith Forbush, for the DREB, to OH, October 13, 1953, DHM, OHP, N-1, 1953 (temporary classification); Joseph Cardinal, for the Dearborn Chamber of Commerce, to OH and Council, December 28, 1951, DHM, OHP, Organizations, "Chamber of Commerce, 1944–64."

55. *DP,* January 20, 1949; *SDCA News,* February 1949, 1 (copies in DHM. OHP, Organizations, "SDCA"); *DG,* November 30, 1949; "Zoning Map, City of Dearborn . . . Amended to September 25, 1956," DHM, Dearborn, Departments, "Zoning Ordinances, 1933–1973." By comparison, the ordinance was amended 118 times between 1933 and 1950. For development history of the Madison parcel, see USCB, *Housing (Supplement to the First Series, Housing Bulletin for Michigan: Dearborn—Block Statistics),* 1940 (Washington, D.C.: GPO, 1942); USCB, *1950 Housing Report* V, pt. 48, *Block Statistics: Dearborn, Michigan* (Washington, D.C.: GPO, 1951), table. 3.

56. Although they did frequently refer to the physical decay and dirtiness of *Detroit* as an example to be avoided. See chap. 8.

57. SDCA to City Council, February 17, 1953, DHM, SDCA; Keith Forbush, for the Dearborn Real Estate Board, to OH, October 13, 1953, DHM, OHP, N-1, 1953 (temporary classification). In 1945, for example, the chair of the Dearborn Board of Assessors, William T. Kronberg, sent a "confidential report" to Hubbard noting that "Mr. Arthur DeVey, colored citizen from Detroit, has acquired title through purchase from the State Land Office Board, of seventy lots in the Herndon's Dearborn Golf Park Subdivision"; Kronberg to OH, September 10, 1945, DHM, OHP, D1, CAN (temporary classification).

58. *SDCA News,* January 1950, 1, March 1950, 2, December 1950, and February 1949. The *News* was distributed door to door by volunteer neighborhood captains. Residents who failed to receive an issue were instructed to call the SDCA.

59. *SDCA News,* February 1949 and October 1950. In 1950, the SDCA published an appeal for "people who will consent to act as area leaders in their immediate neighborhood to see that this bulletin is delivered in their block"; "In Unity . . . There Is Strength," *SDCA News,* October 1950, 1. The *News* served as a bulletin for community activities, as well. In October 1949, the editors invited local organizations,

"Scouts, Churches, PTA, School dances, etc.," to announce "any special event which would be of interest to the area at large"; "Your Bulletin," *SDCA News*, October 1949, 1. Dozens of local merchants advertised in the monthly newsletter.

60. *SDCA News*, October 1950, April 1950, September 1950, and June 1950. Federal appraisers had predicted its potential value as early as 1939.

61. *SDCA News*, June 1950.

62. *SDCA News*, October 1950.

63. *SDCA News*, October 1949.

64. *SDCA News*, April 1950 and October 1950. "To get your share of community betterments and to stop developments that are detrimental to the neighborhood, is the reason for Civic Associations."

65. DPOPA, "Join Your Civic Association," in *SDCA News*, April 1951.

66. *SDCA News*, April 1950 and October 1950. The extant printed record on other Dearborn civic and homeowners' associations, while limited, nonetheless reveals similar activities. *The Springwells Parker* lists street captains, announces meetings, and reports on members' social activities (in DHM, Organizations, Civic Associations, "Springwells"). The Dearborn Woods Association, in a typescript outline of their activities, states that the group was organized to "promote, procure, and enforce building, zoning and other restrictions" and to participate in the DFCA. Among its accomplishments were the maintenance of "a high level of construction and conformity of design of new houses built in the area"; November 13, 1950, DHM, Organizations, Civic Associations, "General."

67. For excellent introductions, see Elaine Tyler May, "Cold War—Warm Hearth: Politics and the Family in Postwar America," in Steve Fraser and Gary Gerstle, eds., *The Rise and Fall of the New Deal Order, 1930–1980* (Princeton: Princeton University Press, 1989); 153–81; Clifford E. Clark, "Ranch House Suburbia: Ideals and Realities," in Lary May, ed., *Recasting America: Culture and Politics in the Age of Cold War* (Chicago: University of Chicago Press, 1989); Lizabeth Cohen, *A Consumers' Republic: The Politics of Mass Consumption in Postwar America* (New York: Knopf, 2003).

68. John T. Flynn, *The Road Ahead: America's Creeping Revolution* (New York: Committee for Constitutional Government, 1949).

69. "'Socialist Planners' Held Real Enemies," *DI*, January 27, 1950. The last quote is from *Road Ahead*, cited in the *Independent*. For a discussion of popular fears about totalitarian threats and other best-selling exposés, see Alan Brinkley, *The End of Reform: New Deal Liberalism in Recession and War* (New York: Knopf, 1995), 154–64.

70. *DI*, February 17, 1950.

CHAPTER EIGHT

1. *DT*, March 1, March 4, and September 2, 1955; December 2, 1954. See also "Why New Cities are Formed," June 6, 1955.

2. "Persistence of Slums," *DT*, August 4, 1958, December 13, 1954, and "Small Cities Serve a Purpose," February 17, 1955. Keeping governments "scaled down to a size individuals can deal with," wrote Philip Miller in 1955, is a "basic human desire."

3. Slagle to *Detroit Times*, April 25, CR/AD, 28–31; letters from "A future Dearbornite," April 19, CR/1956; Miss Joan Calcaterra (ca. June 22), CR/ADb. Slagle told blacks to take care of their own neighborhoods and property, and not "expect the White man to do everything for you." "Get some paint and paint it, put a new roof on it, and if [it] can't be fixed, tare [*sic*] it down and build a new one, that is what the white man would do."

4. Letters from Harry Badarak, April 20, CR/ADb; Martha Molian, May 15, CR/AD, 28–31.

5. Prominent examples of this enormous literature include David M. Potter, *People of Plenty: Economic Abundance and the American Character* (Chicago: University of Chicago Press, 1954); John Keats, *The Crack in the Picture Window* (Boston: Houghton Mifflin, 1957); John Kenneth Galbraith, *The Affluent Society* (Boston: Houghton Mifflin, 1958); William H. Whyte, *The Organization Man* (New York: Simon & Schuster, 1956); and Elaine Tyler May, *Homeward Bound: American Families in the Cold War Era* (New York: Basic Books, 1988). On the racial narrative, in particular, see Charles Abrams, *Forbidden Neighbors: A Study of Prejudice in Housing* (Port Washington, N.Y.: Kennikat Press, 1971); Jonathan Rieder, *Canarsie: The Jews and Italians of Brooklyn against Liberalism* (Cambridge, Mass.: Harvard University Press, 1985); Ronald Formisano, *Boston against Busing: Race, Class, and Ethnicity in the 1960s and 1970s* (Chapel Hill: University of North Carolina Press, 1991). For an introduction to the scholarship exploring the postwar suburb's complicated racial, class, and gender histories, see Jeanne Meyerowitz, ed., *Not June Cleaver: Women and Gender in Postwar America, 1945–1960* (Philadelphia: Temple University Press, 1994); Becky M. Nicolaides, *My Blue Heaven: Life and Politics in the Working-Class Suburbs of Los Angeles, 1920–1965* (Chicago: University of Chicago Press, 2002); Andrew Wiese, *Places of Their Own: African American Suburbanization in the Twentieth Century* (Chicago: University of Chicago Press, 2004); and Kevin M. Kruse and Thomas J. Sugrue, eds., *The New Suburban History* (Chicago: University of Chicago Press, 2006). Barbara Ehrenreich and Stephanie Coontz brilliantly unravel many myths about the postwar suburban good life; see Ehrenreich, *Fear of Falling: The Inner Life of the Middle Class* (New York: Pantheon Books, 1989), and Coontz, *The Way We Never Were: American Families and the Nostalgia Trap* (New York: Basic Books, 1992).

6. Important exceptions are George Lipsitz, *The Possessive Investment in Whiteness: How White People Profit from Identity Politics* (Philadelphia: Temple University Press, 1998), and Eric Avila, *Popular Culture in the Age of White Flight: Fear and Fantasy in Suburban Los Angeles* (Berkeley: University of California Press, 2004). Visual and performing artists have long explored the more complicated, often ambiguous stories of class, gender, and racial identity in postwar America. A *very* small sample of insightful explorations includes *Twelve Angry Men* (Sidney Lumet, 1957); *Faces* (John Cassavetes, 1968); *Color Adjustment* (Marlon Riggs, 1991); *Fires in the Mirror* (George C. Wolfe, written and performed by Anna Deavere Smith, 1993), and *Pleasantville* (Gary Ross, 1998).

7. See Thomas J. Sugrue, *The Origins of the Urban Crisis: Race and Inequality in Postwar Detroit* (Princeton: Princeton University Press, 1996), chap. 7, and Wiese, *Places of Their Own*. Excellent treatments of class and color conflict in black communities include St. Clair Drake and Horace Cayton, *Black Metropolis: A Study of Negro Life in a Northern City*, rev. and enl. ed. (Chicago: University of Chicago Press, 1993); James Grossman, *Land of Hope: Chicago, Black Southerners, and the Great Migration* (Chicago: University of Chicago Press, 1989); Victoria W. Wolcott, *Remaking Respectability: African American Women in Interwar Detroit* (Chapel Hill: University of North Carolina Press, 2001); and *A Question of Color* (Kathe Sandler, 1993).

8. "Statement by the Rt. Rev. Richard S. Emrich, Bishop of the Episcopal Diocese in Michigan," n.d., CR/1956; *DN*, April 18, 1956; *Detroit Times*, April 18, 1956; *DG*, April 19, 1956; *DFP*, April 19, 1956; Dorothy Laviolette and Mary Kosgesi (for the

Dearborn Council of United Church Women) to OH, April 11, CR/ADb, 1956. The council represented twenty-one Protestant churches in the Dearborn area. See also David L. Good, *Orvie, the Dictator of Dearborn: The Rise and Reign of Orville L. Hubbard* (Detroit: Wayne State University Press, 1989), chap. 31.

9. For references to the Lou Gordon television show, see letters from Sally Nicholas, June 6, and Bob and Helen Drewniak, June 6, CR/1957; quote is from Mrs. J. Hagben, April 22, CR/ADb. I am so grateful to the late Winthrop Sears Jr. of the Ford Library and Dearborn Historical Museum, for introducing me to this correspondence, generously providing working drafts of his cataloging notes and, most of all, for years of voluntary work processing the Hubbard Papers.

10. Letters from Mr. and Mrs. Hutchins, April 19, Mr. and Mrs. John Cunningham, April 20, Louis Martin, April 20, Mr. and Mrs. Martin, April 20, and Aloysius W. Schreidel, April 24, CR/ADb. Herman J. Romps thanked the mayor for his "fine stand in defense of community interests"; Romps, May 1, CR/ADb.

11. For examples, see letters from the James Godre family, April 20, "A friend," April 27, G. Machuga, April 20, James Griffin, April 27, and Mellon E. Disser, n.d., CR/ADb; Sam Drueak, April 19, and K. Schmidt, April 18, CR/AD, 6–27; A. L. Goody, April 28, Mr. and Mrs. Charles Reagan, April 28, and Frederick O'Dras, May 5, CR/AD, 28–31.

12. "How many colored ministers does the Bishop have that are the head of our white churches????" Letter from Otis Lijesey and Rosalie Beki, April 24, CR/ADb.

13. Letters from Harry Badarak, April 20; anon., with attached pamphlet and article, n.d.; Mrs. H. Alexander, April 21; Mrs. Anna Holdren, April 27; "Some Disgusted Detroiters," April 26, CR/ADb; K. Schmidt, April 18, and "A friend," April 19, CR/AD, 6–27; Martha Molian, May 15, G. E. Baker, April 28, and "The Public of Detroit," November 28, 1957, CR/AD, 28–31; Mrs. M. Foote, September 16, CR/1957. Suburban whites often spoke on behalf of white Detroiters, explaining that "the rank and file . . . are afraid of the negro." Camp Dearborn, created in 1948, is owned and operated by the city of Dearborn, but located about 25 miles to the northwest in the town of Milford.

14. Letters from anon., April 20, Michael Morgan, April 13, and anon., n.d., with *U.S. News and World Report* article, CR/ADb; J. Monroe, July 5, CR/AD, 28–31. The man who forwarded pictures of Detroit described his family's home as "our pride and joy," adding that "our life time savings are invested there." They were worried about the future, since it was becoming "too expensive to keep moving around in order to stay one jump ahead of the Colored Blight." Residents often referred the mayor to articles in national newspapers and magazines discussing conditions in Chicago, Washington, and other cities.

15. Two revealing explorations are Thomas Cripps, *Making Movies Black: The Hollywood Message Movie from World War II to the Civil Rights Era* (New York: Oxford University Press, 1993) and Riggs, *Color Adjustment.*

16. Letters from Badarak, April 20, "A friend," April 27, and Holdren, April 27, CR/ADb; anon., May 2, and J. Jico, April 29, CR/AD, 28–31.

17. Letters from Molian, May 15, and anon., May 25, CR/AD, 28–31; Mrs. M. Foote, September 16, CR/1957; anon., April 27, Calcaterra, ca. June 22, and Svend Plum, April 21, CR/ADb; Stanley Braun, April 19, and "A future Dearborner," April 19, CR/AD, 6–27; Varga, April 30, CR/AN, 1956. "I moved away [from Detroit] and never have been back in three years now," wrote Varga. "I can't stand the place. It makes me sick to think of it."

18. Letters from Foote, September 16, and L. A. Putnam, December 16, CR/1957; K. Schmidt, April 18, CR/AD, 6–27; anon., April 23, anon., April 20, Eleanor Voldrich, April 24, Mrs. Della F. Peterson, May 2, and [illegible], April 23, CR/ADb; Alma Burch, April 19, CR/AD, 6–27.

19. Good introductions are Clifford Geertz, *The Interpretation of Cultures: Selected Essays* (New York: Basic Books, 1973), and Stuart Hall, "Race, Articulation and Societies Structured in Dominance," in UNESCO, ed., *Sociological Theories: Race and Colonialism* (Paris: UNESCO, 1980). My thinking on this subject is especially indebted to Raymond Williams, *Marxism and Literature* (Oxford: Oxford University Press, 1977); Pierre Bourdieu, *Outline of a Theory of Practice* (Cambridge: Cambridge University Press, 1977); Paul Willis, *Learning to Labor: How Working Class Kids Get Working Class Jobs* (New York: Columbia University Press, 1981); Henri Lefebvre, *The Production of Space* (Cambridge, Mass.: Blackwell, 1991); and Edward Soja, *Postmodern Geographies: The Reassertion of Space in Critical Social Theory* (London: Verso, 1989).

20. Letters from Mrs. Fern Hand, April 17, "Parents of Dearborn," ca. September 26, and George H. Washabaugh, April 28, CR/ADb.

21. Letter from "A neighbor out that way," April 20, CR/ADb.

22. Clifford E. Clark, *The American Family Home: 1800–1960* (Chapel Hill: University of North Carolina Press, 1986), chap. 7; idem, "Ranch House Suburbia: Ideals and Realities," in Lary May, ed., *Recasting America: Culture and Politics in the Age of Cold War* (Chicago: University of Chicago Press, 1989); Coontz, *The Way We Never Were*, esp. chaps. 2 and 4; May, *Homeward Bound*; Ehrenreich, *Fear of Falling*; and Lizabeth Cohen, *A Consumers' Republic: The Politics of Mass Consumption in Postwar America* (New York: Knopf, 2003), esp. 114–29.

23. Letters from John Smith, April 30, and Wm. A. Carey, June 7, CR/AD, 28–31; Ken O. LePard, April 7, Aloysius W. Schriedel, April 24, anon., April 20, and Arthur Schuetzler, to James Eastland, c/c Orville Hubbard, April 20, CR/ADb; anon., June 6, and G. E. Baker, September 11, 1958, CR/1957.

24. Letters from H. Myers, April 20, CR/ADb; Thomas Dunne, May 5, CR/AD, 28–31; Harry Trobaugh, April 18, CR/AD, 6–27; anon., June 6, CR/1957. Correspondents frequently lashed out at the Supreme Court, arguing that "we still have a voting privilege . . . regardless of the highest court"; Foote, September 16, CR/1957.

25. Letters from Allan Norris, April 20 and Washabaugh, April 28, CR/ADb; James Haggerty, January 11, 1958, CR/1957; anon., October 9, CR/1957.

26. Letters from Calcaterra, ca. June 22, Hand, April 17, Peterson, May 2, 1956, and "Mrs. Moore," April 19, CR/ADb.

27. Letters from Mike Luptak, May 8, Stanley Baran, n.d., William O. Brennan, April 29, anon., May 1, and Harry F. Joseph, June 4 and July 7, CR/AD, 28–31; Robert Herndon, April 10, CR/ADb.

28. Letters from G. C. Weyher, April 23, Mrs. H. Alexander, April 21, Holdren, April 27, "A Detroiter," April 27, Mrs. J. Hagben, April 22, and anon., with notes on pamphlet and article, CR/ADb; Peterson, May 2 and Joseph, July 7, CR/AD, 28–31; Haggerty, January 11, CR/1958.

29. Letters from John Smith, April 30, Jico, April 29, Mr. and Mrs. Grover C. Puryear, April 30, and Russell Roberts, April 29, CR/AD, 28–31; Romps, May 1, anon., April 20, and Washabaugh, April 28, CR/ADb; Foote, September 16, CR/1957. Detroit council platform attached to note from a white Detroiter.

30. Letter from Plum, April 21, CR/ADb. See also Braun, April 19, CR/AD, 6–27; and E. Varga, April 30, CR/AN, 1956. Mrs. Charles Bergquist insisted that she was "not

against the Negro and don't want them abused" but was equally certain that they were "naturally low morally and otherwise." From Bay City Michigan came the assertion that "all men are equal, but every man should be in his own place." Thomas Conroy explained that he led an organization of whites promoting voluntary segregation in the metropolitan area to "defend the principle of free enterprise and the other freedoms which are the rightful heritage of Americans." Their other goal was to "uphold the Constitution and the laws of the State of Michigan." Bergquist, April 20, Mrs. Arthur Arndt, April 28, and Thomas Conroy, May 29, CR/AN, 1965.

31. Letters from "A Detroit Housewife," April 20, Mrs. Louis Picklesimer, April 23, Mary Smith, April 24, Hagben, April 22, Albert C. Nute, April 12, and Peterson, May 2, CR/ADb; "A future Dearborner," April 19, and Burch, April 19, CR/AD, 6–27. "Wish you were Mayor of Detroit," wrote Sally Nichols. "Better yet, I wish I could live in Dearborn"; June 6, CR/1957.

32. Letter from Mr. and Mrs. C. L. Shepard, April 21, CR/ADb.

33. Oliver C. Moles Jr., "Voter Characteristics and the Mayor of Dearborn," 60.

34. For an excellent introduction to the "long" history of civil rights protest, see Robin D. G. Kelley and Earl Lewis, eds., *To Make Our World Anew: A History of African Americans* (New York: Oxford University Press, 2000). On the decades-long assault against de jure segregation, see Clement E. Vose, *Caucasians Only: The Supreme Court, the NAACP, and the Restrictive Covenant Cases* (Berkeley: University of California Press, 1959), and Mark V. Tushnet, *Making Civil Rights Law: Thurgood Marshall and the Supreme Court, 1936–1961* (New York: Oxford University Press, 1994), esp. chap. 6.

35. Wiese, *Places of Their Own*, 44–49; Joe T. Darden et al., *Detroit: Race and Uneven Development* (Philadelphia: Temple University Press, 1987), 140–42. In 1970, 30 percent of Warren's workers were black, but only 1 percent of its homeowners.

36. Meanwhile, black organizations, energized by their victory in passing a state fair employment practices law in 1955, stepped up their efforts to end employment discrimination, staging boycotts against public and private enterprises. The MIC became the Commission on Community Relations (CCR) under Detroit mayor Albert Cobo, who undermined its efforts in the early 1950s by staffing it with anti–civil rights housing activists. See Sugrue, *Origins of the Urban Crisis*, 171–77, 190–93 (quoted on 191), 225; John T. McGreevey, *Parish Boundaries: The Catholic Encounter with Race in the Twentieth-Century North* (Chicago: University of Chicago Press, 1996), chaps. 4 and 6; Kathy Cosseboom, *Grosse Pointe, Michigan: Race against Race* (East Lansing: Michigan State University Press, 1972). For excellent discussions of early postwar activism in other cities, see Martha Biondi, *To Stand and Fight: The Struggle for Civil Rights in Postwar New York City* (Cambridge, Mass.: Harvard University Press, 2003), and Robert O. Self, *American Babylon: Race and the Struggle for Postwar Oakland* (Princeton: Princeton University Press, 2003).

37. In Pontiac, the NAACP persuaded FHA and VA officials to insure reclaimed housing units on a nondiscriminatory basis, which in turn introduced black residents to nearly all of the city's census tracts by 1962.

38. James Garrett, Forum Committee, Commission on Community Relations/Coordinating Council on Human Relations, open letter, September 25, 1962, ALUA, NAACP, Box 16, "Housing Discriminator, 1962"; "A Solution for Housing Desegregation," Associate Brokers, ALUA, NAACP, Box 16, "Housing Committee, 1962"; mimeo announcing Dearborn action, June 13, 1963 at Dexter Branch Office; July 3, 1963, announcement regarding Redford march; handwritten notes re plans for the march along Oak Park Blvd. and rally at the Oak Park municipal building; Ulmer

to Elsea Realty, May 17, 1963; Ulmer to F. G. Cherry Realty, May 9, 1963; Ulmer to W. C. Patterson, Michigan Bell, n.d.; "Suggestions for Speakers of NAACP Housing Committee," n.d.: all in ALUA, NAACP, Box 22, "Housing Committee, 1963"; Sugrue, *Origins of the Urban Crisis*, 190–94, 240; Darden et al., *Detroit*, 132–35.

39. Later renamed the Religion and Race Conference.

40. ALUA, NAACP, Box 18, "Metropolitan Conference on Open Occupancy, Sept. 1962"; letters from John P. Breeden Jr., for Christ Episcopal Church, Dearborn, January 7, 1963, and "A twenty-two year Dearbornite," ca. April 17, 1963, CR/1962–3. On organizing against employment discrimination in Detroit, see Sugrue, *Origins of the Urban Crisis*, chaps 4 and 7. On national and regional housing activism, see Wiese, *Places of Their Own*, 219–25, 238–40; Biondi, *To Stand and Fight*, chaps. 6 and 11; and Scott A. Henderson, *Housing and the Democratic Ideal: The Life and Thought of Charles Abrams* (New York: Columbia University Press, 2000).

41. More than 100 people attended the founding meeting of the Dearborn Community Council on October 18, 1963. "Dearborn Community Council, February 7, 1964" (mimeo list of leadership and board of directors, origin unclear); "Dearborn Community Council Newsletter," March 18, 1964; and typescript report on DCC meeting, April 17, 1964 (no attribution): all in CR/Stanz, DCC; *DN*, October 19 and November 30, 1963. On civil rights activism in postwar Detroit, see Dan Georgakas and Marvin Surkin, *Detroit: I Do Mind Dying: A Study in Urban Revolution* (New York: St. Martin's Press, 1975), quoting 43; B. J. Widick, *Detroit: City of Race and Class Violence*, rev. ed. (Detroit: Wayne State University Press, 1989); McGreevey, *Parish Boundaries*; and Grace Lee Boggs, *Living for Change: An Autobiography* (Minneapolis: University of Minnesota Press, 1998).

42. Letters from James Kapple, September 20, CR/Stanz, 1963; John Matle, May 5, "A friend," April 27. Alexander, April 21, anon., April 22, and Holdren, April 27, CR/ADb; "A twenty-two year Dearbornite," ca. April 17, 1963, CR/1962–3; McGreevey, *Parish Boundaries*, 92–93. Kapple was "confident that [ministers] did not speak for [their parishioners]," and Matle was sure that "these church women and Ministers would be the first to squak about it if they got colored or [so] called Negroes to live next door!"

43. "Buyer Beware," *Time* April 16, 1956. In 1963, white homeowners' associations in Detroit responded to the open housing campaign by gathering enough signatures to put a homeowners' rights ordinance designed to secure their right to exclude blacks from their neighborhoods on the 1964 ballot. It passed by a margin of 55 to 45 percent but was ruled unconstitutional the following year. See Sugrue, *Origins of the Urban Crisis*, 226–27.

44. Letters from Martin Kosten, May 12, 1962, with attached form letter, CR/1962–3; Albert Zajac, September 19, 1961, CR/1957–61. Realtors who contacted Hubbard often invoked NAREB's Code of Ethics; some attached copies. See Keith Forbush (for Dearborn Real Estate Board) to OH, March 12, 1953, with attachment ("Code of Ethics"), DHM, OHP, "Business and Industry: Real Estate." Peter W. Vermullen discusses the 1961 session of the Annual Short Course for Assessing Officers (sponsored by the University of Michigan) in a letter of December 7, 1961, DHM, OHP, D1, CAN.

45. Letter from Rev. Robert Fehribach, May 28, CR/1960. According to Alex Pilch, Hubbard often promoted Camp Dearborn by noting that "It's thirty minutes to Belle Isle and 30 hours to Africa and who wants to go to either place." The mayor "wasn't saying anything racial," Pilch added, "but everybody knew what he meant"; Alex Pilch, oral history, transcript, DHM 337. Members of the camp commission did talk

about things "racial" when they planned the facility in consultation with forty-three civic and social organizations between 1947 and 1950. One of the issues addressed was the "problem" of excluding black children. Minutes from a September 1947 meeting explain that "an informal discussion ensued as to whether the camp would be restricted to white people only, or open to other races . . . The resolution creating the Commission speaks only of the 'Citizens of Dearborn,' which should pretty well clarify that point"; Regular Meeting of the Camp Commission, September 8, 1947, DHM, City Commissions, Camp.

46. Letter from Matt and Ruth Zipple, September 23, 1963, DHM, OHP, CR/ "Correspondence: critical, 1963." On the Stanzione affair, see chap. 1.

47. DMARPC, "Residential Construction in the Detroit Region: 1962," January 1963, 1–2, 6–8; "Residential Construction in the Detroit Region: 1963," January 1964, 5–7; "Residential Construction in the Detroit Region: 1964," January 1965, 7–10: all in MHC, DMARPC; Harold Black, "Community Development Study, Big Beaver/ Crooks Rd. Site," table 17 and 37–39, THM, Box 14; City Plan Commission, Royal Oak, "1959–1960, Annual Report," ROHC, "Annual Reports."

48. Local journalists and officials continued to reproduce planners' claim that apartments were not a "residential" use. The *Tribune* noted in the 1964 debate, for example, that planners recommended against "extending the multiple-family zone into the residential area"; *DT,* May 9, 1957, and May 27, 1964.

49. Between 1955 and 1967, at least thirty-five of the cases before the Michigan Supreme court involved Detroit-area suburbs (including two in Warren, five in Troy, seven in Dearborn, and five in Southfield). Supreme Court cases decreased after the ruling in *Brae Burn, Inc v. City of Bloomfield Hills,* 350 Mich. 425, 86 N.W.2d 166 (1957) established a much stricter test for appeal. Andrews, "Michigan Zoning Cases—1949 through 1986," unpublished report, ca. 1986, 2 (copy in MML).

50. *Anchor Steel and Conveyor Co. v. City of Dearborn,* 342 Mich. 361, 70 N.W.2d 753 (1955); *McGiverin v. City of Huntington Woods,* 343 Mich. 413, 72 N.W.2d 105 (1955); *Scholnick v. City of Bloomfield Hills* (1958); *Comer v. City of Dearborn,* 342 Mich. 471, 70 N.W.2d 813 (1955); *Basey v. City of Huntington Woods* (1956); *Alderton v. City of Saginaw,* 367 Mich. 28, 116 N.W.2d 53 (1962). See *Michigan Reports* (14B Mich D), 454.

51. Southfield incorporated in September of 1957; the charter was filed in April of the following year.

52. *White v. Township of Southfield,* 347 Mich. 548, 79 N.W.2d 863 (1956); James Hickey, "The Land in Which the Lawyer Dwells," DMARPC, *Regional Reporter,* January 1957, 2–3, MHC, "SEMCOG publications"; *Wenner v. City of Southfield,* 365 Mich. 563, 113 N.W.2d 918 (1962).

53. "Troy City Council Meeting," minutes, Troy High School, February 11, 1957, 1–2, typescript, THM, Box 14, "Zoning." On neighborhood organizing in Dearborn, see the correspondence in DHM, D1, "Building and Safety, Correspondence," for example, Mr. and Mrs. Alex Stanyar to OH, February 17, 1962.

54. "Meeting 1/14/59, Chrysler Expressway," 4, typescript, THM, Box 14, "Zoning"; Dale Libby to OH, February 14, 1962, DHM, OHP, D1, Building and Safety, C. Residents scrutinized local tax policy and compared it with that in neighboring suburbs and even other states. One Dearborner referred city administrators to J. C. Lincoln's *Ground Rent, Not Taxes: The Natural Source of Revenue for the Government,* first published in 1957, noting that the Dearborn Public Library owned a copy. See letters

from Louis Veith, April 21, 1961; L. Groney, September 5, 1957; Theodore Sahulka, November 15, 1961; Fred Storch, March 4, 1960; Mrs. Iva Smith, July 7, 1962; and Margaret Petrilli, February 16, 1961: all in DHM, OHP, Departments, Box 1, "Assessors, citizens letters."

55. "Troy City Council Meeting," minutes, Troy High School, February 11, 1957, 8, typescript, THM, Box 14, "Zoning."

56. There were initially five designations for single-family dwellings, each with a different minimum lot, square footage, and setback size. The least restrictive zone required a minimum lot width of 60 feet and a minimum lot size of 7,500 square feet. See "City of Troy, Michigan: Zoning Ordinance, Ordinance No. 23"; Ordinance No. 23-1, June 24, 1957; "Zoning District Map, City of Troy Michigan: all in THM, Box 14, "Zoning"; interview with Larry Kiesling, Troy Planning Department, August 10, 1995.

57. Thompson asked why officials had "vilified" a "long-honored improvement organization run by dedicated, selfless individuals under the democratic process of election to office by thousands of interest[ed] property owners," while treating a "community council, organized under the direction of City employees" as "a thing of beauty"; Ralph A. Thompson, for Grandvale Civic Association, to the Common Council, Detroit, April 1, 1963, attached to letter from Thompson, April 2, 1963, CR/1962-3. See Sugrue's discussion of the protective associations, their alliances with local realtors, and their invocations of property owners' rights and "true Americanism" in *Origins of the Urban Crisis,* chap. 8, esp. 220.

58. USBC, *United States Censuses of Population and Housing: 1960 (Census Tracts: Detroit, Mich. Standard Metropolitan Statistical Area)* (Washington, D.C.: GPO, 1961), 17 (table P-1); USBC, *Sixteenth Census of the United States: 1940, Population,* vol. 2, *Characteristics of the Population,* pt. 3, 863–64; Sugrue, *Origins of the Urban Crisis,* 19, 24–31, chap. 2 (esp. 42, 51–55), 140–41, 183–88, 216; *Emergence and Growth of an Urban Region: The Developing Urban Detroit Area,* vol. 1: *Analysis* (Detroit: Detroit Edison Co., 1966), pt. 4, 232 (fig. 138). In 1960, between 10 and 15 percent of Detroit's housing units were considered dilapidated, compared with 0–5 percent or 5–10 percent in virtually every western and northern suburb. The U.S. government invested $353 million in equipment and plant construction in the metropolitan area during the Korean War, of which only 7.5 percent went to Detroit firms.

For an introduction to the extensive scholarship on central-city decline, see Michael Katz, ed., *The Underclass Debate: Views from History* (Princeton: Princeton University Press, 1993); Douglas S. Massey and Nancy A. Denton, *American Apartheid: Segregation and the Making of the Underclass* (Cambridge, Mass.: Harvard University Press, 1993); Sugrue, *Origins of the Urban Crisis;* and John F. Bauman, Roger Biles, and Kristin Szylvian, eds., *From Tenements to Taylor Homes: In Search of an Urban Housing Policy in Twentieth-Century America* (University Park: Pennsylvania State University Press, 2000).

59. R. Stiffler, "An Analysis of The City of Troy, Michigan," prepared for Mrs. Patton's Public Finance Class, Western Michigan University, Kalamazoo, Michigan, December 29, 1958, 1–2, THM, Box 14; Harold Black, "Community Development Study, Big Beaver/Crooks Rd. Site," 4, THM, Box 14.

60. *DT,* March 18, 1966, February 21, 1964, January 18 and March 18, 1955, and January 21, April 17, and December 1, 1964; press release, Dearborn Board of Realtors, "35th Anniversary of the Dearborn Board of Realtors, 1926–1961," DHM,

Organizations, "Dearborn Board of Realtors." On suburban newspaper readership, see report on Publication Research Service study in "Our Readers Speak Up," *DT,* March 25, 1955.

61. Detroiter cited in Sugrue, *Origins of the Urban Crisis,* 62; anon. to OH, ca. August 28, 1962, DHM, OHP, Box 15, Housing, Dept. business, 1949–64. (The correspondent attached a *Detroit Free Press* article regarding Kennedy's plans). Compare Sugrue's discussion of the mortgage programs' reception on 62–63. On Depression-era discussions of selective credit programs, see chap. 4.

62. I located one discussion of the mechanics of federal mortgage programs in Royal Oak, and none in the other suburbs discussed in this study; "Tight Money Worries Builders," *DT,* October 3, 1956. In "Good News in Construction" (*DT,* January 16, 1958), Miller discusses FHA commissioner Norman Mason's strategies to "stimulate the revival of home building," namely, freeing homebuyers from paying closing costs in cash and further adjustment to FHA discount rates. Miller occasionally noted that government intrusion in private markets was required, when special circumstances made this "necessary," for example, to redevelop blighted neighborhoods ("New Plans for Downtown," *DT,* November 13, 1958).

63. On Royal Oak annual reports, see chap. 6; "Building Survey Shows Increase in Size, Cost," "Independent Home of the Week," and "That Old Flame," *DI,* January 20, 1950; Royal Oak *Annual* (Plan), 1959–60, ROHC, "Annual Reports"; "City of Royal Oak Annual Report Section," *DT,* December 1, 1956; "City of Royal Oak Annual Report," *DT,* September 27, 1958; "Annual Report . . . 1960—City of Royal Oak, Michigan," *DT,* September 3, 1960. For discussions of "health, safety, and welfare," see Royal Oak Plan Commission, "1959–60, Annual Report," and "Annual Report, 1965–66," ROHC, "Royal Oak." Suburban planners and publicists throughout the region adopted this language. See Southfield Planning Commission, *Economic Base Study of Southfield: A Master Plan Study* (Southfield, 1960), 17, and "Hazel Park: A Suburban City That Is Growing Up," *Inside Michigan,* March 1953, 35. Beginning in 1960, the *Tribune*'s Annual Report section was reformatted again to resemble an advertising supplement.

64. "Registration Shows Responsibility," *DT,* December 5, 1956, "Incorporation for Madison?" January 13, 1955, and "9th City for Royal Oak Township" and "Creating the Good Community" January 19, 1955. The Michigan Municipal League's journal, the *Michigan Municipal Review,* catalogued the passage of new municipal ordinances and reported on local petition drives regarding annexation, zoning reform, and other development issues. See, for example, "Round Towns," *Michigan Municipal Review,* August 1941, 99. By the early 1950s, the MML, too, was referring to the typical municipal resident as a homeowner ("Dear Property Owner," *MMR,* August 1951, 134). The collaboration between localities (in this case, Dearborn) and both state and national municipal organizations is documented extensively in Alex Pilch's correspondence, in DHM, Alex Pilch papers.

65. *DT,* January 19, June 10, 1955; "Sound Charter for Madison," December 1, 1955; "End HP Controversy," September 14, 1955; "Hazel Park: The Real Issue," February 13, 1956. Other examples include "Small Cities Serve a Purpose," *DT,* February 17, 1955; "Creating the Good Community," January 19, 1955; "Keep Interest in Government," November 8, 1956; and editorials of February 13, 20, and 22, May 26 and 31, 1955, and December 8, 1958.

66. "Why New Cities Are Formed," *DT,* June 6, 1955, and "Parking, Proper Zoning Use," June 16, 1955.

67. "Learning by Living," *DT*, February 9, 1955. See also "Pruning Out Eyesores," May 6, 1955; "Ferndale Parking Lot? Yes!" March 27, 1958; and "How to Blight a Business Section," January 14, 1955.

68. Alex Pilch oral history, July 26 and August 15, 1979, transcript, DHM, 337; "Clean Up, Paint Up, Fix Up" flyer, 1957; "The 1957 Clean-Up Story of Dearborn, Michigan: narration for slide presentation (August 1, 1957)"; viewership tabulated from "1957, City Beautiful Commission, Slide Show: Completed Showings"; letter from the Miller-Bradley Civic Association, n.d.: all in DHM, Commissions, "City Beautiful." The presentation was shown to 3,880 children, 150 members of the Dearborn Kiwanis, and 206 members of local "civic" and "property protective" associations. Some local organizations specifically requested the slide show.

69. "Clean-Up Parade Order," mimeo; "Dearborn Clean Up—Paint Up—Fix Up Program," flyer (1956); and E. J. Salancy to George W. Lewis re poster distribution, April 23, 1958: all in DHM, Commissions, "City Beautiful"; "Dearborn Salutes Progress, Ford Motor Company" (photograph), September 26, 1956, DHM, photofile, "Dearborn Salutes Progress." In 1956, three weeks in May were declared "Clean Up," "Fix Up," and "Paint Up" weeks, respectively. Daily tasks included: "Parade Day," "Attend Church Day," "Clean Your House Day," "Clean Your Garage Day," "Clean Your Yard Day," "Plant Petunias Day," "Home Improvement Survey Day," and "Family Outing Day."

70. Many organizations illustrated their advertisements and publications with "clean-up"–themed images.

71. Huller to Robert Brueck, March 7, 1958; Diane K. and Jim L. Jr., City Beautiful Commission, Ray Junior High to City Beautiful Commission, May 22, 1958; "Miller School News, 'Clean Up' Edition," May 1958; "Report of Clean-Up, Fix-Up, Paint-Up Week at Roulo School, May 1958"; "City Beautiful Commission Awards Night, June 7, 1957"; Richard Rusinki, for the Dearborn Jaycees, to Mayor and Council, October 19, 1956; "City Beautiful Commission Agenda," March 15, 1957; "1957 Clean-Up Campaign Balloon Contest," sponsored by the Dearborn Historical Commission, mimeo; informational flyers for public distribution, including "Dearborn: Clean Up—Paint Up—Fix Up Program, Clean Up Week, May 5–11, 1956"; Grace Smith, for Miller School to Robert Brueck, May 1, 1958; Thornley, for Edsel Ford High School, to Harold G. Odgers, June 6, 1958; Gwinell to "Parents," April 29, 1958; St. Sebastian's' Junior Commissioners' Report (n.d.); Atonement Lutheran School Clean Up, Fix Up, Paint Up Report (n.d.]: all in DHM, Commissions, "City Beautiful." See the extensive photographic record of annual award ceremonies and citywide "Clean Up" parades from the 1950s to 1970s, in DHM, Photofile, Commissions, "City Beautiful Commission." The competition between schools was stiff, and parents were kept apprised of student activities with form letters.

72. "Regular Meeting of the Hazel Park City Council," May 21 and 26, 1947, April 11, 1944, May 9, 1944, HP; "Landis Wins First Place," *DT*, July 22, 1954; and "Encouraging a More Attractive City," May 23, 1952; O. L. Hubbard, "'Operation Eyesore' Stops Urban Decay," *American City*, May 1963, 165–66. Examples of national press coverage include Harry Kursh, "Has Your Town a Gripe Center," *American Mercury*, September 1956, 26–28, and Barbara Holland, "Camping for the Community," *Recreation*, May 1950, 68–69. One example of a solicitation for advice is Hayes A. Richardson, Welfare Department, Kansas City, Missouri to Alex Pilch, March 4, 1957, DHM, 337, "Correspondence 1954–1957."

American City ran at least nineteen features on Dearborn government and services in the 1950s, many of them drafted by Alex Pilch's office. Press releases in DHM, Commissions, "City Beautiful" and DHM, Commissions, "Public Relations." See also the extensive correspondence between Pilch and Pann Dodd Eimon, executive director, Government Public Relations Association, and editor of *American City*. In 1958, the GPRA presented Dearborn with the award for the "best overall public relations program among municipal governments" at the annual banquet of the American Municipal Association.

73. "Why 'Do-It-Yourself'?" *DT*, March 11, 1955. On the national trend of do-it-yourself, see Clark, *American Family Home*, 230–31.

74. DHM, Photofile, "Celebrations."

75. "Persistence of Slums," *DT*, August 4, 1958. See the extensive documentation on the "bulletin board" case in DHM, OHP, CR/Civil Rights, 1965, Civil Rights Commission." Hubbard was acquitted.

76. For example, Miller expressed his frustration with Eisenhower's civil rights stand, supported passage of civil rights legislation, applauded Gunnar Myrdal's work, complained about footdragging by the Civil Rights Commission, applauded religious leaders who supported the civil rights movement, and condemned Barry Goldwater.

77. "On Becoming Americans," *DT*, March 7, 1956, and "Need We Be Hypocrites and Fools?" February 23, 1955.

78. "Minstrels, Musicals and Drama," *DT*, March 30, 1965, and "Royal Oak Lions Club Stages Twentieth Annual Minstrel Show," February 21, 1967. Most of Miller's editorials in defense of civil rights politics appeared in the late winter and early spring of each year, roughly coinciding with the Lions Club's preparations and rehearsals for the annual minstrel show.

79. *DT*, May 27, 1964; Office of Intergovernmental Relations, *Michigan Planning and Zoning; Historical Statistics*, N 171–79.

80. See Sugrue, *Origins of the Urban Crisis*; Nicolaides, *My Blue Heaven*; Self, *American Babylon*; and Matthew D. Lassiter, *The Silent Majority: Suburban Politics in the Sunbelt South* (Princeton: Princeton University Press, 2006).

81. Letters from Jeff Brescoe, December 17, 1964, CR/1964; "And Oblige," March 7, 1960, and Mrs. Ann Santander, Coral Cables, Florida, June 30, 1961, CR/1957–61; I. A. M. Fantomas, September 16, 1963, Mr. and Mrs. G. Belle, ca. September 17, 1963, Mr. and Mrs. Hutchins, ca. September 16, 1963, George Buckenhizer, September 18, 1963, and Mrs. Frances Szczisniak, September 17, 1963, CR, Stanz/1963; "White Church Deserters," March 1962, CR/1962–3; Stanley Braun, March 24, CR/ Stanz, 1964. Santander described herself as the "only woman builder during F.H.A. boom Roosevelt's time," one who built "many a beautiful home in Dearborn Hills, the good old 5 to $6,000 days."

The enormous collection of correspondence and phone messages received between 1961 to 1964 is filled with declarations that local residents and "all their friends" supported Hubbard. They applauded his "judicious manner" in handling the Stanzione case, exhorted him to "keep Dearborn clean," and notified him of local, church-sponsored open housing events. Many correspondents responded directly to news and editorial coverage of racial politics in the local press, radio programming, and television. Hubbard continued to hear from residents throughout the metropolitan area. See CR/1957–61, CR/1962–3, CR/Stanz, 1963, CR/1964, CR/ Stanz, 1964, and CR/Stanz, DCC.

82. Virginia Fox to Thomas L. Poindexter (c/c OH), April 18, CR/Stanz, 1964; letter from Shirley Sraburg, September 19, CR/Stanz, 1963.

83. Letter from Sraburg, September 19, CR/Stanz, 1963. This language was ubiquitous in public conversations about desegregation. See, for example, Dan Wilhoyte, "Hubbard Defended" (letter to the editor), *DN*, June 24, 1965.

84. Letters from Longmoore, December 29, 1964, and Fox, April 18, CR/Stanz, 1964; John G. Bilecke, October 23, CR/Stanz, 1963.

85. For samples of this voluminous correspondence (including those cited here), see letters from Mrs. Stanley Wisniewski, September 18, Fantomas, September 16, Buckenhizer, September 18, Mr. and Mrs. Leon Kobozny, September 13, Lorne A. Putnam, September 16, Vincent Alessi, September 17, and Martin Brennan, September 17, CR/Stanz, 1963; Mr. and Mrs. R. L. Burke, December 29, CR/1964; phone message (from "np"), CR, Stanz/1964. A self-identified "twenty-two-year Dearbornite" asked Hubbard to make an appearance at a church-sponsored meeting on interracial marriage, lamenting that "the Dearborn homeowner has nobody to defend their position"; "A twenty-two-year Dearbornite," ca. April 17, 1963, CR/1962–3.

86. Letters from Kenneth V. Knuth, August 6, CR/1961; "A voter," ca. June 28, 1963, CR/1962–3; anon., ca. December 8, CR/1964; George L. King, September 21, describing his letter to WXYZ radio, CR/Stanz, 1963.

87. H. D. Warren to Romney, September 13, CR/Stanz, 1963; letters from Fox to Poindexter (c/c OH), April 18, and Braun, March 24, CR/Stanz, 1964; "White Church Deserters," March 1962, CR/1962–3. Of the families living in Detroit's public low-rent housing (8 projects) in 1962, only 16.7 percent received aid for dependent children; "Quarterly Report to the Commissioners, Detroit Housing Commission," winter 1962, ALUA, NAACP, Box 16, "Housing Discriminator, 1962."

88. The correspondent asked why Stempian did not "stay on Steel Street where he belonged"; letter from anon., ca. March 31, CR/Stanz. Steel Street is in Detroit, north of Tireman Avenue. Virginia Brickel suspected that one local activist minister "probably doesn't even pay taxes"; phone message, September 19, CR/Stanz, 1963.

89. Letters from Camille De Kose, "April," Sam Leonard, April 29, "White Chicagoan," June 13, Fred Johnson, June 16, Lucille Erickson, April 22, and William Osmond, July 19, CR/AN, 1956; "A Staunch Hubbard Booster," May 1, CR/ADb; Rudy Simpson, July 6, 1961, and Mrs. Paul Roberts, July 14, 1961, CR/1957–61.

90. Letter from Margaret von Walthausen, March 22, 1963, DHM, Departments, "Assessors, citizens letters."

91. Letter from James R. Kapple, September 20, 1963, CR/Stanz, 1963.

CHAPTER NINE

1. U.S. Kerner Commission, *Report of the National Advisory Commission on Civil Disorders* (Washington, D.C.: GPO, 1968), 47–61; U.S. Kerner Commission, *Supplemental Studies for the National Advisory Commission on Civil Disorders* (Washington, D.C.: GPO, 1968), 30, table 111-e; Sidney Fine, *Violence in the Model City: The Cavanaugh Administration, Race Relations, and the Detroit Riot of 1967* (Ann Arbor: University of Michigan Press, 1989), 36, 306–7, 383–84 (citing Lobsinger and letters); John Hersey, *The Algiers Motel Incident* (London: Hamilton, 1968), 331 (citing Lobsinger); Thomas J. Sugrue, *Origins of the Urban Crisis: Race and Inequality in Postwar Detroit* (Princeton: Princeton University Press, 1996), 259–60; Mrs. Donald F. Hagerty describes the scene at a suburban appliance store in letter to OH, August 2, CR/1967; copies of "arrest" warrants in CR/1967, riots. In national surveys conducted after

the riots, 56 percent of white respondents said that blacks, alone, were responsible for the fact that they had "worse jobs, education and housing"; 19 percent of whites argued that discrimination compounded the problems that blacks brought on themselves.

2. Letters from Ernest C. Rix, August 1, Mr. and Mrs. Henry Priestaf, August 2, and Mrs. Jon Chris Smith, August 1, CR/1967. Rix served on the Board of Directors of the Aviation Property Owners Association. One post-riot survey indicated that 9 percent of the whites in Detroit had armed themselves.

    The riots—and the response of white spokespeople like Lobsinger and Hubbard (who publicly encouraged local residents to "learn to shoot and shoot straight")— outraged and energized many white residents, activists, religious leaders, and elected officials. See, for example, letter from Rev. A. R. Heidmann and Rev. Richard Hofmann, August 10, CR/1967.

3. In addition to riots in Detroit, Newark, Chicago, Savannah, Rochester, Tampa, Cincinnati, Atlanta, and other locales, hundreds of acts of race-related violence were recorded during this period; U.S. Kerner Commission, *Report*, 19–61; Bryan T. Downes, "Social and Political Characteristics of Riot Cities: A Comparative Study," in James A. Geschwender, ed., *The Black Revolt: The Civil Rights Movement, Ghetto Uprisings, and Separatism* (Englewood Cliffs, N.J.: Prentice-Hall, 1971).

4. George R. Metcalf, *Fair Housing Comes of Age* (New York: Greenwood Press, 1988), 84–85; Douglas S. Massey and Nancy A. Denton, *American Apartheid: Segregation and the Making of the Underclass* (Cambridge, Mass.: Harvard University Press, 1993), 193–94. For further discussion of the obstacles facing federal "fair housing" efforts at HHFA and HUD, see David M. P. Freund, "'Democracy's Unfinished Business': Federal Policy and the Search for Fair Housing, 1961–1968," in Chester Hartman, ed., *Poverty and Race in America: The Emerging Agendas* (Lanham, Md.: Lexington Books, 2006), and Mara S. Sidney, "Images of Race, Class, and Markets: Rethinking the Origins of U.S. Fair Housing Policy," *Journal of Policy History* 13, no. 2 (2001): 181–214.

5. In 1968, most of the region's suburban municipalities had few if any black inhabitants. Black suburbanites were concentrated in four cities: Mt. Clemens, Ecorse, Inkster, and River Rouge; Louis H. Masotti, John R. Krause Jr., and Sheldon R. Gawiser, *Race and Representation in Detroit and the Six County Metropolitan Region: Regional Governing Bodies, Methods of Selection* (Detroit: Metropolitan Fund, 1968), table 2. Detroit-area whites, meanwhile, knew where black suburban residents "belonged." "I don't want any of them for neighbors and I doubt that any of my Christian friends really want them either," wrote Kathleen Parr, of Dearborn, in February 1965. "If they do, I always say I know of empty houses in Inkster for sale at a bargain and suggest they go up and look them over;" letter from Parr, Feb. 1, CR/BB. On national patterns of settlement and segregation, see Karl E. Taeuber and Alma F. Taeuber, *Negroes in Cities: Residential Segregation and Neighborhood Change* (New York: Atheneum, 1969), chap. 3, and Massey and Denton, *American Apartheid*.

6. Kerner Commission, *Supplemental Studies*, p. 31, table III-f. Two-thirds of those interviewed insisted that "changes in the Negro are possible," while another 25 percent were uncertain about the origins of "Negro conditions." On 1920s housing activism, see chap. 1.

7. Thomas Byrne Edsall and Mary D. Edsall, *Chain Reaction: The Impact of Race, Rights, and Taxes on American Politics* (New York: Norton, 1991), 4, 6, 7, 9, 21, 27–28. For

variations on this argument and an introduction to the literature on the Republican's "Southern Strategy," see Kevin P. Phillips, *The Emerging Republican Majority* (New Rochelle, N.Y.: Arlington House, 1969); Jim Sleeper, *The Closest of Strangers: Liberalism and the Politics of Race in New York* (New York: W. W. Norton, 1990); Jonathan Rieder, "The Rise of the 'Silent Majority,'" in Steve Fraser and Gary Gerstle, eds., *The Rise and Fall of the New Deal Order, 1930–1980* (Princeton: Princeton University Press, 1989), 243–68; Stanley Greenberg, *Middle Class Dreams: The Politics and Power of the New American Majority* (New York: Times Books, 1995); and Dan T. Carter, *From George Wallace to Newt Gingrich: Race in the Conservative Counterrevolution, 1963–1994* (Baton Rouge: Louisiana State University Press, 1996). See also Matthew Lassiter's important challenge in *The Silent Majority: Suburban Politics in the Sunbelt South* (Princeton: Princeton University Press, 2006).

8. Edsall and Edsall, *Chain Reaction*, 11.

9. In a communication with President Kennedy, on the eve of his decision to issue Executive Order 11063 (1962), Congresswoman Martha Griffiths discussed the views of suburban Democrats in the Detroit region. "Most of the white people," she explained, "have resigned themselves to the fact of integration, but the suburbs of Detroit believe it will be years before it applies to their exact areas . . . No Democratic Congressman, from suburbia, to whom I have talked, believes he is in any danger of losing colored votes; but he does feel such an order could cost white votes"; cited in Greenberg, *Middle Class Dreams*, 104. On suburban party affiliation nationwide, see Frederick M. Wirt et al., *On the City's Rim: Politics and Policy in Suburbia* (Lexington, Mass.: D. C. Heath, 1972).

10. For detailed discussion of the "Billboard Case" and the federal trial, see David L. Good, *Orvie, the Dictator of Dearborn: The Rise and Reign of Orville L. Hubbard* (Detroit: Wayne State University Press, 1989), chaps. 36 and 37.

11. See the vast collection of correspondence and phone messages in: CR/BB; CR/CNS, 1–24; CR/CNS, 1–13; and CR/CNS, J–S. Cited here are letters from James O. and Bettie Chappelle, February 6, 1965, Sallie A. Kopp, February 3, 1965, illegible, February 3, 1965, Joe and Charlie, February 3, 1965, Walter and Frances Szczesniak, February 17, 1965, and Fay Haines, March 15, 1965.

12. Letters from James O. and Bettie Chappelle, February 6, CR/BB; W. A. Settle Jr., n.d., anon. to "President Johnson," c/c Mayor Hubbard and the *Detroit News*, ca. February 16, and Mrs. Helen Bodner, February 23, CR/CNS, 1–24; Nell Miller, July 5, CR/CNS, J–S. See also "A disgusted Detroiter" to Judge Machrowicz, c/c Lyndon Johnson, February 17, CR/CNS, 1–24. A fourteen-year-old, self-identified "Proud Citizen of Dearborn" condemned the editors of the *Detroit News* for slandering a man who has "put twenty-three years of excellent service" in for the city; "A Proud Citizen of Dearborn" to *Detroit News*, c/c President Johnson, *Dearborn Press*, and Orville Hubbard, February 16, in CR/CNS, 1–24.

13. Assorted telegrams and letters, citing Mrs. Ford Karr, June 24, and Countz, June 25, CR/Stanz, 24–30; letter from Steve Rohanci, March 18, CR/CNS, 1–13.

14. Letters from Gregory M. Pillon, March 5, and Miss Irma Hemenway, May 11, with copy of John Dingell to Irma Hemenway, March 15, CR/CNS, 1–13; A. C. Walliday, February 19, Frank O'Donnell, February 2, Mrs. Edna Flannery. February 23, Thomas Humphrey, February 17, and "an interested citizen," n.d., plus a memo of January 17, CR/CNS, 1–24. On donations to the legal defense fund, see letters and memos in CR/CNS, J–S and "Donations to defense fund (for donations under $20)" in DHM, OHP, Civil Rights, "Defense Fund, Lists."

15. Robert C. Wood, *1400 Governments: The Political Economy of the New York Metropolitan Region* (Cambridge, Mass.: Harvard University Press, 1961), 171–72; Robert Bruegmann, *Sprawl: A Compact History* (Chicago: University of Chicago Press, 2005), 101–7; David Brooks, *On Paradise Drive: How We Live Now (and Always Have) in Future Tense* (New York: Simon & Schuster, 2004), 3. "How many times in human history," asks Brooks, "have two-hundred-thousand or five-hundred-thousand person communities materialized out of practically nothing in the space of a few years?" See also Lassiter's discussion in *The Silent Majority,* 8.

16. Kenneth R. Mladenka, "The Distribution of an Urban Public Service: The Changing Role of Race and Politics," *Urban Affairs Quarterly* 24, no. 4 (June 1989): 556–83. Compare Kenneth Jackson, *Crabgrass Frontier: The Suburbanization of the United States* (New York: Oxford University Press, 1985); Sugrue, *Origins of the Urban Crisis;* Dolores Hayden, *Building Suburbia, 1820–2000* (New York: Pantheon Books, 2003); Robert O. Self, *American Babylon: Race and the Struggle for Postwar Oakland* (Princeton: Princeton University Press, 2003); and Amanda Seligman's fascinating exploration of the local politics of service provision, infrastructure, neighborhood attachment, and race in *Block by Block: Neighborhoods and Public Policy on Chicago's West Side* (Chicago: University of Chicago Press, 2005).

17. Massey and Denton, *American Apartheid,* 187, 190–92, 220. Much of the best recent work on racial politics acknowledges the "constructed" nature of race but only begins to explore the process of construction and, most important, the ways that racial ideology is embedded in supposedly nonracial systems and institutions.

18. The area bounded by Warren, Tireman, Schaefer, and the industrial property along Dearborn's eastern border.

19. In 1966, the association debated opening membership to tenants. The vote, taken by hand, was 50 to 0; handwritten note on "General Meeting" minutes, 1966, DHM, "Aviation Property Owners Association, 1960–." In June 1967, the APOA reported having 439 paying members.

20. "Minutes of Dearborn Federation of Civic Associations," 1966; APOA, "President's Annual Reports"; letters to members; "Minutes of the Meetings of the Board of Directors," 1960–68, quoting "The Year in Review," typescript notes, January 1965; Herbert B. Gaston, M.D., for the APOA to "Property Owner," February 14, 1964; and "President's Report," May 17, 1960: all in DHM, "Aviation Property Owners Association, 1960–."

21. Paul J. Rice, for APOA to City Council, November 4, 1964; Mrs. Robert Cochell to Gaston and Gaston to Cochell, June 1964; Arthur Nash, for APOA to Zoning Board of Appeals, August 26, 1965 and January 13, 1966; Joseph A. Kosmowski, for APOA to Mr. Ray Brooks, December 29, 1966; "President's Report," 1965 and 1966; handwritten phone messages dated April 20 and May 2, 1966 on back of APOA letterhead; Blaska to Hoeck, March 28, 1964; "Near Neighbor" to APOA president Alex Lebedeff, n.d.: all in DHM, "Aviation Property Owners Association, 1960–." See also message from William Pratt to APOA president George Donaldson calling for opposition to Michigan's Civil Rights Commission, on APOA letter to "Citizen of Dearborn," May 16, 1963.

22. APOA "Minutes," November 7, 1967, untitled draft petition, ca. 1968, and "Minutes," September 10, 1968, DHM, "Aviation Property Owners Association, 1960–."

23. Letter from Arthur Durham, March 1, CR/CNS, 1–13. "We are comparative newcomers to Dearborn," wrote Durham, "although we have lived for many years in the

down river area. We are extremely well pleased with living conditions in Dearborn and are anxious to keep the community as it is."

24. Letters from Dorothy Anderson et al., February 9, and anon., June 10, CR/CNS, 1–24. Charles W. Jones, of Detroit, mentioned that it was "a pleasure to come to Dearborn on shopping tours and other business"; Jones, June 25, CR/DF, 24–30.

25. Many of these letters and note cards accompanied donations to Hubbard's legal defense fund.

26. Assorted telegrams and letters, citing Mrs. Ford Karr, June 24, and Countz, June 25, CR/Stanz, 24–30. "We all want equal rights for Negroes," wrote Lelia Zander, of Florida, "but that does not mean we must give up ours"; February 2, CR/CNS 1–24.

27. Letters from Chester Witkowski, June 29, F. J. Hildebrandt, June 25, Mr. and Mrs. Danner, June 27, Maurice Kaiser, June 28, and Archi Henry Jimmie, June 30, CN/DF, 24–30.

Letters came from long-time supporters and activists ("We have battled with you, in thought and spirit, as well as material effort for the past twenty-three years," wrote an engineer); from newly energized residents ("I have never written a letter of this kind to anyone before, but there is always a first time"); from young fans, including one self-identified "Jr. City Beautiful Commissioner" at Dearborn's St. Clement School; and from adults willing to organize at the workplace, like the employee at Ford's Engineering Center, who promised that he and many of his co-workers were "eager to do whatever they can." Most seemed to feel that they spoke for a silent majority. In a letter to the editor the *Detroit News* mocking him for slandering Hubbard, one of the mayor's supporters noted that he "might have more friends than enemies in this part of Michigan." Citing letters from Greg Popowicz, June 28, Lee [illegible], June 25, Jerry E. Moore, June 25, and George L. King, CN/DF, 24–30.

28. Letter from Nelson Free, June 3, CR/DF, M–J.

29. Letter from Lawrence V. Williams, March 24, CR/DF, M–J.

30. Assorted phone messages, January 30–February 18, CR, Stanz, J–J.

31. Letters from Orville L. Lippert, for the Friends of Hubbard, February 26, CR/DF, 20; Smutek, July 6, CR/Stanz, 1965.

32. Letters from anon., with c/c to Hubbard, the *Dearborn Press*, the Dearborn Community Council, the *Detroit News*, Mayor Cavanaugh, WJBK-TV, the *Detroit Free Press*, Bishop Emrich, Bishop Deardon, and Judge F. W. Kaess, February 15, CR/CNS, 1–24; CR/DF, 20. Another Hubbard supporter volunteered to help the mayor combat his civil rights indictment by going "house to house on Kendal Ave [to] ask everyone to sign up to go to court as witnesses." Correspondents regularly decried the efforts of Detroiters to use the "news media and Federal intervention" to "lower the high standard of our wonderful City of Dearborn." See letters from H. M. Sutt, February 19, CR, CNS, 1–24; Mrs. I. Zink, March 12, Helen Zuchowski, April 4, and Mrs. Irene Petrikowicz, March 15, CR/DF, F–M.

33. Philip Miller, "Home Town Doings Affect Me," *DT*, June 21, 1955.

34. Many correspondents made the link to the Kendal Street incident, noting that they "followed your case from the very beginning (Labor Day, 1963)." Letters from Arnold S. Wiwigacz, February 17, and Richard McCalla, February 18, CR/CNS, 1–24.

35. Herman H. Long and Charles S. Johnson, *People vs. Property: Race Restrictive Covenants in Housing* (Nashville: Fisk University Press, 1947), quoting 6.

36. Robert Weaver, *The Negro Ghetto* (New York: Russell & Russell, 1948); Charles Johnson, *Negro Housing* (President's Conference on Home Building and Home Ownership, Report of the Committee on Negro Housing), edited by John M. Gries and James Ford (1931; reprint New York: Negro Universities Press, 1969); Norman J. Williams, "Planning Law and Democratic Living," *Law and Contemporary Problems* 20, no. 2 (1955): 317–50; Charles Abrams, *Forbidden Neighbors: A Study of Prejudice in Housing* (Port Washington, N.Y.: Kennikat Press, 1971); Clement E. Vose, *Caucasians Only: The Supreme Court, the NAACP, and the Restrictive Covenant Cases* (Berkeley: University of California Press, 1959); St. Clair Drake and Horace R. Cayton, *Black Metropolis: A Study of Negro Life in a Northern City*, rev. ed. (Chicago: University of Chicago Press, 1993). See also Arnold Hirsch, "Searching for a 'Sound Negro Policy': A Racial Agenda for the Housing Acts of 1949 and 1954," *Housing Policy Debate* 11, no. 2 (2000): 393–441; August Meier, *CORE: A Study in the Civil Rights Movement, 1942–1968* (New York: Oxford University Press, 1973); George Lipsitz, *A Life in the Struggle: Ivory Perry and the Culture of Opposition* (Philadelphia: Temple University Press, 1998), esp. chaps. 3 and 6; Self, *American Babylon*; Martha Biondi, *To Stand and Fight: The Struggle for Civil Rights in Postwar New York City* (Cambridge, Mass.: Harvard University Press, 2003); and Freund, "Democracy's Unfinished Business."

37. Secondary and conventional market operations were ignored. The report calculated that "government guarantees helped to stimulate nearly a quarter of the new housing units during the period of 1946 through 1967"; U.S. National Commission on Urban Problems, *Building the American City* (Washington, D.C.: GPO, 1968), 94–95, 99–103.

38. U.S. President's Committee on Urban Housing, *A Decent Home* (Washington, D.C.: GPO, 1969) 45; U.S. President's Task Force on Suburban Problems, *Final Report*, ed. by Charles M. Haar (Cambridge, Mass.: Ballinger, 1974), 9–10, 63, 69, 159–60. The Task Force cited the need to remedy years of discriminatory federal policies, but did not discuss those policies. It also argued that whites' "fear" that integration would undermine property values was real, yet had "no foundation in fact."

39. U.S. President's Task Force on Suburban Problems, *Final Report*, 28–29, 49–50, and 3. The authors criticized suburbs for their "contrived homogeneity," which they viewed as a "violation of the American tradition of pluralism."

40. Massey and Denton, *American Apartheid*, 235.

INDEX